Ford Fiesta
Owners Workshop Manual

Martynn Randall

Models covered

(6407 - 368 - 1B1)

Ford Fiesta Hatchback & Van
Petrol: 1.0 litre (998cc) turbo (EcoBoost), 1.25 litre (1242cc) & 1.6 litre (1596cc)
Turbo-diesel: 1.5 litre (1499cc) & 1.6 litre (1560cc) Duratorq TDCi

Does NOT cover 1.0 litre non-turbo (Duratec) or 1.4 litre petrol engines, or 'Mountune' or 'ST' versions (with 1.6 litre EcoBoost petrol engines)
Does NOT cover new Fiesta range introduced July 2017

© Haynes Group Limited 2017

ABCDE
FGHIJ
KL

A book in the **Haynes Owners Workshop Manual Series**

ISBN **978 1 78521 407 3**

British Library Cataloguing in Publication Data
A catalogue record for this book is available from the British Library.

Printed in India

Haynes Group Limited
Sparkford, Yeovil, Somerset BA22 7JJ, England

Haynes North America, Inc
2801 Townsgate Road, Suite 340, Thousand Oaks, CA 91361

Disclaimer

There are risks associated with automotive repairs. The ability to make repairs depends on the individual's skill, experience and proper tools. Individuals should act with due care and acknowledge and assume the risk of performing automotive repairs.

The purpose of this manual is to provide comprehensive, useful and accessible automotive repair information, to help you get the best value from your vehicle. However, this manual is not a substitute for a professional certified technician or mechanic.

This repair manual is produced by a third party and is not associated with an individual vehicle manufacturer. If there is any doubt or discrepancy between this manual and the owner's manual or the factory service manual, please refer to the factory service manual or seek assistance from a professional certified technician or mechanic.

Even though we have prepared this manual with extreme care and every attempt is made to ensure that the information in this manual is correct, neither the publisher nor the author can accept responsibility for loss, damage or injury caused by any errors in, or omissions from, the information given.

Contents

LIVING WITH YOUR FORD FIESTA

Roadside repairs

Weekly checks

Lubricants and fluids

Tyre pressures

MAINTENANCE

Routine maintenance and servicing – petrol models

Routine maintenance and servicing – diesel models

Contents

The Ford Fiesta model range covered by this manual was introduced into the UK in December 2012, superseding the previous Fiesta range. It is available in 3- and 5-door Hatchback, and 3-door Van versions with 1.25, and 1.6 litre Duretec petrol engines, 1.0 litre EcoBoost (turbocharged) engines, and 1.5 and 1.6 litre Duratorq TDCi diesel engines. The Duratorq diesel engines all feature state-of-the art common-rail injection which meet or exceed the latest emissions standards. Whist the 1.0 litre petrol engine is a 3-cylinder design, the 1.25 and 1.6 litre engines have 4 cylinders. All petrol engines are 4-valves per cylinder, with Double OverHead Camshafts (DOHC). Both the 1.5 and 1.6 litre diesel engines are 4-cylinder, Single OverHead Camshaft (SOHC) design, with 2-valves per cylinder. All engines are mounted transversely at the front of the car.

All models have front-wheel-drive, with a five-speed manual transmission. A 6-speed automated (Powershift) transmission is also optionally available on 1.0 litre EcoBoost and 1.6 litre petrol engine models. The front suspension is of conventional MacPherson strut type, incorporating lower arms, and an anti-roll bar; at the rear, a semi-independent beam axle is combined with compact under-floor springs to provide a more spacious load area.

A wide range of standard and optional equipment is available within the Fiesta range to suit most tastes, including electric power steering, air conditioning, remote central locking, electric windows, electric sunroof, anti-lock braking system, electronic alarm system and supplemental restraint systems.

For the home mechanic, the Fiesta is a relatively straightforward vehicle to maintain, and most of the items requiring frequent attention are easily accessible.

Your Ford Fiesta Manual

The aim of this manual is to help you get the best value from your car. It can do so in several ways. It can help you decide what work must be done (even should you choose to get it done by a garage). It will also provide information on routine maintenance and servicing, and give a logical course of action and diagnosis when random faults occur. However, it is hoped that you will use the manual by tackling the work yourself. On simpler jobs it may even be quicker than booking the car into a garage and going there twice, to leave and collect it. Perhaps most important, a lot of money can be saved by avoiding the costs a garage must charge to cover its labour and overheads.

The manual has drawings and descriptions to show the function of the various components so that their layout can be understood. Tasks are described and photographed in a clear step-by-step sequence.

References to the 'left' and 'right' of the car are in the sense of a person in the driver's seat facing forward.

Project vehicles

The main vehicle used in the preparation of this manual, and which appears in many of the photographic sequences, was a Ford Fiesta 1.5 litre diesel. Additional work was carried out on a Fiesta 1.0, 1.25 and 1.6 litre petrol, along with a 1.6 litre diesel.

Acknowledgements

Thanks are due to Draper Tools Limited, who provided some of the workshop tools, and to all those people at Sparkford who helped in the production of this manual.

We take great pride in the accuracy of information given in this manual, but vehicle manufacturers make alterations and design changes during the production run of a particular vehicle of which they do not inform us. No liability can be accepted by the authors or publishers for loss, damage or injury caused by any errors in, or omissions from, the information given.

Ford Fiesta

Working on your car can be dangerous. This page shows just some of the potential risks and hazards, with the aim of creating a safety-conscious attitude.

General hazards

Scalding

• Don't remove the radiator or expansion tank cap while the engine is hot.
• Engine oil, transmission fluid or power steering fluid may also be dangerously hot if the engine has recently been running.

Burning

• Beware of burns from the exhaust system and from any part of the engine. Brake discs and drums can also be extremely hot immediately after use.

Crushing

• When working under or near a raised vehicle, always supplement the jack with axle stands, or use drive-on ramps. *Never venture under a car which is only supported by a jack.*
• Take care if loosening or tightening high-torque nuts when the vehicle is on stands. Initial loosening and final tightening should be done with the wheels on the ground.

Fire

• Fuel is highly flammable; fuel vapour is explosive.
• Don't let fuel spill onto a hot engine.
• Do not smoke or allow naked lights (including pilot lights) anywhere near a vehicle being worked on. Also beware of creating sparks (electrically or by use of tools).
• Fuel vapour is heavier than air, so don't work on the fuel system with the vehicle over an inspection pit.
• Another cause of fire is an electrical overload or short-circuit. Take care when repairing or modifying the vehicle wiring.
• Keep a fire extinguisher handy, of a type suitable for use on fuel and electrical fires.

Electric shock

• Ignition HT and Xenon headlight voltages can be dangerous, especially to people with heart problems or a pacemaker. Don't work on or near these systems with the engine running or the ignition switched on.

• Mains voltage is also dangerous. Make sure that any mains-operated equipment is correctly earthed. Mains power points should be protected by a residual current device (RCD) circuit breaker.

Fume or gas intoxication

• Exhaust fumes are poisonous; they can contain carbon monoxide, which is rapidly fatal if inhaled. Never run the engine in a confined space such as a garage with the doors shut.
• Fuel vapour is also poisonous, as are the vapours from some cleaning solvents and paint thinners.

Poisonous or irritant substances

• Avoid skin contact with battery acid and with any fuel, fluid or lubricant, especially antifreeze, brake hydraulic fluid and Diesel fuel. Don't syphon them by mouth. If such a substance is swallowed or gets into the eyes, seek medical advice.
• Prolonged contact with used engine oil can cause skin cancer. Wear gloves or use a barrier cream if necessary. Change out of oil-soaked clothes and do not keep oily rags in your pocket.
• Air conditioning refrigerant forms a poisonous gas if exposed to a naked flame (including a cigarette). It can also cause skin burns on contact.

Asbestos

• Asbestos dust can cause cancer if inhaled or swallowed. Asbestos may be found in gaskets and in brake and clutch linings. When dealing with such components it is safest to assume that they contain asbestos.

Special hazards

Hydrofluoric acid

• This extremely corrosive acid is formed when certain types of synthetic rubber, found in some O-rings, oil seals, fuel hoses etc, are exposed to temperatures above 4000C. The rubber changes into a charred or sticky substance containing the acid. *Once formed, the acid remains dangerous for years. If it gets onto the skin, it may be necessary to amputate the limb concerned.*
• When dealing with a vehicle which has suffered a fire, or with components salvaged from such a vehicle, wear protective gloves and discard them after use.

The battery

• Batteries contain sulphuric acid, which attacks clothing, eyes and skin. Take care when topping-up or carrying the battery.
• The hydrogen gas given off by the battery is highly explosive. Never cause a spark or allow a naked light nearby. Be careful when connecting and disconnecting battery chargers or jump leads.

Air bags

• Air bags can cause injury if they go off accidentally. Take care when removing the steering wheel and trim panels. Special storage instructions may apply.

Diesel injection equipment

• Diesel injection pumps supply fuel at very high pressure. Take care when working on the fuel injectors and fuel pipes.

⚠ *Warning: Never expose the hands, face or any other part of the body to injector spray; the fuel can penetrate the skin with potentially fatal results.*

Remember...

DO

• Do use eye protection when using power tools, and when working under the vehicle.

• Do wear gloves or use barrier cream to protect your hands when necessary.

• Do get someone to check periodically that all is well when working alone on the vehicle.

• Do keep loose clothing and long hair well out of the way of moving mechanical parts.

• Do remove rings, wristwatch etc, before working on the vehicle – especially the electrical system.

• Do ensure that any lifting or jacking equipment has a safe working load rating adequate for the job.

DON'T

• Don't attempt to lift a heavy component which may be beyond your capability – get assistance.

• Don't rush to finish a job, or take unverified short cuts.

• Don't use ill-fitting tools which may slip and cause injury.

• Don't leave tools or parts lying around where someone can trip over them. Mop up oil and fuel spills at once.

• Don't allow children or pets to play in or near a vehicle being worked on.

The following pages are intended to help in dealing with common roadside emergencies and breakdowns. You will find more detailed fault finding information at the back of the manual, and repair information in the main chapters.

If your car won't start and the starter motor doesn't turn

☐ If it's a model with manual transmission, make sure that the clutch pedal is fully depressed. On models with Powershift transmission, make sure the selector is in P or N and the brake pedal is fully depressed.

☐ Open the bonnet and make sure that the battery terminals are clean and tight.

☐ Switch on the headlights and try to start the engine. If the headlights go very dim when you're trying to start, the battery is probably flat. Get out of trouble by jump starting using a friend's car.

If your car won't start even though the starter motor turns as normal

☐ Is there fuel in the tank?

☐ Is there moisture on electrical components under the bonnet? Switch off the ignition, then wipe off any obvious dampness with a dry cloth. Spray a water-repellent aerosol product (WD-40 or equivalent) on engine and fuel system electrical connectors like those shown in the photos.

A Check the security and condition of the battery connections

B With the ignition off, check that the wiring connectors are securely connected to the ignition coils (petrol models)

C With the ignition off, check the security of the airflow sensor/pressure sensor connections

Check that electrical connections are secure (with the ignition switched off) and spray them with a water-dispersant spray like WD-40 if you suspect a problem due to damp

D Check that all fuses are still in good condition and none have blown

Jump starting

 Jump starting will get you out of trouble, but you must correct whatever made the battery go flat in the first place. There are three possibilities:

1 *The battery has been drained by repeated attempts to start, or by leaving the lights on.*

2 *The charging system is not working properly (alternator drivebelt slack or broken, alternator wiring fault or alternator itself faulty).*

3 *The battery itself is at fault (electrolyte low, or battery worn out).*

When jump-starting a car, observe the following precautions:

Caution: Remove the key in case the central locking engages when the jump leads are connected.

✓ Before connecting the booster battery, make sure that the ignition is switched off.
✓ Ensure that all electrical equipment (lights, heater, wipers, etc) is switched off.
✓ Take note of any special precautions printed on the battery case.
✓ Make sure that the booster battery is the same voltage as the discharged one in the vehicle.

✓ If the battery is being jump-started from the battery in another vehicle, the two vehicles MUST NOT TOUCH each other.
✓ Make sure that the transmission is in neutral (or PARK, in the case of automatic transmission).

 Budget jump leads can be a false economy, as they often do not pass enough current to start large capacity or diesel engines. They can also get hot.

1 Connect one end of the red jump lead to the positive (+) terminal of the flat battery

2 Connect the other end of the red lead to the positive (+) terminal of the booster battery.

3 Connect one end of the black jump lead to the negative (-) terminal of the booster battery

4 Connect the other end of the black jump lead to a bolt or bracket on the engine block, well away from the battery, on the vehicle to be started.

5 Make sure that the jump leads will not come into contact with the fan, drive-belts or other moving parts of the engine.

6 Start the engine using the booster battery and run it at idle speed. Switch on the lights, rear window demister and heater blower motor, then disconnect the jump leads in the reverse order of connection. Turn off the lights etc.

Flat tyre

Note: *Most Fiesta models are equipped with a puncture repair kit and do not have a spare wheel and jack*

Preparation

- [ ] When a puncture occurs, stop as soon as it is safe to do so.
- [ ] Park on firm level ground, if possible, and well out of the way of other traffic.
- [ ] Use hazard warning lights if necessary.
- [ ] If you have one, use a warning triangle to alert other drivers of your presence.
- [ ] Apply the handbrake and engage first or reverse gear (or Park on models with automatic transmission).

Changing the wheel

- [ ] Chock the wheel diagonally opposite the one being removed – a couple of large stones will do for this.
- [ ] If the ground is soft, use a flat piece of wood to spread the load under the jack.

⚠️ **Warning: Do not change a wheel in a situation where you risk being hit by other traffic. On busy roads, try to stop in a lay-by or a gateway. Be wary of passing traffic while changing the wheel – it is easy to become distracted by the job in hand.**

1 Lift the floor covering and unscrew the spare wheel clamp bolt.

2 Lift out the spare wheel ...

3 then take out the jack and tools located in the spare wheel well.

4 Use the special tool or screwdriver provided to pull the wheel trim from the wheel or wheel nuts, then slacken each wheel nut by half a turn.

5 Locate the jack head below the jacking point nearest the wheel to be changed; the jacking point is indicated by a reinforced section in the sill. Ensure that the slot in the jack head engages with the sill flange at the jacking point. Raise the vehicle until the wheel is clear of the ground, then remove the wheel.

6 Fit the spare wheel and tighten the nuts moderately with the wheelbrace.

7 Lower the vehicle to the ground, then finally tighten the wheel nuts in a diagonal sequence. Refit the wheel trim. Note that the wheel nuts should be tightened to the specified torque at the earliest opportunity.

Finally . . .

- [ ] Remove the wheel chocks.
- [ ] Stow the jack and tools in the correct locations in the car.
- [ ] Check the tyre pressure on the wheel just fitted. If it is low, or if you don't have a pressure gauge with you, drive slowly to the next garage and inflate the tyre to the correct pressure.
- [ ] Have the damaged tyre or wheel repaired as soon as possible, or another puncture will leave you stranded.

Using the puncture repair kit

1 Lift the luggage compartment floor covering and take out the tyre repair kit. Remove the sealant bottle and compressor from the wrapping, then remove the air hose and electrical cable from the underside of the compressor.

2 Screw the air hose onto the sealant bottle connection.

3 Fit the sealant bottle in the retainer on the compressor, then position the compressor near the punctured tyre.

4 Unscrew the dust cap from the punctured tyre, and screw the sealant bottle air hose onto the tyre valve.

5 Ensure that the switch on the compressor is set to O, then plug the compressor electrical cable into the accessory socket or cigarette lighter socket.

Important notes

- [ ] If the correct tyre pressure is not obtained within 10 minutes, it is likely that the tyre is too badly damaged to be repaired with the kit.
- [ ] The maximum speed sticker attached to the sealant bottle should be placed in the driver's field of view. Do not exceed the permitted maximum speed until an undamaged wheel and tyre have been fitted.
- [ ] On completion, disconnect the tyre repair kit and continue driving immediately so that the sealant is evenly distributed around the inside of the tyre.
- [ ] After driving approximately 6 miles (but no more than 10 minutes) stop and check the tyre pressure by connecting the air hose to the tyre valve. As long as the pressure indicated on the gauge is more than 1.0 bar (14.5 psi) it may be adjusted to the prescribed value using the compressor. If the pressure has fallen below 1.0 bar (14.5 psi) the repair has not been successful and the car should not be driven. It will therefore be necessary to seek roadside assistance.

6 Switch on the ignition, then set the compressor switch to I to start the compressor. To avoid discharging the battery when the compressor is running, it is advisable to start the engine. The pump will initially pump the sealant into the tyre which will take approximately 30 seconds, and then start to inflate the tyre. During the initial 30 second period, the pressure gauge on the pump will indicate up to 6 bar (87 psi) and then drop. The correct tyre pressure (see end of Weekly checks) should be obtained within 10 minutes. The compressor can then be switched off by returning the switch to the O position.

7 If it is necessary to release the pressure in the tyre, press the pressure relief valve button on the air hose.

Finally . . .

- [ ] Stow the puncture repair kit in the luggage compartment and refit the floor covering.
- [ ] Remember to obtain a new bottle of sealant at the earliest opportunity.

 Warning: Repair of a tyre using the puncture repair kit must be regarded as a 'get you home' emergency repair only. A new tyre must be fitted as soon as possible.

Towing

When all else fails, you may find yourself having to get a tow home – or of course you may be helping somebody else. Long-distance recovery should only be done by a garage or breakdown service. For shorter distances, DIY towing using another car is easy enough, but observe the following points:

☐ Use a proper tow-rope – they are not expensive. The vehicle being towed must display an ON TOW sign in its rear window.

☐ Always turn the ignition key to the 'on' position when the vehicle is being towed, so that the steering lock is released, and the direction indicator and brake lights work.

☐ A towing eye is provided with the tool kit in the luggage compartment. Only attach the tow-rope to the towing eyes.

☐ To fit the towing eye, remove the cover from the front bumper, then screw in the towing eye anti-clockwise as far as it will go using the handle of the wheel brace to turn the eye. Note that the towing eye has a left-hand thread.

☐ Before being towed, release the handbrake and select neutral on the transmission. On models with Powershift transmission, special precautions apply – do not exceed 12 mph or travel further than 12 miles, and the wheels must always roll forward. If in doubt, do not tow, or transmission damage may result.

☐ Note that greater-than-usual pedal pressure will be required to operate the brakes, since the vacuum servo unit is only operational with the engine running.

☐ Greater-than-usual steering effort will also be required.

☐ The driver of the car being towed must keep the tow-rope taut at all times to avoid snatching.

☐ Make sure that both drivers know the route before setting off.

☐ Only drive at moderate speeds and keep the distance towed to a minimum. Drive smoothly and allow plenty of time for slowing down at junctions.

Identifying leaks

Puddles on the garage floor or drive, or obvious wetness under the bonnet or underneath the car, suggest a leak that needs investigating. It can sometimes be difficult to decide where the leak is coming from, especially if the engine bay is very dirty already. Leaking oil or fluid can also be blown rearwards by the passage of air under the car, giving a false impression of where the problem lies.

 Warning: Most automotive oils and fluids are poisonous. Wash them off skin, and change out of contaminated clothing, without delay.

 HAYNES HiNT *The smell of a fluid leaking from the car may provide a clue to what's leaking. Some fluids are distinctively coloured. It may help to clean the car carefully and to park it over some clean paper overnight as an aid to locating the source of the leak. Remember that some leaks may only occur while the engine is running.*

Sump oil

Engine oil may leak from the drain plug...

Oil from filter

...or from the base of the oil filter.

Gearbox oil

Gearbox oil can leak from the seals at the inboard ends of the driveshafts.

Antifreeze

Leaking antifreeze often leaves a crystalline deposit like this.

Brake fluid

A leak occurring at a wheel is almost certainly brake fluid.

Introduction

There are some very simple checks which need only take a few minutes to carry out, but which could save you a lot of inconvenience and expense.

These checks require no great skill or special tools, and the small amount of time they take to perform could prove to be very well spent, for example:

☐ Keeping an eye on tyre condition and pressures, will not only help to stop them wearing out prematurely, but could also save your life.

☐ Many breakdowns are caused by electrical problems. Battery-related faults are particularly common, and a quick check on a regular basis will often prevent the majority of these.

☐ If your car develops a brake fluid leak, the first time you might know about it is when your brakes don't work properly. Checking the level regularly will give advance warning of this kind of problem.

☐ If the oil or coolant levels run low, the cost of repairing any engine damage will be far greater than fixing the leak, for example.

Underbonnet check points

▲ Petrol engine models

1 *Engine oil level dipstick*
2 *Engine oil filler cap*
3 *Coolant reservoir (expansion tank)*

4 *Brake and clutch fluid reservoir*
5 *Washer fluid reservoir*

6 *Battery*
7 *Engine compartment fuse/relay box*

Underbonnet check points

▲ Diesel engine models

1 *Engine oil level dipstick*
2 *Engine oil filler cap*
3 *Coolant reservoir (expansion tank)*

4 *Brake and clutch fluid reservoir*
5 *Washer fluid reservoir*

6 *Battery*
7 *Engine compartment fuse/relay box*

Engine oil level

HAYNES HiNT *If the oil is checked immediately after driving the vehicle, some of the oil will remain in the upper engine components, resulting in an inaccurate reading on the dipstick.*

Before you start

✔ Make sure that the car is on level ground.
✔ The oil level must be checked with the engine at normal operating temperature, however, wait at least 5 minutes after the engine has been switched off.

The correct oil

Modern engines place great demands on their oil. It is very important that the correct oil for your car is used (see *Lubricants and fluids*).

Car care

● If you have to add oil frequently, you should check whether you have any oil leaks. Place some clean paper under the car overnight, and check for stains in the morning. If there are no leaks, then the engine may be burning oil, or the oil may only be leaking when the engine is running.
● Always maintain the level between the upper and lower dipstick marks (see photo 3). If the level is too low, severe engine damage may occur. Oil seal failure may result if the engine is overfilled by adding too much oil.

1 The dipstick is brightly coloured for easy identification (see Underbonnet check points for exact location). Withdraw the dipstick.

2 Using a clean rag or paper towel remove all oil from the dipstick. Insert the clean dipstick into the tube as far as it will go, then withdraw it again.

3 Note the level on the end of the dipstick, which should be between the upper (MAX) mark and lower (MIN) mark. Approximately 1.0 litre of oil will raise the level from the lower mark to the upper mark.

4 Oil is added through the filler cap. Unscrew the cap and top-up the level. A funnel may help to reduce spillage. Add the oil slowly, checking the level on the dipstick frequently. Avoid overfilling (see Car care).

Brake and clutch fluid level

Note: All manual transmission models have a hydraulically-operated clutch, which uses the same fluid as the braking system.

 Warning: Hydraulic fluid can harm your eyes and damage painted surfaces, so use extreme caution when handling and pouring it.

 Warning: Do not use fluid that has been standing open for some time, as it absorbs moisture from the air, which can cause a dangerous loss of braking effectiveness.

Before you start

✔ Make sure that your car is on level ground.

Safety first!

● If the reservoir requires repeated topping-up this is an indication of a fluid leak somewhere in the system, which should be investigated immediately.

● If a leak is suspected, the car should not be driven until the braking system has been checked. Never take any risks where brakes are concerned

● The fluid level in the reservoir will drop slightly as the brake pads and shoes wear down, but the fluid level must never be allowed to drop below the MIN mark.

1 The MAX and MIN marks are indicated on the side of the reservoir. The fluid level must be kept between the marks at all times.

2 If topping-up is necessary, first wipe clean the area around the filler cap to prevent dirt entering the hydraulic system. Unscrew the reservoir cap.

3 Carefully add fluid, taking care not to spill it onto the surrounding components. Use only the specified fluid; mixing different types can cause damage to the system. After topping-up to the correct level, securely refit the cap and wipe off any spilt fluid.

Coolant level

 Warning: Do not attempt to remove the expansion tank pressure cap when the engine is hot, as there is a very great risk of scalding. Do not leave open containers of coolant about, as it is poisonous.

Car care

● With a sealed-type cooling system, adding coolant should not be necessary on a regular basis. If frequent topping-up is required, it is likely there is a leak. Check the radiator, all hoses and joint faces for signs of staining or wetness, and rectify as necessary.

● It is important that antifreeze is used in the cooling system all year round, not just during the winter months. Don't top-up with water alone, as the antifreeze will become diluted.

1 The coolant level varies with the temperature of the engine, and is visible through the expansion tank. When the engine is cold, the coolant level should be between the MAX and MIN marks on the front of the reservoir. When the engine is hot, the level may rise slightly above the MAX mark.

2 If topping-up is necessary, wait until the engine is cold. Slowly unscrew the expansion tank cap, to release any pressure present in the cooling system, and remove it.

3 Add a mixture of water and antifreeze to the expansion tank until the coolant level is halfway between the level marks. Use only the specified antifreeze – if using Ford antifreeze, make sure it is the same type and colour as that already in the system. Refit the cap and tighten it securely.

Screen washer fluid level

● Screenwash additives not only keep the windscreen clean during bad weather, they also prevent the washer system freezing in cold weather – which is when you are likely to need it most. Don't top-up using plain water, as the screenwash will become diluted, and will freeze in cold weather.

 Warning: On no account use engine coolant antifreeze in the screen washer system – this may damage the paintwork.

1 The reservoir for the windscreen and rear window washer systems is located on the left-hand side of the engine compartment. If topping-up is necessary, open the filler cap.

2 When topping-up the reservoir a screenwash additive should be added in the quantities recommended on the bottle.

Battery

Caution: Before carrying out any work on the vehicle battery, read the precautions given in ',2 !' at the start of this manual. If the battery is to be disconnected, refer to Chapter 5A Section 4, before proceeding.
✔ Make sure that the battery tray is in good condition, and that the clamp is tight. Corrosion on the tray, retaining clamp and the battery itself can be removed with a solution of water and baking soda. Thoroughly rinse all cleaned areas with water. Any metal parts damaged by corrosion should be covered with a zinc-based primer, then painted.
✔ Periodically (approximately every three months), check the charge condition of the battery as described in Chapter 5A Section 3.
✔ If the battery is flat, and you need to jump start your vehicle, see *Jump starting*.

Battery corrosion can be kept to a minimum by applying a layer of petroleum jelly to the clamps and terminals after they are reconnected.

1 The battery is located at the rear, left-hand side of the engine compartment. Check the tightness of battery clamps to ensure good electrical connections. You should not be able to move them. Also check each cable for cracks and frayed conductors.

2 If corrosion (white, fluffy deposits) is evident, remove the cables from the battery terminals, clean them with a small wire brush, then refit them. Automotive stores sell a tool for cleaning the battery post …

3 … as well as the battery cable clamps

Electrical systems

✔ Check all external lights and the horn. Refer to the appropriate Sections of Chapter 12 for details if any of the circuits are found to be inoperative.

✔ Visually check all accessible wiring connectors, harnesses and retaining clips for security, and for signs of chafing or damage.

1 If a single indicator light, brake light or headlight has failed, it is likely that a bulb has blown and will need to be renewed. Refer to Chapter 12 for details. If both brake lights have failed, it is possible that the switch has failed (see Chapter 9).

2 If more than one indicator light or headlight has failed, it is likely that either a fuse has blown or that there is a fault in the circuit. The main fuses are located in the engine compartment fuse/relay box on the left-hand side of the engine compartment. Unclip and remove the cover for access. Refer to the wiring diagrams at the end of this manual for details of fuse locations and circuits protected.

3 Additional fuses are located in the passenger compartment fuse/relay box located behind the glovebox. Open the glovebox and press the sides inwards to release it from the facia.

4 To renew a blown fuse, remove it, where applicable, using the plastic tool provided or needle-nosed pliers. Fit a new fuse of the same rating, available from car accessory shops. It is important that you find the reason that the fuse blew (see Electrical fault finding in Chapter 12).

Wiper blades

1 Check the condition of the wiper blades; if they are cracked or show any signs of deterioration, or if the glass swept area is smeared, renew them. Wiper blades should be renewed annually.

2 To remove a windscreen wiper blade, pull the arm fully away from the screen until it locks. Depress the tab on the side of the wiper arm.

3 Disengage the blade from the end of the arm and lift away the blade.

4 Don't forget to check the tailgate wiper blade as well which is removed by simply disengaging the blade pivot pin from the end of the arm.

Tyre condition and pressure

It is very important that tyres are in good condition, and at the correct pressure – having a tyre failure at any speed is highly dangerous.

Tyre wear is influenced by driving style – harsh braking and acceleration, or fast cornering, will all produce more rapid tyre wear. As a general rule, the front tyres wear out faster than the rears. Interchanging the tyres from front to rear ("rotating" the tyres) may result in more even wear. However, if this is completely effective, you may have the expense of replacing all four tyres at once!

Remove any nails or stones embedded in the tread before they penetrate the tyre to cause deflation. If removal of a nail does reveal that the tyre has been punctured, refit the nail so that its point of penetration is marked. Then immediately change the wheel, and have the tyre repaired by a tyre dealer.

Regularly check the tyres for damage in the form of cuts or bulges, especially in the sidewalls. Periodically remove the wheels, and clean any dirt or mud from the inside and outside surfaces. Examine the wheel rims for signs of rusting, corrosion or other damage. Light alloy wheels are easily damaged by "kerbing" whilst parking; steel wheels may also become dented or buckled. A new wheel is very often the only way to overcome severe damage.

New tyres should be balanced when they are fitted, but it may become necessary to re-balance them as they wear, or if the balance weights fitted to the wheel rim should fall off. Unbalanced tyres will wear more quickly, as will the steering and suspension components. Wheel imbalance is normally signified by vibration, particularly at a certain speed (typically around 50 mph). If this vibration is felt only through the steering, then it is likely that just the front wheels need balancing. If, however, the vibration is felt through the whole car, the rear wheels could be out of balance. Wheel balancing should be carried out by a tyre dealer or garage.

1 Tread Depth - visual check
The original tyres have tread wear safety bands (B), which will appear when the tread depth reaches approximately 1.6 mm. The band positions are indicated by a triangular mark on the tyre sidewall (A).

2 Tread Depth - manual check
Alternatively, tread wear can be monitored with a simple, inexpensive device known as a tread depth indicator gauge.

3 Tyre Pressure Check
Check the tyre pressures regularly with the tyres cold. Do not adjust the tyre pressures immediately after the vehicle has been used, or an inaccurate setting will result.

Tyre tread wear patterns

Shoulder Wear

Underinflation (wear on both sides)
Under-inflation will cause overheating of the tyre, because the tyre will flex too much, and the tread will not sit correctly on the road surface. This will cause a loss of grip and excessive wear, not to mention the danger of sudden tyre failure due to heat build-up.
Check and adjust pressures
Incorrect wheel camber (wear on one side)
Repair or renew suspension parts
Hard cornering
Reduce speed!

Centre Wear

Overinflation
Over-inflation will cause rapid wear of the centre part of the tyre tread, coupled with reduced grip, harsher ride, and the danger of shock damage occurring in the tyre casing.
Check and adjust pressures

If you sometimes have to inflate your car's tyres to the higher pressures specified for maximum load or sustained high speed, don't forget to reduce the pressures to normal afterwards.

Uneven Wear

Front tyres may wear unevenly as a result of wheel misalignment. Most tyre dealers and garages can check and adjust the wheel alignment (or "tracking") for a modest charge.
Incorrect camber or castor
Repair or renew suspension parts
Malfunctioning suspension
Repair or renew suspension parts
Unbalanced wheel
Balance tyres
Incorrect toe setting
Adjust front wheel alignment
Note: *The feathered edge of the tread which typifies toe wear is best checked by feel.*

Lubricants, fluids and tyre pressures

Engine oil:

Petrol engines . . . . Multigrade engine oil, viscosity 5W/20 Ford specification WSS-M2C948-B. Eg. Castrol Magnatec Stop-Start 5W/20

Diesel engines

All except 1.5 litre engine codes XUJA, XUJB,

XVJB and XVJC . . . . Multigrade engine oil, viscosity SAE 5W/30 Ford specification WSS-M2C913-C. Eg. Castrol Magnatec Stop-Start 5W/30

1.5 litre engine codes XUJA, XUJB, XVJB and XVJC . . . . . Multigrade engine oil, viscosity SAE 0W/30 Ford specification WSS-M2C950-A. Eg, Castrol Magnatec Stop-Start 0W/30

Cooling system . . . . Motorcraft SuperPlus pink/red antifreeze Ford specification WSS-M97B44-D

Manual transmission . . . . SAE 75W FE gear oil Ford specification WSD-M2C200-D2 API GL-4 fully synthetic. Eg, Castrol Syntrans FE 75W

Powershift transmission . . . . SAE 75W FE gear oil Ford specification WSD-M2C200-D2 API GL-4 fully synthetic. Eg. Castrol Syntrans FE 75W

Brake and clutch hydraulic system . . . . Super DOT 4, paraffin-free hydraulic fluid Ford specification WSS-M6C65-A2

Tyre pressures (cold)

1 The tyre pressures for your vehicle are given on a sticker affixed to the door pillar (see illustration).

Tyre pressures are given on the door pillar sticker

Chapter 1A
Routine maintenance and servicing – petrol models

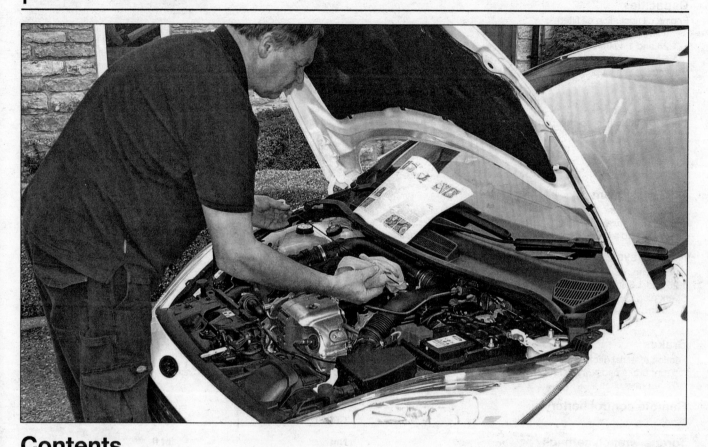

Contents

Degrees of difficulty

Easy, suitable for novice with little experience	**Fairly easy,** suitable for beginner with some experience	**Fairly difficult,** suitable for competent DIY mechanic	**Difficult,** suitable for experienced DIY mechanic	**Very difficult,** suitable for expert DIY or professional

1 Servicing specifications – petrol models

Lubricants and fluids...............................	Refer to end of *Weekly checks*

Capacities

Engine oil (including oil filter)

1.0 litre EcoBoost (turbocharged) engines.....................	4.6 litres
1.25 and 1.4 litre engines...................................	4.1 litres
1.6 litre engine	4.1 litres

Cooling system (approximate)

All models...	5.8 litres

Transmission

Manual transmission.....................................	2.3 litres
Powershift transmission (approximate)	1.7 litres

Washer fluid reservoir

All models...	2.5 litres

Fuel tank

All models...	42.0 litres

Cooling system

Antifreeze mixture:

50% antifreeze	Protection down to -37°C

Note: *Refer to antifreeze manufacturer for latest recommendations.*

Ignition system

1.0 litre engines	NGK SILZNAR8C7H
1.25 and 1.6 litre engines.................................	Motorcraft AYFS 22 C

Spark plug gap:

1.0 litre engines	0.7 mm (preset)
1.25 and 1.6 litre engines.................................	1.3 mm (preset)

Brakes

Friction material minimum thickness:

Front brake pads	1.5 mm
Rear brake shoes	1.0 mm

Remote control battery

Type	CR2032, 3V

Torque wrench settings

	Nm	lbf ft
Engine oil drain plug:		
1.0 litre engines	25	18
1.25 and 1.6 litre engines.................................	28	21
Ignition coils (1.0 litre engines)............................	10	7
Manual transmission filler/level plug	35	26
Roadwheel nuts	135	100
Spark plugs:		
1.0 litre engines	13	10
1.25 and 1.6 litre engines.................................	15	11

2 Maintenance schedule – petrol models

1 The maintenance intervals in this manual are provided with the assumption that you, not the dealer, will be carrying out the work. These are the minimum maintenance intervals based on the standard service schedule recommended by the manufacturer for vehicles driven daily. If you wish to keep your vehicle in peak condition at all times, you may wish to perform some of these procedures more often. We encourage frequent maintenance, because it enhances the efficiency, performance and resale value of your vehicle.

2 If the vehicle is driven in dusty areas, used to tow a trailer, or driven frequently at slow speeds (idling in traffic) or on short journeys, more frequent maintenance intervals are recommended.

3 When the vehicle is new, it should be serviced by a dealer service department (or other workshop recognised by the vehicle manufacturer as providing the same standard of service) in order to preserve the warranty. The vehicle manufacturer may reject warranty claims if you are unable to prove that servicing has been carried out as and when specified, using only original equipment parts or parts certified to be of equivalent quality.

Every 250 miles or weekly
☐ Refer to Weekly checks

Every 6000 miles or 6 months, whichever comes first
☐ Renew the engine oil and filter (Section 6)

Note: *Ford recommend that the engine oil and filter are changed every 12 500 miles or 12 months. However, oil and filter changes are good for the engine, and we recommend that the oil and filter are renewed more frequently, especially if the car is used on a lot of short journeys.*

Every 12 500 miles or 12 months, whichever comes first
In addition to the items listed above, carry out the following:
☐ Renew the pollen filter, where applicable (Section 7)
☐ Check all components, pipes and hoses for fluid leaks (Section 8)
☐ Check the condition of the auxiliary drivebelt (Section 9)
☐ Check the antifreeze/inhibitor strength (Section 30)
☐ Check the condition and operation of the seat belts (Section 10)
☐ Check the front brake pads and discs for wear (Section 11)
☐ Check the condition of the driveshaft gaiters (Section 12)
☐ Check the steering and suspension components for condition and security (Section 13)
☐ Check the rear brake shoes and drums for wear (Section 14)
☐ Check and if necessary adjust the handbrake (Section 15)
☐ Check the condition of the exhaust system components (Section 16)
☐ Check the roadwheel nuts are tightened to the specified torque (Section 17)
☐ Lubricate all door, bonnet and tailgate hinges and locks (Section 18)
☐ Check the operation of the horn, all lights, and the wipers and washers (Section 19)
☐ Carry out a road test (Section 20)

Every 37 500 miles or 3 years, whichever comes first
In addition to the items listed above, carry out the following:
☐ Renew the spark plugs (Section 21)
☐ Renew the air filter (Section 22)
☐ Check the braking system rubber hoses (Section 23)

Every 62 500 miles
In addition to the items listed above, carry out the following:
☐ Renew the timing belt and tensioner – 1.25 and 1.6 litre engines (Section 24)

Note: *Although the normal interval for timing belt renewal is 100 000 miles or 8 years, it is strongly recommended that the interval suggested above is observed, especially on cars which are subjected to intensive use, ie, mainly short journeys or a lot of stop-start driving. The actual belt renewal interval is very much up to the individual owner, but bear in mind that severe engine damage will result if the belt breaks.*

Every 100 000 miles or 8 years, whichever comes first
☐ Adjust the valve clearances (Section 25)
☐ Renew the auxiliary drivebelt – 1.25 and 1.6 litre engines (Section 26)
☐ Renew the timing belt, tensioner and idlers – 1.0 litre engines (Section 24)

Note: *Although the normal interval for timing belt renewal is 150 000 miles or 10 years, it is strongly recommended that the interval suggested above is observed, especially on cars which are subjected to intensive use, ie, mainly short journeys or a lot of stop-start driving. The actual belt renewal interval is very much up to the individual owner, but bear in mind that severe engine damage will result if the belt breaks.*

Every 2 years, regardless of mileage
☐ Renew the brake fluid (Section 27)
☐ Check the manual transmission oil level (Section 28)
☐ Renew the remote control battery (Section 29)

Every 150 000 miles or 10 years, whichever comes first
☐ Adjust the valve clearances – 1.0 litre engines (Section 25)
☐ Renew the auxiliary drivebelt – 1.0 litre engines (Section 26)

Every 2 years, regardless of mileage
☐ Renew the coolant (Section 30)

Note: *Ford state that, if their Super Plus antifreeze is in the system from new, the coolant need only be changed every 10 years. If there is any doubt as to the type or quality of the antifreeze which has been used, we recommend this shorter interval be observed.*

3 Component location – petrol models

Underbonnet view of a 1.0 litre EcoBoost model

1 Engine oil level dipstick
2 Engine oil filler cap
3 Coolant reservoir (expansion tank)
4 Brake and clutch fluid reservoir
5 Air cleaner
6 Battery
7 Fuse/relay box
8 Powertrain Control Module (PCM)
9 Ignition coils
10 Turbocharger
11 High-pressure fuel pump

Underbonnet view of a 1.6 litre model (1.25 litre similar)

1 Coolant reservoir (expansion tank)
2 Brake and clutch fluid reservoir
3 Timing belt upper cover
4 Engine oil filler cap
5 Ignition coil
6 Powertrain control module
7 Battery negative lead
8 Fuse/relay box
9 Windscreen washer fluid reservoir filler
10 Air cleaner
11 Inlet manifold
12 Engine oil level dipstick

Front underbody view

1 Brake caliper
2 Brake hose
3 Auxiliary drivebelt lower cover
4 Radiator bottom hose
5 Air conditioning compressor
6 Engine oil drain plug
7 Engine oil filter
8 Cooling fan
9 Gearchange cable front cover
10 Suspension lower arm
11 Oxygen sensor
12 Driveshaft
13 Subframe
14 Track rod end

Rear underbody view

1 Shock absorber
2 Fuel filler pipe
3 Rear coil spring
4 Rear suspension beam
5 Exhaust rear silencer
6 Fuel tank
7 Handbrake cable
8 Charcoal canister

4 General Information

1 This Chapter is designed to help the home mechanic maintain his/her car for safety, economy, long life and peak performance.

2 The Chapter contains a master maintenance schedule, followed by Sections dealing specifically with each task in the schedule. Visual checks, adjustments, component renewal and other helpful items are included. Refer to the accompanying illustrations of the engine compartment and the underside of the car for the locations of the various components.

3 Servicing your car in accordance with the mileage/time maintenance schedule and the following Sections will provide a planned maintenance programme, which should result in a long and reliable service life. This is a comprehensive plan, so maintaining some items but not others at the specified service intervals, will not produce the same results.

4 As you service your car, you will discover that many of the procedures can – and should – be grouped together, because of the particular procedure being performed, or because of the proximity of two otherwise-unrelated components to one another. For example, if the car is raised for any reason, the exhaust can be inspected at the same time as the suspension and steering components.

5 The first step in this maintenance programme is to prepare yourself before the actual work begins. Read through all the Sections relevant to the work to be carried out, then make a list and gather all the parts and tools required. If a problem is encountered, seek advice from a parts specialist, or a dealer service department.

5 Regular maintenance

1 If, from the time the car is new, the routine maintenance schedule is followed closely, and frequent checks are made of fluid levels and high-wear items, as suggested throughout this manual, the engine will be kept in relatively good running condition, and the need for additional work will be minimised.

2 It is possible that there will be times when the engine is running poorly due to the lack of regular maintenance. This is even more likely if a used car, which has not received regular and frequent maintenance checks, is purchased. In such cases, additional work may need to be carried out, outside of the regular maintenance intervals.

3 If engine wear is suspected, a compression test (refer to Chapter 2A Section 2 or Chapter 2B Section 2) will provide valuable information regarding the overall performance of the main internal components. Such a test can be used as a basis to decide on the extent of

6.3 Engine undershield fasteners

the work to be carried out. If, for example, a compression test indicates serious internal engine wear, conventional maintenance as described in this Chapter will not greatly improve the performance of the engine, and may prove a waste of time and money, unless extensive overhaul work is carried out first.

4 The following series of operations are those most often required to improve the performance of a generally poor-running engine:

Primary operations

a) *Clean, inspect and test the battery (refer to ' Weekly checks').*
b) *Check all the engine-related fluids (refer to ' Weekly checks').*
c) *Check the condition of all hoses, and check for fluid leaks (Section 8).*
d) *Check the condition of the auxiliary drivebelt (Section 9).*
e) *Renew the spark plugs (Section 21).*
f) *Check the condition of the air filter, and renew if necessary (Section 22).*

5 If the above operations do not prove fully effective, carry out the following secondary operations:

Secondary operations

6 All items listed under Primary operations, plus the following:

a) *Check the charging system (Chapter 5A Section 5).*
b) *Check the ignition system (Chapter 5B Section 2).*
c) *Check the fuel system (Chapter 4A Section 10).*

6.5a Slacken the oil drain plug on the back of the sump with a socket ...

6.4 Rotate the oil filler cap anti-clockwise and remove it

6 Engine oil and filter renewal – petrol models

1 Frequent oil and filter changes are the most important preventative maintenance procedures which can be undertaken by the DIY owner. As engine oil ages, it becomes diluted and contaminated, which leads to premature engine wear.

2 Before starting this procedure, gather together all the necessary tools and materials. Also make sure that you have plenty of clean rags and newspapers handy, to mop-up any spills. Ideally, the engine oil should be warm, as it will drain more easily, and more built-up sludge will be removed with it. Take care not to touch the exhaust or any other hot parts of the engine when working under the car. To avoid any possibility of scalding, and to protect yourself from possible skin irritants and other harmful contaminants in used engine oils, it is advisable to wear gloves when carrying out this work.

3 Firmly apply the handbrake, then jack up the front of the car and support it on axle stands (see *Jacking and vehicle support*). Undo the fasteners and remove the engine undershield (where fitted) **(see illustration)**.

4 Remove the oil filler cap **(see illustration)**.

5 Using a spanner, or preferably a socket and bar, slacken the drain plug about half a turn. Position the draining container under the drain plug, then remove the plug completely **(see illustrations)**.

6.5b ... then unscrew it by hand, and allow the oil to drain

6.7 On some engines, the seal is integral with the drain plug

6.8a Oil filter location – 1.0 litre engines...

6.8b ...1.25 and 1.6 litre engines

6 Allow some time for the oil to drain, noting that it may be necessary to reposition the container as the oil flow slows to a trickle.

7 After all the oil has drained, wipe the drain plug with a clean rag. Examine the condition of the drain plug sealing ring, and renew it if it shows signs of flattening or other damage which may prevent an oil-tight seal (it is generally considered good practice to fit a new seal every time). Note that on some engines the seal is integral with the drain plug **(see illustration)**. Clean the area around the drain plug opening, and refit the plug complete with the seal and tighten it to the specified torque.

8 Move the container into position under the oil filter, which is located at the rear of the engine block on 1.0 litre engines, and on the front of the cylinder block on 1.25 and 1.6 litre engines **(see illustrations)**.

9 Use an oil filter removal tool to slacken the filter initially, then unscrew it by hand the rest of the way **(see illustration)**. Empty the oil from the old filter into the container.

10 Use a clean rag to remove all oil, dirt and sludge from the filter sealing area on the engine.

11 Apply a light coating of clean engine oil to the sealing ring on the new filter, then screw the filter into position on the engine **(see illustration)**. Tighten the filter firmly by hand only – do not use any tools.

12 Remove the old oil and all tools from under the car, then lower the car to the ground.

13 Fill the engine through the filler hole, using the correct grade and type of oil (refer to Weekly checks0,5 for details of topping-up). Pour in half the specified quantity of oil first, then wait a few minutes for the oil to drain into the sump. Continue to add oil, a small quantity at a time, until the level is up to the lower mark on the dipstick. Adding approximately a further 0.5 to 1.0 litre will bring the level up to the upper mark on the dipstick.

14 Start the engine and run it for a few minutes, while checking for leaks around the oil filter seal and the sump drain plug. Note that there may be a delay of a few seconds before the oil pressure warning light goes out when the engine is first started, as the oil circulates through the new oil filter and the engine oil galleries before the pressure builds-up.

15 Stop the engine, and wait a few minutes for the oil to settle in the sump once more. With the new oil circulated and the filter now completely full, recheck the level on the dipstick, and add more oil as necessary.

16 Dispose of the used engine oil and filter safely, with reference to General repair procedures in the Reference chapter of this manual. Do not discard the old filter with domestic household waste. The facility for waste oil disposal provided by many local council refuse tips and/or recycling centres generally has a filter receptacle alongside.

Engine oil change warning light/display reset

17 With the oil and filter change completed, if necessary the Oil Change warning light/display can be reset as follows:

Vehicles up to 2013 model year

18 With the ignition turned off, press and hold down the accelerator and brake pedals at the same time. Disconnect the battery negative lead as described in Chapter. **Note:** *On models with push-button start, press and hold down the accelerator pedal only.*

19 Turn the ignition to the 'On' position. **Note:** On models with push-button start, press the Start/Stop button briefly, then whilst still depressing the accelerator pedal, press and hold down the brake pedal.

20 Hold down both pedals for at least 20 seconds.

21 Turn the ignition off, and release the pedals. Verify that the oil change warning is no longer displayed.

6.9 Use a filter removal tool to slacken the filter

6.11 Apply a light coating of engine oil to the sealing ring on the new filter

Vehicles from 2014 model year

22 Turn the ignition on without starting the engine. On models with a push-start button, press and hold the button for 2 seconds without pressing the brake pedal. This will turn the ignition on.

23 Press and hold down the accelerator and brake pedals at the same time.

24 After approximately 3 seconds, 'Service: Oil reset in Prog' is displayed.

25 Continue to hold down the pedals for approximately 25 seconds or until the display reads 'Service: Oil reset complete'.

26 Release the pedals and turn the ignition off.

7 Pollen filter renewal

1 Working in the footwell on the driver's side, unscrew the centre pin and extract the plastic rivet securing the inner trim panel to the base of the facia. Pull the panel away to release the three retaining clips at the rear and remove the trim panel **(see illustration)**.

2 Undo the retaining screws securing the base pollen filter housing cover to the side of the air distribution housing. Disengage and remove the cover from the housing **(see illustrations)**.

3 Slide out the pollen filter, into the driver's footwell, and remove it **(see illustration)**.

7.1 Unscrew the centre pin and pull out the rivet

7.2b ...and remove the cover

4 When fitting the new filter, note the direction-of-airflow arrow marked on its top edge – the arrow should point into the car.

5 Slide the filter fully into position, secure the cover with the retaining screws, then refit the facia inner trim panel.

8 Hose and fluid leak check

Note: *Also refer to Section 23.*

General

1 Visually inspect the engine joint faces, gaskets and seals for any signs of water or oil leaks. Pay particular attention to the areas around the cylinder head cover, cylinder head, oil filter and sump joint faces. Bear in mind that, over a period of time, some very slight seepage from these areas is to be expected – what you are really looking for is any indication of a serious leak. Should a leak be found, renew the offending gasket or oil seal by referring to the appropriate Chapters in this manual.

2 High temperatures in the engine compartment can cause the deterioration of the rubber and plastic hoses used for engine, accessory and emission systems operation. Periodic inspection should be made for cracks, loose clamps, material hardening and leaks.

7.2a Undo the retaining screws...

7.3 Slide out the pollen filter, into the driver's footwell, and remove it

3 When checking the hoses, ensure that all the cable-ties or clips used to retain the hoses are in place, and in good condition. Clips which are broken or missing can lead to chafing of the hoses, pipes or wiring, which could cause more serious problems in the future.

4 Carefully check the large top and bottom radiator hoses, along with the other smaller-diameter cooling system hoses and metal pipes; do not forget the heater hoses/pipes which run from the engine to the bulkhead. Inspect each hose along its entire length, renewing any that is cracked, swollen or shows signs of deterioration. Cracks may become more apparent if the hose is squeezed, and may often be apparent at the hose ends.

5 Make sure that all hose connections are tight. If the large-diameter air hoses from the air cleaner are loose, they will leak air, and upset the engine idle quality. If the spring clamps that are used to secure some of the hoses appear to be slackening, they should be updated with worm-drive clips to prevent the possibility of leaks.

6 Some other hoses are secured to their fittings with clamps. Where clamps are used, check to be sure they haven't lost their tension, allowing the hose to leak. If clamps aren't used, make sure the hose has not expanded and/or hardened where it slips over the fitting, allowing it to leak.

7 Check all fluid reservoirs, filler caps, drain plugs and fittings, etc, looking for any signs of leakage of oil, transmission and/or brake hydraulic fluid and coolant. Also check the clutch hydraulic fluid lines which lead from the fluid reservoir, master cylinder, and the slave cylinder (on the transmission).

8 If the vehicle is regularly parked in the same place, close inspection of the ground underneath it will soon show any leaks; ignore the puddle of water which will be left if the air conditioning system is in use. Place a clean piece of cardboard below the engine, and examine it for signs of contamination after the vehicle has been parked over it overnight – be aware, however, of the fire risk inherent in placing combustible material below the catalytic converter.

9 Remember that some leaks will only occur with the engine running, or when the engine is hot or cold. With the handbrake firmly applied, start the engine from cold, and let the engine idle while you examine the underside of the engine compartment for signs of leakage.

10 If an unusual smell is noticed inside or around the car, especially when the engine is thoroughly hot, this may point to the presence of a leak.

11 As soon as a leak is detected, its source must be traced and rectified. Where oil has been leaking for some time, it is usually necessary to use a steam cleaner, pressure washer or similar, to clean away the accumulated dirt, so that the exact source of the leak can be identified.

8.16 Check the security of the fuel hose where it joins the fuel rail

Vacuum hoses

12 It's quite common for vacuum hoses, especially those in the emissions system, to be colour-coded, or to be identified by coloured stripes moulded into them. Various systems require hoses with different wall thicknesses, collapse resistance and temperature resistance. When renewing hoses, be sure the new ones are made of the same material.

13 Often the only effective way to check a hose is to remove it completely from the vehicle. If more than one hose is removed, be sure to label the hoses and fittings to ensure correct installation.

14 When checking vacuum hoses, be sure to include any plastic T-fittings in the check. Inspect the fittings for cracks, and check the hose where it fits over the fitting for distortion, which could cause leakage.

15 A small piece of vacuum hose (approximately 6 mm inside diameter) can be used as a stethoscope to detect vacuum leaks. Hold one end of the hose to your ear, and probe around vacuum hoses and fittings, listening for the 'hissing' sound characteristic of a vacuum leak.

⚠️ *Warning: When probing with the vacuum hose stethoscope, be very careful not to come into contact with moving engine components such as the auxiliary drivebelt, radiator electric cooling fan, etc.*

Fuel hoses

⚠️ *Warning: There are certain precautions which must be taken when inspecting or servicing fuel system components. Work in a well-ventilated area, and do not allow open flames (cigarettes, appliance pilot lights, etc) or bare light bulbs near the work area. Mop-up any spills immediately, and do not store fuel-soaked rags where they could ignite.*

16 Check all fuel hoses for deterioration and chafing. Check especially for cracks in areas where the hose bends, and also just before fittings, such as where a hose attaches to the fuel rail **(see illustration)**.

17 High-quality fuel line, usually identified by the word 'Fluoroelastomer' printed on the hose, should be used for fuel line renewal. Never, under any circumstances, use non-reinforced vacuum line, clear plastic tubing or water hose as a substitute for fuel lines.

18 Spring-type clamps may be used on fuel lines. These clamps often lose their tension over a period of time, and can be 'sprung' during removal. Renew all spring-type clamps with proper petrol pipe clips whenever a hose is renewed.

Metal pipes

19 Sections of metal piping are often used for fuel line between the fuel tank and the engine, and for most air conditioning applications. Check carefully to be sure the piping has not been bent or crimped, and that cracks have not started in the line; also check for signs of excessive corrosion.

20 If a section of metal fuel line must be renewed, only seamless steel piping should be used, since copper and aluminium piping don't have the strength necessary to withstand normal engine vibration.

21 Check the metal lines where they enter the brake master cylinder, ABS hydraulic unit or clutch master/slave cylinders (as applicable) for cracks in the lines or loose fittings. Any sign of brake fluid leakage calls for an immediate and thorough inspection.

Air conditioning refrigerant

⚠️ *Warning: Refer to the safety information given in 'Safety first!' and Chapter 3, regarding the dangers of disturbing any of the air conditioning system components.*

22 The air conditioning system is filled with a liquid refrigerant, which is retained under high pressure. If the air conditioning system is opened and depressurised without the aid of specialised equipment, the refrigerant will immediately turn into gas and escape into the atmosphere. If the liquid comes into contact with your skin, it can cause severe frostbite. In addition, the refrigerant contains substances which are environmentally damaging; for this reason, it should not be allowed to escape into the atmosphere.

23 Any suspected air conditioning system leaks should be immediately referred to a Ford dealer or air conditioning specialist. Leakage will be shown up as a steady drop in the level of refrigerant in the system.

24 Note that water may drip from the condenser drain pipe, underneath the car, immediately after the air conditioning system has been in use. This is normal, and should not be cause for concern.

9 Auxiliary drivebelt check

1 A single auxiliary drivebelt is fitted at the right-hand side of the engine. The length of the drivebelt varies according to whether air conditioning is fitted. On 1.25 and 1.6 litre engines, a tensioner is not used – the belt is 'elastic' and self-tensioning.

2 Due to their function and material makeup, drivebelts are prone to failure after a long period of time, and should therefore be inspected regularly.

3 Since the drivebelt is located very close to the right-hand side of the engine compartment, it is possible to gain better access by raising the front of the car and removing the right-hand wheel. Undo the two screws and remove the drivebelt lower cover.

4 With the engine stopped, inspect the full length of the drivebelt for cracks and separation of the belt plies. It will be necessary to turn the engine (using a spanner or socket and bar on the crankshaft pulley bolt) in order to move the belt from the pulleys so that the belt can be inspected thoroughly. Twist the belt between the pulleys so that both sides can be viewed. Also check for fraying, and glazing which gives the belt a shiny appearance. Check the pulleys for nicks, cracks, distortion and corrosion.

5 Small cracks in the belt ribs are not usually serious, but look closely to see whether the crack has extended into the belt plies. If the belt is in any way suspect, or is known to have seen long service, renew it as described in Section 26.

6 On 1.25 and 1.6 litre engines, if the belt appears to be too slack (or has actually been slipping in service), this indicates that the 'elastic' belt is over-stretched – possibly as a result of incorrect fitting. Any slipping may also be due to external contamination of the belt (eg, by oil or water).

10 Seat belt check

1 Check the seat belts for satisfactory operation and condition. Pull sharply on the belt to check that the locking mechanism engages correctly. Inspect the webbing for fraying and cuts. Check that they retract smoothly and without binding into their reels.

2 Check the accessible seat belt mountings, ensuring that all bolts are securely tightened.

11 Front brake pad and disc wear check

1 Apply the handbrake, then jack up the front of the car and support it securely on axle stands (see *Jacking and vehicle support*). Remove the front roadwheels.

2 The brake pad thickness, and the condition of the disc, can be assessed roughly with just

11.2 With the wheel removed, the pad thickness can be seen through the front of the caliper

12.1a Check the outer constant velocity (CV) joint gaiters …

12.1b … and, though less prone to wear, check the inner gaiters too

the wheels removed **(see illustration)**. For a comprehensive check, the brake pads should be removed and cleaned. The operation of the caliper can then also be checked, and the condition of the brake disc itself can be fully examined on both sides. Refer to Chapter 9 for further information.

3 On completion, refit the roadwheels and lower the car to the ground.

12 Driveshaft gaiter check

1 With the car raised and securely supported on stands, turn the steering onto full lock, then slowly rotate the roadwheel. Inspect the condition of the outer constant velocity (CV) joint rubber gaiters while squeezing the gaiters to open out the folds. Check for signs of cracking, splits or deterioration of the rubber which may allow the grease to escape and lead to water and grit entry into the joint. Also check the security and condition of the retaining clips. Repeat these checks on the inner CV joints **(see illustrations)**. If any damage or deterioration is found, the gaiters should be renewed as described in Chapter 8.

2 At the same time, check the general condition of the CV joints themselves by first holding the driveshaft and attempting to rotate the wheel. Repeat this check by holding the inner joint and attempting to rotate the driveshaft. Any appreciable movement indicates wear in the joints, wear in the driveshaft splines, or a loose driveshaft retaining nut.

13 Steering and suspension check

Front suspension and steering

1 Raise the front of the car, and securely support it on axle stands (see *Jacking and vehicle support*).

2 Visually inspect the balljoint dust covers and the steering rack-and-pinion gaiters for splits, chafing or deterioration **(see illustration)**. Any wear of these components will cause loss of lubricant, together with dirt and water entry, resulting in rapid deterioration of the balljoints or steering gear.

3 Grasp the roadwheel at the 12 o'clock and 6 o'clock positions, and try to rock it **(see illustration)**. Very slight free play may be felt, but if the movement is appreciable, further

investigation is necessary to determine the source. Continue rocking the wheel while an assistant depresses the footbrake. If the movement is now eliminated or significantly reduced, it is likely that the hub bearings are at fault. If the free play is still evident with the footbrake depressed, then there is wear in the suspension joints or mountings.

4 Now grasp the wheel at the 9 o'clock and 3 o'clock positions, and try to rock it as before. Any movement felt now may again be caused by wear in the hub bearings or the steering track rod balljoints. If the outer balljoint is worn, the visual movement will be obvious. If the inner joint is suspect, it can be felt by placing a hand over the rack-and-pinion rubber gaiter and gripping the track rod. If the wheel is now rocked, movement will be felt at the inner joint if wear has taken place.

5 Using a large screwdriver or flat bar, check for wear in the suspension mounting bushes by levering between the relevant suspension component and its attachment point. Some movement is to be expected, as the mountings are made of rubber, but excessive wear should be obvious. Also check the condition of any visible rubber bushes, looking for splits, cracks or contamination of the rubber.

6 With the car standing on its wheels, have

13.2 Check the steering gaiters for signs of splitting

13.3 Check for wear in the front suspension and hub bearings

an assistant turn the steering wheel back-and-forth, about an eighth of a turn each way. There should be very little, if any, lost movement between the steering wheel and roadwheels. If this is not the case, closely observe the joints and mountings previously described. In addition, check the steering column universal joints for wear, and also check the rack-and-pinion steering gear itself.

Rear suspension

7 Chock the front wheels, then jack up the rear of the car and support securely on axle stands (see *Jacking and vehicle support*).
8 Working as described previously for the front suspension, check the rear hub bearings, the suspension bushes and the shock absorber mountings for wear.

Shock absorber

9 Check for any signs of fluid leakage around the shock absorber body, or from the rubber gaiter around the piston rod **(see illustration)**. Should any fluid be noticed, the shock absorber is defective internally, and should be renewed. Shock absorbers should always be renewed in pairs on the same axle.
10 The efficiency of the shock absorber may be checked by bouncing the car at each corner. Generally speaking, the body will return to its normal position and stop after being depressed. If it rises and returns on a rebound, the shock absorber is probably suspect. Also examine the shock absorber upper and lower mountings for any signs of wear.

14 Rear brake shoe and drum wear check

1 Remove the rear brake drums, and check the brake shoes for signs of wear or contamination. At the same time, also inspect the wheel cylinders for signs of leakage, and the brake drum for signs of wear. Refer to the relevant Sections of Chapter 9 for further information.

15 Handbrake check and adjustment

1 The handbrake should be fully applied (and capable of holding the car on a slope) after approximately three to five clicks of the ratchet. Should adjustment be necessary, refer to Chapter 9 Section 14 for the full adjustment procedure.

16 Exhaust system check

1 With the engine cold (at least three hours after the vehicle has been driven), check the complete exhaust system, from its starting

13.9 Check for signs of fluid leakage from the shock absorbers

point at the engine to the end of the tailpipe. Ideally, this should be done on a hoist, where unrestricted access is available; if a hoist is not available, raise and support the vehicle on axle stands (see *Jacking and vehicle support*).
2 Make sure that all brackets and rubber mountings are in good condition, and tight; if any of the mountings are to be renewed, ensure that the new ones are of the correct type – in the case of the rubber mountings, their colour is a good guide. Those nearest to the catalytic converter are more heat-resistant than the others **(see illustration)**.
3 Check the pipes and connections for evidence of leaks, severe corrosion, or damage. One of the most common points for a leak to develop is around the welded joints between the pipes and silencers. Leakage at any of the joints or in other parts of the system will usually show up as a black sooty stain in the vicinity of the leak. **Note:** *Exhaust sealants should not be used on any part of the exhaust system upstream of the catalytic converter (between the converter and engine) – even if the sealant does not contain additives harmful to the converter, pieces of it may break off and foul the element, causing local overheating.*
4 At the same time, inspect the underside of the body for holes, corrosion, open seams, etc, which may allow exhaust gases to enter the passenger compartment. Seal all body openings with silicone or body putty.
5 Rattles and other noises can often be traced to the exhaust system, especially the rubber mountings. Try to move the system, silencer(s), heat shields and catalytic

16.2 Check the condition of the exhaust rubber mountings

converter. If any components can touch the body or suspension parts, secure the exhaust system with new mountings.
6 Check the running condition of the engine by inspecting inside the end of the tailpipe; the exhaust deposits here are an indication of the engine's state of tune. The inside of the tailpipe should be dry, and should vary in colour from dark grey to light grey/brown; if it is black and sooty, or coated with white deposits, this may indicate the need for a full fuel system inspection.

17 Roadwheel nut tightness check

1 Remove the wheel trims or alloy wheel centre covers, and slacken the roadwheel nuts slightly.
2 Tighten the nuts to the specified torque, using a torque wrench.

18 Hinge and lock lubrication

1 Work around the car and lubricate the hinges of the bonnet, doors and tailgate with light oil.
2 Lightly lubricate the bonnet release mechanism with a smear of grease.
3 Check carefully the security and operation of all hinges, latches and locks, adjusting them where required. Check the operation of the central locking system.
4 Check the condition and operation of the tailgate struts, renewing them both if either is leaking or no longer able to support the tailgate securely when raised.

19 Electrical systems check

1 Check the operation of all the electrical equipment, ie, lights, direction indicators, horn, etc. Refer to the appropriate sections of Chapter for details if any of the circuits are found to be inoperative.
2 Check all accessible wiring connectors, harnesses and retaining clips for security, and for signs of chafing or damage. Rectify any faults found.

20 Road test

Instruments and electrical equipment

1 Check the operation of all instruments and electrical equipment.
2 Make sure that all instruments read correctly,

21.6a The ignition coils are located above the spark plugs

21.6b Slide out the clip and depress it to release the wiring plug

and switch on all electrical equipment in turn, to check that it functions properly.

Steering and suspension

3 Check for any abnormalities in the steering, suspension, handling or road 'feel'.
4 Drive the car, and check that there are no unusual vibrations or noises.
5 Check that the steering feels positive, with no excessive 'sloppiness', or roughness, and check for any suspension noises when cornering and driving over bumps.

Drivetrain

6 Check the performance of the engine, clutch, transmission and driveshafts.
7 Listen for any unusual noises from the engine, clutch and transmission.
8 Make sure that the engine runs smoothly when idling, and that there is no hesitation when accelerating.
9 Check that, where applicable, the clutch action is smooth and progressive, that the drive is taken up smoothly, and that the pedal travel is not excessive. Also listen for any noises when the clutch pedal is depressed.
10 Check that all gears can be engaged smoothly without noise, and that the gear lever action is smooth and not abnormally vague or 'notchy'.
11 Listen for a metallic clicking sound from the front of the car, as the car is driven slowly in a circle with the steering on full-lock. Carry out this check in both directions. If a clicking noise is heard, this indicates wear in a driveshaft joint (see Chapter 8 Section 4).

Braking system

12 Make sure that the car does not pull to one side when braking, and that the wheels do not lock prematurely when braking hard. They should not lock at all on models with ABS.
13 Check that there is no vibration through the steering when braking.
14 Check that the handbrake operates correctly, without excessive movement of the lever, and that it holds the car stationary on a slope.

21.6c Undo the retaining bolts and pull each coil straight upwards

15 Test the operation of the brake servo unit as follows. Depress the footbrake four or five times to exhaust the vacuum, then start the engine. As the engine starts, there should be a noticeable 'give' in the brake pedal as vacuum builds-up. Allow the engine to run for at least two minutes, and then switch it off. If the brake pedal is now depressed again, it should be possible to detect a hiss from the servo as the pedal is depressed. After about four or five applications, no further hissing should be heard, and the pedal should feel considerably harder.

21 Spark plug renewal and ignition system check – petrol models

Spark plug renewal

1 The correct functioning of the spark plugs is vital for the correct running and efficiency of the engine. It is essential that the plugs fitted are appropriate for the engine.
2 If the correct type is used and the engine is in good condition, the spark plugs should not need attention between scheduled intervals. Spark plug cleaning is rarely necessary, and should not be attempted unless specialised equipment is available, as damage can easily be caused to the firing ends.

21.7 Unscrew each spark plug carefully

3 Spark plug removal and refitting requires a spark plug socket, with an extension which can be turned by a ratchet handle or similar. This socket is lined with a rubber sleeve, to protect the porcelain insulator of the spark plug, and to hold the plug while you insert it into the spark plug hole. You may also need feeler blades and/or a spark plug gap checking gauge to check and adjust the spark plug electrode gap, and (ideally) a torque wrench to tighten the new plugs to the specified torque.
4 To remove the spark plugs, first open the bonnet; the plugs are easily reached at the top of the engine.

1.0 litre engines

5 Unscrew the oil filler cap, and pull the plastic cover on the top of the engine upwards from its' mountings (where fitted).
6 Release the clips, disconnect the wiring plugs, then undo the bolts and pull the ignition coils upwards from their locations above the spark plugs (see illustrations).
7 Unscrew the spark plugs, ensuring that the socket is kept in alignment with each plug – if the socket is forcibly moved to either side, the porcelain top of the plug may be broken off. Remove the plug from the engine (see illustration).

21.9 Pull the HT leads from the spark plugs by gripping the rubber boot

21.11 Unscrew the spark plugs using a suitable socket

21.15 Check the electrode gap with a set of feeler gauges

1.25 and 1.6 litre engines

8 Note how the spark plug (HT) leads are routed and secured by the clips on the cylinder head cover; unclip the leads as necessary, to provide enough slack in the lead. To prevent the possibility of mixing up spark plug (HT) leads, it is a good idea to try to work on one spark plug at a time.

9 If the marks on the original-equipment spark plug (HT) leads cannot be seen, mark the leads 1 to 4, to correspond to the cylinder the lead serves (No 1 cylinder is at the timing belt end of the engine). Pull the leads from the plugs by gripping the rubber boot sealing the cylinder head cover opening, not the lead, otherwise the lead connection may be fractured **(see illustration)**.

10 It is advisable to soak up any water in the spark plug recesses with a rag, and to remove any dirt from them using a clean brush, vacuum cleaner or compressed air before removing the plugs, to prevent any dirt or water from dropping into the cylinders.

 Warning: Wear eye protection when using compressed air.

11 Unscrew the spark plugs, ensuring that the socket is kept in alignment with each plug – if the socket is forcibly moved to either side, the porcelain top of the plug may be broken off **(see illustration)**. Remove the plug.

All engines

12 If any undue difficulty is encountered when unscrewing any of the spark plugs, carefully check the cylinder head threads and sealing surfaces for signs of wear, excessive corrosion or damage; if any of these conditions is found, seek the advice of a Ford dealer as to the best method of repair.

13 As each plug is removed, examine it as follows – this will give a good indication of the condition of the engine:

a) *If the insulator nose of the spark plug is clean and white, with no deposits, this is indicative of a weak mixture.*

b) *If the tip and insulator nose are covered with hard black-looking deposits, then this is indicative that the mixture is too rich.*

c) *Should the plug be black and oily, then it is likely that the engine is fairly worn, as well as the mixture being too rich.*

d) *If the insulator nose is covered with light tan to greyish-brown deposits, then the mixture is correct, and it is likely that the engine is in good condition.*

14 If you are renewing the spark plugs, purchase the new plugs, then check each of them first for faults such as cracked insulators or damaged threads. New plugs are supplied with a preset gap. Do not attempt to adjust the gap.

15 If the plugs were removed to inspect them, then the gap can be checked **(see illustration)**. If the gap is not as specified do not attempt to adjust the gap or clean the spark plug. If there is any doubt as to the condition of the spark plugs they should be replaced.

16 Before fitting the spark plugs, check that the threaded connector sleeves at the top of the plugs are tight (where fitted), and that the plug exterior surfaces and threads are clean. Brown staining on the porcelain, immediately above the metal body, is quite normal, and does not necessarily indicate a leak between the body and insulator.

17 On installing the spark plugs, first check that the cylinder head thread and sealing surface are as clean as possible; use a clean rag wrapped around a paintbrush to wipe clean the sealing surface. Apply a smear of copper-based grease or anti-seize compound to the threads of each plug, and screw them in by hand where possible. Take extra care to enter the plug threads correctly, as the cylinder head is made of aluminium alloy – it's often difficult to insert spark plugs into their holes without cross-threading them (see **Haynes Hint**).

18 When each spark plug is started correctly on its threads, screw it down until it just seats lightly, then tighten it to the specified torque wrench setting. If a torque wrench is not available – and this is one case where the use of a torque wrench is strongly recommended – tighten each spark plug through no more than 1/16th of a turn. Do not exceed the specified torque setting, and NEVER overtighten spark plugs.

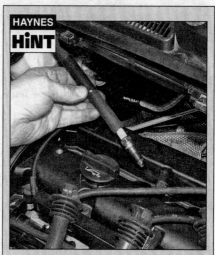

It's often difficult to insert spark plugs into their holes without cross-threading them. To avoid this possibility, fit a short length of rubber or plastic hose over the end of the spark plug. The flexible hose acts as a universal joint, to help align the plug with the plug hole. Should the plug begin to cross thread, the hose will slip on the spark plug, preventing thread damage to the aluminium cylinder head.

19 Refit the coils and tighten the retaining bolts to the specified torque or reconnect the HT leads (in their correct order), using a slight twisting motion as applicable.

22 Air filter element renewal – petrol models

Caution: Never drive the vehicle with the air cleaner filter element removed. Excessive engine wear could result, and backfiring could even cause a fire under the bonnet.

1 The air filter element is located in the air cleaner assembly on the left-hand side of the engine compartment.

22.2a Air cleaner housing cover screws – 1.0 litre engines

22.2b Remove the four bolts securing the cover to the air cleaner housing – 1.25 and 1.6 litre engines

2 Remove the four bolts securing the cover to the air cleaner housing **(see illustrations)**.

3 The cover can now be lifted, and the filter element removed **(see illustration)**.

4 If carrying out a routine service, the element must be renewed regardless of its apparent condition.

5 If you are checking the element for any other reason, inspect its lower surface; if it is oily or very dirty, renew the element. If it is only moderately dusty, it can be re-used by blowing it clean from the upper to the lower surface with compressed air. Because it is a pleated-paper type filter, it cannot be washed or re-oiled. If it cannot be cleaned satisfactorily with compressed air, discard and renew it.

 Warning: Wear eye protection when using compressed air.

23 Braking system rubber hose check

1 Position the car over an inspection pit, on car ramps, or jack it up one wheel at a time (see *Jacking and vehicle support*).

2 Inspect the braking system rubber hoses fitted to each front caliper, and on each side of the rear axle **(see illustration)**. Look for perished, swollen or hardened rubber, and any signs of cracking, especially at the metal end fittings. If there's any doubt as to the condition of any hose, renew it as described in Chapter 9.

24 Timing belt renewal

1 Refer to the procedures contained in Chapter 2A Section 8 (1.0 litre engines) or Chapter 2B Section 8 (1.25 and 1.6 litre engines).

25 Valve clearance check and adjustment – petrol models

1 Refer to the procedures contained in Chapter 2A Section 5 (1.0 litre engines) or Chapter 2B Section 5 (1.25 and 1.6 litre engines).

26 Auxiliary drivebelt renewal

Renewal

1 Firmly apply the handbrake, then jack up the front of the vehicle and support it securely on axle stands (see *Jacking and vehicle support*). Remove the right-hand front wheel.

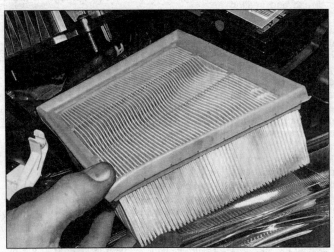

22.3 Lift up the cover and take out the filter element

23.2 Rubber brake hose fitted to the front caliper

26.2 Undo the bolts and remove the lower cover

1.0 litre engines

2 Undo the 2 bolts and remove the lower cover from the inner wheelarch (see illustration).

3 On models with 'Auto-Start-Stop', undo the 4 bolts and remove the auxiliary drivebelt cover (see illustration).

4 If the belt is to be refitted mark the direction of rotation on the belt.

5 Using a ratchet and short extension rotate the tensioner upwards (anti-clockwise) until it is possible to fit an 4 mm drill bit into the hole provided in the tensioner to lock the tensioner in position (see illustration).

6 Note the routing of the belt and then remove it (see illustration).

7 Fit the replacement belt and carefully release the tensioner sufficiently to remove the drill bit. With the drill bit removed slowly release the tensioner. Align the belt with all the pulleys and fully release the tensioner.

8 Using a suitable spanner or socket on the crankshaft pulley, rotate the engine twice in the normal (clockwise) direction, checking that the belt is correctly located on all the pulleys as the engine is rotated.

1.25 and 1.6 litre engines

Note: *No tensioner is fitted on these engines, so the only way to remove an old belt is to cut it off. Even if the old belt could be prised off without damaging it or the pulleys, a belt which has already been fitted has stretched, and may slip if re-used.*

9 Undo the two screws and remove the drivebelt lower cover (see illustrations).

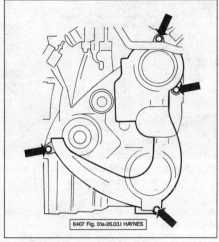

26.3 Auxiliary drivebelt cover bolts

10 Cut off the old drivebelt – take care that no damage is caused to surrounding components as this is done.

11 Due to the fitting method required for this unusual type of belt, it is essential that all the belt pulleys are as clean as possible before installing the new belt.

12 Wipe all the pulleys over with a suitable solvent, to ensure any traces of oil are removed. It's important that the new belt doesn't slip round the pulleys as it is stretched into place.

13 The fitting procedure for the 'elastic' drivebelt is quite lengthy, and involves the use of several plastic tools (which should be provided with a new, genuine Ford belt). Ford state that, if the fitting procedure is not followed, a new belt may suffer premature failure.

14 Using a dab of paint or typist's correction fluid, mark the crankshaft pulley at the 6 o'clock position. It doesn't matter where the engine is positioned (ie, relative to TDC) before starting.

15 Fit the first installation tool to the crankshaft pulley, fitted centrally on the pulley mark you just made (see illustration).

16 Fit the new belt around the alternator pulley, then the air conditioning pump pulley, the coolant pump pulley, and finally, around the plastic installation tool. Make sure the

26.5 Insert the short extension into the square hole, then rotate the tensioner anti-clockwise until a 4 mm drill bit can be inserted

26.6 Auxiliary drivebelt routing – 1.0 litre engines

1 Crankshaft pulley	3 Alternator
2 Air conditioning compressor or idle pulley	4 Coolant pump
	5 Tensioner
	6 Idler pulley

drivebelt is seated properly in the pulley grooves.

17 Turn the engine slowly in the normal direction of rotation (clockwise, as seen from the pulley itself). The engine should only be turned

26.9a Undo the screws …

26.9b … and take off the drivebelt lower cover

26.15 Fit the first installation tool, centrally on the pulley mark

26.18 The second tool fits round the belt and alternator mounting bracket

28.2 Unclip the plastic cover from the front of the transmission

28.3 Unscrew and remove the filler/level plug

so that the mark made earlier moves from the 6 o'clock to the 8 o'clock position. As the engine is turned, guide the belt onto the crankshaft pulley, with the help of the plastic tool.

18 Now fit the second plastic tool to the alternator mounting bracket. The tool clips round the bracket and the new belt, and keeps the belt on the pulley as it is stretched fully over the crankshaft pulley **(see illustration)**.

19 Start turning the engine slowly again, as before. Guide the belt gradually onto the crankshaft pulley, keeping an eye on the other pulleys as this is done. Make sure that the belt goes in to its grooves properly – 'help' it into place if necessary, using a blunt tool.

20 Once the pulley mark comes round to the 3 o'clock position, the belt should be fully fitted onto the crankshaft pulley, and the belt guide tools can be removed.

21 Turn the engine through a full 360°, and check that the belt is sitting correctly in the pulley grooves.

22 Refit the crankshaft pulley lower cover, then refit the roadwheel and lower the car to the ground.

27 Brake fluid renewal

Caution: Brake hydraulic fluid can harm your eyes and damage painted surfaces, so use extreme caution when handling and pouring it. Do not use fluid that has been standing open for some time, as it absorbs moisture from the air. Excess moisture can cause a dangerous loss of braking effectiveness.

1 The procedure is similar to that for bleeding the hydraulic system as described in Chapter 9 Section 2, except that allowance should be made for the old fluid to be expelled when bleeding each section of the circuit.

2 Working as described in Chapter 9 Section 2, open the first bleed screw in the sequence, and pump the brake pedal gently until the level in the reservoir is approaching the MIN mark. Top-up to the MAX level with new fluid, and continue pumping until only new fluid remains in the reservoir, and new fluid can be seen emerging from the bleed screw. Tighten

the screw, and top the reservoir level up to the MAX level line.

3 Work through all the remaining bleed screws in the sequence until new fluid can be seen at all of them. Be careful to keep the master cylinder reservoir topped-up above the MIN level at all times, or air may enter the system. If this happens, further bleeding will be required, to remove the air.

4 When the operation is complete, check that all bleed screws are securely tightened, and that their dust caps are refitted. Wash off all traces of spilt fluid, and recheck the master cylinder reservoir fluid level.

5 Check the operation of the brakes before taking the car on the road.

28 Manual transmission oil level check

1 Position the car over an inspection pit, on car ramps, or jack it up and support it on axle stands (see *Jacking and vehicle support*), but make sure that it is level.

2 Unclip the plastic cover fitted over the gearchange cables at the front of the transmission **(see illustration)**.

3 Remove all traces of dirt, then unscrew the filler/level plug from the front face of the transmission. This will probably be very tight, and a large Allen key or bit will be needed – access is made awkward by the plastic shroud around the gearchange cables **(see illustration)**.

4 The level must be just below the bottom edge of the filler/level plug hole (use a cranked tool such as an Allen key to check the level). If necessary, top-up the level with the specified grade of oil (see Lubricants and fluids0,6) until the oil just starts to run out. Allow any excess oil to flow out until the level stabilises **(see illustrations)**.

5 When the level is correct, clean and refit the filler/level plug (check the condition of the O-ring seal, and renew if necessary), then tighten it to the specified torque.

6 Lower the car to the ground.

29 Remote control battery renewal – petrol models

Note: *All the remote control units described below are fitted with a type CR 2032, 3 volt battery.*

1 Although not in the Ford maintenance schedule, we recommend that the battery is changed every 2 years, regardless of the vehicle's mileage. However, if the door locks repeatedly fail to respond to signals from the remote control at the normal distance, change the battery in the remote control before attempting to troubleshoot any of the vehicle's other systems.

Control with a folding key

2 Insert a small flat-bladed screwdriver fully into the slot on the side of the transmitter unit,

28.4a Top-up the oil level …

28.4b … then allow any excess to flow out before refitting the plug

29.2a Insert a small screwdriver into the slot on the side of the transmitter unit ...

29.2b ... then push the screwdriver towards the key blade and remove the key blade

29.3 Insert the screwdriver at the side and front of the transmitter unit to separate the two halves

push the screwdriver towards the key blade and remove the key blade **(see illustrations)**.

3 Use the screwdriver, inserted at the side and front of the transmitter unit, to separate the two halves of the unit **(see illustration)**.

4 Note the fitted position of the battery (positive side down), then prise the battery from its location, and insert the new one **(see illustration)**. Avoid touching the battery or the terminals with bare fingers.

5 Snap the two halves of the transmitter together, and re-attach it to the key blade.

Control without a folding key

6 Depress the two tabs on the side of the transmitter unit and carefully lift off the cover.

7 Remove the key blade from the transmitter unit.

8 Use a small flat-bladed the screwdriver, inserted at the side of the transmitter unit, to separate the two halves of the unit.

9 Note the fitted position of the battery (positive side down), then prise the battery from its location, and insert the new one. Avoid touching the battery or the terminals with bare fingers.

10 Snap the two halves of the transmitter together, place the key blade in position and refit the cover.

---

30 Coolant strength check and renewal

⚠️ *Warning: Do not allow antifreeze to come in contact with your skin or painted surfaces of the vehicle. Flush contaminated areas immediately with plenty of water. Don't store new coolant, or leave old coolant lying around, where it's accessible to children or pets – they're attracted by its sweet smell. Ingestion of even a small amount of coolant can be fatal. Wipe up garage-floor and drip-pan spills immediately. Keep antifreeze containers covered, and repair cooling system leaks as soon as they're noticed.*

⚠️ *Warning: Never remove the expansion tank filler cap when the engine is running, or has just been switched off, as the cooling*

system will be hot, and the consequent escaping steam and scalding coolant could cause serious injury.*

⚠️ *Warning: Wait until the engine is cold before starting these procedures.*

Strength check

1 Use a hydrometer to check the strength of the antifreeze. Follow the instructions provided with your hydrometer. The antifreeze strength should be approximately 50%. If it is significantly less than this, drain a little coolant from the radiator (see this Section), add antifreeze to the coolant expansion tank, then recheck the strength.

Coolant draining

2 To drain the system, first remove the expansion tank filler cap.

3 Firmly apply the handbrake, then jack up the front of the vehicle and support it securely on axle stands (see *Jacking and vehicle support*). Where applicable, release the fasteners and remove the engine undershield.

4 Place a suitable container beneath the right-hand side of the radiator.

5 Release the retaining clamp and disconnect the bottom hose from the radiator **(see illustration)**. Allow the coolant to drain into the container.

6 Once the coolant has stopped draining from the radiator, reconnect the bottom hose and secure with the retaining clamp.

System flushing

7 With time, the cooling system may

29.4 Note the fitted position of the battery, then prise it out and insert the new one

gradually lose its efficiency, as the radiator core becomes choked with rust, scale deposits from the water, and other sediment. To minimise this, as well as using only good-quality antifreeze and clean soft water, the system should be flushed as follows whenever any part of it is disturbed, and/or when the coolant is renewed.

8 With the coolant drained, refit the radiator bottom hose and refill the system with fresh water. Refit the expansion tank filler cap, start the engine and warm it up to normal operating temperature, then stop it and (after allowing it to cool down completely) drain the system again. Repeat as necessary until only clean water can be seen to emerge, then refill finally with the specified coolant mixture.

9 If only clean, soft water and good-quality antifreeze (even if not to Ford's specification) has been used, and the coolant has been renewed at the suggested intervals, the above procedure will be sufficient to keep the system clean for a considerable length of time. If, however, the system has been neglected, a more thorough operation will be required, as follows.

10 First drain the coolant, then disconnect the radiator top hose. Insert a garden hose into the radiator top hose connection, and allow water to circulate through the radiator until it runs clean from the bottom outlet.

11 To flush the engine, insert the garden hose into the radiator bottom hose, wrap a piece of rag around the garden hose to seal the connection, and allow water to circulate until it runs clear.

12 Try the effect of repeating this procedure in the top hose, although this may not be

30.5 Release the clamp and disconnect the bottom hose

effective, since the thermostat will probably close and prevent the flow of water.

13 In severe cases of contamination, reverse-flushing of the radiator may be necessary. This may be achieved by inserting the garden hose into the bottom outlet, wrapping a piece of rag around the hose to seal the connection, then flushing the radiator until clear water emerges from the top hose outlet.

14 If the radiator is suspected of being severely choked, remove the radiator (Chapter 3 Section 3), turn it upside-down, and repeat the procedure described in paragraph 13.

15 Flushing the heater matrix can be achieved using a similar procedure to that described in paragraph 13, once the heater inlet and outlet hoses have been identified. These two hoses will be of the same diameter, and pass through the engine compartment bulkhead (refer to the procedures contained in Chapter 3 for more details).

16 The use of chemical cleaners is not recommended, and should be necessary only as a last resort; the scouring action of some chemical cleaners may lead to other cooling system problems. Normally, regular renewal of the coolant will prevent excessive contamination of the system.

Coolant filling

17 With the cooling system drained and flushed, ensure that all disturbed hose unions are correctly secured. If it was raised, lower the vehicle to the ground.

18 Set the heater temperature control to maximum heat, but ensure the blower is turned off.

19 Prepare a sufficient quantity of the specified coolant mixture (see below); allow for a surplus, so as to have a reserve supply for topping-up.

20 Slowly fill the system through the expansion tank. Since the tank is the highest point in the system, all the air in the system should be displaced into the tank by the rising liquid. Slow pouring reduces the possibility of air being trapped and forming airlocks.

21 Continue filling until the coolant level reaches the expansion tank MAX level line (see *Weekly checks*), then refit the filler cap.

22 Start the engine and run it at 2500 rpm for 15 minutes. If the level in the expansion tank drops significantly, top-up to the MAX level line, to minimise the amount of air circulating in the system.

23 Increase the engine speed to 5000 rpm, then allow it to return to idle. Repeat this sequence 6 times.

24 Increase the engine speed to 4000 rpm, maintain this speed for 10 seconds, then reduce the engine speed to 2500 rpm and maintain this speed for 10 minutes.

25 Stop the engine, then leave the car to cool down completely (overnight, if possible).

26 With the system cool, open the expansion tank, and top-up the tank to the MAX level line. Refit the filler cap, tightening it securely, and clean up any spillage.

27 After refilling, always check carefully all components of the system (but especially any unions disturbed during draining and flushing) for signs of coolant leaks. Fresh antifreeze has a searching action, which will rapidly expose any weak points in the system.

Antifreeze type and mixture

Caution: Do not use engine antifreeze in the windscreen/tailgate washer system, as it will damage the vehicle's paintwork. A screenwash additive should be added to the washer system in its maker's recommended quantities.

28 If the vehicle's history (and therefore the quality of the antifreeze in it) is unknown, owners are advised to drain and thoroughly reverse-flush the system, before refilling with fresh coolant mixture.

29 If the antifreeze used is to Ford's specification, the levels of protection it affords are indicated in the coolant packaging.

30 To give the recommended standard mixture ratio for antifreeze, 50% (by volume) of antifreeze must be mixed with 50% of clean, soft water; if you are using any other type of antifreeze, follow its manufacturer's instructions to achieve the correct ratio.

31 You are unlikely to fully drain the system at any one time (unless the engine is being completely stripped), and the capacities quoted in the Specifications are therefore slightly academic for routine coolant renewal. As a guide, only two-thirds of the system's total capacity is likely to be needed for coolant renewal.

32 As the drained system will be partially filled with flushing water, in order to establish the recommended mixture ratio, measure out 50% of the system capacity in antifreeze and pour it into the hose/expansion tank as described above, then top-up with water. Any topping-up while refilling the system should be done with water – for Weekly checks0,5 use a suitable mixture.

33 Before adding antifreeze, the cooling system should be drained, preferably flushed, and all hoses checked for condition and security. As noted earlier, fresh antifreeze will rapidly find any weaknesses in the system.

34 After filling with antifreeze, a label should be attached to the expansion tank, stating the type and concentration of antifreeze used, and the date installed. Any subsequent topping-up should be made with the same type and concentration of antifreeze.

General cooling system checks

35 The engine should be cold for the cooling system checks, so perform the following procedure before driving the vehicle, or after it has been shut off for at least three hours.

36 Remove the expansion tank filler cap, and clean it thoroughly inside and out with a rag. Also clean the filler neck on the expansion tank. The presence of rust or corrosion in the filler neck indicates that the coolant should be changed. The coolant inside the expansion tank should be relatively clean and transparent.

If it is rust-coloured, drain and flush the system, and refill with a fresh coolant mixture.

37 Carefully check the radiator hoses and heater hoses along their entire length; renew any hose which is cracked, swollen or deteriorated.

38 Inspect all other cooling system components (joint faces, etc) for leaks. A leak in the cooling system will usually show up as white- or antifreeze-coloured deposits on the area adjoining the leak. Where any problems of this nature are found on system components, renew the component or gasket with reference to Chapter 3.

Airlocks

39 If, after draining and refilling the system, symptoms of overheating are found which did not occur previously, then the fault is almost certainly due to trapped air at some point in the system, causing an airlock and restricting the flow of coolant; usually, the air is trapped because the system was refilled too quickly.

40 If an airlock is suspected, first try gently squeezing all visible coolant hoses. A coolant hose which is full of air feels quite different to one full of coolant when squeezed. After refilling the system, most airlocks will clear once the system has cooled, and been topped-up.

41 While the engine is running at operating temperature, switch on the heater and heater fan, and check for heat output. Provided there is sufficient coolant in the system, lack of heat output could be due to an airlock in the system.

42 Airlocks can have more serious effects than simply reducing heater output – a severe airlock could reduce coolant flow around the engine. Check that the radiator top hose is hot when the engine is at operating temperature – a top hose which stays cold could be the result of an airlock (or a non-opening thermostat).

43 If the problem persists, stop the engine and allow it to cool down completely, before unscrewing the expansion tank filler cap or loosening the hose clips and squeezing the hoses to bleed out the trapped air. In the worst case, the system will have to be at least partially drained (this time, the coolant can be saved for re-use) and flushed to clear the problem. If all else fails, have the system evacuated and vacuum filled by a suitably-equipped garage.

Expansion tank cap check

44 Wait until the engine is completely cold – perform this check before the engine is started for the first time in the day.

45 Place a wad of cloth over the expansion tank cap, then unscrew it slowly and remove it.

46 Examine the condition of the rubber seal on the underside of the cap. If the rubber appears to have hardened, or cracks are visible in the seal edges, a new cap should be fitted.

47 If the car is several years old, or has covered a large mileage, consider renewing the cap regardless of its apparent condition – they are not expensive. If the pressure relief valve built into the cap fails, excess pressure in the system will lead to puzzling failures of hoses and other cooling system components.

Chapter 1B
Routine maintenance and servicing – diesel models

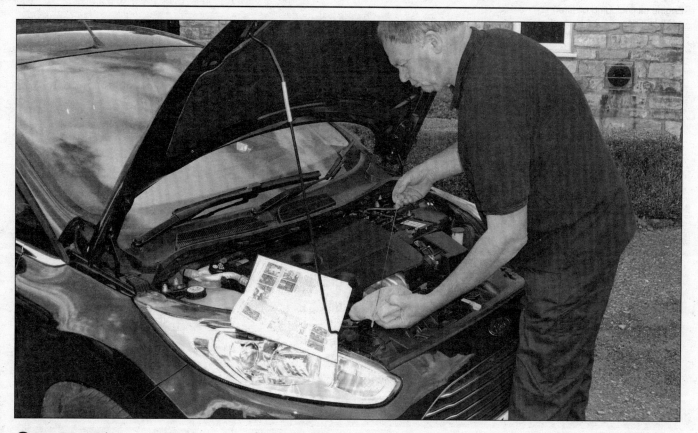

Contents

Degrees of difficulty

| Easy, suitable for novice with little experience | Fairly easy, suitable for beginner with some experience | Fairly difficult, suitable for competent DIY mechanic | Difficult, suitable for experienced DIY mechanic | Very difficult, suitable for expert DIY or professional |

1 Servicing specifications – diesel models

Lubricants and fluids... Refer to *Weekly checks*

Capacities

Engine oil (including oil filter)
   All engines .... 3.9 litres
Cooling system (approximate)
   All models... 6.1 litres
Manual transmission
   All models... 2.3 litres
Washer fluid reservoir
   All models... 2.5 litres
Fuel tank
   All models... 42.0 litres

Cooling system

Antifreeze mixture:
   50% antifreeze .... Protection down to -37°C
Note: Refer to antifreeze manufacturer for latest recommendations.

Brakes

Friction material minimum thickness:
   Front brake pads .... 1.5 mm
   Rear brake shoes .... 1.0 mm

Remote control battery

Type CR2032, 3V

Torque wrench settings

	Nm	lbf ft
Engine oil drain plug...	35	25
Engine oil filter cover	25	18
Manual transmission filler/level plug	35	26
Roadwheel nuts	135	100

2 Maintenance schedule – diesel models

1 The maintenance intervals in this manual are provided with the assumption that you, not the dealer, will be carrying out the work. These are the minimum maintenance intervals based on the standard service schedule recommended by the manufacturer for vehicles driven daily. If you wish to keep your vehicle in peak condition at all times, you may wish to perform some of these procedures more often. We encourage frequent maintenance, because it enhances the efficiency, performance and resale value of your vehicle.

2 If the vehicle is driven in dusty areas, used to tow a trailer, or driven frequently at slow speeds (idling in traffic) or on short journeys, more frequent maintenance intervals are recommended.

3 When the vehicle is new, it should be serviced by a dealer service department (or other workshop recognised by the vehicle manufacturer as providing the same standard of service) in order to preserve the warranty. The vehicle manufacturer may reject warranty claims if you are unable to prove that servicing has been carried out as and when specified, using only original equipment parts or parts certified to be of equivalent quality.

Every 250 miles or weekly
- [ ] Refer to *Weekly checks*

Every 6000 miles or 6 months, whichever comes first
- [ ] Renew the engine oil and filter (Section 6)

Note: *Ford recommend that the engine oil and filter are changed every 12 500 miles or 12 months. However, oil and filter changes are good for the engine, and we recommend that the oil and filter are renewed more frequently, especially if the car is used on a lot of short journeys.*

Every 12 500 miles or 12 months, whichever comes first
In addition to the items listed above, carry out the following:
- [ ] Renew the pollen filter, where applicable (Section 7)
- [ ] Drain any water from the fuel filter (Section 8)
- [ ] Check all components, pipes and hoses for fluid leaks (Section 9)
- [ ] Check the condition of the auxiliary drivebelt (Section 10)
- [ ] Check the antifreeze/inhibitor strength (Section 30)
- [ ] Check the condition and operation of the seat belts (Section 11)
- [ ] Check the front brake pads and discs for wear (Section 12)
- [ ] Check the condition of the driveshaft gaiters (Section 13)
- [ ] Check the steering and suspension components for condition and security (Section 14)
- [ ] Check the rear brake shoes and drums for wear (Section 15)

Every 12 500 miles or 12 months, whichever comes first (continued)
- [ ] Check and if necessary adjust the handbrake (Section 16)
- [ ] Check the condition of the exhaust system components (Section 17)
- [ ] Check the roadwheel nuts are tightened to the specified torque (Section 18)
- [ ] Lubricate all door, bonnet and tailgate hinges and locks (Section 19)
- [ ] Check the operation of the horn, all lights, and the wipers and washers (Section 20)
- [ ] Carry out a road test (Section 21)

Every 37 500 miles or 3 years, whichever comes first
In addition to the items listed above, carry out the following:
- [ ] Renew the fuel filter (Section 22)
- [ ] Renew the air filter (Section 23)
- [ ] Check the braking system rubber hoses (Section 24)

Every 56 250 miles
In addition to the items listed above, carry out the following:
- [ ] Renew the timing belt and tensioner (Section 25)

Note: *Although the normal interval for timing belt renewal is 112 500 miles or 10 years, it is strongly recommended that the interval suggested above is observed, especially on cars which are subjected to intensive use, ie, mainly short journeys or a lot of stop-start driving. The actual belt renewal interval is very much up to the individual owner, but bear in mind that severe engine damage will result if the belt breaks.*

Every 112 500 miles or 10 years, whichever comes first
- [ ] Renew the auxiliary drivebelt (Section 26)

Every 2 years, regardless of mileage
- [ ] Renew the brake fluid (Section 27)
- [ ] Check the manual transmission oil level (Section 28)
- [ ] Renew the remote control battery (Section 29)
- [ ] Renew the coolant (Section 30)

Note: *Ford state that, if their Super Plus antifreeze is in the system from new, the coolant need only be changed every 10 years. If there is any doubt as to the type or quality of the antifreeze which has been used, we recommend this shorter interval be observed.*

3 Component location – diesel models

Underbonnet view of a 1.5 litre model

1 Coolant reservoir (expansion tank)
2 Brake and clutch fluid reservoir
3 Engine oil filler cap
4 Air cleaner
5 Fuel filter
6 Powertrain control module
7 Battery negative lead
8 Fuse/relay box
9 Windscreen washer fluid reservoir filler
10 Airflow sensor
11 Turbocharger
12 Engine oil level dipstick

Underbonnet view of a 1.6 litre model

1 Engine oil filler cap
2 Engine oil level dipstick
3 Coolant reservoir (expansion tank)
4 Brake and clutch fluid reservoir
5 Fuel filter
6 Powertrain control module
7 Battery negative lead
8 Fuse/relay box
9 Windscreen washer fluid reservoir filler
10 Air cleaner
11 Airflow sensor
12 Turbocharger

Front underbody view

1 Brake caliper
2 Auxiliary drivebelt lower cover
3 Air conditioning compressor
4 Intercooler (1.6 litre only)
5 Engine oil drain plug
6 Exhaust system
7 Radiator bottom hose
8 Gearchange cable front cover
9 Suspension lower arm
10 Driveshaft
11 Subframe
12 Track rod end

Rear underbody view

1 Shock absorber
2 Fuel filler pipe
3 Rear coil spring
4 Rear suspension beam
5 Exhaust rear silencer
6 Fuel tank
7 Handbrake cable

4 General Information

1 This Chapter is designed to help the home mechanic maintain his/her car for safety, economy, long life and peak performance.

2 The Chapter contains a master maintenance schedule, followed by Sections dealing specifically with each task in the schedule. Visual checks, adjustments, component renewal and other helpful items are included. Refer to the accompanying illustrations of the engine compartment and the underside of the car for the locations of the various components.

3 Servicing your car in accordance with the mileage/time maintenance schedule and the following Sections will provide a planned maintenance programme, which should result in a long and reliable service life. This is a comprehensive plan, so maintaining some items but not others at the specified service intervals, will not produce the same results.

4 As you service your car, you will discover that many of the procedures can – and should – be grouped together, because of the particular procedure being performed, or because of the proximity of two otherwise-unrelated components to one another. For example, if the car is raised for any reason, the exhaust can be inspected at the same time as the suspension and steering components.

5 The first step in this maintenance programme is to prepare yourself before the actual work begins. Read through all the Sections relevant to the work to be carried out, then make a list and gather all the parts and tools required. If a problem is encountered, seek advice from a parts specialist, or a dealer service department.

5 Regular maintenance

1 If, from the time the car is new, the routine maintenance schedule is followed closely, and frequent checks are made of fluid levels and high-wear items, as suggested throughout this manual, the engine will be kept in relatively good running condition, and the need for additional work will be minimised.

2 It is possible that there will be times when the engine is running poorly due to the lack of regular maintenance. This is even more likely if a used car, which has not received regular and frequent maintenance checks, is purchased. In such cases, additional work may need to be carried out, outside of the regular maintenance intervals.

3 If engine wear is suspected, a compression test or leakdown test (refer to Chapter 2C Section 2 or Chapter 2D Section 2) will provide valuable information regarding the overall performance of the main internal components. Such a test can be used as a basis to decide on the extent of the work to be carried out. If, for example, the test indicates serious internal engine wear, conventional maintenance as described in this Chapter will not greatly improve the performance of the engine, and may prove a waste of time and money, unless extensive overhaul work is carried out first.

4 The following series of operations are those most often required to improve the performance of a generally poor-running engine:

Primary operations

a) Clean, inspect and test the battery (refer to Weekly checks).
b) Check all the engine-related fluids (refer to Weekly checks).
c) Check the condition of all hoses, and check for fluid leaks (Section 9).
d) Check the condition of the auxiliary drivebelt (Section 10).
e) Renew the fuel filter (Section 22).
f) Check the condition of the air filter, and renew if necessary (Section 23).

5 If the above operations do not prove fully effective, carry out the following secondary operations:

Secondary operations

6 All items listed under Primary operations, plus the following:
a) Check the charging system (Chapter 5A Section 5).
b) Check the preheating system (Chapter 5A Section 11).
c) Check the fuel system (Chapter 4B Section 12).

6 Engine oil and filter renewal – diesel models

1 Frequent oil and filter changes are the most important preventative maintenance procedures which can be undertaken by the DIY owner. As engine oil ages, it becomes diluted and contaminated, which leads to premature engine wear.

2 Before starting this procedure, gather together all the necessary tools and materials. Also make sure that you have plenty of clean rags and newspapers handy, to mop-up any spills. Ideally, the engine oil should be warm, as it will drain better, and more built-up sludge will be removed with it. Take care, however, not to touch the exhaust or any other hot parts of the engine when working under the vehicle. To avoid any possibility of scalding, and to protect yourself from possible skin irritants and other harmful contaminants in used engine oils, it is advisable to wear gloves when carrying out this work.

3 Firmly apply the handbrake, then jack up the front of the car and support it on axle stands (see Jacking and vehicle support).

4 Undo the retaining bolts and remove the engine undertray (where fitted) (see illustration).

5 Slacken the drain plug about half a turn, position the draining container under the drain plug, then remove the plug completely (see illustration). If possible, try to keep the plug pressed into the sump while unscrewing it by hand the last couple of turns (see Haynes Hint). Recover the sealing ring from the drain plug.

6 Allow some time for the old oil to drain, noting that it may be necessary to reposition the container as the oil flow slows to a trickle.

7 After all the oil has drained, wipe off the drain plug with a clean rag, and fit a new

HAYNES HINT

As the drain plug releases from the threads, move it away sharply so the stream of oil issuing from the sump runs into the container, not up your sleeve.

6.4 Engine undertray retaining bolts

6.5 Unscrew the drain plug from the base of the sump

6.7 Renew the drain plug sealing washer

6.9a Use a 27 mm socket to slacken the filter cover…

6.9b …then remove it along with the filter element

sealing washer **(see illustration)**. Clean the area around the drain plug opening, and refit the plug. Tighten the plug to the specified torque.

Note: *On some engines, the seal is integral with the sump drain plug. On these engines, the sump plug should be renewed every time the oil is drained.*

8 If the filter is also to be renewed, move the container into position under the oil filter, which is located on the front side of the cylinder block.

9 The filter element is contained within a filter cover. Using a 27 mm socket or spanner, slacken and remove the filter cover from above **(see illustrations)**. Be prepared for oil spillage, and recover the O-ring seal from the cover. If improved access to the filter is required, remove the air filter housing as described in Chapter 4B Section 4.

10 Pull the filter element from the filter housing.

11 Use a clean rag to remove all oil, dirt and sludge from the inside and outside of the filter cover.

12 Fit the new O-ring to the filter cover, then insert the new filter element into the housing, ensuring that the element locating peg engages correctly with the corresponding hole in the housing **(see illustrations)**.

13 Apply a little clean engine oil to the O-ring seal, then refit the filter/cover to the housing and tighten the cover to the specified torque.

14 Remove the old oil and all tools from under the car, refit the engine undertray (where applicable), then lower the car to the ground.

15 Remove the dipstick, then unscrew the oil filler cap. Fill the engine, using the correct grade and type of oil (see *Lubricants and fluids*). An oil can spout or funnel may help to reduce spillage **(see illustrations)**. Pour in half the specified quantity of oil first, then wait a few minutes for the oil to run to the sump. Continue adding oil a small quantity at a time until the level is up to the lower mark on the dipstick. Adding approximately 1.0 litre will bring the level up to the upper mark on the dipstick. Refit the filler cap.

16 Start the engine and run it for a few minutes; check for leaks around the oil filter seal and the sump drain plug. Note that there

may be a delay of a few seconds before the oil pressure warning light goes out when the engine is first started, as the oil circulates through the engine oil galleries and the new oil filter (where fitted) before the pressure builds-up.

17 Switch off the engine, and wait a few minutes for the oil to settle in the sump once more. With the new oil circulated and the filter completely full, recheck the level on the dipstick, and add more oil as necessary.

18 Dispose of the used engine oil and filter safely, with reference to General repair procedures in the Reference chapter of this manual. Do not discard the old filter with domestic household waste. The facility for waste oil disposal provided by many local council refuse tips and/or recycling centres generally has a filter receptacle alongside.

Engine oil change warning light/ display reset

19 With the oil and filter change completed, if necessary the Oil Change warning light/ display can be reset as follows:

Vehicles up to 2013 model year

20 With the ignition turned off, press and hold down the accelerator and brake pedals at the same time. Disconnect the battery negative lead as described in Chapter. **Note:** *On models with push-button start, press and hold down the accelerator pedal only.*

21 Turn the ignition to the 'On' position. Note: On models with push-button start, press the Start/Stop button briefly, then whilst still depressing the accelerator pedal, press and hold down the brake pedal.

22 Hold down both pedals for at least 20 seconds.

6.12a Fit the new O-ring to the cover

6.12b Ensure the filter locating peg locates into the corresponding hole in the housing

6.15a Remove the oil filler cap …

6.15b … and add the engine oil

7.1 Unscrew the centre pin and pull out the rivet

7.2a Undo the retaining screws…

7.2b … and take off the pollen filter housing cover

23 Turn the ignition off, and release the pedals. Verify that the oil change warning is no longer displayed.

Vehicles from 2014 model year

24 Turn the ignition on without starting the engine. On models with a push-start button, press and hold the button for 2 seconds without pressing the brake pedal. This will turn the ignition on.

25 Press and hold down the accelerator and brake pedals at the same time.

26 After approximately 3 seconds, 'Service: Oil reset in Prog' is displayed.

27 Continue to hold down the pedals for approximately 25 seconds or until the display reads 'Service: Oil reset complete'.

28 Release the pedals and turn the ignition off.

7 Pollen filter renewal

1 Working in the footwell on the driver's side, unscrew the centre pin and extract the plastic rivet securing the inner trim panel to the base of the facia. Pull the panel away to release the three retaining clips at the rear and remove the trim panel **(see illustration)**.

2 Undo the retaining screws securing the base pollen filter housing cover to the side of the air distribution housing. Disengage and remove the cover from the housing**(see illustrations)**.

3 Slide out the pollen filter, into the driver's footwell, and remove it **(see illustration)**.

7.3 Slide out the pollen filter, into the driver's footwell, and remove it

4 When fitting the new filter, note the direction-of-airflow arrow marked on its top edge – the arrow should point into the car.

5 Slide the filter fully into position, secure the cover with the retaining screws, then refit the facia inner trim panel.

8 Fuel filter water draining – diesel models

Note: *Various types of fuel filters are fitted to these engines depending on model year and territory. The following procedures depict a typical example. Not all filters are fitted with a drain facility.*

1 The fuel filter is located at the rear of the engine compartment between the air cleaner housing and the battery.

2 Pull up the plastic cover from the top of the engine.

3 A drain pipe is attached to the underside of the filter housing, which exits at the back of the engine. To prevent fuel spillage, position a suitable container under the back of the engine, on the left-hand side.

4 Rotate the centre fitting on the top of the filter clockwise slightly and lift it **(see illustration)**. This opens the drain tap, and allows the fuel/water to drain from the filter. As soon as water-free fuel emerges from the pipe, press down the fitting and rotate it anti-clockwise to secure it.

5 Start the engine. If difficulty is experienced, bleed the fuel system (Chapter 4B Section 3).

8.4 Rotate the centre fitting clockwise and lift it

9 Hose and fluid leak check

Note: *Also refer to Section 24.*

General

1 Visually inspect the engine joint faces, gaskets and seals for any signs of water or oil leaks. Pay particular attention to the areas around the cylinder head cover, cylinder head, oil filter and sump joint faces. Bear in mind that, over a period of time, some very slight seepage from these areas is to be expected – what you are really looking for is any indication of a serious leak. Should a leak be found, renew the offending gasket or oil seal by referring to the appropriate Chapters in this manual.

2 High temperatures in the engine compartment can cause the deterioration of the rubber and plastic hoses used for engine, accessory and emission systems operation. Periodic inspection should be made for cracks, loose clamps, material hardening and leaks.

3 When checking the hoses, ensure that all the cable-ties or clips used to retain the hoses are in place, and in good condition. Clips which are broken or missing can lead to chafing of the hoses, pipes or wiring, which could cause more serious problems in the future.

4 Carefully check the large top and bottom radiator hoses, along with the other smaller-diameter cooling system hoses and metal pipes; do not forget the heater hoses/pipes which run from the engine to the bulkhead. Inspect each hose along its entire length, renewing any that is cracked, swollen or shows signs of deterioration. Cracks may become more apparent if the hose is squeezed, and may often be apparent at the hose ends.

5 Make sure that all hose connections are tight. If the large-diameter air hoses from the air cleaner are loose, they will leak air, and upset the engine idle quality. If the spring clamps that are used to secure some of the hoses appear to be slackening, they should be updated with worm-drive clips to prevent the possibility of leaks.

6 Some other hoses are secured to their fittings with clamps. Where clamps are used, check to be sure they haven't lost their

tension, allowing the hose to leak. If clamps aren't used, make sure the hose has not expanded and/or hardened where it slips over the fitting, allowing it to leak.

7 Check all fluid reservoirs, filler caps, drain plugs and fittings, etc, looking for any signs of leakage of oil, transmission and/or brake hydraulic fluid and coolant. Also check the clutch hydraulic fluid lines which lead from the fluid reservoir, master cylinder, and the slave cylinder (on the transmission).

8 If the vehicle is regularly parked in the same place, close inspection of the ground underneath it will soon show any leaks; ignore the puddle of water which will be left if the air conditioning system is in use. Place a clean piece of cardboard below the engine, and examine it for signs of contamination after the vehicle has been parked over it overnight – be aware, however, of the fire risk inherent in placing combustible material below the catalytic converter.

9 Remember that some leaks will only occur with the engine running, or when the engine is hot or cold. With the handbrake firmly applied, start the engine from cold, and let the engine idle while you examine the underside of the engine compartment for signs of leakage.

10 If an unusual smell is noticed inside or around the car, especially when the engine is thoroughly hot, this may point to the presence of a leak.

11 As soon as a leak is detected, its source must be traced and rectified. Where oil has been leaking for some time, it is usually necessary to use a steam cleaner, pressure washer or similar, to clean away the accumulated dirt, so that the exact source of the leak can be identified.

Vacuum hoses

12 It's quite common for vacuum hoses, especially those in the emissions system, to be colour-coded, or to be identified by coloured stripes moulded into them. Various systems require hoses with different wall thicknesses, collapse resistance and temperature resistance. When renewing hoses, be sure the new ones are made of the same material.

13 Often the only effective way to check a hose is to remove it completely from the vehicle. If more than one hose is removed, be sure to label the hoses and fittings to ensure correct installation.

14 When checking vacuum hoses, be sure to include any plastic T-fittings in the check. Inspect the fittings for cracks, and check the hose where it fits over the fitting for distortion, which could cause leakage.

15 A small piece of vacuum hose (approximately 6 mm inside diameter) can be used as a stethoscope to detect vacuum leaks. Hold one end of the hose to your ear, and probe around vacuum hoses and fittings, listening for the 'hissing' sound characteristic of a vacuum leak.

 Warning: When probing with the vacuum hose stethoscope, be very careful not to come into

contact with moving engine components such as the auxiliary drivebelt, radiator electric cooling fan, etc.

Fuel pipes/hoses

 Warning: Refer to the safety information given in 'Safety first!' and Chapter 4B before disturbing any of the fuel system components.

16 Check all fuel lines at their connections to the injection pump, accumulator rail, injectors and fuel filter housing.

17 Examine each fuel hose/pipe along its length for splits or cracks. Check for leakage from the union nuts and examine the unions between the metal fuel lines and the fuel filter housing. Also check the area around the fuel injectors for signs of leakage.

18 To identify fuel leaks between the fuel tank and the engine bay, the vehicle should raised and securely supported on axle stands. Inspect the fuel tank and filler neck for punctures, cracks and other damage. The connection between the filler neck and tank is especially critical. Sometimes a rubber filler neck or connecting hose will leak due to loose retaining clamps or deteriorated rubber.

19 Carefully check all rubber hoses and metal fuel lines leading away from the fuel tank. Check for loose connections, deteriorated hoses, kinked lines, and other damage. Pay particular attention to the vent pipes and hoses, which often loop up around the filler neck and can become blocked or kinked, making tank filling difficult. Follow the fuel supply and return lines to the front of the vehicle, carefully inspecting them all the way for signs of damage or corrosion. Renew damaged sections as necessary.

Air conditioning refrigerant

 Warning: Refer to the safety information given in 'Safety first!' and Chapter 3, regarding the dangers of disturbing any of the air conditioning system components.

20 The air conditioning system is filled with a liquid refrigerant, which is retained under high pressure. If the air conditioning system is opened and depressurised without the aid of specialised equipment, the refrigerant will immediately turn into gas and escape into the atmosphere. If the liquid comes into contact with your skin, it can cause severe frostbite. In addition, the refrigerant contains substances which are environmentally damaging; for this reason, it should not be allowed to escape into the atmosphere.

21 Any suspected air conditioning system leaks should be immediately referred to a Ford dealer or air conditioning specialist. Leakage will be shown up as a steady drop in the level of refrigerant in the system.

22 Note that water may drip from the condenser drain pipe, underneath the car, immediately after the air conditioning system has been in use. This is normal, and should not be cause for concern.

10 Auxiliary drivebelt check – diesel models

1 A single auxiliary drivebelt is fitted at the right-hand side of the engine. The length of the drivebelt varies according to whether air conditioning is fitted. An automatic tensioner is fitted so setting the drivebelt tension is unnecessary.

2 Due to their function and material makeup, drivebelts are prone to failure after a long period of time, and should therefore be inspected regularly.

3 Since the drivebelt is located very close to the right-hand side of the engine compartment, it is possible to gain better access by raising the front of the car and removing the right-hand wheel. Where fitted, undo the retaining bolts and remove the engine undertray, then undo the two screws and remove the drivebelt lower cover.

4 With the engine stopped, inspect the full length of the drivebelt for cracks and separation of the belt plies. It will be necessary to turn the engine (using a spanner or socket and bar on the crankshaft pulley bolt) in order to move the belt from the pulleys so that the belt can be inspected thoroughly. Twist the belt between the pulleys so that both sides can be viewed. Also check for fraying, and glazing which gives the belt a shiny appearance. Check the pulleys for nicks, cracks, distortion and corrosion.

5 Small cracks in the belt ribs are not usually serious, but look closely to see whether the crack has extended into the belt plies. If the belt is in any way suspect, or is known to have seen long service, renew it as described in Section 26.

6 If the belt appears to be too slack (or has actually been slipping in service), this may indicate a problem with the belt tensioner, or external contamination of the belt (eg, by oil or water).

11 Seat belt check

1 Check the seat belts for satisfactory operation and condition. Pull sharply on the belt to check that the locking mechanism engages correctly. Inspect the webbing for fraying and cuts. Check that they retract smoothly and without binding into their reels.

2 Check the accessible seat belt mountings, ensuring that all bolts are securely tightened.

12 Front brake pad and disc wear check

1 Apply the handbrake, then jack up the front of the car and support it securely on axle stands (see *Jacking and vehicle support*). Remove the front roadwheels.

12.2 With the wheel removed, the pad thickness can be seen through the front of the caliper

13.1a Check the outer constant velocity (CV) joint gaiters ...

13.1b ... and, though less prone to wear, check the inner gaiters too

2 The brake pad thickness, and the condition of the disc, can be assessed roughly with just the wheels removed **(see illustration)**. For a comprehensive check, the brake pads should be removed and cleaned. The operation of the caliper can then also be checked, and the condition of the brake disc itself can be fully examined on both sides. Refer to Chapter 9 for further information.

3 On completion, refit the roadwheels and lower the car to the ground.

13 Driveshaft gaiter check

1 With the car raised and securely supported on stands, turn the steering onto full lock, then slowly rotate the roadwheel. Inspect the condition of the outer constant velocity (CV) joint rubber gaiters while squeezing the gaiters to open out the folds. Check for signs of cracking, splits or deterioration of the rubber which may allow the grease to escape and lead to water and grit entry into the joint. Also check the security and condition of the retaining clips. Repeat these checks on the inner CV joints **(see illustrations)**. If any

damage or deterioration is found, the gaiters should be renewed as described in Chapter 8.

2 At the same time, check the general condition of the CV joints themselves by first holding the driveshaft and attempting to rotate the wheel. Repeat this check by holding the inner joint and attempting to rotate the driveshaft. Any appreciable movement indicates wear in the joints, wear in the driveshaft splines, or a loose driveshaft retaining nut.

14 Steering and suspension check

Front suspension and steering

1 Raise the front of the car, and securely support it on axle stands (see *Jacking and vehicle support*).

2 Visually inspect the balljoint dust covers and the steering rack-and-pinion gaiters for splits, chafing or deterioration **(see illustration)**. Any wear of these components will cause loss of lubricant, together with dirt and water entry, resulting in rapid deterioration of the balljoints or steering gear.

3 Grasp the roadwheel at the 12 o'clock and

6 o'clock positions, and try to rock it **(see illustration)**. Very slight free play may be felt, but if the movement is appreciable, further investigation is necessary to determine the source. Continue rocking the wheel while an assistant depresses the footbrake. If the movement is now eliminated or significantly reduced, it is likely that the hub bearings are at fault. If the free play is still evident with the footbrake depressed, then there is wear in the suspension joints or mountings.

4 Now grasp the wheel at the 9 o'clock and 3 o'clock positions, and try to rock it as before. Any movement felt now may again be caused by wear in the hub bearings or the steering track rod balljoints. If the outer balljoint is worn, the visual movement will be obvious. If the inner joint is suspect, it can be felt by placing a hand over the rack-and-pinion rubber gaiter and gripping the track rod. If the wheel is now rocked, movement will be felt at the inner joint if wear has taken place.

5 Using a large screwdriver or flat bar, check for wear in the suspension mounting bushes by levering between the relevant suspension component and its attachment point. Some movement is to be expected, as the mountings are made of rubber, but excessive wear should be obvious. Also check the

14.2 Check the steering gaiters for signs of splitting

14.3 Check for wear in the front suspension and hub bearings

14.9 Check for signs of fluid leakage from the shock absorbers

17.2 Check the condition of the exhaust rubber mountings

condition of any visible rubber bushes, looking for splits, cracks or contamination of the rubber.

6 With the car standing on its wheels, have an assistant turn the steering wheel back-and-forth, about an eighth of a turn each way. There should be very little, if any, lost movement between the steering wheel and roadwheels. If this is not the case, closely observe the joints and mountings previously described. In addition, check the steering column universal joints for wear, and also check the rack-and-pinion steering gear itself.

Rear suspension

7 Chock the front wheels, then jack up the rear of the car and support securely on axle stands (see *Jacking and vehicle support*).

8 Working as described previously for the front suspension, check the rear hub bearings, the suspension bushes and the shock absorber mountings for wear.

Shock absorber

9 Check for any signs of fluid leakage around the shock absorber body, or from the rubber gaiter around the piston rod **(see illustration)**. Should any fluid be noticed, the shock absorber is defective internally, and should be renewed. **Note:** *Shock absorbers should always be renewed in pairs on the same axle.*

10 The efficiency of the shock absorber may be checked by bouncing the car at each corner. Generally speaking, the body will return to its normal position and stop after being depressed. If it rises and returns on a rebound, the shock absorber is probably suspect. Also examine the shock absorber upper and lower mountings for any signs of wear.

15 Rear brake shoe and drum wear check

1 Remove the rear brake drums, and check the brake shoes for signs of wear or contamination. At the same time, also inspect the wheel cylinders for signs of leakage, and the brake drum for signs of wear. Refer to

the relevant Sections of Chapter 9 for further information.

16 Handbrake check and adjustment

1 The handbrake should be fully applied (and capable of holding the car on a slope) after approximately three to five clicks of the ratchet. Should adjustment be necessary, refer to Chapter 9 Section 14 for the full adjustment procedure.

17 Exhaust system check

1 With the engine cold (at least three hours after the vehicle has been driven), check the complete exhaust system, from its starting point at the engine to the end of the tailpipe. Ideally, this should be done on a hoist, where unrestricted access is available; if a hoist is not available, raise and support the vehicle on axle stands (see *Jacking and vehicle support*).

2 Make sure that all brackets and rubber mountings are in good condition, and tight; if any of the mountings are to be renewed, ensure that the new ones are of the correct type – in the case of the rubber mountings, their colour is a good guide. Those nearest to the catalytic converter are more heat-resistant than the others **(see illustration)**.

3 Check the pipes and connections for evidence of leaks, severe corrosion, or damage. One of the most common points for a leak to develop is around the welded joints between the pipes and silencers. Leakage at any of the joints or in other parts of the system will usually show up as a black sooty stain in the vicinity of the leak. **Note:** *Exhaust sealants should not be used on any part of the exhaust system upstream of the catalytic converter (between the converter and engine) – even if the sealant does not contain additives harmful to the converter, pieces of it may break off and foul the element, causing local overheating.*

4 At the same time, inspect the underside of the body for holes, corrosion, open seams, etc, which may allow exhaust gases to enter the passenger compartment. Seal all body openings with silicone or body putty.

5 Rattles and other noises can often be traced to the exhaust system, especially the rubber mountings. Try to move the system, silencer(s), heat shields and catalytic converter. If any components can touch the body or suspension parts, secure the exhaust system with new mountings.

6 Check the running condition of the engine by inspecting inside the end of the tailpipe; the exhaust deposits here are an indication of the engine's state of tune. The inside of the tailpipe should be dry, and should vary in colour from dark grey to light grey/brown; if it is black and sooty, or coated with white deposits, this may indicate the need for a full fuel system inspection.

18 Roadwheel nut tightness check

1 Remove the wheel trims or alloy wheel centre covers, and slacken the roadwheel nuts slightly.

2 Tighten the nuts to the specified torque, using a torque wrench.

19 Hinge and lock lubrication

1 Work around the car and lubricate the hinges of the bonnet, doors and tailgate with light oil.

2 Lightly lubricate the bonnet release mechanism with a smear of grease.

3 Check carefully the security and operation of all hinges, latches and locks, adjusting them where required. Check the operation of the central locking system.

4 Check the condition and operation of the tailgate struts, renewing them both if either is leaking or no longer able to support the tailgate securely when raised.

20 Electrical systems check

1 Check the operation of all the electrical equipment, ie, lights, direction indicators, horn, etc. Refer to the appropriate sections of Chapter for details if any of the circuits are found to be inoperative.

2 Note that the brake light switch is described in Chapter 9 Section 17.

3 Check all accessible wiring connectors, harnesses and retaining clips for security, and for signs of chafing or damage. Rectify any faults found.

21 Road test

Instruments and electrical equipment

1 Check the operation of all instruments and electrical equipment.
2 Make sure that all instruments read correctly, and switch on all electrical equipment in turn, to check that it functions properly.

Steering and suspension

3 Check for any abnormalities in the steering, suspension, handling or road 'feel'.
4 Drive the car, and check that there are no unusual vibrations or noises.
5 Check that the steering feels positive, with no excessive 'sloppiness', or roughness, and check for any suspension noises when cornering and driving over bumps.

Drivetrain

6 Check the performance of the engine, clutch, transmission and driveshafts.
7 Listen for any unusual noises from the engine, clutch and transmission.
8 Make sure that the engine runs smoothly when idling, and that there is no hesitation when accelerating.
9 Check that the clutch action is smooth and progressive, that the drive is taken up smoothly, and that the pedal travel is not excessive. Also listen for any noises when the clutch pedal is depressed.
10 Check that all gears can be engaged smoothly without noise, and that the gear lever action is smooth and not abnormally vague or 'notchy'.
11 Listen for a metallic clicking sound from the front of the car, as the car is driven slowly in a circle with the steering on full-lock. Carry out this check in both directions. If a clicking noise is heard, this indicates wear in a driveshaft joint (see Chapter 8 Section 5).

Braking system

12 Make sure that the car does not pull to

22.3 Undo the bolts and remove the bracket

one side when braking, and that the wheels do not lock prematurely when braking hard. They should not lock at all on models with ABS.
13 Check that there is no vibration through the steering when braking.
14 Check that the handbrake operates correctly, without excessive movement of the lever, and that it holds the car stationary on a slope.
15 Test the operation of the brake servo unit as follows. Depress the footbrake four or five times to exhaust the vacuum, then start the engine. As the engine starts, there should be a noticeable 'give' in the brake pedal as vacuum builds-up. Allow the engine to run for at least two minutes, and then switch it off. If the brake pedal is now depressed again, it should be possible to detect a hiss from the servo as the pedal is depressed. After about four or five applications, no further hissing should be heard, and the pedal should feel considerably harder.

22 Fuel filter renewal

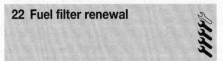

Note: *Various types of fuel filters are fitted to these engines depending on model year and territory. The following procedures depict a typical example.*

22.4 Lift the yellow catch and disconnect the wiring plug

Note: *After renewing the filter it will be necessary to prime and bleed the fuel system, which can occasionally prove troublesome on these engines. Refer to the procedures contained in Chapter 4B Section 3 and ensure you have the necessary equipment before proceeding.*

1 The fuel filter is located at the rear of the engine compartment between the air cleaner housing and the battery . If increased access is required, remove the windscreen cowl panel and bulkhead closure panel as described in Chapter 11 Section 20.
2 Pull up and remove the plastic cover from the top of the engine.
3 Undo the bolts and remove the remove the bracket above the filter location **(see illustration)**.
4 Lift the yellow locking catch and disconnect the wiring plug(s) from the top of the filter **(see illustration)**.
5 Position some rag around the connections to collect the spilt fuel, then depress the release buttons and disconnect the fuel pipes from the filter **(see illustration)**. Plug the openings to prevent contamination.
6 Undo the 2 bolts and lift the filter from place **(see illustration)**.
7 Hold the filter over a suitable container, then rotate the central fitting clockwise, pull it up slightly and drain the fuel **(see illustration)**. When the filter housing is drained, push down the fitting and rotate it fully anti-clockwise.

22.5 Depress the buttons and disconnect the pipes

22.6 Filter retaining bolts

22.7 Rotate the centre fitting clockwise, and pull it upwards

22.8 Fuel filter retaining bolts

22.9 Pull the filter top from the element

22.10 Remove the sealing cap and plug

8 Undo the 3 retaining bolts and lift the top from the filter element **(see illustration)**.
9 Carefully pull the top from the filter element **(see illustration)**.
10 Remove the sealing plug and cap from the new filter element **(see illustration)**.
11 Clean the filter top.
12 Locate the new seal into the groove in the filter element **(see illustration)**.
13 Insert the new element into the filter top, refit the bolts and tighten them securely.
14 Locate the filter into the housing, and tighten the retaining bolts.
15 Reconnect the fuel pipes to their original locations, and reconnect the wiring plug(s).
16 Refit the bracket above the filter and tighten the retaining bolts securely.
17 The remainder of refitting is a reversal of removal, noting the following points:
a) *Ensure that the fuel hose connections are securely remade.*
b) *Where applicable, refit the bulkhead closure panel and windscreen cowl panel as described in Chapter 11 Section 20.*
c) *On completion, prime and bleed the fuel system as described in Chapter 4B Section 3.*
d) *When the engine is running, check for any sign of leakage from the disturbed pipes.*

23 Air filter element renewal – diesel models

Caution: Never drive the vehicle with the air

22.12 Ensure the seal is correctly located

cleaner filter element removed. Excessive engine wear could result, and backfiring could even cause a fire under the bonnet.
1 The air filter element is located in the air cleaner assembly on the left-hand side of the engine compartment.
2 Disconnect the wiring plug from the airflow sensor on the air cleaner cover **(see illustration)**.
3 Undo the four bolts securing the cover to the air cleaner housing **(see illustration)**.
4 The cover can now be lifted, and the filter element removed **(see illustration)**.
5 Clean the filter housing and cover, removing any dirt or debris. A vacuum cleaner is ideal for this.
6 Position the new element in the filter housing and refit the filter cover. Tighten the

23.2 Slide up the locking catch, and disconnect the wiring plug from the airflow sensor

retaining screws securely, and reconnect the wiring plug.

24 Braking system rubber hose check

1 Position the car over an inspection pit, on car ramps, or jack it up one wheel at a time (see *Jacking and vehicle support*).
2 Inspect the braking system rubber hoses fitted to each front caliper, and on each side of the rear axle **(see illustration)**. Look for perished, swollen or hardened rubber, and any signs of cracking, especially at the metal end fittings. If there's any doubt as to the condition of any hose, renew it as described in Chapter 9.

23.3 Undo the four bolts securing the cover to the air cleaner housing

23.4 The cover can now be lifted, and the filter element removed

24.2 Rubber brake hose fitted to the front caliper

26.2 Drivebelt lower cover screws

26.3a Rotate the tensioner arm clockwise...

26.3b ...then insert a 4.0 mm drill bit/rod to lock it in place

25 Timing belt renewal

1 Refer to the procedures contained in Chapter 2C Section 7 or Chapter 2D Section 7.

26 Auxiliary drivebelt renewal

Removal

1 Firmly apply the handbrake, then jack up the front of the vehicle and support it securely on axle stands (see *Jacking and vehicle support*). Remove the right-hand roadwheel.
2 Where fitted, undo the retaining bolts and remove the engine undertray, then undo the two screws and remove the drivebelt lower cover **(see illustration)**.
3 Engage an open-ended spanner with the lug at the top of the tensioner arm, then rotate the tensioner arm clockwise to release the belt tension. Insert a 4.0 mm diameter drill bit or rod into the hole in the tensioner body, so that the tensioner arm rests against it and locks it in this position **(see illustrations)**. It is useful to have a small mirror available to enable the alignment of the locking holes to be more easily seen in the limited space available.
4 Note how the drivebelt is routed, then remove the belt from the pulleys. Note that if the belt is to be re-used, mark the direction

of rotation. The belt must be refitted the same way round.

Refitting

5 Fit the belt around the pulleys, ensuring that the ribs on the belt are correctly engaged with the grooves in the pulleys and the drivebelt is correctly routed.
6 Using an open-ended spanner, hold the tensioner arm so that the locking drill bit/rod can be removed, then release the pressure on the spanner so that the automatic tensioner takes up the slack in the drivebelt.
7 Refit the drivebelt lower cover and, where applicable, the engine undertray. Refit the roadwheel then lower the vehicle to the ground and tighten the wheel nuts to the specified torque.

27 Brake fluid renewal

 Warning: Brake hydraulic fluid can harm your eyes and damage painted surfaces, so use extreme caution when handling and pouring it. Do not use fluid that has been standing open for some time, as it absorbs moisture from the air. Excess moisture can cause a dangerous loss of braking effectiveness.

1 The procedure is similar to that for bleeding the hydraulic system as described in Chapter 9 Section 2, except that allowance should be made for the old fluid to be expelled when bleeding each section of the circuit.

2 Working as described in Chapter 9 Section 2, open the first bleed screw in the sequence, and pump the brake pedal gently until the level in the reservoir is approaching the MIN mark. Top-up to the MAX level with new fluid, and continue pumping until only new fluid remains in the reservoir, and new fluid can be seen emerging from the bleed screw. Tighten the screw, and top the reservoir level up to the MAX level line.
3 Work through all the remaining bleed screws in the sequence until new fluid can be seen at all of them. Be careful to keep the master cylinder reservoir topped-up above the MIN level at all times, or air may enter the system. If this happens, further bleeding will be required, to remove the air.
4 When the operation is complete, check that all bleed screws are securely tightened, and that their dust caps are refitted. Wash off all traces of spilt fluid, and recheck the master cylinder reservoir fluid level.
5 Check the operation of the brakes before taking the car on the road.

28 Manual transmission oil level check

1 Position the car over an inspection pit, on car ramps, or jack it up and support it on axle stands (see *Jacking and vehicle support*), but make sure that it is level. Where fitted, undo the retaining bolts and remove the engine undertray.
2 Unclip the plastic cover fitted over the gearchange cables at the front of the transmission **(see illustration)**.
3 Remove all traces of dirt, then unscrew the filler/level plug from the front face of the transmission. This will probably be very tight, and a large Allen key or bit will be needed – access is made awkward by the plastic shroud around the gearchange cables **(see illustration)**.
4 The level must be just below the bottom edge of the filler/level plug hole (use a cranked tool such as an Allen key to check the level). If necessary, top-up the level with the specified grade of oil (see *Lubricants and fluids*) until the oil just starts to run out. Allow any excess

28.2 Unclip the plastic cover from the front of the transmission

28.3 Unscrew and remove the filler/level plug

28.4a Top-up the oil level ...

28.4b ... then allow any excess to flow out before refitting the plug

29.2a Insert a small screwdriver into the slot on the side of the transmitter unit ...

29.2b ... then push the screwdriver towards the key blade and remove the key blade

29.3 Insert the screwdriver at the side and front of the transmitter unit to separate the two halves

29.4 Note the fitted position of the battery, then prise it out and insert the new one

oil to flow out until the level stabilises (**see illustrations**).
5 When the level is correct, clean and refit the filler/level plug (check the condition of the O-ring seal, and renew if necessary), then tighten it to the specified torque. Clip the plastic cover back into position.
6 Where applicable, refit the engine undertray, then lower the car to the ground.

29 Remote control battery renewal – diesel models

Note: *All the remote control units described below are fitted with a type CR 2032, 3 volt battery.*
1 Although not in the Ford maintenance schedule, we recommend that the battery is changed every 2 years, regardless of the vehicle's mileage. However, if the door locks repeatedly fail to respond to signals from the remote control at the normal distance, change the battery in the remote control before attempting to troubleshoot any of the vehicle's other systems.

Control with a folding key
2 Insert a small flat-bladed screwdriver fully into the slot on the side of the transmitter unit, push the screwdriver towards the key blade and remove the key blade (**see illustrations**).
3 Use the screwdriver, inserted at the side

and front of the transmitter unit, to separate the two halves of the unit (**see illustration**).
4 Note the fitted position of the battery (positive side down), then prise the battery from its location, and insert the new one (**see illustration**). Avoid touching the battery or the terminals with bare fingers.
5 Snap the two halves of the transmitter together, and re-attach it to the key blade.

Control without a folding key
6 Depress the two tabs on the side of the transmitter unit and carefully lift off the cover.
7 Remove the key blade from the transmitter unit.
8 Use a small flat-bladed the screwdriver, inserted at the side of the transmitter unit, to separate the two halves of the unit.
9 Note the fitted position of the battery (positive side down), then prise the battery from its location, and insert the new one. Avoid touching the battery or the terminals with bare fingers.
10 Snap the two halves of the transmitter together, place the key blade in position and refit the cover.

30 Coolant strength check and renewal

⚠ **Warning: Do not allow antifreeze to come in contact with your skin or painted surfaces of the vehicle.**

Flush contaminated areas immediately with plenty of water. Don't store new coolant, or leave old coolant lying around, where it's accessible to children or pets – they're attracted by its sweet smell. Ingestion of even a small amount of coolant can be fatal. Wipe up garage-floor and drip-pan spills immediately. Keep antifreeze containers covered, and repair cooling system leaks as soon as they're noticed.

⚠ *Warning: Never remove the expansion tank filler cap when the engine is running, or has just been switched off, as the cooling system will be hot, and the consequent escaping steam and scalding coolant could cause serious injury.*

⚠ *Warning: Wait until the engine is cold before starting these procedures.*

Strength check
1 Use a hydrometer to check the strength of the antifreeze. Follow the instructions provided with your hydrometer. The antifreeze strength should be approximately 50%. If it is significantly less than this, drain a little coolant from the radiator (see this Section), add antifreeze to the coolant expansion tank, then recheck the strength.

Coolant draining
2 To drain the system, first remove the expansion tank filler cap.

30.5 Squeeze together the tangs, release the clamp and disconnect the bottom hose

3 Firmly apply the handbrake, then jack up the front of the vehicle and support it securely on axle stands (see *Jacking and vehicle support*). Where fitted, undo the retaining bolts and remove the engine undertray.

4 Place a suitable container beneath the right-hand side of the radiator.

5 Release the retaining clamp and disconnect the bottom hose from the radiator **(see illustration)**. Allow the coolant to drain into the container.

6 Once the coolant has stopped draining from the radiator, reconnect the bottom hose and secure with the retaining clamp.

System flushing

7 With time, the cooling system may gradually lose its efficiency, as the radiator core becomes choked with rust, scale deposits from the water, and other sediment. To minimise this, as well as using only good-quality antifreeze and clean soft water, the system should be flushed as follows whenever any part of it is disturbed, and/or when the coolant is renewed.

8 With the coolant drained, refit the radiator bottom hose and refill the system with fresh water. Refit the expansion tank filler cap, start the engine and warm it up to normal operating temperature, then stop it and (after allowing it to cool down completely) drain the system again. Repeat as necessary until only clean water can be seen to emerge, then refill finally with the specified coolant mixture.

9 If only clean, soft water and good-quality antifreeze (even if not to Ford's specification) has been used, and the coolant has been renewed at the suggested intervals, the above procedure will be sufficient to keep the system clean for a considerable length of time. If, however, the system has been neglected, a more thorough operation will be required, as follows.

10 First drain the coolant, then disconnect the radiator top hose. Insert a garden hose into the radiator top hose connection, and allow water to circulate through the radiator until it runs clean from the bottom outlet.

11 To flush the engine, insert the garden hose into the radiator bottom hose, wrap a piece of rag around the garden hose to seal the connection, and allow water to circulate until it runs clear.

12 Try the effect of repeating this procedure in the top hose, although this may not be effective, since the thermostat will probably close and prevent the flow of water.

13 In severe cases of contamination, reverse-flushing of the radiator may be necessary. This may be achieved by inserting the garden hose into the bottom outlet, wrapping a piece of rag around the hose to seal the connection, then flushing the radiator until clear water emerges from the top hose outlet.

14 If the radiator is suspected of being severely choked, remove the radiator (Chapter 3 Section 3), turn it upside-down, and repeat the procedure described in paragraph 13.

15 Flushing the heater matrix can be achieved using a similar procedure to that described in paragraph 13, once the heater inlet and outlet hoses have been identified. These two hoses will be of the same diameter, and pass through the engine compartment bulkhead (refer to the procedures contained in Chapter 3 for more details).

16 The use of chemical cleaners is not recommended, and should be necessary only as a last resort; the scouring action of some chemical cleaners may lead to other cooling system problems. Normally, regular renewal of the coolant will prevent excessive contamination of the system.

Coolant filling

17 With the cooling system drained and flushed, ensure that all disturbed hose unions are correctly secured. Where applicable, refit the engine undertray, then lower the vehicle to the ground.

18 Set the heater temperature control to maximum heat, but ensure the blower is turned off.

19 Prepare a sufficient quantity of the specified coolant mixture (see below); allow for a surplus, so as to have a reserve supply for topping-up.

20 Slowly fill the system through the expansion tank. Since the tank is the highest point in the system, all the air in the system should be displaced into the tank by the rising liquid. Slow pouring reduces the possibility of air being trapped and forming airlocks. Continue filling until the coolant level reaches the top of the expansion tank.

21 With the help of an assistant, start the engine and run it at 2500 rpm until the coolant level stabilises. If the level in the expansion tank drops significantly, top-up to the MAX level line, to minimise the amount of air circulating in the system.

22 Once the coolant level has stabilised, refit the expansion tank filler cap and continue running the engine at 2500 rpm for a further 15 minutes.

23 Increase the engine speed to 5000 rpm, then allow it to return to idle. Repeat this sequence 6 times.

24 Increase the engine speed to 4000 rpm, maintain this speed for 10 seconds, then reduce the engine speed to 2500 rpm and maintain this speed for 15 minutes.

25 Stop the engine, then leave the car to cool down completely (overnight, if possible).

26 With the system cool, open the expansion tank, and top-up the tank to the MAX level line. Refit the filler cap, tightening it securely, and clean up any spillage.

27 After refilling, always check carefully all components of the system (but especially any unions disturbed during draining and flushing) for signs of coolant leaks. Fresh antifreeze has a searching action, which will rapidly expose any weak points in the system.

Antifreeze type and mixture

Note: *Do not use engine antifreeze in the windscreen/tailgate washer system, as it will damage the vehicle's paintwork. A screenwash additive should be added to the washer system in its maker's recommended quantities.*

28 If the vehicle's history (and therefore the quality of the antifreeze in it) is unknown, owners are advised to drain and thoroughly reverse-flush the system, before refilling with fresh coolant mixture.

29 If the antifreeze used is to Ford's specification, the levels of protection it affords are indicated in the coolant packaging.

30 To give the recommended standard mixture ratio for antifreeze, 50% (by volume) of antifreeze must be mixed with 50% of clean, soft water; if you are using any other type of antifreeze, follow its manufacturer's instructions to achieve the correct ratio.

31 You are unlikely to fully drain the system at any one time (unless the engine is being completely stripped), and the capacities quoted in the Specifications are therefore slightly academic for routine coolant renewal. As a guide, only two-thirds of the system's total capacity is likely to be needed for coolant renewal.

32 As the drained system will be partially filled with flushing water, in order to establish the recommended mixture ratio, measure out 50% of the system capacity in antifreeze and pour it into the hose/expansion tank as described above, then top-up with water. Any topping-up while refilling the system should be done with water – for Weekly checks0,5 use a suitable mixture.

33 Before adding antifreeze, the cooling system should be drained, preferably flushed, and all hoses checked for condition and security. As noted earlier, fresh antifreeze will rapidly find any weaknesses in the system.

34 After filling with antifreeze, a label should be attached to the expansion tank, stating the type and concentration of antifreeze used, and the date installed. Any subsequent topping-up should be made with the same type and concentration of antifreeze.

General cooling system checks

35 The engine should be cold for the cooling system checks, so perform the following procedure before driving the vehicle, or after it has been shut off for at least three hours.

36 Remove the expansion tank filler cap, and clean it thoroughly inside and out with a rag. Also clean the filler neck on the expansion tank. The presence of rust or corrosion in the filler neck indicates that the coolant should be changed. The coolant inside the expansion tank should be relatively clean and transparent. If it is rust-coloured, drain and flush the system, and refill with a fresh coolant mixture.

37 Carefully check the radiator hoses and heater hoses along their entire length; renew any hose which is cracked, swollen or deteriorated.

38 Inspect all other cooling system components (joint faces, etc) for leaks. A leak in the cooling system will usually show up as white- or antifreeze-coloured deposits on the area adjoining the leak. Where any problems of this nature are found on system components, renew the component or gasket with reference to Chapter 3.

Airlocks

39 If, after draining and refilling the system, symptoms of overheating are found which did not occur previously, then the fault is almost certainly due to trapped air at some point in the system, causing an airlock and restricting the flow of coolant; usually, the air is trapped because the system was refilled too quickly.

40 If an airlock is suspected, first try gently squeezing all visible coolant hoses. A coolant hose which is full of air feels quite different to one full of coolant when squeezed. After refilling the system, most airlocks will clear once the system has cooled, and been topped-up.

41 While the engine is running at operating temperature, switch on the heater and heater fan, and check for heat output. Provided there is sufficient coolant in the system, lack of heat output could be due to an airlock in the system.

42 Airlocks can have more serious effects than simply reducing heater output – a severe airlock could reduce coolant flow around the engine. Check that the radiator top hose is hot when the engine is at operating temperature – a top hose which stays cold could be the result of an airlock (or a non-opening thermostat).

43 If the problem persists, stop the engine and allow it to cool down completely, before unscrewing the expansion tank filler cap or loosening the hose clips and squeezing the hoses to bleed out the trapped air. In the worst case, the system will have to be at least partially drained (this time, the coolant can be saved for re-use) and flushed to clear the problem. If all else fails, have the system evacuated and vacuum filled by a suitably-equipped garage.

Expansion tank cap check

44 Wait until the engine is completely cold – perform this check before the engine is started for the first time in the day.

45 Place a wad of cloth over the expansion tank cap, then unscrew it slowly and remove it.

46 Examine the condition of the rubber seal on the underside of the cap. If the rubber appears to have hardened, or cracks are visible in the seal edges, a new cap should be fitted.

47 If the car is several years old, or has covered a large mileage, consider renewing the cap regardless of its apparent condition – they are not expensive. If the pressure relief valve built into the cap fails, excess pressure in the system will lead to puzzling failures of hoses and other cooling system components.

Chapter 2 Part A
1.0 litre petrol engine in-car repair procedures

Contents

Degrees of difficulty

Easy, suitable for novice with little experience 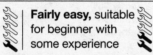	Fairly easy, suitable for beginner with some experience	Fairly difficult, suitable for competent DIY mechanic	Difficult, suitable for experienced DIY mechanic	Very difficult, suitable for expert DIY or professional

Specifications

General

Engine type	Three-cylinder, in-line, double overhead camshafts, with variable valve timing
Designation	EcoBoost
Engine codes	SFJA, SFJB, SFJC, SFJD, M1JE, M1JH, YYJA and YYJB
Capacity 998 cc	
Bore	71.9 mm
Stroke	81.9 mm
Compression ratio:	
All except engine codes YYJA and YYJB	10: 1
Engine codes YYJA and YYJB	9.9: 1
Output:	
Power:	
Codes SFJA, SFJB, SFJC and SFJD	74 kW (100 PS)
Codes M1JE and M1JH	92 kW (125 PS)
Codes YYJA and YYJB	103 kW (140 PS)
Torque:	
All except engine codes YYJA and YYJB	170 Nm
Engine codes YYJA and YYJB	180 Nm
Firing order	1-2-3 (No 1 cylinder at timing belt end)
Emissions level:	
Engine codes SFJA, SFJB, M1JE and YYJA	Stage V
Engine codes SFJC, SFJD, M1JH and YYJB	Stage VI
Direction of crankshaft rotation	Clockwise (seen from right-hand side of car)

Valves

Valve clearances (cold)	
Inlet	0.21 to 0.30 mm
Exhaust:	
CM5G FA, FB and FC camshaft	0.31 to 0.37 mm
All other camshafts	0.38 to 0.47 mm

Lubrication

Oil pressure (minimum, warm engine) at 2000 rpm	2.0 bars
Pressure relief valve opens at.	Not specified
Oil pump clearances	Not specified

Torque wrench settings

	Nm	lbf ft
Air conditioning compressor mounting bolts.	25	18
Alternator mounting bolts.	48	35
Auxiliary drivebelt belt idler pulley bolt.	25	18
Auxiliary drivebelt tensioner bolts	25	18
Camshaft bearing caps bolts*	10	7
Camshaft position sensors.	10	7
Camshaft sprocket bolts		
Stage 1.	30	22
Stage 2.	50	37
Stage 3.	95	70
Stage 4.	Angle-tighten a further 45°	
Coolant outlet to cylinder head	10	7
Coolant outlet at rear of the waterpump	10	7
Crankshaft position sensor	10	7
Crankshaft oil seal carrier*	10	7
Crankshaft pulley/vibration damper: *		
Stage 1.	25	18
Stage 2.	70	52
Install Torque multiplier**		
Stage 1.	60	44
Stage 2.	Angle-tighten a further 90°	
Stage 3.	Angle-tighten a further 90°	
Stage 4.	Angle-tighten a further 90°	
Stage 5.	Angle-tighten a further 90°	
Stage 6.	Angle-tighten a further 90°	
Cylinder head bolts: *		
Stage 1.	10	7
Stage 2.	40	29
Stage 3 (slacken)	Loosen 45°	
Stage 4.	30	22
Stage 5.	Angle-tighten a further 90°	
Stage 6.	Angle-tighten a further 90°	
Cylinder head cover	10	7
Engine mountings:		
Right-hand mounting-to-vehicle body retaining bolts	90	66
Right-hand mounting bracket-to-engine bolts.	80	59
Right-hand mounting studs (on engine).	10	7
Left-hand mounting nuts	48	35
Left-hand mounting bracket to transmission.	82	61
Lower-rear torque rod bolts	48	35
Engine lifting eye	22	16
Exhaust flexible section-to-catalytic converter nuts	25	18
Exhaust manifold heat shield bolts	10	7
Exhaust manifold nuts/bolts.	25	18
Fuel pump bolts:		
Stage 1.	5	3
Stage 2.	13	9
Flywheel bolts*		
Stage 1.	10	7
Stage 2.	25	18
Stage 3.	50	37
Stage 4.	Angle-tighten a further 90°	
Inlet manifold-to-block bolt	10	7
Oil drain plug	25	18
Oil filter connector (to block)	55	41
Oil pressure switch	15	11
Oil pressure control solenoid	10	7
Oil pump to cylinder block	25	18
Spark plugs	15	11
Sump bolts:		
Sump-to-block bolts*	10	7
Sump-to-transmission bolts.	48	35

Torque wrench settings (continued)	Nm	lbf ft
TDC pin hole blanking plug	20	15
Timing belt cover bolts*		
First stage:		
Bolts 1-2	5	3
Bolts 3-6	10	7
Bolts 7-16	5	3
Bolts 17-19	5	3
Bolts 20	5	3
Second stage:		
Bolts 3-6	40	30
Bolts 3-4		
Stage 1	70	52
Stage 2	Angle-tighten a further 90°	
Bolts 5-6		
Stage 1	70	52
Stage 2	Angle-tighten a further 90°	
Bolts 1-2		
Stage 1	9	6.5
Stage 2	Angle-tighten a further 90°	
Bolts 7-20		
Stage 1	15	11
Stage 2	Angle-tighten a further 90°	
Timing belt tensioner bolt	25	18
Turbocharger oil feed pipe:		
To turbocharger	30	22
To cylinder block	10	7
Variable valve timing solenoid	7	6
Variable valve timing units		
Stage 1	30	22
Stage 2	50	37
Stage 3	95	70
Stage 4	Angle-tighten a further 45°	

*Use new fasteners
**See the text for an alternative method that does not require the use of a torque multiplier

1 General Information

How to use this Chapter

1 This Part of Chapter 2 is devoted to in-car repair procedures on the 1.0 litre 3 cylinder petrol engine. All procedures concerning engine removal and refitting, and engine block/cylinder head overhaul can be found in Chapter 2E.

2 Refer to Vehicle identification numbers 13 Section 3 for details of engine code locations.

3 Most of the operations included in this Chapter are based on the assumption that the engine is still installed in the car. Therefore, if this information is being used during a complete engine overhaul, with the engine already removed, many of the steps included here will not apply.

Engine description

4 This engine is a twelve-valve, double overhead camshaft (DOHC), three-cylinder engine, mounted transversely at the front of the car, with the transmission on its left-hand end. The engine features an aluminium cylinder head with an integral exhaust manifold, a cast iron cylinder block and an aluminium sump.

5 All 1.0 litre Ecoboost engines are equipped with a turbocharger.

Caution: When tightening bolts into aluminium castings, it is important to adhere to the specified torque wrench settings, to avoid stripping threads.

6 The crankshaft runs in four main bearings. Due to the very fine bearing clearances and bearing shell tolerances incorporated during manufacture, it is not possible to renew the crankshaft separate to the cylinder block; in fact it is not possible to remove and refit the crankshaft accurately using conventional tooling. This means that if the crankshaft is worn excessively, it must be renewed together with the cylinder block.

Caution: Do not unbolt the main bearing caps from the cylinder block, as it is not possible to refit it accurately using conventional tooling. Additionally, the manufacturers do not supply torque settings for the main bearing cap/ladder retaining bolts.

7 The connecting rods rotate on horizontally-split bearing shells at their big-ends. The pistons are attached to the connecting rods by gudgeon pins which are an interference fit in the connecting rod small-end eyes.

The aluminium alloy pistons are fitted with three piston rings: two compression rings and an oil control ring. After manufacture, the cylinder bores and pistons are measured and classified. These are then matched together, to ensure the correct piston/cylinder clearance. No oversizes or replacement parts are available to rectify any faults with the pistons, piston rings, connecting rods or big end bearings. If there is any fault with the crankshaft, pistons or cylinder bores, a replacement 'short' engine must be fitted.

Caution: Do not unbolt the big end bearing caps from the crankshaft, as it is not possible to refit them accurately using conventional tooling. Additionally, the manufacturers do not supply torque settings or replacement parts.

8 The inlet and exhaust valves are each closed by coil springs; they operate in guides which are shrink-fitted into the cylinder head, as are the valve seat inserts. The exhaust valves are hollow sodium filled valves.

9 Both camshafts are driven by the same toothed timing belt, each operating six valves via bucket tappets. Each camshaft rotates in four main bearings that are line-bored directly in the cylinder head and the (bolted-on) bearing caps; this means that the bearing caps are not available separately from the

cylinder head, and must not be interchanged with caps from another engine.

10 All engines are fitted with variable valve timing on the both the inlet and exhaust camshafts. Engine oil pressure is used to vary the positions of the camshaft sprocket in relation to the camshafts, thus varying the valves opening and closing times. Control of the oil flow is achieved using solenoid valves, which in turn are controlled by the engine management electronic control module (ECM). Varying the valve timing is this manner results in improved driveability and output, whist reducing fuel consumption and exhaust emissions.

11 The timing belt features an automatic tensioner and runs in an oil bath. This reduces noise and frictional loses, thus contributing to improved fuel consumption.

12 The coolant pump is bolted to the right-hand end of the cylinder block and is driven by the auxiliary drivebelt from the crankshaft pulley. Separate cooling circuits for the cylinder head and block enable a faster warm up time.

13 Lubrication is by means of a vane type oil pump with an adjustable outer ring. The oil pump has a variable output, controlled by the ECU, via a solenoid valve. The oil pump is mounted is mounted below the crankshaft right-hand end. The oil pump is belt driven and draws oil through a strainer located in the sump. The pump forces oil through an externally-mounted full-flow cartridge-type filter.

Operations with engine in car

14 The following work can be carried out with the engine in the car:
a) Cylinder head cover – removal and refitting.
b) Timing belt – renewal.
c) Timing belt tensioner and sprockets – removal and refitting.
d) Camshaft oil seals – renewal.
e) Camshafts, tappets and shims – removal and refitting.
f) Cylinder head – removal and refitting.
g) Sump – removal and refitting.
h) Crankshaft oil seals – renewal.
i) Oil pump – removal and refitting.
j) Flywheel/driveplate – removal and refitting.
k) Engine/transmission mountings – removal and refitting.

Note: It is possible to remove the pistons and connecting rods (after removing the cylinder head and sump) without removing the engine. However, this is not recommended. Work of this nature is more easily and thoroughly completed with the engine on the bench, as described in Chapter 2E.

2 Compression test – description and interpretation

Note: Cranking the engine with the coils removed may set a DTC (Diagnostic Trouble Code). Completing several drive cycles after carrying out a compression test may erase the fault codes. If the EML (Engine Management Light) remains illuminated, suitable diagnostic equipment will be required to erase the fault codes.

1 When engine performance is down, or if misfiring occurs which cannot be attributed to the ignition or fuel systems, a compression test can provide diagnostic clues as to the engine's condition. If the test is performed regularly, it can give warning of trouble before any other symptoms become apparent.

2 The engine must be fully warmed-up to operating temperature, the oil level must be correct and the battery must be fully-charged. The help of an assistant will also be required.

3 Remove fuse number 34 from the engine compartment fusebox. This is the fuse for the fuel pump – further details are to be found in Chapter 12 Section 3. Now start the engine and allow it to run until it stalls.

4 Remove the engine cover (where fitted) and the with reference to Chapter 1A Section 21, remove the spark plugs.

5 Fit a compression tester to the No 1 cylinder spark plug hole – the type of tester which screws into the spark plug thread is preferable.

6 Arrange for an assistant to hold the accelerator pedal fully depressed to the floor, while at the same time cranking the engine over for several seconds on the starter motor. Observe the compression gauge reading. The compression will build-up fairly quickly in a healthy engine. Low compression on the first stroke, followed by gradually-increasing pressure on successive strokes, indicates worn piston rings. A low compression on the first stroke which does not rise on successive strokes, indicates leaking valves or a blown head gasket (a cracked cylinder head could also be the cause). Deposits on the underside of the valve heads can also cause low compression. Record the highest gauge reading obtained, then repeat the procedure for the remaining cylinders.

7 Due to the variety of testers available, and the fluctuation in starter motor speed when cranking the engine, different readings are often obtained when carrying out the compression test. For this reason, actual compression pressure figures are not quoted by Ford. However, the most important factor is that the compression pressures are uniform in all cylinders, and that is what this test is mainly concerned with.

8 Add some engine oil (about three squirts from a plunger type oil can) to each cylinder through the spark plug holes, and then repeat the test.

9 If the compression increases after the oil is added, the piston rings are probably worn. If the compression does not increase significantly, the leakage is occurring at the valves or the head gasket. Leakage past the valves may be caused by burned valve seats and/or faces, or warped, cracked or bent valves.

10 If two adjacent cylinders have equally low compressions, it is most likely that the head gasket has blown between them. The appearance of coolant in the combustion chambers or on the engine oil dipstick would verify this condition.

11 If one cylinder is about 20 percent lower than the other, and the engine has a slightly rough idle, a worn lobe on the camshaft could be the cause.

12 On completion of the checks, refit the spark plugs and ignition coils. Refit the fuel pump fuse to the fusebox.

3 Top Dead Centre (TDC) for No 1 piston – locating

Note: The engine must only be rotated in the normal direction of rotation (clockwise).

1 Top dead centre (TDC) is the highest point of the cylinder that each piston reaches as the crankshaft turns. Each piston reaches its TDC position at the end of its compression stroke, and then again at the end of its exhaust stroke. For the purpose of engine timing, TDC on the compression stroke for No 1 piston is used. No 1 cylinder is at the timing belt end of the engine. Proceed as follows.

2 Disconnect the battery negative lead as described in Chapter 5A Section 4, and remove the spark plugs as described in Chapter 1A Section 21.

3 Slacken the right-hand front road wheel nuts, then jack up the front of the vehicle and support it on axle stands (see Jacking and vehicle support). Remove the road wheel

4 Undo the fasteners, remove the engine undershield, then remove the wheel arch liner to improve access to the crankshaft pulley and bolt.

5 Undo the nuts, remove the right-hand driveshaft mid-bearing cap, then undo the 3 bolts and remove the 3 bolts securing the bearing support bracket to the cylinder block **(see illustration)**. Ford insist that the bearing cap is renewed.

6 Remove the blanking plug from the rear of

3.5 Right-hand driveshaft mid-bearing cap retaining nuts

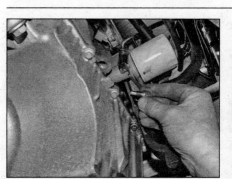

3.6 Remove the blanking plug

3.7 The TDC locating pin

3.9a Slacken the charge air duct clamp at the throttle body…

the engine block – next to the oil pump control solenoid **(see illustration)**.

7 Install the Top Dead Centre (TDC) locating pin. This is Ford special tool 303-1604 **(see illustration)** or equivalent from a reputable manufacturer such as Draper or AST.

8 Release the clamps, disconnect the breather hoses, then undo the 2 nuts and remove the remove the air intake duct from the air cleaner housing to the intake manifold or turbocharger (as applicable) **(see illustrations 4.4a to 4.4g)**.

9 Release the clamps, disconnect the hoses/ wiring plugs, undo the retaining bolt and remove the charge air duct between the intercooler and the throttle body **(see illustrations)**.

10 Undo the nut, and unclip the wiring harness duct from the right-hand end of the engine.

11 Remove the wiring plugs from the variable valve timing control solenoids and then remove the solenoids **(see illustration)**. Recover the O-ring seals.

12 Rotate the crankshaft pulley slowly clockwise until the crankshaft stops against the locating pin. Install Ford special tool 303-1606 to the camshaft Variable Valve Timing units (VVT). If the engine is at TDC with cylinder number 1 on the firing stroke, the tool can easily be fitted and the pointers on the VVT timing tools will be vertical **(see illustration)**. If

3.9b …and the intercooler

this is not the case, remove the TDC locating pin and rotate the crankshaft approximately 340 degrees and then refit the TDC locating pin. Fully rotate the crankshaft until the crankshaft locks against the TDC locating pin. The VVT locking tools should now fit.

13 Once the work requiring the TDC setting has been completed, remove the special tool from the camshaft VVT units and refit the control solenoids – the O-rings can be reused if they are in good condition. Unscrew the TDC locating pin and refit the blanking plug.

14 The remainder of refitting is a reversal of removal.

3.9c Charge air duct retaining bolt

4 Cylinder head cover –
   removal and refitting

Removal

1 Remove fuse 34 (fuel pump relay) from the engine compartment fusebox and then run the engine until it stalls. Crank the engine for a further 5 seconds after it stalls.

2 Disconnect the battery negative lead as described in Chapter 5A Section 4.

3 Disconnect and then remove the fuel rail as described in Chapter 4A Section 11.

3.11 Remove the control solenoids

3.12 Fit the special tools.

4.4a Release the clamp securing the air duct to the air cleaner housing

4.4b Slacken the clamp securing the duct at the rear, and undo the retaining nut…

4.4c … slide out the clip and disconnect the breather pipe at the right-hand rear corner…

4.4d … undo the retaining nut…

4.4e … squeeze together the side of the collar and disconnect the breather pipe…

4.4f … then release the clamp at the turbocharger

4.4g Release the clip and disconnect the vacuum pipe at the rear of the air duct

4.5 Camshaft position sensor wiring plugs

4 Disconnect the breather pipe, then release the clamps and remove the air duct from the air cleaner housing to the turbocharger **(see illustrations)**.

5 Disconnect the wiring plugs, undo the bolts and remove the camshaft position sensors **(see illustration)**.

6 Make a note of its fitted position, then unclip the vacuum pipe assembly from the top/rear of the engine and move it rearwards **(see illustration)**. Disconnect the wiring plug from the solenoid valve as it's withdrawn.

7 Disconnect the wiring plug from the fuel pump and then remove the securing bolts from the fuel pump. Remove each bolt one turn at a time. Lift the pump from place, and move it to one side – there's no need to disconnect the fuel supply pipe. Note that new bolts will be required.

8 Unclip the ignition coils wiring loom from the engine.

9 Disconnect the vacuum pipes from the wastegate actuator, and control valve, then unclip the pipe assembly and move it to one side **(see illustration)**.

10 Undo the nuts/bolt and remove the small heatshield between the turbocharger and cylinder head cover **(see illustration)**.

4.6 Unclip the vacuum pipe assembly and move it to the rear of the engine

4.9 Disconnect the vacuum pipes from the control valve and wastegate actuator

4.10 Undo the nuts/bolt and remove the heatshield

4.11 Squeeze together the sides of the collar and disconnect the breather pipe

4.14 Apply a 5mm diameter bead of sealant at (A) and a 4mm diameter bead at (B)

11 Disconnect the breather pipe **(see illustration)** and then in reverse order to that shown **(see illustration 4.16)**, slacken the cover bolts in turn.
12 Remove the cover from the engine.

Refitting

13 Clean the mating surfaces of the cylinder head and the cover gasket. Inspect the gasket, if it is in good condition it can be reused.
14 Apply sealant at the points shown **(see illustration)**. Note that Ford list 2 different sealants for this application. Ford WSE-M4G323-A4 should be applied at the timing belt end of the engine and Ford WSE-M2G3-A548 should be applied at the fuel pump end of the engine.
15 Lower the cover onto the cylinder head, ensuring that the gasket stays in place.
16 Tighten the bolts in the correct sequence, finger tight at first and then to the specified torque **(see illustration)**.
17 Fit a new O-ring to the high pressure fuel pump and lubricate the O-ring with clean engine oil before refitting. Tighten the bolts half a turn at time to the specified torque.
18 When refitting the camshaft position sensors lubricate the O-rings with clean engine oil and tighten to the specified torque
19 The remainder of refitting is a reversal of removal.

5 Valve clearances – checking and adjustment

Note: *The valve clearances will not normally require checking or adjustment during the life of the vehicle. Checking and adjustment should only be required when work has been undertaken on the cylinder head or the camshafts.*
Note: *If checking the valve clearances with the timing belt removed (eg, after refitting the camshafts), rotate the crankshaft 90° anti-clockwise back from TDC on No 1 cylinder so the pistons are halfway down the cylinder bores. Verify this by inserting a long screwdriver down the spark plug holes.*
1 Remove the cylinder head cover as described in Section 4.
2 Remove the spark plugs as described in Chapter 1A Section 21 in order to make turning the engine easier. The engine may be turned using a spanner on the crankshaft pulley bolt or by raising the front right-hand roadwheel clear of the ground, engaging top gear and turning the wheel. If the former method is used, jack up and support the front

of the car (see *Jacking and vehicle support*) then remove the engine undershield for access to the pulley bolt; if the latter method is used, apply the handbrake then jack up the front right-hand side of the car until the roadwheel is clear of the ground and support with an axle stand.
3 Draw the valve positions on a piece of paper, numbering them 1 to 12 inlet and exhaust, from the timing belt (right-hand) end of the engine (ie, 1E, 1I, 2E, 2I and so on). As there are two inlet and two exhaust valves for each cylinder, draw the cylinders as large circles and the four valves as smaller circles. The inlet valves are at the rear of the cylinder head, and the exhaust valves are at the front. As the valve clearances are checked, cross them off.
Note: *The engine should only ever be turned in the normal (clockwise) direction of rotation.*
4 Turn the engine in a clockwise direction until both inlet valves of No 1 cylinder are fully shut and the apex of the camshaft lobes are pointing upwards away from the valve positions.
5 Insert a feeler blade of the correct thickness (see Specifications) between the heel of the camshaft lobe and the tappet **(see illustration)**. It should be a firm sliding fit. If

4.16 Tighten the bolts in the sequence shown

5.5 Checking the valve clearances

5.10 Measure the thickness of the tappets with a micrometer

5.11 The thickness of each tappet should be etched on its underside

this is the case, the clearance is correct and the valve position can be crossed off. If the clearance is not correct, use feeler blades to determine the exact clearance and record this on the drawing. From this clearance it will be possible to calculate the thickness of the new tappet to be fitted. Note that no shims are fitted between the camshaft and tappet – the complete tappet must be renewed.

6 Check the clearance of the second inlet valve for No 1 cylinder, and if necessary record the existing clearance on the drawing.

7 Now turn the engine until the inlet valves of No 2 cylinder are fully shut and the camshaft lobes pointing away from the valve positions. Check the clearances as described previously, and record any that are incorrect.

8 After checking all of the inlet valve clearances, check the exhaust valve clearances in the same way, but note that the clearances are different.

9 Where adjustment is required, the procedure is to remove the camshafts as described in Section 10.

10 If the recorded clearance was too small, a thinner tappet must be fitted, and conversely if the clearance was too large, a thicker tappet must be fitted. To calculate the thickness of the new tappet, first use a micrometer to measure the thickness of the existing tappet (C) and add this to the measured clearance (B) **(see illustration)**. Deduct the desired clearance (A) to provide the thickness (D) of the new tappet. The thickness of the tappet should be etched on the downward facing surface, however use the micrometer to verify this. The formula is as follows.

Sample calculation	
New tappet thickness D = Existing tappet thickness C + Measured clearance B – Desired clearance A	
Desired clearance (A)	0.20
Measured clearance (B)	0.15
Existing tappet thickness (C)	2.725
Tappet thickness required (D)	2.675
All measurements in mm	

11 The tappets are available in varying thicknesses in increments of 0.025 mm. Note that tappets are only marked with the digits

after the decimal point e.g. a 2.625 will be marked 625 **(see illustration)**.

12 It will be helpful for future adjustment if a record is kept of the thickness of tappet fitted at each position.

13 When all the clearances have been checked and adjusted, refit the camshafts and valve cover. Refit the engine undershield and lower the car to the ground.

---

6 Crankshaft pulley/vibration damper – removal and refitting

Note: The crankshaft pulley/ vibration damper retaining bolt may only be used once. Obtain a new bolt for the refitting procedure.

Removal

1 Remove the auxiliary drivebelt as described in Chapter 1A Section 26.

2 Set the engine to the top dead centre (TDC) position as described in Section 3. Fully tighten both the inner and outer sections of the VVT locating tool.

3 Remove the starter motor as described in Chapter 5A Section 9.

4 Slacken the right-hand road wheel nuts, then jack up and support the front of the vehicle (see *Jacking and vehicle support*). Remove the road wheel.

5 If the correct Ford special tools are available unbolt the driveshaft bearing support bracket from the block.

6 If not already done so, remove the blanking

6.7 Install the flywheel locking tool

plug and install the crankshaft locating pin (303-1604).

7 Ford tool 303-1602 (or equivalent) must now be fitted to lock the crankshaft in position. This tool bolts across the starter motor aperture in the transmission bellhousing, and engages with the teeth of the starter ring gear on the flywheel/driveplate **(see illustration)**. The tool must be firmly locked in position. Do not attempt to improvise this tool, the correct tool must be used due to the high torque figure required to retain the crankshaft pulley bolt

8 Where available, Install Ford special tool 303-1611-01 to the rear of the engine block and then fit Ford special tool 303-1611 to the crankshaft pulley.

9 If the correct Ford tools are not available it is possible to remove the pulley using conventional methods. Note however that the bolt is extremely tight and a very long knuckle bar and a best quality socket will be required.

10 Loosen the crankshaft pulley bolt and discard it. A new one must be used.

11 Remove the crankshaft pulley, and (where applicable) discard the friction washer behind the pulley **(see illustration)**. The washer is only fitted if the pulley has been removed – it is not fitted in the factory. Note that Ford recommend that whenever the pulley is removed, then the crankshaft oil seal should also be replaced as described in Section 15.

Refitting

Caution: The crankshaft pulley locating pin and the crankshaft locating pin are not designed to lock the pulley or the crankshaft in position. The crankshaft must be locked in place with the correct tool (303-1602) fitted to the flywheel ring gear.

Refitting with the Ford special tools

12 Fit a new friction washer, refit the crankshaft pulley and then loosely fit the new bolt. Fit Ford special tool 303-732 and lock the crankshaft pulley in position.

13 The crankshaft pulley bolt requires a very high torque to fully tighten it. Tighten the bolt through the first 2 stages given in the specifications and then remove the crankshaft pulley locating pin.

14 Install the torque multiplier and fully tighten the crankshaft pulley bolt to the

6.11 Renew the friction washer behind the pulley

specified torque and then through the angle tightening stages given in the specifications.

15 Check that the crankshaft pulley locating pin can be fitted. Note that if the pulley has moved in relation to the crankshaft, the bolt will have to be removed (and replaced) and the procedure repeated.

16 Remove the crankshaft locating pin, the VVT locking tools and the flywheel locking tool and then rotate the engine clockwise 2 complete revolutions. Refit the locating tools and check that they fit. If the crankshaft pulley, crankshaft and VVT locking tools do not fit the procedure must be repeated. A replacement crankshaft pulley bolt will be required

17 Refit the remaining components in the reverse order of removal.

Refitting without the Ford special tools

Note: *The crankshaft locating pin, the crankshaft pulley locating pin, the VVT locating tools and the flywheel locking tool will be still be required.*

18 Fit a new friction washer, refit the crankshaft pulley and then loosely fit the new bolt. Fit Ford special tool 303-732 and lock the crankshaft pulley in position **(see illustrations)**.

19 The crankshaft pulley bolt requires a very high torque to fully tighten it. Tighten the bolt through the first 2 stages given in the specifications and then remove the crankshaft pulley locating pin.

20 The torque multiplier specified is a 5: 1 multiplier, so the crankshaft pulley is effectively tightened to 300Nm using conventional tools. A best quality socket and long knuckle bar will be required. Ideally this will be a ¾ drive socket set.

21 Tighten the crankshaft pulley bolt to 300Nm and then fit an angle gauge to the crankshaft pulley bolt **(see illustrations)**. Tighten the bolt through 90 degrees. Note that unless the vehicle is raised sufficiently it will be impossible to attain the required 90 degrees in one movement. A less than ideal solution will be to tighten the bolt 45 degrees and then another 45 degrees.

6.18a Using a new bolt fit the pulley...

22 Check that the crankshaft pulley locating pin can be fitted. Note that if the pulley has moved in relation to the crankshaft, the bolt will have to be removed (and replaced) and the procedure repeated.

23 Remove the crankshaft locating pin, the VVT locking tools and the flywheel locking tool and then rotate the engine clockwise 2 complete revolutions. Refit the locating tools and check that they fit. If the crankshaft pulley, crankshaft and VVT locating tools do not fit the procedure must be repeated. A replacement crankshaft pulley bolt will be required

24 Refit the remaining components in the reverse order of removal.

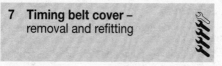

7 Timing belt cover – removal and refitting

Removal

1 Disconnect the battery negative lead as described in Chapter 5A Section 4.

2 Drain the engine oil and remove the oil filter as described in Chapter 1A Section 6.

3 Drain the cooling system as described in Chapter 1A Section 30.

4 Remove the cylinder head cover as described in Section 4.

5 Remove the auxiliary drivebelt as described

6.18b ...and then install the special tool (arrowed)

in Chapter 1A Section 26, then unbolt the drivebelt tensioner.

6 Remove the crankshaft pulley as described in Section 6.

7 Remove the catalytic converter as described in Chapter 4A Section 13.

8 Remove the alternator as described in Chapter 5A Section 7.

9 Remove the throttle body as described in Chapter 4A Section 11.

10 Undo the bolts and remove the engine lifting eye from the right-hand front corner of the engine.

11 Undo the bolts and move the coolant pipe assembly at the front/rear of the engine to one side.

12 The engine must now be supported from below. Using a suitable jack and a block of wood between the jack head and the oil sump to spread the load, raise the engine slightly.

13 Release the clips and move the coolant expansion tank to one side **(see illustration)**. There's no need to disconnect the hoses.

14 With the engine supported from below remove the right-hand engine mount as described in Section 17.

15 The cover can now be removed. It is held in place with a total of 20 bolts that are of varying lengths. Note position of each bolt as it is removed and remove them in reverse order to that shown **(see illustration 7.18)**. The cover is secured to the engine and sump with sealant. Do not use any metal tools to separate the cover. Small wooden wedge can

6.21a Use an angle gauge or...

6.21b ...alternatively mark the bolt and the pulley (arrowed). This Is also useful as a back up In case the gauge moves

7.13 Release the clips and slide up the coolant expansion tank

7.17a Apply a 4mm diameter bead of sealant at (A) and a 6mm diameter bead of sealant at (B)

7.17b Add a 4mm bead of sealant at the join between the cylinder head and block (A) and a 4mm run of sealant along the sump (B)

7.18 Tighten the bolts in the order shown

be used at strategic points around the cover to free it from the engine. Ford insist that the bolts are renewed.

Refitting

16 Clean the gasket material from both surfaces using a plastic or wooden scraper. Do not use a metal scraper or the machined surfaces will be damaged.

17 Apply silicone gasket and sealant (Ford WSE-M4G323-A4) as shown **(see illustrations)**. The sealant must be applied 1mm from the inner edge and must go all the way around the mating surface. Note that the cover must be installed within 10 minutes of applying the sealant.

18 Fit the new bolts to the cover and tighten them finger tight in the order shown. Torque them to the settings given in the specifications in the order shown **(see illustration)**.

19 Refit the remaining components in reverse order.

8 Timing belt – removal and refitting

Removal

1 Set the engine to TDC as described in Section 3.

2 Remove the timing belt cover as described in Section 7.

3 On turbocharged (Ecoboost) engines, remove the oil feed pipe from the turbocharger. Dispose of the washer. A new one must be used.

4 With the engine at TDC install Ford special tool 303-1605 (or equivalent) and lock the camshafts in position **(see illustration)**.

5 Rotate the belt tensioner anti-clockwise and fit the locking pin. This is best accomplished with the aid of an assistant pulling on the long run of the timing belt. Use a pair of waterpump

pliers to finally rotate the tensioner and fit the locking pin **(see illustration)**. Ford list a special tool for this (303-1054) but a drill bit is also suitable. Remove the timing belt.

6 Unbolt and remove the tensioner **(see illustration)**.

Inspection

7 The belt must always be replaced if removed. As a safety measure, the belt should be renewed irrespective of its apparent condition whenever the engine is overhauled.

8 Check the sprockets for signs of wear or damage. Renew any worn or damaged components.

9 When fitting a new belt always fit a new tensioner.

Refitting

10 Locate and then correctly fit the new cambelt tensioner. Tighten the bolt to the specified torque.

8.4 Lock the camshafts in position with the special tools

8.5 Lock the tensioner in position and remove the belt

8.6 Note how the tensioner locates on the engine block, then remove the tensioner locating bolt

9.3 Hold the camshaft on the flats provided with an open ended spanner

9.4a Undo the bolt…

9.4b …remove the sprockets

11 Locate the timing belt on the crankshaft sprocket, then feed it first over the exhaust camshaft sprocket and then the inlet camshaft sprocket. Finally fit the belt over the tensioner pulley.
12 Remove the locking pin and release tensioner. Remove the camshaft locking tool and TDC timing pin. Rotate the engine twice in the normal direction (clockwise) and check that the locking tools can be still be fitted. If necessary remove the belt and repeat the installation procedure
13 The remainder of refitting is a reversal of removal.

9 Timing belt tensioner and sprockets – removal, inspection and refitting

Tensioner pulley

1 Removal of the tensioner pulley is described within the timing belt procedure as described in Section 8.

Camshaft sprockets (VVT units)

Removal

2 Remove the timing belt as described in Section 8.
Caution: Do not use the camshaft locking tools (303-1605) to restrain the camshafts whilst the VVT sprockets are removed.
3 Use a suitable extra long open ended spanner on the camshafts to prevent them

9.5 Lock the camshafts in position

from turning, and then with the aid of an assistant remove the camshaft sprocket bolts **(see illustration)**. Note that the bolts are also the control valves for the variable valve timing.
4 Mark the position of the sprockets and then remove them **(see illustrations)**. Inspect them for damage and replace them if necessary.

Refitting

5 Fit the camshaft locking tools (303-1605, or equivalent) and lock the camshafts in position **(see illustration)**.
6 Refit the sprockets and then install Ford special tool 303-1606 (or equivalent). Tighten the bolts on the tool finger tight only at this point.
7 Install the camshaft sprocket special bolts – finger tight only at this stage. Position the special tools (303-1606) so that the lever arms on the special tool are approximately vertical **(see illustration)**. Remove the special tools.
8 Fit the new timing belt and cover as described in Section 8, then refit the timing belt cover.
9 With the camshaft locking tool still in position, install special tool 303-1606 to the camshaft sprockets. Using the tool rotate the camshaft sprockets anti-clockwise until resistance is felt. Tighten the 6 central bolts and lock the tool in position **(see illustration 3.12)**.
10 Use an open ended spanner on the camshaft flats and tighten the camshaft sprocket bolts to the first stage in the bolt tightening procedure. Do not use the camshaft locking tool to prevent the camshafts from

9.7 Fit the special tools

turning, a spanner must be used on the flat section provided on each camshaft.
11 Use an open ended spanner on the camshaft flats and tighten the camshaft sprocket bolts to the specified torque (stages 2, 3 and 4). Note to prevent any possibility of the camshafts moving it is recommended that an assistant holds the camshaft in position whilst the bolts are tightened.
12 Remove the special tool from the sprockets and then refit the control solenoids to the timing belt cover.
13 Remove the camshaft locking tool (303-1605) and then (using a new washer) refit the oil feed banjo bolt. Tighten the bolt to the specified torque.
14 Refit the rest of the components in reverse order.

Crankshaft sprocket

15 Remove the timing belt as described in Section 8.
16 Slide the sprocket off the end of the crankshaft.
17 Examine the teeth of the sprocket for wear and damage, and renew if necessary.
18 Wipe clean the end of the crankshaft, then slide on the sprocket.
19 Refit the timing belt as described in Section 8.

10 Camshafts and tappets – removal, inspection and refitting

Removal

1 Disconnect the battery negative lead as described in Chapter 5A Section 4.
2 Remove the cylinder head cover as described in Section 4.
3 Before removing the camshafts, it may be useful to check and record the valve clearances as described in Section 5. If any clearance is not within limits, new tappets can be obtained and fitted.
4 Remove the camshaft sprockets/variable valve timing control units as described in Section 9.
5 Note the positions of the camshaft bearing caps (mark them if necessary) and then slacken the retaining bolts in the reverse

10.6a Remove the camshafts...

10.6b ...and then the tappets

10.13 The camshafts are position with the 'QR' code uppermost

order to that shown **(see illustration 10.15)**. Each bolt should be slackened one turn only initially. Repeat this a second time for all 22 bolts and then finally fully slacken the bolts and remove the bearing caps. Keep the caps in the correct order for refitting. Note that Ford insist that new bolts are used upon refitting.

6 Remove the camshafts and then remove the tappets **(see illustrations)**. Store them in the correct order – ideally obtain 12 small containers and label each one appropriately.

Inspection

7 With the camshafts and tappets removed, check each for signs of obvious wear (scoring, pitting, etc) and for ovality, and renew if necessary.

8 Visually examine the camshaft lobes for score marks, pitting, and evidence of

overheating (blue, discoloured areas). Look for flaking away of the hardened surface layer of each lobe. If any such signs are evident, renew the component concerned.

9 Examine the camshaft bearing journals and the cylinder head bearing surfaces for signs of obvious wear or pitting. If any such signs are evident, renew the component concerned.

10 To check camshaft endfloat, remove the tappets, clean the bearing surfaces carefully, and refit the camshafts and bearing caps. Tighten the bearing cap bolts to the specified torque wrench setting, then measure the endfloat using a dial gauge mounted on the cylinder head so that its tip bears on the camshaft right-hand end.

11 Tap the camshaft fully towards the gauge, zero the gauge, then tap the camshaft fully away from the gauge, and note the gauge

reading. At the time of writing no camshaft endfloat specifications were available from Ford, however and play in excess of 0.2mm will require further investigation.

Refitting

12 Clean all the gasket material from the bearing caps and cylinder head before refitting the camshafts.

13 Lubricate the tappets with clean engine oil and refit them. Refit the camshafts **(see illustration)**. Apply engine oil to the camshaft lobes and bearing journals. To avoid any possibility of the valves contacting the pistons rotate the crankshaft anti-clockwise 90° so that the pistons are halfway up (or down) the bores.

14 Each end bearing cap must be have a 3mm bead of Ford sealant (WSK-M2G348-A5) applied to the cap surface. **(see illustrations)**. The camshaft caps must then be fitted within 5 minutes of applying the sealant.

15 With all the caps in position, fit the new bolts and tighten them in the order shown **(see illustration)**. Tighten each bolt finger tight and then each bolt should be tightened two turns only to start with – in the order shown. Finally tighten the bolts to the specified torque.

16 Refit the remaining components in reverse order of removal.

10.14a Applying sealant to the fuel pump housing/bearing cap

10.14b A 3mm diameter bead of sealant must be applied as shown

10.14c Follow the same procedure for the vacuum pump housing

10.14d Fit the cap/housing within 5 minutes of applying the sealant

10.15 Tighten the bolts in the order shown

11.7a Remove the coolant hoses and...

11.7b ...then the coolant outlet

11.18 Check the cylinder head for distortion with a straight edge and a feeler gauge

11 Cylinder head – removal, inspection and refitting

Note: *The cylinder head bolts require a suitable 'Ribe' socket to remove them.*

Removal

1 Jack up and support the front of the vehicle (see *Jacking and vehicle support*).

2 Drain the cooling system as described in Chapter 1A Section 30.

3 Drain the engine oil as described in Chapter 1A Section 6.

4 Disconnect the battery negative lead as described in Chapter 5A Section 4. To improve access, also remove the battery tray.

5 Remove the turbocharger as described in Chapter 4A Section 15.

6 Remove the camshafts and tappets as described in Section 10.

7 At the left-hand end of the cylinder head unbolt and remove both coolant hoses and then unbolt the coolant outlet from the cylinder head (4 bolts) **(see illustrations)**.

8 Remove the vacuum pump as described in Chapter 9 Section 21.

9 Lower the vehicle to the ground.

10 Make a note of their fitted locations and the harness routing, then disconnect any wiring plugs attached to components on the cylinder head. Label the plugs if necessary to aid refitting.

11 Make a last check round the cylinder head, to ensure that nothing remains connected or attached which would prevent the head from being lifted off.

12 Prepare a clean surface to lay the head down on once it has been removed.

13 Working in the reverse of the tightening sequence **(see illustration 11.27)**, slacken the ten cylinder head bolts progressively and by half a turn at a time; a Torx key (TX 50 size) or Ribe polydrive bit will be required. Remove all the bolts and dispose of them.

14 Lift off the cylinder head away. Remove the gasket, noting the two dowels. Although the gasket cannot be re-used, it is advisable to retain it for comparison with the new one, to confirm that the right part has been supplied.

Inspection

15 The mating faces of the cylinder head and cylinder block must be perfectly clean before refitting the head. Use a hard plastic or wood scraper to remove all traces of gasket and carbon; also clean the piston crowns. Take particular care during the cleaning operations, as aluminium alloy is easily damaged.

16 Make sure that the carbon is not allowed to enter the oil and coolant passages – this is particularly important for the lubrication system, as carbon could block the oil supply to the engine's components. Using adhesive tape and paper, seal the coolant, oil and bolt holes in the cylinder block. To prevent carbon entering the gap between the pistons and bores, smear a little grease in the gap. After cleaning each piston, use a small brush to remove all traces of grease and carbon from the gap, then wipe away the remainder with a clean rag.

17 Check the mating surfaces of the cylinder block and the cylinder head for nicks, deep scratches and other damage. If slight, they may be removed carefully with a file, but if excessive, renewal is necessary as it is not permissible to machine the surfaces.

18 If warpage of the cylinder head gasket surface is suspected, use a straight-edge to check it for distortion **(see illustration)**. Refer to Part D of this Chapter if necessary.

19 If possible, clean out the bolt holes in the block using compressed air, to ensure no oil or coolant is present. Screwing a bolt into an oil- or coolant-filled hole can (in extreme cases) cause the block to fracture, due to the hydraulic pressure created.

20 Although not essential, if a suitable tap-and-die set is available, it's worth running the correct-size tap down the bolt threads in the cylinder block. This will clean the threads of any debris, and go some way to restoring any damaged threads. Make absolutely sure the tap is the right size and thread pitch, and lightly oil the tap before starting.

21 Ford insist that the cylinder head bolts must be renewed.

Refitting

22 Wipe clean the mating surfaces of the cylinder head and cylinder block, and check that the two locating dowels are in position in the block **(see illustration)**.

23 Turn the crankshaft anti-clockwise so that pistons are halfway up (or down) the cylinder bores, in order to avoid the risk of valve/piston contact. Turn the crankshaft using a spanner on the pulley bolt.

24 If the old gasket is still available, check that it is identical to the new one. Position the new gasket over the dowels on the cylinder block surface. It can only be fitted one way round – check carefully that the holes in the gasket align with the holes in the block surface, and that none are blocked **(see illustration)**.

25 It is useful when refitting a cylinder head to have an assistant on hand to help guide the head onto the dowels. Take care that the gasket does not get moved as the head is lowered into position. To confirm that the

11.22 Check that the dowels are secure

11.24 Fit the new gasket

11.27 Tighten the bolts to the specified torque

12.5 Gently lever the sump free

head is aligned correctly, once it is in place, temporarily slide in two or more of the head bolts, and check that they fit into the block holes.

26 Fit the new head bolts carefully, and screw them in by hand only until finger-tight.

27 Working progressively and in sequence, tighten the cylinder head bolts to their Stage 1 torque setting **(see illustration)**.

28 Next, go around again in the same sequence, and tighten the bolts to the Stage 2 setting.

29 Stage 3 requires all the bolts to be loosened by 45 degrees – an 'angle tightening gauge' will be required.

30 Next (stage 4) tighten the bolts in sequence to the specified torque.

31 Stage 5 is to tighten all the bolts through 90 degrees in correct order.

32 Finally (stage 6), the bolts should be angle-tightened further, by the specified amount.

33 The remainder of refitting is a reversal of removal, noting the following points:

a) *Refit the camshafts as described in Section 10, and the timing belt as described in Section 8.*

b) *Refit the turbocharger (where applicable) as described in Chapter 4A Section 15.*

c) *Tighten all fasteners to the specified torque, where given.*

12.7 Apply sealant to the inside of the bolt holes

d) *Ensure that all hoses and wiring are correctly routed, and that hose clips and wiring connectors are securely refitted.*

e) *Refill the cooling system as described in Chapter 1A Section 30.*

f) *Replace the engine oil. An oil and filter change is recommended.*

g) *Check all disturbed joints for signs of oil or coolant leakage once the engine has been restarted and warmed-up to normal operating temperature.*

12 Sump – removal and refitting

Removal

1 Drain the engine oil and renew the oil filter as described in Chapter 1A Section 6.

2 Remove the catalytic converter as described in Chapter 4A Section 13.

3 On turbocharged (Ecoboost) models, remove the air conditioning compressor as described in Chapter 3 Section 11. Note there

12.9 Tighten the bolts in the order shown

is no need to disconnect the refrigerant pipes – move the compressor to one side, and secure it with wire/string to the vehicle bodywork etc.

4 Remove the sump retaining bolts in the reverse order to that shown **(see illustration 12.9)**. Note the location of each bolt, as they are of different lengths. Ford insist that the sump-to-cylinder block bolts are discarded, and new ones fitted.

5 A traditional sump gasket is not used – sealant is used instead. Unfortunately, the use of sealant makes removal of the sump more difficult. There are several points around the sump where it is possible to insert a screwdriver or wooden wedges to break the seal and release the sump **(see illustration)**.

Note: *On no account lever between the mating faces, as this will almost certainly damage them, resulting in leaks when finished.*

Refitting

6 Thoroughly clean the contact surfaces of the sump and crankcase. Use a plastic or wooden scraper only. Do not use metal tools or the machined surfaces may be damaged.

7 Apply a 3 to 4 mm diameter bead of sealant (Ford WSE M4G323-A4, or equivalent) to the sump pan, to the inside of the bolt holes **(see illustration)**. The sump bolts must be fitted and tightened within 10 minutes of applying the sealant.

8 Offer the sump up into position and fit all the sump bolts finger tight.

9 Tighten the bolts to the specified torque in the order shown **(see illustration)**. Note that the 2 sump to transmission bolt have a higher torque value than the sump to block bolts.

10 Refit the remaining components in reverse order of removal.

11 Lower the car to the ground. To be on the safe side, wait a further 30 minutes for the sealant to cure before fitting a new oil filter and refilling the engine with fresh oil as described in Chapter 1A Section 6.

12 Finally start the engine and check for signs of oil leaks.

13.2 Remove the cover

13.3a Remove the pump…

13.3b …and recover the belt

13 Oil pump – removal and refitting

Removal

1 Remove the sump as described in Section 12.

2 Unclip the cover plate from the oil pump and remove it **(see illustration)**.

3 Unscrew the 3 bolts securing the oil pump to the block and then rotate the pump towards the timing belt, to enable it to be unhooked from the drive belt **(see illustrations)**.

4 If required the oil pump drive sprocket can now be removed **(see illustration)**.

5 Individual parts are not available for the oil pump. If the oil pump is faulty it must be replaced.

Refitting

6 If the oil pump has been replaced it should be primed with fresh engine before being fitted.

7 Refitting is a reversal of removal, but note that the oil pump cover must be clipped in place and then rotated into position. An audible click will be heard when the cover is correctly positioned **(see illustration)**.

8 Refit the sump as described in Section 12.

9 Ensure that the oil pressure warning light is illuminated before starting the engine. Restart the engine whilst watching the oil pressure warning light. It should go out as soon as the engine starts. Stop the engine immediately if the oil pressure warning light does not go out.

14 Oil pressure switch – removal and refitting

1 The oil pressure switch is a vital early warning of low oil pressure. The switch operates the oil warning light on the instrument panel – the light should come on with the ignition, and go out almost immediately when the engine starts.

2 If the light does not come on, there could be a fault on the instrument panel, the switch wiring, or the switch itself. If the light does not go out, low oil level, worn oil pump (or sump pick-up blocked), blocked oil filter, or worn main bearings could be to blame – or again, the switch may be faulty.

3 If the light comes on while driving, the best advice is to turn the engine off immediately, and not to drive the car until the problem has been investigated – ignoring the light could mean expensive engine damage.

Removal

4 The oil pressure switch is located on the rear face of the engine, above the oil filter **(see illustration)**.

5 Disconnect the wiring plug from the switch.

6 Unscrew the switch from the block, and remove it. There should only be a very slight loss of oil when this is done.

Inspection

7 Examine the switch for signs of cracking or splits. If the top part of the switch is loose, this is an early indication of impending failure.

8 Check that the wiring terminals at the switch are not loose, then trace the wire from the switch connector until it enters the main loom – any wiring defects will give rise to apparent oil pressure problems.

Refitting

9 Refitting is the reverse of the removal procedure, noting the following points:

a) *Coat the switch with thread lock (Loctite 243, Ford WSK-M2G349-A7 or equivilant)*

b) *Tighten the switch securely.*

c) *Reconnect the switch connector, making sure it clicks home properly. Ensure that the wiring is routed away from any hot or moving parts.*

d) *Check the engine oil level and top-up if necessary (see 'Weekly checks').*

e) *Check for signs of oil leaks once the engine has been restarted and warmed-up to normal operating temperature.*

15 Crankshaft oil seals – renewal

Right-hand oil seal

1 Remove the crankshaft pulley as described in Section 6.

2 Note the fitted depth of the oil seal as a guide for fitting the new one.

3 Using a small pry bar or (ideally) an oil seal removal tool, prise the old oil seal from the

13.4 Note the orientation of the drive sprocket

13.7 The cover must clip into place correctly

14.4 The oil pressure switch

15.3 Remove the old seal

15.5 Locate the new seal in position

15.6a Use the correct Ford tool or alternatively...

15.6b ...drive the seal home with a large socket

timing cover **(see illustration)**. Take great care not to damage the timing belt cover or the nose of the crankshaft.

4 Wipe clean the seating and the nose of the crankshaft.

5 Apply a little clean engine oil to the inner lip of the seal, then locate it in position. Make sure that the closed end of the oil seal faces outwards **(see illustration)**.

6 Using a socket or length of metal tubing, drive the oil seal squarely into position to the previously-noted depth. The Ford installation tool (303-1603) can be used together with an old crankshaft pulley bolt to press the oil seal into position **(see illustrations)**. Do not use a new crankshaft pulley bolt, as it is only permissible to use the bolt once. With the oil seal in position, wipe away any excess oil.

7 Refit the crankshaft pulley with reference to Section 6.

Left-hand oil seal

Note: *Once removed the seal must be replaced. It can not be refitted.*

8 Remove the flywheel/driveplate as described in Section 16.

9 Unscrew the 8 bolts and withdraw the oil seal carrier from the end of the crankshaft **(see illustrations)**. The 2 bolts securing the sump to the oil seal carrier are accessed from the underside of the sump. Note that the seal and carrier are made as one unit – it is not possible to obtain the seal separately.

Note: *Ford insist that all 8 oil seal carrier bolts must be discarded, and new ones fitted.*

10 Clean the carrier contact surface on the cylinder block, and the end of the crankshaft.

11 The new oil seal carrier is supplied complete with a fitting sleeve, which ensures that the oil seal lips are correctly located on the crankshaft. Ford state that neither the

crankshaft nor the new oil seal should be lubricated before fitting.

12 Locate the oil seal carrier and fitting sleeve over the end of the crankshaft. Press the carrier into position, noting that the centre bolt holes are formed into locating dowels.

13 Insert the new retaining bolts and progressively tighten them to the specified torque.

14 Remove the fitting sleeve and check that the oil seal lips are correctly located.

15 Refit the flywheel/driveplate as described in Section 16.

16 Flywheel/driveplate – removal, inspection and refitting

Removal

1 Remove the transmission as described in Chapter 7A Section 6 and the clutch as described in Chapter 6 Section 6.

2 Hold the flywheel/driveplate stationary using one of the following methods:

a) *If an assistant is available, insert one of the transmission mounting bolts into the cylinder block and have the assistant engage a wide-bladed screwdriver with the starter ring gear teeth while the bolts are loosened. Alternatively, a piece of angle-iron can be engaged with the ring gear and located against the transmission mounting bolt*

b) *A further method is to fabricate a piece of flat metal bar with a pointed end to engage the ring gear – fit the tool to the transmission bolt and use washers and packing to align it with the ring gear, then tighten the bolt to hold it in position.*

c) *Fit Ford tool 303-1602 (or equivalent) and lock the flywheel in position (see illustration).*

3 Unscrew and remove the bolts, then lift the flywheel/driveplate off the locating dowel on the crankshaft. Dispose of the bolts. New ones must be used

Inspection

4 Clean the flywheel/driveplate to remove

15.9a Remove the bolts...

15.9b ...and withdraw the seal/carrier assembly

16.2 The correct Ford tool locking the flywheel

16.5 Mark the inner and outer sections and check for excessive play

16.8 Fit the new bolts

grease and oil. Inspect the surface for cracks, rivet grooves, burned areas and score marks. Light scoring can be removed with emery cloth. Check for cracked and broken ring gear teeth. Lay the flywheel/driveplate on a flat surface, and use a straight-edge to check for warpage.

5 Where a dual mass flywheel is fitted check for excessive play between the stationary section and the movable section. Make paint marks on the inner and outer sections and then rotate the secondary section of the flywheel. Note the amount of rotation between the two sections **(see illustration)**. As a rule of thumb anything greater than 15mm should be considered excessive. If in doubt (and given the amount of work required to remove the flywheel) a second opinion from a Ford dealer or suitably equipped garage should be sought. Note that special tools are available to accurately asses the condition of the flywheel. If the service history of the vehicle is known and the clutch is being replaced for the second time, then the dual mass flywheel should always be replaced.

6 Clean and inspect the mating surfaces of the flywheel/driveplate and the crankshaft. If the crankshaft oil seal is leaking, renew it (see Section 15) before refitting the flywheel/driveplate. In fact, given the large amount of work needed to remove the flywheel/driveplate, it's probably worth fitting a new seal anyway, as a precaution.

Refitting

7 Make sure that the mating faces of the flywheel/driveplate and crankshaft are clean, then locate the flywheel/driveplate on the crankshaft – it will only fit in one position.
8 Insert the new retaining bolts finger-tight **(see illustration)**.
9 Lock the flywheel/driveplate (see paragraph 2), then tighten the bolts in a diagonal sequence to the specified torque.
10 The remainder of refitting is a reversal of removal.

17 Engine/transmission mountings – inspection and renewal

General

1 The engine/transmission mountings seldom require attention, but broken or deteriorated mountings should be renewed immediately, or the added strain placed on the driveline components may cause damage or wear.
2 While separate mountings may be removed and refitted individually, if more than one is disturbed at a time – such as if the engine/transmission unit is removed from its mountings – they must be reassembled and their fasteners tightened in the position marked on removal.
3 On reassembly, the complete weight of the engine/transmission unit must not be taken by the mountings until all are correctly aligned with the marks made on removal. Tighten the engine/transmission mounting fasteners to their specified torque wrench settings.

Inspection

4 During the check, the engine/transmission unit must be raised slightly, to remove its weight from the mountings.
5 Raise the front of the vehicle, and support it securely on axle stands. Position a jack under the sump, with a large block of wood between the jack head and the sump, then carefully raise the engine/transmission just enough to take the weight off the mountings.

⚠️ *Warning: DO NOT place any part of your body under the engine when it is supported only by a jack.*

6 Check the mountings to see if the rubber is cracked, hardened or separated from the metal components. Sometimes the rubber will split right down the centre.
7 Check for relative movement between each mounting's brackets and the engine/transmission or body (use a large screwdriver or lever to attempt to move the mountings). If movement is noted, lower the engine and check-tighten the mounting fasteners.

Renewal

Note: *The following paragraphs assume the engine is supported beneath the sump as described earlier.*

Right-hand mounting

8 Lift up the coolant expansion tank and position it to one side **(see illustration)**. Note there is no need to disconnect the coolant pipes. On some models a vibration damper is fitted to the rear of the mounting. Where fitted unbolt and remove the damper.
9 Mark the position of the mounting on the vehicle on the right-hand inner wing panel, and then undo the 3 bolts securing the mounting **(see illustration)**.
10 Undo the 3 retaining bolts from the engine side of the mounting and then remove the mounting **(see illustration)**.
11 Re-align the marks made on removal.

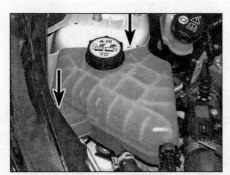

17.8 Release the clips and slide up the coolant expansion tank

17.9 Mounting-to-inner wing bolts

17.10 Mounting-to-engine retaining bolts

17.14 Undo the nuts and remove the battery support tray

17.16 Mounting bracket to transmission bolts – Powershift transmission shown

Tighten all fasteners to the torque wrench settings specified.

Left-hand mounting

12 Remove the air filter housing as described in Chapter 4A Section 5.

13 Remove the battery and battery tray as described in Chapter 5A Section 4.

14 Remove the nuts and withdraw the support tray **(see illustration)**.

15 With the transmission supported, unscrew the 2 bolts securing the mounting to the chassis side member.

16 Undo the bolts securing the mounting bracket to the transmission **(see illustration)**.

17 Refitting is a reversal of removal. Re-align the mounting in the position noted on removal, then tighten all fasteners to the specified torque wrench settings.

Rear mounting (roll restrictor)

18 Remove the mounting bolts and withdraw the mounting **(see illustration)**.

19 With the aid of an assistant pivot the engine (assuming the two main engine mountings are in position) and work the mounting free.

20 On refitting, ensure that the bolts are securely tightened to the specified torque wrench setting.

17.18 Rear mounting bolts

Chapter 2 Part B
1.25 and 1.6 litre petrol engines in-car repair procedures

Contents

Degrees of difficulty

Easy, suitable for novice with little experience | **Fairly easy,** suitable for beginner with some experience | **Fairly difficult,** suitable for competent DIY mechanic | **Difficult,** suitable for experienced DIY mechanic | **Very difficult,** suitable for expert DIY or professional

Specifications

General

Engine type..	Four-cylinder, in-line, double overhead camshafts, variable valve timing on 1.6 litre engines only
Designation:	
1.25 engines...	Duratec 16V
1.6 litre engines	Duratec 16V Ti-VCT
Engine codes:	
1.25 litre engines	STJB, STJC, SNJB, SNJC and SNJD
1.6 litre engines	IQJA, IQJC and IQJE
Capacity:	
1.25 litre engine	1242 cc
1.6 litre engines	1596 cc
Bore:	
1.25 litre engines	71.9 mm
1.6 litre engines	79.0 mm
Stroke:	
1.25 engines...	76.5 mm
1.6 litre engines	81.4 mm
Compression ratio:	
1.25 litre engines	11.0: 1
1.6 litre engines	11.0: 1

General (continued)

Output:
  Power:
    1.25 litre engines:
      Engine codes STJB, STJC and STJD . . . . 44 kW (60 PS)
      Engine codes SNJB, SNJC and SNJD . . . . 60 kW (82 PS)
    1.6 litre engines . . . . 77 kW (105 PS)
  Torque:
    1.25 litre engines:
      Engine codes STJB, STJC and STJD . . . . 109 Nm
      Engine codes SNJB, SNJC and SNJD . . . . 114 Nm
    1.6 litre engines:
      Engine codes IQJA and IQJC . . . . 150 Nm
      Engine code IQJE . . . . 148 Nm
Emissions level:
  1.25 litre engines:
    Engine codes STJB and SNJB . . . . Stage V
    Engine codes STJC, STJD, SNJC and SNJD . . . . Stage VI
  1.6 litre engines:
    Engine codes IQJA and IQJE . . . . Stage V
    Engine codes IQJC . . . . Stage VI
Firing order . . . . 1-3-4-2 (No 1 cylinder at timing belt end)
Direction of crankshaft rotation . . . . Clockwise (seen from right-hand side of car)

Valve clearances (cold)

Inlet . . . . 0.14 to 0.23 mm
Exhaust:
  1.25 engines . . . . 0.24 to 0.33 mm
  1.6 litre engines . . . . 0.28 to 0.37 mm

Camshafts

Camshaft bearing journal diameter . . . . Unavailable at time of writing
Camshaft bearing journal-to-cylinder head running clearance . . . . Unavailable at time of writing
Camshaft endfloat (typical) . . . . 0.05 to 0.13 mm

Lubrication

Oil pressure (minimum, warm engine):
  Idling (800 rpm) . . . . 1.0 bar
  At 2000 rpm . . . . 2.0 bars
Pressure relief valve opens at . . . . 4.0 bars
Oil pump clearances . . . . Not specified

Torque wrench settings

	Nm	lbf ft
Air conditioning compressor mounting bolts	25	18
Alternator mounting bracket bolts	42	31
Camshaft bearing cap:		
1.25 litre engines:		
Stage 1	7	5
Stage 2	Angle-tighten a further 45°	
1.6 litre engines:		
Stage 1	10	7
Stage 2:		
Timing belt end bearing cap outer bolts	Angle-tighten a further 53°	
Timing belt end bearing cap inner bolts	Angle-tighten a further 70°	
All other bearing cap bolts	Angle-tighten a further 45°	
Camshaft position sensor (1.6 litre engines)	9	7
Camshaft sensor ring (1.6 litre engines)	21	15
Camshaft sprocket bolt (1.25 litre engines)*:		
Stage 1	60	44
Stage 2	Angle-tighten a further 45°	
Coolant outlet to cylinder head	20	15
Coolant pump pulley bolts	24	18
Crankcase breather to cylinder block	9	7
Crankshaft position sensor	9	7
Crankshaft oil seal carrier	9	7

Torque wrench settings (continued)

	Nm	lbf ft
Crankshaft pulley/vibration damper: *		
Stage 1	100	74
Stage 2	Angle-tighten a further 90°	
Stage 3	Wait at least 20 seconds	
Stage 4	Angle-tighten a further 15°	
Cylinder head bolts: *		
Stage 1	5	4
Stage 2	15	11
Stage 3	35	26
Stage 4	Angle-tighten a further 75°	
Cylinder head cover	10	7
Driveplate bolts:		
Stage 1	30	22
Stage 2	Angle-tighten a further 80°	
Engine mountings:		
Right-hand mounting bracket to cylinder head	55	41
Right-hand mounting to cylinder head bracket*	80	59
Right-hand mounting to body	48	35
Left-hand mounting bracket to transmission	90	66
Left-hand mounting to transmission bracket	125	92
Left-hand mounting to body	90	66
Roll restrictor/rear mounting bolts	48	35
Engine-to-transmission bolts	48	35
Exhaust flexible section-to-catalytic converter nuts	48	35
Exhaust manifold heat shield bolts	10	7
Exhaust manifold nuts/bolts	54	40
Flywheel bolts: *		
Stage 1	30	22
Stage 2	Angle-tighten a further 80°	
Inlet manifold bolts	18	13
Oil baffle to cylinder block	9	7
Oil drain plug	28	21
Oil filter connector	45	33
Oil intake pipe to oil baffle	9	7
Oil pressure switch	15	11
Oil pump to cylinder block	9	7
Spark plugs	15	11
Sump bolts:		
Sump-to-block bolts:		
Stage 1	10	7
Stage 2	20	15
Sump-to-transmission bolts	48	35
TDC pin hole blanking plug	20	15
Timing belt cover bolts	9	7
Timing belt tensioner bolt	20	15
Torque converter to driveplate*	37	27
VCT solenoid	8	6
VCT unit blanking plugs	16	12
VCT unit retaining bolts: *		
Stage 1	25	18
Stage 2	Angle-tighten a further 75°	

*Use new fasteners

1 General Information

How to use this Chapter

1 This Part of Chapter 2 is devoted to in-car repair procedures on the 1.25 and 1.6 litre Duratec 16V petrol engines. All procedures concerning engine removal, refitting, and overhaul can be found in Chapter 2E.

2 Refer to Vehicle identification 13 Section 3 numbers for details of engine code locations.

3 Most of the operations included in this Chapter are based on the assumption that the engine is still installed in the car. Therefore, if this information is being used during a complete engine overhaul, with the engine already removed, many of the steps included here will not apply.

Engine description

4 The Duratec engine (formerly the Zetec-SE), is a sixteen-valve, double overhead camshaft (DOHC), four-cylinder, in-line unit, mounted transversely at the front of the car, with the transmission on its left-hand end.

5 Apart from the plastic timing belt covers, plastic cylinder head cover, plastic inlet manifold, and the cast-iron cylinder liners, the main engine components (including the sump) are manufactured entirely of aluminium alloy. *Caution: When tightening bolts into aluminium castings, it is important to adhere to the specified torque wrench settings, to avoid stripping threads.*

6 The crankshaft runs in five main bearings, the centre main bearing's upper half incorporating thrustwashers to control crankshaft endfloat.

Note: *On all petrol engines covered by*

this manual, it is not possible to remove the intermediate/main bearing section or to remove the crankshaft or pistons. No separate parts are available, and replacement/exchange units are supplied with crankshaft, pistons, connecting rods, etc, already fitted. Consult a Ford dealer or parts specialist for further information.

7 The connecting rods rotate on horizontally-split bearing shells at their big-ends, however the big-ends are of unusual design in that the caps are sheared from the rods during manufacture thus making each cap individually matched to its own connecting rod. The pistons are attached to the connecting rods by gudgeon pins which are an interference fit in the connecting rod small-end bores. The aluminium alloy pistons are fitted with three piston rings: two compression rings and an oil control ring.

8 The inlet and exhaust valves are each closed by coil springs; they operate in guides which are shrink-fitted into the cylinder head, as are the valve seat inserts.

9 Both camshafts are driven by the same toothed timing belt, each operating eight valves via bucket tappets. Each camshaft rotates in five bearings that are line-bored directly in the cylinder head and the (bolted-on) bearing caps; this means that the bearing caps are not available separately from the cylinder head, and must not be interchanged with caps from another engine.

10 1.6 litre engines are available with variable valve timing on the both the inlet and exhaust camshafts – this engine is known as the Ti-VCT (Twin independent Variable Camshaft Timing). Engine oil pressure is used to vary the positions of the camshaft sprocket in relation to the camshafts, thus varying the valves' opening and closing times. Control of the oil flow is achieved using solenoid valves, which in turn are controlled by the engine management powertrain control module (PCM). Varying the valve timing is this manner results in improved driveability and output, whist reducing fuel consumption and exhaust emissions.

11 The coolant pump is bolted to the right-hand end of the cylinder block, beneath the front run of the timing belt, and is driven by the auxiliary drivebelt from the crankshaft pulley.

12 Lubrication is by means of an eccentric-rotor trochoidal pump, which is mounted on the crankshaft right-hand end, and draws oil through a strainer located in the sump. The pump forces oil through an externally-mounted full-flow cartridge-type filter.

Operations with engine in car

13 The following work can be carried out with the engine in the car:
a) Cylinder head cover – removal and refitting.
b) Timing belt – renewal.
c) Timing belt tensioner and sprockets – removal and refitting.
d) Camshaft oil seals – renewal.
e) Camshafts, tappets and shims – removal and refitting.
f) Cylinder head – removal and refitting.
g) Sump – removal and refitting.
h) Crankshaft oil seals – renewal.
i) Oil pump – removal and refitting.
j) Flywheel/driveplate – removal and refitting.
k) Engine/transmission mountings – removal and refitting.

2 Compression test – description and interpretation

1 When engine performance is down, or if misfiring occurs which cannot be attributed to the ignition or fuel systems, a compression test can provide diagnostic clues as to the engine's condition. If the test is performed regularly, it can give warning of trouble before any other symptoms become apparent.

2 The engine must be fully warmed-up to operating temperature, the oil level must be correct and the battery must be fully-charged. The help of an assistant will also be required.

3 Note that it is necessary to remove the fuel pump relay to allow the compression test to be performed. This will log a fault code in the engine management powertrain control module when the engine is turned over on the starter, and the fault code will have to be cleared, using Ford diagnostic equipment or a compatible alternative, on completion of the test. Unless you have access to the necessary diagnostic equipment it may be preferable to have the compression test carried out by a Ford dealer or suitably-equipped garage. Should you wish to proceed, the procedure is as follows.

4 Refer to Chapter 12 Section 3 and remove the fuel pump relay from the engine compartment fusebox. Now start the engine and allow it to run until it stalls.

5 Disable the ignition system by disconnecting the multiplug from the DIS ignition coil. Remove all the spark plugs with reference to Chapter 1A Section 21.

6 Fit a compression tester to the No 1 cylinder spark plug hole – the type of tester which screws into the spark plug thread is preferable.

7 Arrange for an assistant to hold the accelerator pedal fully depressed to the floor, while at the same time cranking the engine over for several seconds on the starter motor. Observe the compression gauge reading. The compression will build-up fairly quickly in a healthy engine. Low compression on the first stroke, followed by gradually-increasing pressure on successive strokes, indicates worn piston rings. A low compression on the first stroke which does not rise on successive strokes, indicates leaking valves or a blown head gasket (a cracked cylinder head

could also be the cause). Deposits on the underside of the valve heads can also cause low compression. Record the highest gauge reading obtained, then repeat the procedure for the remaining cylinders.

8 Due to the variety of testers available, and the fluctuation in starter motor speed when cranking the engine, different readings are often obtained when carrying out the compression test. For this reason, actual compression pressure figures are not quoted by Ford. However, the most important factor is that the compression pressures are uniform in all cylinders, and that is what this test is mainly concerned with.

9 Add some engine oil (about three squirts from a plunger type oil can) to each cylinder through the spark plug holes, and then repeat the test.

10 If the compression increases after the oil is added, the piston rings are probably worn. If the compression does not increase significantly, the leakage is occurring at the valves or the head gasket. Leakage past the valves may be caused by burned valve seats and/or faces, or warped, cracked or bent valves.

11 If two adjacent cylinders have equally low compressions, it is most likely that the head gasket has blown between them. The appearance of coolant in the combustion chambers or on the engine oil dipstick would verify this condition.

12 If one cylinder is about 20 percent lower than the other, and the engine has a slightly rough idle, a worn lobe on the camshaft could be the cause.

13 On completion of the checks, refit the spark plugs and reconnect the HT leads and the DIS ignition coil multiplug. Refit the fuel pump relay to the fusebox, then clear the fault code from the powertrain control module.

3 Top Dead Centre (TDC) for No 1 piston – locating

1 Top dead centre (TDC) is the highest point of the cylinder that each piston reaches as the crankshaft turns. Each piston reaches its TDC position at the end of its compression stroke, and then again at the end of its exhaust stroke. For the purpose of engine timing, TDC on the compression stroke for No 1 piston is used. No 1 cylinder is at the timing belt end of the engine. Proceed as follows.

2 Disconnect the battery negative terminal as described in Chapter 5A Section 4, then remove the spark plugs as described in Chapter 1A Section 21.

3 Firmly apply the handbrake, then jack up the front of the vehicle and support it securely on axle stands (see Jacking and vehicle support). If the engine is to be turned using the right-hand front roadwheel with top gear engaged (manual transmission models only),

3.7a Undo the blanking plug from the right-hand rear corner of the cylinder block ...

3.7b ... and screw-in the timing pin

3.9 Locate the home-made camshaft setting tool (arrowed) in the slots

it is only necessary to raise the right-hand front roadwheel off the ground.

4 Where necessary, undo the fasteners, remove the engine undershield, then remove the auxiliary drivebelt lower cover for access to the crankshaft pulley and bolt.

1.25 litre engines

5 Remove the cylinder head cover as described in Section 4.

6 The piston of No 1 cylinder must now be positioned just before top dead centre (TDC). To do this, have an assistant turn the crankshaft until the slots in the left-hand ends of the camshafts are parallel with the upper surface of the cylinder head. Note that the slots are slightly offset so make sure that the lower edges of the slots are aligned with the cylinder head, and the lobes of No. 4 cylinder pointing downwards. Turn the crankshaft slightly anti-clockwise (viewed from the right-hand end of the engine).

7 Unscrew the blanking plug from the right-hand rear side of the engine cylinder block. A TDC timing pin must now be inserted and tightened into the hole. It is highly recommended that the special Ford timing pin 303-748 is obtained, or alternatively, a timing pin from a reputable tool manufacturer **(see illustrations)**.

8 With the timing pin in position, turn the crankshaft slowly clockwise until the specially-machined surface on the crank web

just touches the timing pin. No 1 piston is now at TDC on its compression stroke. To confirm this, check that the camshaft lobes for No 4 cylinder are 'rocking' (ie, exhaust valves closing and inlet valves opening).

9 It should now be possible to insert the camshaft setting bar into the slots in the left-hand ends of the camshafts. If the Ford setting tool 303-376B is unavailable, a home-made tool can be fabricated out of a length of flat metal bar 5.00 mm thick. The bar must be a good fit in the slots and should be approximately 180 to 230 mm long by 20 to 30 mm wide **(see illustration)**.

10 If the bar cannot be inserted in the slots with the crankshaft at TDC, the valve timing must be adjusted as described in Section 8 of this Chapter.

11 Once the work requiring the engine to be set at TDC has been completed, remove the metal bar from the camshaft slots then unscrew the timing pin and refit the blanking plug. Refit the spark plugs (Chapter 1A), cylinder head cover (Section 4), auxiliary drivebelt lower cover, and where necessary the engine undershield. Lower the vehicle to the ground and reconnect the battery negative terminal.

1.6 litre engines

12 Remove the upper timing belt cover as described in Section 7.

13 Position a trolley jack under the engine.

Use a block of wood on the jack head to prevent damage to the sump. Take the weight of the engine.

14 Pull the coolant expansion tank upwards and move it to one side. With the engine securely supported, remove the nuts/bolts securing the right-hand engine mounting to the body and engine bracket, then lift off the mounting **(see illustration)**. New nuts should be obtained for refitting the mounting.

15 Rotate the crankshaft pulley clockwise until the marks (dot on the inlet sprocket groove on the exhaust sprocket) of the camshaft VCT units are approaching the 11 o'clock position **(see illustrations)**.

16 Undo the blanking plug from the right-hand rear side of the engine cylinder block **(see illustration 3.7a)**. A TDC timing pin must now be inserted and tightened into the hole. It is highly recommended that the Ford timing pin 303-748 is obtained, or alternatively, a timing pin from a reputable tool manufacturer **(see illustration 3.7b)**. The diameter of the pin is critical as it determines the TDC point where the machined flat on the crankshaft web contacts the shank of the tool – note that the web does not contact the end of the tool.

17 With the timing pin in position, turn the crankshaft slowly clockwise until the specially machined surface on the crank web just touches the timing pin. No 1 piston is now at TDC on its compression stroke.

18 Now it is necessary to fit Ford special tool

3.14 Undo the nuts/bolts (arrowed) and remove the right-hand engine mounting

3.15a The inlet camshaft sprocket is marked with a dot (arrowed) ...

3.15b ... and the exhaust camshaft sprocket with a groove (arrowed)

3.18a Fit the special tool over the VCT units

3.18b The tool is marked with a dot (2) for the inlet camshaft, a line (1) for the exhaust camshaft, and an arrow (3) which must point upwards

303-1097 over the VCT units on the ends of the camshafts. Note that the tool is marked with a line to indicate the exhaust side, a dot to indicate the inlet side, and an arrow which must point upwards **(see illustrations)**.

19 Once the work requiring the engine to be set at TDC has been completed, remove the special tool from the camshaft VCT units then unscrew the timing pin and refit the blanking plug. Refit the spark plugs (Chapter 1A Section 21), upper timing belt cover, auxiliary drivebelt lower cover, and where necessary

the engine undershield. Lower the vehicle to the ground and reconnect the battery negative terminal.

4 Cylinder head cover – removal and refitting

Removal

1 Disconnect the battery negative

lead as described in Chapter 5A Section 4.

2 Disconnect the breather pipe from the front of the cover **(see illustration)**.

3 Disconnect the HT leads from the spark plugs, unclip them from the cover, and position them to the left-hand side of the engine compartment.

4 On 1.6 litre engines, disconnect the wiring plugs from the camshaft position sensors and VCT solenoids on the cylinder head cover, clean around the area, then undo the retaining bolts and remove both VCT oil control solenoids from the top, right-hand end of the cylinder head **(see illustrations)**. Plug the openings to prevent contamination. Examine the O-ring seals, and renew if necessary.

5 Where fitted, undo the nut and bolt and move the wiring connector bracket at the left-hand rear corner of the cylinder head cover to one side.

6 On all engines, the cylinder head cover is secured by a total of twelve bolts. Note their fitted locations and remove the bolts. On 1.6 litre engines, the bolts are integral with the cover.

7 On 1.25 litre engines, remove the centre top bolt from the timing belt upper cover **(see**

4.2 Disconnect the breather pipe

4.4a Disconnect the camshaft position sensors wiring plugs

4.4b Disconnect the VCT solenoid wiring plugs

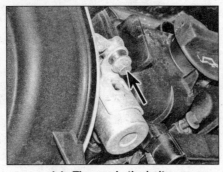

4.4c Then undo the bolt...

4.4d ... and pull the solenoids from their locations

illustration). This bolt secures the timing belt cover to the cylinder head cover.

8 Carefully lift the cover from the top of the cylinder head, unclipping any wiring as necessary. Recover the gasket – this may be re-used if it is not damaged.

Refitting

9 Clean the mating surfaces of the cylinder head and the cover gasket.

10 Lower the cover onto the cylinder head, ensuring that the gasket stays in place.

11 Progressively tighten all bolts to the specified torque.

12 The remainder of refitting is a reversal of removal.

5 Valve clearances – checking and adjustment

1 Remove the cylinder head cover as described in Section 4. **Note:** *If checking the valve clearances with the timing belt removed (eg, after refitting the camshafts), rotate the crankshaft 90° anti-clockwise back from TDC on No 1 cylinder so the pistons are halfway down the cylinder bores. Verify this by inserting a long screwdriver down the spark plug holes.*

2 Remove the spark plugs (Chapter 1A Section 21) in order to make turning the engine easier. The engine may be turned using a spanner on the crankshaft pulley bolt or by raising the front right-hand roadwheel clear of the ground, engaging top gear and turning the wheel (manual transmission models only). If the former method is used, jack up and support the front of the car (see *Jacking and vehicle support*) then unbolt the lower cover for access to the pulley bolt; if the latter method is used, apply the handbrake then jack up the front right-hand side of the car until the roadwheel is clear of the ground and support with an axle stand.

3 Draw the valve positions on a piece of paper, numbering them 1 to 8 inlet and exhaust, from the timing belt (right-hand) end of the engine (ie, 1E, 1I, 2E, 2I and so on). As there are two inlet and two exhaust valves for each cylinder, draw the cylinders as large circles and the four valves as smaller circles. The inlet valves are at

the front of the cylinder head, and the exhaust valves are at the rear. As the valve clearances are adjusted, cross them off.

4 Turn the engine in a clockwise direction until both inlet valves of No 1 cylinder are fully shut and the apex of the camshaft lobes are pointing upwards away from the valve positions.

5 Insert a feeler blade of the correct thickness (see Specifications) between the heel of the camshaft lobe and the tappet **(see illustration).** It should be a firm sliding fit. If this is the case, the clearance is correct and the valve position can be crossed off. If the clearance is not correct, use feeler blades to determine the exact clearance and record this on the drawing. From this clearance it will be possible to calculate the thickness of the new tappet to be fitted. Note that no shims are fitted between the camshaft and tappet – the complete tappet must be renewed.

6 Check the clearance of the second inlet valve for No 1 cylinder, and if necessary record the existing clearance on the drawing.

7 Now turn the engine until the inlet valves of No 2 cylinder are fully shut and the camshaft lobes pointing away from the valve positions. Check the clearances as described previously, and record any that are incorrect.

8 After checking all of the inlet valve clearances, check the exhaust valve clearances in the same way, but note that the clearances are different.

9 Where adjustment is required, the procedure is to remove the camshafts as described in Section 11.

10 If the recorded clearance was too small, a thinner tappet must be fitted, and conversely if the clearance was too large, a thicker tappet must be fitted. To calculate the thickness of the new tappet, first use a micrometer to measure the thickness of the existing tappet (C) and add this to the measured clearance (B) **(see illustrations).** Deduct the desired clearance (A) to provide the thickness (D) of the new tappet. The thickness of the tappet should be etched on the downward facing surface, however use the micrometer to verify this. The formula is as follows.

New tappet thickness D =
Existing tappet thickness C +
Measured clearance B –
Desired clearance A

Sample calculation

Desired clearance (A) = 0.20
Measured clearance (B) = 0.15
Existing tappet thickness (C) = 2.725
Tappet thickness required (D) =
    C+B–A = 2.675
All measurements in mm

11 The tappets are available in varying thicknesses in increments of 0.025 mm.

12 It will be helpful for future adjustment if a record is kept of the thickness of tappet fitted at each position so it is possible to identify which new tappets will be needed before removing the camshafts.

13 When all the clearances have been checked and adjusted, refit the lower cover (where removed), lower the car to the ground and refit the camshafts (Section 11) and the cylinder head cover as described in Section 4.

6 Crankshaft pulley/ vibration damper – removal and refitting

Caution: Removal of the crankshaft pulley/ vibration damper on 1.25 litre engines effectively loses the valve timing setting, and it will be necessary to reset the timing using the procedure and tools described in Section 8.

Note: *The crankshaft pulley/vibration damper retaining bolt may only be used once. Obtain a new bolt for the refitting procedure.*

4.7 Remove the timing belt upper cover centre top bolt

5.5 Insert a feeler gauge between the heel of the camshaft lobe and the tappet

5.10a Measure the thickness of the tappets with a micrometer

5.10b The thickness of each tappet should be etched on its underside

6.3a Ford tool No 303-393A and 303-393-02

6.3b The assembled tools bolt across the starter motor aperture ...

6.3c ... and engages with the teeth on the flywheel ring gear

Removal

1 Remove the auxiliary drivebelt as described in Chapter 1A Section 26.

2 Set the engine to the top dead centre (TDC) position as described in Section 3.

3 Remove the starter motor as described in Chapter 5A Section 9, then use Ford tool 303-393 and 303-393-02 to lock the crankshaft in position. This tool bolts across the starter motor aperture in the transmission bellhousing, and engages with the teeth of the starter ring gear on the flywheel/driveplate **(see illustrations)**.

4 Using a suitable socket and extension bar, undo and remove the crankshaft pulley/

7.2 Remove the nut securing the refrigerant pipe bracket

vibration damper retaining bolt, then slide the pulley/damper off the end of the crankshaft. Discard the bolt – Ford insist that a new bolt is fitted.

Refitting

5 Clean the end of the crankshaft and the crankshaft pulley/vibration damper.

6 Locate the crankshaft pulley/vibration damper on the end of the crankshaft, and press it fully home.

7 Insert the new crankshaft pulley/vibration damper retaining bolt and tighten it to the specified torque setting.

8 Remove the camshaft and crankshaft locking tools.

9 The remainder of refitting is a reversal of removal.

7 Timing belt covers – removal and refitting

Upper cover

Removal

1 Release the clips and pull the coolant expansion tank upwards and move it to one side.

2 On models with air conditioning, undo the refrigerant pipe bracket retaining nut

to prevent any strain on the pipe **(see illustration)**.

3 Slacken the coolant pump pulley bolts, then remove the alternator as described in Chapter 5A Section 7.

4 Unscrew the 4 bolts and remove the coolant pump pulley.

5 On 1.25 litre engines, undo the single bolt securing the upper timing belt cover to the cylinder head cover **(see illustration 4.7)**.

6 On all engines, unscrew the timing belt upper cover retaining bolts **(see illustration)**.

7 Manoeuvre the timing cover from the engine compartment.

Refitting

8 Refitting is a reversal of removal. Fit a new auxiliary drivebelt as described in Chapter 1A Section 26.

Lower cover

Removal

9 The timing belt lower cover is located around the crankshaft. First remove the crankshaft pulley/vibration damper as described in Section 6.

10 Working beneath the right-hand wheel arch, unscrew the retaining bolts and withdraw the timing cover **(see illustration)**.

Refitting

11 Refitting is a reversal of removal.

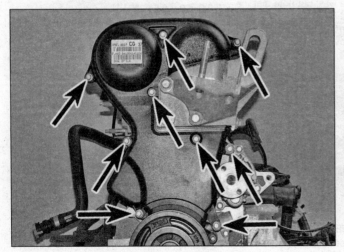

7.6 Timing belt upper cover bolts

7.10 Timing belt lower cover bolts

8.2 Remove the timing belt guide disc (where fitted)

8.4 Support the engine with a trolley jack and block of wood under the sump

8.7 Insert a 4 mm drill bit or rod into the tensioner arms

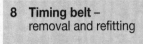

8 Timing belt – removal and refitting

Caution: The camshaft sprockets are made from a type of plastic. Care must be taken to avoid damage to the sprockets during the following procedure.

Removal

1 Remove the upper and lower timing belt covers as described in Section 7.
2 Where fitted, remove the timing belt guide disc from the end of the crankshaft. Note which way round the disc is fitted – the concave side faces outwards **(see illustration)**.
3 Remove the alternator as described in Chapter 5A Section 7.
4 The engine must now be supported, as the right-hand mounting (right as seen from the driver's seat) must be removed. Supporting the engine should ideally be done from above, using an engine crane or a special engine lifting beam. However, in the absence of these tools, the engine can be supported from below, on the cast-aluminium sump, providing a piece of wood is used to spread the load **(see illustration)**.
5 With the engine securely supported, remove the nuts/bolts securing the right-hand mounting to the body and engine bracket, then lift off the mounting **(see illustration 3.14)**. New nuts should be obtained for refitting the mounting.

6 Unbolt the lower half of the engine right-hand mounting bracket from the engine.
7 Push the timing belt eccentric tensioner pulley rearwards to detension the belt, then insert Ford tool No 303-1054 or a suitable equivalent into the pulley arm to lock it in position **(see illustration)**.
8 If the timing belt is to be re-used (this is not recommended), use white paint or similar to mark its direction of rotation, and note from the manufacturer's markings which way round it is fitted. Withdraw the belt from the sprockets and from over the tensioner **(see illustration)**. Do not attempt to turn the crankshaft or camshafts until the timing belt is refitted.

Inspection

9 If the belt is being removed for reasons other than routine renewal, check it carefully for any signs of uneven wear, splitting, cracks (especially at the roots of the belt teeth) or contamination with oil or coolant. Renew the belt if there is the slightest doubt about its condition. As a safety measure, the belt should be renewed irrespective of its apparent condition whenever the engine is overhauled.
10 Check the sprockets for signs of wear or damage, and ensure that the tensioner pulley rotates smoothly on its bearings; renew any worn or damaged components. Ford dealers (and many motor factors) now supply 'cambelt kits', consisting of the belt itself and a new tensioner – for peace of mind, it is recommended that one of these is purchased.
11 If signs of oil or coolant contamination are

found on the old belt, trace the source of the leak and rectify it, then wash down the engine timing belt area and related components to remove all traces of oil or coolant.

Refitting

1.25 litre engines

12 Ensure that the engine is still set to TDC on No 1 cylinder (Section 3).
13 Locate the timing belt on the crankshaft sprocket, then feed it over the two camshaft sprockets and finally, around the tensioner. If the original belt is being refitted, make sure that it is the correct way round as noted during removal **(see illustrations)**.
14 Where applicable, refit the timing belt guide disc on the end of the crankshaft, making sure that the concave side faces outwards.
15 Remove the locking pin from the tensioner, and allow it to tension the belt.
16 Refit the engine mounting bracket to the cylinder block, and tighten the bolts to the specified torque.
17 Refit the upper engine mounting bracket tightening the bolts and the new nuts to the specified torque. Remove the jack from under the engine, or remove the hoist from above, as applicable.
18 Refit the timing belt lower cover, and tighten the bolts to the specified torque.
19 Refit the crankshaft pulley/vibration damper as described in Section 6.
20 Remove the camshaft setting bar, the crankshaft timing pin and flywheel/driveplate locking tool.

8.8 Note the belt may be marked with direction-of-rotation arrows

8.13a Fit the belt around the camshaft sprockets ...

8.13b ... and the crankshaft sprocket

8.23 Timing belt routing

9.9 The lug on the tensioner mounting plate must locate in the square hole in the cylinder block

21 Rotate the crankshaft clockwise 1¾ turns approximately. Refit the crankshaft TDC timing pin then rotate the crankshaft clockwise until it stops against the timing pin. Check to see whether the setting bar will fit in the camshaft slots. If necessary, slacken the crankshaft pulley bolt, and repeat the procedure (using a new pulley bolt). On completion, remove the timing pin and bar and refit the blanking plug.

22 Refit the timing belt upper cover, and the alternator. Refit the coolant pump pulley, and tighten the bolts as far as possible for now – once the auxiliary drivebelt has been fitted it will be easier to tighten the bolts to the specified torque.

1.6 litre engines

23 Ensure the engine's still set to TDC on No 1 cylinder (Section 3), then working clockwise, locate the timing belt on the crankshaft sprocket, then over the camshaft VCT units, then around the tensioner. If the original belt is being refitted, make sure that it is the correct way round as noted during removal (see illustration).

24 Where applicable, refit the timing belt guide disc on the end of the crankshaft, making sure that the concave side faces outwards.

25 Remove the locking pin from the tensioner, and allow it to tension the belt.

26 Refit the lower timing belt cover and tighten the bolts to the specified torque.

27 Refit the crankshaft pulley/vibration damper as described in Section 6.

28 Remove the locking tool from the camshaft VCT units, the crankshaft timing pin, and the flywheel/driveplate locking tool.

29 Rotate the crankshaft clockwise approximately 1¾ turns, until the marks on the camshaft VCT units are in the 11 o'clock position (see illustrations 3.15a and 3.15b).

30 Refit the crankshaft timing pin, and rotate the crankshaft clockwise until it stops against the timing pin. Refit the VCT units locking tool

to check their positions. If the tool cannot be fitted, remove the belt, and carry out the fitting/tensioning procedure again. If the timing is correct, remove the timing pin and VCT locking tool. Refit the cylinder block blanking plug.

31 Refit the engine mounting bracket to the cylinder block, and tighten the bolts to the specified torque.

32 Refit the upper engine mounting bracket tightening the bolts and the new nuts to the specified torque. Remove the jack from under the engine, or remove the hoist from above, as applicable.

33 Refit the timing belt upper cover, and the alternator. Refit the coolant pump pulley, and tighten the bolts as far as possible for now – once the auxiliary drivebelt has been fitted it will be easier to tighten the bolts to the specified torque.

All engines

34 The remainder of refitting is a reversal of removal.

9 Timing belt tensioner and sprockets – removal, inspection and refitting

Tensioner pulley

1 Remove the auxiliary drivebelt as described in Chapter 1A Section 26.

2 Remove the timing belt upper cover as described in Section 7.

3 As a precaution against losing the valve timing, use string to tie the front and rear runs of the timing belt together. This will ensure that the belt remains engaged with the camshaft sprockets while the tensioner pulley is removed.

4 Push the tensioner pulley rearwards to detension the belt, then insert Ford tool No 303-1054 or a suitable equivalent into the pulley arm to lock it in position (see

illustration 8.7).

5 Undo the tensioner pulley centre mounting bolt and withdraw the unit from the engine.

6 While the tensioner pulley is removed, make sure that the timing belt remains fully engaged with the camshaft and crankshaft sprockets.

7 Spin the tensioner pulley, and check that it turns freely without any roughness or tightness. Do not attempt to clean the pulley by immersing in any cleaning fluid. **Note:** *It is recommended that a new tensioner is fitted, regardless of the apparent condition of the old one. If the tensioner were to seize or break up in service, the resulting damage to the timing belt could lead to serious engine damage.*

8 Clean the cylinder block in the area of the tensioner.

9 Locate the tensioner pulley in position ensuring that the lug on the tensioner mounting plate engages with the square hole on the cylinder block (see illustration). Insert the mounting bolt and tighten it to the specified torque.

10 Remove the locking pin from the tensioner, and allow it to tension the belt.

11 Remove the string used to tie the front and rear runs of the timing belt together.

12 Provided that the timing belt has remained fully engaged with the camshaft and crankshaft sprockets, it should not be necessary to check the valve timing. However, if there is any doubt, check the valve timing as described in Section 3.

13 Refit the timing belt upper cover as described in Section 7.

14 Fit a new auxiliary drivebelt as described in Chapter 1A Section 26.

Camshaft sprockets

Caution: The camshaft sprockets are made from a type of plastic. Care must be taken to avoid damage to the sprockets during the following procedure.

15 Remove the timing belt as described in Section 8.

9.16a Use an open-ended spanner on the hexagonal section of the camshaft

9.16b Unscrew the bolt …

9.16c … and remove the camshaft sprocket

9.18 Counterhold the camshaft with a spanner on the hexagonal section, then unscrew the blanking plug from the VCT unit

9.19a Unscrew the Torx bolt …

9.19b … and pull the VCT unit from the camshaft

1.25 litre engines

16 Prevent the camshafts from rotating using an open-ended spanner on the hexagonal section of the camshafts, then unscrew the bolts and remove the sprockets from the camshafts **(see illustrations)**. Discard the bolts – new ones must be fitted.

1.6 litre engines

17 Remove the cylinder head cover as described in Section 4.

18 Counterhold the camshafts using an open-ended spanner on the hexagonal sections, then unscrew the blanking plugs from the centre of the VCT units **(see illustration)**.

19 Still counterholding the camshafts, slacken and remove the VCT units' centre Torx bolts **(see illustrations)**. Remove the VCT units from the ends of the camshafts.

All engines

20 Examine the teeth of the sprockets for wear and damage, and renew them if necessary.

1.25 litre engines

21 Locate the sprockets on the camshafts, and screw in the retaining bolts loosely. It must be possible to rotate the sprockets independently of the camshafts.

22 Fit the timing belt as described in Section 8, but before removing the crankshaft and

camshaft locking tools, tighten the camshaft sprocket bolts to their specified torque, counterholding the camshafts to prevent them rotating as during removal.

1.6 litre engines

23 Insert Ford tool No 303-376B into the slots in the left-hand ends of the camshafts. If the Ford setting tool 303-376B is unavailable, a home-made tool can be fabricated out of a length of flat metal bar 20 mm thick **(see illustrations)**.

24 Locate the VCT units on the ends of the camshafts, but only finger-tighten the retaining bolts at this stage. Ensure the timing marks on the VCT units (dot on the inlet sprocket,

9.23a Camshaft setting tool dimensions
Drawing not to scale

9.23b Fit the setting tool into the slots in the end of the camshafts

9.24 Ensure the groove (1) on the exhaust VCT unit and the dot (2) on the inlet unit are at the 12 o'clock position

9.25 Note how the dots/holes on the VCT units align with the groove/dot on the sprockets

9.29a Renew the seal if necessary ...

9.29b ... then refit the plugs to the VCT units

9.32 Slide the sprocket from the end of the crankshaft

groove on the exhaust sprocket) are at the 12 o'clock position **(see illustration)**.

25 Fit the VCT locking tool (No 303-1097) over the units **(see illustrations 3.18a and 3.18b)**. Note how the dots/holes on the VCT units align with the groove/dot on the sprockets **(see illustration)**.

26 Tighten each VCT unit retaining bolt to the specified Stage 1 torque.

27 Remove the camshaft setting bar and the VCT locking tool, then counterhold the camshafts using a spanner on the hexagonal section, and tighten each VCT unit retaining bolt to the specified Stage 2 angle setting

using an angle-tightening gauge. Do not allow the camshafts to rotate.

28 Refit the VCT locking tool, and check the marks on the sprockets align with the marks on the VCT units **(see illustration 9.25)**. If not, repeat the VCT unit refitting procedure.

29 If the timing is correct, counterhold the camshafts using a spanner on the hexagonal section, and fit the each VCT unit blanking plug. Tighten each plug to the specified torque. Renew the plug seal if necessary **(see illustrations)**.

30 Fit the timing belt as described in Section 8, and the cylinder head cover as described In Section 4.

Crankshaft sprocket

31 Remove the timing belt as described in Section 8.

32 Slide the sprocket off the end of crankshaft **(see illustration)**.

33 Examine the teeth of the sprocket for wear and damage, and renew if necessary.

34 Wipe clean the end of the crankshaft, then slide on the sprocket.

35 Refit the timing belt as described in Section 8.

10 Camshaft oil seals – renewal

1 Remove the camshaft sprockets or VCT units as described in Section 9.

2 Note the fitted depths of the oil seals as a guide for fitting the new ones.

3 Using a screwdriver or similar tool, carefully prise the oil seals from the cylinder head/camshaft bearing caps. Take care not to damage the oil seal contact surfaces on the ends of the camshafts or the oil seal seatings. An alternative method of removing the seals is to drill a small hole, then insert a self-tapping screw and use pliers to pull out the seal **(see illustrations)**.

10.3a Drill a small hole and insert a self-tapping screw ...

10.3b ... then pull out the oil seal using a pair of pliers

10.5 Locate the new oil seal into the cylinder/camshaft bearing cap

10.6 Drive the new seal into position with a socket

4 Wipe clean the oil seal seatings and also the ends of the camshafts.

5 Apply a little clean engine oil to the seal lip, then locate it over the camshaft and into the cylinder head/camshaft bearing cap. Make sure that the closed end of the oil seal faces outwards **(see illustration)**.

6 Using a socket or length of metal tubing, drive the oil seals squarely into position to the previously-noted depths. Wipe away any excess oil **(see illustration)**.

7 Refit the camshaft sprockets or VCT units as described in Section 9.

11 Camshafts and tappets
– removal, inspection and refitting

Removal

1 Before removing the camshafts, it may be useful to check and record the valve clearances as described in Section 5. If any clearance is not within limits, new tappets can be obtained and fitted.

2 Remove the camshaft oil seals as described in Section 10.

3 The camshaft bearing caps are marked for position – the inlet caps have the letter I and exhaust caps have the letter E. On the project car these were not very clear, and if this is the case, mark them using paint or a marker pen. Make sure they are identified for inlet and exhaust camshafts **(see illustrations)**.

4 Position the crankshaft so that No 1 piston is approximately 25 mm before TDC. This can be done by starting from the TDC position; carefully insert a large screwdriver down No 1 cylinder spark plug hole until the tip touches the top of the piston, and turn the engine anti-clockwise until the screwdriver shaft has descended 25 mm.

5 Position the camshafts so that none of the valves are at full lift (ie, fully-open, being heavily pressed down by the cam lobes). To do this, turn each camshaft using a spanner on the hexagon flats provided.

6 Progressively loosen the camshaft bearing cap retaining bolts, working in a diagonal sequence. Work gradually and evenly to release the pressure of the valve springs on the caps **(see illustration)**.

11.3a No 3 inlet camshaft bearing cap

11.3b No 3 exhaust camshaft bearing cap

11.3c Number the bearing caps with paint if they are not clearly marked

11.6 Undo the camshaft bearing cap bolts ...

11.7a ... withdraw the caps ...

11.7b ... then remove the camshafts

11.7c The exhaust camshaft is marked 3A
– 1.6 litre engines

11.7d On 1.6 litre engines, recover the
O-ring seal under the right-hand (No 1)
bearing cap

7 Withdraw the caps, keeping them in order to aid refitting, then lift the camshafts from the cylinder head. The exhaust camshaft can be identified by the reference lobe for the camshaft position sensor on 1.25 litre engines, therefore, there is no need to mark the camshafts; on 1.6 litre engines, the inlet camshaft is marked 7A and the exhaust marked 3A **(see illustrations)**. Note: *On 1.6 litre engines, renew the O-ring between the right-hand bearing cap and the cylinder head* **(see illustration)**.

8 Obtain sixteen small, clean containers, and number them 1 to 8 for both the inlet and exhaust camshafts. Lift the tappets one by one from the cylinder head.

Inspection

9 With the camshafts and tappets removed, check each for signs of obvious wear (scoring, pitting, etc) and for ovality, and renew if necessary.

10 Visually examine the camshaft lobes for score marks, pitting, and evidence of overheating (blue, discoloured areas). Look for flaking away of the hardened surface layer of each lobe. If any such signs are evident, renew the component concerned.

11 Examine the camshaft bearing journals and the cylinder head bearing surfaces for signs of obvious wear or pitting. If any such signs are evident, renew the component concerned.

12 To check camshaft endfloat, remove the tappets, clean the bearing surfaces carefully, and refit the camshafts and bearing caps. Tighten the bearing cap bolts to the specified torque wrench setting, then measure the endfloat using a dial gauge mounted on the cylinder head so that its tip bears on the camshaft right-hand end.

13 Tap the camshaft fully towards the gauge, zero the gauge, then tap the camshaft fully away from the gauge, and note the gauge reading. If the endfloat measured is found to be more than the typical value given, fit a new camshaft and repeat the check; if the clearance is still excessive, the cylinder head must be renewed.

Refitting

14 Lubricate the cylinder head tappet bores and the tappets with engine oil. Carefully refit the tappets to the cylinder head, ensuring each tappet is refitted to its original bore. Some care will be needed to enter the tappets squarely into their bores.

15 Liberally oil the camshaft bearings and lobes. Ensuring that each camshaft is in its original location, refit the camshafts, locating each so that the slot in its left-hand end is approximately parallel to, and just above, the cylinder head mating surface. At this stage, position the camshafts so that none of the valves are at full lift – see paragraph 5 **(see illustration)**.

16 Clean the mating faces of the cylinder head and camshaft bearing caps.

17 Apply a thin smear of suitable sealant (Ford recommend WSK-M2G348-A5 or Loctite 518) to the camshaft bearing caps at the timing belt end of the engine only **(see illustration)**. On 1.6 litre engines, renew the O-ring seal beneath the timing belt end bearing cap **(see illustration 11.7d)**.

11.15 The slots in the end of the camshafts should be just above,
and approximately parallel to the cylinder head upper surface

11.17 Apply a thin bead of sealant (see text) to the underside of
the bearing cap(s) at the timing belt end of the engine as shown

11.18 Oil the camshaft bearing surfaces

12.17 Check the cylinder head gasket face for distortion using a straight-edge

12.23 Locate the new cylinder head gasket over the dowels

18 Oil the bearing surfaces, then locate the camshaft bearing caps on the camshafts and insert the retaining bolts loosely. Make sure that each cap is located in its previously-noted position **(see illustration)**.

19 Ensuring each cap is kept square to the cylinder head as it is tightened down, and working in a diagonal sequence, tighten the camshaft bearing cap bolts slowly and by one turn at a time, until each cap touches the cylinder head. Next, go round again in the same diagonal sequence, tightening the bolts to the specified Stage 1 torque wrench setting. Note that on 1.6 litre engines, the torque wrench setting for the bearing cap bolts at the timing belt end of the engine are different to all the other caps.

20 Still working in a diagonal sequence, tighten the bolts further to the specified Stage 2 angle. It is recommended that an angle gauge is used for this, to ensure accuracy. Again, note that on 1.6 litre engines, the angle settings for the bearing cap bolts at the timing belt end of the engine are different to all the other caps.

21 Wipe off all surplus sealant, and check the valve clearances as described in Section 5.

22 Fit new camshaft oil seals as described in Section 10.

12 Cylinder head – removal, inspection and refitting

Removal

1 Depressurise the fuel system as described in Chapter 4A Section 2.

2 Drain the cooling system as described in Chapter 1A Section 30.

3 Disconnect the battery negative lead as described in Chapter 5A Section 4.

4 Remove the inlet manifold and exhaust manifold as described in Chapter 4A.

5 Remove the camshafts and tappets as described in Section 11.

6 Remove the inlet manifold support bolt from the front of the engine at the timing belt end. Lower the car to the ground.

7 Make a note of their fitted locations and the harness routing, then disconnect any wiring plugs attached to components on the cylinder

head. Label the plugs if necessary to aid refitting.

8 Unbolt the timing belt rear cover, which is secured by three bolts.

9 Release the spring-type clip and disconnect the coolant pipe from the left-hand rear of the cylinder head.

10 Undo the 4 bolts and detach the coolant housing from the left-hand end of the cylinder head.

11 Make a last check round the cylinder head, to ensure that nothing remains connected or attached which would prevent the head from being lifted off. Prepare a clean surface to lay the head down on once it has been removed.

12 Working in the reverse of the tightening sequence **(see illustration 12.26a or 12.26b)**, slacken the ten cylinder head bolts progressively and by half a turn at a time; a Torx key will be required. Remove all the bolts.

13 Lift the cylinder head away; use assistance if possible, as it is a heavy assembly. Remove the gasket, noting the two dowels. Although the gasket cannot be re-used, it is advisable to retain it for comparison with the new one, to confirm that the right part has been supplied.

Inspection

14 The mating faces of the cylinder head and cylinder block must be perfectly clean before refitting the head. Use a hard plastic or wood scraper to remove all traces of gasket and carbon; also clean the piston crowns. Take particular care during the cleaning operations, as aluminium alloy is easily damaged.

15 Make sure that the carbon is not allowed to enter the oil and coolant passages – this is particularly important for the lubrication system, as carbon could block the oil supply to the engine's components. Using adhesive tape and paper, seal the coolant, oil and bolt holes in the cylinder block. To prevent carbon entering the gap between the pistons and bores, smear a little grease in the gap. After cleaning each piston, use a small brush to remove all traces of grease and carbon from the gap, then wipe away the remainder with a clean rag. Note that 1.6 litre engines have a filter fitted into the oil supply galleries feeding the VCT system. This filter is permanently installed and cannot be removed.

16 Check the mating surfaces of the cylinder block and the cylinder head for nicks, deep scratches and other damage. If slight, they may be removed carefully with a file, but if excessive, renewal is necessary as it is not permissible to machine the surfaces.

17 If warpage of the cylinder head gasket surface is suspected, use a straight-edge to check it for distortion **(see illustration)**. Refer to Part E of this Chapter if necessary.

18 If possible, clean out the bolt holes in the block using compressed air, to ensure no oil or coolant is present. Screwing a bolt into an oil- or coolant-filled hole can (in extreme cases) cause the block to fracture, due to the hydraulic pressure created.

19 Although not essential, if a suitable tap-and-die set is available, it's worth running the correct-size tap down the bolt threads in the cylinder block. This will clean the threads of any debris, and go some way to restoring any damaged threads. Make absolutely sure the tap is the right size and thread pitch, and lightly oil the tap before starting.

20 Ford insist that the cylinder head bolts must be renewed.

Refitting

21 Wipe clean the mating surfaces of the cylinder head and cylinder block, and check that the two locating dowels are in position in the block.

22 Turn the crankshaft anti-clockwise so that pistons 1 and 4 are approximately 25 mm before TDC, in order to avoid the risk of valve/piston contact. Turn the crankshaft using a spanner on the pulley bolt.

23 If the old gasket is still available, check that it is identical to the new one – for instance, there are several different thicknesses of gasket, indicated by the number of small holes on one side. Position the new gasket over the dowels on the cylinder block surface. It can only be fitted one way round – check carefully that the holes in the gasket align with the holes in the block surface, and that none are blocked **(see illustration)**.

24 It is useful when refitting a cylinder head to have an assistant on hand to help guide the head onto the dowels. Take care that the gasket does not get moved as the head is lowered into position. To confirm that the

12.26a Cylinder head bolt tightening sequence – 1.25 litre engines

12.26b Cylinder head bolt tightening sequence – 1.6 litre engines

head is aligned correctly, once it is in place, temporarily slide in two or more of the head bolts, and check that they fit into the block holes.

25 Fit the new head bolts carefully, and screw them in by hand only until finger-tight.

26 Working progressively and in sequence, tighten the cylinder head bolts to their Stage 1 torque setting **(see illustrations)**.

27 Next, go around again in the same sequence, and tighten the bolts to the Stage 2 setting, then to the Stage 3 setting.

28 Finally, the bolts should be angle-tightened further, by the specified Stage 4 amount, using an angle-tightening gauge **(see illustration)**.

29 The remainder of refitting is a reversal of removal, noting the following points:

a) *Refit the camshafts and tappets as described in Section 11, and the timing belt as described in Section 8.*

b) *Refit the inlet and exhaust manifolds as described in Chapter 4A.*

c) *Tighten all fasteners to the specified torque, where given.*

d) *Ensure that all hoses and wiring are correctly routed, and that hose clips and wiring connectors are securely refitted.*

e) *Refill the cooling system as described in Chapter 1A Section 30.*

f) *Check all disturbed joints for signs of oil or coolant leakage once the engine has been restarted and warmed-up to normal operating temperature).*

13 Sump – removal and refitting

Removal

1 Apply the handbrake, then jack up the front of the car and support it on axle stands (see *Jacking and vehicle support*).

2 Drain the engine oil, then check the drain plug sealing washer and renew if necessary. Clean and refit the engine oil drain plug together with the washer, and tighten it to the specified torque wrench setting. Although not strictly necessary, as the oil is being drained, it makes sense to fit a new oil filter at the same time (see Chapter 1A Section 6).

3 Release the clip, undo the retaining bolt, and pull the engine oil level dipstick guide tube from the sump. Check the condition of

the seal at the base of the tube, and renew it if necessary.

4 Unscrew the bolts securing the transmission to the sump, then progressively unscrew the sump-to-block bolts.

5 On these models, a sump gasket is not used, and sealant is used instead. Unfortunately, the use of sealant makes removal of the sump more difficult. If care is taken not to damage the surfaces, the sealant can be cut around using a sharp knife.

6 On no account lever between the mating faces, as this will almost certainly damage them, resulting in leaks when finished. Ford technicians have a tool comprising a metal rod which is inserted through the sump drain hole, and a handle to pull the sump downwards. Providing care is taken not to damage the threads, a large screwdriver could be used in the drain hole to prise down the sump.

7 While the sump is removed, take the opportunity to remove the oil pump pick-up/strainer pipe, and clean it with reference to Section 14.

Refitting

8 Thoroughly clean the contact surfaces of the sump and crankcase. Take care not to damage the oil pump gasket or the crankshaft oil seal, both of which are partially exposed when the sump is removed. If necessary, use a cloth rag to clean inside the sump and crankcase. If the oil pump pick-up/strainer pipe was removed, fit a new O-ring and refit the pipe with reference to Section 14.

9 Ford state that, to refit the sump, five M8x20 studs must be screwed into the base of the engine **(see illustration)**. This not only helps to align the sump, ensuring that the bead of sealant is not displaced as the sump is fitted, but also ensures that the sealant does not enter the blind holes. Cut a slot across the end of each stud, to make removal easier when the sump is in place.

10 Apply a 3 to 4 mm diameter bead of sealant (Ford recommend WSE M4G323-A4,

12.28 Use an angle-gauge for the final stage

13.9 Sump alignment stud positions

or equivalent) to the sump pan, to the inside of the bolt holes **(see illustration)**. The sump bolts must be fitted and tightened within 10 minutes of applying the sealant.

11 Offer the sump up into position over the studs, and fully refit the remaining bolts by hand. Unscrew the studs, and refit the sump bolts in their place. The sump should be fitted flush with the block at the transmission end.

12 Insert the four sump-to-transmission bolts and tighten them to the specified torque.

13 The sump-to-crankcase bolts are tightened in two stages. Working in sequence **(see illustration)**, tighten all the sump bolts to the specified Stage 1 torque, then go around again in sequence, and tighten them to the Stage 2 setting.

14 Refit the engine oil level dipstick guide tube, with a new seal where necessary, and tighten the retaining bolt securely. Replace the clip.

15 Lower the car to the ground. To be on the safe side, wait a further 30 minutes for the sealant to cure before filling the sump with fresh oil, as described in Chapter 1A Section 6.

16 Finally start the engine and check for signs of oil leaks.

---

14 Oil pump – removal, inspection and refitting

Removal

1 Remove the crankshaft right-hand oil seal as described in Section 16.
2 Remove the sump as described in Section 13.
3 Undo the timing belt rear cover lower 2 bolts.
4 On models with air conditioning, remove the four bolts securing the air conditioning compressor, and tie it up clear of the engine without disconnecting any of the hoses.
5 Unscrew the bolts securing the oil pump pick-up/strainer pipe to the baffle plate/main bearing cap.
6 Unscrew the bolt securing the oil pump pick-up/strainer pipe to the oil pump, then withdraw the pipe and recover the sealing O-ring **(see illustration)**. Discard the O-ring.
7 Unscrew the bolts securing the oil pump to the cylinder block/crankcase, noting the locations of the three different lengths of bolt **(see illustration)**. Withdraw the pump over the nose of the crankshaft.
8 Recover then discard the gasket **(see illustration)**.
9 If necessary, unbolt and remove the baffle plate from the main bearing cap/ladder **(see illustration)**. Thoroughly clean all components, particularly the mating surfaces of the pump, the sump, and the cylinder block/crankcase.

Inspection

10 It is not possible to obtain individual

13.10 Apply the bead of sealant to the sump mating surface as shown

components of the oil pump, furthermore, there are no torque settings available for tightening the pump cover plate bolts. However, the following procedure is provided for owners wishing to dismantle the oil pump for examination.

11 Take out the bolts, and remove the pump cover plate; noting any identification marks on the rotors, withdraw the rotors.

12 Inspect the rotors for obvious signs of wear or damage, and renew if necessary; if either rotor, the pump body, or its cover plate are scored or damaged, the complete oil pump assembly must be renewed.

13 The oil pressure relief valve can be dismantled as follows.

14 Unscrew the threaded plug, and recover the valve spring and plunger. If the plug's sealing O-ring is worn or damaged, a new one must be obtained, to be fitted on reassembly.

14.6 Remove the O-ring seal from the oil pump pick-up/strainer pipe

14.8 Remove the oil pump gasket

13.13 Sump bolt tightening sequence. Also shows sump-to-transmission bolts (A)

15 Reassembly is the reverse of the dismantling procedure; ensure the spring and valve are refitted the correct way round, and tighten the threaded plug securely.

Refitting

16 If removed, refit the oil baffle plate to the crankcase and tighten the bolts.

14.7 Remove the oil pump-to cylinder block/crankcase bolts

14.9 Unbolt the baffle plate from the main bearing cap/ladder

15.4 Oil pressure switch

16.6 Locate the new right-hand oil seal over the crankshaft

16.15 Locate the new oil seal housing (complete with fitting sleeve) over the end of the crankshaft

17 The oil pump must be primed on installation, by pouring clean engine oil into it and rotating its inner rotor a few turns.

18 Use a little grease to stick the new gasket in place on the cylinder block/crankcase.

19 Offer the oil pump over the nose of the crankshaft, and turn the inner rotor as necessary to align its flats with the flats on the crankshaft. Locate the pump on the dowels, then insert the retaining bolts in their previously-noted locations and progressively tighten them to the specified torque.

20 Locate a new O-ring (dipped in oil) on the pick-up/strainer pipe, then locate the pipe in the oil pump and insert the retaining bolts. Insert the bolts retaining the pipe on the baffle plate/main bearing cap. Tighten the bolts to the specified torque.

21 Where removed, refit the air conditioning compressor, tightening the bolts to the specified torque.

22 Refit the sump as described in Section 13.

23 Fit a new crankshaft oil seal as described in Section 16.

15 Oil pressure switch – removal and refitting

1 The oil pressure switch is a vital early warning of low oil pressure. The switch operates the oil warning light on the instrument panel – the light should come on with the ignition, and go out almost immediately when the engine starts.

2 If the light does not come on, there could be a fault on the instrument panel, the switch wiring, or the switch itself. If the light does not go out, low oil level, worn oil pump (or sump pick-up blocked), blocked oil filter, or worn main bearings could be to blame – or again, the switch may be faulty.

3 If the light comes on while driving, the best advice is to turn the engine off immediately, and not to drive the car until the problem has been investigated – ignoring the light could mean expensive engine damage.

Removal

4 The oil pressure switch is located on the front face of the engine, above the oil filter **(see illustration)**.

5 Disconnect the wiring plug from the switch.

6 Unscrew the switch from the block, and remove it. There should only be a very slight loss of oil when this is done.

Inspection

7 Examine the switch for signs of cracking or splits. If the top part of the switch is loose, this is an early indication of impending failure.

8 Check that the wiring terminals at the switch are not loose, then trace the wire from the switch connector until it enters the main loom – any wiring defects will give rise to apparent oil pressure problems.

Refitting

9 Refitting is the reverse of the removal procedure, noting the following points:
a) *Tighten the switch securely.*
b) *Reconnect the switch connector, making sure it clicks home properly. Ensure that the wiring is routed away from any hot or moving parts.*
c) *Check the engine oil level and top-up if necessary (see ' Weekly checks0,5 ').*
d) *Check for signs of oil leaks once the engine has been restarted and warmed-up to normal operating temperature.*

16 Crankshaft oil seals – renewal

Right-hand oil seal

1 Remove the crankshaft sprocket as described in Section 9.

2 As a safety precaution, refit the engine right- hand mounting upper section and mounting bracket, and tighten the mounting bolts/nuts.

3 Note the fitted depth of the oil seal as a guide for fitting the new one.

4 Using a screwdriver, prise the old oil seal from the oil pump housing. Take great care not to damage the seal contact surface on the nose of the crankshaft, or the seating in the housing.

5 Wipe clean the seating and the nose of the crankshaft.

6 Apply a little clean engine oil to the inner lip of the seal, then locate it over the crankshaft and into the oil pump housing. Make sure that the closed end of the oil seal faces outwards **(see illustration)**.

7 Using a socket or length of metal tubing, drive the oil seal squarely into position to the previously-noted depth. The Ford installation tool (303-395) is used together with an old crankshaft pulley bolt to press the oil seal into position. The same idea may be used with metal tubing and a large washer – do not use a new crankshaft pulley bolt, as it is only permissible to use the bolt once. With the oil seal in position, wipe away any excess oil.

8 With the weight of the engine once more supported, unscrew the nuts and bolts and remove the engine right-hand mounting upper section and mounting bracket.

9 Refit the crankshaft sprocket with reference to Section 9.

Left-hand oil seal

10 Remove the flywheel/driveplate as described in Section 17.

11 Remove the sump as described in Section 13.

12 Unscrew the six bolts and withdraw the oil seal carrier from the end of the crankshaft. Note that the seal and carrier are made as one unit – it is not possible to obtain the seal separately.

13 Clean the carrier contact surface on the cylinder block, and the end of the crankshaft.

14 The new oil seal carrier is supplied complete with a fitting sleeve, which ensures that the oil seal lips are correctly located on the crankshaft. Ford state that neither the crankshaft nor the new oil seal should be lubricated before fitting.

15 Locate the oil seal carrier and fitting sleeve over the end of the crankshaft. Press the carrier into position, noting that the centre bolt holes are formed into locating dowels **(see illustration)**.

16 Insert the retaining bolts and progressively tighten them to the specified torque.

17 Remove the fitting sleeve and check that

the oil seal lips are correctly located **(see illustration)**.
18 Refit the sump as described in Section 13.
19 Refit the flywheel/driveplate as described in Section 17.

17 Flywheel/driveplate – removal, inspection and refitting

Removal

1 Remove the transmission as described in Chapter 7A or 7B, and the clutch as described in Chapter 6 Section 6 on manual transmission models.
2 Hold the flywheel/driveplate stationary using one of the following methods:
a) *If an assistant is available, insert one of the transmission mounting bolts into the cylinder block and have the assistant engage a wide-bladed screwdriver with the starter ring gear teeth while the bolts are loosened. Alternatively, a piece of angle-iron can be engaged with the ring gear and located against the transmission mounting bolt.*
b) *A further method is to fabricate a piece of flat metal bar with a pointed end to engage the ring gear – fit the tool to the transmission bolt and use washers and packing to align it with the ring gear, then tighten the bolt to hold it in position* **(see illustration)**.
3 Unscrew and remove the bolts, then lift the flywheel/driveplate off the locating dowel on the crankshaft **(see illustration)**.

Inspection

4 Clean the flywheel/driveplate to remove grease and oil. Inspect the surface for cracks, rivet grooves, burned areas and score marks. Light scoring can be removed with emery cloth. Check for cracked and broken ring gear teeth. Lay the flywheel/driveplate on a flat surface, and use a straight-edge to check for warpage.
5 Clean and inspect the mating surfaces of the flywheel/driveplate and the crankshaft. If the crankshaft oil seal is leaking, renew it (see Section 16) before refitting the flywheel/driveplate. In fact, given the large amount of work needed to remove the flywheel/driveplate, it's probably worth fitting a new seal anyway, as a precaution.
6 While the flywheel/driveplate is removed, clean carefully its inner face, particularly the recesses which serve as the reference points for the crankshaft speed/position sensor. Clean the sensor's tip, and check that the sensor is securely fastened. The sensor mounting may be removed if necessary by first removing the sensor, then unscrewing the bolt and withdrawing the mounting from the cylinder block **(see illustration)**.

16.17 With the oil seal housing bolted into position, remove the fitting ring

Refitting

7 Make sure that the mating faces of the flywheel/driveplate and crankshaft are clean, then locate the flywheel/driveplate on the crankshaft and engage it with the locating dowel.
8 Insert the retaining bolts finger-tight.
9 Lock the flywheel/driveplate (see paragraph 2), then tighten the bolts in a diagonal sequence to the specified Stage 1 torque setting. Again, working in a diagonal sequence, tighten the bolts through the specified Stage 2 angle using an angle-tightening gauge.
10 Refit the clutch with reference to Chapter 6 Section 6, and the transmission as described in Chapter 7A or 7B.

18 Engine/transmission mountings – inspection and renewal

General

1 The engine/transmission mountings seldom require attention, but broken or deteriorated mountings should be renewed immediately, or the added strain placed on the driveline components may cause damage or wear.
2 While separate mountings may be removed and refitted individually, if more than one is disturbed at a time – such as if the engine/transmission unit is removed from its mountings – they must be reassembled and their fasteners tightened in the position marked on removal.

17.3 Remove the flywheel retaining bolts. Note the dowel in the end of the crankshaft

17.2 Home-made flywheel locking tool

3 On reassembly, the complete weight of the engine/transmission unit must not be taken by the mountings until all are correctly aligned with the marks made on removal. Tighten the engine/transmission mounting fasteners to their specified torque wrench settings.

Inspection

4 During the check, the engine/transmission unit must be raised slightly, to remove its weight from the mountings.
5 Raise the front of the vehicle, and support it securely on axle stands. Position a jack under the sump, with a large block of wood between the jack head and the sump, then carefully raise the engine/transmission just enough to take the weight off the mountings.

⚠ *Warning: DO NOT place any part of your body under the engine when it is supported only by a jack.*

6 Check the mountings to see if the rubber is cracked, hardened or separated from the metal components. Sometimes the rubber will split right down the centre.
7 Check for relative movement between each mounting's brackets and the engine/transmission or body (use a large screwdriver or lever to attempt to move the mountings). If movement is noted, lower the engine and check-tighten the mounting fasteners.

Renewal

Note: *The following paragraphs assume the engine is supported beneath the sump as described earlier.*

17.6 Crankshaft position sensor mounting and retaining bolt

18.9 Right-hand engine mounting retaining nuts/bolts

18.15 Undo the retaining nuts and lift out the battery tray support bracket

18.16 Left-hand engine mounting bracket-to-transmission, and bracket-to-side member retaining bolts

Right-hand mounting

8 Lift up the coolant expansion tank and position it to one side. Note there is no need to disconnect the coolant pipes.
9 Mark the position of the mounting on the vehicle, right-hand inner wing panel, then undo the two nuts securing the mounting to the engine bracket **(see illustration)**. Discard the nuts, new ones must be fitted.
10 Where fitted, undo the bolt securing the wiring harness to the engine mounting.
11 Undo the three retaining bolts securing the mounting to the inner wing panel and withdraw the mounting from the vehicle.
12 On refitting, tighten all fasteners to the torque wrench settings specified. Re-align the marks made on removal, then tighten the new mounting bracket retaining nuts.

Left-hand mounting

13 Remove the air cleaner assembly as described in Chapter 4A Section 5.
14 Remove the battery and battery tray as described in Chapter 5A Section 4. Note that it is not necessary to remove the powertrain control module from the battery tray, just

position the tray clear for access to the mounting.
15 Undo the nuts securing the battery tray support bracket in position. Release the wiring loom from the support bracket and lift the support bracket out of the engine compartment **(see illustration)**.
16 With the transmission supported, mark the position of the mounting bracket on the transmission and on the body sidemember. Undo the bolts securing the mounting bracket to the transmission and the two bolts securing the mounting to the body sidemember **(see illustration)**. Remove the mounting from the engine compartment.
17 On refitting, re-align the mounting in the position noted on removal, then tighten all fasteners to the specified torque wrench settings. Refit the components disturbed for access using a reversal of the removal procedures.

Rear mounting (roll restrictor)

18 To remove the engine rear mounting, apply the handbrake, then jack up the front of the car and support it on axle stands

18.18 Rear mounting/roll restrictor retaining bolts

(see *Jacking and vehicle support*). Unscrew the through-bolts and remove the engine rear mounting link from the bracket on the transmission and from the bracket on the subframe **(see illustration)**. Hold the engine stationary while the bolts are being removed, since the link will be under tension.
19 On refitting, ensure that the bolts are securely tightened to the specified torque wrench setting.

Chapter 2 Part C
1.5 litre SOHC diesel engine in-car repair procedures

Contents

Degrees of difficulty

| Easy, suitable for novice with little experience | | Fairly easy, suitable for beginner with some experience | Fairly difficult, suitable for competent DIY mechanic | Difficult, suitable for experienced DIY mechanic | Very difficult, suitable for expert DIY or professional | |

Specifications

General

Designation	Duratorq-TDCi
Engine codes*	UGLC, XUJA, XUJB, XVJB and XVJC
Capacity	1499 cc
Bore	73.5 mm
Stroke	88.3 mm
Direction of crankshaft rotation	Clockwise (viewed from the right-hand side of vehicle)
No 1 cylinder location.	At the transmission end of block
Maximum power output:	
Engine codes UGLC, XUJA and XUJB.	55 kW (75 PS)
Engine codes XVJB and XVJC	70 kW (95 PS)
Maximum torque output:	
Engine code UGLC.	185 Nm
Engine codes XUJA and XUJB.	190 Nm
Engine codes XVJB and XVJC	215 Nm
Emissions level:	
Engine code UGLC.	Stage V
Engine codes XUJA, XUJB, XVJB and XVJC	Stage VI
Compression ratio	16: 1

*The engine code is stamped on a plate attached to the front of the cylinder block, next to the oil filter

Compression pressures (engine hot, at cranking speed)
Normal . . . . 20 ± 5 bar
Minimum . . . . 15 bar
Maximum difference between any two cylinders. . . . . 5 bar

Camshaft
Camshaft end float. . . . . 0.195 – 0.3 mm

Lubrication system
Oil pump type. . . . . Gear-type, driven directly by the right-hand end of the crankshaft, by two flats machined along the crankshaft journal.

Minimum oil pressure at 80°C:
  Idle speed. . . . . 1.0 to 2.0 bar
  2000 rpm . . . . 2.3 to 3.7 bar

Torque wrench settings

	Nm	lbf ft
Ancillary drivebelt tensioner roller	20	15
Big-end bolts: *		
Stage 1.	10	7
Stage 2.	Slacken 180°	
Stage 3.	10	7
Stage 4.	Angle-tighten a further 130°	
Camshaft bearing caps	10	7
Camshaft bearing ladder:		
Studs	10	7
Bolts	10	7
Camshaft position sensor bolt	5	4
Camshaft sprocket bolt		
Stage 1.	20	15
Stage 2.	Angle-tighten a further 50°	
Coolant outlet housing bolts	8	6
Crankshaft position/speed sensor bolt	10	7
Crankshaft pulley/sprocket bolt: *		
Stage 1.	35	26
Stage 2.	Angle-tighten a further 190°	
Cylinder head bolts: *		
Stage 1.	20	15
Stage 2.	40	30
Stage 3.	Angle-tighten a further 260°	
Cylinder head cover	10	7
EGR valve.	10	7
Engine-to-transmission fixing bolts	47	35
Flywheel bolts: *		
Stage 1.	25	18
Stage 2.	Slacken 1 turn	
Stage 3.	8	6
Stage 4.	18	13
Stage 5.	Angle-tighten a further 75°	
Fuel pump sprocket	50	37
Left-hand engine/transmission mounting:		
Mounting-to-bracket centre nut	148	109
Mounting-to-bracket outer nuts.	48	35
Mounting bracket to transmission	80	59
Main bearing ladder outer seam bolts:		
Stage 1.	5	4
Stage 2.	10	7
Main bearing ladder to cylinder block:		
Stage 1.	10	7
Stage 2.	Slacken 180°	
Stage 3.	30	22
Stage 4.	Angle-tighten a further 140°	
Piston oil jet spray tube bolt.	20	15
Oil cooler retaining bolts.	10	7
Oil filter cover	25	18
Oil pick-up pipe	10	7

Torque wrench settings

	Nm	lbf ft
Oil pressure switch	30	22
Oil pump to cylinder block:		
Stage 1	5	4
Stage 2	9	7
Rear engine mounting:		
Rear through-bolt	70	52
Mounting bracket-to-transmission bolts	63	46
Right-hand engine mounting:		
Mounting to inner wing and mounting bracket (nuts/bolts)	48	35
Mounting bracket to engine block	55	41
Sump drain plug	35	26
Sump bolts/nuts	12	8
Timing belt idler pulley	37	27
Timing belt tensioner pulley	30	22
Timing cover bolts	5	4
Vacuum pump bolts	20	15

*Do not re-use

1 General Information

How to use this Chapter

1 This Part of Chapter 2 describes the repair procedures that can reasonably be carried out on the engine while it remains in the vehicle. If the engine has been removed from the vehicle and is being dismantled as described in Part E, any preliminary dismantling procedures can be ignored.

2 Note that, while it may be possible physically to overhaul items such as the piston/connecting rod assemblies while the engine is in the car, such tasks are not usually carried out as separate operations. Usually, several additional procedures are required (not to mention the cleaning of components and oilways); for this reason, all such tasks are classed as major overhaul procedures, and are described in Part E of this Chapter.

3 Part E describes the removal of the engine/transmission from the car, and the full overhaul procedures that can then be carried out.

4 The 1.5 litre Duratorq-TDCi engine is a 4-cylinder, turbocharged, single overhead cam (SOHC) 8-valve design, with direct injection. The engine is mounting transversely, with the transmission mounted on the left-hand side.

5 A toothed timing belt drives the camshaft, high-pressure fuel pump and coolant pump. The camshaft operates the inlet and exhaust valves via rocker arms which are supported at their pivot ends by hydraulic self-adjusting tappets. The camshaft Is supported by bearings machined directly in the cylinder head and camshaft bearing housing.

6 The high-pressure fuel pump supplies fuel to the fuel rail, and subsequently to the electronically-controlled injectors which inject the fuel direct into the combustion chambers. This design differs from the previous type where an injection pump supplies the fuel at high pressure to each injector. The earlier, conventional type injection pump required fine calibration and timing, and these functions are now completed by the high-pressure pump, electronic injectors and engine management ECM.

7 The crankshaft runs in five main bearings of the usual shell type. Endfloat is controlled by thrustwashers either side of No 2 main bearing.

8 The pistons are selected to be of matching weight, and incorporate fully-floating gudgeon pins retained by circlips.

Repair operations precaution

9 The engine is a complex unit with numerous accessories and ancillary components. The design of the engine compartment is such that every conceivable space has been utilised, and access to virtually all of the engine components is extremely limited. In many cases, ancillary components will have to be removed, or moved to one side, and wiring, pipes and hoses will have to be disconnected or removed from various cable clips and support brackets.

10 When working on this engine, read through the entire procedure first, look at the car and engine at the same time, and establish whether you have the necessary tools, equipment, skill and patience to proceed. Allow considerable time for any operation, and be prepared for the unexpected.

11 Because of the limited access, many of the engine photographs appearing in this Chapter were, by necessity, taken with the engine removed from the vehicle.

 Warning: It is essential to observe strict precautions when working on the fuel system components of the engine, particularly the high-pressure side of the system. Before carrying out any engine operations that entail working on, or near, any part of the fuel system, refer to the special information given in Chapter 4B Section 2.

12 Operations with engine in vehicle

a) *Compression pressure – testing.*

b) *Cylinder head cover – removal and refitting.*

c) *Crankshaft pulley – removal and refitting.*

d) *Timing belt covers – removal and refitting.*

e) *Timing belt – removal, refitting and adjustment.*

f) *Timing belt tensioner and sprockets – removal and refitting.*

g) *Camshaft oil seal – renewal.*

h) *Camshaft, rocker arms and hydraulic tappets – removal, inspection and refitting.*

i) *Sump – removal and refitting.*

j) *Oil pump – removal and refitting.*

k) *Crankshaft oil seals – renewal.*

l) *Engine/transmission mountings – inspection and renewal.*

m) *Flywheel – removal, inspection and refitting.*

2 Compression and leakdown tests – description and interpretation

Compression test

Note: *A compression tester specifically designed for diesel engines must be used for this test.*

1 When engine performance is down, or if misfiring occurs which cannot be attributed to the fuel system, a compression test can provide diagnostic clues as to the engine's condition. If the test is performed regularly, it can give warning of trouble before any other symptoms become apparent.

2 A compression tester specifically intended for diesel engines must be used, because of the higher pressures involved. The tester is connected to an adapter which screws into the glow plug or injector hole. On this engine, an adapter suitable for use in the glow plug holes will be required, so as not to disturb the fuel system components. It is unlikely to be worthwhile buying such a tester for occasional use, but it may be possible to borrow or hire one – if not, have the test performed by a garage.

3 Unless specific instructions to the contrary

are supplied with the tester, observe the following points:

a) *The battery must be in a good state of charge, the air filter must be clean, and the engine should be at normal operating temperature.*

b) *All the glow plugs should be removed, and the glow plug module disconnected as described in Chapter 5A before starting the test.*

4 The compression pressures measured are not so important as the balance between cylinders. Values are given in the Specifications.

5 The cause of poor compression is less easy to establish on a diesel engine than on a petrol one. The effect of introducing oil into the cylinders ('wet' testing) is not conclusive, because there is a risk that the oil will sit in the swirl chamber or in the recess on the piston crown instead of passing to the rings. However, the following can be used as a rough guide to diagnosis.

6 All cylinders should produce very similar pressures; any difference greater than that specified indicates the existence of a fault. Note that the compression should build-up quickly in a healthy engine; low compression on the first stroke, followed by gradually-increasing pressure on successive strokes, indicates worn piston rings. A low compression reading on the first stroke, which does not build-up during successive strokes, indicates leaking valves or a blown head gasket (a cracked head could also be the cause). Deposits on the undersides of the valve heads can also cause low compression.

7 A low reading from two adjacent cylinders is almost certainly due to the head gasket having blown between them; the presence of coolant in the engine oil will confirm this.

8 If the compression reading is unusually high, the cylinder head surfaces, valves and pistons are probably coated with carbon deposits. If this is the case, the cylinder head should be removed and decarbonised.

Note: *After performing this test, a fault code may be generated and stored in the PCM memory. Have the PCM self-diagnosis facility interrogated by a Ford dealer or suitably-equipped specialist, and the fault code erased.*

Leakdown test

9 A leakdown test measures the rate at which compressed air fed into the cylinder is lost. It is an alternative to a compression test, and in many ways it is better, since the escaping air provides easy identification of where pressure loss is occurring (piston rings, valves or head gasket).

10 The equipment needed for leakdown testing is unlikely to be available to the home mechanic. If poor compression is suspected, have the test performed by a suitably-equipped garage.

3 Engine assembly/valve timing holes – general information and usage

Note: *Do not attempt to rotate the engine whilst the crankshaft and camshaft are locked in position. If the engine is to be left in this state for a long period of time, it is a good idea to place suitable warning notices inside the vehicle, and in the engine compartment. This will reduce the possibility of the engine being accidentally cranked on the starter motor, which is likely to cause damage with the locking pins in place.*

1 Timing holes or slots are located in the crankshaft pulley flange and camshaft sprocket hub. This will ensure that the valve timing is maintained during operations that require removal and refitting of the timing belt. When the holes/slots are aligned with their corresponding holes in the cylinder block and cylinder head, suitable diameter bolts/pins can be inserted to lock the crankshaft and camshaft in position, preventing rotation.

2 Note that the fuel system used on these engines does not have a conventional diesel injection pump, but instead uses a high-pressure fuel pump. However, the fuel pump sprocket must be pegged in position in a similar fashion to the camshaft sprocket.

3 To align the engine assembly/valve timing holes, proceed as follows.

4 Apply the handbrake, then jack up the front of the vehicle and support it on axle stands (see *Jacking and vehicle support*). Remove the right-hand front roadwheel.

5 To gain access to the crankshaft pulley, to enable the engine to be turned, the wheel arch plastic liner must be removed. The liner is secured by several plastic expanding rivets/nut/bolts. To remove the rivets, push in the centre pins a little, then prise the clips from place. Remove the liner from under the front wing.

6 Remove the crankshaft pulley as described in Section 5.

7 Remove the upper and lower timing belt covers as described in Section 6.

8 Temporarily refit the crankshaft pulley bolt (without the crankshaft pulley) and then remove the crankshaft locking tool.

9 Turn the crankshaft until the timing hole in the crankshaft sprocket aligns with the hole in the oil pump casing (this is at the 12 o'clock position). Fit the special tool 303-732, or a suitable alternative (5.0 mm drill bit or rod) and lock the crankshaft in position **(see illustration)**.

10 With the crankshaft locked in position fit the camshaft locking tool (303-735 or similar). The hole in the camshaft sprocket should be at approximately the 1 o'clock position **(see illustration)**. If this is not the case remove the crankshaft locking pin and rotate the engine one revolution. Note that the crankshaft must always be turned in a clockwise direction (viewed from the right-hand side of vehicle).

11 When refitting the timing belt, rotate the fuel pump sprocket clockwise and insert a 5.0 mm bolt or drive bit through the slot in the sprocket flange and into the corresponding

3.9 Insert the special tool (or a 5.0 mm drill bit/bolt) through the round hole in the sprocket flange into the hole in the oil pump housing

3.10 Insert the special tool (or an 8.0 mm bolt/rod) through the hole in the camshaft sprocket into the corresponding hole in the cylinder head

3.11 Insert a 5.0 mm rod (or similar) through the slot in the fuel pump sprocket flange

4.1 Pull up and remove the plastic cover

4.2a Release the clamp, undo the bracket nut...

hole in the fuel pump mounting bracket **(see illustration)**.

12 The crankshaft and camshaft are now locked in position, preventing unnecessary rotation.

4 Cylinder head cover – removal and refitting

Removal

1 Pull up and remove the plastic cover from the top of the engine **(see illustration)**.

2 Release the hose clamp, undo the bolts/nut and remove the charge air pipe from the top of the engine **(see illustrations)**.

3 Disconnect the wiring plug, undo the 4 retaining bolts and remove the throttle body **(see illustration)**. The lower, left-hand bolt is accessed from the rear.

4 Disconnect the wiring plugs from the fuel injectors, then undo the retaining bolt and unclip the wiring harness duct from the top of the engine **(see illustrations)**.

5 Release the clips and disconnect the breather hose from the cylinder head cover.

6 Unclip the wiring harness, then unbolt and then remove the timing belt upper cover as described in Section 6.

7 Prise up and remove fuel return pipe assembly plastic rivet **(see illustration)**.

8 Remove the 11 bolts and then remove the cover **(see illustrations)**. Recover the rubber

4.2b ...undo the bolts and remove the charge air pipe

4.3 Throttle body retaining bolts

4.4a Disconnect the injector wiring plugs

4.4b Undo the bolt and unclip the wiring harness duct

4.7 Prise up the rivet securing the fuel return pipe assembly

4.8a Undo the 9 bolts at the top...

4.8b ...and the 2 bolts at the right-hand end of the cover

4.9a Gently push back the clips to release the seal

4.9b Ensure the seal is correctly seated

5.1 Engine undershield fasteners

seal. Examine the seal and renew it if there are any signs of deterioration or damage.

Refitting

9 Refitting is a reversal of removal, but ensure that the seal is correctly located **(see illustration)**.

5 Crankshaft pulley – removal and refitting

Removal

1 Jack up and support the front of the vehicle (see *Jacking and vehicle support*), then undo the fasteners and remove the engine undershield **(see illustration)**.
2 Remove the auxiliary drivebelt as described in Chapter 1B Section 26.
3 To prevent accidental damage, undo the lower timing belt cover lower rear bolt 1.5 turns, then undo the retaining bolt and move the crankshaft position sensor to one side **(see illustrations)**.
4 To lock the crankshaft, working underneath the engine, insert Ford tool No. 303-734 or a 12 mm diameter rod into the hole in the engine block casting over the lower section of the flywheel **(see illustration)**. Note that the hole in the casting and flywheel is provided purely to lock the crankshaft whilst the pulley bolt it undone – it does not position the crankshaft at TDC. Rotate the crankshaft clockwise until the tool engages in the hole in the flywheel – don't rotate the crank pulley anti-clockwise.
5 Pull the central cover from the pulley **(see illustration)**.
6 Using a suitable socket and extension bar, unscrew the retaining bolt, remove the washer, then slide the pulley off the end of the crankshaft **(see illustrations)**. If the pulley is tight fit, it can be drawn off the crankshaft using a suitable puller. If a puller is being used, refit the pulley retaining bolt without the washer, to avoid damaging the crankshaft as the puller is tightened.
Caution: Do not touch the outer magnetic sensor ring of the sprocket with your fingers, or allow metallic particles to come into contact with it.

Refitting

7 Refit the pulley to the end of the crankshaft.
8 Refit the crankshaft pulley. Fit a new bolt and retaining washer. Tighten the bolt to the specified torque, then through the specified angle.
9 Refit the cover to the centre of the pulley.
10 Remove the locking tool.
11 Refit the crankshaft position sensor and tighten the retaining bolt to the specified torque.

5.3a Undo the lower cover rear bolt 1.5 turns

5.3b Note the sensor locating dowel and pin

5.4 Install the flywheel locking tool

5.5 Pull the cover from the pulley

5.6a Remove the bolt and washer

5.6b The key on the crankshaft engages with the slot in the pulley

6.2 Release the clips securing the wiring loom

6.3 Upper cover bolts

6.7 Engine mounting nuts/bolt

6.8a Undo the 2 bolts above the auxiliary drivebelt tensioner…

6.8b... and the bolt at the rear

6.10 Lower timing belt cover bolts

12 Refit and tension the auxiliary drivebelt as described in Chapter 1B Section 26.
13 Refit the remaining components in reverse order of removal.

6 Timing belt covers – removal and refitting

Warning: Refer to the precautionary information contained in Section 1 before proceeding.

Removal

Upper cover

1 Pull the plastic cover on the top of the engine upwards from its' mountings.
2 Unclip the wiring loom from the cover (see illustration).
3 Undo the 4 bolts and remove the timing belt upper cover (see illustration).

Lower cover

4 Remove the crankshaft pulley as described in Section 5.
5 Position a trolley/workshop jack under the engine. Place a block of wood on the jack head (to help spread the load on the sump), then take the weight of the engine.
6 Prise up the coolant expansion tank and move it to one side – there is no need to drain the coolant.
7 Undo the nuts/bolt, and remove the right-hand engine mounting (see illustration).
8 Undo the 3 retaining bolts and move the

wiring harness guide away from the engine (see illustrations). The rear bolt is accessible from underneath the vehicle.
9 Undo the remaining bolt and remove the auxiliary drivebelt tensioner assembly.
10 Undo the 5 bolts and remove the lower cover (see illustration).

Refitting

11 Refitting of all the covers is a reversal of the relevant removal procedure, ensuring that each cover section is correctly located, and that the cover retaining bolts are securely tightened. Ensure that all disturbed hoses are reconnected and retained by their relevant clips.

7 Timing belt – removal, inspection, refitting and tensioning

General

1 The timing belt drives the camshaft, high-pressure fuel pump, and coolant pump from a toothed sprocket on the end of the crankshaft. If the belt breaks or slips in service, the pistons are likely to hit the valve heads, resulting in expensive damage.
2 The timing belt should be renewed at the specified intervals, or earlier if it is contaminated with oil, or at all noisy in operation (a 'scraping' noise due to uneven wear).
3 If the timing belt is being removed, it is a

wise precaution to renew the coolant pump at the same time. This may avoid the need to remove the timing belt again at a later stage, should the coolant pump fail. The timing belt tensioner should always be replaced when a new timing belt is fitted.

Removal

4 Remove the upper and lower timing belt covers, as described in Section 6.
5 Undo the bolts and remove the mounting bracket from the engine (see illustration).
6 Lock the crankshaft and camshaft in the correct position as described in Section 3. If necessary, temporarily refit the crankshaft pulley bolt to enable the crankshaft to be rotated.
7 Insert a hexagon key into the belt tensioner pulley centre, slacken the pulley bolt, and allow the tensioner to rotate clockwise,

7.5 Undo the bolts and remove the bracket

7.7 Slacken the bolt and allow the tensioner to rotate, relieving the tension on the belt

relieving the belt tension **(see illustration)**. With belt slack, temporarily tighten the pulley bolt.

8 Note its routing, then remove the timing belt from the sprockets.

Inspection

9 Renew the belt as a matter of course, regardless of its apparent condition. The cost of a new belt is nothing compared with the cost of repairs should the belt break in service. If signs of oil contamination are found, trace the source of the oil leak and rectify it. Wash down the engine timing belt area and all related components, to remove all traces of oil. The tensioner must always be replaced. Check that the idler pulleys rotate freely without any sign of roughness, and also check that the coolant pump pulley rotates freely. It is highly recommended that both the coolant pump and the idler pulley are replaced at the same time as the timing belt and tensioner.

Refitting and tensioning

10 Commence refitting by ensuring that the crankshaft, camshaft and fuel pump sprocket timing pins are in position as described in Section 3.

11 Locate the timing belt on the crankshaft sprocket, then keeping it taut, locate it around the idler pulley, camshaft sprocket, high-pressure pump sprocket, coolant pump sprocket, and the tensioner roller **(see illustration)**.

12 Slacken the tensioner pulley bolt, and using a hexagonal key, rotate the tensioner anti-clockwise, which moves the index arm clockwise, until the index arm is aligned as shown **(see illustration)**.

13 Remove the camshaft, crankshaft and fuel pump sprocket (where applicable) timing pins and, using a socket on the crankshaft pulley bolt, rotate the crankshaft clockwise 6 complete revolutions. Refit the crankshaft and camshaft locking pins.

14 Check that the tensioner index arm is still aligned **(see illustration 7.12)**. If it is not, remove and belt and begin the refitting process again, starting at Paragraph 11.

15 The remainder of refitting is a reversal of removal. Tighten all fasteners to the specified torque where given.

7.11 Timing belt routing

1 Crankshaft	4 Tensioner
2 Waterpump	5 Fuel pump
3 Idler	6 Camshaft

8 Timing belt sprockets and tensioner – removal and refitting

Camshaft sprocket

Removal

1 Remove the timing belt as described in Section 7.

2 Remove the locking tool from the camshaft sprocket/hub. Slacken the sprocket hub retaining bolt. To prevent the camshaft rotating as the bolt is slackened, a sprocket holding tool will be required. In the absence of

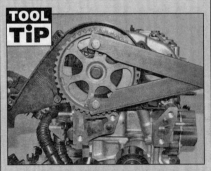

A sprocket holding tool can be made from two lengths of steel strip bolted together to form a forked end. Drill holes and insert bolts in the ends of the fork to engage with the sprocket spokes.

7.12 The index arm must align with the lug

the special Ford tool, an acceptable substitute can be fabricated at home (see **Tool Tip**). Do not attempt to use the engine assembly/valve timing locking tool to prevent the sprocket from rotating whilst the bolt is slackened.

3 Remove the sprocket hub retaining bolt, and slide the sprocket and hub off the end of the camshaft.

4 Clean the camshaft sprocket thoroughly, and renew it if there are any signs of wear, damage or cracks.

Refitting

5 Refit the camshaft sprocket to the camshaft **(see illustration)**.

6 Refit the sprocket hub retaining bolt. Tighten the bolt to the specified torque, preventing the camshaft from turning as during removal.

7 Align the engine assembly/valve timing slot in the camshaft sprocket hub with the hole in the cylinder head and refit the timing pin to lock the camshaft in position.

8 Fit the timing belt around the pump sprocket and camshaft sprocket, and tension the timing belt as described in Section 7.

Crankshaft sprocket

Removal

9 Remove the timing belt as described in Section 7.

10 Check that the engine assembly/valve timing holes are still aligned as described in Section 3, and the camshaft sprocket and flywheel are locked in position.

8.5 Ensure the lug on the sprocket hub engages with the slot on the end of the camshaft

8.11a Slide the sprocket from the crankshaft...

8.11b ...and recover the Woodruff key

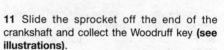

8.31 Timing belt idler pulley retaining nut

11 Slide the sprocket off the end of the crankshaft and collect the Woodruff key **(see illustrations)**.
12 Examine the crankshaft oil seal for signs of oil leakage and, if necessary, renew it as described in Section 13.
13 Clean the crankshaft sprocket thoroughly, and renew it if there are any signs of wear, damage or cracks. Recover the crankshaft locating key.

Refitting

14 Refit the key to the end of the crankshaft, then refit the crankshaft sprocket (with the flange facing the crankshaft pulley).
15 Fit the timing belt around the crankshaft sprocket, and tension the timing belt as described in Section 7.

Fuel pump sprocket

Removal

16 Remove the timing belt as described in Section 7.
17 Using a suitable socket, undo the pump sprocket retaining nut. The sprocket can be held stationary by inserting a suitably-sized locking pin, drill or rod through the slot in the sprocket flange, and into the corresponding hole in the backplate.
18 The pump sprocket is a taper fit on the pump shaft and it will be necessary to use a two-legged puller to release if from the taper.
19 Partially unscrew the sprocket retaining nut, fit the puller and release the sprocket from the taper.
20 Clean the sprocket thoroughly, and renew it if there are any signs of wear, damage or cracks.

Refitting

21 Refit the pump sprocket and retaining nut, and tighten the nut to the specified torque.
22 Refit the timing belt as described in Section 7.

Coolant pump sprocket

23 The coolant pump sprocket is integral with the pump, and cannot be removed. Coolant pump removal is described in Chapter 3 Section 7.

Tensioner pulley

Removal

24 Remove the timing belt as described in Section 7.
25 Remove the tensioner pulley retaining bolt, and then remove the tensioner.
26 Clean the tensioner pulley, but do not use any strong solvent which may enter the pulley bearings. Check that the pulley rotates freely, with no sign of stiffness or free play. The pulley should always be replaced when the timing belt is replaced.
27 Examine the pulley mounting stud for signs of damage and if necessary, renew it.

Refitting

28 Refitting is a reversal of removal.
29 Refit the timing belt as described in Section 7.

Idler pulley

Removal

30 Remove the timing belt as described in Section 7.
31 Undo the retaining bolt/nut and withdraw the idler pulley from the engine **(see illustration)**.
32 Clean the idler pulley, but do not use any strong solvent which may enter the bearings. Check that the pulley rotates freely, with no sign of stiffness or free play. Renew the idler pulley if there is any doubt about its condition, or if there are any obvious signs of wear or damage.

Refitting

33 Locate the idler pulley on the engine, and fit the retaining bolt/nut. Tighten the bolt/nut to the specified torque.
34 Refit the timing belt as described in Section 7.

9 Camshafts, rocker arms and hydraulic tappets – removal, inspection and refitting

Removal

1 Remove the cylinder head cover as described in Section 4.
2 Remove the camshaft position sensor as described in Chapter 4B Section 12.
3 Remove the camshaft sprocket as described in Section 8.
4 Refit the right-hand engine mounting, but only tighten the bolts moderately; this will keep the engine supported during the camshaft removal.
5 Undo the bolts and remove the vacuum pump as described in Chapter 9 Section 21. Recover the pump O-ring seals.
6 Unbolt the fuel filter (see Chapter 1B Section 22) and move it to one side.
7 Working in reverse order to that shown **(see illustration 9.22)** remove the retaining bolts and then remove camshaft bearing cap ladder **(see illustration)**.
8 Lift out the camshaft **(see illustration)** and dispose of the oil seal. A new one will be required.

9.7 Remove the bearing ladder

9.8 Remove the camshaft

9.10 Remove the rocker arms (cam followers)

9.11 Use long nose pliers to remove the hydraulic tappets

9.19 Lubricate the bearing surfaces

9 Obtain 8 small, clean plastic containers, and number them 1 to 4 inlet and 1 to 4 exhaust; alternatively, divide a larger container into 8 compartments.

10 Lift out each rocker arm. Place the rocker arms in their respective positions in the box or containers **(see illustration)**.

11 A compartmentalised container filled with engine oil is now required to retain the hydraulic tappets while they are removed from the cylinder head. Withdraw each hydraulic follower **(see illustration)** and place it in the container, keeping them each identified for correct refitting. The tappets must be totally submerged in the oil to prevent air entering them.

Inspection

12 Inspect the cam lobes and the camshaft bearing journals for scoring or other visible evidence of wear. Once the surface hardening of the cam lobes has been eroded, wear will occur at an accelerated rate. **Note:** *If these symptoms are visible on the tips of the camshaft lobes, check the corresponding rocker arm, as it will probably be worn as well.*

13 Examine the condition of the bearing surfaces in the cylinder head and camshaft bearing housing. If wear is evident, the cylinder head and bearing housing will both have to be renewed, as they are a matched assembly.

14 Inspect the rocker arms and tappets for scuffing, cracking or other damage and renew any components as necessary. Also check the condition of the tappet bores in the cylinder

head. As with the camshafts, any wear in this area will necessitate cylinder head renewal.

Refitting

15 Thoroughly clean the sealant from the mating surfaces of the cylinder head and camshaft bearing housing. Use a suitable liquid gasket dissolving agent (available from Ford dealers) together with a soft putty knife; do not use a metal scraper or the faces will be damaged. As there is no conventional gasket used, the cleanliness of the mating faces is of the utmost importance.

16 Clean off any oil, dirt or grease from both components and dry with a clean lint-free cloth. Ensure that all the oilways are completely clean.

17 Liberally lubricate the hydraulic tappet bores in the cylinder head with clean engine oil.

18 Insert the hydraulic tappets into their original bores in the cylinder head unless they have been renewed.

19 Lubricate the rocker arms and place them over their respective tappets and valve stems. Lubricate the bearing surfaces **(see illustration)** and then refit the camshaft.

20 Apply a thin bead of silicone sealant (Ford part No WSE-M4G323-A4) to the mating surface of the camshaft cover/bearing ladder as shown **(see illustration)**.

21 Assemble the bearing ladder within 10 minutes of applying the sealant. Ford technicians use a special tool (303-245) to align the bearing ladder, however 2 suitable bolts (with their heads and threads cut off) can be used if the tool is not available.

22 Tighten the bolts to the specified torque in sequence **(see illustration)**.

23 Fit a new camshaft oil seal as described in Section 13.

24 Refit the camshaft sprocket, and tighten the retaining bolt.

25 Refit the timing belt and temporarily refit the crankshaft pulley bolt – use the old bolt. Rotate the engine at least 20 revolutions to allow the oil pump to deliver oil to the camshaft and associated components. Refit the timing belt cover.

26 Refit the remainder of the components in the reverse order of removal.

10 Cylinder head – removal and refitting

Removal

1 Apply the handbrake, then jack up the front of the vehicle and support it on axle stands (see *Jacking and vehicle support*).

2 Disconnect the battery negative lead as described in Chapter 5A Section 4.

3 Remove the windscreen cowl panel and bulkhead closure panel as described in Chapter. 11 Section 20

4 Drain the cooling system as described in Chapter 1B Section 30.

5 Release the clamps, undo the 2 bolts, remove the air intake duct between the air cleaner housing and turbocharger, and disconnect the breather hose from the cylinder head cover **(see illustration)**.

9.20 Apply sealant to the camshaft housing

9.22 Bolt tightening sequence

10.5 Remove the air intake duct

10.11 Undo the bolt, disconnect the wiring plugs, then unclip the harness duct

10.13 Depress the buttons, then disconnect the fuel supply and return hoses from the pump

10.16 Remove the coolant outlet housing

6 Remove the timing belt, camshaft, rocker arms and hydraulic tappets as described in Section 9.

7 Remove the diesel particulate filter as described in Chapter 4B Section 18.

8 Remove the EGR cooler assembly as described in Chapter 4C Section 3.

9 Disconnect the hoses and unbolt the fuel filter assembly as described in Chapter 1B Section 22.

10 Undo the upper mounting bolts, and pivot the alternator away from the engine, undo the oil dipstick guide tube bolt, then undo the bolts securing the alternator mounting bracket to the cylinder head/block.

11 Note their fitted positions, then disconnect the wiring plugs as necessary, and unbolt the wiring harness duct from above the fuel rail and injectors **(see illustration)**.

12 Undo the unions and remove the high-pressure pipes between the fuel rail and the injectors. Counterhold the pipe unions with an open-ended spanner on the injector ports to prevent them from rotating. Discard the pipes, new ones must be fitted. Plug the openings to prevent contamination.

13 Disconnect the fuel supply and return hoses from the high-pressure fuel pump, then undo the bolts securing the pump mounting bracket to the cylinder head **(see illustration)**.

14 Remove the fuel injectors as described in Chapter 4B Section 11.

15 With reference to Chapter 4B Section 16, remove the turbocharger oil supply pipe, and disconnect the lower end of the oil return hose. Disconnect the vacuum hose from the wastegate actuator, and the variable vane position sensor.

16 Undo the coolant outlet housing (left-hand end of the cylinder head) retaining bolts, slacken the two bolts securing the housing support bracket to the top of the transmission bellhousing, and move the outlet housing away from the cylinder head a little **(see illustration)**. There is no need to disconnect the hoses.

17 Check that no components or electrical connectors are still fitted to the cylinder head.

18 Working in the reverse of the sequence shown **(see illustration 10.37)** undo the

cylinder head bolts. Discard the bolts – new ones must be fitted.

19 Release the cylinder head from the cylinder block and location dowels by rocking it. The Ford tool for doing this consists simply of two metal rods with 90-degree angled ends **(see illustration)**. Do not prise between the mating faces of the cylinder head and block, as this may damage the gasket faces.

20 Lift the cylinder head from the block, and recover the gasket.

Preparation for refitting

21 The mating faces of the cylinder head and cylinder block must be perfectly clean before refitting the head. Ford recommend the use of a scouring agent for this purpose, but acceptable results can be achieved by using a hard plastic or wood scraper to remove all traces of gasket and carbon. The same method can be used to clean the piston crowns. Take particular care to avoid scoring or gouging the cylinder head/cylinder block mating surfaces during the cleaning operations, as aluminium alloy is easily damaged. Make sure that the carbon is not allowed to enter the oil and water passages – this is particularly important for the lubrication system, as carbon could block the oil supply to the engine's components. Using adhesive tape and paper, seal the water, oil and bolt holes in the cylinder block. To prevent carbon entering the gap between the pistons and bores, smear a little grease in the gap. After cleaning each piston, use a small brush to remove all traces of grease and carbon from the gap, then wipe away the remainder with a clean rag.

22 Check the mating surfaces of the cylinder block and the cylinder head for nicks, deep scratches and other damage. If slight, they may be removed carefully with a file, but if excessive, machining may be the only alternative to renewal. If warpage of the cylinder head gasket surface is suspected, use a straight-edge to check it for distortion. Refer to Part F of this Chapter if necessary.

23 Thoroughly clean the threads of the cylinder head bolt holes in the cylinder block. Ensure that the bolts run freely in their threads, and that all traces of oil and water are removed from each bolt hole.

Gasket selection

24 The gasket thickness is indicated by notches/holes on the front edge of the gasket. If the crankshaft or pistons/connecting rods have not been disturbed, fit a new gasket with the same number of notches/holes as the previous one. If the crankshaft/piston or connecting rods have been disturbed, it's necessary to work out the piston protrusion as follows:

25 Remove the crankshaft timing pin, then turn the crankshaft until pistons 1 and 4 are at TDC (Top Dead Centre). Position a dial test indicator (dial gauge) on the cylinder block adjacent to the rear of No 1 piston, and zero it on the block face. Transfer the probe to the crown of No 1 piston (10.0 mm in from the rear edge), then slowly turn the crankshaft back-and-forth past TDC, noting the highest reading on the indicator. Record this reading as protrusion A.

26 Repeat the check described in paragraph 25, this time 10.0 mm in from the front edge of the No 1 piston crown. Record this reading as protrusion B.

27 Add protrusion A to protrusion B, then divide the result by 2 to obtain an average reading for piston No 1.

28 Repeat the procedure described in paragraphs 25 to 27 on piston 4, then turn

10.19 Free the cylinder head using angled rods

the crankshaft through 180° and carry out the procedure on the piston Nos 2 and 3 **(see illustration)**. Check that there is a maximum difference of 0.07 mm protrusion between any two pistons.

29 If a dial test indicator is not available, piston protrusion may be measured using a straight-edge and feeler blades or Vernier calipers. However, this is much less accurate, and cannot therefore be recommended.

30 Note the greatest piston protrusion measurement, and use this to determine the correct cylinder head gasket from the table below. The series of notches/holes on the side of the gasket are used for thickness identification **(see illustration)**.

10.28 Measure the piston protrusion using a DTI gauge

10.30 Cylinder head gasket thickness identification notches

Piston protrusion (mm)	Gasket thickness (mm)	Notches
0.533 to 0.634	1.25	2
0.634 to 0.684	1.30	3
0.684 to 0.734	1.35	1
0.734 to 0.784	1.40	4
0.784 to 0.886	1.45	5

Refitting

31 Turn the crankshaft and position Nos 1 and 4 pistons at TDC, then turn the crankshaft a quarter turn (90°) anti-clockwise.

32 Thoroughly clean the surfaces of the cylinder head and block.

33 Make sure that the locating dowels are in place, then fit the correct gasket the right way round on the cylinder block **(see illustration)**.

34 Carefully lower the cylinder head onto the gasket and block, making sure that it locates correctly onto the dowels.

35 Apply a smear of grease to the threads, and to the underside of the heads of the new cylinder head bolts.

36 Carefully insert the cylinder head bolts into their holes (do not drop them in) and initially finger-tighten them.

37 Working progressively and in sequence, tighten the cylinder head bolts to their Stage 1 torque setting, using a torque wrench and suitable socket **(see illustration)**.

38 Once all the bolts have been tightened to their Stage 1 torque setting, working again in the specified sequence, tighten each bolt to the specified Stage 2 setting. Finally, angle-tighten the bolts through the specified Stage 3 angle. It is recommended that an angle-measuring gauge is used during this stage of tightening, to ensure accuracy. **Note:** *Retightening of the cylinder head bolts after running the engine is not required.*

39 Refit the hydraulic tappets, rocker arms, and camshaft housing (complete with camshafts) as described in Section 9.

40 Refit the timing belt as described in Section 7.

41 The remainder of refitting is a reversal of removal, noting the following points.

a) *Use a new seal when refitting the coolant outlet housing.*

b) *When refitting a cylinder head, it is good practice to renew the thermostat.*

c) *Tighten all fasteners to the specified torque where given.*

d) *Refill the cooling system as described in Chapter 1B Section 30.*

e) *The engine may run erratically for the first few miles, until the engine management ECM relearns its stored values.*

11 Sump – removal and refitting

Removal

1 Drain the engine oil, then clean and refit the engine oil drain plug, tightening it securely. If the engine is nearing its service interval when the oil and filter are due for renewal, it is recommended that the filter is also removed, and a new one fitted. After reassembly, the engine can then be refilled with fresh oil. Refer to Chapter 1B Section 6 for further information.

2 Apply the handbrake, then jack up the front of the vehicle and support it on axle stands (see *Jacking and vehicle support*). Undo the bolts and remove the engine undershield.

3 Although not strictly necessary, remove the exhaust front pipe as described in Chapter 4B Section 18.

10.33 Ensure the gasket locates over the dowels

10.37 Cylinder head bolt tightening sequence

11.8 Apply a bead of sealant to the sump or crankcase mating surface. Ensure the sealant is applied to the inside of the retaining bolt holes

11.9 Refit the sump and tighten the bolts

4 Where necessary, disconnect the wiring connector from the oil temperature sender unit, which is screwed into the sump.

5 Progressively slacken and remove all the sump retaining bolts/nuts. Since the sump bolts vary in length, remove each bolt in turn, and store it in its correct fitted order by pushing it through a clearly-marked cardboard template. This will avoid the possibility of installing the bolts in the wrong locations on refitting.

6 Try to break the joint by striking the sump with the palm of your hand, then lower and withdraw the sump from under the car. If the sump is stuck (which is quite likely) use a putty knife or similar, carefully inserted between the sump and block. Ease the knife along the joint until the sump is released. While the sump is removed, take the opportunity to check the oil pump pick-up/strainer for signs of clogging or splitting. If necessary, remove the pump as described in Section 12, and clean or renew the strainer.

Refitting

7 Clean all traces of sealant from the mating surfaces of the cylinder block/crankcase and sump, then use a clean rag to wipe out the sump and the engine's interior.

8 Ensure that the sump mating surfaces are clean and dry, then apply a 3mm diameter bead of sealant (Ford part No WSE-M4G323-A4) to the sump mating surface **(see illustration)**. The sealant must be applied to the Inside of the bolt holes. Note that the sump must be installed within 10 minutes of applying the sealant, and the bolts tightened within a further 5 minutes.

9 Offer up the sump to the cylinder block/crankcase. Refit its retaining bolts/nuts, ensuring that each bolt is screwed into its original location. Tighten the bolts evenly and progressively to the specified torque setting **(see illustration)**.

10 Reconnect the wiring connector to the oil temperature sensor (where fitted).

11 Where applicable, refit the exhaust pipe.

12 Lower the vehicle to the ground, wait at least 30 minutes and then refill the engine with oil as described in Chapter 1B Section 6.

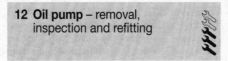

12 Oil pump – removal, inspection and refitting

Removal

1 Remove the sump as described in Section 11.

2 Remove the crankshaft front oil seal as described in Section 13.

3 Disconnect the wiring plug, undo the bolts and remove the crankshaft position sensor, located on the right-hand end of the cylinder block.

4 Undo the three Torx security bolts and remove the oil pump pick-up tube from the pump/block **(see illustration)**. Discard the oil seal, a new one must be fitted.

12.4 Oil pick-up tube bolts

5 Undo the 8 bolts, and remove the oil pump **(see illustration)**.

Inspection

6 Undo and remove the Torx bolts securing the cover to the oil pump **(see illustration)**. Examine the pump rotors and body for signs of wear and damage. If worn, the complete pump must be renewed.

7 Remove the circlip, and extract the cap, valve piston and spring, noting which way

12.5 Oil pump retaining bolts

12.6 Undo the Torx bolts and remove the pump cover

12.7a Remove the circlip...

12.7b ...cap...

12.7c ...spring...

12.7d ...and piston

12.11 Apply a bead of sealant to the cylinder block mating surface

12.12a Fit a new seal...

around they are fitted (see illustrations). The condition of the relief valve spring can only be measured by comparing it with a new one; if there is any doubt about its condition, it should also be renewed.

8 Refit the relief valve piston and spring, then secure them in place with the circlip.

9 Refit the cover to the oil pump, and tighten the Torx bolts securely.

Refitting

10 Remove all traces of sealant, and thoroughly clean the mating surfaces of the oil pump and cylinder block.

11 Apply a 4 mm diameter bead of silicone sealant to the mating face of the cylinder block (see illustration). Ensure that no sealant enters any of the holes in the block.

12 With a new oil seal fitted, refit the oil pump over the end of the crankshaft, aligning the flats in the pump drive gear with the flats machined in the crankshaft (see illustrations). Note that new oil pumps are supplied with the oil seal already fitted, and a seal protector sleeve. The sleeve fits over the end of the crankshaft to protect the seal as the pump is fitted.

13 Install the oil pump bolts and tighten them to the specified torque.

14 Refit the oil pick-up tube to the pump/ cylinder block using a new O-ring seal. Ensure the oil dipstick guide tube is correctly refitted.

15 Refit the woodruff key to the crankshaft, and slide the crankshaft sprocket into place.

16 The remainder of refitting is a reversal of removal.

13 Oil seals – renewal

Crankshaft

Right-hand oil seal

1 Remove the crankshaft sprocket and Woodruff key as described in Section 8.

2 Measure and note the fitted depth of the oil seal.

3 Pull the oil seal from the housing using a screwdriver. Alternatively, drill a small hole in the oil seal, and use a self-tapping screw and a pair of pliers to remove it (see illustration).

12.12b ...align the pump gear flats...

12.12c ...with those of the crankshaft

13.3 Take great care not to mark the crankshaft whilst levering out the oil seal

13.5a Slide the seal and protective sleeve over the end of the crankshaft...

13.5b ...and press the seal into place

13.12 Slide the seal and protective sleeve over the left-hand end of the crankshaft

13.16 Drill a hole, insert a self-tapping screw, and pull the seal from place using pliers

13.18a Use the correct tool to fit the seal...

13.18b ...or a suitable socket

4 Clean the oil seal housing and the crankshaft sealing surface.

5 The new seal should be supplied with a protective sleeve, which fits over the end of the crankshaft to prevent any damage to the seal lip. With the sleeve in place, press the seal (open end first) into the pump to the previously-noted depth, using a suitable tube or socket **(see illustrations)**.

6 Where applicable, remove the plastic sleeve from the end of the crankshaft.

7 Refit the crankshaft sprocket as described in Section 8.

Left-hand oil seal

8 Remove the flywheel, as described in Section 15.

9 Measure and note the fitted depth of the oil seal.

10 Pull the oil seal from the housing using a screwdriver. Alternatively, drill a small hole in the oil seal, and use a self-tapping screw and a pair of pliers to remove it **(see illustration 13.3)**.

11 Clean the oil seal housing and the crankshaft sealing surface.

12 The new seal should be supplied with a protective sleeve, which fits over the end of the crankshaft to prevent any damage to the seal lip **(see illustration)**. With the sleeve in place, press the seal (open end first) into the housing to the previously-noted depth, using a suitable tube or socket.

13 Where applicable, remove the plastic sleeve from the end of the crankshaft.

14 Refit the flywheel, as described in Section 15.

Camshaft

15 Remove the camshaft sprocket as described in Section 8. In principle there is no need to remove the timing belt completely, but remember that if the belt has been contaminated with oil, it must be renewed.

16 Pull the oil seal from the housing using a hooked instrument. Alternatively, drill a small hole in the oil seal and use a self-tapping screw and a pair of pliers to remove it **(see illustration)**.

17 Clean the oil seal housing and the camshaft sealing surface.

18 Press the seal (open end first) into the housing to the previously-noted depth, using either the correct tool (303-684), a suitable

14.3 The oil pressure switch is located on the front face of the cylinder block

tube or a socket which bears only of the outer edge of the seal **(see illustrations)**. If the seal was supplied with a protective sleeve, remove it.

19 Refit the camshaft sprocket as described in Section 8.

20 Where necessary, fit a new timing belt with reference to Section 7.

14 Oil pressure switch and level sensor – removal and refitting

Removal

Oil pressure switch

1 The oil pressure switch is located at the front of the cylinder block, adjacent to the oil dipstick guide tube. Note that on some models, access to the switch may be improved if the vehicle is jacked up and supported on axle stands, then undo the bolts and remove the engine undershield so that the switch can be reached from underneath (see *Jacking and vehicle support*).

2 Remove the protective sleeve from the wiring plug (where applicable), then disconnect the wiring from the switch.

3 Unscrew the switch from the cylinder block, and recover the sealing washer **(see illustration)**. Be prepared for oil spillage, and if the switch is to be left removed from the engine for any length of time, plug the hole in the cylinder block.

14.5 The oil level sensor is located on the rear face of the cylinder block (arrowed)

15.2 Lock the flywheel with a 12mm diameter rod or bolt

15.9 Flywheel retaining bolts

Oil level sensor

4 Where fitted, the oil level sensor is located at the rear of the cylinder block. Jack up the front of the vehicle and support it securely on axle stands (see *Jacking and vehicle support*). Undo the bolts and remove the engine undershield.
5 Reach up between the driveshaft and the cylinder block, and disconnect the sensor wiring plug **(see illustration)**.
6 Using an open-ended spanner, unscrew the sensor and withdraw it from position.

Refitting

Oil pressure switch

7 Examine the sealing washer for any signs of damage or deterioration, and if necessary renew.
8 Refit the switch, complete with washer, and tighten it to the specified torque where given.
9 Refit the engine undershield, and lower the vehicle to the ground.

Oil level sensor

10 Smear a little silicone sealant on the threads and refit the sensor to the cylinder block, tightening it securely.
11 Reconnect the sensor wiring plug.
12 Refit the engine undershield, and lower the vehicle to the ground.

---

15 Flywheel – removal, inspection and refitting

Removal

1 Remove the transmission as described in Chapter 7A Section 6, then remove the clutch assembly as described in Chapter 6 Section 6.
2 Prevent the flywheel from turning. Do not attempt to lock the flywheel in position using the crankshaft pulley locking tool described in Section 3. Insert a 12 mm diameter rod or drill bit through the hole in the flywheel cover casting, and into a slot in the flywheel **(see illustration)**
3 Make alignment marks between the flywheel and crankshaft to aid refitment. Slacken and remove the flywheel retaining bolts, and remove the flywheel from the end of the crankshaft. Be careful not to drop it; it

is heavy. If the flywheel locating dowel (where fitted) is a loose fit in the crankshaft end, remove it and store it with the flywheel for safe-keeping. Discard the flywheel bolts; new ones must be used on refitting.

Inspection

4 Examine the flywheel for scoring of the clutch face, and for wear or chipping of the ring gear teeth. If the clutch face is scored, the flywheel may be surface-ground, but renewal is preferable. Seek the advice of a Ford dealer or engine reconditioning specialist to see if machining is possible. If the ring gear is worn or damaged, the flywheel must be renewed, as it is not possible to renew the ring gear separately.
5 All engines maybe fitted with a dual-mass flywheel. The maximum travel of the primary mass in relation to the secondary must not exceed 15 teeth (or 20 degrees). If in doubt remove the flywheel and have a suitably equipped specialist check the flywheel. Inspect the flywheel for any grease or debris from the interface between the fixed part and the movable part of the flywheel. If any doubt to the condition of the flywheel exists, despite the expense we recommend replacing it.

Refitting

6 Clean the mating surfaces of the flywheel and crankshaft. Remove any remaining locking compound from the threads of the crankshaft holes, using the correct size of tap, if available.
7 If the new flywheel retaining bolts are not supplied with their threads already pre-coated, apply a suitable thread-locking compound to the threads of each bolt.
8 Ensure that the locating dowel is in position. Offer up the flywheel, locating it on the dowel (where fitted), and fit the new retaining bolts. Where no locating dowel is fitted, align the previously-made marks to ensure the flywheel is refitted in its original position.
9 Lock the flywheel using the method employed on dismantling, and tighten the retaining bolts to the specified torque **(see illustration)**.
10 Refit the clutch as described in Chapter 6 Section 6. Remove the flywheel locking tool, and refit the transmission as described in Chapter 7A Section 6.

---

16 Engine/transmission mountings – inspection and renewal

General

1 The engine/transmission mountings seldom require attention, but broken or deteriorated mountings should be renewed immediately, or the added strain placed on the driveline components may cause damage or wear.
2 While separate mountings may be removed and refitted individually, if more than one is disturbed at a time – such as if the engine/transmission unit is removed from its mountings – they must be reassembled and their fasteners tightened in the position marked on removal.
3 On reassembly, the complete weight of the engine/transmission unit must not be taken by the mountings until all are correctly aligned with the marks made on removal. Tighten the engine/transmission mounting fasteners to their specified torque wrench settings.

Inspection

4 During the check, the engine/transmission unit must be raised slightly, to remove its weight from the mountings.
5 Raise the front of the vehicle, and support it securely on axle stands. Position a jack under the sump, with a large block of wood between the jack head and the sump, then carefully raise the engine/transmission just enough to take the weight off the mountings.

⚠ **Warning: DO NOT place any part of your body under the engine when it is supported only by a jack.**

6 Check the mountings to see if the rubber is cracked, hardened or separated from the metal components. Sometimes the rubber will split right down the centre.
7 Check for relative movement between each mounting's brackets and the engine/transmission or body (use a large screwdriver or lever to attempt to move the mountings). If movement is noted, lower the engine and check-tighten the mounting fasteners.

16.9 Right-hand engine mounting-to-
engine bracket retaining nuts

16.10 Right-hand engine mounting-to-inner
wing panel retaining bolts

16.13 Undo the retaining nuts and lift out
the battery tray support bracket

Renewal

Note: *The following paragraphs assume the engine is supported beneath the sump as described earlier.*

Right-hand mounting

8 Release the clips, lift up the coolant expansion tank and position it to one side. Note there is no need to disconnect the coolant pipes.

9 Mark the position of the mounting on the vehicle, right-hand inner wing panel, then undo the three nuts securing the mounting to the engine bracket **(see illustration)**. Discard the nuts, new ones must be fitted.

10 Undo the three retaining bolts securing the mounting to the inner wing panel and withdraw the mounting from the vehicle **(see illustration)**.

11 On refitting, tighten all fasteners to the torque wrench settings specified. Re-align the

marks made on removal, then tighten the new mounting bracket retaining nuts.

Left-hand mounting

12 Remove the battery and battery tray as described in Chapter 5A Section 4. Note that it is not necessary to remove the powertrain control module from the battery tray, just position the tray clear for access to the mounting.

13 Undo the three nuts securing the battery tray support bracket in position. Release the wiring loom from the support bracket and lift the support bracket out of the engine compartment **(see illustration)**.

14 With the transmission supported, mark the position of the mounting bracket on the transmission and on the body side member. Undo the three bolts securing the mounting bracket to the transmission and the two bolts securing the mounting to the body side member **(see illustrations)**. Remove the mounting from the engine compartment.

15 On refitting, re-align the mounting in the position noted on removal, then tighten all fasteners to the specified torque wrench settings. Refit the components disturbed for access using a reversal of the removal procedures.

Rear mounting (roll restrictor)

16 To remove the engine rear mounting, apply the handbrake, then jack up the front of the car and support it on axle stands (see *Jacking and vehicle support*). Unscrew the through-bolts and remove the engine rear mounting link from the bracket on the transmission and from the bracket on the subframe **(see illustration)**. Hold the engine stationary while the bolts are being removed, since the link will be under tension.

17 On refitting, ensure that the bolts are securely tightened to the specified torque wrench setting.

16.14a Left-hand engine mounting
bracket-to-transmission retaining bolts
(arrowed) ...

16.14b ... and mounting-to-body
sidemember retaining bolts (arrowed)

16.16 Rear mounting/roll restrictor
retaining bolts

Notes

Chapter 2 Part D
1.6 litre SOHC diesel engine in-car repair procedures

Contents

Degrees of difficulty

Easy, suitable for novice with little experience	**Fairly easy,** suitable for beginner with some experience ✎	**Fairly difficult,** suitable for competent DIY mechanic ✎	**Difficult,** suitable for experienced DIY mechanic ✎	**Very difficult,** suitable for expert DIY or professional

Specifications

General

Designation	Duratorq-TDCi
Engine codes*	TZJA and TZLB
Capacity	1560 cc
Bore	75.0 mm
Stroke	88.3 mm
Direction of crankshaft rotation	Clockwise (viewed from the right-hand side of vehicle)
No 1 cylinder location	At the transmission end of block
Maximum power output	70 kW (95 PS) @ 3800 rpm
Maximum torque output	200 Nm @ 1750 – 3800 rpm
Compression ratio	16: 1
Emissions level	Stage V

The engine code is stamped on a plate attached to the front of the cylinder block, next to the oil filter

Compression pressures (engine hot, at cranking speed)

Normal	20 ± 5 bar
Minimum	15 bar
Maximum difference between any two cylinders	5 bar

Camshaft

Camshaft end float	0.195 – 0.3 mm

Lubrication system

Oil pump type	Gear-type, driven directly by the right-hand end of the crankshaft, by two flats machined along the crankshaft journal.

Minimum oil pressure at 80°C:

Idle speed	1.0 to 2.0 bar
2000 rpm	2.3 to 3.7 bar

Torque wrench settings

	Nm	lbf ft
Ancillary drivebelt tensioner roller	20	15
Big-end bolts: *		
Stage 1	10	7
Stage 2	Slacken 180°	
Stage 3	10	7
Stage 4	Angle-tighten a further 130°	
Camshaft bearing caps	10	7
Camshaft bearing ladder:		
Studs	10	7
Bolts	10	7
Camshaft position sensor bolt	5	4
Camshaft sprocket bolt		
Stage 1	20	15
Stage 2	Angle-tighten a further 50°	
Coolant outlet housing bolts	8	6
Crankshaft position/speed sensor bolt	10	7
Crankshaft pulley/sprocket bolt: *		
Stage 1	35	26
Stage 2	Angle-tighten a further 190°	
Cylinder head bolts: *		
Stage 1	20	15
Stage 2	40	30
Stage 3	Angle-tighten a further 260°	
Cylinder head cover	10	7
EGR valve	10	7
Engine-to-transmission fixing bolts	47	35
Flywheel bolts: *		
Stage 1	30	22
Stage 2	Angle-tighten a further 90°	
Fuel pump sprocket	50	37
Left-hand engine/transmission mounting:		
Mounting-to-bracket centre nut	148	109
Mounting-to-bracket outer nuts	48	35
Mounting bracket to transmission	80	59
Main bearing ladder outer seam bolts:		
Stage 1	5	4
Stage 2	10	7
Main bearing ladder to cylinder block:		
Stage 1	10	7
Stage 2	Slacken 180°	
Stage 3	30	22
Stage 4	Angle-tighten a further 140°	
Piston oil jet spray tube bolt	20	15
Oil cooler retaining bolts	10	7
Oil filter cover	25	18
Oil pick-up pipe	10	7
Oil pressure switch	30	22
Oil pump to cylinder block:		
Stage 1	5	4
Stage 2	9	7
Rear engine/transmission mounting	25	18
Right-hand engine mounting:		
Mounting to Inner wing (nuts/bolts)	48	35
Mounting bracket to engine block	55	41
Sump drain plug	35	26
Sump bolts/nuts	10	7
Timing belt idler pulley	37	27
Timing belt tensioner pulley	30	22
Vacuum pump bolts	20	15

*Do not re-use

1 General Information

How to use this Chapter

1 This Part of Chapter 2 describes the repair procedures that can reasonably be carried out on the engine while it remains in the vehicle. If the engine has been removed from the vehicle and is being dismantled as described in Part F, any preliminary dismantling procedures can be ignored.

2 Note that, while it may be possible physically to overhaul items such as the piston/connecting rod assemblies while the engine is in the car, such tasks are not usually carried out as separate operations. Usually, several additional procedures are required (not to mention the cleaning of components and oilways); for this reason, all such tasks are classed as major overhaul procedures, and are described in Part E of this Chapter.

3 Part E describes the removal of the engine/transmission from the car, and the full overhaul procedures that can then be carried out.

Duratorq TDCi engines

4 The 1.6 litre Duratorq TDCi engine is a single overhead camshaft (SOHC) 8-valve design, with direct injection. The turbocharged four-cylinder engine is mounted transversely, with the transmission mounted on the left-hand side.

5 A toothed timing belt drives the camshaft, high-pressure fuel pump and coolant pump. The camshaft operates the inlet and exhaust valves via rocker arms which are supported at their pivot ends by hydraulic self-adjusting tappets. The camshaft Is supported by bearings machined directly in the cylinder head and camshaft bearing housing.

6 The high-pressure fuel pump supplies fuel to the fuel rail, and subsequently to the electronically-controlled injectors which inject the fuel direct into the combustion chambers. This design differs from the previous type where an injection pump supplies the fuel at high pressure to each injector. The earlier, conventional type injection pump required fine calibration and timing, and these functions are now completed by the high-pressure pump, electronic injectors and engine management ECM.

7 The crankshaft runs in five main bearings of the usual shell type. Endfloat is controlled by thrustwashers either side of No 2 main bearing.

8 The pistons are selected to be of matching weight, and incorporate fully-floating gudgeon pins retained by circlips.

Repair operations precaution

9 The engine is a complex unit with numerous accessories and ancillary components. The design of the engine compartment is such that every conceivable space has been utilised, and access to virtually all of the engine components is extremely limited. In many cases, ancillary components will have to be removed, or moved to one side, and wiring, pipes and hoses will have to be disconnected or removed from various cable clips and support brackets.

10 When working on this engine, read through the entire procedure first, look at the car and engine at the same time, and establish whether you have the necessary tools, equipment, skill and patience to proceed. Allow considerable time for any operation, and be prepared for the unexpected.

11 Because of the limited access, many of the engine photographs appearing in this Chapter were, by necessity, taken with the engine removed from the vehicle.

⚠️ **Warning: It is essential to observe strict precautions when working on the fuel system components of the engine, particularly the high-pressure side of the system. Before carrying out any engine operations that entail working on, or near, any part of the fuel system, refer to the special information given in Chapter 4B Section 2.**

12 Operations with engine in vehicle
a) *Compression pressure – testing.*
b) *Cylinder head cover – removal and refitting.*
c) *Crankshaft pulley – removal and refitting.*
d) *Timing belt covers – removal and refitting.*
e) *Timing belt – removal, refitting and adjustment.*
f) *Timing belt tensioner and sprockets – removal and refitting.*
g) *Camshaft oil seal – renewal.*
h) *Camshaft, rocker arms and hydraulic tappets – removal, inspection and refitting.*
i) *Sump – removal and refitting.*
j) *Oil pump – removal and refitting.*
k) *Crankshaft oil seals – renewal.*
l) *Engine/transmission mountings – inspection and renewal.*
m) *Flywheel – removal, inspection and refitting.*

2 Compression and leakdown tests – description and interpretation

Compression test

Note: *A compression tester specifically designed for diesel engines must be used for this test.*

1 When engine performance is down, or if misfiring occurs which cannot be attributed to the fuel system, a compression test can provide diagnostic clues as to the engine's condition. If the test is performed regularly, it can give warning of trouble before any other symptoms become apparent.

2 A compression tester specifically intended for diesel engines must be used, because of the higher pressures involved. The tester is connected to an adapter which screws into the glow plug or injector hole. On this engine, an adapter suitable for use in the glow plug holes will be required, so as not to disturb the fuel system components. It is unlikely to be worthwhile buying such a tester for occasional use, but it may be possible to borrow or hire one – if not, have the test performed by a garage.

3 Unless specific instructions to the contrary are supplied with the tester, observe the following points:
a) *The battery must be in a good state of charge, the air filter must be clean, and the engine should be at normal operating temperature.*
b) *All the glow plugs should be removed as described in Chapter 5A Section 12 before starting the test.*
c) *Disconnect the glow plug control module as described in Chapter 5A Section 12.*

4 The compression pressures measured are not so important as the balance between cylinders. Values are given in the Specifications.

5 The cause of poor compression is less easy to establish on a diesel engine than on a petrol one. The effect of introducing oil into the cylinders ('wet' testing) is not conclusive, because there is a risk that the oil will sit in the swirl chamber or in the recess on the piston crown instead of passing to the rings. However, the following can be used as a rough guide to diagnosis.

6 All cylinders should produce very similar pressures; any difference greater than that specified indicates the existence of a fault. Note that the compression should build-up quickly in a healthy engine; low compression on the first stroke, followed by gradually-increasing pressure on successive strokes, indicates worn piston rings. A low compression reading on the first stroke, which does not build-up during successive strokes, indicates leaking valves or a blown head gasket (a cracked head could also be the cause). Deposits on the undersides of the valve heads can also cause low compression.

7 A low reading from two adjacent cylinders is almost certainly due to the head gasket having blown between them; the presence of coolant in the engine oil will confirm this.

8 If the compression reading is unusually high, the cylinder head surfaces, valves and pistons are probably coated with carbon deposits. If this is the case, the cylinder head should be removed and decarbonised.

Note: *After performing this test, a fault code may be generated and stored in the PCM memory. Have the PCM self-diagnosis facility interrogated by a Ford dealer or suitably-equipped specialist, and the fault code erased.*

Leakdown test

9 A leakdown test measures the rate at which compressed air fed into the cylinder is lost. It is an alternative to a compression test, and in many ways it is better, since the escaping air

3.9 Insert a 5.0 mm drill bit/bolt through the round hole in the sprocket flange into the hole in the oil pump housing (lower timing belt removed for clarity)

3.10 Insert an 8.0 mm bolt through the hole in the camshaft sprocket into the corresponding hole in the cylinder head

provides easy identification of where pressure loss is occurring (piston rings, valves or head gasket).

10 The equipment needed for leakdown testing is unlikely to be available to the home mechanic. If poor compression is suspected, have the test performed by a suitably-equipped garage.

3 Engine assembly/valve timing holes – general information and usage

Note: *Do not attempt to rotate the engine whilst the crankshaft and camshaft are locked in position. If the engine is to be left in this state for a long period of time, it is a good idea to place suitable warning notices inside the vehicle, and in the engine compartment. This will reduce the possibility of the engine being accidentally cranked on the starter motor, which is likely to cause damage with the locking pins in place.*

1 Timing holes or slots are located in the crankshaft pulley flange and camshaft sprocket hub. This will ensure that the valve timing is maintained during operations that require removal and refitting of the timing belt. When the holes/slots are aligned with their corresponding holes in the cylinder block and cylinder head, suitable diameter bolts/pins can be inserted to lock the crankshaft and camshaft in position, preventing rotation.

2 Note that the fuel system used on these engines does not have a conventional diesel injection pump, but instead uses a high-pressure fuel pump. However, the fuel pump sprocket must be pegged in position in a similar fashion to the camshaft sprocket.

3 To align the engine assembly/valve timing holes, proceed as follows.

4 Apply the handbrake, then jack up the front of the vehicle and support it on axle stands (see *Jacking and vehicle support*). Remove the right-hand front roadwheel.

5 To gain access to the crankshaft pulley, to enable the engine to be turned, the wheel arch plastic liner must be removed. The liner is secured by several plastic expanding rivets/nut/bolts. To remove the rivets, push in the centre pins a little, then prise the clips from place. Remove the liner from under the front wing.

6 Remove the crankshaft pulley as described in Section 2C Section 5.

7 Remove the upper and lower timing belt covers as described in 2C Section 6.

8 Temporarily refit the crankshaft pulley bolt (without the crankshaft pulley) and then remove the crankshaft locking tool.

9 Turn the crankshaft until the timing hole in the crankshaft sprocket aligns with the hole in the oil pump casing (this is at the 12 o'clock position). Fit the special tool 303-732, or a suitable alternative and lock the crankshaft in position **(see illustration)**.

10 With the crankshaft locked in position fit the camshaft locking tool (303-735 or similar). The hole in the camshaft sprocket should be at approximately the 1 o'clock position **(see illustration)**. If this is not the case remove the crankshaft locking pin and rotate the engine

one revolution. Note that the crankshaft must always be turned in a clockwise direction (viewed from the right-hand side of vehicle).

11 When refitting the timing belt, rotate the fuel pump sprocket clockwise and insert a 5 mm bolt or drive bit through the slot in the sprocket flange and into the corresponding hole in the fuel pump mounting bracket.

12 The crankshaft and camshaft are now locked in position, preventing unnecessary rotation.

4 Cylinder head cover – removal and refitting

Removal

1 Disconnect the battery negative lead as described in Chapter 5A Section 4.

2 Pull up the front edge and remove the plastic cover from the top of the engine **(see illustration)**.

3 Release the hose clamp and disconnect the hose from the throttle body **(see illustration)**.

4 Disconnect the wiring plug from the throttle body and then release the clamp, unbolt and remove the throttle body complete with the

4.2 Pull up the front edge, then pull the cover forwards

4.3 Release the throttle body hose clamp

4.4a Release the clamp, then undo the nut and bolt at the front of the hose...

4.4b... and the nut underneath

4.5 Slacken the clamps and remove the elbow

4.6a Remove the bolt...

4.6b... unclip the wiring harness duct and move it to one side

4.9 Prise up the fuel pipe push-in clip, and release the wiring harness

hose **(see illustrations)**. Plug the openings to prevent contamination.

5 Slacken the clamps, and remove the

turbocharger to intercooler hose elbow **(see illustration)**. Seal the opening to the turbocharger.

6 Disconnect the wiring plugs from the fuel injectors, then undo the retaining bolt and unclip the wiring harness duct from the top of the engine **(see illustrations)**.

7 Release the clips and disconnect the breather hose from the cylinder head cover.

8 Unclip the wiring harness, then unbolt and then remove the timing belt upper cover as described in Section Section.

9 Unclip the fuel pipe assembly and wiring harness from the rear of the cover **(see illustration)**.

10 Undo the 4 retaining bolts and remove the air intake flange from the intake manifold **(see illustration)**. Renew the seal.

11 Remove the 11 bolts and then remove the cover **(see illustrations)**. Recover the rubber seal.

4.10 Undo the bolts and remove the intake flange

4.11a The cylinder head cover is secured by 9 bolts on the top...

4.11b... one bolt in the end behind the camshaft sprocket...

4.11c... and one at the rear of the cover

4.11d Carefully manoeuvre the cover from place

4.12 Renew the seal

5.1 Engine undershield fasteners

Caution: Do not touch the outer magnetic sensor ring of the sprocket with your fingers, or allow metallic particles to come into contact with it.

Refitting

6 Refit the pulley to the end of the crankshaft.
7 Refit the crankshaft pulley. Fit a new bolt and retaining washer. Tighten the bolt to the specified torque, then through the specified angle.
8 Remove the locking tool.
9 Refit and tension the auxiliary drivebelt as described in Chapter 1B Section 26.
10 Refit the remaining components in reverse order of removal.

Refitting

12 Refitting is a reversal of removal, but ensure that the seal is correctly located **(see illustration)**.

5 Crankshaft pulley –
removal and refitting

Removal

1 Jack up and support the front of the vehicle (see *Jacking and vehicle support*). Undo the fasteners and remove the engine undershield **(see illustration)**.
2 Disconnect the battery negative lead as described in Chapter 5A Section 4.
3 Remove the auxiliary drivebelt as described in Chapter 1B Section 26.

4 To lock the crankshaft, working underneath the engine, insert a 12 mm diameter rod or bolt into the hole in the engine block casting over the lower section of the flywheel **(see illustration)**. Note that the hole in the casting and flywheel is provided purely to lock the crankshaft whilst the pulley bolt it undone – it does not position the crankshaft at TDC. Rotate the crankshaft clockwise until the tool engages in the hole in the flywheel – don't rotate the crank pulley anti-clockwise.
5 Using a suitable socket and extension bar, unscrew the retaining bolt, remove the washer, then slide the pulley off the end of the crankshaft **(see illustrations)**. If the pulley is tight fit, it can be drawn off the crankshaft using a suitable puller. If a puller is being used, refit the pulley retaining bolt without the washer, to avoid damaging the crankshaft as the puller is tightened.

6 Timing belt covers –
removal and refitting

⚠ *Warning: Refer to the precautionary information contained in Section 1 before proceeding.*

Removal

Upper cover

1 Remove the engine cover from the top of the engine.
2 Pull the coolant expansion tank upwards from its' mountings **(see illustration)**. Place the tank to one side – there's no need to disconnect the hoses. On models with air conditioning, undo the retaining nut securing the refrigerant pipe bracket to the suspension turret **(see illustration)**.

5.4 Install the flywheel locking tool

5.5a Where fitted remove the cover

5.5b Remove the bolt and...

5.5c ...then the pulley

6.2a Undo the nut securing the refrigerant pipe (where applicable)

6.2b Pull the expansion tank upwards from its' mountings

6.3 Release the clips securing the wiring loom

6.4 Upper cover bolts

6.8 Engine mounting nuts/bolt

6.10a Remove the two bolts at the front of the harness guide...

6.10b... and the bolt at the rear

high-pressure fuel pump, and coolant pump from a toothed sprocket on the end of the crankshaft. If the belt breaks or slips in service, the pistons are likely to hit the valve heads, resulting in expensive damage.

2 The timing belt should be renewed at the specified intervals, or earlier if it is contaminated with oil, or at all noisy in operation (a 'scraping' noise due to uneven wear).

3 If the timing belt is being removed, it is a wise precaution to renew the coolant pump at the same time. This may avoid the need to remove the timing belt again at a later stage, should the coolant pump fail. The timing belt tensioner should always be replaced when a new timing belt is fitted.

Removal

4 Remove the upper and lower timing belt covers, as described in Section 6.

5 Undo the bolt and remove the crankshaft position sensor adjacent to the crankshaft sprocket flange, and move it to one side **(see illustration)**.

6 Undo the retaining bolt and remove the timing belt protection bracket, again, adjacent to the crankshaft sprocket flange **(see illustration)**.

7 Lock the crankshaft and camshaft in the correct position as described in Section 3. If necessary, temporarily refit the crankshaft pulley bolt to enable the crankshaft to be rotated.

8 Insert a hexagon key into the belt tensioner pulley centre, slacken the pulley bolt, and allow the tensioner to rotate, relieving the belt tension **(see illustration)**. With belt slack, temporarily tighten the pulley bolt.

3 Unclip the wiring loom from the cover **(see illustration)**.

4 Undo the 4 bolts and remove the timing belt upper cover **(see illustration)**.

Lower cover

5 Remove the crankshaft pulley as described in Section 5.

6 Position a trolley/workshop jack under the engine. Place a block of wood on the jack head (to help spread the load on the sump), then take the weight of the engine.

7 Prise up the coolant expansion tank and move it to one side – there is no need to drain the coolant.

8 Undo the nuts/bolts, and remove the right-hand engine mounting **(see illustration)**.

9 Remove the engine mounting bracket from the engine.

10 Undo the 3 retaining bolts and move the wiring harness guide away from the engine

(see illustrations). The rear bolt is accessible from underneath the vehicle.

11 Undo the 4 bolts and remove the lower cover.

Refitting

12 Refitting of all the covers is a reversal of the relevant removal procedure, ensuring that each cover section is correctly located, and that the cover retaining bolts are securely tightened. Ensure that all disturbed hoses are reconnected and retained by their relevant clips.

---

7   Timing belt – removal, inspection, refitting and tensioning

General

1 The timing belt drives the camshaft,

7.5 Undo the bolt and remove the crankshaft position sensor

7.6 Remove the timing belt protection bracket

7.8 Slacken the bolt and allow the tensioner to rotate, relieving the tension on the belt

7.12 Timing belt routing

1 Crankshaft	4 Tensioner
2 Waterpump	5 Fuel pump
3 Idler	6 Camshaft

9 Note its routing, then remove the timing belt from the sprockets.

Inspection

10 Renew the belt as a matter of course, regardless of its apparent condition. The cost of a new belt is nothing compared with the cost of repairs should the belt break in service. If signs of oil contamination are found, trace the source of the oil leak and rectify it. Wash down the engine timing belt area and all related components, to remove all traces of oil. The tensioner must always be replaced. Check that the idler pulleys rotate freely without any sign of roughness, and also check

7.14 The index arm must align with the lug

that the coolant pump pulley rotates freely. It is highly recommended that both the coolant pump and the idler pulley are replaced at the same time as the timing belt and tensioner.

Refitting and tensioning

11 Commence refitting by ensuring that the crankshaft, camshaft and fuel pump sprocket timing pins are in position as described in Section.
12 Locate the timing belt on the crankshaft sprocket, then keeping it taut, locate it around the idler pulley, camshaft sprocket, high-pressure pump sprocket, coolant pump sprocket, and the tensioner roller **(see illustration)**.
13 Refit the timing belt protection bracket and tighten the retaining bolt securely.
14 Slacken the tensioner pulley bolt, and using a hexagonal key, rotate the tensioner anti-clockwise, which moves the index arm clockwise, until the index arm is aligned as shown **(see illustration)**.
15 Remove the camshaft, crankshaft and fuel pump sprocket (where applicable) timing pins and, using a socket on the crankshaft pulley bolt, rotate the crankshaft clockwise 10 complete revolutions. Refit the crankshaft and camshaft locking pins.

16 Check that the tensioner index arm is still aligned between the edges of the area shown **(see illustration 7.14)**. If it is not, remove and belt and begin the refitting process again, starting at Paragraph 11.
17 The remainder of refitting is a reversal of removal. Tighten all fasteners to the specified torque where given.

8 Timing belt sprockets and tensioner – removal and refitting

Camshaft sprocket

Removal

1 Remove the timing belt as described in Section 7.
2 Remove the locking tool from the camshaft sprocket/hub. Slacken the sprocket hub retaining bolt. To prevent the camshaft rotating as the bolt is slackened, a sprocket holding tool will be required. In the absence of the special Ford tool, an acceptable substitute can be fabricated at home (see **Tool Tip 1**). Do not attempt to use the engine assembly/valve timing locking tool to prevent the sprocket from rotating whilst the bolt is slackened.
3 Remove the sprocket hub retaining bolt, and slide the sprocket and hub off the end of the camshaft.
4 Clean the camshaft sprocket thoroughly, and renew it if there are any signs of wear, damage or cracks.

Refitting

5 Refit the camshaft sprocket to the camshaft **(see illustration)**.
6 Refit the sprocket hub retaining bolt. Tighten the bolt to the specified torque, preventing the camshaft from turning as during removal.
7 Align the engine assembly/valve timing slot in the camshaft sprocket hub with the hole in the cylinder head and refit the timing pin to lock the camshaft in position.

A sprocket holding tool can be made from two lengths of steel strip bolted together to form a forked end. Drill holes and insert bolts in the ends of the fork to engage with the sprocket spokes.

8.5 Ensure the lug on the sprocket hub engages with the slot on the end of the camshaft (arrowed)

8.11a Slide the sprocket from the crankshaft...

8.11b ...and recover the Woodruff key

8 Fit the timing belt around the pump sprocket and camshaft sprocket, and tension the timing belt as described in Section 7.

Crankshaft sprocket

Removal

9 Remove the timing belt as described in Section 7.
10 Check that the engine assembly/valve timing holes are still aligned as described in Section, and the camshaft sprocket and flywheel are locked in position.
11 Slide the sprocket off the end of the crankshaft and collect the Woodruff key **(see illustrations)**.
12 Examine the crankshaft oil seal for signs of oil leakage and, if necessary, renew it as described in Section 13.
13 Clean the crankshaft sprocket thoroughly, and renew it if there are any signs of wear, damage or cracks. Recover the crankshaft locating key.

Refitting

14 Refit the key to the end of the crankshaft, then refit the crankshaft sprocket (with the flange facing the crankshaft pulley).
15 Fit the timing belt around the crankshaft

sprocket, and tension the timing belt as described in Section 7.

Fuel pump sprocket

Removal

16 Remove the timing belt as described in Section 7.
17 Using a suitable socket, undo the pump sprocket retaining nut. The sprocket can be held stationary by inserting a suitably-sized locking pin, drill or rod through the slot in the sprocket, and into the corresponding hole in the backplate, or by using a suitable forked tool engaged with the holes in the sprocket.
18 The pump sprocket is a taper fit on the pump shaft and it will be necessary to make up another tool to release it from the taper (see **Tool Tip 2**).
19 Partially unscrew the sprocket retaining nut, fit the home-made tool, and secure it to the sprocket with two suitable bolts. Prevent the sprocket from rotating as before, and unscrew the sprocket retaining nut. The nut will bear against the tool as it is undone, forcing the sprocket off the shaft taper. Once the taper is released, remove the tool, unscrew the nut fully, and remove the sprocket from the pump shaft.

20 Clean the sprocket thoroughly, and renew it if there are any signs of wear, damage or cracks.

Refitting

21 Refit the pump sprocket and retaining nut, and tighten the nut to the specified torque. Prevent the sprocket rotating as the nut is tightened using the sprocket holding tool.
22 Refit the timing belt as described in Section 7.

Coolant pump sprocket

23 The coolant pump sprocket is integral with the pump, and cannot be removed. Coolant pump removal is described in Chapter 3 Section 7.

Tensioner pulley

Removal

24 Remove the timing belt as described in Section 7.
25 Remove the tensioner pulley retaining bolt, and then remove the tensioner **(see illustration 7.8)**.
26 Clean the tensioner pulley, but do not use any strong solvent which may enter the pulley bearings. Check that the pulley rotates freely, with no sign of stiffness or free play. The pulley should always be replaced when the timing belt is replaced.
27 Examine the pulley mounting stud for signs of damage and if necessary, renew it.

Refitting

28 Refitting is a reversal of removal.
29 Refit the timing belt as described in Section 7.

Idler pulley

Removal

30 Remove the timing belt as described in Section 7.
31 Undo the retaining bolt/nut and withdraw the idler pulley from the engine **(see illustration)**.

TOOL TiP 2

Make a sprocket releasing tool from a short strip of steel. Drill two holes in the strip to correspond with the two holes in the sprocket. Drill a third hole just large enough to accept the flats of the sprocket retaining nut.

8.31 Timing belt idler pulley retaining nut

32 Clean the idler pulley, but do not use any strong solvent which may enter the bearings. Check that the pulley rotates freely, with no sign of stiffness or free play. Renew the idler pulley if there is any doubt about its condition, or if there are any obvious signs of wear or damage.

Refitting

33 Locate the idler pulley on the engine, and fit the retaining bolt/nut. Tighten the bolt/nut to the specified torque.
34 Refit the timing belt as described in Section 7.

---

9 Camshafts, rocker arms and hydraulic tappets – removal, inspection and refitting

---

Removal

1 Remove the cylinder head cover as described in Section 4.
2 Remove the the camshaft sprocket as described in Section 8.
3 Refit the right-hand engine mounting, but only tighten the bolts moderately; this will keep the engine supported during the camshaft removal.
4 Undo the bolts and remove the vacuum pump (see Section). Recover the pump O-ring seals.
5 Unbolt the fuel filter (see Chapter 1B Section 22) and move it to one side.
6 Disconnect the wiring plug from the camshaft position sensor **(see illustration)**.

Unbolt and remove the sensor from the bearing ladder.
7 Working in reverse order to that shown **(see illustration 9.22)** remove the retaining bolts and then remove camshaft bearing cap ladder **(see illustration)**.
8 Lift out the camshaft **(see illustration)** and dispose of the oil seal. A new one will be required.
9 Obtain 8 small, clean plastic containers, and number them 1 to 4 inlet and 1 to 4 exhaust; alternatively, divide a larger container into 8 compartments.
10 Lift out each rocker arm. Place the rocker arms in their respective positions in the box or containers **(see illustration)**.
11 A compartmentalised container filled with engine oil is now required to retain the hydraulic tappets while they are removed from the cylinder head. Withdraw each hydraulic follower **(see illustration)** and place it in the container, keeping them each identified for correct refitting. The tappets must be totally submerged in the oil to prevent air entering them.

Inspection

12 Inspect the cam lobes and the camshaft bearing journals for scoring or other visible evidence of wear. Once the surface hardening of the cam lobes has been eroded, wear will occur at an accelerated rate. **Note:** *If these symptoms are visible on the tips of the camshaft lobes, check the corresponding rocker arm, as it will probably be worn as well.*
13 Examine the condition of the bearing

surfaces in the cylinder head and camshaft bearing housing. If wear is evident, the cylinder head and bearing housing will both have to be renewed, as they are a matched assembly.
14 Inspect the rocker arms and tappets for scuffing, cracking or other damage and renew any components as necessary. Also check the condition of the tappet bores in the cylinder head. As with the camshafts, any wear in this area will necessitate cylinder head renewal.

Refitting

15 Thoroughly clean the sealant from the mating surfaces of the cylinder head and camshaft bearing housing. Use a suitable liquid gasket dissolving agent (available from Ford dealers) together with a soft putty knife; do not use a metal scraper or the faces will be damaged. As there is no conventional gasket used, the cleanliness of the mating faces is of the utmost importance.
16 Clean off any oil, dirt or grease from both components and dry with a clean lint-free cloth. Ensure that all the oilways are completely clean.
17 Liberally lubricate the hydraulic tappet bores in the cylinder head with clean engine oil.
18 Insert the hydraulic tappets into their original bores in the cylinder head unless they have been renewed.
19 Lubricate the rocker arms and place them over their respective tappets and valve stems. Lubricate the bearing surfaces **(see illustration)** and then refit the camshaft.

9.6 Remove the camshaft position sensor

9.7 Remove the bearing ladder

9.8 Remove the camshaft

9.10 Remove the rocker arms (cam followers)

9.11 Use long nose pliers to remove the hydraulic tappets

9.19 Lubricate the bearing surfaces

9.20 Apply sealant to the camshaft housing

9.21 Refit the bearing ladder

9.22 Tighten the bolts to the specified torque in the order shown

20 Apply a thin bead of silicone sealant (Ford part No WSE-M4G323-A4) to the mating surface of the camshaft cover/bearing ladder as shown **(see illustration)**.
21 Assembly the bearing ladder within 10 minutes of applying the sealant **(see illustration)**. Ford technicians use a special tool (303-245) to align the bearing ladder, however 2 suitable bolts (with their heads and threads cut off) can be used if the tool is not available.
22 Tighten the bolts to the specified torque in sequence **(see illustration)**.
23 Fit a new camshaft oil seal as described in Section 13.
24 Refit the camshaft sprocket, and tighten the retaining bolt.
25 Refit the timing belt and temporarily refit the crankshaft pulley bolt – use the old bolt. Rotate the engine at least 20 revolutions to allow the oil pump to deliver oil to the camshaft and associated components. Refit the timing belt cover.
26 Refit the remainder of the components in the reverse order of removal.

10 Cylinder head – removal and refitting

Removal

1 Apply the handbrake, then jack up the front of the vehicle and support it on axle stands (see *Jacking and vehicle support*).

2 Disconnect the battery negative lead as described in Chapter 5A Section 4.
3 Remove the windscreen cowl panel and bulkhead panel as described in Chapter 11 Section 20.
4 Remove the air cleaner assembly as described in Chapter 4B Section 4.
5 Drain the cooling system as described in Chapter 1B Section 30.
6 Undo the 4 bolts and remove the heatshield above the turbocharger **(see illustration)**.
7 Remove the throttle body as described in Chapter 4B Section 12, then undo the nut/bolt and remove the air duct from the intake manifold.
8 Release the clamp, undo the bolts, remove the charge air pipe between the turbocharger and the intercooler **(see illustrations)**.
9 Undo the 4 nuts and remove the heatshield at the back of the turbocharger **(see illustration)**.

10 Remove the timing belt, camshaft, rocker arms and hydraulic tappets as described in 2C Section 9.
11 Remove the diesel particulate filter as described in Chapter 4B Section 18.
12 Remove the EGR cooler assembly as described in Chapter 4C Section 3.
13 Disconnect the hoses and unbolt the fuel filter assembly as described in Chapter 1B Section 22.
14 Undo the upper mounting bolts, and pivot the alternator away from the engine, undo the oil dipstick guide tube bolt, then undo the bolts securing the alternator mounting bracket to the cylinder head/block **(see illustration)**.
15 Note their fitted positions, then disconnect the wiring plugs as necessary, and unbolt the wiring harness duct from above the fuel rail and injectors.
16 Undo the unions and remove the

10.6 Undo the bolts and remove the turbo heatshield

10.8a Charge air-pipe-to turbocharger bolts

10.8b Slacken the clamp securing the pipe to the intercooler

10.9 Heatshield retaining nuts

10.14 Dipstick guide tube Torx bolt

10.16 Use a crows-foot spanner adapter to slacken and tighten the high-pressure fuel pipe unions

10.17 Depress the release buttons, and disconnect the hoses from the fuel filter

10.20 Access to the coolant outlet housing will be improved if the vacuum pump is removed first

high-pressure pipes between the fuel rail and the injectors **(see illustration)**. Counterhold the pipe unions with an open-ended spanner on the injector ports to prevent them from rotating. Discard the pipes, new ones must be fitted. Plug the openings to prevent contamination.

17 Disconnect the fuel supply and return hoses from the fuel filter assembly, then undo the bolts securing the filter mounting bracket to the cylinder head **(see illustration)**.

18 Remove the fuel injectors as described in Chapter 4B Section 11.

19 With reference to Chapter 4B Section 16, remove the turbocharger oil supply pipe, and disconnect the lower end of the oil return hose. Disconnect the vacuum hose from the wastegate actuator, and the variable vane position sensor.

20 Undo the coolant outlet housing (left-hand end of the cylinder head) retaining bolts, slacken the two bolts securing the housing support bracket to the top of the transmission bellhousing, and move the outlet housing away from the cylinder head a little **(see illustration)**. There is no need to disconnect the hoses.

21 Check that no components or electrical connectors are still fitted to the cylinder head.

22 Working in the reverse of the sequence

shown **(see illustration 10.41)** undo the cylinder head bolts. Discard the bolts – new ones must be fitted.

23 Release the cylinder head from the cylinder block and location dowels by rocking it. The Ford tool for doing this consists simply of two metal rods with 90-degree angled ends **(see illustration)**. Do not prise between the mating faces of the cylinder head and block, as this may damage the gasket faces.

24 Lift the cylinder head from the block, and recover the gasket.

Preparation for refitting

25 The mating faces of the cylinder head and cylinder block must be perfectly clean before refitting the head. Ford recommend the use of a scouring agent for this purpose, but acceptable results can be achieved by using a hard plastic or wood scraper to remove all traces of gasket and carbon. The same method can be used to clean the piston crowns. Take particular care to avoid scoring or gouging the cylinder head/cylinder block mating surfaces during the cleaning operations, as aluminium alloy is easily damaged. Make sure that the carbon is not allowed to enter the oil and water passages – this is particularly important for the lubrication system, as carbon could block the oil supply to the engine's components. Using adhesive tape and paper, seal the water, oil and bolt holes in the cylinder block. To prevent carbon entering the gap between the pistons and bores, smear a little grease in the gap. After

cleaning each piston, use a small brush to remove all traces of grease and carbon from the gap, then wipe away the remainder with a clean rag.

26 Check the mating surfaces of the cylinder block and the cylinder head for nicks, deep scratches and other damage. If slight, they may be removed carefully with a file, but if excessive, machining may be the only alternative to renewal. If warpage of the cylinder head gasket surface is suspected, use a straight-edge to check it for distortion. Refer to Part F of this Chapter if necessary.

27 Thoroughly clean the threads of the cylinder head bolt holes in the cylinder block. Ensure that the bolts run freely in their threads, and that all traces of oil and water are removed from each bolt hole.

Gasket selection

28 The gasket thickness is indicated by notches/holes on the front edge of the gasket. If the crankshaft or pistons/connecting rods have not been disturbed, fit a new gasket with the same number of notches/holes as the previous one. If the crankshaft/piston or connecting rods have been disturbed, it's necessary to work out the piston protrusion as follows:

29 Remove the crankshaft timing pin, then turn the crankshaft until pistons 1 and 4 are at TDC (Top Dead Centre). Position a dial test indicator (dial gauge) on the cylinder block adjacent to the rear of No 1 piston, and zero it on the block face. Transfer the probe to the crown of No 1 piston (10.0 mm in from the rear edge), then slowly turn the crankshaft back-and-forth past TDC, noting the highest reading on the indicator. Record this reading as protrusion A.

30 Repeat the check described in paragraph 29, this time 10.0 mm in from the front edge of the No 1 piston crown. Record this reading as protrusion B.

31 Add protrusion A to protrusion B, then divide the result by 2 to obtain an average reading for piston No 1.

32 Repeat the procedure described in paragraphs 29 to 31 on piston 4, then turn the crankshaft through 180° and carry out the procedure on the piston Nos 2 and 3 **(see illustration)**. Check that there is a maximum

10.23 Free the cylinder head using angled rods

10.32 Measure the piston protrusion using a DTI gauge

10.34 Cylinder head gasket thickness identification notches

difference of 0.07 mm protrusion between any two pistons.

33 If a dial test indicator is not available, piston protrusion may be measured using a straight-edge and feeler blades or Vernier calipers. However, this is much less accurate, and cannot therefore be recommended.

34 Note the greatest piston protrusion measurement, and use this to determine the correct cylinder head gasket from the table below. The series of notches/holes on the side of the gasket are used for thickness identification **(see illustration)**.

Piston protrusion (mm)	Gasket thickness (mm)	Notches
0.533 to 0.634	1.25	2
0.634 to 0.684	1.30	3
0.684 to 0.734	1.35	1
0.734 to 0.784	1.40	4
0.784 to 0.886	1.45	5

Refitting

35 Turn the crankshaft and position Nos 1 and 4 pistons at TDC, then turn the crankshaft a quarter turn (90°) anti-clockwise.

36 Thoroughly clean the surfaces of the cylinder head and block.

37 Make sure that the locating dowels are in place, then fit the correct gasket the right way round on the cylinder block **(see illustration)**.

38 Carefully lower the cylinder head onto the gasket and block, making sure that it locates correctly onto the dowels.

39 Apply a smear of grease to the threads, and to the underside of the heads of the new cylinder head bolts.

40 Carefully insert the cylinder head bolts into their holes (do not drop them in) and initially finger-tighten them.

41 Working progressively and in sequence, tighten the cylinder head bolts to their Stage 1 torque setting, using a torque wrench and suitable socket **(see illustration)**.

42 Once all the bolts have been tightened to their Stage 1 torque setting, working again in the specified sequence, tighten each bolt to the specified Stage 2 setting. Finally, angle-tighten the bolts through the specified Stage 3 angle. It is recommended that an angle-measuring gauge is used during this stage of tightening, to ensure accuracy. **Note:** *Retightening of the cylinder head bolts after running the engine is not required.*

43 Refit the hydraulic tappets, rocker arms, and camshaft housing (complete with camshafts) as described in 2C Section 9.

44 Refit the timing belt as described in 2C Section 7.

45 The remainder of refitting is a reversal of removal, noting the following points.
a) Use a new seal when refitting the coolant outlet housing.
b) When refitting a cylinder head, it is good practice to renew the thermostat.
c) Tighten all fasteners to the specified torque where given.
d) Refill the cooling system as described in Chapter 1B Section 30.
e) The engine may run erratically for the first few miles, until the engine management ECM relearns its stored values.

11 Sump – removal and refitting

Removal

1 Drain the engine oil, then clean and refit the engine oil drain plug, tightening it securely. If the engine is nearing its service interval when the oil and filter are due for renewal, it is recommended that the filter is also removed, and a new one fitted. After reassembly, the engine can then be refilled with fresh oil. Refer to Chapter 1B Section 6 for further information.

2 Apply the handbrake, then jack up the front of the vehicle and support it on axle stands (see *Jacking and vehicle support*). Undo the bolts and remove the engine undershield.

3 Although not strictly necessary, remove the exhaust front pipe as described in Chapter 4B Section 18.

4 Where necessary, disconnect the wiring connector from the oil temperature sender unit, which is screwed into the sump.

5 Progressively slacken and remove all the sump retaining bolts/nuts. Since the sump bolts vary in length, remove each bolt in turn, and store it in its correct fitted order by pushing it through a clearly-marked cardboard template. This will avoid the possibility of installing the bolts in the wrong locations on refitting.

6 Try to break the joint by striking the sump with the palm of your hand, then lower and withdraw the sump from under the car. If the sump is stuck (which is quite likely) use a putty knife or similar, carefully inserted between the sump and block. Ease the knife along the joint until the sump is released. While the sump is removed, take the opportunity to check the oil pump pick-up/strainer for signs of clogging or splitting. If necessary, remove the pump as described in 2C Section 12, and clean or renew the strainer.

10.37 Ensure the gasket locates over the dowels

10.41 Cylinder head bolt tightening sequence

11.8 Apply a bead of sealant to the sump or crankcase mating surface. Ensure the sealant is applied to the inside of the retaining bolt holes

11.9 Refit the sump and tighten the bolts

Refitting

7 Clean all traces of sealant from the mating surfaces of the cylinder block/crankcase and sump, then use a clean rag to wipe out the sump and the engine's interior.

8 Ensure that the sump mating surfaces are clean and dry, then apply a 3mm diameter bead of sealant (Ford part No WSE-M4G323-A4) to the sump mating surface **(see illustration)**. The sealant must be applied to the Inside of the bolt holes. Note that the sump must be installed within 10 minutes of applying the sealant, and the bolts tightened within a further 5 minutes.

9 Offer up the sump to the cylinder block/crankcase. Refit its retaining bolts/nuts, ensuring that each bolt is screwed into its original location. Tighten the bolts evenly and progressively to the specified torque setting **(see illustration)**.

10 Reconnect the wiring connector to the oil temperature sensor (where fitted).

11 Where applicable, refit the exhaust pipe.

12 Lower the vehicle to the ground, wait at least 30 minutes and then refill the engine with oil as described in Chapter 1B Section 6.

---

12 Oil pump – removal, inspection and refitting

Removal

1 Remove the sump as described in Section.

2 Remove the crankshaft sprocket as described in Section 8. Recover the locating key from the crankshaft.

3 Disconnect the wiring plug, undo the bolts and remove the crankshaft position sensor, located on the right-hand end of the cylinder block.

4 Undo the three Torx security bolts and remove the oil pump pick-up tube from the pump/block **(see illustration)**. Discard the oil seal, a new one must be fitted.

5 Undo the 8 bolts, and remove the oil pump **(see illustration)**.

Inspection

6 Undo and remove the Torx bolts securing the cover to the oil pump **(see illustration)**. Examine the pump rotors and body for signs of wear and damage. If worn, the complete pump must be renewed.

12.4 Oil pick-up tube bolts

12.5 Oil pump retaining bolts

12.6 Undo the Torx bolts and remove the pump cover

12.7a Remove the circlip...

12.7b ...cap...

12.7c ...spring...

7 Remove the circlip, and extract the cap, valve piston and spring, noting which way around they are fitted **(see illustrations)**. The condition of the relief valve spring can only be measured by comparing it with a new one; if there is any doubt about its condition, it should also be renewed.

8 Refit the relief valve piston and spring, then secure them in place with the circlip.

9 Refit the cover to the oil pump, and tighten the Torx bolts securely.

Refitting

10 Remove all traces of sealant, and thoroughly clean the mating surfaces of the oil pump and cylinder block.

11 Apply a 4 mm diameter bead of silicone sealant to the mating face of the cylinder block **(see illustration)**. Ensure that no sealant enters any of the holes in the block.

12 With a new oil seal fitted, refit the oil

12.7d ...and piston

pump over the end of the crankshaft, aligning the flats in the pump drive gear with the flats machined in the crankshaft **(see illustrations)**. Note that new oil pumps are supplied with the oil seal already fitted, and a seal protector

12.11 Apply a bead of sealant to the cylinder block mating surface

sleeve. The sleeve fits over the end of the crankshaft to protect the seal as the pump is fitted.

13 Install the oil pump bolts and tighten them to the specified torque.

14 Refit the oil pick-up tube to the pump/ cylinder block using a new O-ring seal. Ensure the oil dipstick guide tube is correctly refitted.

15 Refit the woodruff key to the crankshaft, and slide the crankshaft sprocket into place.

16 The remainder of refitting is a reversal of removal.

13 Oil seals – renewal

Crankshaft

Right-hand oil seal

1 Remove the crankshaft sprocket and Woodruff key as described in Section 8.

2 Measure and note the fitted depth of the oil seal.

3 Pull the oil seal from the housing using a screwdriver. Alternatively, drill a small hole in the oil seal, and use a self-tapping screw and a pair of pliers to remove it **(see illustration)**.

4 Clean the oil seal housing and the crankshaft sealing surface.

5 The new seal should be supplied with a protective sleeve, which fits over the end of the crankshaft to prevent any damage to the seal lip. With the sleeve in place, press the seal (open end first) into the pump to the

12.12a Fit a new seal...

12.12b ...align the pump gear flats...

12.12c ...with those of the crankshaft

13.3 Take great care not to mark the crankshaft whilst levering out the oil seal

13.5a Slide the seal and protective sleeve over the end of the crankshaft...

13.5b ...and press the seal into place

13.12 Slide the seal and protective sleeve over the left-hand end of the crankshaft

13.16 Drill a hole, insert a self-tapping screw, and pull the seal from place using pliers

13.18a Use the correct tool to fit the seal...

13.18b ...or a suitable socket

previously-noted depth, using a suitable tube or socket **(see illustrations)**.

6 Where applicable, remove the plastic sleeve from the end of the crankshaft.

7 Refit the crankshaft sprocket as described in Section 8.

Left-hand oil seal

8 Remove the flywheel, as described in Section 15.

9 Measure and note the fitted depth of the oil seal.

10 Pull the oil seal from the housing using a screwdriver. Alternatively, drill a small hole in the oil seal, and use a self-tapping screw and a pair of pliers to remove it **(see illustration 13.3)**.

11 Clean the oil seal housing and the crankshaft sealing surface.

12 The new seal should be supplied with a protective sleeve, which fits over the end of the crankshaft to prevent any damage to the seal lip **(see illustration)**. With the sleeve in place, press the seal (open end first) into the housing to the previously-noted depth, using a suitable tube or socket.

13 Where applicable, remove the plastic sleeve from the end of the crankshaft.

14 Refit the flywheel, as described in Section 15.

Camshaft

15 Remove the camshaft sprocket as described in Section 8. In principle there is no need to remove the timing belt completely, but remember that if the belt

has been contaminated with oil, it must be renewed.

16 Pull the oil seal from the housing using a hooked instrument. Alternatively, drill a small hole in the oil seal and use a self-tapping screw and a pair of pliers to remove it **(see illustration)**.

17 Clean the oil seal housing and the camshaft sealing surface.

18 Press the seal (open end first) into the housing to the previously-noted depth, using either the correct tool (303-684), a suitable tube or a socket which bears only of the outer edge of the seal **(see illustrations)**. If the seal was supplied with a protective sleeve, remove it.

19 Refit the camshaft sprocket as described in Section 8.

20 Where necessary, fit a new timing belt with reference to Section 7.

14 Oil pressure switch and level sensor – removal and refitting

Removal

Oil pressure switch

1 The oil pressure switch is located at the front of the cylinder block, adjacent to the oil dipstick guide tube. Note that on some models, access to the switch may be improved if the vehicle is jacked up and supported on axle stands, then undo the bolts and remove the engine undershield so that

the switch can be reached from underneath (see *Jacking and vehicle support*).

2 Remove the protective sleeve from the wiring plug (where applicable), then disconnect the wiring from the switch.

3 Unscrew the switch from the cylinder block, and recover the sealing washer **(see illustration)**. Be prepared for oil spillage, and if the switch is to be left removed from the engine for any length of time, plug the hole in the cylinder block.

Oil level sensor

Note: *An oil level sensor is not fitted to all models.*

4 The oil level sensor is located at the rear of the cylinder block. Jack up the front of the vehicle and support it securely on axle stands (see *Jacking and vehicle support*). Undo the bolts and remove the engine undershield.

14.3 The oil pressure switch is located on the front face of the cylinder block

5 Reach up between the driveshaft and the cylinder block, and disconnect the sensor wiring plug **(see illustration)**.

6 Using an open-ended spanner, unscrew the sensor and withdraw it from position.

Refitting

Oil pressure switch

7 Examine the sealing washer for any signs of damage or deterioration, and if necessary renew.

8 Refit the switch, complete with washer, and tighten it to the specified torque where given.

9 Refit the engine undershield, and lower the vehicle to the ground.

Oil level sensor

10 Smear a little silicone sealant on the threads and refit the sensor to the cylinder block, tightening it securely.

11 Reconnect the sensor wiring plug.

12 Refit the engine undershield, and lower the vehicle to the ground.

15 Flywheel – removal, inspection and refitting

Removal

1 Remove the transmission as described in Chapter 7A Section 6, then remove the clutch assembly as described in Chapter 6 Section 6.

2 Prevent the flywheel from turning. Do not attempt to lock the flywheel in position using the crankshaft pulley locking tool described in Section. Insert a 12 mm diameter rod or drill bit through the hole in the flywheel cover casting, and into a slot in the flywheel **(see illustration)**

3 Make alignment marks between the flywheel and crankshaft to aid refitment. Slacken and remove the flywheel retaining bolts, and remove the flywheel from the end of the crankshaft. Be careful not to drop it; it is heavy. If the flywheel locating dowel (where fitted) is a loose fit in the crankshaft end, remove it and store it with the flywheel for safe-keeping. Discard the flywheel bolts; new ones must be used on refitting.

15.2 Lock the flywheel with a 12mm diameter rod or bolt

14.5 The oil level sensor is located on the rear face of the cylinder block

Inspection

4 Examine the flywheel for scoring of the clutch face, and for wear or chipping of the ring gear teeth. If the clutch face is scored, the flywheel may be surface-ground, but renewal is preferable. Seek the advice of a Ford dealer or engine reconditioning specialist to see if machining is possible. If the ring gear is worn or damaged, the flywheel must be renewed, as it is not possible to renew the ring gear separately.

5 All engines are fitted with a dual-mass flywheel. The maximum travel of the primary mass in relation to the secondary must not exceed 15 teeth (or 20 degrees). If in doubt remove the flywheel and have a suitably equipped specialist check the flywheel. Inspect the flywheel for any grease or debris from the interface between the fixed part and the movable part of the flywheel. If any doubt to the condition of the flywheel exists, despite the expense we recommend replacing it.

Refitting

6 Clean the mating surfaces of the flywheel and crankshaft. Remove any remaining locking compound from the threads of the crankshaft holes, using the correct size of tap, if available.

7 If the new flywheel retaining bolts are not supplied with their threads already pre-coated, apply a suitable thread-locking compound to the threads of each bolt.

8 Ensure that the locating dowel is in position. Offer up the flywheel, locating it on the dowel (where fitted), and fit the new retaining bolts.

15.9 Flywheel retaining Torx bolts

Where no locating dowel is fitted, align the previously-made marks to ensure the flywheel is refitted in its original position.

9 Lock the flywheel using the method employed on dismantling, and tighten the retaining bolts to the specified torque **(see illustration)**.

10 Refit the clutch as described in Chapter 6 Section 6. Remove the flywheel locking tool, and refit the transmission as described in Chapter 7A Section 6.

16 Engine/transmission mountings – inspection and renewal

General

1 The engine/transmission mountings seldom require attention, but broken or deteriorated mountings should be renewed immediately, or the added strain placed on the driveline components may cause damage or wear.

2 While separate mountings may be removed and refitted individually, if more than one is disturbed at a time – such as if the engine/transmission unit is removed from its mountings – they must be reassembled and their fasteners tightened in the position marked on removal.

3 On reassembly, the complete weight of the engine/transmission unit must not be taken by the mountings until all are correctly aligned with the marks made on removal. Tighten the engine/transmission mounting fasteners to their specified torque wrench settings.

Inspection

4 During the check, the engine/transmission unit must be raised slightly, to remove its weight from the mountings.

5 Raise the front of the vehicle, and support it securely on axle stands. Position a jack under the sump, with a large block of wood between the jack head and the sump, then carefully raise the engine/transmission just enough to take the weight off the mountings.

⚠ *Warning: DO NOT place any part of your body under the engine when it is supported only by a jack.*

6 Check the mountings to see if the rubber is cracked, hardened or separated from the metal components. Sometimes the rubber will split right down the centre.

7 Check for relative movement between each mounting's brackets and the engine/transmission or body (use a large screwdriver or lever to attempt to move the mountings). If movement is noted, lower the engine and check-tighten the mounting fasteners.

Renewal

Note: *The following paragraphs assume the engine is supported beneath the sump as described earlier.*

16.9 Right-hand engine mounting-to-engine bracket retaining nuts

16.10 Right-hand engine mounting-to-inner wing panel retaining bolts

16.13 Battery tray support bracket and wiring loom retaining nuts

Right-hand mounting

8 Lift up the coolant expansion tank and position it to one side. Note there is no need to disconnect the coolant pipes.

9 Mark the position of the mounting on the vehicle, right-hand inner wing panel, then undo the three nuts securing the mounting to the engine bracket **(see illustration)**. Discard the nuts, new ones must be fitted.

10 Undo the three retaining bolts securing the mounting to the inner wing panel and withdraw the mounting from the vehicle **(see illustration)**.

11 On refitting, tighten all fasteners to the torque wrench settings specified. Re-align the marks made on removal, then tighten the new mounting bracket retaining nuts.

Left-hand mounting

12 Remove the battery and battery tray as

described in Chapter 5A Section 4. Note that it is not necessary to remove the powertrain control module from the battery tray, just position the tray clear for access to the mounting.

13 Undo the three nuts securing the battery tray support bracket in position. Release the wiring loom from the support bracket and lift the support bracket out of the engine compartment **(see illustration)**.

14 With the transmission supported, mark the position of the mounting bracket on the transmission and on the body side member. Undo the three bolts securing the mounting bracket to the transmission and the two bolts securing the mounting to the body side member **(see illustrations)**. Remove the mounting from the engine compartment.

15 On refitting, re-align the mounting in the position noted on removal, then tighten all

fasteners to the specified torque wrench settings. Refit the components disturbed for access using a reversal of the removal procedures.

Rear mounting (roll restrictor)

16 To remove the engine rear mounting, apply the handbrake, then jack up the front of the car and support it on axle stands (see *Jacking and vehicle support*). Unscrew the through-bolts and remove the engine rear mounting link from the bracket on the transmission and from the bracket on the subframe **(see illustration)**. Hold the engine stationary while the bolts are being removed, since the link will be under tension.

17 On refitting, ensure that the bolts are securely tightened to the specified torque wrench setting.

16.14a Left-hand engine mounting bracket-to-transmission retaining bolts...

16.14b ...and mounting-to-body sidemember retaining bolts

16.16 Rear mounting/roll restrictor retaining bolts

Chapter 2 Part E
Engine removal and overhaul procedures

Contents

Degrees of difficulty

| **Easy,** suitable for novice with little experience | | **Fairly easy,** suitable for beginner with some experience | | **Fairly difficult,** suitable for competent DIY mechanic | | **Difficult,** suitable for experienced DIY mechanic | | **Very difficult,** suitable for expert DIY or professional | |

Specifications

Petrol engines

Valves
  Valve length:
    1.0 litre engines . . . .   Not available
    1.25 litre engines:
      Inlet . . . .   97.35 mm
      Exhaust . . . .   99.40 mm
    1.6 litre engines:
      Inlet . . . .   96.95 mm
      Exhaust . . . .   99.40 mm
Cylinder head
  Maximum permissible gasket surface distortion . . . .   0.05 mm
  Camshaft endfloat (typical) . . . .   0.05 to 0.13 mm
Crankshaft end float:
  1.0 litre engines . . . .   0.13 to 0.38 mm
  1.25 and 1.6 litre engines . . . .   Not available
Torque wrench settings . . . .   Refer to Chapter 2A or 2B Specifications

1.5 litre diesel engines

Cylinder head
  Maximum permissible gasket surface distortion . . . . 0.025 mm
Camshaft
  Endfloat . . . . 0.195 to 0.300 mm
  Bearing journal diameter . . . . 23.959 to 23.980 mm
Crankshaft
  Endfloat . . . . 0.100 to 0.300 mm
  Main bearing journal diameter . . . . 49.962 to 49.981 mm
  Connecting rod journal diameter . . . . 44.975 to 44.991 mm
Cylinder block
  Cylinder bore diameter (reboring not possible) . . . . 73.5 mm
  Main bearing radial clearance . . . . 0.017 to 0.043 mm
Connecting rods
  Big-end bore diameter . . . . 48.655 to 48.671 mm
  Small-end bore diameter . . . . 25.000 mm
  Connecting rod bearing clearance . . . . 0.024 to 0.070 mm
  Gudgeon pin length . . . . 59.700 to 60.000 mm
  Gudgeon pin diameter . . . . 24.995 to 25.000 mm
Pistons and piston rings
  Piston diameter . . . . 73.336 mm
  Piston-to-bore clearance . . . . 0.164 to 0.196 mm
  Piston ring end gaps – installed:
    Top compression ring . . . . 0.200 to 0.350 mm
    Second compression ring . . . . 0.200 to 0.400 mm
    Oil control ring . . . . 0.200 to 0.400 mm
  Piston ring gap arrangement . . . . 120° to each other
Valve stem-to-guide clearance:
  Intake valve . . . . 0.103 to 0.118 mm
  Exhaust valve . . . . 0.113 to 0.128 mm
Torque wrench settings . . . . Refer to Chapter 2C Specifications

1.6 litre diesel engines

Valves
  Valve stem diameter:
    Inlet . . . . 5.485 +0.0, -0.015 mm
    Exhaust . . . . 5.475 +0.0, -0.015 mm
  Overall length:
    Inlet . . . . 96.43 ± 0.25 mm
    Exhaust . . . . 96.65 ± 0.2 mm
Cylinder head
  Maximum gasket face distortion . . . . 0.025 mm
Crankshaft
  Endfloat . . . . 0.100 to 0.300 mm
  Main bearing journal diameter . . . . 49.962 to 49.981mm
  Connecting rod journal diameter . . . . 44.975 to 44.991 mm
Cylinder block
  Cylinder bore diameter (reboring not possible) . . . . 75.000 to 75.018 mm
Pistons and piston rings
  Piston diameter . . . . 74.104 to 74.128 mm
  Piston-to-bore clearance . . . . 0.164 to 0.196 mm
  Piston ring end gaps – installed:
    Top compression ring . . . . 0.20 to 0.35 mm
    Second compression ring . . . . 0.20 to 0.40 mm
    Oil control ring . . . . 0.85 to 1.00 mm
  Piston ring gap arrangement . . . . 120° to each other
Torque wrench settings . . . . Refer to Chapter 2D Specifications

1 General Information

Note: *On all petrol engines covered by this manual, it is not possible to remove the intermediate/main bearing section or to remove the crankshaft or pistons. No separate parts are available, and replacement/exchange units are supplied with crankshaft, pistons, connecting rods, etc, already fitted. Consult a Ford dealer or parts specialist for further information.*

1 Included in this Part of Chapter 2 are details of removing the engine/transmission from the car and general overhaul procedures for the cylinder head, cylinder block/crankcase and all other engine internal components.

2 The information given ranges from advice concerning preparation for an overhaul and the purchase of new parts, to detailed step-by-step procedures covering removal, inspection, renovation and refitting of engine internal components (where possible).

3 After Section 6, all instructions are based on the assumption that the engine has been removed from the car. For information concerning in-car engine repair, as well as the removal and refitting of those external components necessary for full overhaul, refer to Parts A to D of this Chapter (as applicable) and to Section 6. Ignore any preliminary dismantling operations described in Parts A to D that are no longer relevant once the engine has been removed from the car.

4 Apart from torque wrench settings, which are given at the beginning of Parts A to D (as applicable), all specifications relating to engine overhaul are at the beginning of this Part of Chapter 2.

2 Engine overhaul – general information

1 It is not always easy to determine when, or if, an engine should be completely overhauled, as a number of factors must be considered.

2 High mileage is not necessarily an indication that an overhaul is needed, while low mileage does not preclude the need for an overhaul. Frequency of servicing is probably the most important consideration. An engine which has had regular and frequent oil and filter changes, as well as other required maintenance, will most likely give many thousands of miles of reliable service. Conversely, a neglected engine may require an overhaul very early in its life.

3 Excessive oil consumption is an indication that piston rings, valve stem oil seals and/or valves and valve guides are in need of attention. Make sure that oil leaks are not responsible before deciding that the rings and/or guides are to blame. Perform a cylinder compression check to determine the likely cause of the problem.

4 Check the oil pressure with a gauge fitted in place of the oil pressure switch, and compare it with the value given in the Specifications. If it is extremely low, the main and big-end bearings and/or the oil pump are probably worn out.

5 Loss of power, rough running, knocking or metallic engine noises, excessive valve gear noise and high fuel consumption may also point to the need for an overhaul, especially if they are all present at the same time. If a complete tune-up does not remedy the situation, major mechanical work is the only solution.

6 An engine overhaul involves restoring the internal parts to the specifications of a new engine. During an overhaul, the pistons and rings are renewed, and the cylinder bores are reconditioned. New main bearings, connecting rod bearings and camshaft bearings are generally fitted, and if necessary, the crankshaft may be reground to restore the journals (note however that this work is not possible on petrol engines). The valves are also serviced as well, since they are usually in less-than-perfect condition at this point. While the engine is being overhauled, other components, such as the starter and alternator, can be overhauled as well. The end result should be a like-new engine that will give many trouble-free miles. **Note:** *Critical cooling system components such as the hoses, drivebelts, thermostat and coolant pump should be renewed when an engine is overhauled. The radiator should be checked carefully, to ensure that it is not clogged or leaking. Also, it is a good idea to renew the oil pump whenever the engine is overhauled.*

7 Before beginning the engine overhaul, read through the entire procedure to familiarise yourself with the scope and requirements of the job. Overhauling an engine is not difficult if you follow all of the instructions carefully, have the necessary tools and equipment, and pay close attention to all specifications; however, it can be time-consuming. Plan on the car being tied up for a minimum of two weeks, especially if parts must be taken to an engineering works for repair or reconditioning. Check on the availability of parts, and make sure that any necessary special tools and equipment are obtained in advance. Most work can be done with typical hand tools, although a number of precision measuring tools are required for inspecting parts to determine if they must be renewed. Often the engineering works will handle the inspection of parts, and offer advice concerning reconditioning and renewal.

8 Always wait until the engine has been completely dismantled, and all components, especially the engine block, have been inspected before deciding what service and repair operations must be performed by an engineering works. Since the condition of the block will be the major factor to consider when determining whether to overhaul the original engine or buy a reconditioned unit, do not purchase parts or have overhaul work done on other components until the block has been thoroughly inspected. As a general rule, time is the primary cost of an overhaul, so it does not pay to fit worn or substandard parts.

9 As a final note, to ensure maximum life and minimum trouble from a reconditioned engine, everything must be assembled with care, and in a spotlessly-clean environment.

3 Engine removal – methods and precautions

1 If you have decided that an engine must be removed for overhaul or major repair work, several preliminary steps should be taken.

2 Locating a suitable place to work is extremely important. Adequate work space, along with storage space for the car, will be needed. If a garage is not available, at the very least a flat, level, clean work surface is required.

3 Cleaning the engine compartment and engine before beginning the removal procedure will help keep tools clean and organised.

4 The engine is removed complete with the transmission by lowering it out of the car; the car's body must be raised and supported securely sufficiently high that the engine/transmission can be unbolted as a single unit and lowered to the ground. An engine hoist will therefore be necessary. Make sure the equipment is rated in excess of the combined weight of the engine and transmission. Safety is of primary importance, considering the potential hazards involved in lifting the engine out of the car.

5 If the engine is being removed by a novice, an assistant should be available. Advice and aid from someone more experienced would also be helpful. There are many instances when one person cannot simultaneously perform all of the operations required when removing the engine from the car.

6 Plan the operation ahead of time. Arrange for, or obtain, all of the tools and equipment you will need, prior to beginning the job. Some of the equipment necessary to perform engine removal and installation safely and with relative ease are (in addition to an engine hoist) a heavy-duty trolley jack, complete sets of spanners and sockets as described at the end of this manual, wooden blocks, and plenty of rags and cleaning solvent for mopping-up spilled oil, coolant and fuel. If the hoist must be hired, make sure that you arrange for it in advance, and perform all of the operations possible without it beforehand. This will save you money and time.

7 Plan for the car to be out of use for quite a while. An engineering works will be required to perform some of the work which the do-it-yourselfer cannot accomplish without special equipment. These places often have a busy schedule, so it would be a good idea

to consult them before removing the engine, in order to accurately estimate the amount of time required to rebuild or repair components that may need work.

8 During the engine/transmission removal procedure, it is advisable to make notes of the locations of all brackets, cable-ties, earthing points, etc, as well as how the wiring harnesses, hoses and electrical connections are attached and routed around the engine and engine compartment. An effective way of doing this is to take a series of photographs of the various components before they are disconnected or removed; the resulting photographs will prove invaluable when the engine/transmission is refitted.

Caution: Always be extremely careful when removing and refitting the engine. Serious injury can result from careless actions. Plan ahead, take your time, and you will find that a job of this nature, although major, can be accomplished successfully.

Note: *Such is the complexity of the power unit arrangement on these vehicles, and the variations that may be encountered according to model and optional equipment fitted, that the procedures given in Sections 4 and 5 should be regarded as a guide to the work involved, rather than an accurate step-by-step procedure. Where differences are encountered, or additional component disconnection or removal is necessary, make notes of the work involved as an aid to refitting.*

4 Petrol engine – removal, separation and refitting

1 Depressurise the fuel system with reference to Chapter 4A Section 2.
2 Remove the windscreen cowl panel and bulkhead closure panel as described in Chapter 11 Section 20.
3 Remove the air cleaner assembly as described in Chapter 4A Section 5.
4 Remove the battery and battery tray as described in Chapter 5A Section 4.
5 Undo the three nuts securing the battery tray support bracket in position. Release the wiring loom from the support bracket and lift the support bracket out of the engine compartment.
6 Jack up the front of the car, and support it on axle stands (see *Jacking and vehicle support*). Although not essential immediately, it would pay at this stage to raise the car sufficiently to allow the engine and transmission to be withdrawn from underneath.
7 Drain the cooling system as described in Chapter 1A Section 30.
8 If the engine is being dismantled, drain the engine oil with reference to Chapter 1A Section 6.
9 Disconnect the fuel supply line quick-release connection from the fuel rail at the front of the engine.
10 Remove the alternator as described in Chapter 5A Section 7.

11 Disconnect the hoses from the coolant expansion tank, then release the two clips and remove the tank.
12 Disconnect the hose from the EVAP valve just below the fuel pressure regulator on the fuel rail.
13 Disconnect the brake servo vacuum hose from the inlet manifold.
14 Disconnect the two coolant hoses from the outlet elbow on the left-hand side of the engine, and also the two hoses from the thermostat housing on the front.
15 Disconnect the coolant hoses from the heater connections at the engine compartment bulkhead and from the oil cooler connection beneath the oil filter.
16 Disconnect the following wiring plugs:
a) *Oxygen sensor wiring plug, located just behind the ignition coil, and the catalyst monitor wiring plug below it.*
b) *Camshaft position sensor wiring plug, which is located on the rear of the cylinder head, at the timing belt end.*
c) *Knock sensor wiring plug, located underneath the inlet manifold.*
d) *Starter motor wiring (refer to Chapter 5A Section 9 if necessary).*
e) *Where applicable, air conditioning compressor wiring plug.*
f) *Oil pressure switch, next to the oil filter.*
g) *Crankshaft position sensor, on the front of the engine, at the transmission end.*
h) *Reversing light switch, on the front of the transmission.*
i) *Coolant temperature sensor, below the ignition coil.*
j) *Ignition coil main wiring plug.*
17 Unbolt the engine earth strap just below the ignition coil, and the engine wiring harness support bracket just in front.
18 Where applicable, remove the four bolts securing the air conditioning compressor to the block, and secure the compressor to one side – do not disconnect any of the hoses.
19 Remove the catalytic converter as described in Chapter 4A Section 13.
20 On 1.0 litre models without air conditioning, unbolt the auxiliary drivebelt idler pulley and bracket from the front of the engine.
21 Disconnect the transmission gearchange/selector cable(s) from the transmission as described in Chapter 7A or Chapter 7B, as applicable.
22 Remove both driveshafts as described in Chapter 8 Section 2.
23 Unbolt the engine rear mounting from under the car, referring to Chapter 2B Section 18 if necessary.
24 On manual transmission models, taking precautions against fluid spillage, prise up the spring clip and disconnect the clutch slave cylinder fluid pipe from on top of the transmission. Unclip the pipe, and tie it up to the bulkhead to reduce further fluid spillage. Check that the rubber seal on the pipe end fitting is as it's withdrawn. Often the seal separates from the fitting and remains in the connection housing. If this happens, carefully

extract the seal using small screwdriver or similar **(see illustration 5.26a and 5.26b)**.
25 Make a final check round the engine and transmission, to make sure nothing (apart from the left- and right-hand mountings) remains attached or in the way which will prevent it from being lowered out. Also make sure there is enough room under the front of the car for the engine/transmission to be lowered out and withdrawn.
26 Securely attach the engine/transmission unit to a suitable engine crane or hoist, and raise it so that the weight is just taken off the two remaining engine mountings. It is helpful at this stage to have an assistant available, either to work the crane or to guide the engine out.
27 With the engine securely supported, remove the three bolts from the engine left-hand mounting (on top of the transmission).
28 Similarly, remove the two nuts from the engine right-hand mounting, on the driver's side of the engine compartment.
29 With the help of an assistant, carefully lower the assembly from the engine compartment, making sure it clears the surrounding components and bodywork. Be prepared to steady the engine when it touches down, to stop it toppling over. Withdraw the assembly from under the car, and remove it to wherever it will be worked on.

Separation

30 To separate the transmission from the engine, first remove the starter motor with reference to Chapter 5A Section 9.
31 Remove the bolts securing the transmission to the engine. Note the fitted positions of any brackets.
32 With the aid of an assistant, draw the transmission off the engine. Once it is clear of the dowels, do not allow it to hang on the input shaft.

Refitting

33 On models with manual transmissions, make sure that the clutch is correctly centred and that the clutch release components are fitted to the bellhousing.
34 Do not apply any grease to the transmission input shaft, the guide sleeve, or the release bearing itself, as these components have a friction-reducing coating which does not require lubrication.
35 Manoeuvre the transmission squarely into position, and engage it with the engine dowels. Refit the bolts securing the transmission to the engine, and tighten them to the specified torque. Refit the starter motor.
36 The remainder of refitting is a reversal of removal, noting the following additional points:
a) *Make sure that all mating faces are clean, and use new gaskets where necessary.*
b) *Tighten all nuts and bolts to the specified torque setting, where given.*
c) *Use new nuts on the engine left- and right-hand mountings, but do not fully-tighten them until the car is resting on its wheels.*

d) Use a new centre bearing cap and locknuts when refitting the intermediate shaft.

e) Fit new circlips to the grooves in the inner end of each driveshaft CV joint, and ensure that they fully engage as they are fitted into the transmission.

f) Check and if necessary adjust the gearchange cables as described in Chapter 7A or 7B, as applicable.

g) Refill the transmission with lubricant if necessary as described in Chapter 1A, 7A or 7B as applicable.

h) Top-up and bleed the clutch hydraulic system as described in Chapter 6.

i) Refill the engine with coolant and oil as described in Chapter 1A.

5 Diesel engine – removal, separation and refitting

Warning: The diesel injection system operates at extremely high pressures when the pump is running. Wait at least one minute after stopping the engine before working on the fuel injection system components.

Removal

1 Remove the windscreen cowl panel and bulkhead closure panel as described in Chapter 11 Section 20.

2 Remove the air cleaner assembly as described in Chapter 4B Section 4.

3 Remove the battery and battery tray as described in Chapter 5A Section 4.

4 Refer to Chapter 4B Section 12 and disconnect the 3 wiring connectors from the engine management PCM attached to the battery tray.

5 Undo the 3 nuts securing the battery tray support bracket in position. Release the wiring loom from the support bracket and lift the support bracket out of the engine compartment.

6 Jack up the front of the car, and support it on axle stands (see Jacking and vehicle support). Although not essential immediately, it would pay at this stage to raise the car sufficiently

5.12a Depress the release button and disconnect the fuel supply hose at the filter...

to allow the engine and transmission to be withdrawn from underneath.

7 Undo the retaining bolts and remove the engine undertray.

8 Drain the cooling system as described in Chapter 1B Section 30.

9 Disconnect the hoses from the coolant expansion tank, then release the two clips and remove the tank. On models with air conditioning, undo the nut securing the refrigerant pipe to the right-hand suspension turret.

10 If the engine is being dismantled, drain the engine oil with reference to Chapter 1B Section 6.

11 Remove the particulate filter as described in Chapter 4B Section 18.

12 Disconnect the fuel supply and return line quick-release connections at the rear of the engine compartment (see illustrations). Plug/cover the openings to prevent contamination.

13 Depress the button each side, and disconnect the brake servo vacuum hose quick-release connection from the vacuum pump (see illustration). Release the cable-ties and clips and move the fuel lines and vacuum hoses clear of the engine.

14 Slacken the retaining clips and disconnect the intercooler hoses from their engine attachments (where applicable).

15 Remove the alternator as described in Chapter 5A Section 7.

16 Disconnect the coolant hoses from the thermostat housing at the left-hand side of the engine.

5.12b ...and the fuel return hose at the right-hand rear of the cylinder head

17 Disconnect the coolant hoses from the heater connections at the engine compartment bulkhead.

18 Disconnect the engine wiring harness at the plug in front of the battery location, and separate the current supply cable from the battery positive clamp assembly (see illustrations).

19 Where applicable, remove the four bolts securing the air conditioning compressor to the block, and secure the compressor to one side – do not disconnect any of the hoses.

20 Remove the radiator cooling fan and shroud – refer to Chapter 3 Section 5 if necessary.

21 Disconnect the transmission gearchange cables from the transmission as described in Chapter 7A Section 3.

22 Loosen the 3 upper mounting nuts on both front suspension struts by 3 turns.

23 On both sides of the car, remove the lower arm balljoint clamp bolt from the swivel hub, and lever down the lower arm to separate it. Unclip the balljoint heat shields, and retain them for refitting.

24 Using the information in Chapter 8 Section 2, disconnect both driveshafts from the transmission, and also remove the intermediate shaft. There is no need to remove the driveshafts from the hubs, providing they can be supported clear so that the engine/transmission can drop down. The inner and outer joints should not be bent through more than 18° and 45° respectively.

25 Unbolt the engine rear mounting from

5.13 Vacuum pump hose release buttons

5.18a Fold-over the lever and disconnect the engine wiring harness plug

5.18b Undo the nut and disconnect the current supply cable

5.26a Prise up the clip and pull out the fluid pipe

5.26b Check that the rubber seal is still in place

under the car, referring to Chapter 2C Section 16 or Chapter 2D Section 16 as necessary.

26 Taking precautions against fluid spillage, prise up the spring clip and disconnect the clutch slave cylinder fluid pipe from on top of the transmission. Unclip the pipe, and tie it up to the bulkhead to reduce further fluid spillage. Check the rubber seal on the pipe end fitting as it's withdrawn. Often the seal separates from the fitting and remains in the connection housing. If this happens, carefully extract the seal using small screwdriver or similar **(see illustrations)**.

27 Make a final check round the engine and transmission, to make sure nothing (apart from the left- and right-hand mountings) remains attached or in the way which will prevent it from being lowered out. Also make sure there is enough room under the front of the car for the engine/transmission to be lowered out and withdrawn.

28 Securely attach the engine/transmission unit to a suitable engine crane or hoist, and raise it so that the weight is just taken off the 2 remaining engine mountings **(see illustration)**. It is helpful at this stage to have an assistant available, either to work the crane or to guide the engine out.

29 With the engine securely supported, remove the 3 bolts from the engine left- hand mounting (on top of the transmission).

30 Similarly, remove the 3 nuts from the engine right-hand mounting, on the driver's side of the engine compartment.

31 With the help of an assistant, carefully lower the assembly from the engine

5.28 Attach a lifting bar to the engine brackets

compartment, making sure it clears the surrounding components and bodywork. Be prepared to steady the engine when it touches down, to stop it toppling over. Withdraw the assembly from under the car, and remove it to wherever it will be worked on.

Separation

32 To separate the transmission from the engine, first remove the starter motor with reference to Chapter 5A Section 9.

33 Remove the bolts securing the transmission to the engine. Note the fitted positions of any brackets.

34 With the aid of an assistant, draw the transmission off the engine. Once it is clear of the dowels, do not allow it to hang on the input shaft.

Refitting

35 Make sure that the clutch is correctly centred and that the clutch release components are fitted to the bellhousing. Do not apply any grease to the transmission input shaft, the guide sleeve, or the release bearing itself, as these components have a friction-reducing coating which does not require lubrication.

36 Manoeuvre the transmission squarely into position, and engage it with the engine dowels. Refit the bolts securing the transmission to the engine, and tighten them to the specified torque. Refit the starter motor.

37 The remainder of refitting is a reversal of removal, noting the following additional points:

a) Make sure that all mating faces are clean, and use new gaskets where necessary.

b) Tighten all nuts and bolts to the specified torque setting, where given.

c) Use new nuts on the engine left- and right-hand mountings, but do not fully-tighten them until the car is resting on its wheels.

d) Use a new centre bearing cap and lock-nuts when refitting the intermediate shaft.

e) Fit new circlips to the grooves in the inner end of each driveshaft CV joint, and ensure that they fully engage as they are fitted into the transmission.

f) Check and if necessary adjust the gearchange cables as described in Chapter 7A Section 2.

g) Refill the transmission with lubricant if necessary as described in Chapter 1B or 7A as applicable.

h) Top-up and bleed the clutch hydraulic system as described in Chapter 6 Section 4.

i) Refill the engine with coolant and oil as described in Chapter 1B.

j) Tighten the suspension strut upper mounting nuts to the specified torque on completion (see Chapter 10 Section 4).

6 Engine overhaul – dismantling sequence

Note: *On all petrol engines covered by this manual, it is not possible to remove the intermediate/main bearing section or to remove the crankshaft or pistons. No separate parts are available, and replacement/ exchange units are supplied with crankshaft, pistons, connecting rods, etc, already fitted. Consult a Ford dealer or parts specialist for further information.*

1 It is much easier to dismantle and work on the engine if it is mounted on a portable engine stand. These stands can often be hired from a tool hire shop. Before the engine is mounted on a stand, the flywheel should be removed from the engine, so that the engine stand bolts can be tightened into the end of the cylinder block.

2 If a stand is not available, it is possible to dismantle the engine with it blocked up on a sturdy workbench or on the floor. Be extra careful not to tip or drop the engine when working without a stand.

3 If you're going to obtain a reconditioned ('recon') engine, all external components must be removed first, to be transferred to the new engine (just as they will if you are doing a complete engine overhaul yourself). **Note:** *When removing the external components from the engine, pay close attention to details that may be helpful or important during refitting. Note the fitted position of gaskets, seals, spacers, pins, washers, bolts and other small items. These external components include the following:*

Petrol engines

a) Ignition coil (s), HT leads and spark plugs.

b) All electrical switches and sensors.

c) Thermostat housing.

d) Fuel injection equipment.

e) Inlet and exhaust manifolds.

f) Oil filter.

g) Engine mountings and lifting brackets.

h) Ancillary component mounting brackets.

i) Oil filler tube and dipstick.

j) Coolant pipes and hoses.

k) Flywheel/driveplate.

Diesel engines

a) All electrical switches and sensors.

b) Fuel injection pump and mounting bracket, and fuel injectors and glow plugs.

c) Thermostat housing.

d) Inlet and exhaust manifolds.

e) Oil cooler.
f) Engine lifting brackets, hose brackets and wiring brackets.
g) Ancillary component mounting brackets.
h) Wiring harnesses and brackets.
i) Coolant pipes and hoses.
j) Oil filler tube and dipstick.
k) Flywheel.

4 If you are obtaining a 'short' motor (which consists of the engine cylinder block, crankshaft, pistons and connecting rods all assembled), then the timing belt, cylinder head, sump and oil pump will have to be removed also.

5 If you are planning a complete overhaul (diesel engines only) the engine can be disassembled and the internal components removed in the following order:
a) Engine external components (including inlet and exhaust manifolds).
b) Timing belt and sprockets.
c) Cylinder head.
d) Flywheel.
e) Sump.
f) Oil pump.
g) Pistons and connecting rods.
h) Crankshaft and main bearings.

6 Before beginning the disassembly and overhaul procedures, make sure that you have all of the correct tools necessary. Refer to the reference section at the end of this manual for further information.

7 Cylinder head – dismantling

Note: New and reconditioned cylinder heads are available from the manufacturers and from engine overhaul specialists. Due to the fact that some specialist tools are required for the dismantling and inspection procedures, and new components may not be readily available, it may be more practical and economical for the home mechanic to purchase a reconditioned head rather than dismantle, inspect and recondition the original head.

1 Remove the cylinder head as described in Part A, B, C or D of this Chapter (as applicable).
2 If not already done, remove the inlet and exhaust manifolds with reference to the relevant Part of Chapter 4A or Chapter 4B.

7.8 Use a labelled plastic bag to store and identify valve components

7.4 Removing the valve spring and upper seat

Also remove all external brackets and elbows.
3 Remove the camshafts and tappets as described in Part A or B of this Chapter as applicable, being careful to store the components as described.
4 Using a valve spring compressor, compress each valve spring in turn until the split collets can be removed. A special valve spring compressor will be required, to reach into the deep wells in the cylinder head without risk of damaging the tappet bores; such compressors are now widely available from most good motor accessory shops. Release the compressor, and lift off the spring upper seat and spring **(see illustration)**.
5 If, when the valve spring compressor is screwed down, the spring upper seat refuses to free and expose the split collets, gently tap the top of the tool, directly over the upper seat, with a light hammer. This will free the seat.
6 Withdraw the valve through the combustion chamber. If it binds in the guide (won't pull through), push it back in, and de-burr the area around the collet groove with a fine file; take care not to mark the tappet bores.
7 Pull the valve stem seals from the valve guides using a pair of pliers. As the seals are removed, note whether they are of different colours for the inlet and exhaust valves – compare with the new parts, and note this for refitting. As a guide, the inlet valve seals are green, and the exhaust seals are red **(see illustration)**.
8 It is essential that the valves are kept together with their collets, spring seats and springs, and in their correct sequence (unless they are so badly worn that they are

8.7 Check the head for warpage using a straight-edge and feeler blades

7.7 Pull the valve stem seals from the guides

to be renewed). If they are going to be kept and used again, place them in a labelled polythene bag or similar small container **(see illustration)**. Note that No 1 valve is nearest to the timing belt end of the engine.

8 Cylinder head and valves – cleaning, inspection and renovation

1 Thorough cleaning of the cylinder head and valve components, followed by a detailed inspection, will enable you to decide how much valve service work must be carried out during the engine overhaul.

Cleaning

2 Scrape away all traces of old gasket material and sealing compound from the cylinder head. Take care not to damage the cylinder head surfaces.
3 Scrape away the carbon from the combustion chambers and ports, then wash the cylinder head thoroughly with paraffin or a suitable solvent.
4 Scrape off any heavy carbon deposits that may have formed on the valves, then use a power-operated wire brush to remove deposits from the valve heads and stems.
5 If the head is extremely dirty, it should be steam cleaned. On completion, make sure that all oil holes and oil galleries are cleaned.

Inspection and renovation

Note: Be sure to perform all the following inspection procedures before concluding that the services of an engine overhaul specialist are required. Make a list of all items that require attention.

Cylinder head

6 Inspect the head very carefully for cracks, evidence of coolant leakage and other damage. If cracks are found, a new cylinder head should be obtained.
7 Use a straight-edge and feeler blade to check that the cylinder head surface is not distorted **(see illustration)**. If the specified distortion limit is exceeded, machining of the gasket face is not recommended by the manufacturers, so the only course of action is to renew the cylinder head.

8.12 Measuring the diameter of a valve stem

8.15 Grinding-in a valve seat

8.18 Checking the valve spring free length

8 Examine the valve seats in each of the combustion chambers. If they are severely pitted, cracked or burned, then they will need to be renewed or recut by an engine overhaul specialist. If they are only slightly pitted, this can be removed by grinding the valve heads and seats together with coarse, then fine, grinding paste as described below.

9 If the valve guides are worn, indicated by a side-to-side motion of the valve in the guide, new guides must be fitted. If necessary, insert a new valve in the guides to determine if the wear is on the guide or valve. If new guides are to be fitted, the valves must be renewed as a matter of course. Valve guides may be renewed using a press and a suitable mandrel, however, the work is best carried out by an engine overhaul specialist, since if it is not done skilfully, there is a risk of damaging the cylinder head.

10 Check the tappet bores in the cylinder head for wear. If excessive wear is evident, the cylinder head must be renewed.

Valves

11 Examine the head of each valve for pitting, burning, cracks and general wear, and check the valve stem for scoring and wear ridges. Rotate the valve, and check for any obvious indication that it is bent. Look for pits and excessive wear on the end of each valve stem.

12 If the valve appears satisfactory at this stage, measure the valve stem diameter at several points using a micrometer **(see illustration)**. Any significant difference in the readings obtained indicates wear of the valve

stem. Should any of these conditions be apparent, the valve(s) must be renewed.

13 If the valves are in satisfactory condition, or if new valves are being fitted, they should be ground (lapped) into their respective seats to ensure a smooth gas-tight seal.

14 Valve grinding is carried out as follows. Place the cylinder head upside-down on a bench, with a block of wood at each end to give clearance for the valve stems. Where applicable, take care to protect the camshaft bearing surfaces.

15 Smear a trace of coarse carborundum paste on the seat face, and press a suction grinding tool onto the valve head. With a semi-rotary action, grind the valve head to its seat, lifting the valve occasionally to redistribute the grinding paste **(see illustration)**.

16 When a dull, matt even surface is produced on both the valve seat and the valve, wipe off the paste and repeat the process with fine carborundum paste. A light spring placed under the valve head will greatly ease this operation.

17 When a smooth unbroken ring of light grey matt finish is produced on both the valve and seat, the grinding operation is complete. Be sure to remove all traces of grinding paste, using paraffin or a suitable solvent, before reassembly of the cylinder head.

Valve components

18 Examine the valve springs for signs of damage and discoloration, and also measure their free length using vernier calipers or a steel rule **(see illustration)** or by comparing the existing spring with a new component.

19 Stand each spring on a flat surface, and check it for squareness. If any of the springs are damaged, distorted or have lost their tension, obtain a complete new set of springs. It is normal to renew the springs as a matter of course during a major overhaul.

20 On petrol engines, inspect the tappet buckets for scoring, pitting (especially on the shims), and wear ridges. Renew any components as necessary. Note that some scuffing is to be expected, and is acceptable provided that the tappets are not scored.

Valve stem oil seals

21 The valve stem oil seals should be renewed as a matter of course.

9 Cylinder head – reassembly

1 Lubricate the valve stem oil seals with clean engine oil, then fit them by pushing into position in the cylinder head using a suitable socket or special tool **(see illustration)**. Ensure that the seals are fully engaged with the valve guide. Note that the inlet and exhaust seals are usually different colours – green for the inlet valves, red for the exhaust valves.

2 Lubricate the valve stems, then insert the valves into their original locations. If new valves are being fitted, insert them into the locations to which they have been ground. Take care not to damage the valve stem oil seal as each valve is fitted **(see illustrations)**.

9.1 Using a special tool to fit the valve stem oil seals

9.2a Oil the valve stems ...

9.2b ... then insert the valves in their guides

3 Locate the spring and cap over the valve stem.
4 Compress the valve spring and locate the split collets in the recess in the valve stem **(see illustrations)**. Release the compressor, then repeat the procedure on the remaining valves.
5 With all the valves installed, place the cylinder head on blocks on the bench and, using a hammer and interposed block of wood, tap the end of each valve stem to settle the components.
6 The previously-removed components can now be refitted.

10 Piston/connecting rod assemblies (diesel engines) – removal

1 Remove the cylinder head, sump, oil pump pick-up tube and baffle plate, as applicable, with reference to Chapter 2C or Chapter 2D.
2 Rotate the crankshaft so that No 1 big-end cap (timing end of the engine) is at the lowest point of its travel. If the big-end cap and rod are not already numbered, mark them with a marker pen. Mark both cap and rod to identify the cylinder they operate in.
3 Remove the main bearing ladder as described in Section 11.
4 Unscrew and remove the big-end bearing cap bolts, and withdraw the cap complete with shell bearing from the connecting rod. Make sure that the shell remains in the cap and if necessary identify it for position.
5 If only the bearing shells are being attended to, push the connecting rod up and off the crankpin, and remove the upper bearing shell. Keep the bearing shells and cap together in their correct sequence if they are to be refitted.
6 If the piston is being removed, push the connecting rod up and remove the piston and rod from the top of the bore. Note that if there is a pronounced wear ridge at the top of the bore, there is a risk of damaging the piston as the rings foul the ridge. However, it is reasonable to assume that a rebore and new pistons will be required in any case if the ridge is so pronounced.
7 Repeat the procedure for the remaining piston/connecting rod assemblies. Ensure that the caps and rods are marked before removal, as described previously, and keep all components in order.

11 Crankshaft (diesel engines) – removal

1 Remove the timing belt, crankshaft sprocket, sump, oil pick-up tube, flywheel and left-hand/flywheel end oil seal housing. The pistons/connecting rods must be free of the crankshaft journals, however it is not essential to remove them completely from the cylinder

9.4a Apply a small dab of grease to each collet before installation – it will hold them in place on the valve stem

block.
2 Before the crankshaft is removed, check the endfloat. Mount a dial gauge with the probe in line with the crankshaft and just touching the crankshaft.
3 Push the crankshaft fully away from the gauge, and zero it. Next, lever the crankshaft towards the gauge as far as possible, and check the reading obtained. The distance that the crankshaft moved is its endfloat; if it is greater than specified, new thrustwashers will be required.
4 If no dial gauge is available, feeler blades can be used. Gently lever or push the crankshaft in one direction, then insert feeler blades between the crankshaft web and the main bearing with the thrustwashers to determine the clearance.
5 Work around the outside of the cylinder block, and unscrew all the small bolts securing the main bearing ladder to the base of the cylinder block. Note the correct fitted depth of the left-hand crankshaft oil seal in the cylinder block/main bearing ladder.
6 Working in a diagonal sequence, evenly and progressively slacken the large main bearing ladder retaining bolts by a turn at a time. Once all the bolts are loose, remove them from the ladder. **Note:** *Prise up the two caps at the flywheel end of the ladder to expose the two end main bearing bolts* **(see illustration)**. *The larger (M11) bolts should be discarded, and new bolts obtained for reassembly.*
7 With all the retaining bolts removed, carefully lift the main bearing ladder casting

11.6 Prise up the two caps to expose the main bearing bolts at the flywheel end

9.4b A dab of grease on a screwdriver will help to fit the collets

away from the base of the cylinder block. Recover the lower main bearing shells, and tape them to their respective locations in the casting. If the two locating dowels are a loose fit, remove them and store them with the casting for safe-keeping. Undo the big-end bolts and remove the pistons/connecting rods as described in Section 10.
8 Lift out the crankshaft, and discard both the oil seals.
9 Recover the upper main bearing shells, and store them along with the relevant lower bearing shell. Also recover the two thrustwashers (one fitted either side of No 2 main bearing) from the cylinder block.

12 Cylinder block/crankcase (diesel engines) – cleaning and inspection

Cleaning

1 For complete cleaning, the core plugs should be removed. Drill a small hole in them, then insert a self-tapping screw and pull out the plugs using pliers or a slide-hammer **(see illustration)**. Also remove all external components and senders (if not already done), noting their locations.
2 Scrape all traces of gasket or sealant from the cylinder block, taking care not to damage the head and sump mating faces.
3 If the block is extremely dirty, it should be steam-cleaned.

12.1 The core plugs should be removed with a slide hammer – don't drive them inwards

4 After the block has been steam-cleaned, clean all oil holes and oil galleries one more time. Flush all internal passages with warm water until the water runs clear, dry the block thoroughly and wipe all machined surfaces with a light rust-preventative oil. If you have access to compressed air, use it to speed up the drying process and to blow out all the oil holes and galleries.

 Warning: Wear eye protection when using compressed air.

5 If the block is not very dirty, you can do an adequate cleaning job with hot soapy water and a stiff brush. Take plenty of time, and do a thorough job. Regardless of the cleaning method used, be sure to clean all oil holes and galleries very thoroughly, dry the block completely and coat all machined surfaces with light oil.

6 The threaded holes in the block must be clean to ensure accurate torque wrench readings during reassembly. Run the proper-size tap into each of the holes to remove rust, corrosion, thread sealant or sludge, and to restore damaged threads. If possible, use compressed air to clear the holes of debris produced by this operation.

7 After coating the mating surfaces of the new core plugs with suitable sealant, refit them in the cylinder block. Make sure that they are driven in straight and seated properly, or leakage could result. Special tools are available for this purpose, but a large socket, with an outside diameter that will just slip into the core plug, will work just as well **(see illustration)**.

8 Where applicable, remove the oil spray jets from their locations in the crankcase and clean them. After cleaning the cylinder block, refit the jets.

9 If the engine is not going to be reassembled right away, cover it with a large plastic bag to keep it clean and prevent it rusting.

Inspection

10 Visually check the block for cracks, rust and corrosion. Look for stripped threads in the threaded holes. It's also a good idea to have the block checked for hidden cracks by an engine reconditioning specialist that has the equipment to do this type of work, especially if the vehicle had a history of overheating or

using coolant. If defects are found, have the block repaired, if possible, or renewed.

11 If in any doubt as to the condition of the cylinder block, have it inspected and measured by an engine reconditioning specialist. If the bores are worn or damaged, a new cylinder block will be required. If the bores are in a satisfactory condition, they will be able to carry out the necessary honing and supply appropriate oversized pistons, etc.

12 Refit all external components and senders in their correct locations, as noted before removal.

13 Piston/connecting rod assemblies (diesel engines) – inspection and reassembly

Inspection

1 Before the inspection process can begin, the piston/connecting rod assemblies must be cleaned, and the original piston rings removed from the pistons.

2 Carefully expand the old rings over the top of the pistons. The use of two or three old feeler blades will be helpful in preventing the rings dropping into empty grooves **(see illustration)**. Note that the oil control scraper ring is in two sections.

3 Scrape away all traces of carbon from the top of the piston. A hand-held wire brush or a piece of fine emery cloth can be used once the majority of the deposits have been scraped away.

4 Remove the carbon from the ring grooves in the piston by cleaning them using an old ring. Break the ring in half to do this. Be very careful to remove only the carbon deposits; do not remove any metal, or scratch the sides of the ring grooves. Protect your fingers – piston rings are sharp.

5 Once the deposits have been removed, clean the piston/connecting rod assembly with paraffin or a suitable solvent, and dry thoroughly. Make sure the oil return holes in the ring grooves are clear.

6 If the pistons and cylinder bores are not damaged or worn excessively, the original pistons can be re-used. Normal piston wear appears as even vertical wear on the piston thrust surfaces, and slight looseness of the

top ring in its groove. New piston rings, however, should always be used when the engine is reassembled.

7 Carefully inspect each piston for cracks around the skirt, at the gudgeon pin bosses, and at the piston ring lands (between the piston ring grooves).

8 Look for scoring and scuffing on the sides of the skirt, holes in the piston crown, and burned areas at the edge of the crown. If the skirt is scored or scuffed, the engine may have been suffering from overheating and/or abnormal combustion, which caused excessively-high operating temperatures. The cooling and lubricating systems should be checked thoroughly.

9 Scorch marks on the sides of the pistons show that blow-by has occurred and the rings are not sealing correctly. A hole in the piston crown is an indication that abnormal combustion (pre-ignition, knocking or detonation) has been occurring. If any of the above problems exist, the causes must be corrected, or the damage will occur again.

10 Corrosion of the piston, in the form of small pits, indicates that coolant is leaking into the combustion chamber and/or the crankcase. Again, the cause must be corrected, or the problem may persist in the rebuilt engine.

11 If in any doubt as to the condition of the pistons and connecting rods, have them inspected and measured by an engine reconditioning specialist. If new parts are required, they will be able to supply and fit appropriate-sized pistons/rings, and hone the cylinder block.

Reassembly

12 Before refitting the rings to the pistons, check their end gaps by inserting each of them in their cylinder bores. Use the piston to make sure that they are square. Using feeler blades, check that the gaps are within the tolerances given in the Specifications. Genuine rings are supplied pre-gapped; no attempt should be made to adjust the gaps by filing.

13 Install the new rings by fitting them over the top of the piston, starting with the oil control scraper ring sections. Use feeler blades in the same way as when removing the old rings. New rings generally have their top surfaces identified, and must be fitted the correct way round **(see illustration)**. Note that

12.7 A large socket on an extension can be used to drive in new core plugs

13.2 Using feeler blades to remove piston rings

13.13 Look for etched markings identifying the piston ring top surface

the first and second compression rings have different sections. Be careful when handling the compression rings; they will break if they are handled roughly or expanded too far. With all the rings in position, space the ring gaps at 120° to each other (unless otherwise specified). The oil control scraper ring expander must also be positioned opposite to the actual ring.

14 Crankshaft (diesel engines) – inspection

1 Clean the crankshaft using paraffin or a suitable solvent, and dry it, preferably with compressed air if available. Be sure to clean the oil holes with a pipe cleaner or similar probe, to ensure that they are not obstructed.

 Warning: Wear eye protection when using compressed air.

2 Check the main and big-end bearing journals for uneven wear, scoring, pitting and cracking.
3 Big-end bearing wear is accompanied by distinct metallic knocking when the engine is running (particularly noticeable when the engine is pulling from low revs), and some loss of oil pressure.
4 Main bearing wear is accompanied by severe engine vibration and rumble – getting progressively worse as engine revs increase – and again by loss of oil pressure.
5 Check the bearing journal for roughness by running a finger lightly over the bearing surface. Any roughness (which will be accompanied by obvious bearing wear) indicates that the crankshaft requires regrinding.
6 Have the crankshaft journals measured by an engine reconditioning specialist. If the crankshaft is worn or damaged, they may be able to regrind the journals and supply suitable undersize bearing shells. If no undersize shells are available and the crankshaft has worn beyond the specified limits, it will have to be renewed. Consult your Ford dealer or engine reconditioning specialist for further information on parts availability.
7 If the crankshaft has been reground, check for burrs around the crankshaft oil holes (the holes are usually chamfered, so burrs should not be a problem unless regrinding has been carried out carelessly). Remove any burrs with a fine file or scraper, and thoroughly clean the oil holes as described previously.

15 Main and big-end bearings (diesel engines) – inspection

1 Even though the main and big-end bearings should be renewed during the engine overhaul, the old bearings should be retained for close

examination, as they may reveal valuable information about the condition of the engine. The size of the bearing shells is stamped on the back metal, and this information should be given to the supplier of the new shells.
2 Bearing failure occurs because of lack of lubrication, the presence of dirt or other foreign particles, overloading the engine, and corrosion. Regardless of the cause of bearing failure, it must be corrected before the engine is reassembled, to prevent it from happening again **(see illustration)**.
3 When examining the bearings, remove them from the engine block, the main bearing caps, the connecting rods and the rod caps, and lay them out on a clean surface in the same general position as their location in the engine. This will enable you to match any bearing problems with the corresponding crankshaft journal.
4 Dirt and other foreign particles get into the engine in a variety of ways. Dirt may be left in the engine during assembly, or it may pass through filters or the crankcase ventilation system. It may get into the oil, and from there into the bearings. Metal chips from machining operations and normal engine wear are often present. Abrasives are sometimes left in engine components after reconditioning, especially when parts are not thoroughly cleaned using the proper cleaning methods.
5 Whatever the source, these foreign objects often end up embedded in the soft bearing material, and are easily recognised. Large particles will not embed in the bearing, and will score or gouge the bearing and journal. The best prevention for this cause of bearing failure is to clean all parts thoroughly, and keep everything spotlessly-clean during engine assembly. Frequent and regular engine oil and filter changes are also recommended.
6 Lack of lubrication (or lubrication breakdown) has a number of interrelated causes. Excessive heat (which thins the oil), overloading (which squeezes the oil from the bearing face) and oil leakage (from excessive bearing clearances, worn oil pump or high engine speeds) all contribute to lubrication breakdown. Blocked oil passages, which usually are the result of misaligned oil holes in a bearing shell, will also oil-starve a bearing and destroy it. When lack of lubrication is the cause of bearing failure, the bearing material is wiped or extruded from the steel backing of the bearing. Temperatures may increase to the point where the steel backing turns blue from overheating.
7 Driving habits can have a definite effect on bearing life. Full-throttle, low-speed operation (labouring the engine) puts very high loads on bearings, which tends to squeeze out the oil film. These loads cause the bearings to flex, which produces fine cracks in the bearing face (fatigue failure). Eventually, the bearing material will loosen in pieces and tear away from the steel backing. Short-trip driving leads to corrosion of bearings, because insufficient engine heat is produced to drive off the

15.2 Typical bearing failures

condensed water and corrosive gases. These products collect in the engine oil, forming acid and sludge. As the oil is carried to the engine bearings, the acid attacks and corrodes the bearing material.
8 Incorrect bearing installation during engine assembly will lead to bearing failure as well. Tight-fitting bearings leave insufficient bearing oil clearance, and will result in oil starvation. Dirt or foreign particles trapped behind a bearing shell result in high spots on the bearing which lead to failure.
9 Do not touch any shell's bearing surface with your fingers during reassembly; there is a risk of scratching the delicate surface, or of depositing particles of dirt on it.
10 As mentioned at the beginning of this Section, the bearing shells should be renewed as a matter of course during engine overhaul; to do otherwise is false economy.

16 Engine overhaul – reassembly sequence

1 Before reassembly begins, ensure that all new parts have been obtained and that all necessary tools are available. Read through the entire procedure to familiarise yourself with the work involved, and to ensure that all items necessary for reassembly of the engine are at hand. In addition to all normal tools and materials, jointing and thread-locking compound will be needed during engine reassembly. Do not use any kind of silicone-based sealant on any part of the fuel system or inlet manifold, and never use exhaust sealants upstream (on the engine side) of the catalytic converter.
2 In order to save time and avoid problems,

1 Bearing shell
2 Main bearing ladder
3 Special tool
4 Aligning pins

H44713

17.4 Main bearing shell refitment

H44820

17.11 Main bearing ladder bolts tightening sequence

engine reassembly can be carried out in the following order.
a) Crankshaft and main bearings (diesel engines).
b) Pistons/connecting rods and main bearing ladder (diesel engines).
c) Oil pump.
d) Sump.
e) Flywheel/driveplate.
f) Cylinder head.
g) Timing sprockets and belt.
h) Engine external components (including inlet and exhaust manifolds).

3 Ensure that everything is clean prior to reassembly. As mentioned previously, dirt and metal particles can quickly destroy bearings and result in major engine damage. Use clean engine oil to lubricate during reassembly.

17 Crankshaft (diesel engines) – refitting

Selection of new bearing shells

1 Have the crankshaft inspected and measured by a Ford dealer or engine reconditioning specialist. They will be able to carry out any regrinding/repairs, and supply suitable main and big-end bearing shells.

Refitting

2 It is assumed at this point that the cylinder block/crankcase and crankshaft have been cleaned and repaired or reconditioned as necessary. Position the engine upside-down.
3 Clean the backs of the bearing shells in both the cylinder block/crankcase and the main bearing ladder. If new shells are being fitted, ensure that all traces of protective grease are cleaned off using paraffin. Wipe dry the shells with a lint-free cloth.
4 Press the bearing shells into their locations, ensuring that the tab (where applicable) on each shell engages in the notch in the cylinder

block/crankcase and bearing ladder. Take care not to touch any shell's bearing surface with your fingers. Note that the upper bearing shells all have a grooved surface, whereas the lower shells have a plain bearing surface. It is essential that the lower bearing shell halves are centrally located in the ladder. To ensure this, a Ford special tool (303-737) is positioned over the ladder, and the bearing shells inserted through the slots in the tool (see illustration). If this tool is not available, use a tape-measure or ruler to ensure the shells are perfectly central on their bearings.
5 Liberally lubricate each bearing shell in the cylinder block with clean engine oil, then lower the crankshaft into position.
6 Insert the thrustwashers to either side of No 2 main bearing upper location, and push them around the bearing journal until their edges are horizontal. Ensure that the oilway grooves on each thrustwasher face outwards (they should be visible).
7 Refit the piston and connecting rod assemblies as described in Section 18.
8 Thoroughly degrease the mating surfaces of the cylinder block/crankcase and the main bearing ladder. Apply a thin bead of RTV sealant to the main bearing ladder mating surface. Ford recommend the use of their WSE-M4G323-A4 sealant for this purpose. Use two aligning pins inserted into the main bearing ladder to ensure the correct positioning of the assembly. Make sure the sealant does not enter the blind holes in the cylinder block or ladder, or damage may result. The ladder should be fitted within four minutes of applying the sealant.
9 Lubricate the lower bearing shells with clean engine oil, then refit the main bearing ladder, ensuring that the shells are not displaced, and that the locating dowels engage correctly. Remove the aligning pins from the bearing ladder.
10 Install the large and small main bearing ladder retaining bolts, and screw them in until they are just making contact with the ladder.

Note that the larger (M11) bolts must not be re-used – a new set should be obtained.
11 Tighten all the main bearing ladder bolts to their Stage 1 torque setting in sequence (see illustration).
12 Slacken (Stage 2) the larger bolts half a turn (180°), then tighten them in sequence to the Stage 3 torque setting, followed by the Stage 4 angle-tightening setting. Apply sealant to the two new bearing ladder bolt caps, and tap them into place over the two flywheel end bolts.
13 Finally, tighten the smaller bearing ladder bolts to their Stage 2 setting.
14 Rotate the crankshaft a number of times by hand, to check for any obvious binding.
15 Check the crankshaft endfloat (refer to Section 11).
16 Fit new crankshaft oil seals as described in Chapter 2C Section 13, or Chapter 2D Section 13 (as applicable).
17 Refit the components removed.

18 Piston/connecting rod assemblies (diesel engines) – refitting

1 Clean the backs of the big-end bearing shells, and the recesses in the connecting rods and big-end caps. If new shells are being fitted, ensure that all traces of the protective grease are cleaned off using paraffin. Wipe the shells and connecting rods dry with a lint-free cloth.
2 Lubricate No 1 piston and piston rings, and check that the ring gaps are spaced at 120° intervals to each other.
3 Fit a ring compressor to No 1 piston, then insert the piston and connecting rod into No 1 cylinder. Make sure that the mark or arrow on the piston crown is facing the timing belt end of the engine. With No 1 crankpin at its lowest point, drive the piston carefully into the cylinder with the wooden handle of a hammer,

at the same time guiding the connecting rod onto the crankpin **(see illustration)**.

4 On these engines, the connecting rod is made in one piece, then the big-end bearing cap is 'cracked' off. This ensures that the cap fits onto the connecting rod only in one position, and with maximum rigidity. Consequently, there are no locating notches for the bearing shells to fit into.

5 To ensure that the big-end bearing shells are centrally located in the connecting rod and cap, two special tools are available from Ford (303-736). These half-moon shaped tools are pressed in from either side of the rod/cap, and locate the shell exactly in the centre **(see illustration)**. Fit the shells into the connecting rods and big-end caps, and lubricate them with plenty of clean engine oil.

6 Tighten the bolts to the Stage 1 torque setting, then slacken them 180° (Stage 2). Tighten the bolts to the Stage 3 setting, followed by the Stage 4 angle-tightening setting.

7 Continue refitting the main bearing shells and ladder as described in Section 17.

8 On completion, refit the oil pump pick-up tube, sump and cylinder head as described in the relevant Chapter.

19 Engine – initial start-up after overhaul

1 With the engine refitted in the vehicle, double-check the engine oil and coolant

18.3 With the compressor fitted, use the handle of a hammer to gently drive the piston into the cylinder

levels. Make a final check that everything has been reconnected, and that there are no tools or rags left in the engine compartment.

2 On diesel engines, prime and bleed the fuel system as described in Chapter 4B Section 3.

3 Start the engine, noting that this may take a little longer than usual. Make sure that the oil pressure warning light goes out.

4 While the engine is idling, check for fuel, water and oil leaks. Don't be alarmed if there are some odd smells and smoke from parts getting hot and burning off oil deposits.

5 Assuming all is well, run the engine until it reaches normal operating temperature, then switch off the engine.

6 After a few minutes, recheck the oil and coolant levels as described in Weekly checks0,5, and top-up as necessary.

H44712

18.5 Big-end bearing shell positioning

1 Special tool   2 Bearing shell

7 Note that there is no need to retighten the cylinder head bolts once the engine has first run after reassembly.

8 If new pistons, rings or crankshaft bearings have been fitted, the engine must be treated as new, and run-in for the first 600 miles. Do not operate the engine at full-throttle, or allow it to labour at low engine speeds in any gear. It is recommended that the oil and filter be changed at the end of this period.

Chapter 3
Cooling, heating and air conditioning systems

Contents

Degrees of difficulty

Easy, suitable for novice with little experience	Fairly easy, suitable for beginner with some experience	Fairly difficult, suitable for competent DIY mechanic	Difficult, suitable for experienced DIY mechanic	Very difficult, suitable for expert DIY or professional

Specifications

General
Maximum system pressure .... 1.4 bars
Thermostat start of opening temperature .... 88°C to 92°C

Air conditioning system
Refrigerant:
  Up to 11.07.2016 .... R134a
  From 11.07.2016 .... R1234yf
Refrigerant quantity:
  1.0 litre petrol engines .... 610 to 630 g
  1.25, 1.6 litre petrol engines, and 1.5 litre diesel engines:
    With 12 mm condenser.............................. 380 to 400 g
    With 16 mm condenser.............................. 510 to 530 g
  1.6 litre diesel engines:
    With 12 mm condenser.............................. 440 to 460 g
    With 16 mm condenser.............................. 560 to 580 g
Refrigerant oil:
  Up to 11.07.2016 .... Ford WSH-M1C231-B
  From 11.07.2016 .... Ford WSS-M2C300-A2
Refrigerant oil capacity:
  1.0 litre petrol, and all diesel engines .... 120 ml
  1.25 and 1.6 litre petrol engines........................... 170 ml

Torque wrench settings

	Nm	lbf ft
Air conditioning compressor mounting bolts	25	18
Coolant pump bolts:		
1.0 litre petrol engines:		
Long bolts:		
Stage 1	15	11
Stage 2	Angle-tighten a further 90°	
Short bolts	10	7
1.25 and 1.6 litre petrol engines.	10	7
Diesel engines:		
Stage 1	3	2
Stage 2	10	7
Coolant pump pulley bolts (petrol engines)	27	20
Refrigerant pipe to compressor	20	15
Refrigerant pipe to expansion valve.	10	7
Steering column shaft universal joint clamp bolt*	34	25
Thermostat cover bolts	10	7
Thermostat housing bolts:		
Petrol engines.	10	7
Diesel engines:		
Stage 1	4	3
Stage 2	7	5

*Use a new bolt

1 General information and precautions

1 The cooling system is of pressurised type, comprising a pump driven by the auxiliary drivebelt (petrol engines) or the timing belt (diesel engines), an aluminium crossflow radiator, electric cooling fan, and a thermostat. The system functions as follows. Cold coolant from the radiator passes through the hose to the coolant pump, where it is pumped around the cylinder block and head passages. After cooling the cylinder bores, combustion surfaces and valve seats, the coolant reaches the underside of the thermostat, which is initially closed. The coolant passes through the heater, and is returned via the cylinder block to the coolant pump.

2 When the engine is cold, the thermostat is shut, and the coolant circulates only through the cylinder block, cylinder head and heater. When the coolant reaches a predetermined temperature, the thermostat opens and the coolant passes through to the radiator. As the coolant circulates through the radiator, it is cooled by the inrush of air when the car is in forward motion. Airflow is supplemented by the action of the electric cooling fan when necessary. Once the coolant has passed through the radiator, and has cooled, the cycle is repeated.

3 On 1.0 litre Duratec petrol engines, an additional thermostat is fitted to the cylinder block. This thermostat controls the flow of coolant around the cylinder head during the warm-up phase, allowing coolant flow only through the exhaust side of the head. This causes rapid temperature increase, bringing the engine up to its normal, most-efficient operating temperature.

4 The electric cooling fan, mounted on the rear of the radiator, is controlled by the engine management ECM,

5 An expansion tank is fitted to allow for the expansion of the coolant when hot.

6 Refer to Section 10 for information on the air conditioning system.

⚠ *Warning: Do not attempt to remove the expansion tank filler cap, or disturb any part of the cooling system, while the engine is hot; there is a high risk of scalding. If the expansion tank filler cap must be removed before the engine and radiator have fully cooled (even though this is not recommended) the pressure in the cooling system must first be relieved. Cover the cap with a thick layer of cloth, to avoid scalding, and slowly unscrew the filler cap until a hissing sound can be heard. When the hissing has stopped, indicating that the pressure has reduced, slowly unscrew the filler cap until it can be removed; if more hissing sounds are heard, wait until they have stopped before unscrewing the cap completely. At all times, keep well away from the filler cap opening and protect your hands.*

⚠ *Warning: Do not allow antifreeze to come into contact with skin, or with the painted surfaces of the car. Rinse off spills immediately, with plenty of water. Never leave antifreeze lying around in an open container, or in a puddle on the driveway or garage floor. Children and pets are attracted by its sweet smell, but antifreeze can be fatal if ingested.*

⚠ *Warning: If the engine is hot, the electric cooling fan may start rotating even if the engine is not running; be careful to keep hands, hair and loose clothing well clear when working in the engine compartment.*

2 Cooling system hoses – disconnection and renewal

Note: *Refer to the warnings given in Section 1 of this Chapter before proceeding. Do not attempt to disconnect any hose while the system is still hot.*

1 If the checks described in the relevant part of Chapter 1A or Chapter 1B reveal a faulty hose, it must be renewed as follows.

2 First drain the cooling system (see Chapter 1A Section 30 or Chapter 1B Section 30). If the coolant is not due for renewal, it may be re-used if it is collected in a clean container.

3 Before disconnecting a hose, first note its routing in the engine compartment, and whether it is secured by any clips or ties. Use a pair of pliers to release the spring clamps (or a screwdriver to slacken screw-type clamps) then move them along the hose, clear of the relevant inlet/outlet union. Carefully work the hose free **(see illustration)**.

2.3 Most of the coolant hoses are of the spring clamp type, which need large pliers to remove

4 Note that the coolant unions are fragile (most are made of plastic); do not use excessive force when attempting to remove the hoses. If a hose proves to be difficult to remove, try to release it by rotating the hose ends before attempting to free it – if this fails, try gently prising up the end of the hose with a small screwdriver to 'break' the seal.

5 When fitting a hose, first slide the clamps onto the hose, then work the hose into position. If spring-type clamps were originally fitted, it is a good idea to use screw-type clamps when refitting the hose (if only to make removal easier, next time). If the hose is stiff, use a little soapy water (washing-up liquid is ideal) as a lubricant, or soften the hose by soaking it in hot water.

6 Work the hose into position, checking that it is correctly routed and secured. Slide each clamp along the hose until it passes over the flared end of the relevant inlet/outlet union, before tightening the clamps securely.

7 Refill the cooling system with reference to Chapter 1A Section 30 or Chapter 1B Section 30.

8 Check thoroughly for leaks as soon as possible after disturbing any part of the cooling system.

3.5 Release the clamp and disconnect the lower hose

3.6a Depress the clip at the rear…

3.6b … and slide out the fastener each side

3.6c Remove the rubber washer each side to give extra clearance

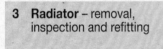

3 Radiator – removal, inspection and refitting

Note: *If leakage is the reason for removing the radiator, bear in mind that minor leaks can often be cured using a radiator sealant with the radiator in situ.*

Removal

1 Firmly apply the handbrake, then jack up the front of the vehicle and support it securely on axle stands (see *Jacking and vehicle support*). Where fitted, remove the engine undershield.

2 Drain the cooling system as described in Chapter 1A Section 30 or Chapter 1B Section 30.

3 On models with air conditioning, to improve access, remove the front bumper as described in Chapter 11 Section 6.

4 Remove the electric cooling fan and shroud as described in Section 5.

5 Release the clamps and disconnect the lower cooling hose from the radiator **(see illustration)**.

6 Remove the fasteners at the top of the radiator, move it rearwards a little, then lift it slightly **(see illustrations)**. In order to create sufficient clearance, remove the rubber washers from the radiator upper mountings. When lifting the radiator, ensure the lower rubber mountings are lifted along with the radiator.

7 On models with air conditioning, release the clips securing the base of the condenser to the radiator, then lower the condenser slightly to disengage it from the radiator at the top **(see illustration)**. Secure the condenser to the vehicle body to prevent straining the refrigerant pipes.

8 Carefully lower the radiator from place.

Inspection

9 If the radiator has been removed due to suspected blockage, reverse-flush it as described in Chapter 1A Section 30 or Chapter 1B Section 30. Clean dirt and debris from the radiator fins, using an airline (in which case, wear eye protection) or a soft brush. Be careful, as the fins are easily damaged, and are sharp.

10 If necessary, a radiator specialist can perform a 'flow test' on the radiator, to establish whether an internal blockage exists.

11 A leaking radiator must be referred to a specialist for permanent repair. Do not attempt to weld or solder a leaking radiator, as damage may result.

Refitting

12 Refitting is a reversal of removal, bearing in mind the following points:
a) Refit the radiator cooling fan as described in Section 5.
b) Ensure that all hoses are correctly reconnected, and their retaining clips securely refitted (or tightened).
c) On models with air conditioning, ensure

3.6d Lift the rubber mountings along with the radiator

3.7 Press up the clip securing the base of the condenser to the radiator

3.12a The rear upper edge of the condenser locates in the slot in the upper mountings…

3.12b … whilst the condenser lower lugs must slide into the slots at the base of the radiator

4.13 Release the clamps and disconnect the air intake duct

that the engages correctly with the radiator **(see illustrations)**.
d) On completion, refill the cooling system as described in Chapter 1A Section 30 or Chapter 1B Section 30.

4 Thermostat – removal, testing and refitting

1 As the thermostat ages, it will become slower to react to changes in water temperature ('lazy'). Ultimately, the unit may stick in the open or closed position, and this causes problems. A thermostat which is stuck open will result in a very slow warm-up; a thermostat which is stuck shut will lead to rapid overheating.
2 Before assuming the thermostat is to blame for a cooling system problem, check the coolant level. If the system is draining due to a leak, or has not been properly filled, there may be an airlock in the system (refer to the coolant renewal procedure in the relevant Part of Chapter 1A or Chapter 1B).
3 If the engine seems to be taking a long time to warm up (based on heater output), the thermostat could be stuck open. Don't necessarily believe the temperature gauge reading – some gauges never seem to register very high in normal driving.
4 A lengthy warm-up period might suggest

that the thermostat is missing – it may have been removed or inadvertently omitted by a previous owner or mechanic. Don't drive the car without a thermostat – the engine management system's PCM will then stay in warm-up mode for longer than necessary, causing emissions and fuel economy to suffer.
5 If the engine runs hot, use your hand to check the temperature of the radiator top hose. If the hose isn't hot, but the engine clearly is, the thermostat is probably stuck closed, preventing the coolant inside the engine from escaping to the radiator – renew the thermostat. Again, this problem may also be due to an airlock (refer to the coolant renewal procedure in the relevant Part of Chapter 1A Section 30 or Chapter 1B Section 30).
6 If the radiator top hose is hot, it means that the coolant is flowing (at least as far as the radiator) and the thermostat is open. Consult the Fault diagnosis section at the end of this manual to assist in tracing possible cooling system faults, but a lack of heater output would now definitely suggest an airlock or a blockage.
7 To gain a rough idea of whether the thermostat is working properly when the engine is warming up, without dismantling the system, proceed as follows.
8 With the engine completely cold, start the engine and let it idle, while checking the temperature of the radiator top hose.

Periodically check the temperature indicated on the coolant temperature gauge – if overheating is indicated, switch the engine off immediately.
9 The top hose should feel cold for some time as the engine warms up, and should then get warm quite quickly as the thermostat opens.
10 The above is not a precise or definitive test of thermostat operation, but if the system does not perform as described, remove and test the thermostat as described below. Note that it is not possible to test the thermostat fitted to the diesel engine.

Petrol engine models

Removal

11 Drain the cooling system as described in Chapter 1A Section 30.

1.0 litre engines

Main thermostat

12 Remove the oil filler cap, and pull the plastic cover (where fitted) on the top of the engine upwards from its' mountings.
13 Release the clamps, and remove the air intake duct from the air cleaner housing **(see illustration)**. Where applicable, disconnect the breather hose from the duct.
14 Loosen the clamps, disconnect the coolant hoses and the wiring from the thermostat housing, located on the left-hand end of the engine **(see illustrations)**.
15 Unscrew the four securing bolts, and

4.14a Disconnect the coolant temperature sensor wiring plug

4.14b Depress the release button and disconnect the quick-release connector

4.14c Disconnect the remaining coolant hoses

remove the thermostat housing from the engine **(see illustration)**. Recover the gasket.

Cylinder block thermostat

16 Remove the alternator as described in Chapter 5A Section 7.

17 Release the clamp and disconnect the hose from the thermostat **(see illustration)**.

18 Undo the 2 retaining bolts and pull the thermostat from the cylinder block **(see illustration)**. Renew the 2 O-ring seals.

1.25 and 1.6 litre models

19 Remove the alternator as described in Chapter 5A Section 7.

20 Release the clamps and disconnect the coolant hoses from the thermostat housing at the front face of the cylinder block.

21 Undo the 4 retaining bolts and remove the thermostat housing.

22 Note its fitted position and pull the thermostat from place.

Note: *When fitting a thermostat, ensure the 'jiggle' pin the the thermostat flange is positioned at the 12 o'clock position.*

Refitting

23 Refitting is a reversal of removal.

Diesel engine models

Removal

24 Drain the cooling system as described in Chapter 1B Section 30.

25 Remove the battery and battery tray as described in Chapter 5A Section 4. **Note:** *It's not necessary to remove the PCM from the battery tray – leave it attached and move the tray to one side.*

26 Disconnect the coolant temperature sensor wiring plug from the thermostat housing **(see illustration)**.

27 Disconnect the four coolant hoses from the thermostat housing, noting their locations. Note that some of the hoses are disconnected after pressing down on the white-coloured release button.

4.15 Remove the thermostat housing

28 At the base of the housing, loosen the screw and detach the mounting bracket for the bypass tube.

29 Remove the four mounting bolts and take off the thermostat housing.

Refitting

30 Refitting is a reversal of removal, noting the following points:

a) *Thoroughly clean the mating faces of the thermostat housing and the engine.*

b) *Use a new gasket when refitting the housing, and tighten the bolts to the specified torque.*

c) *Refit the battery tray and battery as described in Chapter 5A Section 4.*

d) *On completion, refill the cooling system as described in Chapter 1B Section 30.*

Testing

Note: *DIY testing of the thermostat is not possible on the diesel engine, as the thermostat is an integral part of its housing. If there is good reason to suspect the thermostat is not working properly (read the introductory paragraphs in this Section), a new housing will have to be obtained.*

31 If the thermostat remains in the open position at room temperature, it is faulty, and must be renewed as a matter of course.

4.17 Disconnect the hose from the thermostat

32 Check to see if there's an open temperature marking stamped on the thermostat.

33 Using a thermometer and container of water, heat the water until the temperature corresponds with the temperature marking stamped on the thermostat. If no marking is found, start the test with the water hot, and heat slowly until it boils.

34 Suspend the (closed) thermostat on a length of string in the water, and check that maximum opening occurs within two minutes, or before the water boils.

35 Remove the thermostat and allow it to cool down; check that it closes fully.

36 If the thermostat does not open and close as described, or if it sticks in either position, it must be renewed. Frankly, if there is any question about the operation of the thermostat, renew it – they are not expensive items.

5 Radiator cooling fan – testing, removal and refitting

Testing

1 On all models, the cooling fan is controlled by the engine management powertrain control module, using signals provided by the engine coolant temperature sensor.

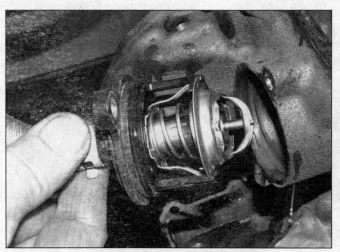

4.18 Pull the thermostat from the block

4.26 Coolant temperature sensor wiring plug

5.7 Unclip the transmission breather from the shroud

5.8 Disconnect the various wiring plugs and unclip the loom

5.9 Disconnect the wiring plugs from the underside of the cooling fan

5.10 Electric coolant pump retaining bolt

5.11a Undo the lower bolt...

5.11b ... and upper bolt, then remove the bracket

2 The fan operation can be checked by connecting the fan motor directly to a 12 volt power supply. Disconnect the motor wiring plug, and apply 12 volts across the motor terminals (the black wire is the earth) – take great care not to short out the power supply wires.

3 If the fan fails to operate, the fan motor is almost certainly at fault.

4 Testing of the fan motor control circuit must be entrusted to a Ford dealer, who will have the necessary specialist diagnostic equipment to test the system – do not attempt to test the system using conventional test equipment, as the PCM may be damaged.

Removal

5 Disconnect the battery negative lead as described in Chapter 5A Section 4.

6 On petrol models and 1.5 litre diesel models, remove the air cleaner assembly as described in Chapter 4A Section 5 or Chapter 4B Section 4 as applicable

7 Unclip the transmission breather from the cooling fan shroud **(see illustration)**.

8 Where applicable, disconnect the wiring plugs, and unclip the wiring loom from above the bonnet slam panel **(see illustration)**.

9 Disconnect the cooling fan wiring plugs, and unclip the wiring harness as necessary **(see illustration)**.

10 On 1.0 litre Ecoboost petrol engines, undo the retaining bolt and move the electric coolant pump to one side **(see illustration)**.

11 On 1.0 litre Ecoboost petrol engines, undo the upper and lower bolts, unclip the coolant hose and remove the bracket

on the right-hand side of the shroud **(see illustrations)**.

12 Apply a clamp to the top radiator coolant hose, then release the clamp and disconnect the hose **(see illustration)**. Be prepared for a small amount of coolant loss.

⚠️ **Warning: Ensure the engine is cold before disconnecting the hose.**

13 Remove the cooling fan motor and mounting frame by releasing the two plastic catches either side at the top, then lift the motor and frame up to disengage the lower mountings. Once released, the motor and frame can be lifted from place **(see illustration)**.

14 If desired, the fan motor can be removed from the frame after undoing the nut and removing the fan, then unscrewing the three motor securing bolts **(see illustration)**.

5.12 Disconnect the upper coolant hose from the radiator

5.13 Release the two plastic catches either side at the top

5.14 Fan motor securing bolts

6.4a Pull out the retaining clip...

6.4b ... followed by the sensor

6.7 Pull out the retaining clip followed by the sensor

Refitting

15 Refitting is a reversal of removal. Reconnect the radiator fan wiring securely, and ensure the harness is routed clear of the fan blades or hot components. If the cooling system was drained, refill or top-up as described in the relevant Part of *Weekly checks*.

6 Coolant temperature sensor – removal and refitting

⚠ **Warning: Do not attempt to remove the sensor while the cooling system is hot and/or pressurised, as there is a great risk of scalding.**

1 Allow the engine to cool, then slowly remove the cap from the coolant expansion tank to depressurise the cooling system. To avoid any chance of coolant spillage, the system can be drained as described in Chapter 1A or 1B, but this is not essential if a new sensor is being fitted, and can quickly be substituted for the old one. Otherwise, if the system is not drained and the sensor will be left out for some time, a plug of some kind should be inserted to reduce coolant loss.

Petrol engine models

1.0 litre models

⚠ **Warning: Ensure the coolant is cold before attempting this procedure.**

2 Remove the engine cover and then remove the air filter housing and inlet duct from the left-hand side of the engine bay.
3 Disconnect the wiring plug from the sensor.
4 The sensor is clipped into place with a horseshoe shaped retaining clip. Pull out the clip and if necessary recover the seal from the thermostat housing – it will normally come away with the sensor **(see illustrations)**. Be prepared for coolant spillage and have rag or a rubber plug handy to force into the sensor aperture – or better still have a replacement sensor to hand. This way only a little coolant will be lost.
5 If required the sensor operation can be checked by using a multi-meter (set to the ohms scale) to check the resistance of the

sensor. Connect the meter to the sensor and gently warm the sensor with a hot air gun (or suspend the sensor in a pan of water that can be brought up to the boil). As the temperature changes the resistance will change. The normal failure mode will be either open circuit (very high resistance) or short circuit (very low resistance). Note however this is not a definitive test, as the sensor may still respond to temperature changes, but the change in resistance may not track the change in coolant temperature.

1.25 and 1.6 litre models

6 The sensor is located in the coolant outlet housing, beneath the ignition coil, at the transmission end of the cylinder head. To improve access, undo the four ignition coil mounting bolts, and move the coil to one side (the wiring can be left attached).
7 Pull out the retaining clip and withdraw the sensor **(see illustration)**. Be prepared for coolant spillage and have rag or a rubber plug handy to force into the sensor aperture – or better still have a replacement sensor to hand. This way only a little coolant will be lost.

Refitting

8 Refitting is a reversal of removal, noting the following points:
a) *Renew the sensor seal if necessary.*
b) *Refit the sensor and insert the clip.*
c) *Either refill or top-up the cooling system as described in Chapter 1A Section 30 or Weekly checks.*

Diesel engine models

Removal

9 The sensor is clipped into the top of the thermostat housing, which is located at the transmission end of the engine.
10 Pull up and remove the plastic cover from the top of the engine.
11 Release the sensor wiring plug, then pull out the spring clip used to retain the sensor, and remove the sensor from the housing **(see illustration 4.26)**.

Refitting

12 Refitting is a reversal of removal, noting the following points:
a) *Renew the sensor seal if necessary.*
b) *Push the sensor fully home, then retain it with the spring clip.*

c) *Either refill or top-up the cooling system as described in Chapter 1B Section 30 or Weekly checks.*

7 Coolant pump – removal and refitting

Petrol engine models

1 Drain the cooling system as described in Chapter 1A Section 30.

Main coolant pump

1.0 litre models

2 Slacken the coolant pump pulley bolts, then remove the auxiliary drivebelt as described in Chapter 1A Section 26.
3 Completely unscrew the bolts and remove the coolant pump pulley.
4 Unbolt and remove the 7 bolts, noting their positions **(see illustration 7.6)**. Dispose of the 2 longer bolts as they must be replaced.
5 Remove the pump and clean the mounting surface. The replacement pump should be supplied with a new gasket, if not, or if you intend to replace the original pump, obtain a replacement gasket.
6 Fit the new pump and tighten the 5 short bolts in a diagonal sequence to the specified torque. Tighten the remaining 2 long bolts to the specified torque **(see illustration)**. On completion refill the cooling system as described in Chapter 1A Section 30 and check for leaks.

7.6 Tighten the bolts 1-5 in the order shown and then tighten bolts 6 and 7

7.9 Coolant pump retaining bolts

7.14 Release the clamps securing the hoses to the pump

1.25 and 1.6 litre models

7 Slacken the coolant pump pulley bolts.

8 Remove the timing belt and tensioner as described in Chapter 2B Section 8.

9 Unscrew the bolts and remove the coolant pump from the cylinder block **(see illustration)**. Remove and discard the gasket.

Refitting

10 Commence refitting by thoroughly cleaning the mating faces of the coolant pump and the cylinder block.

11 Refit the coolant pump, using a new gasket, and tighten the securing bolts to the specified torque.

12 Refit the timing belt tensioner and timing belt as described in Chapter 2B Section 8, then refill the cooling system (Chapter 1A Section 30).

Auxiliary electric coolant pump

Note: *1.0 litre Ecoboost engines only*

13 Raise the front of the vehicle and support it securely on axle stands (see *Jacking and vehicle support*). Where fitted, undo the fasteners and remove the engine undershield.

14 The pump is at the rear of the cooling fan shroud. Working underneath, release the clamps and disconnect the hoses from the pump **(see illustration)**.

15 Disconnect the wiring plug, undo the

7.20 Coolant pump retaining bolts

bolt securing the mounting bracket to the fan shroud, and lower the pump from place **(see illustration 5.10)**.

16 Refitting is a reversal of removal.

17 Refill the cooling system as described in Chapter 1A Section 30.

Diesel engine models

Removal

18 Drain the cooling system as described in Chapter 1B Section 30.

19 Remove the timing belt as described in Chapter 2C Section 7 or Chapter 2D Section 7.

20 Remove the bolts securing the coolant pump to the engine, and remove it **(see illustration)**. Recover the sealing ring or gasket.

Refitting

21 Commence refitting by thoroughly cleaning the mating faces of the coolant pump and the cylinder block. If the old coolant pump is being refitted, check the condition of the sealing ring. Obtain a new one if possible, but it appears that it may not be available separately.

22 Refit the coolant pump, and tighten the securing bolts to the specified torque, in two stages. The pump body is made of plastic, so care is required. The first stage of tightening is a very low torque, which in reality approximates to doing the bolts just up to the surface.

23 Refit the timing belt as described in Chapter 2C Section 7 or Chapter 2D Section 7, then refill the cooling system (Chapter 1B Section 30).

8 Heating and ventilation system – general information

1 The heater/ventilation system consists of a multi-speed blower motor (housed behind the facia), face-level vents in the centre and

at each end of the facia, and air ducts to the front footwells.

2 The control unit is located in the facia, and the controls operate flap valves, to deflect and mix the air flowing through the various parts of the heater/ventilation system. The flap valves are contained in the air distribution housing, which acts as a central distribution unit, passing air to the various ducts and vents.

3 Cold air enters the system through the grille at the rear of the engine compartment.

4 The air (boosted by the blower fan if required) then flows through the various ducts, according to the settings of the controls. Stale air is expelled through ducts at the rear of the car. If warm air is required, the cold air is passed through the heater matrix, which is heated by the engine coolant.

5 On models with air conditioning, a recirculation switch enables the outside air supply to be closed off, while the air inside the car is recirculated. This can be useful to prevent unpleasant odours entering from outside the car, but should only be used briefly, as the recirculated air inside the car will soon deteriorate.

9 Heater/ventilation system components – removal and refitting

Heater/ventilation control panel

Removal

Models with manual temperature control

1 Remove the glovebox as described in Chapter 11 Section 23, then unclip the footwell air ducts on both sides **(see illustrations 9.21a and 9.21b)**.

2 Release the clips and disconnect the operating cables from the levers on the side

9.3 Prise the trim panel rearwards

9.4 Unclip the gear lever trim from the base of the gear lever

9.5a Staring at the top, prise the surround trim panel rearwards...

9.5b ...and remove it

9.6a Control panel retaining screws

9.6b Disconnect the cables and wiring as they become accessible

of the heater housing **(see illustration 9.22a and 9.22b)**.

All models

3 Carefully prise the trim panel above the heater control panel rearwards **(see illustration)**. Disconnect the wiring plug as the panel is withdrawn.

4 Unclip the gear lever or selector lever trim from the base of the gear/selector lever **(see illustration)**.

5 Using a plastic spatula or similar tool, starting at the top, carefully prise the heater control panel surround trim rearwards. Disconnect any wiring plugs as the panel is withdrawn **(see illustrations)**.

6 Undo the 4 screws and gently pull the control panel rearwards slight until the operating cables and wiring become

accessible. Disconnect the wiring plugs/ operating cables as they become accessible **(see illustrations)**.

Refitting

7 Refitting is a reversal of removal.

Heater blower motor

Removal

8 Working in the footwell on the driver's side, unscrew out the centre pin and extract the plastic rivet securing the inner trim panel to the base of the facia. Pull the panel away to release the three retaining clips at the rear and remove the trim panel **(see illustration)**.

9 On manual transmission models remove the clutch pedal as described in Chapter 6 Section 5.

10 On automatic transmission models, set the front wheels in the straight-ahead position, then lock the steering column in position by removing the ignition key. Working in the driver's footwell, undo the clamp bolt securing the steering column shaft lower universal joint to the steering gear pinion **(see illustration)**. Note that a new clamp bolt will be required for refitting. Pull the shaft upwards and off the pinion.

11 Unclip and remove the footwell air duct below the blower motor.

12 Disconnect the blower motor wiring connector.

13 Undo the retaining screw securing the blower motor to the air distribution housing **(see illustration)**.

14 Rotate the blower motor clockwise to

9.8 Unscrew the centre pin and pull out the rivet

9.10 Steering column shaft lower universal joint clamp bolt

9.13 Undo the retaining screw securing the blower motor to the air distribution housing

9.14 Rotate the blower motor clockwise to release it from the housing

9.18 Unscrew the securing screws, and withdraw the resistor from the air distribution housing

release it from the housing then withdraw it down and out from the footwell **(see illustration)**.

Refitting

15 Refitting is a reversal of removal, noting the following points:
a) *On automatic transmission models use a new clamp bolt when reconnecting the steering column shaft universal joint and tighten the clamp bolt to the specified torque.*

b) *On manual transmission models refit the clutch pedal as described in Chapter 6 Section 5.*

Heater blower motor resistor

Removal

16 Working in the footwell on the passenger's side, pull out the centre pin and extract the plastic rivet securing the inner trim panel to the base of the facia. Pull the panel away

to release the three retaining clips at the rear and remove the trim panel **(see illustration 9.8)**.

17 Disconnect the resistor wiring connector.
18 Unscrew the securing screws, and withdraw the resistor from the air distribution housing **(see illustration)**.

Refitting

19 Refitting is a reversal of removal.

Air distribution housing

Note: *On models with air conditioning, it is not possible to remove the air distribution housing without opening the refrigerant circuit (see Sections 10 and 11). Have the refrigerant discharged at a dealer service department or an automotive air conditioning repair facility before proceeding.*

Note: *The air distribution housing is removed together with the complete facia assembly and is then separated from it on the bench. This is an involved and complex operation and it is suggested that the contents of this Section and the relevant Section in Chapter 11 are studied carefully to gain an understanding of the work involved, before proceeding.*

20 Remove the facia assembly as described in Chapter 11 Section 25. Turn the facia assembly upside down on the bench to improve access to the air distribution housing and attachments on the underside of the facia.

21 Unclip and remove the footwell air ducts on each side of the air distribution housing **(see illustrations)**.

22 On models with manual temperature control, release the two control cables from the clips on the air distribution housing, and disconnect the cable ends from the operating levers **(see illustrations)**.

23 Disconnect the wiring connectors at

9.21a Unclip and remove the footwell air ducts on the left-hand side ...

9.21b ... and right-hand side of the air distribution housing

9.22a Release the control cable...

9.22b ...from each side of the housing

9.23a Disconnect the wiring connectors at the air inlet blend control motor...

9.23b ... heater blower motor and sunlight sensor...

9.23c ... heater blower motor resistor and air distribution control motor...

9.23d ... temperature control motor...

9.23e ... and air temperature sensor

9.26a Undo the 3 nuts at the rear...

the following components, where fitted (see illustrations):

a) Air inlet blend control motor.
b) Heater blower motor.
c) Sunlight sensor.
d) Heater blower motor resistor.
e) Air distribution control motor.
f) Temperature control motor.
g) Air temperature sensor.

24 Release the disconnected wiring harness from the cable clips on the air distribution housing and move it to one side.

25 Remove the heater/ventilation control panel as described previously in this Section.

26 Undo the 3 nuts at the rear and the single bolt at the front securing the air distribution housing to the facia and crossmember (see illustrations).

27 Make a final check that all wiring has been disconnected from the air distribution housing components, and that the harness has been released from the various cable clips and ties. Lift the housing up and off the retaining studs, and remove it from the facia.

Refitting

28 Refitting is a reversal of removal. On completion, refill the cooling system as described in Chapter 1A Section 30 or Chapter 1B Section 30. On models with air conditioning, have the system evacuated, charged and leak-tested by the specialist who discharged it.

Heater matrix

Removal

29 Remove the air distribution housing as described previously in this Section.

30 Lift off the foam insulation pad over the heater matrix pipe stubs (see illustration).

31 Undo the two screws securing the two halves of the bulkhead closure plate together (see illustration).

9.26b ... and the single bolt at the front securing the air distribution housing to the facia and crossmember

9.30 Lift off the foam insulation pad over the heater matrix pipe stubs

9.31 Undo the two screws securing the two halves of the bulkhead closure plate together

9.32a Cut through the foam sealing strip at the join of the bulkhead closure plate ...

9.32b ... and separate the two halves of the plate

9.34 Undo the securing screw and remove the heater matrix retainer

9.35 Carefully slide out the heater matrix and heater pipe assembly from the air distribution housing

9.38 Depress the clip and disconnect the ambient temperature sensor wiring plug

32 Using a sharp knife, cut through the foam sealing strip at the join of the bulkhead closure plate and separate the two halves of the plate **(see illustrations)**.

33 Undo the two screws and remove the pipe cover.

34 Undo the securing screw and remove the heater matrix retainer **(see illustration)**.

35 Carefully slide out the heater matrix and heater pipe assembly from the air distribution housing **(see illustration)**.

Refitting

36 Refitting is a reversal of removal.

Ambient temperature sensor

37 Remove the front bumper as described in Chapter 11 Section 6.

38 Disconnect the wiring plug and unclip the sensor from the cowling **(see illustration)**.

39 Refitting is a reversal of removal.

10 Air conditioning system – general information and precautions

1 Air conditioning is available on certain models. It enables the temperature of incoming air to be lowered, and also dehumidifies the air, which makes for rapid demisting and increased comfort.

2 The cooling side of the system works in the same way as a domestic refrigerator. Refrigerant gas is drawn into a belt-driven compressor, and passes into a condenser mounted in front of the radiator, where it loses heat and becomes liquid. The liquid passes through an expansion valve to an evaporator, where it changes from liquid under high pressure to gas under low pressure. This change is accompanied by a drop in temperature, which cools the evaporator. The refrigerant returns to the compressor, and the cycle begins again.

3 Air blown through the evaporator passes to the heater assembly, where it is mixed with hot air blown through the heater matrix, to achieve the desired temperature in the passenger compartment.

4 The heating side of the system works in the same way as on models without air conditioning (see Section 8).

5 The operation of the system is controlled electronically. Any problems with the system should be referred to a Ford dealer or an air conditioning specialist.

Air conditioning service ports

Note: *The air conditioning service port location varies slightly according to model. The following is a general description of service port location.*

6 The service ports are located on the right-hand side of the engine compartment **(see illustrations)**.

7 The low-pressure service port is located at the rear right-hand side of the engine compartment **(see illustration 10.6)**.

10.6a On 1.0 litre Ecoboost models, one of the ports is beneath the intercooler-to-throttle body duct

10.6b Air conditioning service ports – 1.25 and 1.6 litre petrol models

10.6c Air conditioning service ports – 1.6 litre diesel models

11.3 Undo the nuts and disconnect the refrigerant pipes

11.8a Undo the two retaining bolts...

11.8b ... and remove the expansion valve from the refrigerant pipe stubs

Precautions

8 It is necessary to observe special precautions whenever dealing with any part of the system, its associated components, and any items which necessitate disconnection of the system.

 Warning: The refrigeration circuit contains a liquid refrigerant. This refrigerant is potentially dangerous, and should only be handled by qualified persons. If it is splashed onto the skin, it can cause frostbite. It is not itself poisonous, but in the presence of a naked flame it forms a poisonous gas; inhalation of the vapour through a lighted cigarette could prove fatal. Uncontrolled discharging of the refrigerant is dangerous, and potentially damaging to the environment. Do not disconnect any part of the system unless it has been discharged by a Ford dealer or an air conditioning specialist.
Caution: Do not operate the air conditioning system if it is known to be short of refrigerant, as this may damage the compressor.

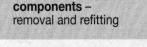

11 Air conditioning system components – removal and refitting

 Warning: The air conditioning system is under high pressure. Do not loosen any fittings or remove

any components until after the system has been discharged. Air conditioning refrigerant should be properly discharged into an approved type of container at a dealer service department or an automotive air conditioning repair facility capable of handling R134a refrigerant. Cap or plug the pipe lines as soon as they are disconnected, to prevent the entry of moisture. Always wear eye protection when disconnecting air conditioning system fittings.
Note: *This Section refers to the components of the air conditioning system itself – refer to Sections 8 and 9 for details of components common to the heating/ventilation system.*

Compressor

Note: *If the compressor is being removed as part of another procedure, it may not be necessary to have the system discharged. Usually, the compressor can be unbolted and tied to one side without the need to disturb the refrigerant lines.*

Removal

1 Remove the auxiliary drivebelt as described in Chapter 1A Section 26 or Chapter 1B Section 26.
2 Disconnect the compressor wiring plug.
3 With the system discharged, disconnect the refrigerant pipes from the compressor **(see illustration)**. Discard the O-ring seals – new ones must be used when refitting.
4 Support the compressor, then remove the

three mounting bolts (petrol engines) or four mounting bolts (diesel engines) and lower the compressor out of the engine bay.

Refitting

5 Refitting is a reversal of removal, noting the following points:
a) *Use new O-rings, coated with refrigerant oil, when reconnecting the refrigerant pipes.*
b) *Tighten the compressor mounting bolts to the specified torque.*
c) *Have the system evacuated, charged and leak-tested by the specialist that discharged it.*

Evaporator

6 Have the refrigerant discharged at a dealer service department or an automotive air conditioning repair facility.
7 Remove the air distribution housing as described in Section 9.
8 Undo the two retaining bolts and remove the expansion valve from the refrigerant pipe stubs **(see illustrations)**. Note that new seals for the refrigerant pipes will be required for refitting. Suitably plug or cover the disconnected pipes.
9 Remove the expansion valve retaining plate, then lift off the foam pad **(see illustrations)**.
10 Undo the two screws securing the two halves of the bulkhead closure plate together **(see illustration)**.
11 Using a sharp knife, cut through the foam sealing strip at the join of the bulkhead closure

11.9a Remove the expansion valve retaining plate ...

11.9b ... then lift off the foam pad

11.10 Undo the two screws securing the two halves of the bulkhead closure plate together

11.11a Cut through the foam sealing strip at the join of the bulkhead closure plate …

11.11b … then release the retaining tabs and separate the two halves of the plate

11.12a Undo the retaining screw…

11.12b … lift off the pollen filter cover from the side of the air distribution housing …

11.12c … then slide out the filter

plate. Release the retaining tabs and separate the two halves of the plate **(see illustrations)**.
12 Undo the retaining screw and lift off the pollen filter cover from the side of the air distribution housing, then slide out the filter **(see illustrations)**.
13 Undo the retaining screws and separate the two halves of the air distribution housing **(see illustrations)**.
14 Lift out the evaporator retaining plate, then carefully withdraw the evaporator and pipe assembly from the air distribution housing **(see illustrations)**.

Refitting

15 Refitting is a reversal of removal, ensuring that all disturbed pipe seals are renewed.

Condenser

Removal

16 Have the refrigerant discharged at a dealer service department or an automotive air conditioning repair facility.
17 Remove the radiator as described in Section 3.
18 Undo the retaining nuts and disconnect the upper and lower refrigerant pipe connector blocks from the right-hand side of

11.13a Undo the retaining screws…

11.13b … and separate the two halves of the air distribution housing

11.14a Lift out the evaporator retaining plate …

11.14b … then carefully withdraw the evaporator and pipe assembly

11.18a Undo the refrigerant pipe connector block upper retaining nut...

11.18b ... and lower retaining nut, and disconnect the connector blocks

the condenser **(see illustrations)**. Discard the seals – new ones must be used when refitting. Suitably cap the open fittings immediately to keep moisture and contamination out of the system.

19 Where applicable, disconnect the wiring connector from the pressure sensor on the right-hand side of the condenser.

20 Carefully lower the condenser and remove it from under the car.

Refitting

21 Refitting is the reverse of removal ensuring that all disturbed pipe seals are renewed.

22 Have the system evacuated, charged and leak-tested by the specialist who discharged it.

Receiver dryer

Note: *The following procedure is only applicable to 1.6 litre diesel engine models. On all other models, the receiver dryer is an integral part of the condenser.*

Removal

23 Have the refrigerant discharged at a dealer service department or an automotive air conditioning repair facility.

24 Remove the front bumper as described in Chapter 11 Section 6.

25 Undo the retaining nuts and disconnect the refrigerant pipe connector blocks from the base of the receiver dryer **(see illustration)**. Discard the seals – new ones must be used when refitting. Suitably cap the open fittings immediately to keep moisture and contamination out of the system.

26 Disconnect the wiring plug from the air conditioning pressure switch.

27 Undo the receiver dryer retaining clamp nut and withdraw the receiver dryer from under the wheel arch.

Refitting

28 Refitting is a reversal of removal, noting the following points:

a) Use new O-rings, coated with refrigerant

11.25 Receiver/dryer refrigerant pipe connector block nuts and pressure switch wiring plug

   oil, when reconnecting the refrigerant lines.

b) Refit the front bumper as described in Chapter 11 Section 6.

c) Have the system evacuated, charged and leak-tested by the specialist who discharged it.

Chapter 4 Part A
Fuel and exhaust systems – petrol models

Contents

Degrees of difficulty

Easy, suitable for novice with little experience | **Fairly easy,** suitable for beginner with some experience | **Fairly difficult,** suitable for competent DIY mechanic | **Difficult,** suitable for experienced DIY mechanic | **Very difficult,** suitable for expert DIY or professional

Specifications

General
System type . . . . Sequential multi-port fuel injection
Fuel octane requirement. . . . . 95 RON unleaded
Regulated fuel pressure (nominal) . . . . 3.6 to 4.0 bar

Torque wrench settings

	Nm	lbf ft
Catalytic converter support bracket:		
Support bracket to cylinder block:		
1.0 litre models	24	18
1.25 and 1.6 litre models	50	37
Support bracket to catalytic converter	24	18
Exhaust centre section flange joint	48	35
Exhaust manifold heat shield bolts	10	7
Exhaust manifold to cylinder head:		
Stage 1	20	15
Stage 2	55	41
Fuel rail mounting bolts	8	6
Fuel tank strap retaining bolts	25	18
Throttle housing bolts	8	6
Inlet manifold bolts/nuts:		
1.0 litre engines	10	7
1.25 and 1.6 litre engines	18	13
Turbocharger-to-cylinder head nuts: *		
Stage 1	19	14
Stage 2	25	18
Stage 3	Wait 30 seconds	
Stage 4	25	18
Turbocharger oil supply pipe:		
Upper banjo bolt	30	22
Lower bolt	10	7
Turbocharger oil return upper bolts	10	7
Variable camshaft timing oil control solenoids	8	6

Do not re-use

---

1 General information and precautions

General information

1 The fuel system consists of a fuel tank (mounted under the floor, beneath the rear seats), fuel hoses, an electric fuel pump mounted in the fuel tank, and a sequential electronic fuel injection system controlled by an engine management electronic control unit (Powertrain Control Module).

2 On 1.25 and 1.6 litre models, the electric fuel pump supplies fuel under pressure to the fuel rail, which distributes fuel to the injectors. A pressure regulator integral with the pump controls the system pressure. From the fuel rail, fuel is injected into the inlet ports, just above the inlet valves, by four fuel injectors. The fuel rail is mounted to the cylinder head, just above the plastic inlet manifold.

3 1.0 litre models feature a high pressure direct injection fuel system. Fuel is supplied by the tank mounted pump to a camshaft driven high pressure fuel pump. From here fuel is supplied (via a fuel rail) to fuel injectors mounted in the cylinder head.

4 The amount of fuel supplied by the injectors is precisely controlled by the Powertrain Control Module (PCM). The module uses the signals from the crankshaft position sensor and the camshaft position sensor to trigger each injector separately in cylinder firing order (sequential injection), with benefits in terms of better fuel economy and leaner exhaust emissions.

5 The Powertrain Control Module is the heart of the entire engine management system, controlling the fuel injection, ignition and emissions control systems. The module receives information from various sensors which is then computed and compared with preset values stored in its memory to determine the required period of injection.

6 Information on crankshaft position and engine speed is generated by a crankshaft position sensor. On 1.25 and 1.6 litre models the inductive head of the sensor runs just above the engine flywheel and scans a series of protrusions on the flywheel periphery. On 1.0 litre models the sensor is located behind the crankshaft pulley. On 1.25 and 1.6 litre models, as the crankshaft rotates, the sensor transmits a pulse to the system's ignition module every time a protrusion passes it. There is one missing protrusion in the flywheel periphery at a point corresponding to 90° BTDC. The ignition module recognises the absence of a pulse from the crankshaft position sensor at this point to establish a reference mark for crankshaft position. Similarly, the time interval between absent pulses is used to determine engine speed. On 1.0 litre models an inductive sensor is fitted that picks up the variation in the magnetic field in the pick up ring fitted to the rear of the crankshaft pulley. The information from the crankshaft position sensors is then fed to the Powertrain Control Module for further processing.

7 On all engines 2 camshaft position sensors are fitted, as each camshaft is fitted with variable timing units. The camshaft position sensor functions in the same way as the crankshaft position sensor, producing a series of pulses. The output from the sensors provides the Powertrain Control Module with a reference point, to enable it to determine the firing order and operate the injectors in the appropriate sequence.

8 Engine temperature information is supplied by the coolant temperature sensor. The sensor is an NTC (Negative Temperature Coefficient) thermistor – that is, a semi-conductor whose electrical resistance decreases as its temperature increases. The sensor provides the Powertrain Control Module with a constantly-varying (analogue) voltage signal, corresponding to the temperature of the engine coolant. This is used to refine the calculations made by the module when determining the correct amount of fuel required to achieve the ideal air/fuel mixture ratio.

9 Inlet air temperature and density information for air/fuel mixture ratio calculations is provided by a temperature and manifold absolute pressure (TMAP) sensor. The TMAP sensor is located on the throttle housing, and consists of a pressure transducer and a temperature sensor which directly supersedes the mass airflow and inlet air temperature sensors. The TMAP sensor provides information to the Powertrain Control Module relating to inlet manifold vacuum and barometric pressure, and the temperature of the air in the inlet manifold. When the ignition is switched on with the engine stopped, the sensor calculates barometric pressure and, when the engine is running, the sensor calculates inlet manifold vacuum. All engines are fitted with a mass airflow sensor in the outlet duct from the air cleaner housing.

10 The throttle valve inside the throttle housing is controlled by the driver with the accelerator pedal. As the valve opens, the amount of air that can pass through the system increases. As the throttle valve opens further, the TMAP sensor signal alters, and the Powertrain Control Module opens each injector for a longer duration, to increase the amount of fuel delivered to the inlet ports.

11 All models features a throttle which is electronically-controlled – an accelerator cable is not fitted. Instead, a throttle position sensor fitted to the accelerator pedal provides the Powertrain Control Module with the throttle opening signal, and this is relayed to a motor-driven throttle valve. This system also enables the PCM to control the engine idle speed, varying the throttle opening as required by changes in engine temperature and load.

12 To improve performance and economy 1.0 litre EcoBoost models have a low inertia turbocharger and intercooler fitted.

13 On all models, road speed is monitored by the ABS wheel sensors.

14 The clutch pedal position is monitored by a switch fitted to the pedal bracket. This sends a signal to the Powertrain Control Module.

15 Oxygen sensors in the exhaust system provides the module with constant feedback – 'closed-loop' control – which enables it to adjust the mixture to provide the best possible operating conditions for the catalytic converter. A further sensor is fitted, downstream of the converter, to monitor the converter's operation, and this provides an even finer degree of emission control.

16 The air inlet side of the system consists of an air cleaner housing, an inlet hose, a throttle housing and on EcoBoost models a turbocharger.

17 Both the idle speed and mixture are under the control of the Powertrain Control Module, and cannot be adjusted.

Precautions

 Warning: Many of the procedures in this Chapter require the removal of fuel lines and connections, which may result in

some fuel spillage. Before carrying out any operation on the fuel system, refer to the precautions given in ' Safety first !' at the beginning of this manual, and follow them implicitly. Petrol is a highly-dangerous and volatile liquid, and the precautions necessary when handling it cannot be overstressed.

Residual pressure will remain in the fuel lines long after the car was last used. When disconnecting any fuel line, first depressurise the fuel system as described in Section 2.

Before disconnecting any of the fuel injection system sensor wiring plugs, ensure at least that the ignition is switched off (ideally, disconnect the battery). If this is not done, it could result in a fault code being logged in the system memory, and may even cause damage to the component concerned.

2 Fuel system – depressurisation

 Warning: The following procedure will merely relieve the pressure in the fuel system – remember that fuel will still be present in the system components, and take precautions accordingly before disconnecting any of them.

Note: *Refer to the warnings in Section 1 before proceeding.*

1 The fuel system referred to in this Chapter is defined as the fuel tank and tank-mounted fuel pump/fuel gauge sender unit, the fuel injectors, fuel pressure regulator, and the metal pipes and flexible hoses of the fuel lines between these components. All these contain fuel, which will be under pressure while the engine is running and/or while the ignition is switched on.

2 The pressure will remain for some time after the ignition has been switched off, and must be relieved before any of these components is disturbed for servicing work.

3 The simplest depressurisation method is to disconnect the fuel pump electrical supply by removing the fuel pump fuse (refer to the wiring diagrams or the label on the engine compartment fusebox for exact location) and starting the engine; allow the engine to idle until it stops through lack of fuel. Turn the engine over once or twice on the starter to ensure that all pressure is released, then switch off the ignition; do not forget to refit the fuse when work is complete.

4 Note that, once the fuel system has been depressurised and drained (even partially), it will take significantly longer to restart the engine – perhaps several seconds of cranking – before the system is refilled and pressure restored.

3 Unleaded petrol – general information and usage

1 All petrol models are designed to run on fuel with a minimum octane rating of 95 (RON). All models have a catalytic converter, and so must be run on unleaded fuel only. Under no circumstances should leaded fuel (UK '4-star' or LRP) be used, as this will damage the converter.

2 Super unleaded petrol (98 or 99 octane) can also be used in all models if wished, though there is no advantage in doing so.

4 Fuel pipes and fittings – general information and disconnection

1 Depressurise the fuel system (Section 2) and disconnect the cable from the negative battery terminal (Chapter 5A Section 4) before proceeding.

2 The fuel supply pipe connects the fuel pump in the fuel tank to the fuel rail on the engine.

3 Whenever you're working under the vehicle, be sure to inspect all fuel and evaporative emission pipes for leaks, kinks, dents and other damage. Always replace a damaged fuel pipe immediately.

4 If you find signs of dirt in the pipes during disassembly, disconnect all pipes and blow them out with compressed air. Inspect the fuel strainer on the fuel pump pick-up unit for damage and deterioration.

Steel tubing

5 It is critical that the fuel pipes be replaced with pipes of equivalent type and specification.

6 Some steel fuel pipes have threaded fittings. When loosening these fittings, hold the stationary fitting with a spanner while turning the union nut.

Plastic tubing

 Warning: When removing or installing plastic fuel tubing, be careful not to bend or twist it too much, which can damage it. Also, plastic fuel tubing is NOT heat resistant, so keep it away from excessive heat.

7 When replacing fuel system plastic tubing, use only original equipment replacement plastic tubing.

Flexible hoses

8 When replacing fuel system flexible hoses, use original equipment replacements, or hose to the same specification.

9 Don't route fuel hoses (or metal pipes) within 100 mm of the exhaust system or within 280 mm of the catalytic converter. Make sure that no rubber hoses are installed directly against the vehicle, particularly in places where there is any vibration. If allowed to touch some vibrating part of the vehicle, a hose can easily become chafed and it might start leaking. A good rule of thumb is to maintain a minimum of 8.0 mm clearance around a hose (or metal pipe) to prevent contact with the vehicle underbody.

Disconnecting Fuel pipe Fittings

10 Typical fuel pipe fittings:

4.10a Two-tab type fitting; depress both tabs with your fingers, then pull the fuel pipe and the fitting apart

4.10b On this type of fitting, depress the two buttons on opposite sides of the fitting, then pull it off the fuel pipe

4.10c Threaded fuel pipe fitting; hold the stationary portion of the pipe or component (A) while loosening the union nut (B) with a flare-nut spanner

4.10d Plastic collar-type fitting; rotate the outer part of the fitting

4.10e Metal collar quick-connect fitting; pull the end of the retainer off the fuel pipe and disengage the other end from the female side of the fitting ...

4.10f ... insert a fuel pipe separator tool into the female side of the fitting, push it into the fitting and pull the fuel pipe off the pipe

4.10g Some fittings are secured by lock tabs. Release the lock tab (A) and rotate it to the fully-opened position, squeeze the two smaller lock tabs (B) ...

4.10h ... then push the retainer out and pull the fuel pipe off the pipe

4.10i Spring-lock coupling; remove the safety cover, install a coupling release tool and close the tool around the coupling ...

4.10j ... push the tool into the fitting, then pull the two pipes apart

4.10k Hairpin clip type fitting: push the legs of the retainer clip together, then push the clip down all the way until it stops and pull the fuel pipe off the pipe

5.1 Slacken the outlet duct clamp

5.2 Slide up the red locking clip and disconnect the wiring plug

5.3 Pull the hose collar away from the air cleaner assembly

5.4 Prise the air duct over the retaining tab

5.5 Pull the air cleaner upwards from its' mountings

5 Air cleaner assembly – removal and refitting

Removal

1 Release the clamp securing the outlet duct to the air cleaner housing **(see illustration)**.
2 On 1.0 litre EcoBoost (turbocharged) and 1.6 litre models, disconnect the airflow sensor wiring plug from the housing **(see illustration)**.
3 On 1.25 and 1.6 litre models, pull the collar away from the air cleaner assembly, and disconnect the crankcase ventilation hose **(see illustration)**.
4 On all models, prise up the end of the air inlet duct over the retaining tab, and disconnect it from the front body panel **(see illustration)**.
5 Pull the air cleaner upwards to remove it

(see illustration). The pegs on the base of the cleaner fit into rubber grommets. These pegs may prove troublesome to release, and some effort may be needed. Disconnect the air outlet duct as the air cleaner housing is withdrawn.

Refitting

6 Refitting is a reversal of the removal procedure. Locate the air cleaner pegs into the grommets and push down firmly to engage them in the grommets.

6 Accelerator pedal – removal and refitting

Removal

1 Disconnect the wiring plug from the accelerator pedal position sensor, then unscrew the two mounting nuts and

remove the pedal/sensor assembly from the brake pedal mounting bracket studs **(see illustration)**.

Refitting

2 Refitting is a reversal of the removal procedure.

7 Fuel tank – removal, inspection and refitting

Note: *Refer to the warnings in Section 1 before proceeding.*

Removal

1 Run the fuel level as low as possible prior to removing the tank.
2 Relieve the residual pressure in the fuel system (see Section 2), and equalise tank pressure by removing the fuel filler cap.
3 Disconnect the battery negative lead as described in Chapter. 5A Section 4
4 Chock the front wheels, then jack up the rear of the vehicle, and support it securely on axle stands (see *Jacking and vehicle support*). Remove the rear roadwheels.
5 Unhook the exhaust system mounting rubbers from the rear hangers, and allow the exhaust system to rest on the rear axle.
6 Undo the 5 retaining nuts and remove the exhaust system heat shield from the base of the fuel tank **(see illustration)**.
7 Release the handbrake cables from the underbody retaining clips on the fuel tank **(see illustration)**.

6.1 Accelerator pedal mounting nuts

7.6 Undo the nuts and remove the heat shield

7.7 Unclip the handbrake cables

7.9 Release the clips and disconnect the fuel tank filler and vent pipes

7.12 Fuel tank strap rear retaining bolts

7.15 Slide out the collars, then disconnect the fuel supply and return (diesel models) hoses

8 Release the fuel lines from the four underbody retaining clips nearest to the fuel tank.

9 Release the clips and disconnect the fuel tank filler and vent pipes **(see illustration)**. Do not use any sharp-edged tools to release the pipes from their stubs, as the pipes are easily damaged. Discard the pipe clips and obtain worm-drive hose clips for refitting. Be prepared for fuel spillage and observe all relevant safety precautions.

10 Support the tank using a trolley jack and a large sheet of wood to spread the load.

11 Note exactly how the fuel tank retaining straps are arranged, to make refitting easier. In particular, note their fitted order under the retaining bolt head, at the front fixing.

12 Unbolt and remove the two fuel tank retaining straps **(see illustration)**.

13 Partially lower the tank on the jack, taking care that no strain is placed on any fuel lines or wiring. As soon as the wiring connector for the fuel pump/gauge sender on top of the tank is accessible, reach in and disconnect it.

14 On petrol models, squeeze the quick-release fitting, and disconnect the fuel tank vent pipe from the evaporative emissions charcoal canister at the side of the tank.

15 Disconnect the fuel supply line (and return line on diesel models) from the top of the tank **(see illustration)**.

16 Lower the fuel tank to the ground, checking all the way down that no pipes or wiring are under any strain. Remove the tank from under the car.

17 If required the fuel pump/fuel gauge sender unit can be removed as described in Section 8,

8.3 Alignment marks on the fuel pump/ gauge sender unit and fuel tank

and the charcoal canister can be removed as described in Chapter 4C Section 2.

Inspection

18 Whilst removed, the fuel tank can be inspected for damage or deterioration. Removal of the fuel pump/fuel gauge sender unit (see Section 8) will allow a partial inspection of the interior. If the tank is contaminated with sediment or water, swill it out with clean fuel. Do not under any circumstances undertake any repairs on a leaking or damaged fuel tank; this work must be carried out by a professional who has experience in this critical and potentially-dangerous work.

19 Whilst the fuel tank is removed from the car, it should be placed in a safe area where sparks or open flames cannot ignite the fumes coming out of the tank. Be especially careful inside garages where a natural-gas type appliance is located, because the pilot light could cause an explosion.

Refitting

20 Refitting is a reversal of the removal procedure, noting the following points:
a) Ensure that all pipe and wiring connections are securely fitted.
b) When refitting the quick-release couplings, press them together until the locking lugs snap into their groove.
c) Tighten the tank strap retaining bolts to the specified torque.
d) If evidence of contamination was found, do not return any previously-drained fuel to the tank unless it is carefully filtered first.

| 8 | Fuel pump/fuel gauge sender unit – removal and refitting | |

Note: *Refer to the warnings in Section 1 before proceeding. Ford specify the use of their service tool 310-069 (a large socket with projecting teeth to engage the fuel pump/ sender unit retaining ring's raised edges) for this task. Suitable alternatives to this tool are readily available from accessory stores and motor factor outlets.*

Removal

1 A combined fuel pump and fuel gauge sender unit is located in the top face of the fuel tank. The combined unit can only be detached and withdrawn from the tank after the tank is released and lowered from under the car. Refer to Section 7 and remove the fuel tank, then proceed as follows.

2 Unscrew and remove the special retaining ring, by unscrewing it with the Ford tool (No. 310-069) or a suitable alternative.

3 Check that alignment marks are visible on the fuel pump/gauge sender unit and fuel tank. There should be an arrow on the sender unit aligned with raised projections on the tank **(see illustration)**. If no marks are visible, suitably mark the tank and sender unit with paint.

4 Carefully lift out the fuel pump/gauge sender unit from the tank. Take care that the sender unit float and arm are not damaged as the unit is removed.

5 Lift out the rubber seal from the tank aperture, and obtain a new seal for refitting.

6 If required, the fuel gauge sender unit can be removed from the pump by disconnecting the wiring connector, releasing the retaining catch and withdrawing the unit from the side of the pump.

Refitting

7 Refitting is a reversal of removal, but fit a new rubber seal and tighten the retaining ring securely. Refit the fuel tank as described in Section.

| 9 | Fuel tank filler neck – removal and refitting |

Note: *Refer to the warnings in Section 1 before proceeding.*

Removal

1 Chock the front wheels, then jack up the rear of the vehicle, and support it securely on axle stands (see *Jacking and vehicle support*). Remove the left-hand rear wheel.

2 Remove the left-hand rear wheel arch liner, which is secured by a combination of screws and push-in clips.

9.3 Undo the bolt securing the filler neck and vent pipe support bracket to the wheel arch

9.5 Undo the bolt securing the filler pipe lower support bracket

10.2 Open the storage compartment in the facia to access the 16-pin diagnostic plug

3 Remove the single bolt securing the filler neck and vent pipe support bracket to the wheel arch (see illustration).

4 Release the clips and disconnect the fuel tank filler and vent pipes (see illustration 7.9). Do not use any sharp-edged tools to release the pipes from their stubs, as the pipes are easily damaged. Discard the pipe clips and obtain worm-drive hose clips for refitting. Be prepared for fuel spillage and observe all relevant safety precautions.

5 Unscrew the single bolt securing the pipe lower support bracket (see illustration), and remove the filler neck from under the car.

6 Check the condition of the filler neck and vent pipe, and renew if necessary.

Refitting

7 Refitting is a reversal of removal.

10 Fuel injection system – checking

Note: *Refer to the warnings in Section 1 before proceeding.*

1 If a fault appears in the fuel injection system, first ensure that all the system wiring connectors are securely connected and free of corrosion – also refer to paragraphs 5 to 8 below. Then ensure that the fault is not due to poor maintenance; ie, check that the air cleaner filter element is clean, the spark plugs are in good condition and correctly gapped, the cylinder compression pressures are correct,

the ignition system wiring is in good condition and securely connected, and the engine breather hoses are clear and undamaged.

2 If these checks fail to reveal the cause of the problem, the car should be taken to a suitably-equipped Ford dealer or specialist for testing. A diagnostic connector is fitted into the facia on the driver's side into which dedicated electronic test equipment can be plugged (see illustration). The test equipment is capable of 'interrogating' the engine management system powertrain control module (PCM) electronically and accessing its internal fault log (reading fault codes).

3 Fault codes can only be extracted from the PCM using a dedicated fault code reader. A Ford dealer will obviously have such a reader, but they are also available from other suppliers. It is unlikely to be cost-effective for the private owner to purchase a fault code reader, but a well-equipped local garage or auto-electrical specialist will have one.

4 Using this equipment, faults can be pinpointed quickly and simply, even if their occurrence is intermittent. Testing all the system components individually in an attempt to locate the fault by elimination is a time-consuming operation that is unlikely to be fruitful (particularly if the fault occurs dynamically), and carries a high risk of damage to the PCM's internal components.

Limited Operation Strategy

5 Certain faults, such as failure of one of the engine management system sensors, will cause the system to revert to a backup (or

'limp-home') mode, referred to by Ford as 'Limited Operation Strategy' (LOS). This is intended to be a 'get-you-home' facility only – the engine management warning light will come on when this mode is in operation.

6 In this mode, the signal from the defective sensor is substituted with a fixed value (it would normally vary), which may lead to loss of power, poor idling, and generally-poor running, especially when the engine is cold.

7 However, the engine may in fact run quite well in this situation, and the only clue (other than the warning light) would be that the exhaust CO emissions (for example) will be higher than they should be.

8 Bear in mind that, even if the defective sensor is correctly identified and renewed, the engine will not return to normal running until the fault code is erased, taking the system out of LOS. This also applies even if the cause of the fault was a loose connection or damaged piece of wire – until the fault code is erased, the system will continue in LOS.

11 Fuel injection system components – removal and refitting

Note: *Refer to the warnings in Section 1 before proceeding.*

Throttle housing

1 Unscrew the oil filler cap (where applicable), then pull up and remove the plastic cover on the top of the engine.

All except 1.0 litre EcoBoost engines

2 Release the retaining clips and disconnect the air inlet duct from the air cleaner and throttle housing (see illustration). Where applicable, disconnect the breather hose from the duct.

3 Undo the four mounting bolts, then disconnect the throttle control motor wiring plug, and remove the throttle housing (see illustration). Recover the seal – a new one should be used when refitting.

4 Do not attempt to clean the inside of the throttle housing. The inner surfaces are specially coated during manufacture, and this coating should not be removed.

11.2 Release the clamp securing the air duct to the throttle housing

11.3 Throttle housing mounting bolts

11.6 Slide out the clip, disconnect the breather hose, then disconnect the MAPT sensor wiring plug

11.7a Release the clamp securing the hose to the intercooler…

11.7b … and the clamp at the throttle housing end…

11.7c … then undo the retaining bolt and remove the charge air duct

11.8a Slide out the locking clip and disconnect the wiring plug

11.8b Throttle housing retaining bolts

5 Refitting is a reversal of removal. Use a new seal, and tighten the mounting bolts securely, to prevent air leaks. On completion, switch on the ignition to position II, without touching any of the pedals and leave it switched on for one minute to initialise the throttle housing.

11.11a Slacken and then…

11.11b …remove the high pressure pipe

11.12 Disconnect the wiring plug from the fuel rail pressure sensor

11.13 Remove the fuel rail bolts

1.0 litre EcoBoost engines

6 Disconnect the MAPT sensor wiring plug, and the breather hose from the charge air duct between the intercooler and throttle housing **(see illustration)**.
7 Release the clamp at each end, undo the retaining bolt and remove the charge air duct **(see illustrations)**.
8 Disconnect the wiring plug, undo the 3 retaining bolts and remove the throttle housing **(see illustrations)**. Renew the seal.
9 Refitting is a reversal of removal. On completion, switch on the ignition to position II, without touching any of the pedals and leave it switched on for one minute to initialise the throttle housing.

Fuel rail and injectors

1.0 litre engines

10 Remove the ignition coils as described in Chapter 5B Section 3.
11 Place an absorbent cloth beneath the fuel pipe and disconnect the pipe at the fuel rail and the fuel pump **(see illustrations)**. Dispose of the pipe – it must be replaced.
12 Disconnect the wiring plug from the fuel rail pressure sensor **(see illustration)**.
13 Remove the 2 bolts from the fuel rail **(see illustration)** – the injectors will stay in place. If the injectors start to come out with the rail, ease them back into the cylinder head. Seal the injectors with suitable blanking plugs.
14 Disconnect the wiring loom from the injectors. This can either be done at the

11.15 Remove the injectors

11.16a Cut off the old seal

11.16b Renew the clip at the top of the injector

injector, or at the multi-plug at the rear of the valve cover.

15 Pull up the injectors to remove them **(see illustration)**. Ford list a set of special tools (205-047, 205-047-08 and 310-206) to aid removal of the injectors. These tools are a small slide hammer and an adapter that locks over the injector. We removed then using a small pry bar (to lever the injector out) and a block of wood to act as a fulcrum for the pry bar. The block of wood also helps to spread the load over the valve cover.

16 With the injectors on the bench cut off the seal with a sharp knife **(see illustration)**. The seals must always be replaced if the injectors are removed, along with the push-on clip at the top of the injector **(see illustration)**.

17 Ford special tool 310-128 (or equivalent)

will be required to fit the new seal **(see illustrations)**. Fit the new seal to the taper and holding the taper against the injector use the other half of the tool to push the seal up the taper and on to the injector. Push the seal into the groove and then use the special tool to settle the seal into position.

18 Replace the upper seals and fit a new spring clip. Fit the injectors to the fuel rail ensuring that the cut out in the rail aligns with the electrical connector **(see illustrations)**.

19 Check that the injector holes in the cylinder head are clean and free of debris before refitting the fuel rail and injectors.

20 Align the injectors with the holes in the cylinder head **(see illustration)** and push down evenly on the fuel rail. Tighten the fuel rail bolts to the specified torque.

21 Fit a new high pressure pipe to the fuel rail and tighten it to the specified torque **(see illustration)**.

22 Refit the remainder of the components in reverse order to removal. Start the engine and check carefully for fuel leaks.

1.25 and 1.6 litre engines

23 Relieve the residual pressure in the fuel system (see Section 2), and equalise tank pressure by removing the fuel filler cap.

⚠ *Warning: This procedure will merely relieve the increased pressure necessary for the engine to run – remember that fuel will still be present in the system components, and take precautions accordingly before disconnecting any of them.*

11.17a The special tool needed to fit the new seals

11.17b Slide the seal into position with a rotary motion

11.18a The washer must be fitted with the narrow side towards the injector

11.18b Fit the refurbished injectors to the fuel rail

11.20 Fit the fuel rail to the cylinder head

11.21 A crows foot wrench will be required to tighten the fuel pipe

11.25 Prise out the locking catch then depress the release button

11.26a Push the locking clips forwards...

11.26b ... and gently pull the connector assembly from the injectors

24 Disconnect the crankcase breather hose from the cylinder head cover.

25 Unclip the fuel supply pipe from the support bracket, then prise out the locking catch, depress the release button and disconnect the pipe from the fuel rail **(see illustration)**.

26 Depress the wire locking clips and pull the wiring connectors assembly up from the injectors **(see illustrations)**. If necessary, on 1.6 litre engines, disconnect the wiring plug from the camshaft position sensor to allow the harness assembly to be moved to one side.

27 Release the coolant hose and, where applicable, the fuel supply hose from the clips on the fuel rail.

28 Unscrew and remove the two fuel rail mounting bolts. Carefully pull the fuel rail upwards to release the injectors from place – there will be some resistance from the injector O-ring seals **(see illustrations)**.

29 Remove the retaining clips and carefully pull the injectors from the fuel rail **(see illustrations)**.

30 Using a screwdriver, prise the O-rings from the grooves at each end of the injectors **(see illustration)**. Discard the O-rings and obtain new ones.

31 If required, the fuel pulse damper can be removed after the retaining clip has been removed **(see illustration)**. When refitting the damper, lubricate the new O-ring seals with clean engine oil.

32 Refitting is the reverse of the removal procedure, noting the following points:
a) *Fit new injector O-rings, and lubricate them with clean engine oil to aid refitting.*
b) *Tighten the fuel rail mounting bolts to the specified torque.*
c) *Ensure that the hoses and wiring are routed correctly, and secured on reconnection by any clips or ties provided.*
d) *On completion, switch the ignition on to activate the fuel pump and pressurise the system, without cranking the engine. Check for signs of fuel leaks around all disturbed unions and joints before attempting to start the engine.*

11.28a Undo the fuel rail mounting bolts...

11.28b ... and pull the fuel upwards from place

11.29a Release the retaining clips from the rail ...

11.29b ... and pull the injector from the rail

11.30 Renew the injector O-rings seals

11.31 Prise out the clip and remove the fuel pulse damper

11.33a MAPT sensor location on the inlet manifold – 1.25 litre engines

11.33b MAPT sensor on the charge air pipe – 1.0 litre Ecoboost engines

11.37 Slide up the red locking catch and disconnect the sensor wiring plug

MAPT sensor

33 The MAPT (Manifold Absolute Pressure and Temperature) sensor is only fitted to 1.0 and 1.25 litre engines **(see illustrations)**.

34 With the ignition switched off, disconnect the sensor wiring plug, then undo the mounting bolt and withdraw it from the manifold. Check the condition of the sensor O-ring seal, and obtain a new one if necessary.

35 Refitting is a reversal of removal. Use a new seal if necessary, and tighten the mounting bolt securely, to prevent air leaks.

Airflow sensor

36 The airflow sensor is only fitted to 1.0 and 1.6 litre engines and is located in the air cleaner cover.

37 Disconnect the wiring plug from the airflow sensor **(see illustration)**.

38 Undo the two bolts and pull the sensor from the air cleaner cover.

39 Refitting is a reversal of removal. Note the arrow on the top of the sensor indicating airflow.

Powertrain Control Module (PCM)

Note: *The module is fragile. Take care not to drop it, or subject it to any other kind of impact. Do not subject it to extremes of temperature, or allow it to get wet.*

Note: *If a new PCM is to be fitted, the configuration information stored within the module must be uploaded to Ford diagnostic equipment prior to the module being removed, and downloaded to the new PCM once*

installed. Entrust this task to a Ford dealer or suitably-equipped specialist.

40 Disconnect the battery negative lead as described in Chapter 5A Section 4.

41 Remove the plastic cover from the top of the engine (where fitted).

42 Release the clamps, disconnect the breather tube (where applicable) and remove the air duct above the PCM. The PCM is located on the right-hand side of the battery.

43 On models without a security shield over the PCM, pull out the retaining clip and remove the cover from the PCM **(see illustration)**.

44 On models with a security shield, drill out the two shear-bolts securing the security shield over the PCM upper wiring connector. A 3.5 mm drill bit will be required. With the shear bolts removed, withdraw the shield.

45 Disconnect the wiring plugs from the PCM.

46 Undo the four retaining nuts and remove the PCM from the mounting plate.

47 Refitting is a reversal of removal. Strictly speaking, new shear-bolts should be obtained for refitting, and tightened until the head shears off. However, as this is only a deterrent to 'chipping' the module, an ordinary bolt can be used instead.

Crankshaft position sensor

48 On 1.0 litre engines, the sensor is located adjacent to the crankshaft pulley at the right-hand end of the engine. For improved access, apply the handbrake, then jack up the front of the vehicle and support it securely on axle stands (see *Jacking and vehicle support*).

Where applicable, undo the 2 screws and remove the lower cover from the wheelarch aperture **(see illustration)**.

49 On 1.25 and 1.6 litre engines, the sensor is located on the front left-hand side of the engine, close to the transmission. For improved access, apply the handbrake, then jack up the front of the car and support it on axle stands (see *Jacking and vehicle support*).

50 With the ignition switched off, disconnect the wiring plug, then unscrew the mounting bolt and withdraw the sensor **(see illustrations)**.

51 Refitting is a reversal of removal. Ensure

11.43 Remove the retaining clip followed by the PCM cover

11.48 Undo the screws and remove the lower cover

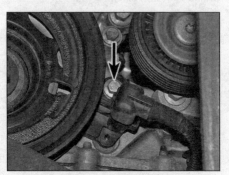

11.50a Crankshaft position sensor – 1.0 litre engines

11.50b Crankshaft position sensor – 1.25 and 1.6 litre engines

11.54a Camshaft position sensors wiring plugs – 1.0 litre engines

11.54b Disconnect the wiring from the camshaft position sensor – 1.25 litre engines

11.54c Disconnect the wiring from the camshaft position sensors – 1.6 litre engines

11.62 Disconnect the VCT solenoids wiring plugs

11.63 Undo the bolts and remove the solenoids

that the sensor is clean when refitting, and tighten the bolt securely.

Camshaft position sensor(s)

52 On 1.25 litre engines, one sensor is fitted, located on the right-hand rear of the cylinder head. On 1.0 and 1.6 litre engines, there are two sensors fitted – one over each of the camshafts at the end of the cylinder head cover.
53 Remove the plastic cover from the top of the engine (where fitted).
54 With the ignition switched off, disconnect the wiring from the camshaft position sensor(s) **(see illustrations)**.
55 Unscrew the mounting bolt(s) and withdraw the sensor(s) from the cylinder head or cylinder head cover (as applicable).
56 Refitting is a reversal of removal, but use a new seal. Smear a little engine oil on the seal before fitting the sensor, and tighten the bolt(s) securely.

Coolant temperature sensor

57 Refer to Chapter 3 Section 6.

Clutch pedal position switch

58 Removal and refitting of the clutch pedal switch(es) is described in Chapter 12 Section 4.

Variable camshaft timing oil control solenoids

Note: *The solenoids are only fitted to 1.0 and 1.6 litre engines.*

1.0 litre engines

59 Disconnect the battery negative lead as described in Chapter 5A Section 4.
60 Unscrew the oil filler cap and pull the plastic cover on the top of the engine upwards from its' mountings.
61 On EcoBoost (turbocharged) models, disconnect the breather pipes, undo the retaining nuts, slacken the clamps and

remove the air intake duct between the air cleaner housing and the turbocharger **(see illustration 11.7a to 11.7c)**.
62 Disconnect the oil control solenoids wiring plugs, and unclip the wiring harness from the right-hand end of the cylinder head cover **(see illustration)**.
63 Undo the 6 retaining bolts (3 per solenoid) and pull the solenoids from place **(see illustration)**. Renew the O-ring seals.

1.6 litre models

64 Disconnect the solenoid wiring plug, then undo the retaining bolt and pull the solenoid from place **(see illustrations)**.

All models

65 Refitting is a reversal of removal. Ensure the solenoid and aperture are scrupulously clean prior to refitting. Apply a little clean engine oil to the solenoid O-rings. Tighten bolt to the specified torque.

MAP sensor

Note: *1.0 litre EcoBoost (turbocharged) models only.*
66 Remove the plastic cover from the top of the engine (where fitted).
67 Release the clamps, disconnect the breather pipe, undo the 2 retaining nuts and remove the centre section of the air intake duct above the intake manifold **(see illustration 11.7a to 11.7c)**.
68 The sensor is located on the top of the inlet manifold. Disconnect the wiring plug, undo the retaining bolt and pull the sensor from place **(see illustration)**.

11.64a Camshaft timing oil control solenoids

11.64b Undo the bolt and pull the solenoid from place

11.68 Manifold Absolute Pressure (MAP) sensor retaining bolt

69 Refitting is a reversal of removal.

Oxygen sensor

70 Refer to Chapter 4C Section 2.

Knock sensor

71 Refer to Chapter 5B Section 6.

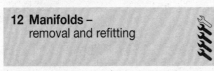

12 Manifolds –
removal and refitting

Note: *Refer to the warnings in Section 1 before proceeding.*

Inlet manifold

1 Depressurise the fuel system as described in Section 2.
2 Disconnect the battery negative lead as described in Chapter 5A Section 4.

1.0 litre EcoBoost engines

3 Slacken the hose clamps and remove the air ducts from the top of the engine (from the air filter to the turbocharger) and then remove the inlet air duct from the throttle body – as described for throttle body in Section 11 of this Chapter.
4 Trace the pipe work and remove the EVAP pipe work from the valve cover **(see illustration)**. Release the vacuum pipes from the control solenoid at the rear of the inlet manifold.
5 Disconnect the breather pipes from the inlet manifold **(see illustration)** and then unclip the coolant hoses. Disconnect the wiring plug from the MAP sensor.
6 Unclip the wiring harness from the right-hand end of the cylinder head cover.
7 Raise the front of the vehicle and support it securely on axle stands (see *Jacking and vehicle support*). Undo the fasteners and remove the engine undershield.
8 Workng underneath the vehicle, note their fitted positions, then disconnect all necessary hoses/wiring from the manifold. On models manufactured before 09/2011, undo the 3 nuts and move the EVAP purge valve and mounting bracket to one side.
9 Remove the support bracket from the right-hand end of the manifold and then remove the main manifold bolts in the reverse order to that shown **(see illustration 12.11)**.
10 Remove the seals and inspect the manifold for cracks or damage.
11 Fit new seals and then tighten the manifold bolts in the order shown **(see illustration)** to the specified torque.

1.25 and 1.6 litre engines

12 Remove the alternator as described in Chapter 5A Section 7.
13 Remove the throttle housing as described in Section 11.
14 Disconnect the breather hose from the cylinder head cover, and unclip it from the inlet manifold.
15 Undo the bolt securing the vacuum

12.4 Release the EVAP solenoid and pipe work from the valve cover

12.11 Tighten the manifold bolts in the order shown

hose and purge valve support bracket to the manifold, and disconnect the hoses from the manifold **(see illustration)**.
16 Remove the fuel rail and injectors as described in Section 11.
17 Where applicable, disconnect the wiring plug from the MAPT sensor on top of the manifold.
18 Undo the bolt securing the engine oil level dipstick guide tube to the manifold.
19 Note their fitted locations and disconnect any remaining vacuum hoses/pipes/wiring harnesses attached to the manifold.
20 Undo the seven retaining bolts and remove the manifold. Renew the manifold-to-cylinder head seals/gasket **(see illustration)**.
21 Refitting is a reversal of removal, noting the following points:
a) *Ensure that the mating faces are clean, and use new manifold gaskets if necessary.*

12.20 Renew the manifold-to-cylinder head seals

12.5 Squeeze together the sides of the collar and disconnect the breather pipe

12.15 Undo the bolt securing the support bracket to the manifold

b) *Tighten the manifold retaining bolts in sequence (see illustration).*
c) *Tighten all fixings to the specified torque.*
d) *On completion, switch the ignition on to activate the fuel pump and pressurise the system, without cranking the engine. Check for signs of fuel leaks around all disturbed unions and joints before attempting to start the engine.*

Exhaust manifold

1.0 litre models

22 On theses engines the exhaust manifold is integrated into the cylinder head. If a fault develops then the cylinder head will have to be removed and replaced.

12.21 Inlet manifold bolts tightening sequence

1.25 and 1.6 litre models

23 Disconnect the battery negative lead as described in Chapter 5A Section 4.

24 Disconnect the oxygen sensor at the wiring connector behind the ignition coil.

25 Undo the four bolts and remove the exhaust manifold upper heat shield.

26 Undo the bolt and four nuts securing the exhaust manifold to the cylinder head.

27 Firmly apply the handbrake, then jack up the front of the vehicle and support it securely on axle stands (see *Jacking and vehicle support*).

28 To prevent damage to the exhaust flexible section, support it by attaching a pair of splints either side (two scrap strips of wood, plant canes, etc) using some cable-ties.

29 Unscrew the two nuts securing the exhaust flexible section to the catalytic converter. Unhook the rubber mounting block and separate the joint. Recover the gasket.

30 Disconnect the catalyst monitor sensor at the wiring connector on the transmission.

31 Undo the four bolts and remove the catalytic converter lower support bracket.

32 Slide the manifold off the cylinder head studs and lower it down to remove it. Take care not to damage the sensors or their wiring. Recover the gasket and discard it

All models

33 Refitting is a reversal of removal, noting the following points:

a) Ensure that the mating faces are clean, and use a new manifold gasket.

b) Tighten all fixings to the specified torque.

13.7 Unscrew the upper oxygen sensor

13 Exhaust system – general information, removal and refitting

Caution: Any work on the exhaust system should only be attempted once the system is completely cool – this may take several hours, especially in the case of the forward sections, such as the manifold and catalytic converter.

General information

1 On 1.0 litre models, the exhaust system consists of a catalytic converter incorporating the front exhaust pipe with a flexible section to allow for engine movement.

2 On 1.25 and 1.6 litre models, the exhaust system consists of the exhaust manifold with integral catalytic converter, and the centre section incorporating the silencer. On 1.6 litre engine models, the centre section incorporates an additional silencer at the front. A flexible ('mesh') section is fitted to allow for engine movement.

3 When fitted in the factory, the exhaust system from the centre section flange joint to the end of the tail pipe is one piece. However, if the rear silencer is to be renewed, new silencers should be available – check with your parts supplier. It will be necessary to cut through the centre section using a hacksaw if a new rear silencer is to be fitted.

4 The system is suspended throughout its entire length by rubber mountings.

Removal

5 To remove a part of the system, first jack up the front or rear of the car, and support it on axle stands (see *Jacking and vehicle support*). Alternatively, position the car over an inspection pit, or on car ramps.

Catalytic converter

1.0 litre EcoBoost models

6 Release the clamps and remove the air outlet pipe from the air cleaner assembly.

7 Disconnect the wiring plug, then using a special 'split' socket, unscrew the upper oxygen sensor from the catalytic converter

(see illustration), Unclip the wiring harness.

8 Disconnect the lower oxygen sensor wiring plug and unclip the harness.

9 Disconnect the wiring plug, undo the mounting bolt and move the electric coolant pump (fitted on the cooling fan shroud) to one side. There's no need to disconnect the hoses.

10 Remove the auxiliary drivebelt as described in Chapter 1A Section 26.

11 Disconnect the wiring plug, undo the 3 mounting bolts and move the air conditioning compressor (where fitted) to one side. Secure it to the vehicle body using cable ties etc. There's no need to disconnect the refrigerant pipes.

12 Undo the 6 bolts and remove the heatshield over the catalytic converter (see illustration).

13 Undo the 3 bolts, and 1 nut securing the catalytic converter to the turbocharger (see illustration).Discard the bolts/nut – new ones must be fitted.

14 Remove the bolt(s) securing the catalytic converter to the cylinder block.

15 Undo the 2 nuts securing the exhaust pipe bracket to the sump (see illustration).

16 To prevent damage to the exhaust flexible section, support it by attaching a pair of splints either side (two scrap strips of wood, plant canes, etc) using some cable-ties.

17 Undo the 2 nuts securing the exhaust centre section to the front section, then manoeuvre the catalytic converter, with the front section, from place.

1.25 and 1.6 litre models

18 Refer to Section 12.

Centre section

19 To prevent damage to the exhaust flexible section, support it by attaching a pair of splints either side (two scrap strips of wood, plant canes, etc) using some cable-ties. If a new centre section is being fitted, this precaution only applies to the new section of exhaust.

20 From under the car, undo the nuts and remove the underfloor cross-brace beneath the exhaust centre section.

13.12 Remove the heatshield over the catalytic converter/turbocharger

13.13 Catalytic converter-to-turbocharger bolts/nut

13.15 Sump-to-exhaust pipe bracket nuts

21 Unscrew the nuts securing the centre section to the catalytic converter, and separate the joint. Recover the gasket (see illustration).

22 Unhook the centre section's rubber mountings, and remove it from under the car (see illustration).

Rear silencer

23 If the original one-piece exhaust system is still fitted, it will be necessary to cut off the old rear silencer to enable fitment of the new unit. Using the new rear silencer as a pattern, mark the exhaust centre section to determine the cut point. Ensure that the cut point will allow a sufficient length of centre section to fit into the new rear silencer.

24 Using a hacksaw, cut through the centre section at the marked cut point. Unhook the rear silencer's rubber mountings, and remove it from under the car.

25 If a replacement rear silencer has already been fitted, unbolt the clamp securing the silencer to the centre section, and separate the pipes. Usually, this will require some effort – the most successful method involves twisting the silencer from side to side, to break the joint. Unfortunately, if the pipe at the rear of the centre section has suffered from corrosion, it's very likely that the centre section will be damaged beyond repair in removing the silencer. A less-destructive method of removal involves heating the two pipes, but this carries the risk of damaging the underbody components, and even a risk of fire from the fuel tank and lines.

26 Unhook the silencer rubber mountings, and remove it from under the car.

13.21 Separate the centre section from the catalytic converter, and recover the gasket

Heat shields

27 The heat shields are secured to the underside of the body by special nuts. Each shield can be removed separately, but note that they may overlap, making it necessary to loosen another section first. If a shield is being removed to gain access to a component located behind it, it may prove sufficient in some cases to remove the retaining nuts and/or bolts, and simply lower the shield, without disturbing the exhaust system. Otherwise, remove the exhaust section as described earlier.

Refitting

28 In all cases, refitting is a reversal of removal, but note the following points:

a) *Always use new gaskets, nuts and clamps (as applicable), and coat all threads with copper grease. Make sure any new clamps*

13.22 Unhook the rubber mountings and remove the centre section

are the same size as the original – over-tightening a clamp which is too big will not seal the joint.

b) *On a sleeved joint (such as that between the centre section and rear silencer), use a smear of exhaust jointing paste to achieve a gas-tight seal.*

c) *If any of the exhaust mounting rubbers are in poor condition, fit new ones.*

d) *Make sure that the exhaust is suspended properly on its mountings, and will not come into contact with the floor or any suspension parts. The rear silencer especially must be aligned correctly before tightening the clamp nuts.*

e) *Tighten all nuts/bolts to the specified torque, where given.*

14 Intercooler – removal and refitting

Note: *1.0 litre EcoBoost engines only.*

Removal

1 The intercooler is located to the right-hand side of the radiator, at the front of the engine compartment. Slacken the clamp and disconnect the air hose from the top of the intercooler (see illustration).

2 Slacken the clamps, undo the retaining nut, disconnect the breather hoses, and remove the air intake duct from the turbocharger (see illustrations).

14.1 Release the clamp and disconnect the top hose from the intercooler

14.2a Slacken the clamp securing the duct to the turbocharger

14.2b Squeeze together the sides of the collar and disconnect the breather hose

14.2c Slide out the clip and disconnect the breather hose

14.2d Undo the retaining nut and move the air intake duct to one side

14.5a Use 2 screwdrivers…

14.5b … to squeeze together the side of the clip…

14.5c … then pull the top of the intercooler rearwards, and lift it from place

3 Undo the 2 nuts securing the outlet duct to the turbocharger, then release the clamp, undo the retaining bolt(s) and remove the duct **(see illustration 15.6a, 15.6b and 15.6c)**.
4 Unclip the coolant hose adjacent to the intercooler.
5 Squeeze together the clip each side, then pull the top of the intercooler rearwards, and lift it from place **(see illustrations)**.

Refitting

6 Refitting is a reversal of removal.

15 Turbocharger – removal and refitting

Note: *1.0 litre EcoBoost models only.*

Removal

1 Disconnect the battery negative lead as described in Chapter 5A Section 4.
2 Drain the cooling system as described in Chapter 1A Section 30.

3 Remove the catalytic converter as described in Section 13.
4 Release the hose clamps and disconnect the turbocharger air inlet duct.
5 Release the spring clips and remove the coolant supply and return hoses **(see illustration)**.
6 Slacken the hose clamp and then remove the turbocharger air outlet pipe to the intercooler. Alternatively unbolt the pipe from the turbocharger **(see illustrations)**.

15.5 Remove the coolant hoses

15.6a Unbolt the outlet pipe…

15.6b … undo the retaining bolt…

15.6c …and remove it

15.8 Remove the 'banjo' bolt from the oil feed pipe

15.9 Remove the vacuum hose

15.10a Remove the main mounting nuts

15.10b Remove the turbocharger

15.11 Remove the combined heat shield
and gasket mounting bolt

7 From below the turbocharger remove the 2 bolts and release the oil drain pipe.

8 Unbolt and remove the oil supply pipe **(see illustration)**. Dispose of the pipe – a new one must be fitted.

9 Compress the spring clamp and remove the vacuum hoses from the diverter valve and waste gate **(see illustration)**.

10 Remove the 4 main mounting bolts, check that all components have been disconnected and then remove the turbocharger **(see illustrations)**. Discard the nuts – new ones must be fitted.

11 Unbolt and recover the combined heat shield and cylinder head to turbocharger gasket **(see illustration)**. Dispose of the gasket, a new one must be fitted.

Refitting

12 Refitting is a reversal of removal. Tighten the new main turbocharger to cylinder head nuts in a diagonal sequence to the specified torque. Refill the cooling system, check the oil level and then restart the engine, checking for coolant and oil leaks.

Chapter 4 Part B
Fuel and exhaust systems – diesel models

Contents

Degrees of difficulty

Easy, suitable for novice with little experience | **Fairly easy,** suitable for beginner with some experience | **Fairly difficult,** suitable for competent DIY mechanic | **Difficult,** suitable for experienced DIY mechanic | **Very difficult,** suitable for expert DIY or professional

Specifications

General

System type . . . . TDCi (Turbo-Diesel Common-rail injection) with full electronic control, direct injection, turbocharger and intercooler
Firing order . . . . 1-3-4-2 (No 1 at flywheel end)
Fuel system operating pressure . . . . 200 to 1350 bars (according to engine speed)
Idle speed . . . . Controlled by PCM
Engine cut-off speed . . . . 5000 rpm (controlled by PCM)

High-pressure fuel pump

Type . . . . Bosch
Direction of rotation . . . . Clockwise, viewed from sprocket end

Injectors

Type . . . . Electromagnetic

Turbocharger

Type . . . . KKK
Boost pressure (approximate) . . . . 1 bar at 3000 rpm

Torque wrench settings

	Nm	lbf ft
Accumulator rail mounting bolts/nuts	20	15
Accumulator rail/injector fuel pipe unions: *		
Stage 1	20	15
Stage 2	25	18
Camshaft position sensor bolt	5	4
Catalytic converter lower mounting bolts	25	18
Catalytic converter-to-turbocharger clamp bolt nut	15	11
Diesel particulate filter (DPF) temperature sensor	15	11
Exhaust centre section flange joint	48	35
Exhaust gas temperature sensor	15	11
Exhaust manifold nuts	25	18
Fuel injector:		
Stage 1	7	5
Stage 2	Angle-tighten a further 85°	
Heated oxygen sensor	48	35
High-pressure fuel pump:		
Front mounting bolts	20	15
Rear mounting bolts:		
M6	8	6
M8	20	15
Turbocharger mounting bolts/nuts†	25	18
Turbocharger oil feed pipe banjo bolts	30	22

*These torque settings are using special crow's-foot adapter – see Section 11
† Do not re-use

1 General information and system operation

1 The fuel system consists of a rear-mounted fuel tank, a fuel filter with integral water separator and fuel heater (to avoid fuel waxing in cold conditions), and an electronically-controlled high-pressure diesel injection system, together with a turbocharger and intercooler.

2 The exhaust system is conventional, but to meet the latest emission levels, all models are fitted with a diesel particulate filter and catalytic converter.

3 The high-pressure diesel injection system (generally known as a 'common-rail' system) derives its name from the fact that a common-rail (referred to as an accumulator rail), or fuel reservoir, is used to supply fuel to all the fuel injectors. Instead of an in-line or distributor type injection pump, which distributes the fuel directly to each injector, a high-pressure pump is used, which generates a very high fuel pressure (1500 bars at high engine speed) in the accumulator rail. The accumulator rail stores fuel, and maintains a constant fuel pressure with the aid of a pressure control valve. Each injector is supplied with high-pressure fuel from the accumulator rail, and the injectors are individually controlled via signals from the system electronic control unit (Powertrain Control Module, or PCM). The injectors are electromagnetically-operated.

4 In addition to the various sensors used on previous diesel engines with a conventional fuel injection pump, common-rail systems also have a fuel pressure sensor. The fuel pressure sensor allows the PCM to maintain the required fuel pressure, via the pressure control valve.

System operation

5 For the purposes of describing the operation of a common-rail injection system, the components can be divided into three sub-systems; the low-pressure fuel system, the high-pressure fuel system, and the electronic control system.

Low-pressure fuel system

6 The low-pressure fuel system consists of the following components:
a) Fuel tank.
b) Fuel transfer pump.
c) Fuel filter/water trap/heater.
d) Low-pressure fuel lines.

7 The low-pressure system (fuel supply system) is responsible for supplying clean fuel to the high-pressure fuel system.

High-pressure fuel system

8 The high-pressure fuel system consists of the following components:
a) High-pressure fuel pump with pressure control valve.
b) High-pressure fuel accumulator rail.
c) Fuel injectors.
d) High-pressure fuel lines.

9 Fuel is drawn from the fuel tank, through the fuel filter, by means of a fuel transfer pump incorporated into the high-pressure pump. After passing through the transfer pump, the fuel is supplied through internal passages to the high-pressure pump, which forces it into the accumulator rail. As diesel fuel has a certain elasticity, the pressure in the accumulator rail remains constant, even though fuel leaves the rail each time one of the injectors operates. Additionally, a pressure control valve mounted on the high-pressure pump ensures that the fuel pressure is maintained within preset limits.

10 The pressure control valve is operated by the PCM. When the valve is opened, fuel is returned from the high-pressure pump to the tank, via the fuel return lines, and the pressure in the accumulator rail falls. To enable the PCM to trigger the pressure control valve correctly, the pressure in the accumulator rail is measured by a fuel pressure sensor.

11 The electromagnetically-controlled fuel injectors are operated individually, via signals from the PCM, and each injector injects fuel directly into the relevant combustion chamber. The fact that high fuel pressure is always available allows very precise and highly flexible injection in comparison to a conventional injection pump: for example combustion during the main injection process can be improved considerably by the pre-injection of a very small quantity of fuel.

Electronic control system

12 The electronic control system consists of the following components:
a) Electronic control unit (PCM).
b) Crankshaft speed/position sensor.
c) Camshaft position sensor.
d) Accelerator pedal position sensor.
e) Coolant temperature sensor.
f) Fuel temperature sensor.
g) Airflow sensor.
h) Fuel pressure sensor.
i) Fuel injectors.
j) Fuel pressure control valve.
k) EGR solenoid valve.
l) ABS wheel speed sensors
m) Intake air shutoff throttle housing

n) *Inlet manifold absolute pressure/ temperautre sensor*
o) *Brake and clutch pedal position switches*
p) *Pre- and post-particulate filter temperature and pressure sensors*
q) *Oxygen sensors*

13 The information from the various sensors is passed to the PCM, which evaluates the signals. The PCM contains electronic 'maps' which enable it to calculate the optimum quantity of fuel to inject, the appropriate start of injection, and even pre- and post-injection fuel quantities, for each individual engine cylinder under any given condition of engine operation.

14 Additionally, the PCM carries out monitoring and self-diagnostic functions. Any faults in the system are stored in the PCM memory, which enables quick and accurate fault diagnosis using appropriate diagnostic equipment (such as a suitable fault code reader).

System components

High-pressure pump

15 The high-pressure pump is mounted on the engine in the position normally occupied by the conventional distributor fuel injection pump. The pump is driven at half engine speed by the timing belt, and is lubricated by the fuel which it pumps.

16 The fuel transfer pump (integral with the high-pressure pump) forces the fuel into the high-pressure pump chamber, via a safety valve.

17 The high-pressure pump consists of three radially-mounted pistons and cylinders. The pistons are operated by an eccentric cam mounted on the pump drive spindle. As a piston moves down, fuel enters the cylinder through an inlet valve. When the piston reaches bottom dead centre (BDC), the inlet valve closes, and as the piston moves back up the cylinder, the fuel is compressed. When the pressure in the cylinder matches the pressure in the accumulator rail, an outlet valve opens, and fuel is forced into the accumulator rail. When the piston reaches top dead centre (TDC), the outlet valve closes, due to the pressure drop, and the pumping cycle is repeated. The use of multiple cylinders provides a steady flow of fuel, minimising pulses and pressure fluctuations.

18 As the pump needs to be able to supply sufficient fuel under full-load conditions, it will supply excess fuel during idle and part-load conditions. This excess fuel is returned from the high-pressure circuit to the low-pressure circuit (to the tank) via the pressure control valve.

19 The pump incorporates a facility to effectively switch off one of the cylinders to improve efficiency and reduce fuel consumption when maximum pumping capacity is not required. When this facility is operated, a solenoid-operated needle holds the inlet valve in the relevant cylinder open during the delivery stroke, preventing the fuel from being compressed.

Accumulator rail

20 As its name suggests, the accumulator rail acts as an accumulator, storing fuel and preventing pressure fluctuations. Fuel enters the rail from the high-pressure pump, and each injector has its own connection to the rail. The fuel pressure sensor is mounted in the rail, and the rail also has a connection to the fuel pressure control valve on the pump.

Pressure control valve

21 The pressure control valve is operated by the PCM, and controls the system pressure. The valve is integral with the high-pressure pump and cannot be separated.

22 If the fuel pressure is excessive, the valve opens, and fuel flows back to the tank. If the pressure is too low, the valve closes, enabling the high-pressure pump to increase the pressure.

23 The valve is an electromagnetically-operated ball valve. The ball is forced against its seat, against the fuel pressure, by a powerful spring, and also by the force provided by the electromagnet. The force generated by the electromagnet is directly proportional to the current applied to it by the PCM. The desired pressure can therefore be set by varying the current applied to the electromagnet. Any pressure fluctuations are damped by the spring.

Fuel pressure sensor

24 The fuel pressure sensor is mounted in the accumulator rail, and provides very precise information on the fuel pressure to the PCM.

Fuel injector

25 The injectors are mounted on the engine in a similar manner to conventional diesel fuel injectors. The injectors are electro-magnetically-operated via signals from the PCM, and fuel is injected at the pressure existing in the accumulator rail. The injectors are high-precision instruments and are manufactured to very high tolerances.

26 Fuel flows into the injector from the accumulator rail, via an inlet valve and an inlet throttle, and an electromagnet causes the injector nozzle to lift from its seat, allowing injection. Excess fuel is returned from the injectors to the tank via a return line. The injector operates on a hydraulic servo principle: the forces resulting inside the injector due to the fuel pressure effectively amplify the effects of the electromagnet, which does not provide sufficient force to open the injector nozzle directly. The injector functions as follows. Five separate forces are essential to the operation of the injector:
a) *A nozzle spring forces the nozzle needle against the nozzle seat at the bottom of the injector, preventing fuel from entering the combustion chamber.*
b) *In the valve at the top of the injector, the valve spring forces the valve ball against the opening to the valve control chamber. The fuel in the chamber is unable to escape through the fuel return.*
c) *When triggered, the electromagnet exerts a force which overcomes the valve spring force, and moves the valve ball away from its seat. This is the triggering force for the start of injection. When the valve ball moves off its seat, fuel enters the valve control chamber.*
d) *The pressure of the fuel in the valve control chamber exerts a force on the valve control plunger, which is added to the nozzle spring force.*
e) *A slight chamfer towards the lower end of the nozzle needle causes the fuel in the control chamber to exert a force on the nozzle needle.*

27 When these forces are in equilibrium, the injector is in its rest (idle) state, but when a voltage is applied to the electromagnet, the forces work to lift the nozzle needle, injecting fuel into the combustion chamber. There are four phases of injector operation as follows:
a) *Rest (idle) state – all forces are in equilibrium. The nozzle needle closes off the nozzle opening, and the valve spring forces the valve ball against its seat.*
b) *Opening – the electromagnet is triggered which opens the nozzle and triggers the injection process. The force from the electromagnet allows the valve ball to leave its seat. The fuel from the valve control chamber flows back to the tank via the fuel return line. When the valve opens, the pressure in the valve control chamber drops, and the force on the valve plunger is reduced. However, due to the effect of the input throttle, the pressure on the nozzle needle remains unchanged. The resulting force in the valve control chamber is sufficient to lift the nozzle from its seat, and the injection process begins.*
c) *Injection – within a few milliseconds, the triggering current in the electromagnet is reduced to a lower holding current. The nozzle is now fully open, and fuel is injected into the combustion chamber at the pressure present in the accumulator rail.*
d) *Closing – the electromagnet is switched off, at which point the valve spring forces the valve ball firmly against its seat, and in the valve control chamber, the pressure is the same as that at the nozzle needle. The force at the valve plunger increases, and the nozzle needle closes the nozzle opening. The forces are now in equilibrium once more, and the injector is once more in the idle state, awaiting the next injection sequence.*

PCM and sensors

28 The PCM and sensors are described earlier in this Section – see Electronic control system.

Air inlet sensor and turbocharger

29 An airflow sensor is fitted downstream of the air filter to monitor the quantity of air supplied to the turbocharger. The turbocharger itself is a variable-nozzle geometry type.

Intake air shutoff throttle housing

30 The intake air shutoff throttle housing controls the volume of air drawn into the engine according to driving conditions, and thus influences the composition of the recirculated exhaust gases. It is activated by the PCM. In addition, the unit ensures that the engine does not run-on after switching off the ignition.

2 High-pressure diesel injection system – special information

Warnings and precautions

1 It is essential to observe strict precautions when working on the fuel system components, particularly the high-pressure side of the system. Before carrying out any operations on the fuel system, refer to the precautions given in *Safety first!* at the beginning of this manual, and to the following additional information.

- Do not carry out any repair work on the high-pressure fuel system unless you are competent to do so, have all the necessary tools and equipment required, and are aware of the safety implications involved.
- Before starting any repair work on the fuel system, wait at least 30 seconds after switching off the engine to allow the fuel circuit pressure to reduce.
- Never work on the high-pressure fuel system with the engine running.
- Keep well clear of any possible source of fuel leakage, particularly when starting the engine after carrying out repair work. A leak in the system could cause an extremely high-pressure jet of fuel to escape, which could result in severe personal injury.
- Never place your hands or any part of your body near to a leak in the high-pressure fuel system.

- Do not use steam-cleaning equipment or compressed air to clean the engine or any of the fuel system components.

Procedures and information

2 Strict cleanliness must be observed at all times when working on any part of the fuel system. This applies to the working area in general, the person doing the work, and the components being worked on.

3 Before working on the fuel system components, they must be thoroughly cleaned with a suitable degreasing fluid. Specific cleaning products may be obtained from dealers. Alternatively, a suitable brake cleaning fluid may be used. Cleanliness is particularly important when working on the fuel system connections at the following components:

a) Fuel filter.
b) High-pressure fuel pump.
c) Accumulator rail.
d) Fuel injectors.
e) High-pressure fuel pipes.

4 After disconnecting any fuel pipes or components, the open union or orifice must be immediately sealed to prevent the entry of dirt or foreign material. Plastic plugs and caps in various sizes are available in packs from motor factors and accessory outlets, and are particularly suitable for this application (see illustration). Fingers cut from disposable rubber gloves should be used to protect components such as fuel pipes, fuel injectors and wiring connectors, and can be secured in place using elastic bands. Suitable gloves of this type are available at no cost from most filling station forecourts.

5 Whenever any of the high-pressure fuel pipes are disconnected or removed, new pipes must be obtained for refitting.

6 On the completion of any repair on the high-pressure fuel system, the use of a leak-detecting compound is recommended. This is a powder which is applied to the fuel pipe unions and connections, which is white when dry. Any leak in the system will cause the product to darken, indicating the source of the leak.

7 The torque wrench settings given in the Specifications must be strictly observed when tightening component mountings and connections. This is particularly important when tightening the high-pressure fuel pipe unions. To use a torque wrench on the fuel pipe unions, two crow's-foot adapters are required – these are available from motor factors and accessory outlets (see illustration).

3 Fuel system – priming and bleeding

1 After disconnecting any part of the fuel system or running out of fuel, it is necessary to prime the fuel system and bleed off any air which may have entered the system components.

2 In many circumstances, the system will self-bleed by operating the starter for a maximum of 30 seconds. If the engine does not start within this time, wait 5 seconds and repeat the procedure. If, after a reasonable number of attempts, the engine still will not start, proceed as follows.

3 It will be necessary to obtain the special Ford priming hose (kit No.310-110) or a suitable alternative with a hand-priming function, and temporarily connect it into the fuel supply line from the fuel filter (see illustration).

4 On some models, a clear plastic fuel pipe is fitted in the fuel return line in the engine compartment, and the pump should be operated until fuel appears in the pipe – on other models, operate the pump until the fuel reaches the pump. Continue to squeeze the pump until it becomes firm, then squeeze and hold the pump for a further 10 seconds. Release the pump, then squeeze and hold it a further 10 seconds.

5 Where applicable, disconnect the temporary hand priming pump, and reconnect the supply pipe to the fuel filter.

6 Operate the starter until the engine starts.

2.4 Typical plastic plug and cap set for sealing disconnected fuel pipes and components

2.7 Two crow's-foot adapters will be necessary for tightening the fuel pipe unions

3.3 Using a hand priming kit to assist with fuel system bleeding

4.1 Slacken the clamp and disconnect the ducting

4.3 Disconnect the rubber hose

4.4 Remove the bolt

4 Air cleaner assembly – removal and refitting

Removal

1 Slacken the clamp and disconnect the inlet ducting from the turbocharger (see illustration).
2 Disconnect the wiring plug from the airflow sensor.
3 Pull the small bore rubber hose from the air cleaner cover (see illustration).
4 Remove the Torx bolt at the right-hand front corner securing the particulate filter pressure differential sensor (where fitted) (see illustration).
5 Lift the edge of intake ducting over the clip at the bonnet slam panel (see illustration).
6 Pull the housing upwards from the rubber grommets.
7 Refitting is a reversal of removal.

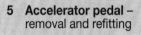

5 Accelerator pedal – removal and refitting

Removal

1 Disconnect the wiring plug from the accelerator pedal position sensor, then unscrew the two mounting nuts and remove the pedal/sensor assembly from the brake pedal mounting bracket studs (see illustration).

Refitting

2 Refitting is a reversal of removal.

6 Fuel tank – removal, inspection and refitting

1 Refer to the warnings and precautions in Section 2 before proceeding.
2 Refer to Chapter 4A Section 7. Fuel tank removal and refitting is the same as for petrol models, with the exception that an evaporative emissions charcoal canister is not

4.5 Lift the edge of the ducting over the clip

fitted to diesel models. Note also that there is a fuel return line as well as a supply line on the top of the tank.

7 Fuel gauge sender unit – removal and refitting

Note: Refer to the warnings in Section 2 before proceeding. Ford specify the use of their service tool 310-069 (a large socket with projecting teeth to engage the sender unit retaining ring's raised edges) for this task. Suitable alternatives to this tool are readily available from accessory stores and motor factor outlets.

Removal

1 The fuel gauge sender unit is located in the

7.3 Alignment marks on the fuel gauge sender unit and fuel tank

5.1 Accelerator pedal mounting nuts

top face of the fuel tank. The unit can only be detached and withdrawn from the tank after the tank is released and lowered from under the car. Refer to Section 6 and remove the fuel tank, then proceed as follows.
2 Unscrew and remove the special retaining ring, by unscrewing it with the Ford tool or a suitable alternative.
3 Check that alignment marks are visible on the gauge sender unit and fuel tank. There should be an arrow on the sender unit aligned with the raised projections on the tank (see illustration). If no marks are visible, suitably mark the tank and sender unit with paint.
4 Carefully lift out the gauge sender unit housing from the tank. Take care that the sender unit float and arm are not damaged as the unit is removed.
5 Lift out the rubber seal and obtain a new seal for refitting (see illustration).

7.5 Renew the seal

7.6 Release the catches and slide up the sender unit

7.7 Measure the resistance of the sender unit with the arm fully raised, then lowered

7.8 Align the ring thread start point with the mark on the tank

6 If required, the fuel gauge sender unit can be removed from the housing by disconnecting the wiring connector, releasing the retaining catches and withdrawing the unit from the side of the housing **(see illustration)**.
7 The function of the sender unit can be checked using a digital multimeter, set to measure resistance in Ohms. At full deflection (tank full) the resistance measured was approximately 10 Ohms, and at zero deflection (tank empty), the resistance was approximately 180 Ohms **(see illustration)**.

Refitting

8 Refitting is a reversal of removal, but fit a new rubber seal and tighten the retaining ring securely Note that when refitting the retaining ring, align the ring thread start point (indicated by an triangle) with the mark on the tank adjacent to the aperture **(see illustration)**. Refit the fuel tank as described in Section.

8 Fuel tank filler neck – removal and refitting

Note: *Refer to the warnings and precautions in Section 2 before proceeding.*
1 Refer to Chapter 4A Section 9.

9 High-pressure fuel pump – removal and refitting

Warning: Refer to the information contained in Section 2 before proceeding.
Note: *A new fuel pump-to-accumulator rail high-pressure fuel pipe will be required for refitting.*

Removal

1 Disconnect the battery negative lead as described in Chapter 5A Section 4.
2 Drain the cooling system as described in Chapter 1B Section 30.
3 Remove the timing belt as described in Chapter 2C Section 7 or Chapter 2D Section 7. After removing the timing belt, temporarily refit the right-hand engine mounting.
4 Remove the diesel particulate filter as described in Section 18.

5 Remove the fuel pump sprocket as described in Chapter 2C Section 8 or Chapter 2D Section 8.
6 Undo the 2 bolts and move the vacuum solenoid and bracket assembly beneath the high-pressure pump to one side.
7 Undo the bolts, release the hoses and remove the coolant pipe assembly from the rear of the engine **(see illustration)**.
8 Where fitted, remove the plastic cover over the pump.
9 Depress the quick-release connector buttons and disconnect the fuel supply and return hoses from the pump **(see illustration)**. Plug the end of the hoses to prevent dirt ingress.
10 Clean carefully around the unions at either end of the pump-to-accumulator rail metal

pipe – it is very important that no dirt enters the system. Counterhold the pump union with a second spanner where applicable – the union screwed into the pump must not be allowed to unscrew **(see illustration)**. Keep the pipe in place until both unions have been fully loosened, and the pipe can be removed – this reduces the chance of dirt getting in. Plug the open ends on the pump and accumulator rail – this is most important. Discard the pipe – a new one must be fitted.
11 Disconnect the wiring plugs from the fuel flow and pressure control valves, noting their locations for refitting. Detach the wiring loom as necessary.
12 On 1.6 litre models, undo the 3 bolts and remove the support bracket at the rear of the pump.

9.7 Remove the coolant pipe assembly to access the pump

9.9 Depress the buttons and disconnect the fuel supply and return hoses

9.10 Pump-to-fuel rail pipe

Caution: The high-pressure fuel pump is manufactured to extremely close tolerances, and must not be dismantled in any way. Do not unscrew the fuel pipe male union on the rear of the pump, or attempt to remove the sensor, piston de-activator switch, or the seal on the pump shaft. No parts for the pump are available separately, and if the unit is in any way suspect, it must be renewed.

Refitting

13 Locate the pump in the mounting bracket, and refit the three mounting bolts, hand-tight. Refit the pump rear support bracket, tightening the bolts to the specified torque, then tighten the three pump mounting bolts to the specified torque.

14 Fit a new metal fuel pipe between the pump and the accumulator rail. The unions at each end of the pipe must be tightened to the specified torque in two stages. Use a second spanner to counterhold the union screwed into the pump. Do not allow the union to move.

15 The remainder of refitting is a reversal of removal.

16 With everything reassembled and reconnected, prime the fuel system as described in Section 3. Observing the precautions listed in Section 2, start the engine and allow it to idle. Check for leaks at the high-pressure fuel pipe unions with the engine idling. If satisfactory, increase the engine speed to 4000 rpm and check again for leaks.

17 Take the car for a short road test, and check for leaks once again on return. If any leaks are detected, obtain and fit another new high-pressure fuel pipe. Do not attempt to cure even the slightest leak by further tightening of the pipe unions.

10 Accumulator (common) rail – removal and refitting

Warning: Refer to the information contained in Section 2 before proceeding.
Note: *A complete new set of high-pressure fuel pipes will be required for refitting.*

Removal

1.5 litre engines

1 Remove the starter motor as described in Chapter 5A Section 9.

1.6 litre engines

2 Disconnect the battery negative lead as described in Chapter 5A Section 4.
3 Remove the windscreen grille cowl as described in Chapter 11 Section 20.
4 Remove the air cleaner as described in Section 4.
5 Slacken the clamps, undo the retaining bolts/nuts and remove the air intake ducting assembly from the top of the engine.
6 Remove the fuel filter as described in Chapter 1B Section 22.

7 Remove the EGR valve assembly as described in Chapter 4C Section 3.
8 Undo the bolts/nut and remove the throttle body/duct assembly from the intake manifold.

All engines

9 Clean the area around the high-pressure fuel pipes to and from the accumulator rail, then unscrew the pump-to-accumulator rail pipe unions. Use a second spanner to counterhold the union screwed in to the pump body as described in Section 9. The screwed-in union must not be allowed to move. Remove the pipe and discard it – a new one must be fitted. Plug the openings to prevent contamination.

10 Repeat the procedure on the accumulator rail-to-injector fuel pipes. Use a second spanner to counterhold the unions screwed into the injectors **(see illustration)** – these unions must not be allowed to move. Note their fitted locations and remove the pipes.

11 Plug the openings in the accumulator rail and fuel pump to prevent dirt ingress.

12 Disconnect the pressure sensor wiring plug from the accumulator rail.

13 Unscrew the two accumulator rail mounting bolts/nuts, and manoeuvre it out. **Note:** *The fuel pressure sensor on the accumulator rail must not be removed.*

Refitting

14 Locate the accumulator rail in position, refit and finger-tighten the mounting bolts.
15 Reconnect the accumulator pressure sensor wiring plug.
16 Fit the new pump-to-rail high-pressure pipe, and only finger-tighten the unions at first, then tighten the unions to the Stage 1 torque setting, followed by the Stage 2 torque setting. Use a second spanner to counterhold the union screwed into the pump body.
17 Fit the new set of rail-to-injector high-pressure pipes, and finger-tighten the unions.
18 Tighten the accumulator mounting bolts to the specified torque.
19 Tighten the rail-to-injector pipe unions to the Stage 1 torque setting, followed by the Stage 2 setting. Use a second spanner to counterhold the injector unions.
20 The remainder of refitting is a reversal of removal, noting the following points:
a) *Ensure all wiring connectors and harnesses are correctly refitting and secured.*
b) *Prime and bleed the fuel system as described in Section 3.*
c) *Observing the precautions listed in Section 2, start the engine and allow it to idle. Check for leaks at the high-pressure fuel pipe unions with the engine idling. If satisfactory, increase the engine speed to 4000 rpm and check again for leaks. Take the car for a short road test, and check for leaks once again on return. If any leaks are detected, obtain and fit additional new high-pressure fuel pipes as required. Do not attempt to cure even the slightest leak by further tightening of the pipe unions.*

10.10 Use a second spanner to counterhold the fuel injector unions whilst slackening the pipe unions

During the road test, initialise the engine management PCM as follows – engage third gear and stabilise the engine at 1000 rpm, then accelerate fully up to 3500 rpm.

11 Fuel injectors – removal and refitting

Warning: Refer to the information contained in Section 2 before proceeding.
Note: *The following procedure describes the removal and refitting of the injectors as a complete set. However, each injector may be removed individually if required. New copper washers, upper seals, injector clamp retaining nuts/bolts and a high-pressure fuel pipe will be required for each disturbed injector when refitting.*

Removal

1 Disconnect the battery as described in Chapter 5A Section 4.
2 Release the clamp, undo the nuts/bolt and move the intake ducting/throttle body from above the cylinder head cover to one side.
3 Disconnect the wiring plugs from the injectors **(see illustration)**.
4 Undo the retaining bolt, then unclip the wiring harness tray and move it to one side for access to the injectors.
5 Hold down the black central union, pull up the green collar, and pull the fuel return hose from the top of each injector. Plug the openings to prevent dirt ingress then move

11.3 Disconnect the wiring plugs

11.5a Pull up the green collar...

11.5b... then pull the return union from each injector

11.7 Use a second spanner to prevent the injector port from rotating

the return hose assembly to one side **(see illustrations)**. Plug the openings to prevent contamination.

6 Remove the starter motor as described in Chapter 5A Section 9.

7 Clean the area around the high-pressure fuel pipe unions on the accumulator rail-to-injector fuel pipes then unscrew the pipe unions. Use a second spanner to counterhold the unions screwed into the injectors – these unions must not be allowed to move **(see illustration)**. Note their fitted locations and remove the pipes.

8 Plug the openings in the accumulator rail and fuel injectors to prevent dirt ingress.

9 Unscrew the injector retaining bolt, remove the clamp and carefully pull or lever the injector from place. If necessary, use an open-ended spanner and twist the injector to free it from position **(see illustrations)**. Do not lever against or pull on the solenoid housing at the top of the injector. Note down the

injectors position – if the injectors are to be refitted, they must be refitted to their original locations.

10 Remove the copper washer from each injector, or from the cylinder head if they remained in place during injector removal. New copper washers will be required for refitting. Cover the injector hole in the cylinder head to prevent dirt ingress.

11 Remove the seal from each of the cylinder head injector recesses or injector body. New ones will be required.

12 Examine each injector visually for any signs of obvious damage or deterioration. If any defects are apparent, renew the injector(s). Note down the injector classification number – this may be needed during the refitting procedure if the injectors have been renewed. *Caution: The injectors are manufactured to extremely close tolerances and must not be dismantled in any way. Do not unscrew the fuel pipe union on the side of the injector,*

or separate any parts of the injector body. Do not attempt to clean carbon deposits from the injector nozzle or carry out any form of ultrasonic or pressure testing.

13 Use a vacuum cleaner to remove any debris from the cylinder head recesses, and the surrounding areas.

Refitting

14 Renew the copper seals on the injectors, and the seals in the cylinder head recesses **(see illustrations)**.

15 Insert the injectors into the cylinder head. If the injectors are being refitted, they must be inserted into their original locations.

16 Refit the injector clamps, but don't tighten the retaining bolts at this stage.

17 Working on one fuel injector at a time, remove the blanking plugs from the fuel pipe unions on the accumulator rail and the relevant injector. Locate a new high-pressure fuel pipe over the unions and screw on the union nuts. Take care not to cross-thread the nuts or strain the fuel pipes as they are fitted. Once the union nut threads have started, finger-tighten the nuts only at this stage, to the ends of the threads.

18 When all the fuel pipes are in place, tighten the injector clamp retaining bolts to the specified torque and through the specified angle.

19 Using an open-ended spanner, hold each fuel pipe union in turn and tighten the union nut to the specified torque using a torque wrench and crow's-foot adapter **(see illustration)**. Tighten all the union nuts in the same way.

11.9a Injector clamp retaining bolt

11.9b Carefully remove the injector

11.14a Renew the copper seals on the injectors...

11.14b...and the seals in the cylinder head

11.19 Use a crow's-foot adapter to tighten the fuel pipe union

20 If new injectors have been fitted, their classification numbers must be programmed into the engine management PCM using dedicated diagnostic equipment/scanner. If this equipment is not available, entrust this task to a Ford dealer or suitably-equipped repairer. Note that it should be possible to drive the vehicle, albeit with reduced performance/increased emissions, to a repairer for the numbers to be programmed.
21 The remainder of refitting is a reversal of removal.

12 Electronic control system components – testing, removal and refitting

Testing

1 If a fault is suspected in the electronic control side of the system, first ensure that all the wiring connectors are securely connected and free of corrosion. Ensure that the suspected problem is not of a mechanical nature, or due to poor maintenance; ie, check that the air cleaner filter element is clean, the engine breather hoses are clear and undamaged, and that the cylinder compression pressures are correct, referring to Chapter, Chapter or Chapter 2D for further information.
2 If these checks fail to reveal the cause of the problem, the car should be taken to a suitably-equipped Ford dealer for testing. A diagnostic connector is fitted under the facia on the driver's side into which dedicated electronic test equipment can be plugged **(see illustration)**. The test equipment is capable of 'interrogating' the engine management system powertrain control module (PCM) electronically and accessing its internal fault log (reading fault codes). This will allow the fault to be quickly and simply traced, alleviating the need to test all the system components individually, which is a time-consuming operation that carries a risk of damaging the PCM.

Powertrain Control Module (PCM)

Caution: The module is fragile. Take care not to drop it, or subject it to any other kind

12.2 Open the drivers side facia storage compartment to access the 16-pin diagnostic connector

of impact. Do not subject it to extremes of temperature, or allow it to get wet.
Note: *If a new PCM is to be fitted, the configuration information stored within the module must be uploaded to Ford diagnostic equipment prior to the module being removed, and downloaded to the new PCM once installed. Entrust this task to a Ford dealer or suitably-equipped specialist.*
3 Remove the battery as described in Chapter 5A Section 4.
4 Slide forward and remove the cover over the PCM **(see illustration)**.
5 Drill out the shear-bolt securing the security shield over the PCM upper wiring connector **(see illustration)**. A 6 mm drill bit will be required, and the hole must be drilled centrally, to avoid damaging the PCM – Ford dealers use a special guide tool (418-537) to

12.5 Drill out the shear-bolt securing the security shield over the PCM wiring connector

ensure this, which is a short tube with a 6 mm internal diameter.
6 Remove the security shield, then disconnect the 3 wiring connectors from the PCM **(see illustrations)**.
7 Undo the 2 retaining nuts, remove the rear section of the cover, then undo the 2 remaining nuts and remove the PCM from the mounting plate **(see illustrations)**.
8 Refitting is a reversal of removal. Strictly speaking, a new shear-bolt should be obtained for refitting, and tightened until the head shears off. However, as this is only a deterrent to 'chipping' the module, an ordinary bolt can be used instead.

Crankshaft position sensor

9 Raise the front of the vehicle and support it securely on axle stands (see *Jacking and*

12.4 Slide forwards the PCM cover

12.6a Remove the security shield

12.6b Depress the clip, then fold-over the catch and disconnect the wiring plugs

12.7a Undo the 2 nuts, remove the rear section of the cover…

12.7b …then undo the remaining nuts and remove the PCM

12.10 Viewed from underneath, undo the 2 Torx screws securing the cover

12.11 Slacken the timing belt cover lower bolt 1.5 turns

12.12 Crankshaft position sensor wiring plug

vehicle support). Release the fasteners and remove the engine undershield.

10 Undo the fasteners and remove the cover beneath the auxiliary drivebelt **(see illustration)**.

11 Using an open-ended spanner, slacken the lower, rearmost bolt securing the timing belt lower cover 1.5 turns **(see illustration)**.

12 Disconnect the wiring plug from the crankshaft position sensor **(see illustration)**.

13 Unbolt and remove the crankshaft sensor from the engine.

14 Refitting is a reversal of removal. Ensure that the sensor is clean when refitting, and tighten its mounting bolt securely.

Camshaft position sensor

15 The camshaft position sensor is mounted on the right-hand end of the cylinder head cover, directly behind the camshaft sprocket.

16 Remove the upper timing belt cover as described in Chapter 2C Section 6 or Chapter 2D Section 6.

17 Unplug the sensor wiring connector **(see illustration)**.

18 Undo the bolt and pull the sensor from position **(see illustration)**.

19 Refit the sensor and tighten the retaining bolt to the specified torque.

20 The remainder of refitting is a reversal of removal.

Accelerator pedal position sensor

21 The sensor is integral with the accelerator pedal assembly. Refer to Section 5 for the pedal removal procedure.

Coolant temperature sensor

22 Refer to Chapter 3 Section 6.

Fuel temperature sensor

 Warning: Refer to the information contained in Section 2 before proceeding.

23 Disconnect the battery negative terminal (refer to Chapter 5A Section 4).

24 The sensor is clipped in to the plastic fuel manifold at the right-hand rear end of the cylinder head. To remove the sensor, disconnect the wiring plug, then unclip the sensor from the manifold. Be prepared for fuel spillage **(see illustration)**.

25 Refitting is a reversal of removal.

26 Observing the precautions listed in Section 2, start the engine and allow it to idle. Check for leaks at the fuel temperature sensor with the engine idling. If satisfactory, increase the engine speed to 4000 rpm and check again for leaks. Take the car for a short road test and check for leaks once again on return. If any leaks are detected, obtain and fit a new sensor.

Airflow sensor

27 The mass airflow sensor is bolted to the air cleaner cover outlet, and an outlet duct connects it to the turbocharger.

28 Unplug the wiring connector from the airflow sensor **(see illustration)**.

29 Undo the two retaining bolts and withdraw the sensor from the air cleaner cover.

30 Suitably plug or cover the turbocharger air duct, using clean rag to prevent any dirt or foreign material from entering.

31 Refitting is a reverse of the removal procedure. Check the condition of the O-ring seal, and fit a new one if necessary.

Fuel pressure sensor

32 The fuel pressure sensor is integral with the accumulator rail, and is not available separately. The sensor must not be removed from the rail.

Fuel pressure control valve

33 The fuel pressure control valve is integral with the high-pressure fuel pump, and cannot be separated.

EGR valve

34 Refer to Chapter 4C Section 3.

12.17 Disconnect the camshaft position sensor wiring plug

12.18 Camshaft position sensor retaining bolt

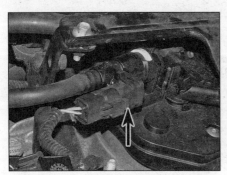

12.24 Depress the clip and disconnect the fuel temperature sensor wiring plug

12.28 Slide up the red locking clip and disconnect the airflow sensor wiring plug

12.38 Disconnect the valve wiring plug

12.39 Air shutoff throttle retaining bolts

12.41 Depress the clip and disconnect the wiring plug

Intake air shutoff throttle

35 The intake air shutoff throttle is located on the right-hand front of the cylinder head, between the inlet air duct between the intercooler and inlet manifold. Its purpose is to prevent engine run-on when switching off, and to vary the volume air drawn into the engine in order to control the composition of recirculated exhaust gas.

1.5 litre engines

36 Pull up and remove the plastic cover from the top of the engine.

37 Slacken the clamps, undo the retaining nut/bolt, and remove the air duct from the right-hand end of the cylinder head cover.

38 Disconnect the air shutoff throttle valve wiring plug **(see illustration)**.

39 Undo the 4 retaining bolts and remove the air shutoff throttle valve **(see illustration)**. Note that the lower, right-hand bolt is accessed from the rear. Examine the seal and renew if necessary.

40 Refitting is a reversal of removal.

1.6 litre engines

41 Disconnect the wiring connector from the side of the intake air shutoff throttle **(see illustration)**.

42 Slacken the clip and disconnect the intercooler air duct from the base of the intake air shutoff throttle **(see illustration)**.

43 Undo the three flange retaining bolts and remove the intake air shutoff throttle from the inlet manifold.

44 If necessary, slacken the retaining clip and disconnect the upper air duct from the shutoff throttle.

45 Refitting is a reversal of removal, however, check the condition of the O-ring seal, and fit a new one if necessary.

Manifold absolute pressure (MAP) sensor

46 On some models, the MAP sensor is combined with an intake air temperature sensor, and is known as a MAPT (Manifold Absolute Pressure and Temperature) sensor. On other models, a separate intake air temperature sensor is fitted as described later in this Section.

47 Pull up and remove the plastic cover from the top of the engine.

MAPT sensor

48 Disconnect the wiring plug from the sensor located on the top of the intake manifold.

49 Undo the retaining bolt and remove the sensor.

50 Refitting is a reversal removal.

MAP sensor

51 Disconnect the wiring plug, and unclip the wiring loom **(see illustration)**.

52 Disconnect the pressure hose from the underside of the sensor, then undo the retaining stud, and remove the sensor.

53 Refitting is a reversal of removal.

Intake air temperature sensor

54 Remove the plastic cover from the top of the engine.

12.42 Slacken the clip and disconnect the intercooler air duct

55 The sensor is located at the right-hand rear of the intake manifold **(see illustration)**.

56 Disconnect the wiring plug, undo the retaining bolt and withdraw the sensor.

57 Refitting is a reversal of removal.

Diesel particulate filter (DPF) pressure differential sensor

58 The DPF pressure differential sensor is located on the right-hand side of the air cleaner housing **(see illustration)**.

59 Release the clamp and disconnect the rubber hose from the metal pressure pipe.

60 Disconnect the wiring plug, undo the retaining nut and remove the sensor.

61 Refitting is a reversal of removal.

Exhaust gas temperature sensor(s)

62 Depending on model, upto 3 temperature sensors may be fitted into the exhaust system.

12.51 MAP sensor

12.55 Intake air temperature sensor

12.58 DPF pressure differential sensor

2 may be fitted into the diesel particulate filter/catalytic converter, whilst a 3rd one may be fitted into the front exhaust pipe behind the engine.

63 Remove the plastic cover from the top of the engine, or raise the front of the vehicle and support is securely on axle stands as applicable (see *Jacking and vehicle support*).

64 Trace the sensor wiring back to the wiring plug, disconnect it, then release the wiring from any retaining clips.

65 Using a split-type socket or open-ended spanner, slacken and remove the sensor **(see illustration)**.

66 Refitting is a reversal of removal. Tighten the sensor to the specified torque.

DPF (diesel particulate filter) gas temperature sensor

67 Remove the plastic cover from the top of the engine, or raise the front of the vehicle and support is securely on axle stands as applicable (see *Jacking and vehicle support*).

68 Trace the sensor back to the wiring plug, disconnect it then release the wiring from any retaining clips.

69 Using a split-type socket or open-ended spanner, slacken and remove the sensor **(see illustration)**.

70 Refitting is a reversal of removal. Tighten the sensor to the specified torque.

Heated oxygen sensor(s)

71 On some models, 1 or 2 heated oxygen sensors are fitted into the exhaust system. The first is fitted into the turbocharger outlet pipe, whilst the second is fitted into the front section of the exhaust pipe at the rear of the engine.

72 Pull up and remove the plastic cover from the top of the engine, or raise the front of the vehicle and support it securely on axle stands as applicable (see *Jacking and vehicle support*). Where necessary, undo the fasteners and remove the engine undershield.

73 Trace the sensor wiring back to the wiring plug, disconnect it, then release the wiring from any retaining clips.

74 Using a split-type socket slacken and remove the sensor.

75 Refitting is a reversal of removal. Tighten the sensor to the specified torque.

12.65 Pre-filter exhaust gas temperature sensor

13 Inlet manifold – removal and refitting

Removal

1 Pull up and remove plastic cover from the top of the engine.

2 Slacken the clamp, undo the nuts/bolts and remove the air intake pipe from the top of the engine.

3 Remove the windscreen cowl panels as described in Chapter 11 Section 20.

4 Disconnect the wiring plug from the MAP sensor on the manifold.

5 Remove the EGR valve as described in Chapter 4C Section 3.

6 Undo the 3 retaining bolts/studs securing the manifold to the cylinder head, and manoeuvre it from place.

Refitting

7 Refitting is a reversal of removal, Renew the manifold seals.

14 Exhaust manifold – removal and refitting

Removal

1 Remove the turbocharger as described in Section 16.

2 Undo the retaining nut and move the heatshield at the left-hand end of the manifold to one side.

3 Where applicable, undo the bolt and pull the engine oil level dipstick guide tube from the sump. Examine the O-ring seal and replace if necessary.

4 Undo the retaining nuts, recover the spacers, and remove the manifold. Recover the gasket.

Refitting

5 Refitting is a reverse of the removal procedure, bearing in mind the following points:

a) *Ensure that the manifold and cylinder head mating faces are clean, with all traces of old gasket removed.*

12.69 DPF gas temperature sensor

b) *Use a new gasket when refitting the manifold to the cylinder head.*

c) *Tighten the exhaust manifold retaining nuts to the specified torque.*

d) *Refit the turbocharger as described in Section 16.*

15 Turbocharger – description and precautions

Description

1 A turbocharger is fitted to increase engine efficiency by raising the pressure in the inlet manifold above atmospheric pressure. Instead of the air simply being sucked into the cylinders, it is forced in.

2 Energy for the operation of the turbocharger comes from the exhaust gas. The gas flows through a specially-shaped housing (the turbine housing) and, in so doing, spins the turbine wheel. The turbine wheel is attached to a shaft, at the end of which is another vaned wheel known as the compressor wheel. The compressor wheel spins in its own housing, and compresses the inlet air on the way to the inlet manifold.

3 Boost pressure (the pressure in the inlet manifold) is limited by a wastegate, which diverts the exhaust gas away from the turbine wheel in response to a pressure-sensitive actuator. The turbocharger incorporates a variable intake nozzle to improve boost pressure at low engine speeds.

4 The turbo shaft is pressure-lubricated by an oil feed pipe from the main oil gallery. The shaft 'floats' on a cushion of oil. A drain pipe returns the oil to the sump.

Precautions

5 The turbocharger operates at extremely high speeds and temperatures. Certain precautions must be observed, to avoid premature failure of the turbo, or injury to the operator.

● Do not operate the turbo with any of its parts exposed, or with any of its hoses removed. Foreign objects falling onto the rotating vanes could cause excessive damage, and (if ejected) personal injury.

● Do not race the engine immediately after start-up, especially if it is cold. Give the oil a few seconds to circulate.

● Always allow the engine to return to idle speed before switching it off – do not blip the throttle and switch off, as this will leave the turbo spinning without lubrication.

● Allow the engine to idle for several minutes before switching off after a high-speed run.

● Observe the recommended intervals for oil and filter changing, and use a reputable oil of the specified quality. Neglect of oil changing, or use of inferior oil, can cause carbon formation on the turbo shaft, leading to subsequent failure.

16.2a Intake duct clamp

16.2b Undo the bolts securing the outlet duct to the turbocharger…

16.2c …then undo the nut, and release the clamp

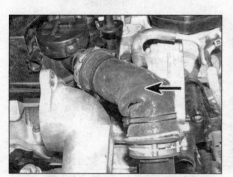

16.3 Disconnect the breather pipe

16.4a Undo the 3 nuts along the top…

16.4b …and slacken the nut at the front of the heatshield

16 Turbocharger – removal, inspection and refitting

Removal

1 Remove the particulate filter/catalytic converter as described in Section 18.
2 Slacken the clamps, undo the retaining bolts/nut and remove the turbocharger inlet and outlet air ducts **(see illustrations)**.
3 Release the clamps and disconnect the breather pipe from the cylinder head cover to the turbocharger intake duct **(see illustration)**.
4 Undo the nuts and remove the heatshield above the turbocharger **(see illustrations)**.
5 Unscrew the oil supply pipe banjo bolts and remove the pipe from the turbocharger and

cylinder block **(see illustrations)**. Recover the sealing washers.
6 Slacken the hose clip and disconnect the turbocharger oil return hose from the cylinder block.
7 Disconnect the vacuum hose and wiring

plug from the turbocharger wastegate capsule **(see illustration)**.
8 Unscrew the four nuts, and remove the turbocharger from the exhaust manifold **(see illustrations)**. Discard the nuts – new ones must be fitted.

16.5a Oil supply pipe-to-turbocharger banjo bolt

16.5b Oil supply pipe-to-cylinder block banjo bolt

16.7 Disconnect the wiring plug and vacuum hose

16.8a The turbocharger is secured by 2 nuts below…

16.8b …and 2 nuts above

Inspection

9 With the turbocharger removed, inspect the housing for cracks or other visible damage.

10 Spin the turbine or the compressor wheel, to verify that the shaft is intact and to feel for excessive shake or roughness. Some play is normal, since in use the shaft is 'floating' on a film of oil. Check that the wheel vanes are undamaged.

11 If oil contamination of the exhaust or induction passages is apparent, it is likely that turbo shaft oil seals have failed.

12 No DIY repair of the turbo is possible, and none of the internal or external parts are available separately. If the turbocharger is suspect in any way, a complete new (or reconditioned) unit must be obtained.

Refitting

13 Refitting is a reverse of the removal procedure, bearing in mind the following points:
a) Renew the turbocharger retaining nuts/ bolts and gaskets.
b) If a new turbocharger is being fitted, change the engine oil and filter. Also renew the filter in the oil feed pipe.
c) Prime the turbocharger by injecting clean engine oil through the oil feed pipe union before reconnecting the union.

17 Intercooler – removal and refitting

Note: An intercooler is only fitted to 1.6 litre models.

Removal

1 The intercooler is located at the front of the car alongside the right-hand side of the radiator. Pull the plastic cover on the top of the engine upwards from its' mountings.

2 Slacken the retaining clips and disconnect the inlet and outlet hoses from the intercooler, intake air resonator and intake air shutoff throttle (see illustrations).

3 Using two small screwdrivers, depress the sides of the intercooler upper retaining collar, located on the top centre of the intercooler, to compress the locating lugs each side. With

17.4 Lift the intercooler up and out from the engine compartment

17.2a Disconnect the inlet hose from the intercooler and intake air resonator ...

17.3a Depress the sides of the intercooler upper retaining collar (shown with intercooler removed) ...

the retaining collar lugs compressed, pull the top of the intercooler towards the engine to disengage the upper retaining collar from its location (see illustrations).

4 Lift the intercooler up to disengage the lower mounting lugs and manipulate the intercooler out from the engine compartment (see illustration).

Refitting

5 Refitting is a reversal of removal.

18 Exhaust system – general information and component renewal

Caution: Any work on the exhaust system should only be attempted once the system is completely cool – this may take

18.6 Heatshield retaining bolts

17.2b ... and outlet hose from the intercooler

17.3b ... then pull the top of the intercooler towards the engine

several hours, especially in the case of the forward sections, such as the manifold and catalytic converter.

General information

1 The exhaust system consists of the particulate filter/catalytic converter and the centre section incorporating the silencer. A flexible ('mesh') section is fitted to allow for engine movement.

2 When fitted in the factory, the exhaust system from the centre section flange joint to the end of the tail pipe is one piece. However, if the silencer is to be renewed, new silencers should be available – check with your parts supplier. It will be necessary to cut through the centre section using a hacksaw if a new rear silencer is to be fitted.

3 The system is suspended throughout its entire length by rubber mountings.

Removal

4 To remove a part of the system, first jack up the front or rear of the car, and support it on axle stands (see *Jacking and vehicle support*). Alternatively, position the car over an inspection pit, or on car ramps. Undo the screws and remove the engine undershield.

Catalytic converter/diesel particulate filter

5 Pull up and remove the plastic cover from the top of the engine (where applicable).

6 Undo the bolts and remove the heatshield over the turbocharger (see illustration).

7 To prevent damage to the exhaust flexible

18.7 Attach a pair of splints to prevent damage to the flexible section.

18.8 Unhook the exhaust rubber mounting

18.9 Slacken the filter-to-turbocharger clamp nut

section, support it by attaching a pair of splints either side (two scrap strips of wood, plant canes, etc) using some cable-ties **(see illustration)**.

8 Unscrew the two nuts securing the exhaust system centre section to the catalytic converter/particulate filter. Unhook the centre section's rubber mounting, then separate the flange joint **(see illustration)**. Recover the gasket.

9 Slacken the nut on the retaining clamp, securing the catalytic converter/particulate filter to the turbocharger **(see illustration)**.

10 Trace the temperature sensors and oxygen sensor wiring back to the plugs and disconnect them. Unclip the wiring from any retaining clips.

11 Release the clamp and disconnect the the particulate filter pressure differential sensor hose **(see illustration)**.

12 Undo the two catalytic converter/particulate filter lower mounting nuts from the brackets on the front of the engine, then lower the assembly carefully from the engine compartment **(see illustration)**.

Flexible section

13 Using a hacksaw, cut the catalytic converter pipe 10 mm in front of the flexible section; the converter can then be connected to the new flexible section with a clamping sleeve (supplied with the new flexible section).

14 Unscrew the two nuts securing the exhaust system centre section to the catalytic converter. Unhook the centre section's

rubber mounting, then separate the flange joint. Recover the gasket and remove the cut (flexible) section from under the car.

Centre section

15 To prevent damage to the exhaust flexible section, support it by attaching a pair of splints either side (two scrap strips of wood, plant canes, etc) using some cable-ties. If a new centre section is being fitted, this precaution only applies to the new section of exhaust.

16 From under the car, undo the nuts and remove the underfloor cross-brace beneath the exhaust centre section.

17 Unscrew the nuts securing the centre section to the catalytic converter/particulate filter, and separate the joint. Recover the gasket.

18 Unhook the centre section's rubber mountings, and remove it from under the car.

Rear silencer

19 If the original one-piece exhaust system is still fitted, it will be necessary to cut off the old rear silencer to enable fitment of the new unit. Using the new rear silencer as a pattern, mark the exhaust centre section to determine the cut point. Ensure that the cut point will allow a sufficient length of centre section to fit into the new rear silencer.

20 Using a hacksaw, cut through the centre section at the marked cut point. Unhook the rear silencer's rubber mountings, and remove it from under the car.

21 If a replacement rear silencer has already been fitted, unbolt the clamp securing the silencer to the centre section, and separate the pipes. Usually, this will require some effort – the most successful method involves twisting the silencer from side to side, to break the joint. Unfortunately, if the pipe at the rear of the centre section has suffered from corrosion, it's very likely that the centre section will be damaged beyond repair in removing the silencer. A less-destructive method of removal involves heating the two pipes, but this carries the risk of damaging the underbody components, and even a risk of fire from the fuel tank and lines.

22 Unhook the silencer rubber mountings, and remove it from under the car.

Heat shields

23 The heat shields are secured to the underside of the body by special nuts. Each shield can be removed separately, but note that they may overlap, making it necessary to loosen another section first. If a shield is being removed to gain access to a component located behind it, it may prove sufficient in some cases to remove the retaining nuts and/or bolts, and simply lower the shield, without disturbing the exhaust system. Otherwise, remove the exhaust section as described earlier.

Refitting

24 In all cases, refitting is a reversal of removal, but note the following points:

a) *Always use new gaskets, nuts and clamps (as applicable), and coat all threads with copper grease. Make sure any new clamps are the same size as the original – over-tightening a clamp which is too big will not seal the joint.*

b) *If any of the exhaust mounting rubbers are in poor condition, fit new ones.*

c) *Make sure that the exhaust is suspended properly on its mountings, and will not come into contact with the floor or any suspension parts. The rear silencer especially must be aligned correctly before tightening the clamp nuts.*

d) *Tighten all nuts/bolts to the specified torque, where given.*

18.11 Pressure differential hose clamp – viewed from beneath

18.12 Particulate filter left-hand lower mounting nut

Notes

Chapter 4 Part C
Emission control systems

Contents

Degrees of difficulty

Easy, suitable for novice with little experience ⚡	**Fairly easy,** suitable for beginner with some experience ⚡	**Fairly difficult,** suitable for competent DIY mechanic ⚡	**Difficult,** suitable for experienced DIY mechanic ⚡	**Very difficult,** suitable for expert DIY or professional ⚡

Specifications

Torque wrench settings	Nm	lbf ft
Petrol engines		
Oxygen (lambda) sensors.	48	35
Diesel engines		
EGR valve mounting bolts	10	7

1 General information and precautions

Petrol engines

Crankcase emission control

1 To reduce the emission of unburned hydrocarbons from the crankcase into the atmosphere, the engine is sealed and the blow-by gases and oil vapour are drawn from inside the crankcase, through an oil separator and regulating (PCV – positive crankcase ventilation) valve, into the inlet manifold to be burned by the engine during normal combustion.

2 Under all conditions the gases are forced out of the crankcase by the (relatively) higher crankcase pressure.

Exhaust emission control

3 To minimise the amount of pollutants which escape into the atmosphere, all models are fitted with a catalytic converter in the exhaust system. The system is of the closed-loop type, in which an oxygen (lambda) sensor in the exhaust manifold provides the fuel injection/ignition system Powertrain Control Module (PCM) with constant feedback, enabling the PCM to adjust the mixture to provide the best possible conditions for the converter to operate.

4 The oxygen sensor has a heating element built-in that is controlled by the PCM through a relay to quickly bring the sensor's tip to an efficient operating temperature. The sensor's tip is sensitive to oxygen and sends the PCM a varying voltage depending on the amount of oxygen in the exhaust gases; if the intake air/fuel mixture is too rich, the exhaust gases are low in oxygen so the sensor sends a low-voltage signal, the voltage rising as the mixture weakens and the amount of oxygen rises in the exhaust gases.

5 Peak conversion efficiency of all major pollutants occurs if the intake air/fuel mixture is maintained at the chemically-correct ratio for the complete combustion of petrol of 14.7 parts (by weight) of air to 1 part of fuel (the 'stoichiometric' ratio). The sensor output voltage alters in a large step at this point, the PCM using the signal change as a reference point and correcting the intake air/fuel mixture accordingly by altering the fuel injector pulse width.

6 A second sensor is fitted downstream of the catalytic converter, to monitor the converter's efficiency, and to fine-tune the information being sent back to the PCM, so that emissions are kept even more tightly under control.

Evaporative emission control

7 To minimise the escape into the atmosphere of unburned hydrocarbons, an evaporative emissions control system is also fitted to all

models. The fuel tank filler cap is sealed, and a charcoal canister is mounted on the side of the fuel tank. The canister collects the petrol vapours generated in the tank when the car is parked, and stores them until they can be cleared from the canister (under the control of the fuel injection/ignition system PCM) via the purge valve into the inlet tract to be burned by the engine during normal combustion. The purge (or EVAP) valve is located on the inlet manifold.

8 To ensure that the engine runs correctly when it is cold and/or idling and to protect the catalytic converter from the effects of an over-rich mixture, the EVAP valve is not opened by the PCM until the engine has warmed-up, and the engine is under load; the valve solenoid is then modulated on and off to allow the stored vapour to pass into the inlet tract.

Diesel engines

Crankcase emission control

9 To reduce the emission of unburned hydrocarbons from the crankcase into the atmosphere, the engine is sealed and the blow-by gases and oil vapour are drawn from inside the crankcase, through an oil separator and regulating (PCV – positive crankcase ventilation) valve, into the inlet manifold to be burned by the engine during normal combustion.

Exhaust emission control

10 To minimise the level of exhaust pollutants released into the atmosphere, a catalytic converter/particulate filter is fitted in the exhaust system of all models.

11 The catalytic converter consists of a canister containing a fine mesh impregnated with a catalyst material, over which the hot exhaust gases pass. The catalyst speeds up the oxidation of harmful carbon monoxide, unburnt hydrocarbons and soot, effectively reducing the quantity of harmful products released into the atmosphere via the exhaust gases.

12 A diesel particulate filter is incorporated in the catalytic converter and contains a silicon carbide honeycomb block containing microscopic channels in which the exhaust gases flow. As the gases flow through the honeycomb channels, soot particles are deposited on the channel walls. To prevent clogging of the honeycomb channels, the soot particles are burned off at regular intervals during what is known as a 'regeneration phase'. Under the control of the engine management system PCM, the injection characteristics are altered to raise the temperature of the exhaust gases to approximately 600°C. At this temperature, the soot particles are effectively burned off the honeycomb walls as the exhaust gases pass through. A differential pressure sensor and temperature sensor are used to inform the PCM of the condition of the particulate filter, and the temperature of the exhaust gases during the regeneration phase. When the PCM detects that soot build-up is reducing the efficiency of the particulate filter, it will instigate the regeneration process. This occurs at regular intervals under certain driving conditions and will normally not be detected by the driver.

Exhaust gas recirculation system

13 This system is designed to recirculate small quantities of exhaust gas into the inlet tract, and therefore into the combustion process. This process reduces the level of oxides of nitrogen present in the final exhaust gas which is released into the atmosphere.

14 The volume of exhaust gas recirculated is controlled by the engine management PCM.

15 The EGR valve is mounted on the rear of the cylinder head, and is connected by an internal channel to the exhaust manifold on the front of the engine. It incorporates a stepper motor to regulate the quantity of exhaust gas recirculated, and the valve is controlled directly by the engine management PCM.

Catalytic converter precautions

16 For long life and satisfactory operation of the catalytic converter, certain precautions must be observed. These are as follows.

17 For petrol engines, only use unleaded fuel. Leaded fuel will damage the catalyst and the oxygen sensor.

18 Do not run the engine for long periods if it is misfiring. Unburnt fuel entering the catalytic converter can cause it to overheat, resulting in permanent damage. For the same reason, do not try to start the engine by pushing or towing the car, nor crank it on the starter motor for long periods.

19 Do not strike or drop the catalytic converter. The ceramic honeycomb which forms part of its internal structure may be damaged.

20 Always renew seals and gaskets upstream of the catalytic converter (between the engine and converter) whenever they are disturbed.

---

2   Petrol engine emission control systems – testing and component renewal

---

Crankcase emission control

1 The components of this system require no attention, other than to check that the hoses are clear and undamaged at regular intervals.

Evaporative emission control

Testing

2 If the system is thought to be faulty, disconnect the hoses from the charcoal canister and purge control (EVAP) valve and check that they are clear by blowing through them. If the purge control valve or charcoal canister are thought to be faulty, they must be renewed.

Charcoal canister renewal

3 The charcoal canister is located under the rear of the car, in a recess in the side of the fuel tank **(see illustration)**. Referring to Chapter 4A Section 7, remove the fuel tank as far as necessary for access to the canister.

4 Disconnect the hoses and back-pressure valve from the canister, then unscrew the mounting bolt and remove it from the recess in the tank.

5 Fit the new canister using a reversal of the removal procedure.

EVAP purge valve renewal

6 The EVAP purge valve is mounted on the inlet manifold **(see illustration)**.

7 To renew the valve, first disconnect the wiring plug.

8 Disconnect the hoses from the valve noting their locations, then detach the valve from its mounting bracket.

9 Fit the new valve using a reversal of the removal procedure.

Exhaust emission control

Testing

10 The performance of the catalytic converter can be checked only by measuring the exhaust gases using a good-quality, carefully-calibrated exhaust gas analyser.

11 If the CO level at the tailpipe is too high, the car should be taken to a Ford dealer so that the complete fuel injection and ignition systems, including the oxygen sensor, can be thoroughly checked using the special diagnostic equipment. Once these have been checked and are known to be free from faults, the fault must be in the catalytic converter, which must be renewed.

Catalytic converter renewal

12 Refer to Chapter 4A Section 12 for details.

Oxygen (lambda) sensor renewal

Note: *The oxygen sensor is delicate and will not work if it is dropped or knocked, if its power supply is disrupted, or if any cleaning materials are used on it.*

13 Trace the wiring back from the oxygen sensor to the connector and disconnect the wiring **(see illustration)**.

14 Unscrew the sensor and remove it from

2.3 The charcoal canister is located in a recess in the side of the fuel tank

2.6 EVAP purge valve location (arrowed) on the inlet manifold

2.13 Oxygen sensor wiring connector (1.25 and 1.6 litre engines shown)

2.14 Unscrew the oxygen sensor and remove it from the manifold

2.18a Disconnect the converter monitor sensor wiring plug...

2.18b ... then unscrew the sensor

the exhaust manifold **(see illustration)**. A special slotted socket may be needed (if a spanner cannot be used), to make allowance for the sensor's wiring.

15 Clean the threads of the sensor and the threads in the exhaust manifold.

16 Insert the sensor in the manifold and tighten to the specified torque.

17 Reconnect the wiring, making sure that it is in no danger of contacting the exhaust manifold.

Converter monitor sensor renewal

18 This sensor is very similar to the oxygen sensor, and renewal details are virtually identical. Since the sensor is fitted further down the exhaust manifold than the oxygen sensor, access to the sensor itself will be easier from below **(see illustrations)**.

3 Diesel engine emission control systems – testing and component renewal

Crankcase emission control

1 The components of this system require no attention, other than to check that the hoses are clear and undamaged at regular intervals. The separator and positive crankcase ventilation valve (PCV) are incorporated into the cylinder head cover.

Exhaust emission control

Testing

2 The performance of the catalytic converter can be checked only by measuring the exhaust gases using a good-quality, carefully-calibrated exhaust gas analyser.

3 Before assuming that the catalytic converter is faulty, it is worth checking the problem is not due to a faulty injector. Refer to your Ford dealer for further information.

Catalytic converter/particulate filter renewal

4 Refer to Chapter 4B Section 18.

Exhaust gas recirculation

Testing

5 Testing of the system should be entrusted to a Ford dealer.

EGR valve renewal

6 Pull up and remove the plastic cover from the top of the engine (where applicable).

7 Unclip the fuel supply and return hoses to gain access to the valve, located on the top of the inlet manifold.

8 Where necessary, disconnect the wiring plugs from the fuel injectors etc., undo the retaining bolt and move the wiring harness guide on the top of the cylinder head to one side.

9 Disconnect the wiring plug, undo the 2 retaining bolts and detach the EGR valve from the cooler assembly **(see illustration)**. Renew the gasket/seal.

10 Refitting is a reversal of removal.

EGR cooler renewal

11 The EGR cooler assembly is located on the rear of the engine. Remove the windscreen cowl panel as described in Chapter 11 Section 20.

12 Drain the cooling system as described in Chapter 1B Section 30.

13 Remove the air cleaner assembly as described in Chapter 4B Section 4.

14 Remove the battery and battery tray as described in Chapter 5A Section 4.

15 Disconnect the wiring plugs from the fuel injectors etc., then undo the retaining bolt and move the wiring harness guide on the top of the cylinder head to one side.

16 Move the fuel filter assembly to one side with reference to Chapter 1B Section 22.

17 Move any coolant pipes aside to gain access to the EGR cooler assembly.

3.9 EGR valve retaining bolts

18 Note their fitted positions, then disconnect the various hoses and wiring plugs from the EGR cooler.

19 Undo the 2 bolts securing the EGR pipe to the intake manifold, and the EGR cooler mounting bolts **(see illustration)**.

20 Refitting is a reversal of removal.

4 Catalytic converter – general information and precautions

General information

1 The catalytic converter reduces harmful exhaust emissions by chemically converting the more poisonous gases to ones which (in theory at least) are less harmful. The chemical reaction is known as an 'oxidising' reaction, or one where oxygen is 'added'.

2 Inside the converter is a honeycomb structure, made of ceramic material and coated with the precious metals palladium, platinum and rhodium (the 'catalyst' which promotes the chemical reaction). The chemical reaction generates heat, which itself promotes the reaction – therefore, once the car has been driven several miles, the body of the converter will be very hot.

3 The ceramic structure contained within the converter is understandably fragile, and will not withstand rough treatment. Since the converter runs at a high temperature, driving through deep standing water (in flood conditions, for example) is to be avoided, since the thermal stresses imposed when

3.19 EGR pipe-to-manifold bolts

plunging the hot converter into cold water may well cause the ceramic internals to fracture, resulting in a 'blocked' converter – a common cause of failure. A converter which has been damaged in this way can be checked by shaking it (do not strike it) – if a rattling noise is heard, this indicates probable failure.

Precautions

4 The catalytic converter is a reliable and simple device which needs no maintenance in itself, but there are some facts of which an owner should be aware if the converter is to function properly for its full service life:

Petrol engines

a) *DO NOT use leaded petrol (or lead-replacement petrol, LRP) in a car equipped with a catalytic converter – the lead (or other additives) will coat the precious metals, reducing their converting efficiency and will eventually destroy the converter.*

b) *b) Always keep the ignition and fuel systems well-maintained in accordance with the manufacturer's schedule (see Chapter 1A).*

c) *If the engine develops a misfire, do not drive the car at all (or at least as little as possible) until the fault is cured.*

d) *DO NOT push- or tow-start the car – this will soak the catalytic converter in unburned fuel, causing it to overheat when the engine does start.*

e) *DO NOT switch off the ignition at high engine speeds – ie, do not 'blip' the throttle immediately before switching off the engine.*

f) *DO NOT use fuel or engine oil additives*

– *these may contain substances harmful to the catalytic converter.*

g) *DO NOT continue to use the car if the engine burns oil to the extent of leaving a visible trail of blue smoke.*

h) *Remember that the catalytic converter operates at very high temperatures. DO NOT, therefore, park the car in dry undergrowth, over long grass or piles of dead leaves after a long run.*

i) *As mentioned above, driving through deep water should be avoided if possible. The sudden cooling effect may fracture the ceramic honeycomb, damaging it beyond repair.*

j) *Remember that the catalytic converter is FRAGILE – do not strike it with tools during servicing work, and take care handling it when removing it from the car for any reason.*

k) *In some cases, a sulphurous smell (like that of rotten eggs) may be noticed from the exhaust. This is common to many catalytic converter-equipped cars, and has more to do with the sulphur content of the brand of fuel being used than the converter itself.*

l) *If a substantial loss of power is experienced, remember that this could be due to the converter being blocked. This can occur simply as a result of high mileage, but may be due to the ceramic element having fractured and collapsed internally (see paragraph 3). A new converter is the only cure in this instance.*

m) *The catalytic converter, used on a well-maintained and well-driven car, should last at least 100 000 miles – if the converter is no longer effective, it must be renewed.*

Diesel engines

5 The catalytic converter fitted to diesel models is simpler than that fitted to petrol models, but it still needs to be treated with respect to avoid problems:

a) *DO NOT use fuel or engine oil additives – these may contain substances harmful to the catalytic converter.*

b) *DO NOT continue to use the car if the engine burns (engine) oil to the extent of leaving a visible trail of blue smoke.*

c) *Remember that the catalytic converter operates at very high temperatures. DO NOT, therefore, park the car in dry undergrowth, over long grass or piles of dead leaves after a long run.*

d) *As mentioned above, driving through deep water should be avoided if possible. The sudden cooling effect will fracture the ceramic honeycomb, damaging it beyond repair.*

e) *Remember that the catalytic converter is FRAGILE – do not strike it with tools during servicing work, and take care handling it when removing it from the car for any reason.*

f) *If a substantial loss of power is experienced, remember that this could be due to the converter being blocked. This can occur simply as a result of high mileage, but may be due to the ceramic element having fractured and collapsed internally (see paragraph 3). A new converter is the only cure in this instance.*

g) *The catalytic converter, used on a well-maintained and well-driven car, should last at least 100 000 miles – if the converter is no longer effective, it must be renewed.*

Chapter 5 Part A
Starting and charging systems

Contents

Degrees of difficulty

Easy, suitable for novice with little experience	**Fairly easy,** suitable for beginner with some experience	**Fairly difficult,** suitable for competent DIY mechanic	**Difficult,** suitable for experienced DIY mechanic	**Very difficult,** suitable for expert DIY or professional

Specifications

System type... 12 volt, negative earth

Battery

Type .... Low-maintenance or maintenance-free sealed for life
Charge condition:
  Poor .... 12.5 volts
  Normal .... 12.6 volts
  Good .... 12.7 volts

Torque wrench settings	**Nm**	**lbf ft**
Alternator mounting bolts/nuts.	48	35
Alternator mounting stud (1.25 and 1.6 litre petrol engines)	10	7
Glow plugs	6	5
Starter motor mounting bolts:		
Petrol engines	35	26
Diesel engines	25	18

1 General information and precautions

General information

1 The engine electrical system consists mainly of the charging and starting systems. Because of their engine-related functions, these components are covered separately from the body electrical devices such as the lights, instruments, etc (which are covered in Chapter 12). Information on the ignition system is covered in Part B of this Chapter.
2 The electrical system is of 12 volt negative earth type.
3 The battery is of the low-maintenance or 'maintenance-free' (sealed for life) type and is charged by the alternator, which is belt-driven from the crankshaft pulley.
4 The starter motor is of the pre-engaged type incorporating an integral solenoid. On starting, the solenoid moves the drive pinion into engagement with the flywheel ring gear before the starter motor is energised. Once the engine has started, a one-way clutch prevents the motor armature being driven by the engine until the pinion disengages from the flywheel.

Precautions

5 It is necessary to take extra care when working on the electrical system to avoid damage to semi-conductor devices (diodes and transistors), and to avoid the risk of personal injury. In addition to the precautions given in *Safety first!* at the beginning of this manual, observe the following when working on the system:

● Always remove rings, watches, etc, before working on the electrical system. Even with the battery disconnected, capacitive discharge could occur if a component's live terminal is earthed through a metal object. This could cause a shock or nasty burn.
● Do not reverse the battery connections. Components such as the alternator, electronic control units, or any other components having semi-conductor circuitry could be irreparably damaged.
● If the engine is being started using jump leads and a slave battery, connect the batteries positive-to-positive and negative-to-negative (see Jump starting). This also applies when connecting a battery charger.
● Never disconnect the battery terminals, the alternator, any electrical wiring or any test instruments when the engine is running.
● Do not allow the engine to turn the alternator when the alternator is not connected.
● Never 'test' for alternator output by 'flashing' the output lead to earth.
● Never use an ohmmeter of the type incorporating a hand-cranked generator for circuit or continuity testing.
● Always ensure that the battery negative lead is disconnected when working on the electrical system.

● Before using electric-arc welding equipment on the car, disconnect the battery, alternator and components such as the fuel injection/ignition electronic control unit to protect them from the risk of damage.

2 Electrical fault finding – general information

1 Refer to Chapter 12 Section 2.

3 Battery – testing and charging

Testing

Standard and low-maintenance battery

1 If the car covers a small annual mileage, it is worthwhile checking the specific gravity of the electrolyte every three months to determine the state of charge of the battery. Use a hydrometer to make the check and compare the results with the following table. Note that the specific gravity readings assume an electrolyte temperature of 15°C; for every 10°C below 15°C subtract 0.007. For every 10°C above 15°C add 0.007.
2 Ambient temperature

	Above 25°C	Below 25°C
Fully-charged	1.210 to 1.230	1.270 to 1.290
70% charged	1.170 to 1.190	1.230 to 1.250
Discharged	1.050 to 1.070	1.110 to 1.130

3 If the battery condition is suspect, first check the specific gravity of electrolyte in each cell. A variation of 0.040 or more between any cells indicates loss of electrolyte or deterioration of the internal plates.
4 If the specific gravity variation is 0.040 or more, the battery should be renewed. If the cell variation is satisfactory but the battery is discharged, it should be charged as described later in this Section.

Maintenance-free battery

5 In cases where a 'sealed for life' maintenance-free battery is fitted, topping-up and testing of the electrolyte in each cell is not possible. The condition of the battery can therefore only be tested using a battery condition indicator or a voltmeter.
6 Certain models are fitted with a maintenance-free battery with a built-in charge condition indicator. The indicator is located in the top of the battery casing, and indicates the condition of the battery from its colour. The charge conditions denoted by the colour of the indicator should be printed on a label attached to the battery – if not, consult a Ford dealer or automotive electrician for advice.

All battery types

7 If testing the battery using a voltmeter, connect the voltmeter across the battery and note the voltage. The test is only accurate if the battery has not been subjected to any kind of charge for the previous six hours. If this is not the case, switch on the headlights for 30 seconds, then wait four to five minutes before testing the battery after switching off the headlights. All other electrical circuits must be switched off, so check that the doors and tailgate are fully shut when making the test.
8 If the voltage reading is less than 12.2 volts, then the battery is discharged, whilst a reading of 12.2 to 12.4 volts indicates a partially-discharged condition.
9 If the battery is to be charged, remove it from the vehicle and charge it as described later in this Section.

Charging

Note: *The following is intended as a guide only. Always refer to the manufacturer's recommendations (often printed on a label attached to the battery) before charging a battery.*

Standard and low-maintenance battery

10 Charge the battery at a rate equivalent to 10% of the battery capacity (eg, for a 45 Ah battery charge at 4.5 A) and continue to charge the battery at this rate until no further rise in specific gravity is noted over a four-hour period.
11 Alternatively, a trickle charger charging at the rate of 1.5 amps can safely be used overnight.
12 Specially rapid boost charges which are claimed to restore the power of the battery in 1 to 2 hours are not recommended, as they can cause serious damage to the battery plates through overheating. If the battery is completely flat, recharging should take at least 24 hours.
13 While charging the battery, note that the temperature of the electrolyte should never exceed 38°C.

Maintenance-free battery

14 This battery type takes considerably longer to fully recharge than the standard type, the time taken being dependent on the extent of discharge, but it can take anything up to three days.
15 A constant voltage type charger is required, to be set, when connected, to 13.9 to 14.9 volts with a charger current below 25 amps. Using this method, the battery should be useable within three hours, giving a voltage reading of 12.5 volts, but this is for a partially-discharged battery and, as mentioned, full charging can take far longer.
16 If the battery is to be charged from a fully-discharged state (condition reading less than 12.2 volts), have it recharged by your Ford dealer or local automotive electrician, as the charge rate is higher, and constant supervision during charging is necessary.

4 Battery and battery tray
– disconnection, removal and refitting

Note: *Refer to the warnings given in ' Safety first!' and in Section 1 of this Chapter before starting work.*

Battery disconnection

1 Numerous systems fitted to the vehicle require battery power to be available at all times, either to ensure their continued operation (such as the clock) or to maintain control unit memories which would be erased if the battery were to be disconnected. Whenever the battery is to be disconnected therefore, first note the following, to ensure that there are no unforeseen consequences of this action:

a) *First, on any vehicle with central locking, it is a wise precaution to remove the key from the ignition, and to keep it with you, so that it does not get locked in, if the central locking should engage accidentally when the battery is reconnected.*

b) *If the battery is disconnected while the alarm system is armed or activated, the alarm will remain in the same state when the battery is reconnected. The same applies to the engine immobiliser system.*

c) *If a Ford 'Keycode' audio unit is fitted, and the unit and/or the battery is disconnected, the unit will not function again on reconnection until the correct security code is entered. Details of this procedure, which varies according to the unit and model year, are given in the 'Ford Audio Systems Operating Guide' supplied with the car when new, with the code itself being given in a 'Radio Passport' and/or a 'Keycode Label' at the same time. Ensure you have the correct code before you disconnect the battery. For obvious security reasons, the procedure is not given in this manual. If you do not have the code or details of the correct procedure, but can supply proof of ownership and a legitimate reason for wanting this information, the car's selling dealer may be able to help.*

d) *The engine management powertrain control module (PCM) is of the 'self-*

4.3 Loosen the clamp nut and disconnect the battery negative lead

learning' type, meaning that as it operates, it also monitors and stores the settings which give optimum engine performance under all operating conditions. When the battery is disconnected, these settings are lost and the PCM reverts to the base settings programmed into its memory at the factory. On restarting, this may lead to the engine running/idling roughly for a short while, until the PCM has re-learned the optimum settings. This process is best accomplished by taking the vehicle on a road test (for approximately 15 minutes), covering all engine speeds and loads, concentrating mainly in the 2500 to 3500 rpm region,

e) *On models with electric windows, it will be necessary to reprogramme the motors to restore the one-touch function of the buttons, after reconnection of the battery. To do this, fully close both front windows. With the windows closed, depress the up button of the driver's side window for approximately 5 seconds, then release it and depress the passenger side window up button for approximately 5 seconds.*

f) *On all models, when reconnecting the battery after disconnection, switch on the ignition and wait 10 seconds to allow the electronic vehicle systems to stabilise and re-initialise.*

2 The battery is located on the left-hand side of the engine compartment, on a platform above the transmission.

3 Loosen the clamp nut, then detach the earth lead from the battery negative (earth)

4.4 Loosen the clamp nut and disconnect the battery positive lead

terminal post **(see illustration)**. This is the terminal to disconnect before working on, or disconnecting, any electrical component on the car. Position the lead away from the battery.

4 Pivot up the plastic cover from the positive terminal, then loosen the positive lead clamp nut **(see illustration)**. Detach the positive lead from the terminal, and position it away from the battery.

Battery removal

5 Undo the nuts/bolt securing the battery top clamp plate, and lift it off **(see illustration)**. On certain models, one or two vacuum hoses may be clipped to the clamp plate – if so, detach them before removal.

6 Slide up the front panel of the battery tray or lift away the battery retaining bracket (as applicable), then lift out the battery, keeping it as level as possible **(see illustrations)**. Take care, as the battery is heavy.

Battery refitting

7 Refitting is a reversal of removal. Reconnect the battery negative lead last. Make sure the battery terminals and clamps are clean before refitting, and that the clamp nuts are tightened securely.

Battery tray removal

8 If required, once the battery has been removed, the battery tray and its support bracket can also be removed, as follows.

9 Remove the PCM as described in Chapter 4A Section 11 or Chapter 4B Section 12.

4.5 Undo the nuts/bolt securing the battery top clamp plate, and lift it off

4.6a Slide up and remove the front panel of the battery tray…

4.6b … or remove the retaining bracket

4.10 Undo the three bolts and lift the battery tray off its support bracket

4.11 Undo the two screws on the underside and separate the PCM mounting bracket from the battery tray

4.12 Undo the nuts, release the wiring loom and lift out the support bracket

Note: *It is possible to undo the battery tray bolts (see next paragraph), then undo the screws and detach the PCM bracket from the battery tray without disconnecting the wiring plugs. The PCM and wiring harness must then be carefully moved to one side. Take care not to damage the wiring harness.*

10 The battery tray is secured by three bolts at the base. Undo the bolts, and lift the battery tray off its support bracket **(see illustration)**.

11 Undo the two Torx screws on the underside and separate the PCM mounting bracket from the battery tray **(see illustration)**. Remove the battery tray from the engine compartment.

12 Undo the nuts securing the battery tray support bracket in position. Release the wiring loom from the support bracket and lift the support bracket out of the engine compartment **(see illustration)**.

Battery tray refitting

13 Refitting is a reversal of removal.

5 Charging system – testing

Note: *Refer to the warnings given in ' Safety first!' and in Section 1 of this Chapter before starting work.*

1 If the ignition warning light fails to illuminate when the ignition is switched on, first check

the alternator wiring connections for security. If all is satisfactory, the alternator may be at fault and should be renewed or taken to an auto-electrician for testing and repair.

2 If the ignition warning light illuminates when the engine is running, stop the engine and check that the drivebelt is intact and correctly tensioned (see Chapter 1A Section 9 or Chapter 1B Section 10) and that the alternator connections are secure. If all is so far satisfactory, have the alternator checked by an auto-electrician for testing and repair.

3 If the alternator output is suspect even though the warning light functions correctly, the regulated voltage may be checked as follows.

4 Connect a voltmeter across the battery terminals and start the engine.

5 Increase the engine speed until the voltmeter reading remains steady; the reading should be between 13.5 and 14.8 volts.

6 Switch on as many electrical accessories (eg, the headlights, heated rear window and heater blower) as possible, and check that the alternator maintains the regulated voltage between 13.5 and 14.8 volts.

7 If the regulated voltage is not as stated, the fault may be due to worn brushes, weak brush springs, a faulty voltage regulator, a faulty diode, a severed phase winding, or worn or damaged slip-rings. At the time of writing, it would appear that no parts were available for the alternator. If faulty the complete assembly must be renewed. If in doubt, the alternator

should be renewed or taken to an auto-electrician for testing.

6 Alternator drivebelt – removal, refitting and tensioning

1 Refer to the procedure given for the auxiliary drivebelt in Chapter 1A Section 9, 26 or Chapter 1B Section 26, as applicable.

7 Alternator – removal and refitting

Note: *Refer to the warnings given in ' Safety first!' and in Section 1 of this Chapter before starting work.*

1 Disconnect the battery negative lead as described in Section 4.

Petrol engines

Removal

2 Remove the auxiliary drivebelt as described in Chapter 1A Section 26.

1.0 litre engines

3 Unbolt and remove the auxiliary drivebelt tensioner.

4 On models with air conditioning, disconnect the wiring plugs, undo the 3 mounting bolts and move the compressor to one side (see Chapter 3 Section 11). There's no need to disconnect the refrigerant pipes. Secure the compressor to the vehicle body to prevent straining the pipes.

5 Disconnect the crankshaft position sensor wiring plug, and unclip the wiring.

6 Prise up the plastic cap and disconnect the alternator battery cable, then disconnect the field wiring multiplug behind it **(see illustration)**. Note the fitted positions and routing of the wiring.

7 Unclip the alternator wiring harness guide and move it to one side.

8 Undo and remove the alternator mounting bolts **(see illustration)**.

9 Lower the alternator from place.

7.6 Prise out the plastic cap, and disconnect the battery positive cable from the alternator terminal

7.8 Alternator mounting bolts

7.11 Remove the upper mounting bolt and nut

7.12 Alternator lower mounting bolt

7.19 Disconnect the wiring plugs above the alternator

1.25 and 1.6 litre engines

10 Prise out the plastic cap, undo the nut securing the battery positive cable to the alternator, then disconnect the wiring plug.

11 Undo and remove the alternator upper mounting nut and bolt **(see illustration)**.

12 Undo the lower mounting bolt **(see illustration)**.

13 Unscrew the alternator upper mounting stud. Ideally use Torx socket to unscrew the stud, although if necessary, this can be done using two nuts locked together on the stud's threads. Support the alternator as the stud is removed, then lift the alternator from place.

Refitting

14 Refitting is a reversal of removal. Remembering to tighten the various fasteners to their specified torque where given.

Diesel engines

Removal

15 The alternator is located on the right-hand front of the engine. First, remove the auxiliary drivebelt as described in Chapter 1B Section 26.

16 Pull up and remove the plastic cover from the top of the engine.

17 Access to the alternator is limited. Although not strictly necessary, if improved access is required, remove the particulate filter as described in Chapter 4B Section 18.

7.20 Prise out the cover, then disconnect the alternator wiring and plug

18 If the particulate filter has been removed, undo the retaining bolt and pull the engine oil level dipstick guide tube from place. Examine the tube O-ring seal and replace if necessary.

19 If the filter has not been removed, disconnect the 2 wiring plugs from the temperature sensors at the bracket above the alternator **(see illustration)**. Where applicable, disconnect the air conditioning compressor wiring plug at the same time.

20 Prise up the plastic cap and disconnect the alternator battery cable, then disconnect the field wiring multiplug next to it **(see illustration)**. Note the fitted positions and routing of the wiring.

21 Disconnect the wiring plug from the

7.22 Drivebelt tensioner/wiring harness guide bolts

oil pressure sensor, then unclip the wiring harness from the alternator.

22 Undo the 3 bolts and remove the auxiliary drivebelt tensioner, along with the wiring harness guide **(see illustration)**.

23 Undo the 4 mounting bolts securing the air conditioning compressor (where fitted), and move the compressor forward. Secure it to the front of the vehicle using cable ties or similar. There is no need to disconnect the refrigerant pipes.

24 Undo the nuts and remove the right-hand front engine cover bracket **(see illustration)**.

25 Remove the alternator left-hand mounting bolts **(see illustration)**.

26 Support the alternator, then remove the right-hand mounting bolts **(see illustration)**.

7.24 Engine cover bracket nuts

7.25 Alternator left-hand mounting bolts

7.26 Alternator right-hand mounting bolts

7.27 Rotate the alternator, and lift it from place

27 Manoeuvre the alternator from place **(see illustration)**.

Refitting

28 Refitting is a reversal of removal, noting the following points:
a) Tighten the mounting bolts to the specified torque, including those for the air conditioning compressor, where applicable.
b) Ensure that the wiring is reconnected correctly, and that the retaining nuts are tight.
c) Refit the auxiliary drivebelt as described in Chapter 1B Section 26.

8 Starting system – testing

Note: *Refer to the precautions given in ' Safety first!' and in Section 1 of this Chapter before starting work.*

1 If the starter motor fails to operate when the ignition key is turned to the appropriate position, the following possible causes may be to blame.
a) The engine immobiliser is faulty.
b) The battery is faulty.
c) The electrical connections between the switch, solenoid, battery and starter motor are somewhere failing to pass the necessary current from the battery through the starter to earth.
d) The solenoid is faulty.
e) The starter motor is mechanically or electrically defective.

2 To check the battery, switch on the headlights. If they dim after a few seconds, this indicates that the battery is discharged – recharge (see Section 3) or renew the battery. If the headlights glow brightly, operate the ignition switch and observe the lights. If they dim, then this indicates that current is reaching the starter motor, therefore the fault must lie in the starter motor. If the lights continue to glow brightly (and no clicking sound can be heard from the starter motor solenoid), this indicates that there is a fault in the circuit or solenoid – see following paragraphs. If the starter motor turns slowly when operated, but the battery is in good condition, then this indicates that either the starter motor is faulty, or there is considerable resistance somewhere in the circuit.

3 If a fault in the circuit is suspected, disconnect the battery leads (including the earth connection to the body), the starter/solenoid wiring and the engine/transmission earth strap. Thoroughly clean the connections, and reconnect the leads and wiring, then use a voltmeter or test lamp to check that full battery voltage is available at the battery positive lead connection to the solenoid, and that the earth is sound. Smear petroleum jelly around the battery terminals to prevent corrosion – corroded connections are amongst the most frequent causes of electrical system faults.

4 If the battery and all connections are in good condition, check the circuit by disconnecting the wire from the solenoid terminal. Connect a voltmeter or test lamp between the wire end and a good earth (such as the battery negative terminal), and check that the wire is live when the ignition switch is turned to the 'start' position. If it is, then the circuit is sound – if not, the circuit wiring can be checked as described in Chapter 12 Section 2.

5 The solenoid contacts can be checked by connecting a voltmeter or test lamp between the battery positive feed connection on the starter side of the solenoid, and earth. When the ignition switch is turned to the 'start' position, there should be a reading or lighted bulb, as applicable. If there is no reading or lighted bulb, the solenoid is faulty and should be renewed.

6 If the circuit and solenoid are proved sound,

the fault must lie in the starter motor. In this event, it may be possible to have the starter motor overhauled by a specialist, but check on the cost of spares before proceeding, as it may prove more economical to obtain a new or exchange motor.

9 Starter motor – removal and refitting

Note: *Refer to the warnings given in ' Safety first!' and in Section 1 of this Chapter before starting work.*

Removal

1 Disconnect the battery negative lead as described in Section 4.

Petrol engines

1.0 litre engines

2 Unscrew the engine oil filler cap, and pull the plastic cover on the top of the engine upwards from its' mountings.
3 Release the clamps, disconnect the breather pipe and remove the air outlet duct from the air cleaner housing.
4 Undo and remove the starter motor upper mounting bolt, along with the bracket.
5 Apply the handbrake, then jack up the front of the car and support on axle stands (see *Jacking and vehicle support*).
6 Working beneath the left-hand rear of the engine, unscrew the two nuts and disconnect the wiring assembly from the starter motor. Note the location of each wire, for refitting.
7 Support the starter motor, then unscrew the lower mounting bolt, and withdraw the motor **(see illustration)**.

1.25 and 1.6 litre engines

8 Raise the front of the vehicle and support is securing on axle stands (see *Jacking and vehicle support*). Undo the fasteners and remove the engine undershield (where applicable).
9 Disconnect the wiring plug from the crankshaft position sensor at the front of the engine, adjacent to transmission bellhousing.
10 Undo the nuts securing the wiring to the starter motor **(see illustrations)**.

9.7 Withdraw the starter motor

9.10a Undo the nuts...

9.10b ...and pull the wiring from the starter motor terminals

9.11a Undo the mounting bolts...

9.11b ...and withdraw the starter motor

9.16 Undo the nuts and disconnect the wiring

11 Undo the mounting bolts and remove the starter motor **(see illustrations)**. Note that on some models, the wiring harness guide is also secured by the starter motor mounting bolts. On models with Powershift transmission, undo the two bolts and remove the selector cable support bracket from the top of the transmission.

Diesel engines

12 The starter motor is located on the left-hand rear of the engine.

13 To gain access to the upper mounting bolts, remove the fuel filter assembly as described in Chapter 1B Section 22. Move the filter assembly to one side, there's no need to disconnect the hoses.

14 Undo the bolts and remove the fuel filter mounting bracket.

15 Apply the handbrake, then jack up the front of the car and support on axle stands (see *Jacking and vehicle support*). Undo the fasteners and remove the engine undershield, where applicable.

16 Working beneath the vehicle, unscrew the two nuts and disconnect the wiring from the starter motor **(see illustration)**. Note the location of each wire, for refitting.

17 Support the starter motor, then unscrew and remove the 3 mounting bolts, and withdraw the motor **(see illustrations)**.

Refitting

18 Refitting is a reversal of removal, but tighten the mounting bolts to the specified torque.

9.17a Starter motor lower mounting bolt...

10 Starter motor – testing and overhaul

1 If the starter motor is thought to be suspect, it should be removed from the car and taken to an auto-electrician for testing. Most auto-electricians will be able to supply and fit brushes at a reasonable cost. However, check on the cost of repairs before proceeding as it may prove more economical to obtain a new or exchange motor.

11 Preheating system – description and testing

Description

1 To assist cold starting, diesel engines are fitted with a preheating system, which consists of four glow plugs (one per cylinder), a glow plug relay, a facia-mounted warning light, the engine management PCM, and the associated electrical wiring.

2 The glow plugs are miniature electric heating elements, encapsulated in a metal case with a probe at one end and electrical connection at the other. Each combustion chamber has one glow plug threaded into it, with the tip of the glow plug probe positioned directly in line with incoming spray of fuel from the injectors. When the glow plug is energised,

9.17b ...and upper mounting bolts

it heats up rapidly, causing the fuel passing over the glow plug probe to be heated to its optimum temperature, ready for combustion. In addition, some of the fuel passing over the glow plugs is ignited and this helps to trigger the combustion process.

3 The preheating system begins to operate as soon as the ignition key is switched to the second position, but only if the engine coolant temperature is below 20ºC and the engine is turned at more than 70 rpm for 0.2 seconds. A facia-mounted warning light informs the driver that preheating is taking place. The light extinguishes when sufficient preheating has taken place to allow the engine to be started, but power will still be supplied to the glow plugs for a further period until the engine is started. If no attempt is made to start the engine, the power supply to the glow plugs is switched off after 10 seconds, to prevent battery drain and glow plug burn-out.

4 With the electronically-controlled diesel injection system fitted to models in this manual, the glow plug relay is controlled by the engine management system PCM, which determines the necessary preheating time based on inputs from the various system sensors. The system monitors the temperature of the intake air, then alters the preheating time (the length for which the glow plugs are supplied with current) to suit the conditions.

5 Post-heating takes place after the ignition key has been released from the 'start' position, but only if the engine coolant temperature is below 20ºC, the injected fuel flow is less than a certain rate, and the engine speed is less than 2500 rpm. The glow plugs continue to operate for a maximum of 30 seconds, helping to improve fuel combustion whilst the engine is warming-up, resulting in quieter, smoother running and reduced exhaust emissions.

Testing

6 The preheating system is controlled by the PCM, which is equipped with a sophisticated self-diagnosis system. Should a fault develop, have the system interrogated by a Ford dealer or suitably equipped repairer. The diagnostic equipment plugs into a socket under the drivers side of the facia – See Chapter 4B Section 12.

7 If the system malfunctions, testing is ultimately by substitution of known good units, but some preliminary checks may be made as follows.

8 Connect a voltmeter or 12 volt test light between the glow plug supply cable and earth (engine or car body). Make sure that the live connection is kept clear of the engine and bodywork.

9 Have an assistant switch on the ignition, and check that voltage is applied to the glow plugs. Note the time for which the warning light is lit, and the total time for which voltage is applied before the system cuts out. Switch off the ignition.

10 Warning light time will increase with lower temperatures and decrease with higher temperatures.

11 If there is no supply at all, the module or associated wiring is at fault.

12 Disconnect the main supply cable (behind the fuel filter) and the interconnecting wire from the top of the glow plugs. Be careful not to drop the nuts and washers.

13 Use a continuity tester, or a 12 volt test light connected to the battery positive terminal, to check for continuity between each glow plug terminal and earth. The resistance of a glow plug in good condition is very low (less than 1 ohm), so if the test light does not light or the continuity tester shows a high resistance, the glow plug is certainly defective.

14 If an ammeter is available, the current draw of each glow plug can be checked. After an initial surge of 15 to 20 amps, each plug should draw 12 amps. Any plug which draws much more or less than this is probably defective.

15 As a final check, the glow plugs can be removed and inspected as described in the following Section. On completion, refit any components removed for access.

12 Glow plugs – removal, inspection and refitting

Caution: If the preheating system has just been energised, or if the engine has been running, the glow plugs will be very hot.

Removal

1 Pull the plastic cover on the top of the engine upwards from its' mountings.

2 Work at the rear of the engine, pull off the wiring connector from the top of each glow plug and move the wiring harness to one side. Access is extremely limited.

3 Where applicable, carefully move any obstructing pipes or wires to one side to enable access to the relevant glow plug(s).

4 Unscrew the glow plug(s) and remove from the cylinder head.

Inspection

5 Inspect each glow plug for physical damage. Burnt or eroded glow plug tips can be caused by a bad injector spray pattern. Have the injectors checked if this sort of damage is found.

6 If the glow plugs are in good physical condition, check them electrically using a 12 volt test light or continuity tester as described in the previous Section.

Refitting

7 Refit by reversing the removal operations. Apply a smear of copper-based anti-seize compound to the plug threads, and tighten the glow plugs to the specified torque. Do not overtighten, as this can damage the glow plug element.

8 Refit any components removed for access.

Chapter 5 Part B
Ignition system – petrol models

Contents

Degrees of difficulty

| **Easy,** suitable for novice with little experience | **Fairly easy,** suitable for beginner with some experience | **Fairly difficult,** suitable for competent DIY mechanic | **Difficult,** suitable for experienced DIY mechanic | **Very difficult,** suitable for expert DIY or professional |

Specifications

General
System type . . . .   Electronic distributorless ignition system (DIS) with ignition module controlled by engine management system (Powertrain control module)

Firing order:
  1.0 litre engines   1-2-3
  1.25 and 1.6 litre engines   1-3-4-2
Location of No 1 cylinder . . . .   Timing belt end of engine

Torque wrench settings

	Nm	lbf ft
Ignition coils:		
1.0 litre engines	10	6
1.25 and 1.6 litre engines	6	4
Knock sensor(s):		
1.0 litre engines	20	15
1.25 and 1.6 litre engines	18	14

3.2 Slide out and depress the locking clips, then disconnect the wiring plugs

3.3 Ignition coil retaining bolts

1 Ignition system – general information and precautions

General information

1 The ignition system is integrated with the fuel injection system to form a combined engine management system under the control of the Powertrain control module (PCM) (see Chapter 4A Section 11 for further information). The main ignition system components include the ignition switch, the battery, the crankshaft speed/position sensor, the ignition coil (or coils), and the spark plugs.

2 A Distributorless Ignition System (DIS) is fitted where the main functions of the conventional distributor are superseded by a computerised module within the Powertrain Control Module. On 1.25 and 1.6 litre engines, the remote ignition coil unit combines a double-ended pair of coils – each time a coil receives an ignition signal, two sparks are produced, one at each end of the secondary windings. One spark goes to a cylinder on its compression stroke and the other goes to the corresponding cylinder on its exhaust stroke. The first will give the correct power stroke, but the second spark will have no effect (a 'wasted spark'), occurring as it does during exhaust conditions. On 1.0 litre engines, one coil is fitted for each spark plug. The coil fits above the spark plug, and has an integral power stage and HT cap. This system is often referred as a 'COP' (Coil On Plug) ignition system.

3 The information contained in this Chapter concentrates on the ignition-related components of the engine management system. Information covering the fuel, exhaust and emission control components can be found in the applicable Parts of Chapter 4A.

Precautions

4 The following precautions must be observed, to prevent damage to the ignition system components and to reduce risk of personal injury.

a) *Do not keep the ignition on for more than 10 seconds if the engine will not start.*
b) *Ensure that the ignition is switched off before disconnecting any of the ignition wiring.*
c) *Ensure that the ignition is switched off before connecting or disconnecting any ignition test equipment.*
d) *Do not earth the coil primary or secondary circuits.*

Warning: Due to the high voltages produced by the electronic ignition system, extreme care must be taken when working on the system with the ignition switched on. Persons with surgically-implanted cardiac pacemaker devices should keep well clear of the ignition circuits, components and test equipment.

2 Ignition system – testing

1 If a fault appears in the engine management system, first ensure that all the system wiring connectors are securely connected and free of corrosion. Ensure that the fault is not due to poor maintenance; ie, check that the air cleaner filter element is clean, the spark plugs are in good condition and correctly gapped, the cylinder compression pressures are correct and that the engine breather hoses are clear and undamaged.

2 If these checks fail to reveal the cause of the problem, the car should be taken to a suitably-equipped Ford dealer or engine management diagnostic specialist for testing. A diagnostic socket is incorporated in the engine management circuit into which a fault code reader or other suitable test equipment can be connected (see Chapter 4A Section 10). By using the code reader or test equipment, the engine management PCM can be interrogated, and any stored fault codes can be retrieved. This will allow the fault to be quickly and simply traced, alleviating the need to test all the system components individually, which is a time-consuming operation that carries a risk of damaging the PCM.

3 HT ignition coil – removal and refitting

Removal

1.0 litre engines

1 Unscrew the oil filler cap, then pull the plastic cover (where fitted) on the top of the engine upwards from its' mountings.

2 Disconnect the ignition coil(s) wiring plug(s) **(see illustration)**. It is safest to work on one coil at a time. However, if the coils and the wiring plugs are marked for position, all 3 could be removed at once.

3 Undo the 2 retaining bolts and pull the coil upwards from place **(see illustration)**.

1.25 and 1.6 litre engines

4 The ignition coil is bolted to the coolant outlet elbow on the left-hand end of the cylinder head **(see illustration)**.

3.4 The ignition coil is bolted to the left-hand end of the cylinder head

3.5 Disconnecting the coil wiring plug

3.6 Make sure the HT lead positions are marked on the coil before disconnecting

3.7a Unscrew the four mounting bolts …

3.7b … then remove the ignition coil and heat shield/mounting plate from the engine

6.3 Note the fitted position of the knock sensor

6.7 The knock sensors are located under the inlet manifold – 1.6 litre engine

5 Make sure the ignition is switched off, then disconnect the main wiring plug from the coil **(see illustration)**.
6 Identify the HT leads for position (mark the leads and the coil terminals) then carefully pull them from the terminals on the coil **(see illustration)**.
7 Unscrew the four mounting bolts and remove the ignition coil from the engine compartment. Where applicable, recover the heat shield/mounting plate **(see illustrations)**.

Refitting

7 Refitting is a reversal of removal.

4 Crankshaft position sensor – removal and refitting

1 Refer to Chapter 4A Section 11.

5 Ignition timing – checking and adjustment

1 Due to the nature of the ignition system, the ignition timing is constantly being monitored and adjusted by the engine management PCM, and nominal values cannot be given. Therefore, it is not possible for the home mechanic to check the ignition timing.
2 The only way in which the ignition timing can be checked is using special electronic test equipment, connected to the engine management system diagnostic socket (refer to Chapter). No adjustment of the ignition timing is possible. Should the ignition timing be incorrect, then a fault must be present in the engine management system.

6 Knock sensor – removal and refitting

Removal

1.0 litre engines

1 Remove the starter motor as described in Chapter 5A Section 9.
2 Disconnect the wiring plug from the sensor.
3 Note its fitted position, then undo the bolt and remove the sensor **(see illustration)**.

Note: *It's essential that the sensor is refitted to its original position* – *the wiring plug should be horizontal, pointing towards the timing belt of the engine.*

1.25 and 1.6 litre engines

4 Remove the inlet manifold as described in Chapter 4A Section 12.
5 The knock sensor(s) is located on the front facing side of the cylinder block under the inlet manifold.
6 Trace the wiring back from the sensor to the connector, then slide the retaining clip down and disconnect the wiring plug.
7 Note its fitted position, then undo the bolt and remove the sensor **(see illustration)**.

Refitting

8 Refitting is a reversal of removal, noting the following points:
a) The sensor(s) must be refitted in their original positions, with the wiring harness angle exactly as before.
b) Tightening the retaining bolt to the specified torque is absolutely essential. Failure to do so could impair the performance of the sensor, causing engine damage.

Chapter 6
Clutch

Contents

Degrees of difficulty

Easy, suitable for novice with little experience	Fairly easy, suitable for beginner with some experience	Fairly difficult, suitable for competent DIY mechanic	Difficult, suitable for experienced DIY mechanic	Very difficult, suitable for expert DIY or professional

Specifications

General
Clutch type. . . . . Single dry plate, diaphragm spring, hydraulically-operated release mechanism

Friction disc
Friction material thickness (minimum):
  1.0 litre EcoBoost engines . . . . 5.4 mm
  1.25 litre petrol engines . . . . 5.2 mm
  1.5 litre diesel engines . . . . 5.15 mm
  1.6 litre diesel engines . . . . 5.15 mm

Torque wrench settings

	Nm	lbf ft
Clutch master cylinder nuts/bolts	27	20
Clutch pedal bracket nuts	25	18
Clutch slave cylinder bolts *	10	7
Pressure plate-to-flywheel bolts*	29	21
Steering column shaft universal joint clamp bolt*	35	26

*Use new fasteners

1 General Information

1 The clutch consists of a friction disc, a pressure plate assembly, a release bearing and hydraulic slave cylinder; all of these components are contained in the large cast-aluminium alloy bellhousing, sandwiched between the engine and the transmission.

2 The hydraulic master cylinder is located in the pedal bracket on the bulkhead, and the clutch fluid reservoir is shared with the brake fluid reservoir on the top of the brake master cylinder. Inside the reservoir each circuit has its own compartment, so that in the event of fluid loss in the clutch circuit, the brake circuit remains fully operational.

3 The clutch disc (friction disc) is fitted between the engine flywheel and the clutch pressure plate, and is allowed to slide on the transmission input shaft splines.

4 The pressure plate assembly is bolted to the engine flywheel. When the engine is running, drive is transmitted from the crankshaft, via the flywheel, to the friction disc (these components being clamped securely together by the pressure plate assembly) and from the friction disc to the transmission input shaft.

5 To interrupt the drive, the spring pressure must be relaxed by the hydraulically-operated release mechanism. Depressing the clutch pedal operates the master cylinder which in turn operates the slave cylinder and presses the release bearing against the pressure plate spring fingers. This causes the springs to deform and releases the clamping force on the friction disc.

6 When the pedal is released, the diaphragm spring forces the pressure plate into contact with the friction linings on the friction disc. The disc is now firmly sandwiched between the pressure plate and the flywheel, thus transmitting engine power to the transmission.

7 Wear of the friction material on the friction disc is automatically compensated for by the operation of the hydraulic system. As the friction material on the disc wears, the pressure plate moves towards the flywheel causing the clutch diaphragm spring inner

2.2 Hose connections to the master cylinder on the bulkhead

fingers to move outwards. When the clutch pedal is released, excess fluid is expelled through the master cylinder into the fluid reservoir.

2 Clutch master cylinder – removal and refitting

Removal

1 Remove the filler cap from the brake master cylinder reservoir on top of the brake master cylinder, and siphon the hydraulic fluid from the reservoir until it is at the MIN mark (below the outlet to the clutch master cylinder). Alternatively, open the slave cylinder bleed screw, and gently pump the clutch pedal to expel the fluid through a plastic tube connected to the screw; tighten the screw when all the fluid has been removed.

Warning: Do not siphon the fluid by mouth, as it is poisonous; use a syringe or an old poultry baster.

2 Trace the fluid supply hose to the master cylinder connection on the bulkhead. Depress the release button, pull back and disconnect the hose from the master cylinder **(see illustration)**. There will be some loss of fluid as the hose is removed – wipe up any spillage, and rinse any painted surfaces with water (avoid getting water inside the clutch master cylinder, however).

3 Similarly, extract the retaining clip and disconnect the supply pipe to the clutch slave

2.6 Steering column shaft universal joint clamp bolt

cylinder from the master cylinder connection on the bulkhead (this is the connection below the one just removed).

4 From inside the car, disconnect the wiring connector at the clutch pedal position sensor located at the top of the pedal mounting bracket, and the switch at the base. Release the wiring from the clips on the pedal bracket.

5 Turn the steering wheel to position the roadwheels in the straight-ahead position, then remove the ignition key to engage the steering column lock.

6 Unclip the cover (where fitted), the undo the clamp bolt securing the steering column shaft universal joint to the steering gear pinion **(see illustration)**. Pull the shaft upwards and off the pinion and move it to one side, clear of the clutch pedal. Note that a new clamp bolt will be required for refitting.

7 Undo the three nuts and manoeuvre the clutch pedal assembly out from under the facia **(see illustration)**.

8 Undo the nuts and pull out the 2 bolts securing the master cylinder to the pedal bracket **(see illustration)**.

9 Use a 2 mm diameter punch to drive out the master cylinder pushrod pivot pin, and separate the master cylinder from the pedal bracket **(see illustration)**. Discard the pin – a new one must be fitted.

Refitting

10 Refitting is a reversal of removal, noting the following points:

a) Use a new clamp bolt when reconnecting the steering column shaft universal joint.

2.7 Clutch pedal mounting bracket retaining nuts

2.8 Undo the nuts and pull out the bolts

2.9 Use a small punch to drive out the pushrod pivot pin

b) Fit a new master cylinder pivot pin. Ensure the end of the pushrod is correctly aligned with the pedal before inserting the new pin.

c) Tighten all nuts and bolts to the specified torque, where given.

d) Ensure that all fluid hose connections are clean, and are securely made.

e) Bleed the clutch hydraulic system on completion, as described in Section 4.

3 Clutch slave cylinder – removal and refitting

Removal

1 Remove the transmission as described in Chapter 7A Section 6.

2 Inside the bellhousing, unscrew and remove the three mounting bolts, then withdraw the slave cylinder over the transmission input shaft **(see illustration)**.

3 With the slave cylinder removed, it is recommended that the transmission input shaft oil seal is renewed. Use a suitable tool to hook it out of the transmission casing and over the input shaft. Refer to Chapter 7A Section 5 if necessary.

4 The release bearing is an interference fit in the slave cylinder, and cannot be renewed separately.

5 If the slave cylinder is faulty it must be renewed, as repair kits are not available.

Refitting

6 Do not apply grease to any part of the slave cylinder or release bearing.

7 Locate a new oil seal over the input shaft and into the transmission housing (refer to Chapter 7A Section 5), then slide the slave cylinder onto the shaft.

8 Insert the mounting bolts and tighten them progressively to the specified torque. As the bolts are tightened, make sure that the oil seal enters the transmission housing correctly.

9 Refit the transmission as described in Chapter 7A Section 6.

10 Refill the master cylinder reservoir with fresh fluid, then bleed the hydraulic system as described in Section 4.

3.2 Slave cylinder and mounting bolts

4 Clutch hydraulic system – bleeding

Warning: Hydraulic fluid is poisonous; wash off immediately and thoroughly in the case of skin contact, and seek immediate medical advice if any fluid is swallowed or gets into the eyes. Certain types of hydraulic fluid are flammable, and may ignite when allowed into contact with hot components; when servicing any hydraulic system, it is safest to assume that the fluid is flammable, and to take precautions against the risk of fire as though it is petrol that is being handled. Hydraulic fluid is also an effective paint stripper, and will attack plastics; if any is spilt, it should be washed off immediately, using copious quantities of fresh water. Finally, it is hygroscopic (it absorbs moisture from the air) – old fluid may be contaminated and unfit for further use. When topping-up or renewing the fluid, always use the recommended type, and ensure that it comes from a freshly-opened sealed container.

1 The correct operation of any hydraulic system is only possible after removing all air from the components and circuit; this is achieved by bleeding the system.

2 During the bleeding procedure, add only clean, unused hydraulic fluid of the recommended type; never re-use fluid that has already been bled from the system. Ensure that sufficient fluid is available before starting work.

3 If there is any possibility of incorrect fluid being already in the system, the hydraulic circuit must be flushed completely with uncontaminated, correct fluid.

4 If hydraulic fluid has been lost from the system, or air has entered because of a leak, ensure that the fault is cured before continuing further.

5 The bleed screw is screwed into the slave cylinder extension which is positioned on the top of the transmission bellhousing – the bleed screw is behind the fluid supply pipe. Access to the screw is difficult, but may be improved by removing the air cleaner assembly (see Chapter 4A Section 5 or Chapter 4B Section 4).

6 First check that all the hydraulic hoses are securely fitted to the master and slave cylinders. Clean any dirt from around the bleed screw.

7 Unscrew the brake master cylinder fluid reservoir cap, and top-up the fluid level to the upper (MAX) level line; refit the cap loosely, and remember to maintain the fluid level at least above the lower (MIN) level line throughout the procedure, or there is a risk of further air entering the system.

8 There are a number of one-man, do-it-yourself bleeding kits currently available from motor accessory shops. It is recommended that one of these kits is used whenever possible, as they greatly simplify the bleeding operation, and reduce the risk of expelled air and fluid being drawn back into the system. If such a kit is not available, the basic (two-man) method must be used, which is described in detail below.

9 If a kit is to be used, prepare the vehicle as described previously, and follow the kit manufacturer's instructions, as the procedure may vary slightly according to the type being used; generally, they are as outlined below in the relevant sub-section.

Bleeding

Ford method

10 The Ford method for bleeding is to attach a hand vacuum pump and a container of fluid to the slave cylinder bleed screw (in front of the fluid supply pipe on top of the gearbox). Open the bleed screw, and then suck the fluid out of the system until no air bubbles are visible in the connecting tubing (the brake fluid reservoir must be kept topped-up with fluid the whole time). On completion, and before removing the vacuum, close the bleed screw. This is obviously the preferred method if suitable tools are available – if not, the more conventional methods described below should also be successful.

Basic (two-man) method

11 Collect a clean glass jar, a suitable length of plastic or rubber tubing which is a tight fit over the bleed screw. The help of an assistant will also be required. Ensure that the fluid level is maintained at least above the outlet to the clutch master cylinder in the reservoir throughout the procedure.

12 Remove the protective cap from the slave cylinder bleed screw. Fit the tube to the screw, place the other end of the tube in the jar, and pour in sufficient fluid to cover the end of the tube.

13 Loosen the bleed screw (this should be possible by hand) half a turn, then have the assistant slowly depress and release the clutch pedal several times until fluid free of air bubbles emerges. On the final stroke, have the assistant hold the pedal fully depressed. Note that the pedal must be fully depressed and fully released each time.

14 With the pedal held down, tighten the bleed screw and have the assistant fully release the pedal slowly. Check the reservoir fluid level and top-up if necessary, then check the operation of the pedal. After the initial free movement, increased pressure should be felt as the clutch pressure plate diaphragm spring is operated.

15 If the pedal feels spongy, air still remains in the hydraulic system and the bleeding operation must be repeated as described in the previous paragraphs.

16 With the hydraulic system bled, tighten the bleed screw securely, then remove the tube and spanner and refit the dust cap. Do not overtighten the bleed screw.

Using a one-way valve kit

17 As the name implies, these kits consist of a length of tubing with a one-way valve fitted, to prevent expelled air and fluid being drawn back into the system; some kits include a translucent container, which can be positioned so that the air bubbles can be more easily seen flowing from the end of the tube.

18 The kit is connected to the bleed screw, which is then opened **(see illustrations)**. The user returns to the driver's seat, depresses the clutch pedal with a smooth, steady stroke, and slowly releases it; this is repeated until the expelled fluid is clear of air bubbles.

19 Note that these kits simplify work so much that it is easy to forget the fluid reservoir level; ensure that this is maintained at least above the outlet to the clutch master cylinder at all times.

Using a pressure-bleeding kit

20 These kits are usually operated by the reservoir of pressurised air contained in the spare tyre. However, note that it will probably be necessary to reduce the pressure to a lower level than normal; refer to the instructions supplied with the kit.

21 By connecting a pressurised, fluid-filled container to the fluid reservoir, bleeding can be carried out simply by opening the bleed screw and allowing the fluid to flow out until no more air bubbles can be seen in the expelled fluid.

22 This method has the advantage that the large reservoir of fluid provides an additional safeguard against air being drawn into the system during bleeding.

All methods

23 When bleeding is complete, and correct pedal feel is restored, check that the bleed screw is securely tightened and wash off any spilt fluid. Refit the dust cap to the bleed screw.

24 Check the hydraulic fluid level in the reservoir, and top-up if necessary.

4.18a Bleeding the clutch using a one-way valve kit – attach the hose to the bleed screw

4.18b Rotate the bleed screw anti-clockwise to open it

25 Discard any hydraulic fluid that has been bled from the system; it will not be fit for re-use.

26 If the clutch is not operating correctly after carrying out the bleeding procedure, the master cylinder or slave cylinder may be faulty.

5 Clutch pedal – removal and refitting

1 The clutch pedal is removed as an assembly with the clutch master cylinder – refer to Section 2.

6 Clutch assembly – removal, inspection and refitting

⚠️ *Warning: Dust created by clutch wear and deposited on the clutch components may contain asbestos, which is a health hazard. DO NOT blow it out with compressed air, or inhale any of it. DO NOT use petrol or petroleum-based solvents to clean off the dust. Brake*

system cleaner or methylated spirit should be used to flush the dust into a suitable receptacle. After the clutch components are wiped clean with rags, dispose of the contaminated rags and cleaner in a sealed, marked container.

Removal

1 Unless the complete engine/transmission unit has to be removed from the car (see Chapter 2E Section 4, 5), the clutch can be reached by removing the transmission as described in Chapter 7A Section 6.

2 Before disturbing the clutch, use chalk or a marker pen to mark the relationship of the pressure plate assembly to the flywheel.

3 Hold the flywheel stationary using a suitable tool engaged with the starter ring gear teeth – a piece of metal can be tightened to one of the bolt holes, or alternatively an assistant can use a wide-bladed screwdriver engaged with the teeth **(see illustration)**.

4 Working in a diagonal sequence, slacken the pressure plate bolts by half a turn at a time, until spring pressure is released and the bolts can be unscrewed by hand **(see illustration)**. Discard the bolts – new ones should be used when refitting.

6.3 Home-made tool for holding the flywheel stationary

6.4 Slacken and remove the pressure plate bolts

6.5 Prise the pressure plate off its dowels and remove it with the friction disc

6.14a Clutch friction disc FLYWHEEL SIDE markings should face the flywheel

5 Prise the pressure plate assembly off its locating dowels, and collect the friction disc, noting which way round the disc is fitted **(see illustration)**.

Inspection

Note: *Due to the amount of work necessary to remove and refit clutch components, it is usually considered good practice to renew the clutch friction disc, pressure plate assembly and release bearing (slave cylinder) as a matched set, even if only one of these is actually worn enough to require renewal. It is also worth considering the renewal of the clutch components on a preventive basis if the engine and/or transmission have been removed for some other reason.*

6 When cleaning clutch components, read first the warning at the beginning of this Section; remove the dust using a clean, dry cloth, and working in a well-ventilated atmosphere.

7 Check the friction disc linings for signs of wear, damage or oil contamination. If the friction material is cracked, burnt, scored or damaged, or if it is contaminated with oil or grease (shown by shiny black patches), the friction disc must be renewed. Check the depth of the rivets below the friction material surface. If any are at or near the surface of the friction material, then the friction disc must be renewed.

8 If the friction material is still serviceable, check that the centre boss splines are unworn, that the torsion springs are in good condition and securely fastened, and that all the rivets are tight. If any wear or damage is found, the friction disc must be renewed.

9 If the friction material is fouled with oil, this must be due to an oil leak from the crankshaft oil seal, from the sump-to-cylinder block joint, or from the transmission input shaft. Renew the seal or repair the joint, as appropriate, as described in the appropriate part of Chapter 2A, Chapter 2B, Chapter 2C, Chapter 2D or Chapter 7A, before installing the new friction disc.

6.14b Fit the friction disc, then use a centralising tool to align it

10 Check the pressure plate assembly for obvious signs of wear or damage; shake it to check for loose rivets or worn or damaged fulcrum rings, and check that the drive straps securing the pressure plate to the cover do not show signs of overheating (such as a deep yellow or blue discoloration). If the diaphragm spring is worn or damaged, or if its pressure is in any way suspect, the pressure plate assembly should be renewed.

11 Examine the machined bearing surfaces of the pressure plate and of the flywheel; they should be clean, completely flat, and free from scratches or scoring. If either is discoloured from excessive heat, or shows signs of cracks, it should be renewed – although minor damage of this nature can sometimes be polished away using emery paper.

12 Check that the release bearing contact surface rotates smoothly and easily, with no sign of noise or roughness. Also check that the surface itself is smooth and unworn, with no signs of cracks, pitting or scoring. If there is any doubt about its condition, the bearing (and slave cylinder) must be renewed.

Refitting

13 On reassembly, ensure that the disc contact surfaces of the flywheel and pressure plate are completely clean, smooth, and free

6.15 Fit the pressure plate onto its dowels

from oil or grease. Use solvent to remove any protective grease from new components.

14 Fit the friction disc so that its spring hub assembly faces away from the flywheel; there may also be a marking showing which way round the plate is to be refitted. Depending on the type of centralising tool being used, the friction disc may be held in position at this stage **(see illustrations)**.

15 Refit the pressure plate assembly, aligning the marks made on dismantling (if the original pressure plate is re-used), and locating the pressure plate on its locating dowels **(see illustration)**. Fit the pressure plate bolts, but tighten them only finger-tight, so that the friction disc can still be moved.

16 The friction disc must now be centralised, so that when the transmission is refitted, its input shaft will pass through the splines at the centre of the friction disc.

17 Centralisation can be achieved by passing a screwdriver or other long bar through the friction disc and into the hole in the crankshaft; the friction disc can then be moved around until it is centred on the crankshaft hole. Alternatively, a clutch-aligning-tool can be used to eliminate the guesswork; these can be obtained from most accessory shops. The normal type consists of a spigot bar with several different adapters, but a more

6.18 Tighten the pressure plate bolts to the specified torque

6.19 Apply a little grease to the transmission input shaft splines

recent type consists of a tool which clamps the friction disc to the pressure plate before locating the two items on the flywheel. A home-made aligning tool can be fabricated from a length of metal rod or wooden dowel which fits closely inside the crankshaft hole, and has insulating tape wound around it to match the diameter of the friction disc splined hole.

18 When the friction disc is centralised, tighten the pressure plate bolts evenly and in a diagonal sequence to the specified torque setting **(see illustration)**.

19 Apply a thin smear of molybdenum disulphide grease to the splines of the friction disc and the transmission input shaft **(see illustration)**.

Caution: Do not apply too much grease, as

there is a risk that it will contaminate the friction disc material.

20 Refit the transmission as described in Chapter 7A Section 6.

7 Clutch release bearing – removal, inspection and refitting

Removal

1 For access to the clutch release bearing, the transmission must be removed as described in Chapter 7A Section 6.

2 Remove the slave cylinder as described in Section 3. The release bearing is an interference fit in the slave cylinder, and cannot be renewed separately.

Inspection

3 Note that it is often considered worthwhile to renew the release bearing as a matter of course regardless of its condition, considering the amount of work necessary to access it. Check that the contact surface rotates smoothly and easily, with no sign of noise or roughness, and that the surface itself is smooth and unworn, with no signs of cracks, pitting or scoring. If there is any doubt about its condition, the bearing (and slave cylinder) must be renewed.

Refitting

4 Refit the slave cylinder as described in Section 3.

5 Refit the transmission with reference to Chapter 7A Section 6.

Chapter 7 Part A
Manual transmission

Contents

Degrees of difficulty

Easy, suitable for novice with little experience		**Fairly easy,** suitable for beginner with some experience		**Fairly difficult,** suitable for competent DIY mechanic		**Difficult,** suitable for experienced DIY mechanic		**Very difficult,** suitable for expert DIY or professional	

Specifications

General

Transmission type...	Five forward speeds, one reverse. Synchromesh on all forward gears Gearchange linkage operated by twin cables
Transmission code	iB5
Transmission oil capacity...................................	See Chapter 1A or 1B Specifications

Torque wrench settings

	Nm	lbf ft
Left-hand engine mounting to transmission.....................	80	59
Neutral position sensor	9	7
Oil filler/level plug...	35	26
Rear engine mounting bolts.................................	48	35
Reversing light switch	12	9
Selector lever securing bolt	25	18
Slave cylinder pressure pipe bracket.........................	28	21
Transmission to engine.....................................	48	35

1 General Information

1 The transmission is contained in a cast-aluminium alloy casing bolted to the engine's left-hand end, and consists of the gearbox and final drive differential – often called a transaxle. The transmission unit type is stamped on a plate attached to the transmission.

2 The iB5 unit is identical to that used in the previous Fiesta range, albeit with improved synchromesh components to improve the quality of gearchange. The transmission is intended to be sealed for life – no oil changes are required, and no drain plug is fitted. Provided that the oil level is maintained as described in Chapter 1A Section 28 or Chapter 1B Section 28, no routine maintenance is necessary.

3 Drive is transmitted from the crankshaft via the clutch to the input shaft, which has a splined extension to accept the clutch friction disc. From the input shaft, drive is transmitted to the output shaft, from where the drive is transmitted to the differential crownwheel, which rotates with the differential and planetary gears, thus driving the sun gears and driveshafts. The rotation of the planetary gears on their shaft allows the inner roadwheel to rotate at a slower speed than the outer roadwheel when the car is cornering.

4 The input and output shafts are arranged side-by-side, parallel to the crankshaft and driveshafts, so that their gear pinion teeth are in constant mesh. In the neutral position, the output shaft gear pinions rotate freely, so that drive cannot be transmitted to the crownwheel.

5 Gear selection is via a floor-mounted lever and selector cable mechanism.

6 The transmission selector mechanism causes the appropriate selector fork to move its respective synchro-sleeve along

2.2 Unclip the cover from the front of the transmission

the output shaft, to lock the gear pinion to the synchro-hub. Since the synchro-hubs are splined to the output shaft, this locks the pinion to the shaft, so that drive can be transmitted. To ensure that gearchanging can be made quickly and quietly, a synchromesh system is fitted to all forward gears, consisting of baulk rings and spring-loaded fingers, as well as the gear pinions and synchro-hubs. The synchromesh cones are formed on the mating faces of the baulk rings and gear pinions. The transmission has dual synchromesh on 1st and 2nd gears for even smoother gearchanging.

Transmission overhaul

7 Because of the complexity of the assembly, possible unavailability of new parts and special tools necessary, internal repair procedures for the transmission are not recommended for the home mechanic. The bulk of the information in this Chapter is devoted to removal and refitting procedures.

2 Gearchange cables – adjustment

1 Apply the handbrake, then jack up the front of the car, supporting it on axle stands

2.4 Unlock the selector cable by prising the coloured insert towards the engine

(see *Jacking and vehicle support*). Where applicable, remove the engine undershield.

2 At the front face of the transmission housing, remove the selector mechanism cover by working around the edge, releasing a total of seven clips **(see illustration)**.

3 Only the selector cable is to be adjusted during this procedure – this is the cable which comes to the lowest point on the front of the transmission, with its end fitting nearest the engine.

4 Unlock the selector cable by prising the coloured insert towards the engine, then prise the selector cable end fitting from the lever on the transmission **(see illustration)**.

5 Check that the selector lever on the transmission (the lever with the disconnected selector cable) to the central neutral position **(see illustration)**. The lever is sprung-loaded, and should in the neutral position when at rest.

6 Move the shift lever on the transmission (the lever with the other cable still attached) to the fully upwards to the 4th gear position **(see illustration)**.

7 Refit the selector cable end fitting to the transmission selector lever, then lock the selector cable in position by moving the coloured insert away from the engine.

8 Refit the selector mechanism cover, ensuring that the clips engage correctly.

2.5 Check that the selector lever is in the central, neutral position

2.6 Move the shift lever fully upwards

3.3 Prise the 2 gearchange cable end fittings from the levers on the gear lever housing

3.4 Pull back the retaining collars and detach the gearchange outer cables from the gear lever housing

3.5 Gear lever housing retaining nuts

Where applicable refit the engine undershield and lower the car to the ground.

9 Start the engine, keeping the clutch pedal depressed, and check for correct gear selection.

3 Gearchange cables and gear lever – removal and refitting

Removal

Gear lever

1 Disconnect the battery as described in Chapter 5A Section 4.

2 Remove the centre console as described in Chapter 11 Section 24.

3 Prise the 2 gearchange cable end fittings from the levers on the gear lever housing **(see illustration)**.

4 Pull back the retaining collars and detach the gearchange outer cables from their locations on the gear lever housing **(see illustration)**.

5 Undo the 4 nuts and lift out the gear lever housing assembly **(see illustration)**.

Cables

6 Remove the gear lever as described previously.

7 Remove the air cleaner assembly as described in Chapter 4A Section 5 or Chapter 4B Section 4 as applicable.

8 Remove the battery and battery tray as

3.11a Prise the cable end fittings from their levers

3.11b Pull back the collars and detach the outer cables from the brakcets

described in Chapter 5A Section 4.

9 Apply the handbrake, then jack up the front of the car, supporting it on axle stands (see *Jacking and vehicle support*). Where applicable, remove the engine undershield.

10 At the front face of the transmission housing, remove the selector mechanism cover by working around the edge, releasing a total of seven clips **(see illustration 2.2)**.

11 Prise the shift cable and selector cable end fittings from their levers on the transmission – note their fitted locations. Pull back the retaining collars and detach both cables from the transmission support bracket **(see illustrations)**.

12 Unclip the cables from the bracket above the transmission **(see illustration)**.

13 From under the car, undo the nuts and remove the underfloor cross-brace beneath

the exhaust centre section **(see illustration)**. Release the exhaust system from the rubber mounting block just in front of the cross-brace.

14 Remove the six washer-type fasteners, and slide the exhaust heat shield rearwards.

15 Undo the two nuts securing the cable guide plate to the underbody.

16 Withdraw the cables downwards from the engine compartment, releasing them from their retaining clips and noting how they are routed. Take care not to kink or bend the cables during removal.

17 Undo the bolts and remove the bracket each side between the facia crossmember centre supports and the floor **(see illustration)**. Take care as the edges of the brackets are extremely sharp.

18 The cable entry point into the car should now be visible, but the cables themselves are

3.12 Unclip the cables

3.13 Undo the nuts and remove the underfloor cross-brace

3.17 Undo the bolts and remove the facia crossmember support brackets each side

4.3 Unscrew and remove the reversing light switch from the front of the transmission

4.6 Unclip the cover from the transmission

4.7 Disconnect the neutral position sensor wiring plug

hidden under the carpet. To gain access to them it will be necessary to cut the carpet and sound-deadening material. Take great care not to cut through the wiring harness when cutting the carpet.

19 Have an assistant unclip the cable guide from the underbody and guide the cables out of the engine compartment. Withdraw the cables into the car, again, taking care not to kink or bend them.

Refitting

20 Refitting is a reversal of removal. On completion, adjust the cables as described in Section 2.

4 Transmission switches – removal and refitting

Reversing light switch

1 The switch is located on the front of the transmission, next to the selector cable front cover. To improve access, jack up the front left-hand side of the car (see *Jacking and vehicle support*). Where fitted, remove the engine undershield.

2 Disconnect the wiring plug from the switch.

3 Unscrew and remove the switch from the front of the transmission – anticipate a little oil spillage as this is done **(see illustration)**.

4 Refitting is a reversal of removal. Tighten the switch to the specified torque.

Neutral position sensor

Note: *A neutral position sensor is only fitted to models equipped with the auto 'Stop-Start' system.*

5 The neutral position sensor is located on the rear/underside of the transmission, adjacent to the end cover. Raise the front of the vehicle and support it securely on axle stands (see *Jacking and vehicle support*). Release the fasteners and remove the engine undershield where fitted.

6 Unclip the front and rear cover from the transmission **(see illustration)**.

7 Disconnect the sensor wiring plug, undo the retaining bolt and withdraw the sensor from the transmission **(see illustration)**.

8 Refitting is a reversal of removal. Tighten the sensor retaining bolt to the specified torque.

5 Oil seals – renewal

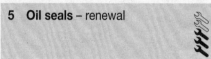

1 Oil leaks frequently occur due to wear or deterioration of the driveshaft oil seals, or the selector shaft oil seal. Renewal of these seals is relatively easy, since the repairs can be performed without removing the transmission from the vehicle.

Driveshaft oil seals

2 The driveshaft oil seals are located at the sides of the transmission, where the driveshaft or intermediate shaft enters the transmission. If leakage at the seal is suspected, raise the vehicle and support it securely on axle stands. If the seal is leaking, oil will be found on the side of the transmission below the driveshaft/intermediate shaft.

3 Refer to Chapter 8 Section 2 and remove the appropriate driveshaft/intermediate shaft.

4 Using a large screwdriver or lever, carefully prise the oil seal out of the transmission casing, taking care not to damage the transmission casing **(see illustration)**.

5 Wipe clean the oil seal seating in the transmission casing.

6 Dip the new oil seal in clean oil, then press it a little way into the casing by hand, making sure that it is square to its seating.

5.4 Prise out the oil seal using a suitable lever

7 Using suitable tubing or a large socket, carefully drive the oil seal fully into the casing until it contacts the seating **(see illustration)**.

8 When refitting the left-hand driveshaft, use the protective sleeve which should be provided with genuine parts. The sleeve is fitted into the seal, and the driveshaft is then fitted through it – the sleeve is then withdrawn and cut free.

9 Refit the driveshaft/intermediate shaft (see Chapter 8 Section 2).

Selector shaft oil seal

10 Apply the handbrake, then jack up the front of the car, supporting it on axle stands (see *Jacking and vehicle support*). Where fitted, remove the engine undershield.

11 At the front face of the transmission housing, remove the selector mechanism cover by working around the edge, releasing a total of seven clips.

12 Prise the shift cable and selector cable end fittings from their levers on the transmission – note their fitted locations. Pull back the retaining collars and detach both cables from the transmission support bracket.

13 Unscrew and remove the four bolts securing the selector mechanism rear cover to the transmission housing.

14 Remove the transmission shift lever by prising off the protective cap and extracting the retaining clip.

15 With the shift lever removed, unscrew the securing bolt and take off the selector lever and dust cover.

16 The selector shaft oil seal can now be

5.7 Drive the oil seal into place using a tube or socket

prised out of its location. If using a screwdriver or similar sharp tool, take great care not to mark or gouge the selector shaft or the seal housing as this is done, or the new seal will also leak.

17 Before fitting the new oil seal, carefully clean the visible part of the selector shaft, and the oil seal housing. Wrap a little tape around the end of the shaft, to protect the seal lips as they pass over it.

18 Smear the new oil seal with a little oil, then carefully fit it over the end of the selector shaft, lips facing inwards (towards the transmission).

19 Making sure that the seal stays square to the shaft, press it fully along the shaft (if available, a 16 mm ring spanner is ideal for this).

20 Press the seal fully into its housing, again using the ring spanner or perhaps a deep socket. Remove the tape from the end of the shaft.

21 Further refitting is a reversal of removal, tightening the selector lever securing bolt to the specified torque.

22 On completion, check and if necessary adjust the selector cable as described in Section 2.

Input shaft seal

23 Remove the clutch slave cylinder as described in Chapter 6 Section 3.

24 The input shaft oil seal can now be prised out of its location. If using a screwdriver or similar sharp tool, take great care not to mark or gouge the input shaft or the seal housing as this is done, or the new seal will also leak.

25 Before fitting the new oil seal, carefully clean the visible part of the input shaft, and the oil seal housing. Wrap a little tape around the end of the shaft, to protect the seal lips as they pass over it.

26 Smear the new oil seal with a little oil, then carefully fit it over the end of the input shaft, lips facing inwards (towards the transmission).

27 Making sure that the seal stays square to the shaft, press it fully along the shaft (if available, a suitable diameter tube is ideal for this).

28 Press the seal fully into its housing, again using the tube. Remove the tape from the end of the shaft.

29 Refit the slave cylinder as described in Chapter 6 Section 3.

6 Transmission – removal and refitting

Warning: The hydraulic fluid used in the clutch system is brake fluid, which is poisonous. Take care to keep it off bare skin, and in particular out of your eyes. The fluid also attacks paintwork, and may discolour carpets, etc – keep spillages to a minimum, and wash any off immediately with cold water. Finally, brake fluid is highly inflammable, and should be handled with the same care as petrol.

Note: *Read through this procedure before starting work to see what is involved, particularly in terms of lifting equipment. Depending on the facilities available, the home mechanic may prefer to remove the engine and transmission together, then separate them on the bench, as described in Chapter 2E. The help of an assistant is highly recommended if the transmission is to be removed (and later refitted) on its own.*

Removal

1 Remove the air cleaner and inlet ducts as described in Chapter 4A Section 5 or Chapter 4B Section 4 as applicable.

2 Remove the battery, battery tray and support bracket as described in Chapter 5A Section 4.

3 Undo the retaining bolt and disconnect the earth cable from the top of the transmission **(see illustration)**. Release the clutch slave cylinder hydraulic pipe from the support plate and remove the support plate.

4 Disconnect the transmission breather hose from the top of the transmission.

5 Undo the transmission-to-engine bolts which are accessible from above.

6 Firmly apply the handbrake, then jack up the front of the vehicle and support it securely on axle stands (see *Jacking and vehicle support*). Where applicable, remove the engine undershield.

7 Disconnect the gearchange cables from the transmission as described in Section 3.

Release the cables from their support bracket.

8 Remove the starter motor as described in Chapter 5A Section 9.

9 To prevent damage to the exhaust flexible section, support it by attaching a pair of splints either side (two scrap strips of wood, plant canes, etc) using some cable-ties. Undo the nuts securing the flexible section to the exhaust manifold, and separate the joint. Recover the gasket, and discard it. Release the exhaust front rubber mounting block and move the system to one side.

10 On diesel models, undo the nuts securing the particulate filter/catalytic converter to the cylinder block, and move it towards the timing belt end of the engine to enable access to the transmission retaining bolts. Refer to Chapter 4B Section 18 if necessary.

11 Taking adequate precautions against brake fluid spillage (refer to the Warning at the start of this Section), pull out the securing clip, then pull the pipe fitting out of the clutch slave cylinder at the top of the transmission **(see illustration)**. Plug or tape over the pipe end, to avoid losing fluid, and to prevent dirt entry.

12 Check that the rubber seal on the pipe end fitting as it's withdrawn. Often the seal separates from the fitting and remains in the connection housing. If this happens, carefully extract the seal using small screwdriver or similar **(see illustration)**.

13 Unbolt the engine rear mounting completely from under the car.

14 Disconnect the reversing light switch and neutral position sensor (where applicable) wiring plugs.

15 Remove both driveshafts from the transmission as described in Chapter 8 Section 2.

16 The engine/transmission must now be supported, as the left-hand mounting must be dismantled and removed. Ford technicians use a support bar which locates in the tops of the inner wings – proprietary engine support bars are available from tool outlets.

17 If a support bar is not available, an engine hoist should be used. With an engine hoist, the engine/transmission can be manoeuvred more easily and safely. In the workshop, we found the best solution was to move the engine to the required position, and support it from

6.3 Undo the retaining bolt and disconnect the earth cable from the top of the transmission

6.11 Extract the retaining clip and disconnect the slave cylinder hydraulic pipe

6.12 Check that the rubber seal is in place

6.19 Left-hand engine mounting retaining bolts

below – using the hoist on the transmission then gave excellent manoeuvrability, and total control for lowering out.

18 Supporting both the engine and transmission from below should be considered a last resort, and should only be done if a heavy-duty hydraulic ('trolley') jack is used, with a large, flat piece of wood on the jack head to spread the load and avoid damage to the sump. A further jack will be needed to lower the transmission out. **Note:** *Always take care when using a hydraulic jack, as it is possible for this type to collapse under load – generally, a scissor-type jack avoids this problem, but is also less stable, and offers no manoeuvrability.*

19 With the engine securely supported, remove the three bolts from the engine left-hand mounting (on top of the transmission) **(see illustration)**.

20 Taking care that nothing which is still attached to the engine is placed under strain, lower the transmission as far as possible.

21 Remove the lower transmission-to-engine bolts. The bolts are of different lengths, so note their positions carefully for refitting.

22 Swing the transmission forwards, and wedge it in position with a stout piece of wood, about 300 mm long, between the engine and the subframe.

23 Check that, apart from the remaining flange bolts, there is nothing preventing the transmission from being lowered and removed. Make sure that any wiring or hoses lying on top of the transmission are not going to get caught up and stretched as the transmission is lowered.

24 Unscrew the remaining flange bolts. If the transmission does not separate on its own, it must be rocked from side-to-side, to free it from the locating dowels. As the transmission is withdrawn from the engine,

make sure its weight is supported at all times – the transmission input shaft (or the clutch) may otherwise be damaged as it is withdrawn through the clutch assembly bolted to the engine flywheel. Recover the adapter plates (where fitted) between the engine and transmission, as they may fall out when the two are separated.

25 Keeping the transmission steady, carefully lower it down and remove it from under the car.

26 The clutch components can now be inspected with reference to Chapter 6, and renewed if necessary. Unless they are virtually new, it is worth renewing the clutch components as a matter of course, even if the transmission has been removed for some other reason.

Refitting

27 If removed, refit the clutch components (see Chapter 6 Section 6). Also ensure that the engine-to-transmission adapter plates (where fitted) are in position on the engine.

28 Apply a very thin smear of high-temperature anti-seize grease to the splines of the transmission input shaft. Take care not to apply too much or the clutch plates may become contaminated.

29 Where a block of wood was used to wedge the engine forwards for transmission removal, make sure that it is in place for refitting.

30 With the transmission secured to the hoist/trolley jack as on removal, raise it into position, and then carefully slide it onto the engine, at the same time engaging the input shaft with the clutch friction disc splines.

31 Do not use excessive force to refit the transmission – if the input shaft does not slide into place easily, readjust the angle of the transmission so that it is level, and/or turn the input shaft so that the splines engage properly with the disc. If problems are still experienced, check that the clutch disc is correctly centred (Chapter 6 Section 6).

32 Once the transmission is successfully mated to the engine, insert as many of the flange bolts as possible, and tighten them progressively to draw the transmission fully onto the locating dowels.

33 Where applicable, remove the wedge fitted between the engine and subframe. Raise the transmission into position, then refit the engine left-hand mounting bolts. Tighten the bolts to the specified torque.

34 Refit the remaining transmission-to-engine bolts, and tighten all of them to the specified torque.

35 Refit the engine/transmission rear mounting and tighten the bolts to the specified torque.

36 Once the engine/transmission mountings have been refitted, the support bar, engine hoist or supporting jack can be removed.

37 Further refitting is a reversal of removal, noting the following points:
a) *Refit the driveshafts as described in Chapter 8 Section 2.*
b) *On completion, adjust the gearchange cables as described in Section 2.*

7 Transmission overhaul – general information

1 The overhaul of a manual transmission is a complex (and often expensive) engineering task for the DIY home mechanic to undertake, which requires access to specialist equipment. It involves dismantling and reassembly of many small components, measuring clearances precisely and if necessary, adjusting them by the selection shims and spacers. Internal transmission components are also often difficult to obtain and in many instances, extremely expensive. Because of this, if the transmission develops a fault or becomes noisy, the best course of action is to have the unit overhauled by a specialist repairer or to obtain an exchange reconditioned unit.

2 Nevertheless, it is not impossible for the more experienced mechanic to overhaul the transmission if the special tools are available and the job is carried out in a deliberate step-by-step manner, to ensure that nothing is overlooked.

3 The tools necessary for an overhaul include internal and external circlip pliers, bearing pullers, a slide hammer, a set of pin punches, a dial test indicator, and possibly a hydraulic press. In addition, a large, sturdy workbench and a vice will be required.

4 During dismantling of the transmission, make careful notes of how each component is fitted to make reassembly easier and accurate.

5 Before dismantling the transmission, it will help if you have some idea of where the problem lies. Certain problems can be closely related to specific areas in the transmission which can make component examination and renewal easier. Refer to Fault finding at the end of this manual for more information.

Chapter 7 Part B
Powershift transmission

Contents

Degrees of difficulty

Easy, suitable for novice with little experience	**Fairly easy,** suitable for beginner with some experience	**Fairly difficult,** suitable for competent DIY mechanic	**Difficult,** suitable for experienced DIY mechanic	**Very difficult,** suitable for expert DIY or professional

Specifications

General

Transmission type.	Fully automatic, dry dual clutch, electronically-controlled transmission with 6 forward speeds and reverse with sequential manual gear selection capability
Transmission code	DPS6/6DCT250
Fluid capacity	See Chapter 1A Section 1 or Chapter 1B Section 1

Gear ratios

1st	3.917: 1
2nd	2.429: 1
3rd	1.436: 1
4th	1.021: 1
5th	0.867: 1
6th	0.702: 1
Reverse	1.444: 1

Torque wrench settings

	Nm	lbf ft
Clutch unit-to-driveplate/flywheel nuts*		
Stage 1	12	8
Stage 2	25	18
Engine/transmission left-hand mounting to body	90	66
Engine/transmission left-hand mounting bracket to transmission.	90	66
Engine/transmission left-hand mounting to transmission bracket.	125	92
Engine/transmission rear mounting bolts.	48	35
Fluid level and drain plugs	43	32
Input shaft speed sensor	10	7
Transmission control module (TCM) bolts	27	20
Transmission to engine.	48	35
Transmission range sensor	10	7

*Use new fasteners

1 General Information

1 The Ford DS6 dual clutch transmission has six-forward speeds (and one reverse). In contrast to traditional automatic transmissions where a fluid flywheel (torque converter) transmits the power from the engine to the gearbox, the DS6 has two dry clutches.

2 This transmission features two input shafts driven by the dry dual clutch system. These two shafts are used in conjunction with each other to provide seamless shifting through the 6 gears. As each gear is selected, the appropriate clutch is activated to drive the vehicle. Each consecutive gear is then preselected for the next "shift" operation as power is shifted from one clutch to the other and back again as moving up and down through the individual gears.

3 Essentially, the transmission is 2 gearboxes within the same housing, that share the same differential, sensors and electronic control module.

4 The selector process within the transmission is controlled by electric stepper motors incorporated into the TCM (Transmission Control Module) located on the front of the transmission housing. The TCM receives information from the transmission range sensor, output shaft speed sensor, and two input shaft sensors. As the TCM is in constant communication with the engine management PCM (Powertrain Control Module), the TCM selects the most appropriate gear to match the driving conditions and demands. The result is seamless gearchanging with high levels of efficiency.

5 The clutch is of a dual-clutch dry plate type, which has two friction discs and a spring loaded centre hub. The clutch friction disc nearest the engine operates 1st, 3rd and 5th gears. The clutch friction disc nearest the transmission operates 2nd, 4th, 6th & Reverse gears. The operation of the clutches is controlled by a brushless DC electric motor, under the control of the TCM.

6 A fault diagnosis system is integrated into the control unit, but analysis can only be undertaken with specialised equipment. It is important that any transmission fault be identified and rectified at the earliest possible opportunity. A Ford dealer or suitable equipped specialist can 'interrogate' the TCM fault memory for stored fault codes, enabling the fault to be pinpointed quickly. Once the fault has been corrected and any fault codes have been cleared, normal transmission operation is restored.

7 Because of the need for special test equipment, the complexity of some of the parts, and the need for scrupulous cleanliness when these transmissions, the work which the owner can do is limited. Most major repairs and overhaul operations should be left to a Ford dealer or specialist, who will be

2.3 The level plug is easier to access through the left-hand front wheelarch aperture

equipped with the necessary equipment for fault diagnosis and repair.

8 In the event of a transmission problem occurring, consult a Ford dealer or transmission specialist before removing the transmission from the vehicle, since the majority of fault diagnosis is best carried out with the transmission still in the vehicle.

2 Transmission fluid – level check, drain and refill

Level check

1 Apply the handbrake, then jack up the front of the car, supporting it on axle stands (see *Jacking and vehicle support*). Undo the fasteners and remove the engine undershield.

2 Position a suitable container beneath the transmission to collect any surplus fluid.

3 Unscrew the fluid level plug **(see illustration)**. An 8 mm Allen (hexagonal) bit will be required.

4 The fluid level should be up to the bottom edge of the hole.

5 If necessary, add the correct specification of fluid (see Lubricants and fluids 0 Section 6) through the hole until fluid just begins to emerge **(see illustration)**.

6 Allow any surplus to drain, then refit the level check plug and tighten it to the specified torque.

7 Refit the undershield, and lower the vehicle to the ground.

2.9 Transmission drain plug

2.5 Using a large syringe to add transmission fluid

Drain and refill

8 Remove the fluid level check plug as described previously in this Section.

9 Reposition the container under the drain plug, then slacken and remove the plug **(see illustration)**.

10 Once the fluid has finished draining, refit the drain plug and tighten it to the specified torque.

11 Add the correct specification of fluid through the level check hole as described previously in this Section.

12 With the fluid level upto the lower edge of the check hole, refit the plug and tighten it to the specified torque.

13 Refit the undershield, and lower the vehicle to the ground.

3 Selector cable – adjustment, removal and refitting

Adjustment

1 Ensure the parking brake is fully applied.

2 Disconnect the servo vacuum hose from the vacuum pump.

3 Release the clamps and remove the air outlet duct from the air cleaner housing.

4 Prise the selector cable end fitting from the lever on the transmission **(see illustration)**.

5 Move the selector lever inside the vehicle to position 'D'. Note that in an emergency, the selector lever can be moved without vehicle electrical power being available (flat battery).

3.4 Prise the cable end fitting from the transmission lever

3.5a Carefully prise up the surround panel…

3.5b … and depress the release catch

3.6 Lift the clip and slide the fitting away a little

3.7 Align the mark on the arm with the raised section adjacent to the 'D'

3.8 Press the fitting onto the shaft pin, then slide the locking end fitting/clip downwards

3.13 Press the clip each side forwards a little

In order to move the lever, carefully prise up the lever surround panel, then depress the release catch on the side of the lever housing (see illustrations).

6 At the transmission end of the selector cable, lift the centre clip slightly, then slide the adjuster end fitting away a little (see illustration).

7 Rotate the transmission selector shaft so the mark on the end of the arm is in line with the raised section of the casing with 'D' cast next to it (see illustration).

8 Press the cable end fitting onto the selector shaft pin, then slide the locking clip onto the cable fitting to secure it (see illustration).

9 The remainder of refitting is a reversal of removal. Ensure the engine will only start in position 'P' or 'N', and the reversing lights illuminate in position 'R'.

Removal

10 Raise the front of the vehicle and support it securely on axle stands (see *Jacking and vehicle support*). Release the fasteners and remove the engine undershield.

11 Disconnect the selector cable from the transmission selector shaft as described previously in this Section.

12 Release the cable from the support bracket on the transmission.

13 Press the clip each side forwards a little, then slide up the cable fitting from the bracket on the transmission (see illustration).

14 Work along the cable and release it from any retaining clips.

15 Remove the centre console as described in Chapter 11 Section 24.

16 Release the clips, and slide out the cable retaining clip at the lever housing.

17 Prise the cable end fitting from the selector lever.

18 Release the centre of the exhaust system from its' rubber mountings.

19 Undo the 4 retaining bolts and remove the crossbrace beneath the exhaust system.

20 Undo the 6 fasteners and slide the heatshield above the exhaust system rearwards to expose the selector cable.

21 Squeeze together the sides of the retaining clip, and undo the 2 nuts securely the cable fitting plate to the vehicle floor.

22 Attach a length of string/cable to the forward end of the selector cable. This string/cable will be left in place to aid refitting.

23 Pull away the carpet slightly, then pull the selector cable and fitting plate in to the vehicle cabin. As the string/cable emerges, untie it and leave it in place.

Refitting

24 Attach the string/cable to the forward end of the new selector cable, then with the help of an assistant, carefully pull the new cable into position.

25 With the new cable correctly routed, untie the string/cable.

26 The remainder of refitting is a reversal of removal. Upon completion, adjust the cable as described previously in this Section.

4 Transmission sensors – removal and refitting

Transmission range sensor

1 Ensure the parking brake is fully applied, then move the selector lever to position 'D'.

2 The range sensor is located on the top of the transmission. Slide up the locking catch and disconnect the sensor wiring plug (see illustration).

3 Undo the 2 retaining bolts and pull the sensor from place.

4 Ensure the mating surfaces of the sensor and casing are clean, then push the sensor into place, and tighten the retaining bolts to the specified torque.

4.2 The range sensor is located on the top of the transmission

4.7 Output shaft speed sensor location

4.13 Input shafts speed sensors retaining bolts

Note: *Note that if a new sensor has been fitted, the sensor 'adaptive learning' steps must be performed using Ford diagnostic equipment. Enstrust this task to a Ford dealer or suitably equipped repairer.*

5 Upon completion, verify that the engine will only start in position 'P' or 'N', and the reversing light illuminates when in position 'R'.

Output shaft speed sensor

6 Raise the front of the vehicle and support it securely on axle stands (see *Jacking and vehicle support*). Undo the fasteners and remove the engine undershield.
7 The sensor is located at the rear of the transmission, behind the driveshafts **(see illustration)**.
8 Where applicable, remove the protective covering from the sensor, then disconnect the sensor wiring plug.
9 Unscrew the sensor securing bolt, and slowly withdraw the sensor from its location.
10 Check the condition of the O-ring seal fitted to the sensor body – fit a new seal if the old one is in poor condition.
11 Refitting is a reversal of the removal procedure, but clean the sensor location and lightly oil the O-ring before inserting the assembly in the transmission casing.

Turbine (input) shafts speed sensors

12 Raise the front of the vehicle and support it securely on axle stands (see *Jacking and vehicle support*). Undo the fasteners and remove the engine undershield. Two

sensors are fitted, located on the rear of the transmission casing.
13 Disconnect the sensor(s) wiring plug(s), then undo the retaining bolt(s) and pull the sensor(s) from place **(see illustration)**. Be prepared for fluid spillage.
14 Examine the condition of the O-ring seal on the sensor, and renew if necessary.
15 Ensure the mating faces of the sensor and casing are clean, apply a little clean transmission fluid to the O-ring seal, then press the sensor into position, and tighten the retaining bolt to the specified torque.
16 Upon completion, check the fluid level as described in Section 2.

5 Oil seals – renewal

Driveshaft

1 The procedure is the same as that for the manual transmission (refer to Chapter 7A Section 5).

Input shaft seal

2 Renewal of the input shaft seal is only possible once the clutch unit has been removed. Removal of the clutch unit requires several complex (and expensive) Ford special tools. Consequently, we recommend this task is entrusted to a Ford dealer or suitably equipped repairer.

6 Transmission control module (TCM) – removal and refitting

Note: *If a new transmission control module is to be fitted, it must be configured prior to use, using Ford diagnostic equipment. Entrust this task to a Ford dealer or suitably equipped repairer.*

Removal

1 Remove the battery and battery tray as described in Chapter 5A Section 4.
2 Release the wiring loom, undo the 3 nuts and remove the battery tray support bracket.
3 Detach the earth lead from the chassis member, and release the wiring harness guide from the top of the transmission.
4 Disconnect the wiring plugs from the TCM, and release the wiring from any retaining clips **(see illustration)**.
5 Undo the 3 retaining bolts and pull the TCM from the casing **(see illustration)**. Discard the O-ring seals – new ones must be fitted.
Caution: Do not attempt to rotate the TCM selector motor shafts. Their original positions will be lost, and the mechanisms may be damaged.

Refitting

6 Ensure the mating surfaces of the TCM and the casing are clean.
7 Fit new O-ring seals to the TCM, and lubricate them with a little clean transmission fluid.
8 Press the TCM into position, and tighten the retaining bolts to the specified torque.
9 Reconnect the wiring plugs and secure the wiring harness.
10 The remainder of refitting is a reversal of removal. If a new TCM has been fitted (or the original one does not perform as expected), have the unit configured using Ford diagnostic equipment by a dealer or suitably equipped repairer.

7 Powershift transmission – removal and refitting

Note: *Read through this procedure before starting work to see what is involved, particularly in terms of lifting equipment. Depending on the facilities available, the home mechanic may prefer to remove the engine and transmission together, then separate them on the bench, as described in Chapter 2E. The help of an assistant is highly recommended if the transmission is to be removed (and later refitted) on its own.*

Removal

1 Remove the air cleaner and inlet ducts as described in Chapter 4A Section 5.
2 Remove the battery, battery tray and support bracket as described in Chapter 5A Section 4.

6.4 Pivot over the locking catches to disconnect the TCM wiring plugs

6.5 TCM retaining bolts

7.3 Pull the breather tube upwards out from the transmission

7.5 Earth connection at the front of the transmission casing

7.10 Remove the rubber insert from the starter motor aperture – 1.6L models

3 Pull the breather tube from the top of the transmission **(see illustration)**.

4 Detach the selector cable from the transmission as described in Section 3.

5 Disconnect the wiring plugs/earth lead and wiring harness guide from the transmission **(see illustration)**.

6 Remove both driveshafts as described in Chapter 8 Section 2.

7 Undo the transmission-to-engine bolts which are accessible from above.

8 Remove the starter motor as described in Chapter 5A Section 9.

9 Using paint, or permanent marker, working through the starter motor aperture, make alignment marks between one of the the clutch unit mounting nuts/studs and the flywheel/driveplate.

10 On 1.6 litre models, remove the insert from the starter motor aperture, then rotating the crankshaft pulley clockwise as necessary, undo the 6 nuts securing the clutch unit to the flywheel/driveplate **(see illustration)**. Discard the nuts – new ones must be fitted.

11 To prevent damage to the exhaust flexible section, support it by attaching a pair of splints either side (two scrap strips of wood, plant canes, etc) using some cable-ties. Undo the nuts securing the flexible section to the exhaust manifold, and separate the joint. Recover the gasket, and discard it. Release the exhaust front rubber mounting block and move the system to one side.

12 Unbolt the engine rear mounting completely from under the car, referring to Chapter 2A Section 17 or Chapter 2B Section 18 if necessary.

13 The engine/transmission must now be supported, as the left-hand mounting must be removed. Ford technicians use a support bar which locates in the tops of the inner wings – proprietary engine support bars are available from tool outlets.

14 If a support bar is not available, an engine hoist should be used. With an engine hoist, the engine/transmission can be manoeuvred more easily and safely. In the workshop, we found the best solution was to move the engine to the required position, and support it from below – using the hoist on the transmission then gave excellent manoeuvrability, and total control for lowering out. If necessary, remove the windscreen cowl panel as described in Chapter 11 Section 20.

15 Supporting both the engine and transmission from below should be considered a last resort, and should only be done if a heavy-duty hydraulic ('trolley') jack is used, with a large, flat piece of wood on the jack head to spread the load and avoid damage to the sump. A further jack will be needed to lower the transmission out. **Note:** *Always take care when using a hydraulic jack, as it is possible for this type to collapse under load – generally, a scissor-type jack avoids this problem, but is also less stable, and offers no manoeuvrability.*

16 With the engine securely supported, undo the three nuts securing the left-hand engine/transmission mounting bracket to the transmission and the two bolts securing the mounting to the body sidemember. Remove the mounting from the engine compartment.

17 Swing the transmission forwards, and wedge it in position with a stout piece of wood, about 300 mm long, between the engine and the subframe.

18 Support the transmission from below, ideally using a trolley jack (if one is not available, a sturdy jack with a large, flat piece of wood on top of the jack head will suffice).

19 Have an assistant ready to help steady the transmission as the flange bolts are removed – attempting to remove the transmission single-handed is not recommended, as it is a heavy assembly which can be awkward to handle.

20 Check that, apart from the remaining flange bolts, there is nothing preventing the transmission from being lowered and removed. Make sure that any wiring or hoses lying on top of the transmission are not going to get caught up and stretched as the transmission is lowered.

21 Unscrew and remove the bolts securing the transmission bell housing to the engine. Note the bolt locations carefully, as they are of different lengths.

22 If the transmission does not separate on its own, it must be rocked from side-to-side, to free it from the locating dowels. As the transmission is withdrawn from the engine, make sure its weight is supported at all times.

23 Keeping the transmission steady on the jack head, carefully lower it and remove it from under the car.

Refitting

24 Prior to refitting, clean the contact surfaces of the transmission and cylinder block/sump.

1.0 litre EcoBoost engines

25 Insert a flat-bladed screwdriver into each slot in the clutch adjustment plate, twist the screwdrivers 90° anti-clockwise, then rotate the adjustment plate anti-clockwise until the locking tangs are fully depressed **(see illustrations)**.

26 As for removal, use a block of wood to wedge the engine forwards for refitting.

27 With the help of an assistant, raise the transmission, insert the input shaft into the centre of the clutch unit.

28 Keeping the transmission straight, and level with the engine, refit the transmission-to-engine flange bolts to their original locations,

7.25a Insert 2 screwdrivers, twist them 90°, then rotate the adjustment plate...

7.25b ...and ensure the locking tangs are fully depressed

6407 Fig. 07b-07.30.i HAYNES

7.30 Align the installation mark on the driveplate/flywheel with the mark on the clutch unit

then simultaneously tighten the bolts to draw the transmission evenly and gradually into place. Tighten the bolts to their specified torque.

1.6 litre engines

29 As for removal, use a block of wood to wedge the engine forwards for refitting.

30 With the help of an assistant, raise the transmission, and align the installation marks on the driveplate/flywheel and clutch unit **(see illustration)**.

31 Slide the transmission into place, with the clutch retaining studs feeding through the holes in the driveplate/flywheel.

32 Refit the transmission-to-engine bolts and tighten them to the specified torque. Draw the transmission up to the engine as evenly as possible.

33 Fit the new clutch unit-to-driveplate/ flywheel retaining nuts, and working in a diagonal pattern, tighten them to the specified torque. Using a socket/spanner on the crankshaft pulley, rotate the crankshaft clockwise only to access the studs and fit the nuts. Tighten the nuts to the Stage 1 torque setting, then go round again and tighten them to the Stage 2 setting.

All engines

34 Remove the wedge fitted between the engine and subframe. Raise the transmission into position, then refit the engine/ transmission left-hand mounting. Tighten the nuts/bolts to the specified torque.

35 Working from below, refit the engine/ transmission rear mounting, and tighten the bolts to the specified torque.

36 Once the engine/transmission mountings

have been refitted, the support bar, engine hoist or supporting jack can be removed.

37 Further refitting is a reversal of removal, noting the following points:

a) *Refit the starter motor as described in Chapter 5A Section 9.*

b) *Refit the driveshafts as described in Chapter 8 Section 2.*

c) *Tighten all fasteners to the specified torque (where given).*

d) *On completion, adjust the selector cable as described in Section 2, and top-up the fluid level as described in Section 2.*

e) *Recheck the transmission fluid level once the car has been driven.*

8 Powershift transmission overhaul – general information

1 Overhaul of the Powershift transmission should be left to a transmission specialist or a Ford dealer. Refer to the information given in Section before removing the unit.

2 Note that, if the vehicle is still within the warranty period, in the event of a fault it is important to take it to a Ford dealer who will carry out a comprehensive diagnosis procedure using specialist equipment. Failure to do this will invalidate the warranty.

Chapter 8
Driveshafts

Contents

Degrees of difficulty

Easy, suitable for novice with little experience	**Fairly easy,** suitable for beginner with some experience	**Fairly difficult,** suitable for competent DIY mechanic	**Difficult,** suitable for experienced DIY mechanic	**Very difficult,** suitable for expert DIY or professional

Specifications

General

Driveshaft type	Solid steel shafts with inner and outer constant velocity (CV) joints, both outer joints are of the ball-and-cage type and the inner joints of the tripod (spider-and-yoke) type. Right-hand driveshaft is fitted with a support bearing

Lubricant

Type/specification	Special grease (Ford specification WSS-M1C259-A1) supplied in sachets with gaiter kits – joints are otherwise prepacked with grease and sealed

Quantity per joint (approximate):

Inner joint	100 g
Outer joint	100 g

Torque wrench settings

	Nm	lbf ft
Driveshaft (front hub) nut*	255	188
Lower arm balljoint clamp bolt nut*	52	38
Right-hand driveshaft support bearing cap nuts*	25	18
Roadwheel nuts	135	100

Use new fasteners

1 General Information

1 Drive is transmitted from the differential to the front wheels by means of two solid-steel, equal-length driveshafts equipped with constant velocity (CV) joints at their inner and outer ends. Due to the position of the transmission, an intermediate shaft and support bearing are incorporated into the right-hand driveshaft assembly.

2 A ball-and-cage type CV joint is fitted to the outer end of each driveshaft. The joint has an outer member, which is splined at its outer end to accept the wheel hub, and is threaded so that it can be fastened to the hub by a large nut. The joint contains six balls within a cage, which engage with the inner member. The complete assembly is protected by a flexible gaiter secured to the driveshaft and joint outer member.

3 At the inner end, the driveshaft is splined to engage a tripod type CV joint, containing needle roller bearings and cups. On the left-hand side, the driveshaft inner CV joint engages directly with the differential sun wheel. On the right-hand side, the inner joint is integral with the intermediate shaft, the inner end of which engages with the differential sun wheel. As on the outer joints, a flexible gaiter secured to the driveshaft and CV joint outer member protects the complete assembly.

2 Driveshafts – removal and refitting

Note: *The driveshaft outer joint splines may be a tight fit in the hub, and it is possible that a puller/extractor will be required to draw the hub assembly off of the driveshaft during removal.*

Removal

1 Firmly apply the handbrake, then jack up the front of the car and support it securely on axle stands (see *Jacking and vehicle support*). Remove the relevant front roadwheel. Where applicable, remove the engine undershield.

2 Refit at least two roadwheel nuts to the

2.2 Using a fabricated tool to hold the front hub stationary whilst the driveshaft retaining nut is slackened

front hub, and tighten them securely. Have an assistant firmly depress the brake pedal to prevent the front hub from rotating, then using a socket and extension bar, slacken the driveshaft retaining nut. Alternatively, a tool can be fabricated from two lengths of steel strip (one long, one short) and a nut and bolt; the nut and bolt forming the pivot of a forked tool. Attach the tool to the hub using two wheel nuts, and hold the tool to prevent the hub from rotating as the driveshaft retaining nut is slackened **(see illustration)**. Loosen the nut almost to the end of its threads, but do not remove it at this stage.

⚠️ *Warning: The driveshaft nut is done up extremely tight, and considerable effort will be required to loosen it. Do not use poor-quality, badly-fitting tools for this task, due to the risk of personal injury.*

3 Unscrew the bolt and release the brake hydraulic hose from the suspension strut **(see illustration)**.

4 Unscrew and remove the lower arm balljoint clamp bolt nut, and withdraw the clamp bolt from the swivel hub **(see illustration)**. Note that a new nut and bolt will be required for refitting.

5 Use a chisel or screwdriver as a wedge to expand the lower portion of the swivel hub.

6 Lever down the lower arm to free the balljoint from the swivel hub **(see illustration)**, then move the swivel hub to one side, taking

2.3 Release the brake hydraulic hose from the suspension strut

care not to damage the balljoint rubber boot.

7 If removing the left-hand driveshaft, turn the steering wheel to full right-hand lock. If removing the right-hand driveshaft, turn it to full left-hand lock.

8 The splined end of the driveshaft now has to be released from its location in the hub. It's likely that the splines will be very tight (corrosion may even be a factor, if the driveshaft has not been disturbed for some time), and considerable force may be needed to push the driveshaft out. Ford recommend using a four-legged puller for this, but if one is not available, the shaft will have to be tapped out with a hammer. If a hammer is used, place a small piece of wood over the end of the driveshaft – in addition to the loosened hub nut, this will protect the threads from damage.

9 Once the splines have been released, remove the hub nut and discard it – a new nut must be used for refitting.

10 The driveshaft can be separated from the hub by having an assistant pull the base of the suspension strut outwards, while the splined end of the shaft is pulled clear of the hub **(see illustration)**. Do not bend the driveshaft excessively at any stage, or the joints may be damaged – the inner and outer joints should not be bent through more than 18° and 45° respectively. Do not let the driveshaft hang down under its own weight – tie it up level if necessary.

11 Proceed as follows, according to which driveshaft is being removed.

2.4 Unscrew the nut and remove the lower arm balljoint clamp bolt

2.6 Home-made method of releasing the lower arm – wood block, long pole and length of chain

2.10 Pull the base of the strut outwards, and pull the driveshaft splines through to the inside

2.12a Use a lever to prise the driveshaft out – this may take some time and effort

2.12b Once the driveshaft comes free, support the inner joint and remove the shaft completely

2.15 Unscrew the intermediate shaft bearing cap nuts

Left-hand driveshaft

12 Insert a lever between the driveshaft inner joint and the transmission housing, positioning a thin piece of wood between the lever and housing to protect it. Also position a container below the inner joint, to catch the transmission oil which will be lost as the driveshaft is removed. Carefully lever the driveshaft inner joint out of the differential, taking great care not to damage the transmission housing or the oil seal **(see illustrations)**.

13 Manoeuvre the driveshaft out of position, ensuring that the constant velocity joints are not placed under excessive strain, and remove the driveshaft from underneath the car. Whilst the driveshaft is removed, plug the differential aperture with a clean, lint-free cloth to prevent the entry of dirt.

14 Extract the circlip from the groove on the inner end of the driveshaft, and obtain a new one.

Right-hand driveshaft

15 Unscrew the nuts securing the intermediate shaft support bearing cap to the rear of the cylinder block. On diesel engine models, remove the support bearing cap from the studs. On petrol engine models, lift the support bearing cap and heat shield (where fitted) from the studs and slide it down the intermediate shaft **(see illustration)**. On all models, a new bearing cap and nuts must be used when refitting.

16 Position a container below the transmission, to catch the oil which will be lost as the driveshaft is removed. Withdraw the complete driveshaft from the transmission and from the bearing bracket, and remove it from under the car. On petrol engine models, remove the support bearing cap and heat shield from the intermediate shaft. Whilst the driveshaft is removed, plug the differential aperture with a clean, lint-free cloth to prevent the entry of dirt.

Both driveshafts

17 Check the condition of the differential oil seals, and if necessary renew them as described in Chapter 7A Section 5.

Refitting

Right-hand driveshaft

18 On petrol engine models, fit the new support bearing cap and heat shield (where fitted) to the intermediate shaft.

19 Use a special sleeve to protect the differential oil seal as the intermediate shaft is inserted. If the sleeve is not used, take great care to avoid damaging the seal (installation sleeves are supplied with new oil seals, where required).

20 Carefully refit the intermediate shaft in the support bearing and into the transmission. Turn the intermediate shaft until it engages the splines on the differential gears.

21 Tighten the new nuts securing the new support bearing cap to the cylinder block to the specified torque. Proceed to paragraph 25.

Left-hand driveshaft

22 Locate the new circlip in the groove on the inner end of the driveshaft **(see illustration)**.

23 Use a special sleeve to protect the differential oil seal as the driveshaft is inserted. If the sleeve is not used, take great care to avoid damaging the seal. (Installation sleeves are supplied with new oil seals, where required.)

24 Insert the driveshaft into the transmission, and push it fully home. Try pulling the shaft out, to make sure the circlip is fully engaged.

Both driveshafts

25 Pull the suspension strut outwards, and insert the outer end of the driveshaft through the hub. Turn the driveshaft to engage the splines in the hub, and fully push on the hub. Ford use a special tool to draw the driveshaft into the hub, but it is unlikely that the splines will be tight. However, if they are, it will be necessary to obtain the tool, or to use a similar home-made tool.

26 Screw on the new driveshaft nut, and use it to draw the driveshaft fully through the hub.

27 Locate the front suspension lower arm balljoint stub in the bottom of the swivel hub. Insert the new clamp bolt in the previously-noted position, screw on the new nut, and tighten it to the specified torque.

2.22 Fit a new circlip to the driveshaft groove

28 Refit the brake hydraulic hose to the suspension strut and tighten the retaining bolt securely.

29 Using the method employed on removal to prevent rotation, tighten the driveshaft retaining nut to the specified torque.

30 Fill the transmission, and check the level as described in Chapter 1A or Chapter 1B.

31 Where applicable, refit the engine undershield, then refit the wheel, and lower the car to the ground. Tighten the wheel nuts to the specified torque.

3 Outer constant velocity joint gaiter – renewal

1 Dismantle the inner constant velocity joint as described in Section 4.

2 On models with a vibration damper, after removing the inner CV joint, measure and note the distance from the end of the shaft to the edge of the damper. The damper must then be pressed from the shaft, the outer joint boot renewed, then the damper pressed back into its original position using the dimensions previously-noted. If access to a hydraulic press in not available, most engineering workshops (automotive or otherwise) would be prepared to carry out this task for a modest fee.

3 Cut off the gaiter retaining clips, then slide

3.3 Cut the gaiter retaining clips

3.7 Pack the outer CV joint with about half the grease supplied

3.10a Locate the outer clip on the gaiter ...

3.10b ... then using a special pair of pliers ...

3.10c ... remove any slack in the clip

Note: Ensure no grease is on the surfaces between the gaiter and the joint housing.

11 Use a small screwdriver to lift the inner lip of the gaiter, allowing the air pressure inside the gaiter to equalise, then fit the inner clip to the gaiter **(see illustration)**.

12 Where applicable, press the damper into its original position.

13 Reassembly the inner constant velocity joint as described in Section 4.

4 Inner constant velocity joint gaiter – renewal

1 Remove the driveshaft(s) as described in Section 2.

2 Cut through the metal clips, and slide the gaiter from the inner CV joint.

3 Clean out some of the grease from the joint, then make alignment marks between the housing and the shaft, to aid reassembly **(see illustration)**.

4 Carefully pull the housing from the tripod, twisting the housing so the tripod rollers come out one at a time. If necessary, use a soft-faced hammer or mallet to tap the housing off.

5 Clean the grease from the tripod and housing.

the gaiter down the shaft to expose the outer constant velocity joint **(see illustration)**.

Caution: Do not disassemble the outer CV joint.

4 Scoop out as much grease as possible from the joint.

5 Inspect the ball tracks on the inner and outer members. If the tracks have widened, the balls will no longer be a tight fit. At the same time, check the ball cage windows for wear or cracking between the windows. If the joints appear worn, complete renewal may be the only option – check with a Ford dealer or specialist.

6 If the joint is in satisfactory condition, obtain

a repair kit from your Ford dealer, consisting of a new gaiter, retaining clips, driveshaft nut, circlip and grease.

7 Pack the joint with the half of the grease supplied, working it well into the ball tracks, and into the driveshaft opening in the inner member **(see illustration)**.

8 Slide the rubber gaiter onto the shaft.

9 Apply the remaining grease to the joint and the inside of the gaiter.

10 Locate the outer lip of the gaiter in the groove on the joint outer member, then fit the retaining clip. Remove any slack in the clips by carefully compressing the raised section using a special pair of pincers **(see illustrations)**.

3.11 Lift the inner edge of the gaiter to equalise the air pressure

4.3 Make alignment marks between the shaft and housing

4.6a Remove the circlip from the end of the shaft ...

4.6b ... then carefully drive the tripod from the shaft

4.7 Slide the new gaiter and smaller diameter clip onto the shaft

6 Remove the circlip, and carefully drive the tripod from the end of the shaft **(see illustrations)**. Discard the circlip, a new one (supplied in the repair kit) must be fitted. Remove the gaiter if still on the shaft.

7 Slide the new gaiter onto the shaft along with the smaller clip **(see illustration)**.

8 Refit the tripod with the bevelled edge towards the driveshaft, and drive it fully into place, until the new circlip can be installed **(see illustrations)**.

9 Lubricate the tripod rollers with some of the grease supplied in the gaiter kit, then fill the housing and gaiter with the remainder.

10 Refit the housing to the tripod, tapping it gently into place using a soft-hammer or mallet if necessary.

11 Slide the new gaiter into place ensuring the smaller diameter of the gaiter locates over the grooves in the shaft **(see illustration)**.

12 Fit the new retaining clips **(see illustration)**.

13 Refit the driveshaft(s) as described in Section 2.

4.8a Fit the tripod with the bevelled edge towards the shaft...

4.8b ... then fit the new circlip

5 Driveshaft overhaul – general information

1 Road test the car, and listen for a metallic clicking from the front as the car is driven slowly in a circle with the steering on full-lock. Repeat the check on full-left and full-right lock. This noise may also be apparent when pulling away from a standstill with lock applied. If a clicking noise is heard, this indicates wear in the outer constant velocity joints.

2 If vibration, consistent with roadspeed, is felt through the car when accelerating, there is a possibility of wear in the inner constant velocity joints.

3 If the joints are worn or damaged, it would appear at the time of writing that no parts are available, other than gaiter renewal kits, and the complete driveshaft must be renewed. Exchange driveshafts may be available – check with a Ford dealer or specialist.

4 Continual noise from the right-hand driveshaft, increasing with roadspeed, may indicate wear in the support bearing. To renew this bearing, the driveshaft and intermediate shaft must be removed, and the bearing extracted using a puller.

5 Remove the bearing dust cover, and obtain a new one.

6 Drive or press on the new bearing, applying the pressure to the inner race only. Similarly drive or press on the new dust cover.

4.11 The smaller diameter of the gaiter must locate over the groove in the shaft

4.12 Equalise the air pressure before tightening the gaiter clip

Notes

Chapter 9
Braking system

Contents

Degrees of difficulty

| **Easy,** suitable for novice with little experience | | **Fairly easy,** suitable for beginner with some experience | | **Fairly difficult,** suitable for competent DIY mechanic | | **Difficult,** suitable for experienced DIY mechanic | | **Very difficult,** suitable for expert DIY or professional | |

Specifications

Front disc brakes

Type	Ventilated disc, with single-piston sliding caliper
Minimum disc thickness	21.0 mm
Maximum disc thickness variation	0.025 mm
Maximum disc/hub run-out (installed)	0.050 mm
Brake pad friction material minimum thickness	1.5 mm

Rear drum brakes

Type	Leading and trailing shoes, with automatic adjusters
Maximum drum internal diameter	201.5 mm
Brake shoe friction material minimum thickness	1.0 mm

Torque wrench settings

	Nm	lbf ft
ABS hydraulic modulator mounting bracket bolts	23	17
Brake caliper guide pin bolts*	26	19
Brake caliper mounting bracket bolts	70	52
Brake fluid pipe unions	18	13
Brake hydraulic hose banjo union bolt	26	19
Brake master cylinder retaining nuts	20	15
Brake pedal mounting bracket nuts	25	18
Engine rear mounting through-bolt	48	35
Engine right-hand mounting to body	48	35
Exhaust flexible section-to-catalytic converter nuts	48	35
Handbrake lever retaining nuts	30	22
Rear wheel cylinder retaining bolt	12	9
Roadwheel nuts	135	100
Steering column shaft universal joint clamp bolt*	34	25
Underfloor cross-brace retaining nuts	40	30
Vacuum pump mounting bolts (diesel engine models)	20	15
Vacuum servo unit to brake pedal mounting bracket	25	18

*Use a new bolt

1 General Information

1 The braking system is of servo-assisted, dual-circuit hydraulic type split diagonally. The arrangement of the hydraulic system is such that each circuit operates one front and one rear brake from a tandem master cylinder. Under normal circumstances, both circuits operate in unison. However, in the event of hydraulic failure in one circuit, full braking force will still be available at two wheels.

2 All models are fitted with front disc and rear drum brakes. The front disc brakes are actuated by single-piston sliding type calipers, which ensure that equal pressure is applied to each disc pad. The rear drum brakes are of the leading and trailing shoe type, and are self-adjusting.

3 The vacuum servo unit uses inlet manifold depression (generated only when a petrol engine is running) to boost the effort applied by the driver at the brake pedal and transmits this increased effort to the master cylinder pistons. Because there is no throttling of the inlet manifold on a diesel engine, it is not a suitable source of vacuum for brake servo operation. Vacuum is therefore derived from a separate camshaft driven vacuum pump.

4 An Anti-lock Braking System (ABS) is fitted as standard equipment. On higher specification models, the ABS may also incorporate traction control or an electronic stability program. Refer to Section 19 for further information on ABS operation.

5 The cable-operated handbrake provides an independent mechanical means of rear brake application.

Warning: When servicing any part of the system, work carefully and methodically; also observe scrupulous cleanliness when overhauling any part of the hydraulic system. Always renew components (in axle sets, where applicable) if in doubt about their condition, and use only genuine Ford parts, or at least those of known good quality. Note the warnings given in ' Safety first, !' and at relevant points in this Chapter concerning the dangers of asbestos dust and hydraulic fluid.

2 Hydraulic system – bleeding

Warning: Hydraulic fluid is poisonous; wash off immediately and thoroughly in the case of skin contact, and seek immediate medical advice if any fluid is swallowed or gets into the eyes. Certain types of hydraulic fluid are inflammable, and may ignite when allowed into contact with hot components; when servicing any hydraulic system, it is safest to assume that the fluid is inflammable, and to take precautions against the risk of fire as though it is petrol that is being handled. Hydraulic fluid is also an effective paint stripper, and will attack plastics; if any is spilt, it should be washed off immediately, using copious quantities of fresh water. Finally, it is hygroscopic (it absorbs moisture from the air) – old fluid may be contaminated and unfit for further use. When topping-up or renewing the fluid, always use the recommended type, and ensure that it comes from a freshly-opened sealed container.

General

1 The correct operation of any hydraulic system is only possible after removing all air from the components and circuit; this is achieved by bleeding the system.

2 During the bleeding procedure, add only clean, unused hydraulic fluid of the recommended type; never re-use fluid that has already been bled from the system. Ensure that sufficient fluid is available before starting work.

3 If there is any possibility of incorrect fluid being already in the system, the brake components and circuit must be flushed completely with uncontaminated, correct fluid, and new seals should be fitted to the various components.

4 If hydraulic fluid has been lost from the system, or air has entered because of a leak, ensure that the fault is cured before proceeding further.

5 Park the vehicle over an inspection pit or on car ramps. Alternatively, apply the handbrake then jack up the front and rear of the vehicle and support it on axle stands (see Jacking and vehicle support). For improved access with the vehicle jacked up, remove the roadwheels.

6 Check that all pipes and hoses are secure, unions tight and bleed screws closed. Clean any dirt from around the bleed screws.

7 Unscrew the master cylinder reservoir cap, and top the master cylinder reservoir up to the MAX level line; refit the cap loosely, and remember to maintain the fluid level at least above the MIN level line throughout the procedure, otherwise there is a risk of further air entering the system.

8 There are a number of one-man, do-it-yourself brake bleeding kits currently available from motor accessory shops. It is recommended that one of these kits is used whenever possible, as they greatly simplify the bleeding operation, and also reduce the risk of expelled air and fluid being drawn back into the system. If such a kit is not available, the basic (two-man) method must be used, which is described in detail below.

9 If a kit is to be used, prepare the vehicle as described previously, and follow the kit manufacturer's instructions, as the procedure may vary slightly according to the type being used; generally, they are as outlined below in the relevant sub-section.

10 Whichever method is used, the same sequence should be followed (paragraphs 11 and 12) to ensure the removal of all air from the system.

Note: *Ford suggest that vehicles equipped with the Stablilty Assist system, should have the hydraulic system bled using the BleedMASTER function in their diagnostic tool. If the following procedure produces less than satisfactory results, entrust this task to a Ford Dealer or suitably equipped repairer.*

Bleeding sequence

11 If the system has been only partially disconnected, and suitable precautions were taken to minimise fluid loss, it should only be necessary to bleed that part of the system (ie, the primary or secondary circuit). If the master cylinder or main brake lines have been disconnected, then the complete system must be bled.

12 If the complete system is to be bled, then it should be done in the following sequence:

a) Left-hand rear brake.
b) Right-hand rear brake.
c) Left-hand front brake.
d) Right-hand front brake.

Bleeding

Basic (two-man) method

13 Collect together a clean glass jar, a suitable length of plastic or rubber tubing which is a tight fit over the bleed screw, and a ring spanner to fit the screw. The help of an assistant will also be required.

14 Remove the dust cap from the first bleed screw in the sequence **(see illustration)**. Fit the spanner and tube to the screw, place the other end of the tube in the jar, and pour in sufficient fluid to cover the end of the tube.

15 Ensure that the master cylinder reservoir fluid level is maintained at least above the MIN level line throughout the procedure.

16 Have the assistant fully depress the brake pedal several times to build-up pressure, then maintain it on the final downstroke.

17 While pedal pressure is maintained, unscrew the bleed screw (approximately one turn) and allow the compressed fluid and air to flow into the jar. The assistant should maintain pedal pressure, following it down to the floor if necessary, and should not release

2.14 Rear wheel cylinder bleed screw

it until instructed to do so. When the flow stops, tighten the bleed screw again, have the assistant release the pedal slowly, and recheck the reservoir fluid level.

18 Repeat the steps given in paragraphs 16 and 17 until the fluid emerging from the bleed screw is free from air bubbles. If the master cylinder has been drained and refilled, and air is being bled from the first screw in the sequence, allow approximately five seconds between cycles for the master cylinder passages to refill.

19 When no more air bubbles appear, securely tighten the bleed screw, remove the tube and spanner, and refit the dust cap. Do not overtighten the bleed screw.

20 Repeat the procedure on the remaining screws in the sequence, until all air is removed from the system and the brake pedal feels firm again.

Using a one-way valve kit

21 As the name implies, these kits consist of a length of tubing with a one-way valve fitted, to prevent expelled air and fluid being drawn back into the system; some kits include a translucent container, which can be positioned so that the air bubbles can be more easily seen flowing from the end of the tube.

22 The kit is connected to the bleed screw, which is then opened. The user returns to the driver's seat, depresses the brake pedal with a smooth, steady stroke, and slowly releases it; this is repeated until the expelled fluid is clear of air bubbles.

23 Note that these kits simplify work so much that it is easy to forget the master cylinder reservoir fluid level; ensure that this is maintained at least above the MIN level line at all times.

Using a pressure-bleeding kit

24 These kits are usually operated by a reservoir of pressurised air contained in the spare tyre. However, note that it will probably be necessary to reduce the pressure to a lower level than normal; refer to the instructions supplied with the kit. You may have to borrow a friend's spare tyre if your car has a puncture kit instead of a spare tyre.

25 By connecting a pressurised, fluid-filled container to the master cylinder reservoir, bleeding can be carried out simply by opening each screw in turn (in the specified sequence), and allowing the fluid to flow out until no more air bubbles can be seen in the expelled fluid.

26 This method has the advantage that the large reservoir of fluid provides an additional safeguard against air being drawn into the system during bleeding.

27 Pressure-bleeding is particularly effective when bleeding 'difficult' systems, or when bleeding the complete system at the time of routine fluid renewal.

All methods

28 When bleeding is complete, and firm pedal feel is restored, wash off any spilt fluid,

securely tighten the bleed screws, and refit the dust caps.

29 Check the hydraulic fluid level in the master cylinder reservoir, and top-up if necessary (see Weekly checks0,5).

30 Discard any hydraulic fluid that has been bled from the system; it will not be fit for re-use.

31 Check the feel of the brake pedal. If it feels at all spongy, air must still be present in the system, and further bleeding is required. Failure to bleed satisfactorily after a reasonable repetition of the bleeding procedure may be due to worn master cylinder seals.

3 Hydraulic pipes and hoses – renewal

Note: *Before starting work, refer to the note at the beginning of Section 2 concerning the dangers of hydraulic fluid.*

1 If any pipe or hose is to be renewed, minimise fluid loss by first removing the master cylinder reservoir cap and screwing it down onto a piece of polythene. Alternatively, flexible hoses can be sealed, if required, using a proprietary brake hose clamp. Metal brake pipe unions can be plugged (if care is taken not to allow dirt into the system) or capped immediately they are disconnected. Place a wad of rag under any union that is to be disconnected, to catch any spilt fluid.

2 If a flexible hose is to be disconnected, unscrew the brake pipe union nut before removing the spring clip which secures the hose to its mounting bracket. Where applicable, unscrew the banjo union bolt securing the hose to the caliper and recover the copper washers.

3 To unscrew union nuts, it is preferable to obtain a brake pipe spanner of the correct size; these are available from most motor accessory shops. Failing this, a close-fitting open-ended spanner will be required, though if the nuts are tight or corroded, their flats may be rounded-off if the spanner slips. In such a case, a self-locking wrench is often the only way to unscrew a stubborn union, but it follows that the pipe and the damaged nuts must be renewed on reassembly. Always clean a union and surrounding area before disconnecting it. If disconnecting a component with more than one union, make a careful note of the connections before disturbing any of them.

4 If a brake pipe is to be renewed, it can be obtained, cut to length and with the union nuts and end flares in place, from Ford dealers. All that is then necessary is to bend it to shape, following the line of the original, before fitting it to the car. Alternatively, most motor accessory shops can make up brake pipes from kits, but this requires very careful measurement of the original, to ensure that the new one is of the correct length. The safest answer is usually to take the original to the shop as a pattern.

5 On refitting, do not overtighten the union nuts.

6 When refitting hoses to the calipers, always use new copper washers and tighten the banjo union bolts to the specified torque. Make sure that the hoses are positioned so that they will not touch surrounding bodywork or the roadwheels.

7 Ensure that the pipes and hoses are correctly routed, with no kinks, and that they are secured in the clips or brackets provided. After fitting, remove the polythene from the reservoir, and bleed the hydraulic system as described in Section. Wash off any spilt fluid, and check carefully for fluid leaks.

4 Front brake pads – renewal

⚠️ *Warning: Renew BOTH sets of front brake pads at the same time – NEVER renew the pads on only one wheel, as uneven braking may result. Note that the dust created by wear of the pads may contain asbestos, which is a health hazard. Never blow it out with compressed air, and do not inhale any of it. An approved filtering mask should be worn when working on the brakes. DO NOT use*

petroleum-based solvents to clean brake parts – use brake cleaner or methylated spirit only.

1 Apply the handbrake, then jack up the front of the vehicle and support it on axle stands (see *Jacking and vehicle support*). Remove the front roadwheels.

2 Follow the accompanying photos (illustrations 4.2a to 4.2u) for the pad renewal procedure, bearing in mind the additional points listed below. Be sure to stay in order and read the caption under each illustration. Note that if the old pads are to be refitted, ensure that they are identified so that they can be returned to their original position.

4.2a Unscrew the lower guide pin bolt while holding the guide pin with a second spanner …

4.2b … remove the upper guide pin bolt in the same way

4.2c Unscrew the retaining bolt …

4.2d … and free the brake hose support bracket from the suspension strut

4.2e Lift the caliper off the mounting bracket …

4.2f … and suspended it from the coil spring using wire or a cable-tie

4.2g Remove the outer pad from the caliper mounting bracket …

4.2h … followed by the inner pad

4.2i Remove the anti-rattle plates from the top …

4.2j … and bottom of the caliper mounting bracket

4.2k Measure the thickness of the pad friction material. If any are worn down to the specified minimum, or fouled with oil or grease, all four pads must be renewed

4.2l Clean the dust and dirt from the caliper piston and mounting bracket using aerosol brake cleaner and a soft brush

4.2m If new pads are to be fitted, before refitting the caliper, push back the caliper piston, ideally with a piston retraction tool. Keep an eye on the fluid level in the reservoir, and remove any surplus with a syringe

4.2n Fit the upper anti-rattle plate …

4.2o … and lower anti-rattle plate to the caliper mounting bracket

4.2p Note the pad orientation before fitting. Outer pad (A) and inner pad (B)

4.2q Fit the inner and outer pads to the caliper mounting bracket, ensuring that the friction material is facing the brake disc

4.2r Slide the caliper into position in the mounting bracket

4.2s Fit the new upper and lower guide pin bolts…

4.2t … and tighten the guide pin bolts to the specified torque

4.2u Refit the brake hose bracket and tighten the bolt securely

3 If the original brake pads are still serviceable, carefully clean them using a clean, fine wire brush or similar, paying particular attention to the sides and back of the metal backing plate. Clean out the grooves in the friction material, and pick out any large embedded particles of dirt or debris. Carefully clean the pad locations in the caliper mounting bracket.

4 Prior to fitting the pads, check that the guide pins are a snug fit in the caliper mounting bracket. Inspect the dust seal around the piston for damage, and the piston for evidence of fluid leaks, corrosion or damage. If attention to any of these components is necessary, refer to Section 5.

5 With the brake pads installed, depress the brake pedal repeatedly, until normal (non-assisted) pedal pressure is restored, and the pads are pressed into firm contact with the brake disc.

6 Repeat the above procedure on the remaining front brake caliper.

7 Refit the roadwheels, then lower the vehicle to the ground and tighten the roadwheel nuts to the specified torque setting.

8 Check the hydraulic fluid level as described in Weekly checks0,5.

Caution: New pads will not give full braking efficiency until they have bedded-in. Be prepared for this, and avoid hard braking as far as possible for the first hundred miles or so after pad renewal.

5 Front brake caliper – removal, overhaul and refitting

Note: *New brake hose copper washers will be required when refitting. Before starting work, refer to the warnings at the beginning of Sections 2 and 4 concerning the dangers of hydraulic fluid and asbestos dust.*

Removal

1 Apply the handbrake, then jack up the front of the vehicle and support it on axle stands (see *Jacking and vehicle support*). Remove the roadwheel.

2 Minimise fluid loss by first removing the master cylinder reservoir cap and screwing it down onto a piece of polythene. Alternatively, use a brake hose clamp to clamp the flexible hose leading to the brake caliper.

3 Clean the area around the caliper brake hose union. Unscrew and remove the union bolt, and recover the copper sealing washer from each side of the hose union. Discard the washers; new ones must be used on refitting. Plug the hose end and caliper hole, to minimise fluid loss and prevent the ingress of dust and dirt into the hydraulic system.

4 Undo the caliper upper and lower guide pin bolts then remove the caliper from mounting bracket **(see illustrations 4.2a and 4.2b).**

Overhaul

Note: *Before starting work, check on the availability of parts (caliper overhaul kit/ seals).*

5 With the caliper on the bench, brush away all traces of dust and dirt, but take care not to inhale any dust, as it may be harmful to your health.

6 Pull the dust cover rubber seal from the end of the piston.

7 Apply low air pressure to the fluid inlet union, to eject the piston. Only low air pressure is required for this, such as is produced by a foot-operated tyre pump.

Caution: The piston may be ejected with some force. Position a thin piece of wood between the piston and the caliper body, to prevent damage to the end face of the piston, in the event of it being ejected suddenly.

8 Using a suitable blunt instrument, prise the piston seal from the groove in the cylinder bore. Take care not to scratch the surface of the bore.

9 Clean the piston and caliper body with methylated spirit, and allow to dry. Examine the surfaces of the piston and cylinder bore for wear, damage and corrosion. If the piston alone is unserviceable, a new piston must be obtained, along with seals. If the cylinder bore is unserviceable, the complete caliper must be renewed. The seals must be renewed, regardless of the condition of the other components.

10 Coat the piston and seals with clean brake fluid, then manipulate the piston seal into the groove in the cylinder bore.

11 Push the piston squarely into its bore, taking care not to damage the seal.

12 Fit the dust cover rubber seal onto the piston and caliper, then depress the piston fully.

Refitting

13 Place the caliper in position over the brake pads on the mounting bracket. Fit the upper and lower guide pin bolts and tighten the bolts to the specified torque.

14 Position a new copper sealing washer on each side of the hose union, and connect the brake hose to the caliper. Ensure that the hose is correctly positioned against the caliper body lug, then install the union bolt and tighten it to the specified torque setting.

15 Remove the brake hose clamp or polythene, and bleed the hydraulic system as described in Section 2. Note that, providing the precautions described were taken to minimise brake fluid loss, it should only be necessary to bleed the relevant front brake circuit.

16 Refit the roadwheel, then lower the vehicle to the ground and tighten the roadwheel nuts to the specified torque.

6 Front brake disc – inspection, removal and refitting

Note: *Before starting work, refer to the warning at the beginning of Section 4 concerning the dangers of asbestos dust. If either disc requires renewal, both should be renewed at the same time together with new pads, to ensure even and consistent braking.*

Inspection

1 Firmly apply the handbrake, then jack up the front of the vehicle and support it securely on axle stands (see *Jacking and vehicle support*). Remove the roadwheel.

2 Unscrew the bolt and release the brake hydraulic hose from the suspension strut **(see illustration).**

3 Unscrew the bolts securing the brake caliper mounting bracket to the hub carrier, then slide the caliper/bracket assembly from the hub carrier and brake disc (there is no need to remove the brake pads) **(see illustration).** Suspend the caliper/bracket assembly from the strut coil spring using wire or a cable-tie – do not allow the caliper to hang on the brake hose.

4 Temporarily refit two of the wheel nuts to diagonally-opposite studs, with the flat sides of the nuts against the disc. Tighten the nuts progressively, to hold the disc firmly.

5 Scrape any corrosion from the disc. Rotate the disc, and examine it for deep scoring, grooving or cracks. Using a micrometer, measure the thickness of the disc in several

6.2 Unscrew the bolt and release the brake hydraulic hose from the suspension strut

6.3 Unscrew the bolts securing the brake caliper mounting bracket to the hub carrier

6.5 Using a micrometer to measure the thickness of the brake disc

6.6 Measuring the disc run-out with a dial gauge

places **(see illustration)**. The minimum thickness is given in the Specifications. Light wear and scoring is normal, but if excessive, the disc should be removed, and either reground by a specialist, or renewed. If regrinding is undertaken, the minimum thickness must be maintained. Obviously, if the disc is cracked, it must be renewed.

6 Using a dial gauge or a flat metal block and feeler gauges, check that the disc run-out 10 mm from the outer edge does not exceed the limit given in the Specifications. To do this, fix the measuring equipment, and rotate the disc, noting the variation in measurement as the disc is rotated **(see illustration)**. The difference between the minimum and maximum measurements recorded is the disc run-out.

7 If the run-out is greater than the specified amount, check for variations of the disc thickness as follows. Mark the disc at eight positions 45° apart then, using a micrometer, measure the disc thickness at the eight positions, 15 mm in from the outer edge. If the variation between the minimum and maximum readings is greater than the specified amount, the disc should be renewed.

8 The hub face run-out can also be checked in a similar way. First remove the disc

as described later in this Section, fix the measuring equipment, then slowly rotate the hub, and check that the run-out does not exceed the amount given in the Specifications. If the hub face run-out is excessive, this should be corrected (by renewing the hub bearings – see Chapter 10 Section 3) before rechecking the disc run-out.

Removal

9 With the wheel and caliper removed, remove the wheel nuts which were temporarily refitted in paragraph 4.

10 Mark the disc in relation to the hub, if it is to be refitted, then withdraw the disc over the wheel studs **(see illustration)**.

Refitting

11 Make sure that the disc and hub mating surfaces are clean, then locate the disc on the wheel studs. Align the previously-made marks if the original disc is being refitted.

12 Refit the caliper mounting bracket complete with caliper and pads and tighten the bolts to the specified torque.

13 Locate the brake hydraulic hose bracket on the suspension strut, refit the retaining bolt and tighten it securely.

14 Refit the wheel, and lower the car to

the ground. Tighten the wheel nuts to the specified torque.

15 Test the brakes carefully before returning the car to normal service.

7 Rear brake drum – removal, inspection and refitting

Note: *Before starting work, refer to the warning at the beginning of Section 8 concerning the dangers of asbestos dust. If either drum requires renewal, both should be renewed at the same time together with new brake shoes, to ensure even and consistent braking.*

Removal

1 Chock the front wheels, then jack up the rear of the vehicle, and support it securely on axle stands (see *Jacking and vehicle support*). Remove the roadwheel.

2 Remove the centre console panels as described in Section 14, then release the handbrake, remove the retaining clip then slacken the handbrake cable adjustment nut 6 turns **(see illustrations)**.

3 Undo the two retaining screws and

6.10 Withdraw the disc from the hub

7.2a Remove the clip...

7.2b ...and slacken the adjuster nut 6 turns

7.3a Undo the two retaining screws…

7.3b … and withdraw the drum from the wheel hub

7.3c If necessary, screw a bolt into the threaded hole and tighten the bolt to draw off the drum

withdraw the drum from the wheel hub. If the drum is initially tight, screw a suitable bolt into the threaded hole on the front face of the drum. Tighten the bolt to draw off the drum while tapping around the periphery with a copper mallet (see illustrations).

4 With the brake drum removed, clean the dust from the drum, brake shoes, wheel cylinder and backplate, using brake cleaner or methylated spirit. Take care not to inhale the dust, as it may contain asbestos.

Inspection

5 Clean the inside surfaces of the brake drum, then examine the internal friction surface for signs of scoring or cracks. If it is cracked, deeply scored, or has worn to a diameter greater than the maximum given in the Specifications, then it should be renewed, together with the drum on the other side.

6 Regrinding of the brake drum is not recommended.

Refitting

7 Refitting is a reversal of removal, noting the following points:

a) If the handbrake adjuster nut was slackened to allow removal of the drum, tighten the adjuster nut six turns to return it to its original position.

b) Adjust the handbrake as described in Section 14.

c) Refit the centre console trim panel and gear/selector lever trim panel after adjusting the handbrake.

d) Test the brakes carefully before returning the car to normal service.

8 Rear brake shoes – renewal

⚠ Warning: Brake shoes must be renewed on BOTH rear wheels at the same time – NEVER renew the shoes on only one wheel, as uneven braking may result. The dust created as the shoes wear may contain asbestos, which is a health hazard. Never blow it out with compressed air, and don't

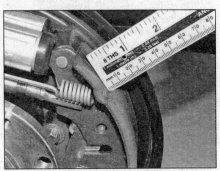

8.3a Measure the thickness of the brake shoe friction material at several points. If any are worn down to the specified minimum, or fouled with oil or grease, all four shoes must be renewed

inhale any of it. An approved filtering mask should be worn when working on the brakes. DO NOT use petroleum-based solvents to clean brake parts – use brake cleaner or methylated spirit only.

1 Remove the brake drum as described in Section 7.

2 Working carefully and taking the necessary precautions, remove all traces of brake dust from the brake drum, backplate and shoes.

3 Follow the accompanying photos (illustrations 8.3a to 8.3ac) for the brake shoe renewal procedure, bearing in mind the additional points listed below. Be sure to stay in order and read the caption under each illustration.

8.3b Using a screwdriver, disengage the upper return spring from the leading shoe, then remove it from the trailing shoe

8.3c Depress and pull off the leading shoe retaining spring clip …

8.3d … then remove the retainer pin from the rear of the backplate

8.3e Pull the lower end of the leading shoe outward and disengage it from the abutment bracket

8.3f Disengage the adjuster lever from the brake shoe peg and tension spring then remove the adjuster lever and adjuster strut

8.3g Disengage and remove the tension spring from the leading shoe

8.3h Disengage the lower return spring from the leading shoe and remove the shoe

8.3i Disengage the lower return spring from the trailing shoe and remove the spring

8.3j Depress and pull off the trailing shoe retaining spring clip ...

8.3k ... then remove the retainer pin from the rear of the backplate

8.3l Pull back the spring and disengage the handbrake cable end from the handbrake lever on the trailing shoe, then remove the shoe

8.3m Use a cable-tie or elastic band to retain the wheel cylinder pistons

8.3n Thoroughly clean the backplate, then apply a smear of high-temperature brake grease to the contact surfaces

8.3o Engage the handbrake cable with the handbrake lever on the trailing shoe and position the shoe on the backplate

8.3p Insert the trailing shoe retainer pin ...

8.3q ... then refit the trailing shoe retaining spring clip

8.3r Engage the lower return spring with the trailing shoe …

8.3s … and leading shoe …

8.3t … then engage the leading shoe with the abutment bracket

8.3u Engage the adjuster strut fork with the handbrake lever on the trailing shoe…

8.3v … and over the peg on the leading shoe

8.3w Place the adjuster lever over the peg on the leading shoe and under the adjuster strut fork

8.3x Engage the tension spring with the leading shoe and adjuster lever

8.3y Insert the leading shoe retainer pin …

8.3z … then refit the leading shoe retaining spring clip

8.3aa Engage the upper return spring with the trailing shoe …

8.3ab … then pull it into engagement with the leading shoe. Cut off the cable-tie or elastic band used to retain the wheel cylinder pistons

8.3ac Pull adjuster lever away from the adjuster fork and turn the adjuster wheel as necessary until the drum can be refitted

4 If both brake assemblies are dismantled at the same time, take care not to mix up the components. Note that the left-hand and right-hand adjuster components are 'handed' and must not be interchanged.

5 Prior to refitting the adjuster mechanism, lift the adjuster lever and turn the adjuster strut wheel to shorten the overall length of the mechanism slightly **(see illustration 8.3ac)**. This will compensate for the additional thickness of the new brake shoes, and allow the brake drum to be fitted easily.

6 On completion, place the brake drum in position over the brake shoes. It is not necessary to refit the two retaining screws at this stage as the drums must be removed again later to adjust the handbrake.

7 Repeat the operation on the remaining brake.

8 Once both sets of rear shoes have been renewed, with the handbrake fully released, adjust the lining-to-drum clearance by repeatedly depressing the brake pedal 20 to 25 times. Whilst depressing the pedal, have an assistant listen to the rear drums, to check that the adjuster mechanism is functioning correctly; if so, a clicking sound will be emitted by the adjuster as the pedal is depressed.

9 Adjust the handbrake as described in Section 14.

10 Refit the roadwheels, then lower the vehicle to the ground and tighten the roadwheel nuts to the specified torque.

11 Check the hydraulic fluid level as described in Weekly checks0,5.

Caution: New brake shoes will not give full braking efficiency until they have bedded-in. Be prepared for this, and avoid hard braking as far as possible for the first hundred miles or so after shoe renewal.

9 Rear wheel cylinder – removal, overhaul and refitting

Note: Before starting work, refer to the warnings at the beginning of Sections 2 and 8 concerning the dangers of hydraulic fluid and asbestos dust.

Removal

1 Remove the brake drum as described in Section 7. If the wheel cylinders have been leaking, there will probably be a significant build-up of brake dust on the failed seals (the dust sticks to the leaking fluid). A leak can be confirmed by carefully prising up the outer lip of the seal – any wetness means a new cylinder will be needed.

2 In recent years, the availability of wheel cylinder repair kits has greatly decreased, but it may still be worth asking. Wheel cylinders do not have to be fitted in pairs (providing they are the same size), but if one is leaking, it's reasonable to assume the other one soon will be. If the leak has been going on for some time, it may be serious enough to have contaminated the brake shoes, in which case new shoes should be fitted on BOTH sides.

3 Minimise fluid loss either by removing the master cylinder reservoir cap, and then tightening it down onto a piece of polythene to obtain an airtight seal, or by using a brake hose clamp, a G-clamp, or similar tool, to clamp the flexible hose at the nearest convenient point to the wheel cylinder.

4 Pull the brake shoes apart at their top ends, so that they are just clear of the wheel cylinder. The automatic adjuster will hold the shoes in this position, so that the cylinder can be withdrawn.

5 Wipe away all traces of dirt around the hydraulic union at the rear of the wheel cylinder, then undo the union nut **(see illustration)**.

6 Unscrew the bolt securing the wheel cylinder to the backplate.

7 Withdraw the wheel cylinder from the backplate so that it is clear of the brake shoes. Plug the open hydraulic unions, to prevent the entry of dirt, and to minimise further fluid loss whilst the cylinder is detached.

Overhaul

8 No overhaul procedures or parts were available at the time of writing – check availability of spares before dismantling. Renewing a wheel cylinder as a unit is recommended.

Refitting

9 Wipe clean the backplate and remove the plug from the end of the hydraulic pipe. Fit the cylinder onto the backplate and screw in the hydraulic union nut by hand, being careful not to cross-thread it.

10 Tighten the mounting bolt, then fully tighten the hydraulic union nut.

11 Retract the automatic brake adjuster mechanism, so that the brake shoes engage with the pistons of the wheel cylinder. To do this, pull adjuster lever away from the adjuster fork and turn the adjuster wheel as necessary until the drum can slide over the brake shoes **(see illustration 8.3ac)**.

12 Remove the clamp from the flexible brake hose, or the polythene from the master cylinder (as applicable).

13 Refit the brake drum (see Section 7).

14 Bleed the hydraulic system as described in Section 2. Providing suitable precautions were taken to minimise loss of fluid, it should only be necessary to bleed the relevant rear brake.

15 Test the brakes carefully before returning the car to normal service.

10 Master cylinder – removal and refitting

Note: Before starting work, refer to the warning at the beginning of Section 2 concerning the dangers of hydraulic fluid.

Removal

1 Remove the master cylinder reservoir cap, and siphon the hydraulic fluid from the reservoir. **Note:** *Do not siphon the fluid by mouth, as it is poisonous; use a syringe or an old hydrometer. Alternatively, open any convenient bleed screw in the system, and gently pump the brake pedal to expel the fluid through a plastic tube connected to the screw (see Section 2).*

2 Depress the tabs of the quick-release connector and disconnect the clutch master cylinder hydraulic hose from the rear of the master cylinder reservoir **(see illustration)**.

3 Disconnect the brake fluid level sensor wiring connector from the underside of the reservoir **(see illustration)**.

9.5 Undo the brake hydraulic pipe union nut from the wheel cylinder

10.2 Clutch hydraulic hose and brake fluid level sensor wiring connector on the master cylinder reservoir

10.3 Disconnect the level sensor wiring plug

10.4 Brake hydraulic pipe union nuts at the master cylinder

10.5 Master cylinder mounting nuts

4 Place cloth rags beneath the master cylinder to collect escaping brake fluid. Identify the brake lines for position, then unscrew the union nuts and move the lines to one side **(see illustration)**. Tape over or plug the line outlets.

5 Unscrew the mounting nuts and withdraw the master cylinder from the vacuum servo unit **(see illustration)**. Take care not to spill fluid on the vehicle paintwork.

6 No further dismantling of the master cylinder is possible as the internal components are not available separately.

Refitting

7 Fit the master cylinder to the servo unit, ensuring that the servo unit pushrod enters the master cylinder piston centrally. Fit the retaining nuts and tighten them to the specified torque setting.

8 Refit the brake lines and tighten the union nuts securely.

9 Reconnect the clutch master cylinder hydraulic hose and the brake fluid level sensor wiring connector to the reservoir.

10 Remove the reservoir filler cap and top-up the reservoir with fresh hydraulic fluid to the MAX mark (see Weekly checks0,5).

11 Bleed the hydraulic systems as described in Section 2 and Chapter 6 Section 4 then refit the filler cap. Thoroughly check the operation of the brakes and clutch before using the vehicle on the road.

11 Brake pedal –
removed and refitting

Note: *The brake pedal is an integral part of the pedal mounting bracket assembly and cannot be individually removed. Should renewal of the pedal, due to wear of the pivot bushes or the pedal itself, be required, it will be necessary to renew the complete mounting bracket assembly.*

Removal

1 Disconnect the battery negative lead as described in Chapter 5A Section 4.

2 Remove the steering column shrouds as described in Chapter 11 Section 25.

3 Set the front wheels in the straight-ahead position, then lock the steering column in position by removing the ignition key.

4 Working in the driver's footwell, undo the clamp bolt securing the steering column shaft lower universal joint to the steering gear pinion **(see illustration)**. Note that a new clamp bolt will be required for refitting. Pull the shaft upwards and off the pinion.

5 Disconnect the wiring connectors from the brake pedal position switch and brake light switch at the top of the pedal mounting bracket. Release the wiring harness from the clips and ties on the pedal bracket.

6 Using a screwdriver, prise out the plastic clevis pin securing the brake pedal to the servo unit pushrod **(see illustration)**. Note that the clevis pin will be damaged during removal and a new clevis pin will be required for refitting.

7 Undo the nuts securing the accelerator pedal to the brake pedal mounting bracket, and the nuts securing the mounting bracket to the bulkhead. Lift off the accelerator pedal and place it to one side.

8 Withdraw the brake pedal mounting bracket off the studs and remove it from inside the car.

Refitting

9 Refitting is a reversal of removal, noting the following points:

a) *Tighten the mounting bracket retaining nuts to the specified torque.*

b) *Reconnect the brake pedal to the servo unit pushrod using a new clevis pin.*

c) *Use a new clamp bolt when reconnecting the steering column shaft universal joint and tighten the clamp bolt to the specified torque.*

12 Vacuum servo unit –
testing, removal and refitting

Testing

1 To test the operation of the servo unit, with the engine off, depress the footbrake several times to exhaust the vacuum. Now start the engine, keeping the pedal firmly depressed. As the engine starts, there should be a noticeable 'give' in the brake pedal as the vacuum builds-up. Allow the engine to run for at least two minutes, then switch it off. The brake pedal should now feel normal, but further applications should result in the pedal feeling firmer, the pedal stroke decreasing with each application.

2 If the servo does not operate as described, first inspect the servo unit check valve as described in Section 13.

3 If the servo unit still fails to operate satisfactorily, the fault lies within the unit itself. Repairs to the unit are not possible; if faulty, the servo unit must be renewed.

Removal

4 Disconnect the battery negative terminal (refer to Chapter 5A Section 4).

5 On models with air conditioning, have the refrigerant discharged at a dealer service department or an automotive air conditioning repair facility.

6 Remove the brake master cylinder as described in Section 10.

7 Working in the driver's footwell, using a screwdriver, prise out the plastic clevis pin securing the brake pedal to the servo unit pushrod **(see illustration 11.6)**. Note that the clevis pin will be damaged during removal and a new clevis pin will be required for refitting.

11.4 Undo the clamp bolt securing the steering column shaft universal joint to the steering gear pinion

11.6 Prise out the plastic clevis pin securing the brake pedal to the servo unit pushrod

12.8 Vacuum servo unit retaining nuts

12.11 Unscrew and remove the engine lower mounting link through-bolt

12.12 Undo the nuts securing the refrigerant pipes to the expansion valve on the bulkhead

8 Undo the four nuts securing the vacuum servo unit to the brake pedal mounting bracket **(see illustration)**.

9 Firmly apply the handbrake, then jack up the front of the vehicle and support it securely on axle stands (see *Jacking and vehicle support*). Where applicable, remove the engine undershield.

10 To prevent damage to the exhaust flexible section in subsequent operations, support it by attaching a pair of splints either side (two scrap strips of wood, plant canes, etc) using some cable-ties. Undo the nuts securing the flexible section to the catalytic converter, and separate the joint. Recover the gasket, and discard it, a new gasket must be used for refitting.

11 Unscrew and remove the engine lower mounting link through-bolt **(see illustration)**.

12 On models with air conditioning, undo the two nuts securing the refrigerant pipes to the expansion valve on the bulkhead and withdraw the pipes from the valve **(see illustration)**. Discard the O-ring seals – new ones must be used when refitting. Suitably cap the open fittings immediately to keep moisture and contamination out of the system.

13 On models with air conditioning, undo the nut at the upper refrigerant pipe connector adjacent to the brake master cylinder reservoir. Undo the support bracket nut on the front suspension strut tower and remove the refrigerant pipe from the car **(see illustration)**. Discard the refrigerant pipe O-ring seals

– new ones must be used when refitting. Suitably cap the open fittings immediately to keep moisture and contamination out of the system.

14 Lift the cooling system expansion tank from its mountings and place it to one side.

15 The engine must now be supported, as the right-hand mounting (right as seen from the driver's seat) must be unbolted from the body. Supporting the engine should ideally be done from above, using an engine crane or a special engine lifting beam. However, in the absence of these tools, the engine can be supported on the sump, using a trolley jack, providing a piece of wood is used to spread the load.

16 With the engine securely supported, undo the three bolts securing the right-hand engine mounting to the body **(see illustration)**.

17 Carefully ease the vacuum hose out of the servo unit, taking care not to displace the sealing grommet **(see illustration)**.

18 Withdraw the servo unit from the bulkhead as far as the initial working clearance will allow. With the engine securely supported on the jack or crane, pull the engine forward on the right-hand side, until sufficient clearance exists to remove the servo unit from the engine compartment.

Refitting

19 Locate the vacuum servo unit in position on the bulkhead ensuring that the servo unit pushrod locates correctly around the brake pedal.

20 Refit the vacuum hose to the servo grommet, ensuring that the hose is correctly seated.

21 Move the engine back to its fitted position and refit the engine mounting retaining bolts. Tighten the bolts to the specified torque. Remove the jack or crane used to support the engine.

22 Place the cooling system expansion tank back in its mountings.

23 On models with air conditioning, reconnect the refrigerant pipes using new O-ring seals and tighten the pipe retaining nuts securely. Refit the upper refrigerant pipe support bracket to the suspension strut turret.

24 Using a new gasket, reconnect the exhaust flexible section to the catalytic converter and tighten the retaining nuts to the specified torque. Remove the support splints from the flexible section.

25 Where applicable, refit the engine undershield, then lower the car to the ground.

26 Refit the four nuts securing the vacuum servo unit to the brake pedal mounting bracket and tighten the nuts to the specified torque.

27 Reconnect the brake pedal to the servo unit pushrod using a new clevis pin.

28 Refit the brake master cylinder as described in Section 10, then reconnect the battery negative terminal.

29 On models with air conditioning, have the system evacuated, charged and leak-tested by the specialist who discharged it.

12.13 Undo the nuts at the refrigerant pipe connector and support bracket and remove the refrigerant pipe

12.16 Undo the three bolts securing the engine mounting to the body

12.17 Ease the vacuum hose out of the servo unit grommet

13 Vacuum servo unit check valve and hose – removal, testing and refitting

Removal

1 Carefully ease the vacuum hose out of the servo unit, taking care not to displace the sealing grommet **(see illustration 12.17)**.
2 Disconnect the hose quick-release fitting from the inlet manifold (petrol engines) or vacuum pump (diesel engines).
3 Release the vacuum hose from its clips and support brackets in the engine compartment, then remove the hose and check valve from the car **(see illustration)**.

Testing

4 Examine the check valve and hose for signs of damage, and renew if necessary. The valve may be tested by blowing through it in both directions. Air should flow through the valve in one direction only – when blown through from the servo unit end. If air flows in both directions, or not at all, renew the valve and hose as an assembly.
5 Examine the servo unit rubber sealing grommet for signs of damage or deterioration, and renew as necessary.

Refitting

6 Refitting is a reversal of removal ensuring that the quick-release connector audibly locks in position, and that the hose is correctly seated in the servo grommet.

13.3 Servo check valve

7 On completion, start the engine and check that there are no air leaks.

14 Handbrake – adjustment

1 Remove both rear brake drums as described in Section 7.
2 Prise the top edge of the passengers airbag warning light surround trim rearwards and remove it **(see illustration)**. Disconnect the wiring plug as the panel is withdrawn.
3 Prise up the gear lever surround along with the gaiter **(see illustration)**. If required, unscrew the gear knob and remove the gaiter assembly.

14.2 Prise the panel rearwards, and disconnect the wiring plug

4 Starting at the top, prise rearwards/up the gear lever surround panel **(see illustrations)**.
5 Prise the panels from the front of the console **(see illustrations)**. Disconnect any wiring plugs as the panels are withdrawn.
6 Working through the aperture at the base of the handbrake lever, remove the retaining clip from the handbrake adjuster nut on the end of the handbrake cable **(see illustrations 7.2a and 7.2b)**.
7 Working on one side of the car at a time, lift the adjuster lever on each leading brake shoe and slacken the adjuster strut wheel to shorten the overall length of the brake shoe adjuster mechanism slightly **(see illustration)**.
8 Working on the brake shoe assembly on the right-hand side of the car, wrap a cable-tie around the trailing brake shoe and the

14.3 Prise up the gear/selector lever surround

14.4a Prise the top of the panel rearwards, then up…

14.4b …and remove it

14.5a Prise up the lever aperture panel…

14.5b …and the console top section

14.7 Pull adjuster lever away from the adjuster fork and turn the adjuster wheel to shorten the adjuster assembly

14.8 Fit a cable-tie to the trailing shoe to hold the stop-peg on the handbrake lever against the brakeshoe

14.9 Insert a 3 mm Allen key between the stop-peg on the handbrake lever, and the edge of the brake shoe

14.10 Tighten the adjuster nut on the handbrake cable until the Allen key falls out

handbrake operating lever on the brake shoe. Tighten the cable-tie until the stop-peg on the handbrake operating lever is in contact with the edge of the brake shoe **(see illustration)**.

9 Working on the brake shoe assembly on the left-hand side of the car, insert a 3 mm Allen key between the stop-peg on the trailing brake shoe handbrake operating lever, and the edge of the brake shoe**(see illustration)**.

10 Working through the aperture at the base of the handbrake lever, and using a socket and extension bar, tighten the adjuster nut on the handbrake cable until the Allen key falls out **(see illustration)**.

11 Remove the cable-tie from the right-hand brake shoe assembly and refit both brake drums, referring to Section 7 if necessary.

12 With the handbrake fully released, adjust the lining-to-drum clearance by repeatedly depressing the brake pedal at least 10 times. Whilst depressing the pedal, have an assistant listen to the rear drums, to check that the adjuster strut is functioning correctly; if so, a clicking sound will be emitted by the strut as the pedal is depressed.

13 Apply the handbrake and check that the after approximately three to five clicks of the ratchet, both rear brake drums are locked. Now fully release the handbrake lever and check that the drums rotate freely.

14 Place the retaining clip back into position on the handbrake adjuster nut, then refit the centre console trim panel and gear/selector lever trim panel.

15 Refit the roadwheels and lower the car to the ground.

15 Handbrake lever – removal and refitting

Removal

1 Disconnect the battery negative lead as described in Chapter 5A Section 4.

2 Remove the centre console (Chapter 11 Section 24) and the front seat on the driver's side (Chapter 11 Section 21).

3 Chock the front wheels, then fully release the handbrake lever.

4 Working through the aperture at the base of the handbrake lever, remove the retaining clip from the handbrake adjuster nut on the end of the handbrake cable. Using a socket and extension bar, slacken the adjuster nut on the handbrake cable five turns to introduce some slack in the cable.

5 Jack up the rear of the vehicle, and support it securely on axle stands (see *Jacking and vehicle support*).

6 From under the car, undo the nuts and remove the underfloor cross-brace beneath the exhaust centre section.

7 Release the exhaust system from the centre and rear rubber mountings and allow the system to rest on the rear axle.

8 Undo the washer-type fasteners, and remove the rear and centre exhaust system heat shields.

9 Depress the retaining tabs and push the handbrake cables rearwards out of the support bracket **(see illustration)**.

10 Detach the short (front) handbrake cable from the compensator plate by sliding the end fitting up and out of the elongated hole in the plate.

11 Disconnect the wiring connector from the handbrake lever warning light switch.

12 Undo the two retaining nuts and remove the centre console rear mounting bracket from the floor.

13 Undo the retaining nuts and release the handbrake cable guide from the floor.

14 Undo the retaining bolt and two retaining nuts and remove the handbrake lever assembly from inside the car **(see illustration)**.

Refitting

15 Refitting is a reversal of removal, noting the following points:

a) Tighten all nuts/bolts to the specified torque (where given).

b) Adjust the handbrake as described in Section 14.

c) Refit the centre console and front seat as described in Chapter.

16 Handbrake cables – removal and refitting

Note: *The handbrake cables are supplied as one part, together with the compensator plate.*

Removal

1 Remove the centre console as described in Chapter 11 Section 24.

2 Working through the aperture at the base of the handbrake lever, remove the retaining clip from the handbrake adjuster nut on the end of the handbrake cable **(see illustrations 7.2a and 7.2b)**. Using a socket and extension bar, slacken the adjuster nut on the handbrake cable five turns to introduce some slack in the cable.

15.9 Depress the retaining tabs and push the handbrake cables out of the support bracket

15.14 Undo the bolt and two nuts and remove the handbrake lever assembly

16.9a Depress the tab in the centre of the connector link ...

16.9b ... then push the handbrake cable end fitting out of the link

16.10 Depress the tabs and pull the handbrake cable out of the trailing arm support bracket

3 Chock the front wheels, then jack up the rear of the vehicle, and support it securely on axle stands (see *Jacking and vehicle support*).

4 From under the car, undo the eight nuts and remove the underfloor cross-brace beneath the exhaust centre section **(see illustration 15.6)**.

5 Release the exhaust system from the centre and rear rubber mountings and allow the system to rest on the rear axle.

6 Undo the washer-type fasteners, and remove the rear and centre exhaust system heat shields.

7 Depress the retaining tabs and push the handbrake cables rearwards out of the support bracket **(see illustration 15.9)**.

8 Detach the short (front) handbrake cable from the compensator plate by sliding the end fitting up and out of the elongated hole in the plate.

9 Working on one side of the car at a time, locate the handbrake cable connector link just forward of the rear brake assembly. Using a small screwdriver, depress the tab in the centre of the connector link, then push the handbrake cable end fitting out of the link **(see illustrations)**.

10 Depress the tabs on the handbrake outer cables and pull the disconnected cables out of the support brackets on the trailing arms **(see illustration)**.

11 Undo the nut and release the handbrake cable support brackets adjacent to the rear axle pivot mountings on each side.

12 Release the cables from the underbody

retaining clips around the fuel tank and remove the cables from under the car.

Refitting

13 Refitting is a reversal of removal, noting the following points:
a) *Adjust the handbrake as described in Section 14.*
b) *Refit the centre console trim panel and gear/selector lever trim panel after adjusting the handbrake.*

17 Brake switches – removal, refitting and adjustment

Removal

Brake light switch

1 Disconnect the battery negative lead as described in Chapter 5A Section 4.

2 Working in the driver's footwell, disconnect the wiring connector from the brake light switch, located on the brake pedal mounting bracket. This is the switch on the right-hand side of the pedal mounting bracket, and is coloured black.

3 Rotate the switch clockwise by a quarter-turn, and withdraw it from the pedal bracket **(see illustration)**. Do not depress the brake pedal during the removal or refitting procedure – the pedal must be 'at rest'.

Brake pedal position switch

4 Disconnect the battery negative lead as described in Chapter 5A Section 4.

5 Working in the driver's footwell, disconnect the wiring connector from the brake pedal position switch, located on the brake pedal mounting bracket. This is the switch on the left-hand side of the pedal mounting bracket, and is coloured blue and white **(see illustration)**.

6 Rotate the switch anti-clockwise by a quarter-turn, and withdraw it from the pedal bracket. Do not depress the brake pedal during the removal or refitting procedure – the pedal must be 'at rest'.

Refitting and adjustment

7 Refitting is a reversal of the removal procedure. Both switches are automatically adjusted/calibrated by the vehicle system.

18 Handbrake warning light switch – removal and refitting

Removal

1 Remove the centre console as described in Chapter 11 Section 24.

2 Disconnect the wiring plug from the warning light switch on the side of the handbrake lever **(see illustration)**.

3 Unscrew the mounting bolt and remove the switch from the handbrake lever bracket.

Refitting

4 Refitting is a reversal of removal.

17.3 Rotate the brake light switch clockwise by a quarter-turn to remove it

17.5 Brake pedal position switch

18.2 Disconnect the wiring plug from the warning light switch

19 Anti-lock Braking and Traction Control systems – general information

1 ABS is fitted as standard equipment. On higher specification models, the ABS may also incorporate traction control or an electronic stability program as additional safety features.
2 The ABS system comprises a hydraulic modulator and electronic control unit together with four wheel speed sensors. The hydraulic modulator contains the electronic control unit (ECU), the hydraulic solenoid valves (one set for each brake) and the electrically-driven pump. The purpose of the system is to prevent the wheel(s) locking during heavy braking. This is achieved by automatic release of the brake on the relevant wheel, followed by re-application of the brake.
3 The solenoid valves are controlled by the ECU, which itself receives signals from the four wheel speed sensors which monitor the speed of rotation of each wheel. By comparing these signals, the ECU can determine the speed at which the vehicle is travelling. It can then use this speed to determine when a wheel is decelerating at an abnormal rate, compared to the speed of the vehicle, and therefore predicts when a wheel is about to lock. During normal operation, the system functions in the same way as a conventional braking system.
4 If the ECU senses that a wheel is about to lock, it operates the relevant solenoid valve(s) in the hydraulic unit, which then isolates from the master cylinder the relevant brake(s) on the wheel(s) which is/are about to lock, effectively sealing-in the hydraulic pressure.
5 If the speed of rotation of the wheel continues to decrease at an abnormal rate, the ECU operates the electrically-driven pump which pumps the hydraulic fluid back into the master cylinder, releasing the brake. Once the speed of rotation of the wheel returns to an acceptable rate, the pump stops, and the solenoid valves switch again, allowing the hydraulic master cylinder pressure to return to the caliper, which then re-applies the brake. This cycle can be carried out many times a second.
6 The action of the solenoid valves and return pump creates pulses in the hydraulic circuit. When the ABS system is functioning, these pulses can be felt through the brake pedal.
7 On models with traction control, the ABS hydraulic modulator incorporates an additional set of solenoid valves which operate the traction control system. The system operates at speeds up to approximately 30 mph using the signals supplied by the wheel speed sensors. If the ECU senses that a driving wheel is about to lose traction, it prevents this by momentarily applying the relevant front brake. The ABS ECU also communicates with the engine management powertrain control module during traction control operation. In severe cases of traction loss the engine

management ECU will reduce engine power to assist with traction recovery.
8 The electronic stability program (ESP) is a further development of ABS and traction control. Using additional sensors to monitor steering wheel position, vehicle yaw rate, acceleration and deceleration, in conjunction with the ABS sensors, the ECU can intervene under conditions of vehicle instability. Using the signals from the various sensors, the ECU can determine driver intent (steering wheel position, throttle position, vehicle speed and engine speed). From the sensor inputs from the wheel speed sensors, yaw rate sensors and acceleration sensors the ECU can calculate whether the vehicle is responding to driver input, or whether an unstable driving situation is occurring. If instability is detected, the ECU will intervene by applying or releasing the relevant front or rear brake, in conjunction with a power reduction, until vehicle stability returns.
9 The operation of the ABS, traction control, and stability programs is entirely dependent on electrical signals. To prevent the system responding to any inaccurate signals, a built-in safety circuit monitors all signals received by the ECU. If an inaccurate signal or low battery voltage is detected, the system is automatically shut down, and the relevant warning light on the instrument panel is illuminated, to inform the driver that the system is not operational. Normal braking is still available, however.
10 If a fault develops in the ABS/traction control/ESP system, the vehicle must be taken to a Ford dealer or suitably equipped repairer for fault diagnosis and repair.

20 Anti-lock Braking and Traction Control system components – removal and refitting

Note: Faults on the ABS system can only be diagnosed using Ford diagnostic equipment or compatible alternative equipment.
Note: Before starting work, refer to the note at the beginning of Section 2 concerning the dangers of hydraulic fluid.

Hydraulic modulator and ECU

Removal

1 The hydraulic modulator and ECU are located at the rear left-hand corner of the engine compartment. To gain access, remove the battery and battery tray as described in Chapter 5A Section 4.
2 Minimise fluid loss by first removing the master cylinder reservoir cap and screwing it down onto a piece of polythene.
3 Pull out the locking bar and disconnect the wiring harness plug from the ABS ECU on the hydraulic modulator **(see illustration)**. Release the wiring harness from the cable-tie on the modulator mounting bracket.
4 Note and record the fitted position of the brake pipes at the modulator, then unscrew

the union nuts and release the pipes. As a precaution, place absorbent rags beneath the brake pipe unions when unscrewing them. Suitably plug or cap the disconnected unions to prevent dirt entry and fluid loss.
5 Unscrew the three mounting bracket retaining bolts and remove the hydraulic modulator together with the mounting bracket.

Refitting

6 Refitting is the reverse of the removal procedure, noting the following points:
a) Tighten the modulator mounting bracket retaining bolts to the specified torque.
b) Refit the brake pipes to their respective locations, and tighten the union nuts to the specified torque.
c) Ensure that the wiring is correctly routed, and that the ECU wiring harness plug is firmly pressed into position and secured with the locking bar.
d) Refit the battery tray and battery as described in Chapter 5A Section 4.
e) On completion, bleed the complete hydraulic system as described in Section 2. Ensure that the system is bled in the correct order, to prevent air entering the modulator return pump.

Electronic control unit (ECU)

Note: If a new ECU is to be fitted, this work must be entrusted to a Ford dealer or suitably-equipped specialist as it is necessary to programme the new ECU after installation. This work requires the use of dedicated Ford diagnostic equipment or a compatible alternative.

Removal

7 Remove the hydraulic modulator from the car as described previously in this Section.
8 Undo the two retaining bolts and carefully withdraw the ECU from the base of the hydraulic modulator.
9 Thoroughly clean the mating face of the hydraulic modulator and also check the condition of the ECU gasket. If the gasket is damaged it will be necessary to obtain a new ECU.

Refitting

10 Ensuring that the seal is correctly located, carefully place the ECU in position, keeping it square and level.

20.3 ABS ECU wiring harness plug

20.17 Slide the wheel speed sensor wiring grommet out of the strut support bracket

20.18a Unscrew the wheel speed sensor retaining bolt...

20.18b ... then withdraw the wheel speed sensor from the top of the hub

11 Fit and moderately tighten the two retaining bolts.

12 On completion, refit the hydraulic modulator as described previously in this Section.

Front wheel speed sensors

Removal

13 Disconnect the battery negative lead as described in Chapter 5A Section 4.

14 Firmly apply the handbrake, then jack up the front of the car and support it securely on axle stands (see *Jacking and vehicle support*). Remove the appropriate front roadwheel.

15 Undo the retaining screws, release the clips and remove the wheel arch liner from under the wheel arch.

16 Trace the wheel speed sensor wiring back to its wiring connector on the inner wheel arch, and disconnect the connector. Depress the tab and pull the wiring connector end from the support clip on the wheel arch. Release the wiring harness from the cable-tie and support bracket on the wheel arch.

17 Slide the wheel speed sensor wiring grommet out of the support bracket on the suspension strut **(see illustration)**. Where applicable, also release the wiring from the clip at the base of the strut.

18 Unscrew the wheel speed sensor retaining bolt, then withdraw the wheel speed sensor from the top of the swivel hub **(see illustrations)**. **Note:** *The sensors can prove difficult to remove, due to corrosion – try soaking the sensor in maintenance spray. Do not use any great force to remove a sensor, or it may be damaged.*

Refitting

19 Ensure that the sensor and swivel hub sealing faces are clean, then fit the sensor to the hub. Refit the retaining bolt, and tighten it securely.

20 Ensure that the sensor wiring is correctly routed, and retained by all the necessary clips. Reconnect it to its wiring connector, and fit the connector into the retaining clip.

21 Refit the wheel arch liner and roadwheel, then lower the vehicle to the ground and tighten the roadwheel nuts to the specified torque. On completion, reconnect the battery negative terminal.

Rear wheel speed sensors

Removal

22 Disconnect the battery negative lead as described in Chapter 5A Section 4.

23 Chock the front wheels, then jack up the rear of the vehicle, and support it securely on axle stands (see *Jacking and vehicle support*). Remove the appropriate rear roadwheel.

24 Undo the retaining screws and nuts and remove the wheel arch liner from under the wheel arch.

25 Trace the wheel speed sensor wiring back to the rubber grommet on the inner wheel arch. Prise out the grommet, and disconnect the wiring plug **(see illustration)**. Depress the tab and pull the wiring connector end from the support clip on the wheel arch. Release the wiring harness from the cable-tie and support bracket on the wheel arch.

26 Release the sensor wiring harness from the grommets and clips on the inner wheel arch and rear suspension trailing arm.

27 Undo the retaining bolt and remove the wheel speed sensor from the rear of the brake backplate **(see illustration)**.

Refitting

28 Ensure that the sensor and brake backplate sealing faces are clean, then fit the sensor to the backplate. Refit the retaining bolt, and tighten it securely.

29 Ensure that the sensor wiring is correctly routed, and retained by all the necessary

20.25 Disconnect the sensor wiring plug

20.27 Undo the bolt and withdraw the sensor

21.1 The vacuum control solenoid on the 1.0 litre engine

21.5a Remove the main vacuum hose...

21.5b ...and the smaller hose

clips. Reconnect it to its wiring connector, and press the rubber grommet back into place.

30 Refit the wheel arch liner and roadwheel, then lower the vehicle to the ground and tighten the roadwheel nuts to the specified torque. On completion, reconnect the battery negative terminal.

Yaw rate sensor

Note: *The yaw rate sensor is only fitted to vehicles with electronic stability control (ESP). The sensor is located beneath the driver's seat on the right-hand side of the car.*

Removal

31 Disconnect the battery negative lead as described in Chapter 5A Section 4.

32 Remove the driver's seat as described in Chapter 11 Section 21.

33 Disconnect the sensor wiring connector, then undo the three bolts and remove the sensor from the car.

Refitting

34 Refitting is the reverse of the removal procedure.

Steering angle sensor

35 The steering angle sensor is an integral part of the EPS steering column and cannot be individually removed.

21 Vacuum pump – removal and refitting

Removal

1 A camshaft driven vacuum pump is fitted to all models except 1.25 and 1.6 litre petrol models. The pump primarily supplies vacuum for the brake servo, but it also supplies vacuum to the various engine controls **(see illustration)** that are vacuum operated, e.g. the turbocharger wastegate.

2 Pull up and remove the engine cover (where fitted).

3 To improve access remove the air filter housing and associated pipe work – as described in Chapter 4A Section 5 or Chapter 4B Section 4.

4 On 1.0 litre engines remove the control solenoid and earth lead.

5 Disconnect the hoses from the vacuum pump **(see illustrations)**.

6 Undo the retaining bolts and remove the vacuum pump **(see illustrations)**. Discard the gasket, new ones must be fitted.

Refitting

7 Refitting is a reversal of removal, noting the following points:

f) *Ensure the pump and cylinder head mating surfaces are clean and dry. Fit a new gasket.*

g) *Ensure the drive coupling is aligned with the slot in the camshaft (see illustration 21.6b).*

h) *Start the engine and check for correct operation of the pump (check brakes have servo action) as described in Section 12.*

i) *Make sure all the hose connections are secure, and check for leaks.*

21.6a Remove the bolts...

21.6b ...and then remove the pump

Chapter 10
Suspension and steering

Contents

Degrees of difficulty

Easy, suitable for novice with little experience	**Fairly easy,** suitable for beginner with some experience	**Fairly difficult,** suitable for competent DIY mechanic	**Difficult,** suitable for experienced DIY mechanic	**Very difficult,** suitable for expert DIY or professional

Specifications

Front suspension

Type .... Independent, with MacPherson struts, gas-filled shock absorbers and anti-roll bar

Rear suspension

Type .... Semi-independent torsion beam, with trailing arms, coil springs and telescopic shock absorbers

Steering

Type .... Rack-and-pinion with electric power steering (EPS)
Wheel alignment

	Total toe	Caster angle	Camber angle
Front wheel			
Normal suspension........................	1.33 mm Toe-in ± 1.5 mm	2.37° to 4.37°	-0.70°
Sports suspension	1.56 mm Toe-in ± 1.5 mm	2.51° to 4.51°	-0.85°
Rear wheel			
Normal suspension........................	2.06 mm ± 1.50 mm		-1.54°
Sports suspension	2.41 mm ± 1.50 mm		-0.64°

Torque wrench settings

	Nm	lbf ft
Front suspension		
Anti-roll bar clamp bolts	48	35
Anti-roll bar connecting link nuts	48	35
Brake caliper carrier bracket bolts	70	52
Driveshaft (front hub) nut*	255	188
Lower arm balljoint clamp bolt nut*	52	38
Lower arm mounting bolts: *		
Rear bolt:		
Stage 1	65	48
Stage 2	Angle-tighten a further 180°	
Front bolt:		
Stage 1	103	76
Stage 2	Angle-tighten a further 180°	
Rear engine mounting through-bolt	48	35
Subframe bolts:		
Front bolts*	60	44
Rear bolts: *		
Stage 1	100	74
Stage 2	Angle-tighten a further 240°	
Subframe brace	52	38
Suspension strut piston rod nut	48	35
Suspension strut top mounting nuts	30	22
Suspension strut to hub carrier: *		
Stage 1	82	61
Stage 2	Angle-tighten a further 90°	
Rear suspension		
Rear axle mounting bolts	125	92
Rear axle pivot through-bolt and nut: *		
Stage 1	80	59
Stage 2	Angle-tighten a further 120°	
Rear hub bearing assembly to trailing arm: *		
Stage 1	65	48
Stage 2	Slacken by 90°	
Stage 3	65	48
Stage 4	Slacken by 90°	
Stage 5	65	48
Stage 6	Slacken by 90°	
Stage 7	65	48
Stage 8	Slacken by 90°	
Stage 9	65	48
Shock absorber lower mounting bolt	115	85
Shock absorber upper mounting bolts	25	18
Steering		
Steering column retaining nuts*	22	16
Steering column shaft:		
Upper clamp bolt*	32	24
Lower clamp bolt*	34	25
Steering gear securing bolts	90	66
Steering wheel securing bolt	48	35
Track rod end locknuts	79	58
Track rod end-to-hub carrier nuts*	53	39
Roadwheels		
Roadwheel nuts	135	100

*Use new fasteners

1 General Information

1 The front suspension is of independent type, with a subframe, MacPherson struts, lower arms, and an anti-roll bar. The struts, which incorporate coil springs and integral shock absorbers, are attached at their upper ends to the reinforced strut mountings on the body shell. The lower end of each strut is bolted to the top of a cast hub carrier, which carries the hub, and the brake disc and caliper. The hubs run within non-adjustable bearings in the hub carriers. The lower end of each hub carrier is attached, via a balljoint, to a pressed-steel lower arm assembly. The balljoints are integral with the lower arms. Each lower arm is attached at its inboard end to the subframe, via flexible rubber bushes, and controls both lateral and fore-and-aft movement of the front wheels. An anti-roll bar is fitted to all models. The anti-roll bar is mounted on the subframe, and is connected to the suspension struts via vertical connecting links.

2 The rear suspension is of semi-independent type, consisting of a torsion beam and trailing arms, with double-conical coil springs and telescopic shock absorbers. The front ends of the trailing arms are attached to the vehicle underbody by horizontal bushes, and the rear ends are located by the shock absorbers, which are bolted to the underbody at their upper ends. The coil springs are mounted independently of the shock absorbers, and act directly between the trailing arms and the underbody. Each rear wheel bearing, hub and stub axle assembly is manufactured as a sealed unit, and cannot be dismantled.

3 The steering column is linked to the steering gear by a steering column shaft. The shaft has a universal joint fitted to its upper end, and is secured to the column by a clamp bolt. The lower end of the shaft is attached to the steering gear pinion by means of a universal joint and clamp bolts.

4 The rack-and-pinion type steering gear is

2.2 Using a fabricated tool to hold the front hub stationary whilst the driveshaft retaining nut is slackened

mounted on the front suspension subframe, and is connected by two track rods, with balljoints at their outer ends, to the steering arms projecting rearwards from the hub carriers. The track rod ends are threaded, to facilitate adjustment.

5 Electric power-assisted steering is fitted as standard, whereby an electric motor, drive gear assembly and torque sensor incorporated in the steering column provide a variable degree of power assistance according to roadspeed. The system is controlled by an electronic control unit with self-diagnostic capability, integral with the electric motor.

2 Front hub carrier –
removed and refitting

Removal

1 Firmly apply the handbrake, then jack up the front of the car and support it securely on axle stands (see *Jacking and vehicle support*). Remove the relevant front roadwheel. Where applicable, remove the engine undershield.

2 Refit at least two roadwheel nuts to the front hub, and tighten them securely. Have an assistant firmly depress the brake pedal to prevent the front hub from rotating, then

2.3 Unscrew the bolt and release the brake hydraulic hose from the suspension strut

using a socket and extension bar, slacken the driveshaft retaining nut. Alternatively, a tool can be fabricated from two lengths of steel strip (one long, one short) and a nut and bolt; the nut and bolt forming the pivot of a forked tool. Attach the tool to the hub using two wheel nuts, and hold the tool to prevent the hub from rotating as the driveshaft retaining nut is slackened **(see illustration)**. Loosen the nut almost to the end of its threads, but do not remove it at this stage.

⚠ *Warning: The driveshaft nut is done up extremely tight, and considerable effort will be required to loosen it. Do not use poor-quality, badly-fitting tools for this task, due to the risk of personal injury.*

3 Unscrew the bolt and release the brake hydraulic hose from the suspension strut **(see illustration)**.

4 Unscrew the bolts securing the brake caliper carrier bracket to the swivel hub, then slide the caliper/bracket assembly from the swivel hub and brake disc (there is no need to remove the brake pads) **(see illustration)**. Suspend the caliper/bracket assembly from the strut coil spring using wire or string – do not allow the caliper to hang on the brake hose.

5 Mark the brake disc in relation to the hub (assuming it is to be refitted), and withdraw it from the hub **(see illustration)**.

2.4 Unscrew the bolts securing the brake caliper carrier bracket to the swivel hub

2.5 Withdraw the brake disc from the hub

2.6a Unscrew the wheel speed sensor retaining bolt...

2.6b ... then withdraw the wheel speed sensor from the top of the hub

2.7 Loosen the track rod end balljoint nut, using an Allen key to stop the pin turning

6 Unscrew the wheel speed sensor retaining bolt, then withdraw the wheel speed sensor from the top of the hub carrier **(see illustrations)**. Provided the sensor is placed out of the way, there is no need to disconnect its wiring. **Note:** *The sensors can prove difficult to remove, due to corrosion – try soaking the sensor in maintenance spray. Do not use any great force to remove a sensor, or it may be damaged.*

7 Slacken the track rod end balljoint nut, and unscrew it as far as the ends of the threads. Counterhold the balljoint pin using a 5 mm Allen key **(see illustration)**.

8 Disconnect the track rod end balljoint from the hub carrier using a balljoint separator tool (leave the nut fitted to protect the threads),

taking care not to damage the balljoint rubber seal **(see illustration)**. Once the balljoint has been released, remove the balljoint nut and discard it – a new one should be used for refitting.

9 Unscrew and remove the lower arm balljoint clamp bolt nut, and withdraw the clamp bolt from the hub carrier **(see illustration)**. Note that a new nut and bolt will be required for refitting.

10 Use a chisel or screwdriver as a wedge to slightly expand the lower portion of the hub carrier.

11 Lever down the lower arm to free the balljoint from the hub carrier **(see illustration)**, then move the hub carrier to one side, taking care not to damage the balljoint rubber boot.

12 The splined end of the driveshaft now has to be released from its location in the hub. It's likely that the splines will be very tight (corrosion may even be a factor, if the driveshaft has not been disturbed for some time), and considerable force may be needed to push the driveshaft out. Ford recommend using a four-legged puller for this, but if one is not available, the shaft will have to be tapped out with a hammer. If a hammer is used, place a small piece of wood over the end of the driveshaft – in addition to the loosened hub nut, this will protect the threads from damage.

13 Once the splines have been released, remove the driveshaft nut and discard it – a new nut must be used for refitting.

14 The driveshaft can be separated from the hub by having an assistant pull the base of the suspension strut outwards, while the splined end of the shaft is pulled clear of the hub **(see illustration)**. Do not bend the driveshaft excessively at any stage, or the joints may be damaged – the inner and outer joints should not be bent through more than 18° and 45° respectively. Do not let the driveshaft hang down under its own weight – tie it up level if necessary.

15 Slacken and remove the two nuts and bolts securing the suspension strut to the hub carrier **(see illustration)**. Discard the nuts and bolts; they should be renewed whenever they are disturbed.

16 Pull the upper part of the hub carrier out of the suspension strut and remove it from under the wheel arch.

2.8 Using a balljoint separator tool to free the track rod end

2.9 Unscrew the lower arm balljoint clamp bolt nut, and withdraw the clamp bolt from the hub carrier

2.11 Home-made method of releasing the lower arm – wood block, long pole and length of chain

2.14 Pull the hub outwards, and pull the driveshaft through inside

2.15 Slacken and remove the two nuts and bolts securing the suspension strut to the hub carrier

3.3a We used a large bolt and washer ...

3.3b ... and a large hammer to drive out the hub flange

Refitting

17 Refitting is a reversal of removal, bearing in mind the following points:
a) *Tighten all fixings to the specified torque.*
b) *Use a new driveshaft retaining nut, strut-to-hub carrier nuts and bolts, lower arm balljoint clamp bolt and nut and track rod end nut.*
c) *When inserting the bolts securing the hub carrier to the base of the strut, note that the bolt heads on the left-hand side must be toward the rear of the vehicle and the bolt heads on the right-hand side must be toward the front of the vehicle.*
d) *Use the method employed on removal to prevent rotation of the driveshaft as the retaining nut is tightened.*

3 Front hub bearings – renewal

Note: *A press, a suitable puller, or similar improvised tools will be required for this operation. Obtain a bearing overhaul kit before proceeding.*

1 With the hub carrier removed as described in Section 2, proceed as follows.
2 The hub flange must now be removed from the bearing/hub carrier assembly. It is preferable to use a press to do this, but it is possible to drive out the hub using a metal tube of suitable diameter. Alternatively a suitable puller can be used.
3 Securely support the hub carrier, on two metal bars for instance, with the inner face uppermost then, using a metal bar or tube of suitable diameter, press or drive out the hub flange – we used a bolt and large washer (the same diameter as the end of the hub's splined end) **(see illustrations)**. Alternatively, use the puller to separate the hub from the bearing. Note that the bearing inner race will remain on the hub.

4 Now the bearing itself must be removed. Start by extracting the retaining circlip from the hub carrier using circlip pliers. After applying a generous amount of spray lubricant, we were able to drive the bearing out using a suitable mandrel**(see illustrations)**. Alternatively use another old bearing, together with the same large bolt and hammer used previously. Mount the hub carrier across two large blocks of wood – putting it across the open jaws of a vice might result in damage to the vice,

owing to the amount of force which will be necessary.
5 The bearing inner race left on the hub flange must now be removed. To do this, grip the edge of the flange in a vice, and begin tapping the race off with a chisel. Tap the race at the top and both sides (even turn the flange over in the vice) to stop it jamming as it frees. Once the race has moved down the hub flange slightly, a suitable puller, together with a bolt and washer for the puller centre screw to bear

3.4a Extract the retaining circlip from the hub carrier...

3.4b ... then using a suitable drift ...

3.4c ... and several sharp blows from the hammer ...

3.4d ... tap out the old bearing

3.5a Mount the hub flange in a vice, and tap the inner race with a chisel ...

3.5b ... then use a suitable puller to draw it off the rest of the way ...

3.5c ... until it comes off

against, can be used to draw it off the rest of the way **(see illustrations)**.

6 Using emery paper, clean off any burrs or raised edges from the hub flange and hub carrier, which might stop the components going back together.

7 Apply a light coat of lubricant to the inside of the hub carrier, and to the outside of the new bearing. Start fitting the bearing by offering it squarely into the hub, with the pink-coloured ABS wheel speed sensor ring towards the

transmission side of the swivel hub. Give it a few light taps with the hammer all round to locate it – keep the bearing square as this is done, or it will jam **(see illustrations)**.

8 Fitting the bearing by tapping it in all the way with a hammer will likely damage it. We used a length of threaded bar (available from motor factors, DIY stores, etc) with a nut, some large washers and a drilled plate on the inside of the hub carrier. With another large washer (or the old bearing and a washer) and

a nut on the outside, the whole assembly was mounted in a vice, and the nut tightened to press the new bearing in place. The actual method was to tighten the nut slightly, give the old bearing a few taps round its edge, tighten the nut some more, and so on until the bearing was fully home **(see illustrations)**.

9 Once the bearing is fully seated in the hub carrier, refit the retaining circlip, ensuring that it fully engages with its groove **(see illustration)**.

3.7a Fit the bearing with the pink-coloured wheel speed sensor ring towards the transmission side of the hub carrier...

3.7b ... then give it a few light taps with the hammer all round to locate it

3.8a Home-made arrangement of threaded rod, nuts and washers ...

3.8b ... used to gradually draw the new bearing into place

3.9 Refit the retaining circlip, ensuring that it fully engages with its groove

3.10a Locate the hub flange in the bearing ...

3.10b ... then use the same arrangement of threaded rod, nuts and washers to draw the flange into place ...

3.10c ... ensuring that the washer used to draw in the flange rests against the bearing inner race

10 The hub flange can be pressed into the new bearing using a very similar method to the one just used. Ensure that the washer used to draw in the flange rests against the bearing inner race **(see illustrations)**.
11 On completion, refit the hub carrier as described in Section 2.

4 Front suspension strut – removal, overhaul and refitting

Removal

1 Remove the windscreen cowl panel and bulkhead closure panel as described in Chapter 11 Section 20.
2 Working in the engine compartment, loosen the 3 suspension strut top mounting nuts by 3 turns each, on the side concerned **(see illustration)**. Do not loosen the centre nut.
3 Slacken the relevant front wheel nuts, then jack up the front of the car, and support securely on axle stands (see *Jacking and vehicle support*). Remove the roadwheel.
4 Unscrew the bolt and release the brake hydraulic hose from the suspension strut **(see illustration 2.3)**.
5 Unclip the ABS wheel speed sensor wiring from the suspension strut **(see illustration)**.
6 Unscrew and remove the nut securing the

anti-roll bar connecting link to the suspension strut, while holding the link stub with an Allen key/bit. Release the link from the strut and move it to one side **(see illustration)**.
7 Slacken and remove the 2 nuts and bolts securing the suspension strut to the hub carrier **(see illustration 2.15)**. Discard the nuts and bolts; they should be renewed whenever they are disturbed.
8 Support the strut from under the wheel arch then, working in the engine compartment, unscrew the suspension strut top mounting nuts. Disengage the base of the strut from the hub carrier, lower the strut out, and remove it under the wheel arch **(see illustration)**.

Overhaul

Note: *A spring compressor tool will be required for this operation. Before overhaul, mark the position of each component in relationship with each other for reassembly.*
9 With the suspension strut resting on a bench, or clamped in a vice, fit a spring compressor tool, and compress the coil spring to relieve the pressure on the spring seats. Ensure that the compressor tool is securely located on the spring, in accordance with the tool manufacturer's instructions **(see illustration)**.
10 Counterhold the strut piston rod with an

4.2 Loosen the 3 suspension strut top mounting nuts by 3 turns each

4.5 Unclip the wheel speed sensor wiring from the strut support bracket

4.6 Unscrew the connecting link nut, using an Allen key/bit to stop the pin turning

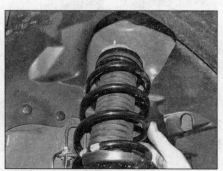

4.8 Fully unscrew the three upper mounting nuts, then remove the strut from under the wheel arch

4.9 Ensure that the compressor tool is securely located on the spring

4.10 Counterhold the piston rod with an Allen key or hexagon bit and unscrew the piston rod nut

4.11a Remove the strut bearing...

4.11b ...followed by upper spring seat...

4.11c ...dust cover...

Allen key or hexagon bit and unscrew the piston rod nut **(see illustration)**.

11 Remove the piston rod nut, followed by the strut bearing, upper spring seat, dust cover, the spring (with compressor tool still fitted) and the rubber bump stop**(see illustrations)**.

12 With the strut assembly now completely dismantled, examine all the components for wear, damage or deformation, and check the strut bearing for smoothness of operation. Renew any of the components as necessary.

13 Examine the strut for signs of fluid leakage. Check the strut piston for signs of pitting along its entire length, and check the strut body for signs of damage. While holding it in an upright position, test the operation of the strut by moving the piston through a full stroke, and then through short strokes of 50 to 100 mm. In both cases, the resistance felt should be smooth and continuous. If the resistance is jerky or uneven or if there is any visible sign of wear or damage to the strut, renewal is necessary.

14 If any doubt exists as to the condition of the coil spring, carefully remove the spring compressors and check the spring for distortion and signs of cracking. Renew the spring if it is damaged or distorted, or if there is any doubt as to its condition.

15 Inspect all other components for damage or deterioration, and renew any that are suspect.

16 Slide the rubber bump stop onto the strut piston.

17 If the spring compressor tool has been removed from the spring, refit it and compress

4.11d ...bump stop...

4.11e ...and spring

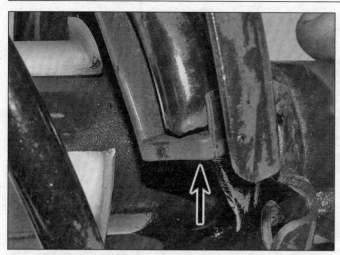

4.18 Ensure the end of the spring is against the stop on the lower seat

4.21a Position the upper spring seat and strut bearing so that the lug on the upper spring seat...

the spring sufficiently to enable it to be refitted to the strut.

18 Slide the spring over the strut, and position it so that the lower end of the spring is resting against the stop on the lower seat **(see illustration)**.

19 Refit the dust cover, upper spring seat and the strut bearing.

20 Refit the piston rod nut, and tighten it to the specified torque. Counterhold the piston rod using an Allen key or hexagon bit as during removal.

21 Position the upper spring seat and strut bearing so that the lug on the upper spring seat is directly in line with the notch at the base of the strut. If necessary, use a straight-edge to check this **(see illustrations)**. Slowly slacken the spring compressor tool to relieve the tension in the spring. Check that the lower end of the spring locates correctly against the stop on the spring seat and the alignment between the lug on the upper

seat and notch on the strut is maintained. If necessary, turn the spring and the upper seat so that the components locate correctly before the compressor tool is removed. Remove the compressor tool when the spring is fully seated.

Refitting

22 Refitting is a reversal of removal, bearing in mind the following points:

a) *Tighten all fixings to the specified torque.*
b) *Use new strut-to-hub carrier nuts and bolts.*
c) *When inserting the bolts securing the hub carrier to the base of the strut, note that the bolt heads on the left-hand side must be toward the rear of the vehicle and the bolt heads on the right-hand side must be toward the front of the vehicle.*
d) *Refit the bulkhead closure panel and windscreen cowl panel as described in Chapter 11 Section 20.*

5 Front anti-roll bar –
    removal and refitting

Removal

1 Remove the front suspension subframe as described in Section 8.

2 Note the position and orientation of the anti-roll bar mounting clamps, then unscrew the four bolts securing the mounting clamps to the subframe. Lift the anti-roll bar off the subframe.

3 Inspect the mounting clamp rubbers for signs of damage and deterioration, and renew if necessary.

4 If desired, the connecting links can be removed from the anti-roll bar after unscrewing the securing nuts. If necessary, counterhold the drop link pins using a spanner on the flats provided.

4.21b ... is directly in line with the notch at the base of the strut

4.21c If necessary, use a straight-edge to check this

6.4 Lever down the lower arm using a bar, block of wood and chain

6.5a Suspension lower arm front mounting bolt...

6.5b ... and rear mounting bolt

Refitting

5 Refitting is a reversal of removal, bearing in mind the following points:

a) *Ensure that the anti-roll bar mounting clamps are refitted with the bevelled side facing the centre of the car.*

b) *Tighten all fixings to the specified torque.*

c) *Refit the front suspension subframe as described in Section 8.*

6 Front lower arm – removal and refitting

Removal

1 Firmly apply the handbrake, then jack up the front of the vehicle and support it securely on axle stands (see *Jacking and vehicle support*). Remove the relevant roadwheel.

2 Unscrew and remove the lower arm balljoint clamp bolt nut, and withdraw the clamp bolt from the hub carrier **(see illustration 2.9)**. Note that a new nut and bolt will be required for refitting.

3 Use a chisel or screwdriver as a wedge to slightly expand the lower portion of the hub carrier.

4 Lever down the lower arm to free the balljoint from the hub carrier **(see illustration)**, then move the hub carrier to one side, taking care not to damage the balljoint rubber boot.

5 Undo the two lower arm mounting bolts and remove the lower arm from the subframe **(see illustrations)**. Note that new bolts will be required for refitting.

Overhaul

6 Examine the rubber bushes and the suspension lower balljoint for wear and damage. See Section 7.

Refitting

7 Refitting is a reversal of removal, bearing in mind the following points:

a) *Use new lower arm mounting bolts and lower arm balljoint clamp bolt and nut.*

b) *Use a trolley jack under the lower arm outer balljoint to simulate vehicle weight prior to tightening the arm's front mounting bolt.*

c) *Tighten all fixings to the specified torque and, where applicable, through the specified angle.*

7 Front lower arm balljoint – renewal

1 If the lower arm balljoint is worn, or the rubber seal is damaged, the complete lower arm must be renewed. Check the latest parts availability situation with Ford, and with reputable motor factors, before deciding.

8 Front subframe – removal and refitting

Note: *Special tools (Ford Tool No 205-870) will be required to align the subframe with the body when refitting (see text).*

Removal

1 Disconnect the battery negative lead as described in Chapter 5A Section 4.

2 Make sure the front wheels (and steering wheel) are in the straight-ahead position. Lock the steering in this position using the steering column lock.

3 Working in the driver's footwell, undo the clamp bolt securing the steering column shaft universal joint to the steering gear pinion **(see illustration)**. Pull the shaft upwards and off the pinion and move it to one side. Note that a new clamp bolt will be required for refitting.

4 Firmly apply the handbrake, then jack up the front of the vehicle and support it securely on axle stands (see *Jacking and vehicle support*). Remove both front roadwheels.

5 Slacken the track rod end balljoint nut on each side, and unscrew it as far as the ends of the threads. Counterhold the balljoint pin using a 5 mm Allen key **(see illustration 2.7)**.

6 Disconnect the track rod end balljoint from the hub carrier on each side using a balljoint separator tool (leave the nut fitted to protect the threads), taking care not to damage the balljoint rubber seal **(see illustration 2.8)**. Once the balljoint has been released, remove the balljoint nut and discard it – a new one should be used for refitting.

7 Working on each side of the car in turn, unscrew and remove the lower arm balljoint clamp bolt nut, and withdraw the clamp bolt from the hub carrier **(see illustration 2.9)**. Note that a new nut and bolt will be required for refitting.

8 Use a chisel or screwdriver as a wedge to slightly expand the lower portion of the hub carrier.

9 Lever down the lower arm to free the balljoint from the hub carrier **(see illustration 2.11)**, then move the hub carrier to one side, taking care not to damage the balljoint rubber boot.

10 Again, working on each side of the car in turn, unscrew the nut securing the anti-roll bar connecting link to the anti-roll bar. If necessary, counterhold the connecting link pin using a 5 mm Allen key.

11 Where applicable, remove the engine undershield.

12 Unscrew and remove the engine lower mounting link through-bolt.

13 Unhook the exhaust system front mounting rubber.

14 Undo the four retaining bolts and remove the subframe brace on each side.

15 If the Ford special tools required for accurate realignment of the subframe are not available, make several accurate marks between the subframe and the car body now, using paint or a sharp tool. If the car has been in service for some time, it may be obvious where the subframe sat, from the clean and dirty paint, but this is a rather hit-and-miss

8.3 Undo the clamp bolt securing the steering column shaft universal joint to the steering gear pinion

approach. If the subframe is not properly aligned on refitting, the car may steer and handle strangely (pulling to one side), and quickly wear out its tyres.

16 Support the subframe from below, using at least two substantial jacks (one either side).

17 With the subframe securely supported, progressively loosen the four subframe mounting bolts. There are two each side – one at the rear corner and one accessible through a hole in the suspension lower arm **(see illustration)**. Note that new bolts will be required for refitting.

18 When all the bolts have been removed, check once more that nothing is still attached to the subframe, and that nothing is still fitted which would hinder it from being lowered. With the help of an assistant, lower the subframe and remove it from under the car.

Refitting

19 With the help of an assistant, position the subframe on the jacks, then raise the jack to lift the subframe into position under the car. Ensure that the subframe is securely supported.

20 If available, fit the Ford alignment tool into the subframe holes and the holes on each side on the underbody. If not, align the marks made prior to removal. Fit the four new retaining bolts and tighten them to the specified Stage 1 torque setting, then through the specified Stage 2 angle.

21 The remainder of refitting is a reversal of removal, noting the following points:
a) Tighten all fixings to the specified torque.
b) Have the front wheel toe setting checked, and if necessary adjusted, at the earliest opportunity (see Section 20)

9 Rear hub and bearings – inspection and renewal

Inspection

1 The rear hub bearings are non-adjustable.

2 To check the bearings for excessive wear, chock the front wheels, then jack up the rear of the vehicle and support it on axle stands. Fully release the handbrake.

3 Grip the rear wheel at the top and bottom, and attempt to rock it. If excessive movement is noted, or if there is any roughness or vibration felt when the wheel is spun, it is indicative that the hub bearings are worn.

Renewal

4 The rear hub bearings cannot be renewed separately, and are supplied with the rear hub as a complete assembly.

5 Remove the rear brake shoes as described in Chapter 9 Section 8.

6 On models with ABS, undo the bolt and remove the ABS wheel speed sensor from the rear of the brake backplate.

7 Undo the four Torx bolts and withdrawn the

8.17 Subframe left-hand rear mounting bolt

bearing assembly from the trailing arm **(see illustration)**. Discard the bolts – new ones must be fitted.

8 Fit the new assembly to the trailing arm then insert the new retaining bolts. Working in a diagonal sequence, tighten the bolts to the specified torque.

9 Refit the ABS wheel speed sensor and brake shoes as described in Chapter 9.

10 Rear shock absorber – removal and refitting

Removal

1 Chock the front wheels, then jack up the rear of the vehicle, and support it securely on axle stands (see *Jacking and vehicle support*). Remove the relevant roadwheel.

2 Remove the plastic wheel arch liner for access to the shock absorber upper mounting bolts. The liner is secured by a combination of screws and clips.

3 Support the trailing arm section of the beam axle using a trolley jack, then unscrew the shock absorber lower mounting bolt. Counterhold the bolt using a second spanner as the nut is unscrewed. Withdraw (or tap out) the bolt, then lower the jack supporting the trailing arm. Slide the bottom end of the shock absorber out of its mounting **(see illustration)**.

4 Support the shock absorber, remove the two upper mounting bolts inside the wheel arch, and remove the unit **(see illustration)**.

10.3 With the trailing arm supported, unscrew and remove the lower bolt

9.7 Rear hub assembly retaining bolts (2 of 4 arrowed)

Refitting

5 Refitting is a reversal of removal, noting the following points:
a) *Fit the upper mounting bolts first, and tighten them to the specified torque.*
b) *The lower mounting bolt should be fitted hand-tight only, then tightened fully once the roadwheel has been refitted and the car is back on the ground.*

11 Rear spring – removal and refitting

Note: *A spring compressor tool will be required for this operation.*

Removal

1 Chock the front wheels, then jack up the rear of the vehicle, and support it securely on axle stands (see *Jacking and vehicle support*). Remove the rear roadwheels.

2 Compress the spring using the spring compressor tool.

3 Place a substantial jack under the end of the trailing arm section of the axle, and lift it slightly, so the shock absorber is just compressed.

4 Unbolt the rear shock absorber lower mounting, and detach the shock absorber from the rear axle (see Section 10).

5 Lower the jack slightly, then lift the (compressed) rear spring off its lower mounting, and remove it from under the car.

10.4 Shock absorber upper mounting bolts

11.5a Lift the compressed spring off its lower mounting ...

11.5b ... and check that the rubber top mounting comes away with it

Recover the rubber top mounting if it sticks to the car **(see illustrations)**.

6 If a new spring is being fitted, carefully release the spring compressors, and transfer to the new spring, which should be compressed prior to fitting.

Refitting

7 Refitting is a reversal of removal, noting the following points:
a) Make sure the spring is properly engaged in the upper and lower mounts.
b) Delay fully tightening the shock absorber lower mounting to its specified torque until the car is resting on its wheels.

12 Rear axle assembly – removal and refitting

Removal

1 Chock the front wheels, then jack up the rear of the vehicle, and support it securely on axle stands (see *Jacking and vehicle support*). Remove the rear roadwheels.

2 Disconnect both handbrake cables from the rear hubs, and release them from the brackets on the trailing arms as described in Chapter 9 Section 16.

3 Remove both rear springs as described in Section 11.

4 Using brake hose clamps, clamp both flexible brake hoses just forward of the brake pipe-to-hose connection on each trailing arm.

5 Clean the area around the brake pipe-to-hose union on each trailing arm, then unscrew the union nuts and disconnect the brake pipes from the brake hoses. Be prepared for fluid spillage. Extract the retaining clips and pull the brake hoses out of the support brackets each side **(see illustration)**.

6 Undo the bolt and remove the ABS wheel speed sensor from the rear of the brake backplate on each side. Pull out the rubber grommet and detach the ABS wiring from the support brackets.

7 Undo the nut and release the handbrake cable support brackets adjacent to the rear axle pivot mountings on each side.

8 Support the rear axle using two substantial jacks, one at each side.

9 The rear axle is secured by three bolts each side, around the pivot points **(see illustration)**. Make sure the axle is well-supported (have an assistant on hand to keep the axle steady), then start loosening the bolts. Leave one bolt loosely in place each side until the axle is ready to come down, then support the axle,

remove the last bolt each side, and let the axle rest on the jacks. Lower the jacks equally until the axle can be lifted out from under the car.

Refitting

10 Refitting of the axle assembly is a reversal of removal, bearing in mind the following points:
a) Tighten the handbrake adjuster nut five turns to return it to its original position.
b) Do not fully tighten the axle mounting bolts, or the shock absorber lower mounting bolts, until the weight of the car is resting on its wheels.
c) Tighten all fixings to the specified torque.
d) Bleed the brake hydraulic system and adjust the handbrake as described in Chapter 9.

13 Rear axle pivot bushes – renewal

1 Chock the front wheels, then jack up the rear of the vehicle, and support it securely on axle stands (see *Jacking and vehicle support*).

2 Support the rear axle assembly using a jack positioned beneath the axle beam. Use a block of wood between the jack and the axle beam to spread the load.

3 Undo the nut and release the handbrake cable support bracket from the rear axle pivot mounting.

4 Unscrew the through-bolt from the rear axle pivot mounting and withdraw it from the pivot bush. Note that a new pivot bolt will be required for refitting. If necessary, lower the jack slightly and withdraw the pivot bush from the pivot mounting.

5 Make an alignment mark on the bush housing on the trailing arm corresponding to the position of the alignment arrow on the end of the bush. If an alignment arrow is not visible, accurately record the fitted position of the bush in the trailing arm.

12.5 Brake pipe-to-hose connection on the trailing arm

12.9 Rear axle mounting bolts

6 Using a metal tube of suitable diameter, flat washers and a long bolt and nut, draw the bush out of its location in the trailing arm.

7 Thoroughly clean the bush housing in the trailing arm.

8 Lubricate the bush housing, and the new bush, with a soapy solution (eg, washing-up liquid) to aid fitting.

9 Locate the new bush in the trailing arm, ensuring that it is positioned correctly as noted during removal, together with the metal tube, washers, bolt and nut used for removal. Draw the bush into the trailing arm until it is fully engaged.

10 Fit the new pivot through-bolt and tighten by hand only at this stage.

11 If desired, repeat the procedure given in paragraphs 3 to 10 for the remaining bush.

12 Further refitting is a reversal of removal, noting the following points:

a) Do not fully tighten the pivot through-bolts until the weight of the car is resting on its wheels.

b) Tighten all fixings to the specified torque.

14 Steering wheel – removal and refitting

 Warning: Make sure that the airbag safety recommendations given in Chapter 12 Section 22 are followed, to prevent personal injury.

Removal

1 Remove the driver's airbag as described in Chapter 12 Section 23.

2 Set the front wheels in the straight-ahead position, then lock the column in position by removing the ignition key.

3 Disconnect the wiring connector for the steering wheel switches (see illustration).

4 Prevent the steering wheel turning by grasping the rim firmly, then unscrew and remove the steering wheel securing bolt (see illustration). Do not rely on the steering column lock to prevent the wheel turning, as this may damage the lock.

5 Grip the steering wheel with both hands and carefully rock it from side-to-side to release it from the splines on the steering column. As the steering wheel is being removed, guide the wiring for the airbag through the aperture in the wheel, taking care not to damage the wiring connectors.

6 With the steering wheel removed, place a strip of adhesive tape across the top and front of the airbag rotary connector to prevent the connector rotating.

Refitting

7 Make sure that the front wheels are pointing in the straight-ahead position, then remove the adhesive tape from the airbag rotary connector.

8 Refit the steering wheel, routing the airbag wiring connectors through the steering wheel aperture.

9 Refit the steering wheel securing bolt, and tighten to the specified torque – again, do not rely on the steering column lock to hold the wheel as the bolt is tightened.

10 Reconnect the wiring connector for the steering wheel switches.

11 Release the steering lock, and refit the airbag as described in Chapter 12 Section 23.

15 Steering column shaft – removal and refitting

Removal

1 Make sure the front wheels (and steering wheel) are in the straight-ahead position. Lock the steering in this position using the steering column lock.

2 Working in the driver's footwell, undo the clamp bolt securing the steering column shaft lower universal joint to the steering gear pinion (see illustration 8.3). Note that a new clamp bolt will be required for refitting. Pull the shaft upwards and off the pinion.

3 Similarly, undo the clamp bolt securing the steering column shaft upper universal joint to the EPS motor pinion. Note that a new clamp bolt will be required for refitting. Pull the shaft downwards off the pinion and remove it from the car.

Refitting

4 Refitting is a reversal of removal, using new universal joint clamp bolts, tightened to the specified torque.

16 Steering column – removal and refitting

Note: The steering column comprises the electric power steering (EPS) motor, the EPS electronic control unit and the steering column itself. All these components form one assembly and cannot be individually separated or dismantled.

Note: The steering column is removed together with the complete facia assembly and is then separated from it on the bench. This is an involved and complex operation and it is suggested that the contents of this Section, and the relevant Section in Chapter 11 are studied carefully to gain an understanding of the work involved, before proceeding.

Removal

1 Remove the facia assembly as described in Chapter 11 Section 25.

2 Remove the steering wheel as described in Section 14.

3 On models equipped with a knee airbag on the driver's side, remove the knee airbag as described in Chapter 12 Section 23.

4 On models without a knee airbag on the driver's side, remove the trim panel beneath the steering column by pulling the panel away

14.3 Disconnect the wiring connector for the steering wheel switches

14.4 Unscrew and remove the steering wheel securing bolt

16.7 Undo the clamp bolt securing the steering column stalk switch housing to the column

from the facia to release the three retaining clips each side.

5 Remove the steering column shrouds as described in Chapter 11 Section 23.

6 Disconnect the wiring connectors at the steering column stalk switches, ignition switch, anti-theft immobiliser transceiver unit and airbag rotary connector. Release the wiring harness from the cable-ties on the steering column and move the harness to one side.

7 Undo the clamp bolt securing the steering column stalk switch housing to the column. Using a small screwdriver, lift the retaining tab at the rear of the switch housing and withdraw the housing from the steering column **(see illustration)**.

8 It is advisable to turn the facia assembly upside down at this stage to improve access to the steering column attachments on the underside of the facia.

9 Using a small screwdriver, depress the retaining tabs and release the plastic wiring harness trough from the support brackets on the steering column.

10 On models equipped with a knee airbag on the driver's side, undo the two nuts and two bolts and remove the support brace from the underside of the facia.

11 Disconnect the three wiring connectors from the side of the EPS motor housing.

12 Check that all wiring connectors to the steering column components have been disconnected and that the wiring harness has been released from any remaining cable clips or ties.

13 Undo the two lower nuts and two upper nuts securing the steering column to the facia crossmember **(see illustration)**. Note that new nuts will be required for refitting.

14 Lift the steering column assembly off the mounting studs and withdraw it from the underside of the facia.

Refitting

15 Refitting is a reversal of removal, bearing in mind the following points:
a) *Use new steering column securing nuts.*
b) *Tighten all fixings to the specified torque, where given.*
c) *Where applicable, refit the driver's knee airbag as described in Chapter 12 Section 23.*
d) *Refit the steering wheel as described in Section 14.*
e) *Refit the facia assembly as described in Chapter 11 Section 25.*

17 Steering gear rubber gaiters – renewal

1 Remove the relevant track rod end as described in Section 19.

2 Count and record the number of exposed threads from the track rod end locknut to the end of the track rod, then unscrew the locknut.

3 Remove the inboard and, where fitted, the outboard securing clips, then slide the gaiter off the end of the track rod.

4 Thoroughly clean the track rod, then slide the new gaiter into position.

5 Fit the gaiter securing clip(s), using new clips if necessary, making sure that the gaiter is not twisted.

6 Screw the track rod end locknut back onto the track rod and position it so that the same number of threads are exposed as was noted during removal.

7 Refit the track rod end as described in Section 19.

8 Have the front wheel toe setting checked, and if necessary adjusted, at the earliest opportunity (see Section 20).

18 Steering gear – removal and refitting

Removal

1 Using the information in Section 8, lower the front subframe to access the steering gear. There is no need to disconnect the lower arm balljoints, and the subframe only needs to be lowered approximately 150 mm, not removed completely.

2 Slacken the track rod end balljoint nut each side, and unscrew it as far as the ends of the threads. Counterhold the balljoint pin using a 5 mm Allen key **(see illustration 2.7)**.

3 Disconnect the track rod end balljoint from the swivel hub using a balljoint separator tool (leave the nut fitted to protect the threads), taking care not to damage the balljoint rubber seal **(see illustration 2.8)**. Once the balljoint has been released, remove the balljoint nut and discard it – a new one should be used for refitting.

4 Unbolt the steering gear from the 3 mountings on the subframe, and lower it out **(see illustration)**. Recover the rubber seal from the bulkhead.

Refitting

5 Refitting is a reversal of removal, noting the following points:
a) *Tighten all fixings to the specified torque.*
b) *Refit the subframe as described in Section 8.*

16.13 Steering column upper retaining nuts

18.4 Steering gear mounting bolts

19.4 Slacken the track rod end locknut, and unscrew the track rod end

19 Track rod end –
removal and refitting

Note: *A balljoint separator tool will be required for this operation. Where applicable, Nyloc-type self-locking nuts must be renewed on refitting.*

Removal

1 Firmly apply the handbrake, then jack up the front of the vehicle and support it securely on axle stands (see *Jacking and vehicle support*). Remove the relevant roadwheel.
2 Slacken the track rod end balljoint nut, and unscrew it as far as the ends of the threads. Counterhold the balljoint pin using a 5 mm Allen key **(see illustration 2.7)**.
3 Disconnect the track rod end balljoint from the hub carrier using a balljoint separator tool (leave the nut fitted to protect the threads), taking care not to damage the balljoint rubber seal**(see illustration 2.8)**. Once the balljoint has been released, remove the balljoint nut and discard it – a new one should be used when refitting.
4 Slacken the track rod end locknut a quarter of a turn, then unscrew the track rod end from the track rod, counting the number of turns necessary to remove it **(see illustration)**.

Refitting

5 Screw the track rod end onto the track rod the number of turns noted during removal, then tighten the locknut while holding the track rod end in position.
6 Engage the track rod end balljoint pin with the hub carrier, then fit a new securing nut. Tighten the nut to the specified torque, while counterholding the balljoint pin as during removal.

7 Refit the roadwheel, then lower the car to the ground, and tighten the wheel nuts.
8 Have the front wheel toe setting checked, and if necessary adjusted, at the earliest opportunity (see Section).

20 Wheel alignment and steering angles –
general information

Definitions

1 A car's steering and suspension geometry is defined in four basic settings – all angles are expressed in degrees (toe settings are also expressed as a measurement); the steering axis is defined as an imaginary line drawn through the axis of the suspension strut, extended where necessary to contact the ground.
2 Camber is the angle between each roadwheel and a vertical line drawn through its centre and tyre contact patch, when viewed from the front or rear of the car. Positive camber is when the roadwheels are tilted outwards from the vertical at the top; negative camber is when they are tilted inwards. The camber angle is not adjustable.
3 Castor is the angle between the steering axis and a vertical line drawn through each roadwheel's centre and tyre contact patch, when viewed from the side of the car. Positive castor is when the steering axis is tilted so that it contacts the ground ahead of the vertical; negative castor is when it contacts the ground behind the vertical. The castor angle is not adjustable.
4 Toe is the difference, viewed from above, between lines drawn through the roadwheel centres and the car's centre-line. 'Toe-in' is when the roadwheels point inwards, towards each other at the front, while 'toe-out' is when they splay outwards from each other at the front.
5 The front wheel toe setting is adjusted by screwing the track rod in or out of its track rod ends, to alter the effective length of the track rod assembly **(see illustration)**. The rear wheel toe setting is not adjustable.

Checking and adjustment

6 Due to the special measuring equipment necessary to check the wheel alignment and steering angles, and the skill required to use it properly, the checking and adjustment of these settings is best left to a Ford dealer or similar expert. Note that most tyre-fitting shops now possess sophisticated checking equipment.

20.5 Wheel alignment details

Chapter 11
Bodywork and fittings

Contents

Degrees of difficulty

| **Easy,** suitable for novice with little experience | **Fairly easy,** suitable for beginner with some experience | **Fairly difficult,** suitable for competent DIY mechanic | **Difficult,** suitable for experienced DIY mechanic | **Very difficult,** suitable for expert DIY or professional |

Specifications

Torque wrench settings	Nm	lbf ft
Air conditioning refrigerant pipe to expansion valve	10	7
Bonnet hinge nuts	12	9
Bonnet lock bolts	20	15
Door hinge bolts	25	18
Facia retaining bolts	25	18
Facia support strut retaining bolts	25	18
Front seat bolts	35	26
Rear seat bolts	40	30
Seat belts:		
Front seat belt inertia reel lower mounting bolt	25	18
Front seat belt inertia reel upper mounting nut	8	6
Front seat belt lower anchor rail bolt (3-door models)	40	30
Front seat belt lower anchorage bolt (5-door models)	40	30
Front seat belt stalk retaining bolt	50	37
Front seat belt upper anchorage bolt	40	30
Rear seat belt buckle bolts	55	41
Rear seat belt inertia reel mounting bolt	40	30
Rear seat belt lower anchorage bolt	40	30
Rear seat belt upper anchorage bolt	40	30
Steering column shaft universal joint clamp bolt*	34	25
Tailgate hinge bolts	12	9

*Use a new bolt

1 General Information

1 The bodyshell is of 3- and 5-door Hatchback (and 3-door Van) configurations, and is made of pressed-steel sections. Most components are welded together, but some use is made of structural adhesives. The front wings are bolted on.
2 The bonnet, doors and some other vulnerable panels are made of zinc-coated metal, and are further protected by being coated with an anti-chip primer prior to being sprayed.
3 Extensive use is made of plastic materials, mainly in the interior, but also in exterior components. The front and rear bumpers and the front grille are injection-moulded from a synthetic material which is very strong, and yet light. Plastic components such as wheel arch liners are fitted to the underside of the car, to improve the body's resistance to corrosion.

2 Maintenance – bodywork and underframe

1 The general condition of a car's bodywork is the one thing that significantly affects its value. Maintenance is easy, but needs to be regular. Neglect, particularly after minor damage, can lead quickly to further deterioration and costly repair bills. It is important also to keep watch on those parts of the car not immediately visible, for instance the underside, inside all the wheel arches, and the lower part of the engine compartment.
2 The basic maintenance routine for the bodywork is washing – preferably with a lot of water, from a hose. This will remove all the loose solids which may have stuck to the car. It is important to flush these off in such a way as to prevent grit from scratching the finish. The wheel arches and underframe need washing in the same way, to remove any accumulated mud which will retain moisture and tend to encourage rust. Paradoxically enough, the best time to clean the underframe and wheel arches is in wet weather, when the mud is thoroughly wet and soft. In very wet weather, the underframe is usually cleaned of large accumulations automatically, and this is a good time for inspection.
3 Periodically, except on models with a wax-based underbody protective coating, it is a good idea to have the whole of the underframe of the car steam-cleaned, engine compartment included, so that a thorough inspection can be carried out to see what minor repairs and renovations are necessary. Steam-cleaning is available at many garages, and is necessary for the removal of the accumulation of oily grime, which sometimes is allowed to become thick in certain areas.

If steam-cleaning facilities are not available, there are one or two excellent grease solvents available, which can be brush-applied; the dirt can then be simply hosed off. Note that these methods should not be used on cars with wax-based underbody protective coating, or the coating will be removed. Such cars should be inspected annually, preferably just prior to Winter, when the underbody should be washed down, and any damage to the wax coating repaired. Ideally, a completely fresh coat should be applied. It would also be worth considering the use of such wax-based protection for injection into door panels, sills, box sections, etc, as an additional safeguard against rust damage, where such protection is not provided by the manufacturer.
4 After washing paintwork, wipe off with a chamois leather to give an unspotted clear finish. A coat of clear protective wax polish will give added protection against chemical pollutants in the air. If the paintwork sheen has dulled or oxidised, use a cleaner/polisher combination to restore the brilliance of the shine. This requires a little effort, but such dulling is usually caused because regular washing has been neglected. Care needs to be taken with metallic paintwork, as special non-abrasive cleaner/polisher is required to avoid damage to the finish. Always check that the door and ventilator opening drain holes and pipes are completely clear, so that water can be drained out. Brightwork should be treated in the same way as paintwork. Windscreens and windows can be kept clear of the smeary film which often appears, by the use of proprietary glass cleaner. Never use any form of wax, or other body or chromium polish, on glass.

3 Maintenance – upholstery and carpets

1 Mats and carpets should be brushed or vacuum-cleaned regularly, to keep them free of grit. If they are badly stained, remove them from the car for scrubbing or sponging, and make quite sure they are dry before refitting. Seats and interior trim panels can be kept clean by wiping with a damp cloth. If they do become stained (which can be more apparent on light-coloured upholstery), use a little liquid detergent and a soft nail brush to scour the grime out of the grain of the material. Do not forget to keep the headlining clean in the same way as the upholstery. When using liquid cleaners inside the car, do not over-wet the surfaces being cleaned. Excessive damp could get into the seams and padded interior, causing stains, offensive odours or even rot. If the inside of the car gets wet accidentally, it is worthwhile taking some trouble to dry it out properly, particularly where carpets are involved. Do not leave oil or electric heaters inside the car for this purpose.

4 Minor body damage – repair

Repair of minor scratches

1 If the scratch is very superficial, and does not penetrate to the metal of the bodywork, repair is very simple. Lightly rub the area of the scratch with a paintwork renovator, or a very fine cutting paste, to remove loose paint from the scratch, and to clear the surrounding bodywork of wax polish. Rinse the area with clean water.
2 In the case of metallic paint, the most commonly-found scratches are not in the paint, but in the lacquer top coat, and appear white. If care is taken, these can sometimes be rendered less obvious by very careful use of paintwork renovator (which would other-wise not be used on metallic paintwork); otherwise, repair of these scratches can be achieved by applying lacquer with a fine brush.
3 Apply touch-up paint to the scratch using a fine paint brush; continue to apply fine layers of paint until the surface of the paint in the scratch is level with the surrounding paintwork. Allow the new paint at least two weeks to harden, then blend it into the surrounding paintwork by rubbing the scratch area with a paintwork renovator or a very fine cutting paste. Finally, apply wax polish.
4 Where the scratch has penetrated right through to the metal of the bodywork, causing the metal to rust, a different repair technique is required. Remove any loose rust from the bottom of the scratch with a penknife, then apply rust-inhibiting paint, to prevent the formation of rust in the future. Using a rubber or nylon applicator, fill the scratch with bodystopper paste. If required, this paste can be mixed with cellulose thinners, to provide a very thin paste which is ideal for filling narrow scratches. Before the stopper-paste in the scratch hardens, wrap a piece of smooth cotton rag around the top of a finger. Dip the finger in cellulose thinners, and quickly sweep it across the surface of the stopper-paste in the scratch; this will ensure that the surface of the stopper-paste is slightly hollowed. The scratch can now be painted over as described earlier in this Section.

Repairs of dents

5 When deep denting of the bodywork has taken place, the first task is to pull the dent out, until the affected bodywork almost attains its original shape. There is little point in trying to restore the original shape completely, as the metal in the damaged area will have stretched on impact, and cannot be reshaped fully to its original contour. It is better to bring the level of the dent up to a point which is about 3 mm below the level of the surrounding bodywork. In cases where the dent is very shallow anyway, it is not worth trying to pull it out at all. If the underside of the dent is accessible,

it can be hammered out gently from behind, using a mallet with a wooden or plastic head. Whilst doing this, hold a suitable block of wood firmly against the outside of the panel, to absorb the impact from the hammer blows and thus prevent a large area of the bodywork from being 'belled-out'.

6 Should the dent be in a section of the bodywork which has a double skin, or some other factor making it inaccessible from behind, a different technique is called for. Drill several small holes through the metal inside the area – particularly in the deeper section. Then screw long self-tapping screws into the holes, just sufficiently for them to gain a good purchase in the metal. Now the dent can be pulled out by pulling on the protruding heads of the screws with a pair of pliers.

7 The next stage of the repair is the removal of the paint from the damaged area, and from an inch or so of the surrounding 'sound' bodywork. This is accomplished most easily by using a wire brush or abrasive pad on a power drill, although it can be done just as effectively by hand, using sheets of abrasive paper. To complete the preparation for filling, score the surface of the bare metal with a screwdriver or the tang of a file, or alternatively, drill small holes in the affected area. This will provide a really good 'key' for the filler paste.

8 To complete the repair, see the Section on filling and respraying.

Repairs of rust holes or gashes

9 Remove all paint from the affected area, and from an inch or so of the surrounding 'sound' bodywork, using an abrasive pad or a wire brush on a power drill. If these are not available, a few sheets of abrasive paper will do the job most effectively. With the paint removed, you will be able to judge the severity of the corrosion, and therefore decide whether to renew the whole panel (if this is possible) or to repair the affected area. New body panels are not as expensive as most people think, and it is often quicker and more satisfactory to fit a new panel than to attempt to repair large areas of corrosion.

10 Remove all fittings from the affected area, except those which will act as a guide to the original shape of the damaged bodywork (eg body side mouldings etc). Then, using tin snips or a hacksaw blade, remove all loose metal and any other metal badly affected by corrosion. Hammer the edges of the hole inwards, in order to create a slight depression for the filler paste.

11 Wire-brush the affected area to remove the powdery rust from the surface of the remaining metal. Paint the affected area with rust-inhibiting paint; if the back of the rusted area is accessible, treat this also.

12 Before filling can take place, it will be necessary to block the hole in some way. This can be achieved by the use of aluminium or plastic mesh, or aluminium tape.

13 Aluminium or plastic mesh, or glass-fibre matting, is probably the best material to use for a large hole. Cut a piece to the approximate size and shape of the hole to be filled, then position it in the hole so that its edges are below the level of the surrounding bodywork. It can be retained in position by several blobs of filler paste around its periphery.

14 Aluminium tape should be used for small or very narrow holes. Pull a piece off the roll, trim it to the approximate size and shape required, then pull off the backing paper (if used) and stick the tape over the hole; it can be overlapped if the thickness of one piece is insufficient. Burnish down the edges of the tape with the handle of a screwdriver or similar, to ensure that the tape is securely attached to the metal underneath.

Filling and respraying

15 Before using this Section, see the Sections on dent, deep scratch, rust holes and gash repairs.

16 Many types of bodyfiller are available, but generally speaking, those proprietary kits which contain a tin of filler paste and a tube of resin hardener are best for this type of repair. A wide, flexible plastic or nylon applicator will be found invaluable for imparting a smooth and well-contoured finish to the surface of the filler.

17 Mix up a little filler on a clean piece of card or board – measure the hardener carefully (follow the maker's instructions on the pack), otherwise the filler will set too rapidly or too slowly. Using the applicator, apply the filler paste to the prepared area; draw the applicator across the surface of the filler to achieve the correct contour and to level the surface. As soon as a contour that approximates to the correct one is achieved, stop working the paste – if you carry on too long, the paste will become sticky and begin to 'pick-up' on the applicator. Continue to add thin layers of filler paste at 20-minute intervals, until the level of the filler is just proud of the surrounding bodywork.

18 Once the filler has hardened, the excess can be removed using a metal plane or file. From then on, progressively-finer grades of abrasive paper should be used, starting with a 40-grade production paper, and finishing with a 400-grade wet-and-dry paper. Always wrap the abrasive paper around a flat rubber, cork, or wooden block – otherwise the surface of the filler will not be completely flat. During the smoothing of the filler surface, the wet-and-dry paper should be periodically rinsed in water. This will ensure that a very smooth finish is imparted to the filler at the final stage.

19 At this stage, the 'dent' should be surrounded by a ring of bare metal, which in turn should be encircled by the finely 'feathered' edge of the good paintwork. Rinse the repair area with clean water, until all of the dust produced by the rubbing-down operation has gone.

20 Spray the whole area with a light coat of – this will show up any imperfections in the surface of the filler. Repair these imperfections with fresh filler paste or bodystopper, and once more smooth the surface with abrasive paper. If bodystopper is used, it can be mixed with cellulose thinners, to form a really thin paste which is ideal for filling small holes. Repeat this spray-and-repair procedure until you are satisfied that the surface of the filler, and the feathered edge of the paintwork, are perfect. Clean the repair area with clean water, and allow to dry fully.

21 The repair area is now ready for final spraying. Paint spraying must be carried out in a warm, dry, windless and dust-free atmosphere. This condition can be created artificially if you have access to a large indoor working area, but if you are forced to work in the open, you will have to pick your day very carefully. If you are working indoors, dousing the floor in the work area with water will help to settle the dust which would otherwise be in the atmosphere. If the repair area is confined to one body panel, mask off the surrounding panels; this will help to minimise the effects of a slight mis-match in paint colours. Bodywork fittings (eg chrome strips, door handles etc) will also need to be masked off. Use genuine masking tape, and several thicknesses of newspaper, for the masking operations.

22 Before commencing to spray, agitate the aerosol can thoroughly, then spray a test area (an old tin, or similar) until the technique is mastered. Cover the repair area with a thick coat of primer; the thickness should be built up using several thin layers of paint, rather than one thick one. Using 400 grade wet-and-dry paper, rub down the surface of the primer until it is really smooth. While doing this, the work area should be thoroughly doused with water, and the wet-and-dry paper periodically rinsed in water. Allow to dry before spraying on more paint.

23 Spray on the top coat, again building up the thickness by using several thin layers of paint. Start spraying at the top of the repair area, and then, using a side-to-side motion, work downwards until the whole repair area and about 2 inches of the surrounding original paintwork is covered. Remove all masking material 10 to 15 minutes after spraying on the final coat of paint.

24 Allow the new paint at least two weeks to harden, then, using a paintwork renovator or a very fine cutting paste, blend the edges of the paint into the existing paintwork. Finally, apply wax polish.

Plastic components

25 With the use of more and more plastic body components by the car manufacturers (eg bumpers. spoilers, and in some cases major body panels), rectification of more serious damage to such items has become a matter of either entrusting repair work to a specialist in this field, or renewing complete components. Repair of such damage by the DIY owner is not really feasible, owing to the cost of the equipment and materials required for effecting such repairs. The basic technique involves making a groove along the line of the crack in the plastic, using a rotary cutter in a power drill. The damaged part is then welded back together, using a hot air gun to heat up and fuse a plastic filler rod into the groove. Any excess plastic is then removed, and the area rubbed down to a smooth finish. It is important that a filler rod of the correct plastic is used, as body components can be made of a variety of different types (eg polycarbonate, ABS, polypropylene).

26 Damage of a less serious nature (abrasions, minor cracks etc) can be repaired by the DIY owner using a two-part epoxy filler repair. Once mixed in equal, this is used in similar fashion to the bodywork filler used on metal panels. The filler is usually cured in twenty to thirty minutes, ready for sanding and painting.

27 If the owner is renewing a complete component himself, or if he has repaired it with epoxy filler, he will be left with the problem of finding a suitable paint for finishing which is compatible with the type of plastic used. At one time, the use of a universal paint was not possible, owing to the complex range of plastics encountered in body component applications. Standard paints, generally speaking, will not bond to plastic or rubber satisfactorily, but suitable paints to match any plastic or rubber finish, can be obtained from dealers. However, it is now possible to obtain a plastic body parts finishing kit which consists of a preprimer treatment, a primer and coloured top coat. Full instructions are normally supplied with a kit, but basically, the method of use is to first apply the preprimer to the component concerned, and allow it to dry for up to 30 minutes. Then the primer is applied, and left to dry for about an hour before finally applying the special-coloured top coat. The result is a correctly-coloured component, where the paint will flex with the plastic or rubber, a property that standard paint does not normally posses.

5 Major body damage – repair

1 Where serious damage has occurred, or large areas need renewal due to neglect,

6.5 Prise down the centre pin, and lever out the plastic rivet each side

it means that complete new panels will need welding-in, and this is best left to professionals. If the damage is due to impact, it will also be necessary to check completely the alignment of the bodyshell, and this can only be carried out accurately by a Ford dealer or accident repair specialist, using special jigs. If the body is left misaligned, it is primarily dangerous, as the car will not handle properly, and secondly, uneven stresses will be imposed on the steering, suspension and possibly transmission, causing abnormal wear, or complete failure, particularly to such items as the tyres.

6 Bumpers – removal and refitting

Front bumper

Removal

1 Remove the headlights as described in Chapter 12 Section 7.

2 Firmly apply the handbrake, then jack up the front of the vehicle and support it securely on axle stands (see *Jacking and vehicle support*).

3 Undo the 2 bolts at the rear edge of the bumper in the wheelarch aperture **(see illustration)**.

4 From within the engine compartment, undo the three bolts each side securing the bumper to the front wing **(see illustration)**.

6.3 Undo the bolts securing the bumper in the wheelarch aperture

6.8a Disengage the two lower plastic retaining tangs...

5 Working under the wheel arch each side, extract the lower plastic rivet **(see illustration)**.

6 On models equipped with front parking sensors. Trace the parking sensor wiring back to the connectors and disconnect them, then release the wiring from the cable clips and ties.

7 Where applicable, disconnect the wiring plugs from the front foglights.

8 Disengage the two lower plastic retaining tangs then, with the help of an assistant, pull the bumper forwards to disengage the side locating pegs and lower it to the ground **(see illustrations)**.

Refitting

9 Refitting is a reversal of removal. Have an assistant available to help align the bumper with the side locating pegs, and tighten the six mounting bolts securely.

Rear bumper

Removal

10 Chock the front wheels, then jack up the rear of the vehicle, and support it securely on axle stands (see *Jacking and vehicle support*).

11 On models with mudflaps, remove the mudflaps each side by extracting the three retaining clips, then removing the two plastic rivets by prising up the centre section and withdrawing the rivet body.

12 Remove the two plastic rivets each side securing the wheel arch liner to the bumper, by

6.4 Undo the three bolts each side securing the bumper to the front wing

6.8b ... then pull the bumper forwards to disengage the side locating pegs

6.12 Remove the two plastic rivets each side securing the wheel arch liner to the rear bumper

6.13 Remove the rear foglight bulb holder from the light unit, and disconnect the parking sensor wiring plug

6.14 Undo the bolt each side securing the upper corner of the bumper to the rear wing

6.15 Remove the two lower plastic rivets securing the bumper to the body

6.16 Undo the Torx screw each side of the tailgate aperture

6.17 Pull the bumper rearwards to disengage the side locating tabs

prising up the centre section and withdrawing the rivet body (see illustration).
13 Where fitted, reach in behind the wheel arch liner and disconnect the parking sensor wiring plug under the right-hand wheel arch, then rotate the fog light bulbholder anti-clockwise and withdraw it from the light unit (see illustration).
14 Undo the bolt each side securing the upper corner of the bumper to the rear wing (see illustration).
15 Remove the two lower plastic rivets securing the bumper to the body, by prising out the centre section and withdrawing the rivet body (see illustration).
16 Open the tailgate and undo the Torx screw each side in the tailgate aperture (see illustration).
17 With the help of an assistant, pull out

the side locating tabs, and manoeuvre the bumper rearwards (see illustration).

Refitting

18 Refitting is a reversal of removal. Have an assistant available to help align the bumper with the side locating tabs, and tighten the mounting bolts securely.

7 Bonnet – removal, refitting and adjustment

Removal

1 Open the bonnet, and support it on its stay.
2 Using a marker pen or paint, mark around the hinge positions on the bonnet.

7.3 Disconnect the washer jet hose

7.4 Bonnet-to-hinge retaining nuts

3 Disconnect the windscreen washer jet hose at the connection at the left-hand side inner wing (see illustration).
4 With the aid of an assistant, support the bonnet, and unscrew the four nuts securing the bonnet to the hinges (see illustration).
5 Lift off the bonnet.

Refitting

6 Align the marks made on the bonnet before removal with the hinges, then refit and tighten the bonnet securing nuts.
7 Feed the washer hose back across the bonnet, and reconnect it to the washer jet T-piece, then refit the sound deadening pad.
8 Check the bonnet adjustment as follows.

Adjustment

9 Close the bonnet, and check that there is an equal gap at each side, between the bonnet and the wing panels. Check that the bonnet sits flush in relation to the surrounding body panels.
10 The bonnet should close smoothly and positively without excessive pressure. If this is not the case, adjustment will be required.
11 To adjust the bonnet alignment, slacken the bonnet securing nuts, and move the bonnet on the studs as required (the holes in the hinges are elongated). To adjust the bonnet closure, adjustable bump stops are fitted to the body front panel. These may be raised or lowered by screwing in or out as necessary. If desired, the bonnet lock can be adjusted as described in Section 9.

8.3a Disengage the bonnet release outer cable from the release lever ...

8.3b ... then slip the inner cable end fitting out of the lever handle

9.2 Undo the three bolts (arrowed) and lift off the bonnet lock top plate

8 Bonnet release cable – removal and refitting

Removal

1 The bonnet release lever is located under the facia on the right-hand side.
2 Working in the driver's footwell, depress the tab in the centre of the release lever, then slide it to the rear to disengage the locating lugs.
3 Disengage the bonnet release outer cable from the release lever, then slip the inner cable end fitting out of the lever handle (see illustrations).
4 Remove the windscreen cowl panel and bulkhead closure panel as described in Section 20.
5 Undo the three bolts securing the bonnet lock top plate and lift the plate from its location (see illustration 9.2).
6 Prise out the outer cable end fitting from its slot in the bonnet lock, then unhook the inner cable from the lock operating lever.
7 Release the cable from the clips and brackets in the engine compartment, noting its routing.
8 Tie a length of string to the end of the cable at the release lever inside the car, then carefully pull the cable through the bulkhead grommet into the engine compartment.
9 Untie the string from the end of the cable, and leave it in position to aid refitting.

Refitting

10 Refitting is a reversal of removal, but tie the string to the release lever end of the cable, and use the string to pull the cable into position. Ensure that the cable is routed as noted before removal, and make sure that the bulkhead grommet is correctly seated.

9 Bonnet lock – removal and refitting

Removal

1 Open the bonnet and disconnect the two wiring connectors from the bonnet lock, then release the wiring loom from the cable clips on the lock platform.
2 Undo the three bolts securing the bonnet lock top plate and lift the plate from its location (see illustration).
3 Prise out the bonnet release outer cable end fitting from its slot in the bonnet lock and unhook the inner cable from the lock operating lever.
4 Depress the four upper retaining tabs and lift up the embellishment panel from the top of the bumper. Depress the four lower retaining tabs and remove the embellishment panel.
5 Undo the two retaining bolts and remove the lock assembly.

Refitting

6 Refitting is a reversal of removal. If necessary, the position of the lock can be altered to adjust the lock operation by moving the lock within the elongated holes.

10 Door – removal and refitting

Removal

1 Release the rubber grommet from the door pillar and withdraw the wiring block connector (see illustration).
2 Disconnect the wiring connector(s) (see illustration).
3 Unbolt the door check strap from the door pillar (see illustration).
4 Ensure that the door is adequately supported, with the aid of an assistant, or using wooden blocks or similar under the bottom edge of the door (take care not to damage the paintwork).
5 Mark the position of the hinges on the door, then unscrew the bolts and remove the door from the car (see illustration).

10.1 Release the rubber grommet from the door pillar and withdraw the wiring block connector

10.2 ... then depress the tabs and disconnect the wiring connectors

10.3 Unbolt the door check strap from the door pillar

10.5 Door upper hinge bolts

11.1a Carefully prise free and remove the door pull handle trim surround

11.1b Note the hook at the rear of the trim surround

11.2 Pull out the recess trim piece

Refitting

6 Refitting is a reversal of removal.

11 Door inner trim panel – removal and refitting

Front door

Removal

1 Starting at the front, using a plastic spatula or similar, carefully prise free and remove the door pull handle trim surround **(see illustrations)**. Note the hook at the rear edge of the trim surround.
2 Pull out the hand recess trim piece **(see illustration)**.
3 Undo the 2 screws, then starting at the rear, carefully prise up the door switch panel **(see illustrations)**. Disconnect the switch panel wiring plug as it becomes accessible.
4 Starting at the rear edge, prise out the circular trim button from the centre of the door interior handle **(see illustration)**.
5 With the trim button removed, undo the

panel retaining screw now exposed **(see illustration)**.
6 Prise rearwards the trim piece/reflector at the rear edge of the door panel, and remove the screw exposed **(see illustration)**.
7 Using a wide-bladed screwdriver or removal tool, carefully prise the bottom and sides of the panel away from the door to release the internal clips **(see illustration)**.
8 Lift the panel upward to release it from the window aperture. From inside the panel, prise open the locking catch using a small screwdriver, and disconnect the interior handle

11.3a Undo the 2 Torx screws...

11.3b ...lift up the rear edge and remove the switch panel

11.4 Remove the circular trim button from the centre of the door interior handle ...

11.5 ... and undo the panel retaining Torx screw now exposed

11.6 Slide the trim piece/reflector rearwards and undo the screw

11.7 Prise the panel away from the door

11.8a Disconnect the wiring connector(s)

11.8b Push the clip at the back rearwards, and disconnect the cable

11.10a Locate a cloth rag between the handle and the trim panel and pull it back and forth to release the spring clip

11.10b Remove the handle from the splined shaft …

11.10c … then remove the circular spacer

11.11 Remove the circular trim button from the centre of the door interior handle

release cable from the panel. Disconnect the wiring connector(s) and remove the panel **(see illustrations)**.

Refitting

9 Refitting is a reversal of removal. Before starting, check to see whether any trim clips have been left on the door, and transfer them to the trim panel.

Rear door

Removal

10 Where a manual window regulator is fitted, locate a cloth rag between the handle and the trim panel and pull it back and forth to release the spring clip. Alternatively use a proprietary regulator spring clip removal tool. Remove the handle from the splined shaft then remove the circular spacer **(see illustrations)**. Refit the spring clip to the handle.

11 Remove the circular trim button from the centre of the door interior handle. The best way to do this is to stick a small piece of

adhesive tape (or similar) to the trim button and pull on the tape to remove the button **(see illustration)**.

12 With the trim button removed, undo the panel retaining screw now exposed.

13 Undo the two screws below the door pull handle **(see illustration)**.

14 Carefully prise free the triangular inner trim panel at the rear of the door **(see illustration)**.

15 Using a wide-bladed screwdriver or removal tool, carefully prise the bottom and sides of the panel away from the door to release the internal clips **(see illustration)**.

16 Lift the panel upward to release it from the window aperture. From inside the panel, prise open the locking catch using a small screwdriver, and disconnect the interior handle release cable from the panel **(see illustration)**. On models with electrically-operated windows, disconnect the wiring connectors and remove the panel.

11.13 Undo the two screws below the door pull handle

11.14 Carefully prise free the triangular inner trim panel at the rear of the door

11.15 Carefully prise the bottom and sides of the panel away from door

11.16 Press the locking catch rearwards, and disconnect the release handle cable

12.2a Prise out the rear edge to release the lug...

12.2b ...then prise the outer waist seal upwards from the door...

12.2c ...and release the seal locating pin at the inside-front

Refitting

17 Refitting is a reversal of removal. Before starting, check to see whether any trim clips have been left on the door, and transfer them to the trim panel.

---

12 Door window glass – removal and refitting

Front door

3-door models

1 Remove the door inner trim panel as described in Section 11.

2 Carefully prise rear edge of the outer waist seal outwards from the door a little, then prise it upwards (**see illustrations**). Use a blunt trim removal tool to prevent damaging the paint work.

3 Disconnect the wiring connector, undo the three screws and remove the loudspeaker from the door (**see illustration**).

4 Carefully pull off the circular foam pad from the door panel for access to the window glass-to-regulator rear attachment (**see illustration**).

5 Reconnect the door window switch wiring connector.

6 Operate the window switch and align the window glass rear attachment with the aperture exposed by removing the circular foam pad.

7 Insert a screwdriver through the circular aperture and disengage the regulator rear attachment by firmly pushing the regulator locating peg, at the same time as pulling the glass upwards slightly. Disengage the regulator front attachment from the window glass in the same way, but working through the loudspeaker aperture (**see illustrations**).

8 Lift the window glass from the door while tilting it up at the rear, and withdraw it from the outside of the door frame.

9 Refitting is a reversal of removal, making sure that the glass is correctly located in the regulator attachments.

5-door models

10 Remove the door inner trim panel as described in Section 11.

12.3 Speaker retaining Torx screws

12.4 Carefully peel away the circular foam pad

12.7a Use a screwdriver...

12.7b ...to push out the pin whilst lifting the glass

11 Carefully prise free the outer waist seal from the door (**see illustration 2.2**).

12 Carefully pull off the circular rubber pads from the centre of the door panel to access the window glass clamps (**see illustration**).

12.12 Peel away the rubber pads

13 Reconnect the door window switch wiring connector, and lower the glass until the window glass clamp nuts are visible in the apertures exposed by removing the circular rubber pads (**see illustration**).

12.13 Lower the glass until the window glass clamp nuts are accessible

12.14 Withdraw the window glass from the door while tilting it up at the rear

12.18a Carefully prise up the outer waist seal...

12.18b ... and inner waist seal from the door

14 Unscrew the window glass clamp nuts, then lift the glass to release the plastic locating peg from the regulator clip. Withdraw the window glass from the door while tilting it up at the rear, and withdraw it from the outside of

12.19 Release the window guide rubber from the front and rear of the door frame

the door frame **(see illustration)**. If necessary, insert a steel ruler down the outside of the window to release the rubber clamp pads from the glass surface **(see illustration 12.23a)**.
15 Refitting is a reversal of removal, noting the following points:
a) Line up the plastic locating peg in the centre of the regulator guide clip, and push down to locate it.
b) Tighten the glass retaining nuts securely.

Rear door

16 Remove the door inner trim panel as described in Section 11.
17 Temporarily refit the regulator handle, or reconnect the door window switch wiring connector, and lower the window glass all the way.
18 Carefully prise free the inner and outer waist seals from the door **(see illustrations)**.
19 Release the window guide rubber from

the front and rear of the door frame **(see illustration)**.
20 Undo the two screws securing the triangular trim panel to the rear of the door frame. Disengage the lower locating peg and remove the panel from the door **(see illustrations)**.
21 Carefully peel off the circular rubber pads from the centre of the door panel to access the window glass clamps **(see illustration)**.
22 Raise the window until the window glass clamp nuts are visible in the apertures exposed by removing the circular rubber pads **(see illustration)**.
23 Slacken the window glass clamp nuts, then lift the glass to release the plastic locating peg from the regulator clip. Withdraw the window glass upwards from the door, and withdraw it from the outside of the door frame. If necessary, insert a steel ruler down the outside of the window to release the rubber clamp pads from the glass surface **(see illustrations)**.

12.20a Undo the two Torx screws...

12.20b ... then disengage the lower locating peg and remove the panel

12.21 Pull off the circular rubber pads from the centre of the door panel

12.22 Raise the window until the window glass clamp nuts are accessible

12.23a Insert a steel ruler (or similar) to release the rubber clamp pads from the glass

12.23b Withdraw the glass from the outside of the door frame

13.4 Door control unit retaining bolts

13.5 Undo the Torx screw securing the handle frame

13.6 Undo the bolts securing the lock to the door

24 Refitting is a reversal of removal, noting the following points:
a) *Line up the plastic locating peg in the centre of the regulator guide clip, and push down to locate it.*
b) *Tighten the glass retaining nuts securely.*

13 Door window regulator – removal and refitting

Front door

1 Remove the door inner trim panel as described in Section 11.
2 Remove the door window glass as described in Section 12 – the glass can be raised and taped to the door frame, as it does not have to be removed completely.

3 Remove the door exterior handle as described in Section 14.
4 Undo the bolts securing the control unit (where applicable), and disconnect the wiring plug(s) **(see illustration)**.
5 Undo the Torx screw securing the handle frame to the door skin **(see illustration)**.
6 Undo the 3 bolts securing the door lock at the rear edge of the door **(see illustration)**.
7 Accurately note and record how the wiring loom is routed over the inner door panel. Disconnect the door mirror wiring connector, then release all the clips and cable-ties securing the loom to the panel.

3-door models

8 Undo the 12 bolts securing the inner door panel to the door frame, then pull the panel away from the door at the upper rear corner, and manoeuvre it from place **(see illustration)**. Disconnect the door lock wiring plug as the panel is withdrawn.
9 Undo the 3 bolts and detach the window motor, or handle assembly **(see illustration)**.
10 Undo the 3 bolts securing the front lifting channel and the four bolts securing the rear lifting channel and remove the regulator assembly from the panel.

5-door models

11 Undo the 9 bolts securing the inner door panel to the door frame, then pull the panel away from the door, and slide it forwards a little until the lock wiring plug can be disconnected. Manoeuvre the panel from place **(see illustrations)**.
12 Undo the 3 bolts and detach the window motor, or handle assembly **(see illustration)**.
13 Undo the 2 bolts securing the lifting

13.8 Door panel retaining bolts

13.9 Window motor retaining bolts

13.11a Undo the 9 bolts…

13.11b …disconnect the lock wiring plug as it becomes accessible…

13.11c …then manoeuvre the panel from the door

13.12 Window motor retaining bolts

13.13 Lifting channel/regulator retaining bolts

13.18a Disconnect the loudspeaker wiring connector ...

13.18b ... then release the clips and cable-ties securing the wiring loom to the door panel

13.19a Inner door panel retaining bolts

13.19b Slide the panel forwards to disengage the securing tabs

channel and remove the regulator assembly from the panel (see illustration).

All models

14 Refitting is a reversal of removal, noting the following points:
a) Secure the wiring loom with the clips and cable-ties in the correct positions as noted during removal.
b) Refit the exterior door handle as described in Section 14.
c) Refit the door window glass as described in Section 12.
d) Refit the door inner trim panel as described in Section 11.

Rear door

15 Remove the door inner trim panel as described in Section 11.

16 Remove the door window glass as described in Section 12 – the glass can be raised and taped to the door frame, as it does not have to be removed completely.
17 On models with electric windows, disconnect the wiring connector then undo the three bolts securing the regulator motor to the inner door panel. Release the motor wiring from the cable clips and remove the motor from the door panel.
18 Accurately note and record how the wiring loom is routed over the inner door panel. Disconnect the loudspeaker wiring connector, then release all the clips and cable-ties securing the loom to the panel (see illustrations).
19 Undo the 8 bolts securing the inner door panel to the door frame, then lift the panel slightly, and pull the panel away from

the door at the upper rear corner. Reach in behind the upper rear corner and insert a screwdriver between inner door panel and the door lock support bracket to release the retaining lug. Now slide the inner door panel forward to allow the three securing tabs to disengage through the elongated openings (see illustrations).
20 Prise free the lock interior handle operating cable grommet from the inner door panel.
21 Withdraw the inner door panel until sufficient clearance exists to reach behind and disconnect the wiring connector from the door lock. Prise free the door lock wiring grommet from the door panel and pull the wiring through to the outside (see illustration).
22 Remove the inner door panel, feeding the interior handle operating cable through the opening as the panel is removed.
23 From the outside of the door panel on models with manually-operated windows, undo the 3 screws securing the regulator to the panel (see illustration).
24 From the inside of the door panel, undo the 2 bolts securing the regulator lifting channel to the panel. Disengage the front of the regulator from the 3 retaining lugs and remove the regulator assembly from the panel (see illustration).
25 Refitting is a reversal of removal, noting the following points:
a) Ensure that the three tabs on the upper rear corner of the inner door panel

13.21 Disconnect the wiring connector from the door lock then prise free the grommet and pull the wiring through to the outside

13.23 Undo the 3 screws securing the window regulator to the panel

13.24 Undo the bolts securing the lifting channel to the panel then disengage the regulator from the retaining lugs

14.1 Prise out the rubber grommet from the end of the door

14.2a Slacken the handle retaining bolt ...

14.2b ... until the lock cylinder can be pulled from the door

correctly engage with the elongated slots on the door lock support bracket.
b) *Secure the wiring loom with the clips and cable-ties in the correct positions as noted during removal.*
c) *Refit the door window glass as described in Section 12.*
d) *Refit the door inner trim panel as described in Section 11.*

14 Door handles and lock components – removal and refitting

Front door exterior handle

Removal

1 Prise out the rubber grommet from the end

of the door adjacent to the exterior handle **(see illustration)**.
2 Working through the aperture, slacken the handle retaining Torx bolt until the lock cylinder can be pulled from the door **(see illustrations)**.
3 Pull the exterior handle rearwards, and manoeuvre it from the door. Recover the seal between the handle and the door skin **(see illustrations)**.
4 On models with the Keyless Entry system, gently pull the handle wiring harness until an audible click is heard, and the harness connector is in the horizontal position. Disconnect the wiring plug.

Refitting

5 Refitting is a reversal of removal. When refitting the exterior handle on models with the

Keyless Entry system, reconnect the wiring connector and push it into the holder.

Rear door exterior handle

Removal

6 Prise out the rubber grommet from the end of the door adjacent to the exterior handle **(see illustration)**.
7 Working through the aperture, slacken the handle retaining Torx bolt until the rear portion of the handle can be pulled from the door **(see illustrations)**.
8 Pull the exterior handle rearwards, and manoeuvre it from the door. Recover the seal between the handle and the door skin **(see illustration)**.

Refitting

9 Refitting is a reversal of removal.

14.3a Pull the exterior handle rearwards, and manoeuvre it from the door ...

14.3b ... then recover the seal between the handle and the door skin

14.6 Prise out the rubber grommet from the end of the door

14.7a Slacken the handle retaining bolt ...

14.7b ... until the rear portion of the handle can be pulled from the door

14.8 Pull the exterior handle rearwards, and manoeuvre it from the door

14.12a Undo the 3 Torx screws at the rear edge...

14.12b ...undo the screw on the outside...

14.12c ...and release the clips

14.13a Disengage the lock button cable...

14.13b ...and the interior handle cable

Front/rear door lock

Removal

10 Remove the door window regulator as described in Section 13.

Rear door

11 Remove the door exterior handle as described previously in this Section.
12 Undo the 3 screws at the rear end of the door, and the screw in the exterior handle aperture, release the clips at the front, and manoeuvre the lock assembly from the door **(see illustrations)**.

All doors

13 Release the operating cables from the lock support brackets, then disengage the inner cable ends from the lock lever **(see illustrations)**.
14 Undo the two screws securing the lock to the support bracket **(see illustration)**.

Refitting

15 Refitting is a reversal of removal.

Front lock cylinder

Removal

16 Prise out the rubber grommet from the

end of the door adjacent to the exterior handle **(see illustration 14.1)**.
17 Working through the aperture, slacken the handle retaining bolt until the lock cylinder can be pulled from the door **(see illustrations 14.2a and 14.2b)**. If required, release the clip each side with a small screwdriver, and separate the lock cylinder from the trim

Refitting

18 Refitting is a reversal of removal.

---

15 Tailgate and support struts
– removal, refitting and adjustment

Tailgate

Removal

1 Remove the tailgate trim panel as described in Section 23.
2 Remove the high-level brake light as described in Chapter 12 Section 7.
3 Disconnect the tailgate wiring harness at the connector on the left-hand side of the tailgate **(see illustration)**.
4 Undo the 3 bolts each side and carefully

14.14 Undo the two screws securing the lock to the support bracket

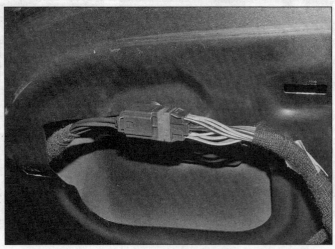

15.3 Disconnect the wiring harness at the connector on the left-hand side of the tailgate

15.4 Undo the bolts securing the spoiler – right-hand bolts arrowed

15.5a Prise out the rubber gaiters inside the top of the tailgate each side…

15.5b …and the ones on the outside of the tailgate

detach the spoiler from the outside of the tailgate **(see illustration)**.

5 Prise out the rubber gaiters inside and outside at the top of the tailgate, and carefully start to pull through the wiring and washer tube **(see illustrations)**. If the same tailgate is being refitted, tie on a length of string to the wiring harness and washer tube beforehand – the string can then be untied when it emerges from the top of the tailgate, and left in place to pull the harness and washer tube back through.

6 Using a pencil or marker pen, mark the position of the hinges on the tailgate to aid refitting.

7 Support the tailgate, and disconnect the support struts as described later in this Section.

8 Ensure that the tailgate is adequately supported, ideally with the aid of an assistant, then unscrew the bolts securing the hinges to the tailgate, and lift the tailgate from the car **(see illustration)**.

Refitting

9 Refitting is a reversal of removal, bearing in mind the following points:

a) *Make sure that the hinges are aligned with the marks made before removal.*

b) *Use the string to pull the wiring harness and the washer fluid hose into position in the tailgate.*

c) *On completion, check the alignment of the tailgate with the surrounding body panels and, if necessary, adjust the position of the tailgate hinges and/or tailgate lock striker plate within the elongated holes until satisfactory alignment is achieved.*

Support struts

Removal

10 Open the tailgate, and support it in the open position, using a wooden prop or similar tool. Note that the tailgate is heavy, and will fall closed if either of the support struts are disconnected.

11 Working at the top end of the strut, lever off the retaining clip a little, and prise off the end of the strut from the lug on the tailgate **(see illustration)**.

15.8 Unscrew the bolts each side, securing the hinges to the tailgate

12 Repeat the procedure at the bottom end of the strut, and withdraw the strut.

Refitting

13 Refitting is a reversal of removal.

16 Tailgate lock components – removal and refitting

Lock assembly

Removal

1 Remove the tailgate trim panel as described in Section 23.

16.2 Tailgate lock wiring plug and mounting bolts

15.11 Lever out the metal clip and prise off the strut

2 Disconnect the wiring plug from the lock assembly **(see illustration)**.

3 Unscrew the two lock mounting bolts, and withdraw the lock.

Refitting

4 Refitting is a reversal of removal, but check the operation of the lock mechanism before refitting the tailgate trim panel.

Release switch

Removal

5 Remove the tailgate trim panel as described in Section 23.

6 Undo the 6 nuts securing the number plate light panel to the tailgate and withdraw the panel **(see illustration)**.

16.6 Undo the 6 nuts securing the number plate light panel to the tailgate (left-hand nuts arrowed)

16.8 Depress the tabs (arrowed) on the side of the release switch

7 Disconnect the release switch wiring plug.
8 Depress the retaining tabs on the side of the release switch and remove the switch from the number plate light panel **(see illustration)**.

Refitting

9 Refitting is a reversal of removal, but check the operation of the lock mechanism before refitting the tailgate trim panel.

---

17 Central locking system – testing, reprogramming, removal and refitting

Testing/reprogramming

1 Testing of the central locking/alarm system can only be carried out using Ford diagnostic test equipment.
2 Prior to reprogramming a remote locking transmitter, ensure the vehicle battery is fully-charged, and the alarm is not armed or triggered. Close all doors to ensure conflicting chimes do not sound during programming.
3 Turn the ignition switch from position 0 to position II four times within 6 seconds, then turn it back to position 0 (off).
4 A chime will be heard to indicate that the 'learning mode' has begun.
5 Within 10 seconds of the previous step, press and hold any button on the remote transmitter until a further chime is heard. This indicates the process has been successful.
6 The system will now return to the 'learning mode' for a further 10 seconds and additional transmitters (up to a maximum of 4) can be programmed as described in paragraph 5. If no further transmitters are programmed, the system will return to normal mode after 10 seconds.
Note: *Additional information, including creating 'My Key' settings are included in the Ford Owners Handbook supplied with the vehicle.*

Removal

Body Control Module (BCM)

Note: *If the BCM is to be renewed, the unit settings must be saved prior to removal, then initialised using Ford diagnostic test equipment.*
7 Removal and refitting of the BCM is described in Chapter 12 Section 12.

Keyless entry system module

Note: *If the module is to be renewed, the unit settings must be saved prior to removal, then initialised using Ford diagnostic test equipment.*
8 Disconnect the battery negative lead as described in Chapter 5A Section 4.
9 Remove the driver's side front seat as described in Section 21.
10 Fold back the carpet, undo the 2 retaining bolts, and remove the module. Disconnect the wiring plugs as the module is withdrawn.

Door lock motors

11 The door lock motors are integral with the locks. Refer to Section 14.

Tailgate lock motor

12 The tailgate lock motor is integral with the lock. Refer to Section 16.

Refitting

13 In all cases, refitting is a reversal of removal.

---

18 Mirrors and associated components – removal and refitting

Door mirror assembly

Removal

1 Remove the front door inner trim panel as described in Section 11.

2 Disconnect the mirror wiring from the connector on the inside of the door, then release the wiring grommet from the door panel **(see illustration)**. Tie a length of string to the wiring connector – the string can then be untied when it emerges from the top of the door, and left in place to pull the wiring back through when refitting
3 Remove the grommet from the top of the door for access to the mirror retaining nut **(see illustration)**.
4 Undo the mirror retaining nut and withdraw the mirror and wiring harness from the outside of the door.

Refitting

5 Refitting is a reversal of removal.

Door mirror motor

6 The motor is integral with the mirror, and cannot be renewed separately. If faulty, the complete mirror assembly must be renewed.

Door mirror switch

Removal

7 Removal of the mirror switch assembly is described within the door inner trim panel procedure (see Section 11).

Refitting

8 Refitting is a reversal of removal.

Door mirror glass

⚠️ **Warning: If the mirror glass is broken, wear gloves to protect your hands.**

Removal

9 Pull the outer edge of the glass rearwards, insert a flat-bladed screwdriver or trim removal tool, and gently prise the glass from place **(see illustration)**.
10 Withdraw the mirror glass and, where fitted, disconnect the wiring connectors for the heated mirrors.

Refitting

11 Refitting is a reversal of removal.

Door mirror cover

Removal

12 Remove the mirror glass as previously described in this Section.

18.2 Disconnect the mirror wiring connector, then release the wiring grommet from the door panel

18.3 Remove the grommet from the door for access to the mirror retaining nut

18.9 Gently prise the mirror glass from place

18.13a Prise up the 3 clips...

18.13b ...and gently lever the cover forwards

18.16 Depress the clip at the front of the mirror base

13 Release the 3 internal clips and withdraw the cover from the mirror body **(see illustrations)**.

Refitting

14 Refitting is a reversal of removal.

Direction indicator side repeater

15 Refer to Chapter 12 Section 7.

Interior mirror

Basic mirror

16 Press the retaining clip at the front of the mirror base downwards **(see illustration)**.
17 Slide the mirror rearwards from the mounting.
18 Refitting is a reversal of removal.

Mirror with autolamps and rain sensor

19 No information was available at the time of writing. Consequently, we recommend you consult your local Ford dealer or repairer.

19 Windscreen, tailgate and fixed window glass – general information

1 These areas of glass are secured by the tight fit of the weatherseal in the body aperture, and are bonded in position with a special adhesive. Renewal of such fixed glass is a difficult, messy and time-consuming task, which is considered beyond the scope of the home mechanic. It is difficult, unless one has plenty of practice, to obtain a secure, waterproof fit. Furthermore, the task carries a high risk of breakage; this applies especially to the laminated glass windscreen. In view of this, owners are strongly advised to have this sort of work carried out by one of the many specialist windscreen fitters.

20 Body exterior fittings – removal and refitting

Radiator grille panel

Removal

1 Remove the front bumper as described in Section 6.

2 The radiator grille panel and the other detachable panels on the bumper are retained by a series of plastic clips, the location of which will become obvious on visual inspection.
3 Carefully disengage all the relevant clips using a small screwdriver, while at the same time pulling the panel from its location.

Refitting

4 Push the panel carefully into place ensuring that all the retaining clips engage fully.

Bumpers

5 Refer to Section 6.

Windscreen cowl panel

Removal

6 Remove the windscreen wiper arms as described in Chapter 12 Section 14.
7 Using a small screwdriver prise out the six clips securing the front edge of the windscreen

20.7 Prise out the clips securing the windscreen cowl panel to the bulkhead closure panel

20.9 Lift the cowl panel up and remove it from its location

cowl panel to the bulkhead closure panel **(see illustration)**.
8 Lift up the lower corners of the windscreen trim surround to disengage the tabs from the slots in the windscreen cowl panel **(see illustration)**.
9 Lift the cowl panel up and remove it from its location **(see illustration)**.

Refitting

10 Refitting is a reversal of removal.

Bulkhead closure panel

Removal

11 Remove the windscreen cowl panel as described previously.
12 Remove both headlights as described in Chapter 12 Section 7.
13 Release the vacuum hose support bracket from the front of the bulkhead closure panel **(see illustration)**.

20.8 Lift up the windscreen trim surround to disengage the tabs from the slots in the cowl panel

20.13 Release the vacuum hose support bracket from the bulkhead closure panel

20.14 Undo the 2 bolts (arrowed) each side securing the bulkhead closure panel to the body

20.15 Lift the panel up, disengage the 4 rear retaining tangs and remove the panel from the car

21.2 Front seat front retaining bolts

14 Undo the 2 bolts each side securing the bulkhead closure panel to the body **(see illustration)**.
15 Lift the panel up, disengage the 4 rear retaining tangs and remove the panel from the car **(see illustration)**.

Refitting

16 Refitting is a reversal of removal.

Wheel arch liners

17 The wheel arch liners are secured by a combination of self-tapping screws and push-fit clips.
18 The push-pin clips are removed by prising out the centre expanding pin, then prising out the main clip body.

19 The metal star clips used to unscrew from their mounting studs – now the metal tabs have to be prised up`at the centre with a small screwdriver to release them.
20 With all the fasteners removed, pull the liner down from the arch and remove it.

Body trim strips and badges

21 The various body trim strips and badges are held in position with a special adhesive. Removal requires the trim/badge to be heated, to soften the adhesive, and then cut away from the surface. Due to the high risk of damage to the paintwork during this operation, it is recommended that this task should be entrusted to a Ford dealer.

21 Seats – removal and refitting

Front seat

⚠️ *Warning: Side airbags may be built into the outer sides of the front seats. Where side airbags are fitted, refer to Chapter 12 Section 22 for the precautions which should be observed when dealing with an airbag system.*

1 Disconnect the battery negative lead as described in Chapter 5A Section 4, then wait a minimum of three minutes before proceeding to allow any residual electrical energy to dissipate.
2 Slide the seat fully rearwards, then unscrew the two front Torx bolts securing the seat rails to the floor **(see illustration)**.
3 Slide the seat fully forwards, then unscrew the two rear Torx bolts **(see illustration)**.
4 Undo the retaining bolt and pull the wiring plug from the front of the seat base **(see illustration)**.
5 Lift the seat, complete with mounting rails, and remove it from the car.
6 Refitting is a reversal of removal, but tighten the seat mounting bolts to the specified torque.

21.3 Front seat rear retaining bolts

21.4 Undo the bolt and pull the wiring plug from the socket

Rear seat

Cushion

7 Lift the seat cushion sharply upwards at the front to disengage the wire retaining hoops from the floor grommets each side **(see illustration)**.
8 Push the cushion rearwards slightly to disengage it from the 3 rear hooks and remove it from the car **(see illustration)**.
9 Refitting is a reversal of removal, but tighten the seat mounting bolts to the specified torque.

Backrest

10 Remove the rear seat cushion as described previously.
11 Fold the backrest forward.

21.7 Lift the rear seat cushion upwards at the front to disengage the retaining hoops from the floor grommets

21.8 Push the cushion rearwards to disengage the hooks

21.12a Use a screwdriver to force the locking catch rearwards ...

21.12b ... and lift the outer end of the backrest from the hinge

21.13 Pull the backrest from the centre pivot to disengage the mounting pin

12 Use a screwdriver to force the locking catch rearwards, and lift the outer end of the backrest from the hinge **(see illustrations)**.
13 Pull the backrest from the centre pivot to disengage the mounting pin **(see illustration)**.
14 Refitting is a reversal of removal, but tighten the seat mounting bolts to the specified torque.

22 Seat belts –
removal and refitting

Front seat belt

1 Disconnect the battery negative lead as described in Chapter 5A Section 4.

⚠️ *Warning: Before proceeding, wait a minimum of 3 minutes, as a precaution against accidental firing of the seat belt tensioner, incorporated in the inertia reel. This period ensures that any residual electrical energy is dissipated.*

⚠️ *Warning: There is a potential risk of the seat belt tensioning device firing during removal, so it should be handled carefully. Once removed, treat it with care – do not allow use chemicals*

on or near it, and do not expose it to high temperatures, as it may detonate.

3-door models

2 Remove the rear quarter trim panel and B-pillar trim panel as described in Section 23.
3 Undo the seat belt upper anchorage Torx bolt **(see illustration)**. Note that the spacer and washer are integral with the bolt.
4 Rotate the seat belt guide loop anti-clockwise and remove it from the B-pillar **(see illustration)**.
5 Undo the inertia reel mounting bolt/nut and withdraw the reel from the base of the pillar **(see illustrations)**. Squeeze together the sides and disconnect the seat belt tensioner

22.3 Undo the seat belt upper anchorage bolt

wiring connector, then remove the belt and reel from the car.
6 Refitting is a reversal of the removal procedure, tightening the mounting bolts to the specified torque.

5-door models

7 Lift up the trim cover and undo the seat belt upper anchorage bolt **(see illustration 23.30)**. Note that the spacer and washer are integral with the bolt.
8 Remove the B-pillar lower trim panel as described in Section 23.
9 Rotate the seat belt guide loop anti-clockwise and remove it from the B-pillar.

22.4 Rotate the seat belt guide loop anti-clockwise and remove it from the B-pillar

22.5a Undo the inertia reel mounting bolt/nut

22.5b Squeeze together the sides and pull the wiring plug upwards

22.11a Squeeze together the sides and disconnect the wiring plug

22.11b Inertia reel upper mounting nut and lower mounting bolt

22.14 Undo the rear side seat belt upper anchorage bolt

10 Undo the seat belt lower anchorage bolt. Note that the spacer and washer are integral with the bolt.
11 Undo the two inertia reel mounting bolts

22.15 Undo the inertia reel mounting bolt and withdraw the seat belt and reel from the car

and withdraw the reel from the base of the pillar (see illustrations). Disconnect the seat belt tensioner wiring connector and remove the belt and reel from the car.
12 Refitting is a reversal of the removal procedure, tightening the mounting bolts to the specified torque.

Rear side seat belt

13 Remove the parcel shelf support as described in Section 23.
14 Undo the seat belt upper anchorage bolt (see illustration). Note that the spacer and washer are integral with the bolt.
15 Undo the inertia reel mounting bolt and withdraw the seat belt and reel from the car (see illustration).
16 Refitting is a reversal of the removal procedure, tightening the mounting bolts to the specified torque.

Rear centre seat belt

17 The centre rear seat belt reel is attached to the rear seat backrest. Remove the backrest as described in Section 21.
18 Use a screwdriver to prise up the backrest release button surround trim, releasing the clips.
19 Push down the backrest padding and use a screwdriver to depress the clip on the side of the headrest guide tubes (see illustrations). Pull the guide tubes from the backrest.
20 Prise free the front of the seat belt guide trim from the top of the backrest, then disengage the two rear locating tangs. Feed the seat belt through the slot in the trim (see illustrations).
21 Gently prise out the beading securing the top half of the backrest seat fabric (see illustration).
22 Undo the bolt securing the inertia reel to the backrest (see illustration).

22.19a Push in the clip and pull the headrest guide tube from the backrest

22.19b Depress the headrest guide tube clip – shown with the tube removed

22.20a Prise free the seat belt guide trim from the top of the backrest ...

22.20b ... then feed the seat belt through the slot in the trim

22.21 Gently prise out the beading securing the top half of the backrest seat fabric

22.22 Undo the bolt securing the inertia reel to the backrest

22.23 Pull the seat foam padding from the backrest and manoeuvre the seat belt reel from the seat backrest

23 Carefully pull the seat foam padding from the top part of the backrest and manoeuvre the seat belt reel from the seat backrest (see illustration). Feed the seat belt through the seat backrest bracket as the reel is withdrawn.
24 Refitting is a reversal of the removal procedure, tightening the mounting bolts to the specified torque.

Front seat belt stalks

25 The front seat belt stalks are bolted to the seat frame and can be removed after removing the front seat as described in Section 21.
26 Refitting is a reversal of the removal procedure, tightening the mounting bolt to the specified torque.

Rear seat belt buckles

27 Remove the rear seat cushion as described in Section 21.

22.28 Rear seat belt buckle retaining bolt

28 Undo the retaining bolt and remove the buckle(s) from the car (see illustration).
29 Refitting is a reversal of the removal procedure, tightening the mounting bolt to the specified torque.

23 Interior trim and fittings – removal and refitting

General

1 The interior trim panels are secured by a combination of clips and screws, with easily-broken plastic clips featuring heavily. Removal and refitting is generally self-explanatory, noting that it may be necessary to remove or loosen surrounding panels to allow a particular panel to be removed. The

following paragraphs describe the removal and refitting of the major panels in more detail.

Door inner trim panels

2 Refer to Section 11.

Steering column shrouds

3 Remove the steering wheel as described in Chapter 10 Section 14.
4 The lower shroud is clipped to the upper shroud at either side, and is further secured by three screws.
5 Undo the 3 retaining screws, then lower the steering column height adjuster lever, and remove the lower shroud (see illustrations)
6 If required, unclip and remove the upper shroud (see illustrations).
7 Refitting is a reversal of removal.

Driver's lower facia trim

Warning: A knee airbag may be incorporated in the lower facia trim panel. Where an airbag is fitted, refer to Chapter 12 Section 22 for the precautions which should be observed when dealing with an airbag system.

8 On models equipped with a knee airbag, disconnect the battery negative terminal as described in Chapter 5A Section 4 and wait a minimum of three minutes before proceeding.
9 On models equipped with a knee airbag, reach up under the facia and undo the two nuts securing the airbag to the facia frame (see illustration).
10 Carefully prise the trim panel away from the facia to release the three retaining clips

23.5a Undo the lower shroud upper retaining screws...

23.5b ... and lower retaining screw ...

23.5c ... then remove the lower shroud

23.6a Unclip the upper shroud...

23.6b ...and detach it from the facia

23.9 Reach up and remove the two nuts securing the airbag to the facia frame

23.10 Squeeze together the clips and disconnect the airbag wiring plug

23.12 Remove the two plastic rivets from the passenger's lower facia trim panel

23.13 Disconnect the wiring plugs as the panel is withdrawn

each side. Where applicable, disconnect the airbag wiring connector and remove the panel **(see illustration)**. Check whether any of the clips pull out of the panel, to be left on the car – transfer them back to the panel before refitting.

11 Refitting is a reversal of removal.

Passenger's lower facia trim

12 Remove the two plastic rivets from the underside of the panel by prising up the centre section, then withdrawing the rivet body **(see illustration)**.

13 Disengage the tabs at the front edge of the panel and remove the panel from under

the facia **(see illustration)**. Disconnect any wiring plugs as the panel is withdrawn.

14 Refitting is a reversal of removal.

Sill trim panels

15 Pull away the rubber door seals in the vicinity of the sill trim panel to be removed.

16 The sill trim panels are clipped in place. Several clips are used, and some are quite stiff to release – start at one end of the panel, and pull the panel back as it is released. Check whether any of the clips pull out of the panel, to be left on the car – transfer them back to the panel before refitting **(see illustration)**.

17 Refitting is a reversal of removal.

A-pillar trim panel

Upper panel

18 Open the door, and carefully prise the rubber door seal from the edge of the door aperture.

19 Pull the panel away from the A-pillar at the top and work down to disengage the upper retaining clips. Once the panel is free, disengage the two locating tabs at the front and remove the panel **(see illustrations)**. Check whether any of the clips pull out of the panel, to be left on the car – transfer them back to the panel before refitting.

20 Refitting is a reversal of removal.

Lower panel

21 Remove the adjacent sill trim panel as described previously in this Section.

22 Unscrew the plastic retaining stud at the top of the panel **(see illustration)**.

23 Pull the panel up at the rear to release the retaining clips and remove the panel from the car **(see illustration)**.

24 Refitting is a reversal of removal.

B-pillar trim panels

25 Detach the rubber weatherstrip from the B-pillar as necessary to free the edges of the trim panel.

3-door models

26 Remove the rear quarter trim panel as described later in this Section.

23.16 Pull the sill trim panels up to release the clips

23.19a Pull the trim panel away from the A-pillar at the top and work down to disengage the upper clips...

23.19b ... then disengage the two locating tabs at the front and remove the panel

23.22 Unscrew the plastic retaining stud at the top of the A-pillar lower panel

23.23 Pull the panel up at the rear to release the clips and remove the panel from the car

23.27a Prise out the trim cap at the top of the B-pillar...

23.27b ...and undo the screw

23.28 Pull the panel away to release the clips, then feed the seat belt through the panel slot

27 Carefully prise out the trim cap at the top of the B-pillar and undo the retaining screw now exposed (see illustrations).

28 Pull the panel away from the pillar to release the internal clips, then feed the seat belt through the panel and remove the panel from the car (see illustration). Check whether any of the clips pull out of the panel, to be left on the car – transfer them back to the panel before refitting.

29 Refitting is a reversal of removal.

5-door models – lower panel

30 Remove the sill trim panels on either side of the B-pillar as described previously in this Section.

31 Pull the panel away from the pillar to release the internal clips, then remove the panel from the car (see illustration). Check whether any of the clips pull out of the panel, to be left on the car – transfer them back to the panel before refitting.

32 Refitting is a reversal of removal.

5-door models – upper panel

33 Remove the B-pillar lower panel as described previously in this Section.

34 Lift up the trim cover and undo the seat belt upper anchorage bolt (see illustration). Note that the spacer and washer are integral with the bolt.

35 Carefully prise out the trim cap at the top of the B-pillar and undo the retaining screw now exposed (see illustrations).

36 Pull the panel away from the pillar to release the internal clips, then remove the panel from the car (see illustration). Check whether any of the clips pull out of the panel, to be left on the car – transfer them back to the panel before refitting.

37 Refitting is a reversal of removal. Tighten the seat belt upper anchorage bolt to the specified torque.

C-pillar trim panel

3-door models

38 Carefully prise free and remove the trim covering above the rear side window (see illustration).

39 Undo the three retaining screws

23.31 Pull the lower B-pillar panel away to release the clips

23.34 Lift up the trim cover and undo the seat belt upper anchorage Torx bolt

23.35a Prise out the trim cap at the top of the B-pillar ...

23.35b ... and undo the retaining screw now exposed

23.36 Pull the upper panel away to release the clips

23.38 Prise free and remove the trim covering above the window

23.39a Undo the retaining screws...

23.39b ... and remove the upper trim plate

23.42 Pull the C-pillar trim panel away to release the clips, then feed the seat belt through the panel slot

and remove the upper trim plate **(see illustrations)**.
40 Remove the rear seat cushion as described in Section 21.
41 Undo the seat belt lower anchorage bolt. Note that the spacer and washer are integral with the bolt.
42 Pull the panel away from the pillar to release the internal clips, then feed the seat belt through the panel and remove the panel from the car **(see illustration)**. Check whether any of the clips pull out of the panel, to be left on the car – transfer them back to the panel before refitting.
43 Refitting is a reversal of removal. Tighten the rear seat belt lower anchorage bolt to the specified torque.

5-door models

44 Pull off the rubber seals from the rear door

and tailgate apertures, in the area adjoining the trim panel.
45 Remove the rear seat cushion as described in Section 21.
46 Undo the seat belt lower anchorage bolt **(see illustration)**. Note that the spacer and washer are integral with the bolt.
47 Carefully prise out the trim cap at the top of the C-pillar and undo the retaining screw now exposed **(see illustration)**.
48 Pull the panel away from the pillar to release the internal clips, then feed the seat belt through the panel and remove the panel from the car **(see illustration)**. Check whether any of the clips pull out of the panel, to be left on the car – transfer them back to the panel before refitting.
49 Refitting is a reversal of removal. Tighten the rear seat belt lower anchorage bolt to the specified torque.

Rear quarter trim panel

Note: *The rear quarter trim panels are only fitted to 3-door models*
50 Remove the C-pillar trim panel and the sill trim panel as described previously in this Section.
51 Pull off the rubber seal from the door aperture, in the area adjoining the trim panel.
52 Unscrew the bolt at the front of the seat belt lower anchor rail, remove the washer and spacer from the bolt, then remove the bolt from the rail **(see illustration)**.
53 Disengage the rear end of the rail from its location and collect the locating collar **(see illustration)**. Disengage the seat belt from the rail.
54 Prise out the plastic fastener at the lower rear corner of the panel **(see illustration)**. If

23.46 Undo the rear seat belt lower anchorage bolt

23.47 Prise out the trim cap at the top of the C-pillar and undo the retaining screw now exposed – 5-door models

23.48 Pull the panel away to release the clips, then feed the seat belt through the panel slot – 5-door models

23.52 Unscrew the seat belt lower anchor rail bolt, then remove the washer, spacer and bolt from the rail

23.53 Disengage the rear end of the rail from its location, and prise out the locating collar

23.54 Prise out the plastic fastener at the lower rear corner of the panel

improved access is required, remove the rear seat backrest as described in Section 21.

55 Unclip the quarter trim panel at the base, then work round the edges of the panel, freeing the remaining clips until the panel can be lifted out **(see illustration)**. Check whether any of the clips pull out of the panel, to be left on the car – transfer them back to the panel before refitting.

56 Refitting is a reversal of removal, noting the following points:

a) Make sure the seat belt anchor rail locating collar is in position before refitting the anchor rail.

b) Refit the spacer and washer to the anchor rail retaining bolt.

c) Tighten the mounting bolts to the specified torque.

Rear door aperture trim panel

57 Remove the C-pillar trim panel and the sill trim panel as described previously in this Section.

58 Prise out the plastic fastener at the lower rear corner of the panel **(see illustration)**.

59 Pull the panel away from the door aperture to release the internal clips, then remove the panel from the car **(see illustration)**. Check whether any of the clips pull out of the panel, to be left on the car – transfer them back to the panel before refitting.

60 Refitting is a reversal of removal.

Parcel shelf support

3-door models

61 Remove the rear quarter trim panel as described previously in this Section.

62 Pull off the rubber seal from the tailgate aperture, in the area adjoining the parcel shelf support.

63 Prise out the luggage compartment light and disconnect the wiring plug (where applicable).

64 Undo the upper and lower retaining screws, then pull the support away from the body to release the internal clips, and remove the support from the car **(see illustration)**. Check whether any of the clips pull out of the support, to be left on the car – transfer them back to the support before refitting.

65 Refitting is a reversal of removal.

23.55 The rear quarter panel is secured by 10 clips

23.59 Pull the panel away to release the clips, then remove the panel from the car – 5-door models

5-door models

66 Remove the C-pillar trim panel as described previously in this Section.

67 Pull off the rubber seal from the tailgate aperture, in the area adjoining the parcel shelf support.

68 Undo the parcel shelf support upper and lower retaining screws **(see illustration)**.

69 Pull the rear door aperture trim panel out slightly, then pull the parcel shelf support away from the body to release the internal retaining clips **(see illustration)**. Where applicable, release the interior light bulbholder then remove the support from the car. Check whether any of the clips pull out of the support, to be left on the car – transfer them back to the support before refitting.

70 Refitting is a reversal of removal.

23.58 Prise out the plastic fastener at the lower rear corner of the panel – 5-door models

23.64 Undo the parcel shelf upper and lower retaining screws

Tailgate aperture lower trim

71 Pull off the rubber seal from the tailgate aperture, in the area adjoining the trim panel.

72 Where fitted, prise out the plastic fasteners at each inner side of the trim panel.

73 Pull the panel upwards from the tailgate aperture to release the internal clips, then remove the panel from the car **(see illustration)**. Check whether any of the clips pull out of the panel, to be left on the car – transfer them back to the panel before refitting.

74 Refitting is a reversal of removal.

Loadspace side trim

75 Remove the parcel shelf support and tailgate aperture trim panel as described previously in this Section.

23.68 Undo the parcel shelf support retaining screws

23.69 Release the bulbholder as the parcel shaft support is withdrawn

23.73 Pull the panel upwards to release the clips

23.76 Lift the loadspace side trim from its location and remove it from the car

23.79a Undo the retaining screw...

23.79b ...and pull the upper trim panel side from the tailgate

23.80 Undo the screw in the handle recess

23.87 Squeeze together the sides to release the lugs

23.88 Depress the retaining tabs and withdraw the two hinge pins from the base of the glovebox

76 Lift the trim from its location and remove it from the car **(see illustration)**.
77 Refitting is a reversal of removal.

Tailgate trim panel

78 Disengage the parcel shelf lifting cords from the studs on the upper trim panel sides.
79 Undo the retaining screw each side and pull the upper trim panel sides away from the tailgate to release the internal clips **(see illustrations)**.
80 Undo the trim panel retaining screw in the grab handle recess **(see illustration)**.
81 Pull the main panel away from the tailgate to release the internal retaining clips and remove the panel from the car. Check whether any of the clips pull out of the panel, to be left on the car – transfer them back to the panel before refitting.
82 Refitting is a reversal of removal.

Carpets

83 The passenger compartment floor carpet is in several pieces, and is secured along the edges by various types of clips.
84 Carpet removal and refitting is reasonably straightforward, but time-consuming, due to the fact that all adjoining trim panels must be released, and the seats and centre console must be removed.

Headlining

85 The headlining is clipped to the roof, and can be withdrawn only once all fittings such as the grab handles, sunvisors, front, centre and rear pillar trim panels, and associated components have been removed. The door and tailgate weatherseals will also have to be prised clear.

86 Note that headlining removal requires considerable skill and experience if it is to be carried out without damage, and is therefore best entrusted to an expert.

Glovebox

87 Open the glovebox, squeeze together the sides to release the lugs, and fully lower the glovebox **(see illustration)**.
88 Depress the retaining tabs and withdraw the two hinge pins from the base of the glovebox **(see illustration)**.
89 Press the sides of the glovebox inwards and remove the glovebox from the facia.
90 Refitting is a reversal of removal.

24 Centre console – removal and refitting

Removal

1 Working in the footwell on the driver's and passenger's side, unscrew the centre pins and extract the plastic rivets securing the inner trim panels to the base of the facia. Pull the panels away to release the three retaining clips at the rear and remove the trim panels **(see illustrations)**.
2 Prise the top edge of the passengers airbag warning light surround trim rearwards and

24.1a Extract the 'scrivets' securing the inner trim panels to the base of the facia...

24.1b ... then pull the panels away to release the retaining clips

24.2 Use a trim removal tool to prise the warning light trim from place

24.3 Prise up the gear lever gaiter surround

24.4 On automatic transmission models, carefully prise up the selector lever trim panel

remove it **(see illustration)**. Disconnect the wiring plug as the panel is withdrawn.

3 On manual transmission models, prise up the gear lever gaiter surround from the centre console and if required, unscrew the gear knob from the lever **(see illustration)**.

4 On automatic transmission models, carefully prise up the selector lever trim panel and surround from the centre console **(see illustration)**.

5 Starting at the top, prise rearwards/up the gear lever surround panel **(see illustrations)**.

6 Prise the panels from the front of the console **(see illustrations)**. Disconnect any wiring plugs as the panels are withdrawn.

7 Undo the screw each side of the centre console at the rear **(see illustration)**.

8 Undo the screw each side at the front, lower section of the console **(see illustration)**.

9 Undo the two screws securing the front of the centre console to the facia **(see illustration)**.

10 Pull the console to the rear to disengage the two front locating lugs. Disconnect any wiring plugs as they become accessible, then lift the console up and over the handbrake lever and remove it from the car.

Refitting

11 Refitting is a reversal of removal.

24.5a Starting at the top, prise the panel reawards, then up…

24.5b …and remove it

24.6a Prise up the panel around the gear lever aperture…

24.6b …and the upper console panel

24.7 Undo the screw from each side of the centre console at the rear

24.8 Remove the screw each side at the front, lower section

24.9 Undo the two screws securing the front of the centre console to the facia

25 Facia assembly –
removal and refitting

Note: *This is an involved procedure which entails removal of the facia in virtually its totally assembled condition, containing the steering column, heater/air conditioning assembly and all the main facia attachments and controls. Once the facia is removed, it can be dismantled by referring to the procedures contained in Chapters 3, 10 and 12 of this manual. It is strongly recommended that this Section is read through thoroughly before starting the procedure.*

Removal

1 On models equipped with air conditioning, have the refrigerant discharged at a dealer service department or an automotive air conditioning repair facility.

2 Set the steering wheel and roadwheels in the straight-ahead position, then remove the ignition key and engage the steering lock. On vehicles with keyless entry, make sure the passive key is outside the vehicle to allow the steering lock to engage.

3 Disconnect the battery negative lead as described in Chapter 5A Section 4, then wait a minimum of three minutes before proceeding.

⚠️ **Warning: Driver's and passenger's airbags are incorporated in the steering wheel and facia. Refer to Chapter 12 Section 22 for the precautions which should be observed when dealing with an airbag system.**

4 Drain the cooling system as described in Chapter 1A Section 30 or Chapter 1B Section 30.

5 Remove the centre console as described in Section 24.

6 Remove the windscreen cowl panel and bulkhead closure panel as described in Section 20.

7 Remove the windscreen wiper motor and linkage as described in Chapter 12 Section 15.

8 Undo the bolt behind the windscreen wiper location securing the facia crossmember to the bulkhead **(see illustration)**.

9 Release the retaining clip and disconnect the upper coolant hose from the heater matrix pipe stub on the engine compartment

25.8 Undo the bolt behind the windscreen wiper location securing the facia crossmember to the bulkhead

25.10 Refrigerant pipe connector block retaining nuts at the expansion valve

bulkhead. Disconnect the lower coolant hose from the matrix pipe stub by pressing together the tabs on the side of the quick-release fitting **(see illustration)**.

10 On models with air conditioning, undo the retaining nuts and disconnect the refrigerant pipe connector blocks from the expansion valve on the engine compartment bulkhead **(see illustration)**. Discard the seals – new ones must be used when refitting. Suitably cap the open fittings immediately to keep moisture and contamination out of the system.

11 Unscrew the plastic nut adjacent to the heater matrix coolant hose attachments on the engine compartment bulkhead **(see illustration)**.

12 Remove the driver's side front door and the driver's seat as described in Sections 10 and 21 respectively.

13 On models with manual transmission,

25.9 Coolant hose connections at the heater matrix pipe stubs

25.11 Unscrew the plastic nut adjacent to the heater matrix coolant hose attachments

remove the gear lever housing assembly as described in Chapter 7A, Section 3.

14 On models with PowerShift transmission, disconnect the selector cable from the lever housing as described in Chapter 7B Section 3, then undo the 4 nuts and remove the housing.

15 Remove the passenger's lower facia trim panel, and the upper and lower A-pillar trim panels each side, as described in Section 23.

16 Working under the facia on the passenger's side, disconnect the wiring plugs from the body control module **(see illustration)**.

17 Undo the retaining bolt and disconnect the wiring harness connector on the passenger's side lower A-pillar **(see illustration)**.

18 Lift up the locking bar and disconnect the wiring harness connector on the driver's side lower A-pillar **(see illustration)**.

25.16 Disconnect the body control module wiring plugs

25.17 Undo the retaining bolt and disconnect the wiring harness connector on the passenger's side lower A-pillar

25.18 Lift up the locking bar and disconnect the wiring harness connector on the driver's side lower A-pillar

25.19 Carefully prise off the facia end panels on each side

25.20 Release the tab and slide the bonnet release lever rearwards

25.21 Undo the clamp bolt securing the steering column shaft lower universal joint to the steering gear pinion

19 Using a plastic spatula or similar tool, carefully prise off the facia end panels on each side to release the 4 internal clips **(see illustration)**.

20 Working under the facia on the driver's side, depress the tab in the centre of the bonnet release lever, then slide the lever to the rear to disengage the locating lugs **(see illustration)**.

21 Undo the clamp bolt securing the steering column shaft lower universal joint to the steering gear pinion **(see illustration)**. Note that a new clamp bolt will be required for refitting. Pull the shaft upwards and off the pinion.

22 Disconnect the wiring from the warning light switch on the side of the handbrake lever **(see illustration)**. Free the wiring from the clips on the plastic cover over the airbag control unit.

23 Lift off the cover (where fitted) over the airbag control unit and disconnect the airbag wiring connectors **(see illustration)**.

24 Open the tabs on the plastic wiring trough and lift out the upper wiring harness so that it's free to be removed with the facia **(see illustration)**.

25 Undo the two bolts each side and remove the two facia support struts **(see illustration)**.

26 Undo the bolt securing the earth lead at the right-hand facia support bracket, and release the wiring harness from the clip at the heater housing **(see illustration)**.

27 Insert a small screwdriver into the slot in the front face of the overhead reading light. Depress the clip and carefully prise the light unit from its location. Disconnect the wiring connectors and remove the light unit **(see illustration)**.

28 Undo the 2 screws in the light aperture securing the headlining to the roof panel **(see illustration)**.

25.22 Disconnect the wiring connector from the warning light switch on the side of the handbrake lever

29 Using a small screwdriver, open the locking flap and remove the driver's side sunvisor. Now carefully open the trim tab,

25.23 Fold over the locking bars and disconnect the wiring plugs

25.24 Open the tabs on the plastic wiring trough and lift out the upper harness

25.25 Undo the two bolts each side and remove the two facia support struts

25.26 Disconnect the earth lead and release the wiring harness

25.27 Using a small screwdriver, depress the clip and carefully prise the light unit from its location

25.28 Undo the screws in the light aperture

25.29a Open the locking flap ...

25.29b ... and remove the driver's side sunvisor ...

25.29c ... then open the trim tab, undo the retaining screw, and remove the sunvisor pivot mounting

undo the retaining screw and remove the sunvisor pivot mounting **(see illustrations)**.

30 Working through the reading light aperture, undo the nut securing the radio aerial and aerial cable to the roof panel, then remove the aerial **(see illustration)**.

31 Tie a suitable length of string to the end of the aerial lead to aid refitting. Carefully pull the headliner down slightly at the front, then reach in and release the aerial lead from the clips on the roof. Take great care not to crease the headliner.

32 Pull the aerial lead out from its roof location until the string emerges at the top of the A-pillar. Untie the string and leave it in place to enable the lead to be drawn back through when refitting.

33 Release the aerial lead from the clips on the A-pillar so that the lead is free to be removed with the facia **(see illustration)**.

34 Disconnect the wiring plug at the base of the upper A-pillar on the drivers side.

35 Extract the rubber grommet from the A-pillar on the driver's side, then using a socket and extension bar, undo and remove the facia side retaining bolt **(see illustrations)**.

36 Using a suitable marker pen, make an alignment mark on the pillar in the centre of the oval hole on the facia mounting bracket each side.

37 Undo the two bolts each side securing the facia to the A-pillars **(see illustration)**.

38 With the help of an assistant, carefully pull the facia rearwards a little, then lift it from its location. Check that all wiring has been disconnected, then remove the facia out from the driver's side of the car.

Refitting

39 Refitting is a reversal of removal, noting the following points:

a) *Tighten all retaining bolts to the specified torque (where given).*

b) *Rotate the tolerance absorber at the drivers end of the facia fully anti-clockwise prior to refitting the facia assembly. As the right-hand retaining bolt is tightened, the tolerance absorber will 'unscrew' to take up any clearance between the crossmember and vehicle body shell* **(see illustration)**.

c) *Use a new clamp bolt when reconnecting the steering column shaft universal joint and tighten the clamp bolt to the specified torque.*

d) *Refill the cooling system as described in Chapter 1A Section 30 or Chapter 1B Section 30.*

e) *On models equipped with air conditioning, use new O-rings, coated with refrigerant oil, when reconnecting the refrigerant lines.*

f) *On models equipped with air conditioning, have the system evacuated, charged and leak-tested by the specialist that discharged it.*

25.30 Undo the nut securing the radio aerial and aerial cable to the roof panel

25.33 Release the aerial lead from the clips on the A-pillar so that the lead is free to be removed with the facia

25.35a Extract the rubber grommet from the A-pillar on the driver's side ...

25.35b ... then using a socket and extension bar, undo the facia side retaining bolt

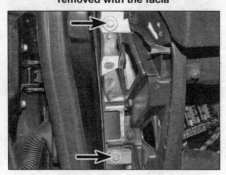

25.37 Undo the two bolts each side securing the facia to the A-pillars

25.39 Rotate the tolerance absorber fully anti-clockwise

Chapter 12
Body electrical system

Contents

Degrees of difficulty

| Easy, suitable for novice with little experience | Fairly easy, suitable for beginner with some experience | Fairly difficult, suitable for competent DIY mechanic | Difficult, suitable for experienced DIY mechanic | Very difficult, suitable for expert DIY or professional |

Specifications

General

System type . . . . 12 volt, negative earth

Fuses

Refer to label on fuse/relay box cover and back of glovebox

Bulbs
	Type/Wattage
Front direction indicator light	PY21
Front direction indicator side repeater light	WY5
Front foglight	H11 55
Front sidelight.	W5
Glovebox light	W5
Headlight dipped beam	H7 55
Headlight main beam	H15 55/15
Interior light	W6
Luggage compartment light	W5
Map reading lights	W5
Number plate light	W5
Rear direction indicator light	PY21
Rear foglight.	P21
Reversing light	W16
Brake/tail light	P21/5

Torque wrench settings
	Nm	lbf ft
Crash sensor(s) nut	10	7
Passengers air bag nuts.	8	6
Restraints Control Module (RCM) nuts.	10	7

1 General information and precautions

⚠️ **Warning: Before carrying out any work on the electrical system, read through the precautions given in 'Safety first!' at the beginning of this manual, and in Chapter 5A.**

1 The electrical system is of the 12 volt negative earth type. Power for the lights and all electrical accessories is supplied by a lead-acid type battery, which is charged by the engine-driven alternator.

2 This Chapter covers repair and service procedures for the various electrical components not associated with the engine. Information on the battery, alternator and starter motor can be found in Chapter 5A.

3 It should be noted that, prior to working on any component in the electrical system, the battery negative terminal should first be disconnected, to prevent the possibility of electrical short-circuits and/or fires. *Caution: Before proceeding, refer to Chapter 5A Section 4 for further information.*

2 Electrical fault finding – general information

Note: *Refer to the precautions given in 'Safety first!' and in Section 1 before starting work. The following tests relate to testing of the main electrical circuits, and should not be used to test delicate electronic circuits (such as the anti-lock braking system or fuel injection system), particularly where an electronic control unit is used.*

General

1 A typical electrical circuit consists of an electrical component, any switches, relays, motors, fuses, fusible links or circuit breakers related to that component, and the wiring and connectors which link the component to both the battery and the vehicle body. To help to pinpoint a problem in an electrical circuit, wiring diagrams are shown at the end of this Chapter.

2 Before attempting to diagnose an electrical fault, first study the appropriate wiring diagram to obtain a complete understanding of the components included in the particular circuit concerned. The possible sources of a fault can be narrowed down by noting if other components related to the circuit are operating properly. If several components or circuits fail at one time, the problem is likely to be related to a shared fuse or earth connection.

3 Electrical problems usually stem from simple causes, such as loose or corroded connections, a faulty earth connection, a blown fuse, a melted fusible link, or a faulty

relay. Inspect the condition of all fuses, wires and connections in a problem circuit before testing the components. Use the wiring diagrams to determine which terminal connections will need to be checked in order to pinpoint the trouble-spot.

4 The basic tools required for electrical fault finding include a circuit tester or voltmeter (a 12 volt bulb with a set of test leads can also be used for certain tests); a self-powered test light (sometimes known as a continuity tester); an ohmmeter (to measure resistance); a battery and set of test leads; and a jumper wire, preferably with a circuit breaker or fuse incorporated, which can be used to bypass suspect wires or electrical components. Before attempting to locate a problem with test instruments, use the wiring diagram to determine where to make the connections.

5 To find the source of an intermittent wiring fault (usually due to a poor or dirty connection, or damaged wiring insulation), a 'wiggle' test can be performed on the wiring. This involves wiggling the wiring by hand to see if the fault occurs as the wiring is moved. It should be possible to narrow down the source of the fault to a particular section of wiring. This method of testing can be used in conjunction with any of the tests described in the following sub-Sections.

6 Apart from problems due to poor connections, two basic types of fault can occur in an electrical circuit – open-circuit, or short-circuit.

7 Open-circuit faults are caused by a break somewhere in the circuit, which prevents current from flowing. An open-circuit fault will prevent a component from working, but will not cause the relevant circuit fuse to blow.

8 Short-circuit faults are caused by a 'short' somewhere in the circuit, which allows the current flowing in the circuit to 'escape' along an alternative route, usually to earth. Short-circuit faults are normally caused by a breakdown in wiring insulation, which allows a feed wire to touch either another wire, or an earthed component such as the bodyshell. A short-circuit fault will normally cause the relevant circuit fuse to blow.

Finding an open-circuit

9 To check for an open-circuit, connect one lead of a circuit tester or voltmeter to either the negative battery terminal or a known good earth.

10 Connect the other lead to a connector in the circuit being tested, preferably nearest to the battery or fuse.

11 Switch on the circuit, bearing in mind that some circuits are live only when the ignition switch is turned to a particular position.

12 If voltage is present (indicated either by the tester bulb lighting or a voltmeter reading, as applicable), this means that the section of the circuit between the relevant connector and the battery is problem-free.

13 Continue to check the remainder of the circuit in the same fashion.

14 When a point is reached at which no voltage is present, the problem must lie between that point and the previous test point with voltage. Most problems can be traced to a broken, corroded or loose connection.

Finding a short-circuit

15 To check for a short-circuit, first disconnect the load(s) from the circuit (loads are the components which draw current from a circuit, such as bulbs, motors, heating elements, etc).

16 Remove the relevant fuse from the circuit, and connect a circuit tester or voltmeter to the fuse connections.

17 Switch on the circuit, bearing in mind that some circuits are live only when the ignition switch is turned to a particular position.

18 If voltage is present (indicated either by the tester bulb lighting or a voltmeter reading, as applicable), this means that there is a short-circuit.

19 If no voltage is present, but the fuse still blows with the load(s) connected, this indicates an internal fault in the load(s).

Finding an earth fault

20 The battery negative terminal is connected to 'earth' – the metal of the engine/transmission unit and the car body – and most systems are wired so that they only receive a positive feed, the current returning via the metal of the car body. This means that the component mounting and the body form part of that circuit. Loose or corroded mountings can therefore cause a range of electrical faults, ranging from total failure of a circuit, to a puzzling partial fault. In particular, lights may shine dimly (especially when another circuit sharing the same earth point is in operation), motors (eg, wiper motors or the radiator cooling fan motor) may run slowly, and the operation of one circuit may have an apparently-unrelated effect on another. Note that on many vehicles, earth straps are used between certain components, such as the engine/transmission and the body, usually where there is no metal-to-metal contact between components, due to flexible rubber mountings, etc **(see illustrations).**

2.20a The main earth strap is between the battery negative terminal and the vehicle body

2.20b Other earth connections may be found at the left-hand front suspension turret...

2.20c ... front of the transmission casing (Powershift transmission)...

2.20d ...top of the transmission (manual transmission)...

2.20e ...front inner wings (both sides)...

2.20f ...nearside front chassis member...

2.20g ...and the drivers side inner sill

21 To check whether a component is properly earthed, disconnect the battery, and connect one lead of an ohmmeter to a known good earth point. Connect the other lead to the wire or earth connection being tested. The resistance reading should be zero; if not, check the connection as follows.

22 If an earth connection is thought to be faulty, dismantle the connection, and clean back to bare metal both the bodyshell and the wire terminal or the component earth connection mating surface. Be careful to remove all traces of dirt and corrosion, then use a knife to trim away any paint, so that a clean metal-to-metal joint is made. On reassembly, tighten the joint fasteners securely; if a wire terminal is being refitted, use serrated washers between the terminal

and the bodyshell, to ensure a clean and secure connection. When the connection is remade, prevent the onset of corrosion in the future by applying a coat of petroleum jelly or silicone-based grease. Alternatively, at regular intervals, spray on a proprietary ignition sealer or a water-dispersant lubricant.

3 Fuses, relays and Body Control Module (BCM) – general information

Fuses

1 Fuses are designed to break a circuit when a predetermined current is reached, in order to protect the components and wiring which could

be damaged by excessive current flow. Any excessive current flow will be due to a fault in the circuit, usually a short-circuit (see Section 2).

2 The main fuses are located in the engine compartment fuse/relay box on the left-hand side of the engine compartment. Unclip and remove the cover for access (see illustration). Refer to the information on the fuse/relay box lid and to the wiring diagrams at the end of Chapter 12 for details of the fuse locations and circuits protected.

3 Additional fuses are located in the passenger compartment fuse/relay box located behind the glovebox. Open the glovebox and press the sides inwards to release it from the facia (see illustration).

4 A blown fuse can be recognised from its melted or broken wire (see illustration).

3.2 Unclip and remove the cover for access to the engine compartment fuse/relay box

3.3 Additional fuses are located in the passenger compartment fuse/relay box located behind the glovebox

3.4 The fuses can be checked visually to determine if they have blown

3.6 Pull the fuse from its location, using thin-nosed pliers if necessary

3.14 Pull open the storage compartment to access the 16-pin diagnostic connector

5 To remove a fuse, first ensure that the relevant circuit is switched off – for maximum safety, disconnect the battery as described in Chapter 5A Section 4.

6 Pull the fuse from its location, using thin-nosed pliers if necessary **(see illustration)**.

7 Before renewing a blown fuse, trace and rectify the cause, and always use a fuse of the correct rating. Never substitute a fuse of a higher rating, or make temporary repairs using wire or metal foil; more serious damage, or even fire, could result.

8 If a new fuse blows immediately, find the cause before renewing it again; a short to earth as a result of faulty insulation is most likely. Where a fuse protects more than one circuit, try to isolate the defect by switching on each circuit in turn (if possible) until the fuse blows again. Always carry a supply of spare fuses of each relevant rating on the vehicle, a spare of each rating should be clipped into the base of the fuse/relay box.

Relays

9 The main relays are located in the engine compartment fuse/relay box on the left-hand side of the engine compartment, and in the passenger compartment fuse/relay box located behind the glovebox. Refer to paragraphs 2 and 3 for further information.

10 If a circuit or system controlled by a relay develops a fault, and the relay is suspect, operate the system. If the relay is functioning, it should be possible to hear it 'click' as it is energised. If this is the case, the fault lies

with the components or wiring of the system. If the relay is not being energised, then either the relay is not receiving a main supply or a switching voltage, or the relay itself is faulty. Testing is by the substitution of a known good unit, but be careful – while some relays are identical in appearance and in operation, others look similar but perform different functions.

11 To remove a relay, first ensure that the relevant circuit is switched off. The relay can then simply be pulled out from the socket, and pushed back into position.

Body Control Module (BCM)

12 This module, which is fitted behind the facia on the passenger's side, controls many of the car's electrical functions:
a) *Direction indicators and hazard lights.*
b) *Interior lighting, including battery saver function (the interior lights and chimes are automatically shut off after a predetermined period of inactivity).*
c) *Heated windscreen and rear window.*
d) *Electric mirrors.*
e) *Wipers and washers.*
f) *Lights-on and door-ajar warnings.*
g) *Central locking.*
h) *Tailgate release.*
i) *Alarm system.*
j) *Autolamp system.*
13 Removal and refitting of the module is described in Section 12.
14 The BCM is equipped with an extensive self-diagnosis capability. Should a fault

develop, have the system interrogated using Ford diagnostic equipment (or generic equivalent), via the 16-pin diagnostic connector under the drivers side of the facia **(see illustration)**.

4 Switches – removal and refitting

1 Disconnect the battery negative terminal as described in Chapter 5A Section 4 before removing any switch, and reconnect the terminal after refitting.

Ignition switch/steering lock cylinder

Steering column lock cylinder

2 Remove the steering column shrouds as described in Chapter 11, Section 23.
3 Disconnect the wiring plug, then unclip and withdraw the anti-theft immobiliser transceiver unit from the ignition switch/steering lock assembly **(see illustration)**.
4 Insert the ignition key, and turn it to position I.
5 Using small screwdrivers/punches, depress the 2 locking pins at the top of the lock housing, then insert a screwdriver/punch into the hole on the underside of the housing and lever the catch withing the housing rearwards. Pull out the lock cylinder using the key **(see illustration)**.
6 To refit the lock cylinder, push the assembly into the lock housing, until the locking pin engages, then turn the ignition key to position 0 and withdraw the key.

Ignition switch

Caution: Do not remove the ignition switch whilst the steering column lock cylinder is removed.
7 Remove the steering column shrouds as described in Chapter 11, Section 23.
8 Use a small screwdriver to lift the locking tab on the wiring connector at the back of the switch, then disconnect it.
9 Depress the switch retaining tabs at the top and bottom, then the switch is withdrawn from the steering column **(see illustration)**.

4.3 Disconnect the wiring plug and unclip the immobiliser unit

4.5 Depress the locking pins at the top of the lock housing, release the catch on the underside, and pull out the lock cylinder using the key

4.9 Release the switch retaining tabs then withdraw the ignition switch from the steering column

4.15 Disconnect the wiring connector from the underside of the relevant switch

4.16a Release the plastic catch at the top...

4.16b ...and slide the switch upwards

10 Refitting is a reversal of removal, but make sure that the switch engages correctly.

Starter control unit (where fitted)

11 Remove the facia centre switch/vent panel as described later in this Section.

12 Reach through the aperture, disconnect the wiring plug, squeeze together the clips and push the control unit from the facia.

13 Refitting is a reversal of removal.

Steering column switches

14 Remove the steering column shrouds as described in Chapter 11, Section 23.

15 Disconnect the wiring connector from the underside of the relevant switch (see illustration).

16 Using a screwdriver if necessary, release the plastic catch at the top of the relevant switch, then slide the switch upwards to remove it (see illustrations).

17 Refitting is a reversal of removal.

Exterior light switch

18 Using a plastic spatula or similar tool, carefully prise off the facia end panel on the driver's side to release the four internal clips (see illustration).

19 Insert a screwdriver through the slot in the side of the facia and push down the light switch upper retaining bar. Pull the switch out slightly at the top to stop the retaining bar re-engaging, then push up on the lower retaining bar (see illustration).

20 Withdraw the light switch from the facia, disconnect the wiring connector and remove the switch (see illustration).

21 Refitting is a reversal of removal.

Facia centre switch/vent panel

22 Using a plastic spatula or similar tool, carefully prise up and remove the multifunction display trim panel in the centre of the facia (see illustration).

23 Undo the 4 screws securing the upper centre switch/vent panel to the facia (see illustration).

24 Using a plastic spatula or similar tool, carefully prise free the top of the panel located above the heater/ventilation control panel. Disengage the two lower pegs and remove the panel (see illustration). Disconnect any wiring plugs as the panel is withdrawn.

25 Pull the upper centre switch/vent panel rearwards from the facia to release the

4.18 Using a plastic spatula or similar tool, carefully prise off the facia end panel

4.19 Insert a screwdriver through the slot in the side of the facia and push switch retaining bars down/up to release it

4.20 Withdraw the light switch from the facia and disconnect the wiring connector

4.22 Carefully prise up and remove the multifunction display trim panel

4.23 Undo the screws securing the upper centre switch/vent panel to the facia

4.24 Carefully prise the top of the panel rearwards

4.25a Pull the upper centre switch/vent panel away from the facia to release the lower clips ...

4.25b ... then disconnect the wiring connector and remove the panel

4.26 The switch pack can be removed from the panel by undoing the four screws

lower retaining clips, then disconnect the wiring connector and remove the panel **(see illustrations)**.

26 If required, the switch pack can be removed from the panel by undoing the four screws at the rear **(see illustration)**.

27 Refitting is a reversal of removal.

Heated rear window and windscreen switches

28 The switches are part of the heater control panel, which is removed as described in Chapter 3 Section 9.

Air conditioning and recirculation switches

29 The switches are part of the heater control panel, which is removed as described in Chapter 3 Section 9.

Electric window switches

30 Using a plastic spatula or similar instrument, carefully prise away the trim at the edge of the door pull handle **(see illustration)**.

31 Pull out the door pull handle recess trim piece **(see illustration)**.

32 Undo the 2 screws, lift the rear edge and remove the switch panel **(see illustrations)**. Disconnect the wiring plugs as they become accessible.

33 Refitting is a reversal of removal.

Electric mirror switch

34 The electric window switch is integral with the electric window switch panel. Removal of the panel is described previously in this Section.

35 Refitting is a reversal of removal.

Steering wheel switches

36 Remove the driver's airbag as described in Section 23.

37 Turn the steering wheel as necessary for access, then undo the three screws securing the switch panel to the steering wheel **(see illustration)**.

38 Disconnect the steering wheel switch wiring connectors, then undo the earth lead retaining screw. Lift the switch panel off the steering wheel.

39 Disconnect the wiring connector from the relevant switch module, then undo the three screws and remove the relevant module from the switch panel.

40 Refitting is a reversal of removal.

Handbrake-on warning switch

41 Remove the centre console as described in Chapter 11, Section 24.

42 Disconnect the wiring connector, then undo the retaining bolt and remove the switch from the side of the handbrake lever **(see illustration)**.

43 Refitting is a reversal of removal.

4.30 Prise inwards the handle trim

4.31 Pull out the handle recess trim piece

4.32a Undo the 2 screws...

4.32b ...lift the rear edge and remove the switch panel

4.37 Switch panel retaining screws

4.42 Disconnect the wiring connector, then undo the bolt and remove the handbrake-on warning switch

4.48 Reach through the aperture and rotate the switch 45° anti-clockwise

4.52a Depress the clip and disconnect the wiring plug

4.52b Lift the clip and slide the switch from place

Brake light switch

44 Refer to Chapter 9, Section 17.

Brake pedal position switch

45 Refer to Chapter 9, Section 17.

Clutch pedal position switch

All models

46 To improve access, remove the drivers side lower facia panel (below the steering column) as described in Chapter 11 Section 23.
47 Reach under the drivers side of the facia, undo the fasteners and remove the panel over the pedals (where fitted).
48 Reach through the aperture to the top of the pedal bracket, disconnect the wiring plug, rotate the switch 45° anti-clockwise and withdraw it from the bracket **(see illustration)**.
49 To refit, with the pedal in the 'at rest' position, insert the switch rotate it 45° clockwise and reconnect the wiring plug.
50 Where applicable, refit the panel above the pedals.

Models with 'Auto-Start-Stop'

51 Reach under the drivers side of the facia, and disconnect the switch wiring plug. The switch is located on the lower part of the clutch pedal bracket.
52 Gently bend the retaining clip, and slide the switch rearwards from the bracket **(see illustrations)**.
53 To refit, with the pedal in the 'at rest' position, slide the switch gently into the bracket, and reconnect the wiring plug.

Glovebox light switch

54 Open the glovebox, then squeeze together the tabs and release the switch from the facia **(see illustration)**. Disconnect the wiring plug as the switch is withdrawn.
55 Refitting is a reversal of removal.

5   Bulbs (exterior lights) – renewal

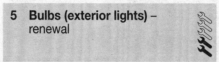

1 Whenever a bulb is renewed, note the following points:
a) *Make sure the switch is in the OFF position, for the bulb you are working on.*
b) *Remember that if the light has just been in use, the bulb may be extremely hot.*
c) *Always check the bulb contacts and holder, ensuring that there is clean metal-to-metal contact between the bulb and its live(s) and earth. Clean off any corrosion or dirt before fitting a new bulb.*
d) *Wherever bayonet-type bulbs are fitted, ensure that the live contact(s) bear firmly against the bulb contact.*
e) *Always ensure that the new bulb is of the correct rating, and that it is completely clean before fitting it; this applies particularly to headlight/foglight bulbs.*

Headlight

2 Remove the relevant headlight as described in Section 7.

4.54 Squeeze together the tabs and remove the switch

Dipped beam bulb

3 Remove the cover from the rear of the headlight unit **(see illustration)**.
4 Pull the wiring plug from the rear of the bulb, then pull the bulb from the reflector **(see illustration)**.
5 When handling the new bulb, use a tissue or clean cloth, to avoid touching the glass with the fingers; moisture and grease from the skin can cause blackening and rapid failure of this type of bulb. If the glass is accidentally touched, wipe it clean using methylated spirit.
6 Install the new bulb into the reflector, aligning the tabs on the bulb flange with the slots in the reflector socket **(see illustration)**.
7 Push the bulb firmly into the reflector.
8 Push the wiring plug firmly onto the bulb terminals.
9 Refit the headlight as described in Section 7.

5.3 Pull the rubber cover from the rear of the headlight unit

5.4 Pull the bulb from the reflector

5.6 Align the tab at the base of the flange with the reflector slot

5.10 Remove the cover from the rear of the headlight unit

5.12 Pull the wiring plug from the rear of the bulb

5.20 Pull the sidelight bulbholder from the light unit

5.21 Pull out the capless bulb from the holder

Main beam bulb

10 Remove the cover from the rear of the headlight unit **(see illustration)**.

11 Pull the side light bulbholder from place **(see illustration 5.20)**.

12 Rotate the main beam bulb anti-clockwise and withdraw it from the reflector **(see illustration)**.

13 When handling the new bulb, use a tissue or clean cloth, to avoid touching the glass with the fingers; moisture and grease from the skin can cause blackening and rapid failure of this type of bulb. If the glass is accidentally touched, wipe it clean using methylated spirit.

14 Insert the new bulb into the reflector, then rotate it clockwise to secure it.

15 Press the sidelight bulbholder back into place.

16 Refit the cover to the rear of the light unit.

5.24 Twist the direction indicator bulbholder anti-clockwise and withdraw it from the headlight

17 Refit the headlight as described in Section 7.

Front sidelight

18 Remove the headlight as described in Section 7.

19 Remove the cover from the rear of the headlight unit **(see illustration 5.10)**.

20 Pull the sidelight bulbholder from the light unit **(see illustration)**.

21 Pull out the capless bulb from the holder, and fit a new one firmly into place **(see illustration)**.

22 Refit the bulbholder and rear cover, then refit the headlight as described in Section 7.

Front direction indicator light

23 Remove the headlight as described in Section 7.

24 Twist the bulbholder anti-clockwise

and withdraw it from the headlight **(see illustration)**.

25 Depress and twist the bulb anti-clockwise to remove it **(see illustration)**.

26 Fit the new bulb, then twist the bulbholder clockwise into the back of the headlight.

27 Refit the headlight as described in Section 7.

Front foglight

28 Firmly apply the handbrake, then jack up the front of the vehicle and support it securely on axle stands (see *Jacking and vehicle support*). Remove the relevant front roadwheel.

29 Undo the fasteners and pull back the front section of the wheelarch liner **(see illustration)**.

30 Disconnect the wiring plug from the bulb/holder assembly.

31 Twist the bulb/holder assembly anti-clockwise to remove it from the back of the light unit **(see illustration)**.

32 Note that the bulb is integral with the holder, and must be renewed as a complete unit.

33 When handling the new bulb, use a tissue or clean cloth, to avoid touching the glass with the fingers; moisture and grease from the skin can cause blackening and rapid failure of this type of bulb. If the glass is accidentally touched, wipe it clean using methylated spirit.

34 Fit the new bulb, twisting it clockwise into the back of the light unit to secure, then reconnect the wiring plug.

35 Refit the wheelarch liner and secure it with the fasteners.

5.25 Depress and twist the bulb anti-clockwise to remove it

5.29 Undo the fasteners and pull back the wheelarch liner

5.31 Twist the foglight bulb anti-clockwise to remove it from the light unit

5.39a Pull the bulbholder from the side repeater

5.39b Release the clip and remove the side repeater

5.42 Remove the two rear light unit retaining screws

36 Refit the roadwheel, lightly tighten the retaining nuts, and lower the vehicle to the ground.
37 Tighten the roadwheel nuts to the specified torque.

Indicator side repeater light

38 Remove the mirror cover as described in Chapter 11 Section 18.
39 Pull the bulbholder from the side repeater **(see illustration)**. If improved access is required, release the clip and remove the side repeater assembly **(see illustration)**.
40 Pull out the capless bulb, and press a new one into place.
41 Refitting is a reversal of removal.

Rear lights

42 Open the tailgate, and remove the two cross-head screws in the tailgate aperture securing the light unit **(see illustration)**.
43 Carefully prise the rubber seal from the edge of the tailgate aperture in the vicinity of the light unit.
44 Pull away the loadspace trim for access to the rear of the light unit.
45 Reach in behind the light unit and unscrew the plastic wing nut securing the light unit to the body **(see illustration)**.
46 Withdraw the light unit from the rear wing, disconnect the wiring connector and remove the light unit **(see illustration)**.
47 Rotate the relevant bulbholder anti-clockwise and withdraw it from the light unit **(see illustration)**.
48 Gently press the bulb into the holder, turn it anti-clockwise and remove it **(see illustrations)**. The capless reversing light bulb

can be simply pulled from its bulbholder and a new bulb pressed in.
49 Fit the new bulb(s) into the holder(s) using a reversal of the removal technique.
50 Reconnect the wiring connector then offer the light unit back into place, engaging the two pegs on the rear with the holes in the vehicle body **(see illustration)**. Refit the wingnut and tighten it securely.
51 Fit the loadspace trim back into position then re-engage the rubber seal in the tailgate aperture.
52 Refit the two outer screws and tighten them securely.

Number plate light

53 To make access easier, open the tailgate and hold it approximately half-open.
54 Insert a small screwdriver into the slot on

5.45 Reach in behind the light unit and unscrew the plastic nut

5.46 Withdraw the light unit from the rear wing and disconnect the wiring connector

5.47 Rotate the bulbholder anti-clockwise and withdraw it

5.48a Remove the bayonet-fitting bulbs by pressing and turning them anti-clockwise

5.48b The capless reversing light bulb simply pulls from the bulbholder

5.50 Engage the locating pegs with the holes in vehicle body

5.54 Insert a small screwdriver into the slot and carefully prise the number plate light unit from the tailgate

5.55 Remove the bulbholder from the light unit

5.56 Pull out the capless bulb from the bulbholder

5.60 Remove the two plastic rivets securing the wheel arch liner to the bumper

5.61 Reach in under the wheel arch and remove the rear foglight bulbholder

6.2 Using a small screwdriver, depress the clip and remove the light unit

the side of the light unit and carefully prise the light unit from the tailgate **(see illustration)**.
55 Remove the bulbholder from the light unit **(see illustration)**.
56 Pull out the capless bulb, and press a new one into place **(see illustration)**.
57 Refitting is a reversal of removal.

High-level brake light

58 The high-level brake light bulbs are of the LED (light emitting diode) type and cannot be individually renewed. Remove the complete light unit as described in Section 7.

Rear foglight

59 On models with rear mudflaps, remove them by extracting the three retaining clips, then removing the two plastic rivets by prising up the centre section and withdrawing the rivet body.

60 On models without mudflaps, remove the two plastic rivets securing the wheel arch liner to the bumper by prising up the centre section and withdrawing the rivet body **(see illustration)**.
61 Reach in under the right-hand wheel arch and remove the rear foglight bulb holder from the light unit **(see illustration)**. The bulbholder is retained by plastic tabs around its periphery.
62 Remove the bulb by pressing and turning anti-clockwise.
63 Refitting is a reversal of removal.

6 Bulbs (interior lights) – renewal

General

1 Refer to Section 5, paragraph 1.

Interior and map reading lights

2 Insert a small screwdriver into the slot in the front face of the light unit. Depress the clip and carefully prise the light unit from its location **(see illustration)**.
3 Turn the relevant bulbholder anti-clockwise and remove it from the light unit **(see illustration)**.
4 Pull out the capless bulb, and press a new one into place.
5 Refitting is a reversal of removal.

Luggage compartment light

6 Carefully prise the light unit out from the trim panel **(see illustration)**.
7 Pull out the capless bulb from the bulbholder **(see illustration)**.
8 Fit the new bulb using a reversal of the removal procedure.

6.3 Rotate the bulbholders anti-clockwise

6.6 Carefully prise the light unit out from the trim panel

6.7 Pull out the capless bulb from the bulbholder

6.12 Pull the footwell illumination bulb from the holder

7.1a Undo the screw each side (A), then unscrew the centre pins (B)...

7.1b ... and withdrawing the rivet body

Instrument panel illumination

9 It is not possible to renew the instrument panel bulbs individually as they are of LED design and soldered to a printed circuit board. Where an LED is not functioning, the complete instrument panel must be renewed.

Switch illumination

10 The switches are illuminated by LEDs, and cannot be renewed separately. Refer to Section 4 and remove the relevant switch.

Heater control unit illumination

11 The control panel is illuminated by non-renewable LEDs. If defective, the control panel may need to be renewed.

Footwell illumination

12 Pull the capless bulb from the bulbholder under the facia **(see illustration)**.
13 Fit the new bulb using a reversal of the removal procedure.

7 Exterior light units – removal and refitting

Headlight

1 Open the bonnet and remove the screws and plastic rivets securing the front bumper upper edge by prising up the centre section and withdrawing the rivet body **(see illustrations)**.
2 Undo the headlight upper and lower retaining screws **(see illustrations)**.

7.2a Undo the headlight upper retaining screw ...

7.2b ... and lower retaining screw

3 Disconnect the wiring connector at the rear of the headlight **(see illustration)**.
4 Slide the headlight forwards slightly, and lift it upwards to release the lower mounting lug and remove the headlight from the car **(see illustration)**.
5 Refitting is a reversal of removal.

Front foglight

6 Firmly apply the handbrake, then jack up the front of the vehicle and support it securely on axle stands (see *Jacking and vehicle support*). Remove the relevant front roadwheel.
7 Undo the fasteners and pull back the front section of the wheelarch liner **(see illustration 5.29)**.
8 Disconnect the wiring plug, then undo the two screws and remove the light unit from the rear of the bumper.
9 Refitting is a reversal of removal.

Rear foglight

10 Remove the rear bumper as described in Chapter 11, Section 6.
11 Undo the two Torx screws and remove the light unit from the rear of the bumper **(see illustration)**.
12 Refitting is a reversal of removal.

Indicator side repeater light

13 The procedure is described as part of the bulb renewal procedure in Section 5.

Rear lights

14 The procedure is described as part of the bulb renewal procedure in Section 5.

Rear number plate light

15 The procedure is described as part of the bulb renewal procedure in Section 5.

7.3 Disconnect the wiring connector at the rear of the headlight

7.4 Pull the headlight forwards slightly, and lift it from the mounting lug

7.11 Undo the Torx screws and remove the fog light

7.16 Undo the two screws and withdraw the high-level brake light from the tailgate

7.17 Pull off the washer hose

7.18 Disconnect the wiring connector and remove the light unit

High-level brake light

16 Undo the two screws securing the light unit to the tailgate and withdraw the unit from its location **(see illustration)**.

17 Pull off the washer hose, and tape the end of the hose up to the tailgate, end upwards, to reduce fluid spillage **(see illustration)**.

18 Disconnect the wiring connector and remove the light unit from the car **(see illustration)**.

19 Refitting is a reversal of removal.

8 Headlight adjuster components – removal and refitting

Adjuster switch

1 Refer to Section 4.

Adjuster motor

2 The motor is integral with the headlight, and is not available separately. The headlight is removed as described in Section 7.

9 Headlight beam alignment – general information

1 All models are equipped with an electrical vertical beam adjuster unit – this can be used to adjust the headlight beam, to compensate for the relevant load which the car is carrying. An adjuster switch is provided on the facia.

Refer to the car's handbook for further information.

2 Accurate adjustment of the headlight beam is only possible using optical beam-setting equipment, and this work should therefore be carried out by a Ford dealer or suitably-equipped workshop.

3 For reference, the headlights can be finely adjusted by rotating the adjuster screws fitted to the top of each light unit.

10 Instrument panel – removal and refitting

Note: *If a new instrument panel is to be fitted, the configuration information stored within the unit must be uploaded to Ford diagnostic equipment prior to removal, and downloaded to the new unit once installed. Entrust this*

task to a Ford dealer or suitably-equipped specialist.

Removal

1 Disconnect the battery negative lead as described in Chapter 5A Section 4.

2 Fully extend the steering column and move the steering wheel to its lowest position.

3 Unclip and remove the steering column upper shroud **(see illustrations)**.

4 Remove the circular trim button from the upper centre of the instrument panel. The best way to do this is to stick a small piece of adhesive to the trim button and pull on the tape to remove the button **(see illustration)**.

5 With the trim button removed, undo the panel retaining Torx screw now exposed **(see illustration)**.

6 Remove the two Torx screws at the base of the instrument panel, then withdraw it from the facia **(see illustration)**.

10.3a Unclip the rear edge…

10.3b …and disengage the upper shroud from the facia

10.4 Use a small piece of adhesive tape to pull off the circular trim button

10.5 Undo the instrument panel upper retaining screw

10.6 Undo the two screws at the base of the instrument panel, then withdraw it from the facia

10.7 Release the hinged locking catch and disconnect the wiring plugs

11.2 Undo the two screws securing the unit to the top of the facia

12.2 The BCM is located behind the facia on the passenger's side

7 Release the hinged locking catch on the wiring plugs at the rear, disconnect the plugs, and remove the instrument panel **(see illustration)**.

Refitting

8 Refitting is a reversal of removal.

11 Front Control/Display Interface Module (FCDIM) – removal and refitting

Removal

1 Using a plastic spatula or similar tool, carefully prise up and remove the FCDIM trim panel in the centre of the facia **(see illustration 4.22)**.
2 Undo the two screws securing the FCDIM to the top of the facia **(see illustration)**.
3 Withdraw the unit from the facia, disconnect the wiring connector and remove the unit from the car.

Refitting

4 Refitting is a reversal of removal.

12 Body Control Module (BCM) – removal and refitting

Note: If a new module is to be fitted, the configuration information stored within the unit must be uploaded to Ford diagnostic

equipment prior to removal, and downloaded to the new unit once installed. Entrust this task to a Ford dealer or suitably-equipped specialist.

Removal

1 Disconnect the battery negative lead as described in Chapter 5A Section 4.
2 The BCM is located behind the facia on the passenger's side **(see illustration)**. To gain access, remove the passenger's lower facia trim panel as described in Chapter 11, Section 23.
3 Lift up the locking bars, where necessary, and disconnect the wiring harness connectors from the front of the BCM.
4 Undo the two nuts securing the BCM mounting bracket to the floor, then remove the module and mounting bracket from the car.
5 Release the two tabs on the rear of the unit and separate the BCM from the mounting bracket.

Refitting

6 Refitting is a reversal of removal.

13 Horns – removal and refitting

Removal

1 The horns is located under the front bumper on the right-hand side.

2 Remove the front bumper as described in Chapter 11, Section 6.
3 Disconnect the wiring plug from the horns, and unclip the wiring loom.
4 Unscrew the retaining bolt, and remove the horns along with their mounting bracket **(see illustration)**.

Refitting

5 Refitting is a reversal of removal.

14 Wiper arm – removal and refitting

Removal

1 Operate the wiper motor, then switch it off so that the wiper arm returns to the park position.
2 Before removing an arm, mark its parked position on the glass with a strip of adhesive tape **(see illustration)**.
3 Prise up the wiper arm spindle nut cover, then slacken and remove the spindle nut **(see illustration)**. Recover the washer.
4 Lift the blade off the glass, and pull the wiper arm off its spindle. Note that on some models, the wiper arms may be very tight on the spindle splines – it should be possible to lever the arm off the spindle, using a flat-bladed screwdriver (take care not to damage the windscreen cowl panel). In extreme cases, it

13.4 Unscrew the bolt and remove the horns along with the mounting bracket

14.2 Mark the parked position of the blade with tape

14.3 Prise up the wiper arm spindle nut cover, then remove the spindle nut

may even be necessary to use a small puller to free the arm (see illustration).

Refitting

5 Ensure that the wiper arm and spindle splines are clean and dry, then refit the arm to the spindle. Align the wiper blade with the tape fitted on removal.

6 Refit the spindle nut, tightening it securely, and clip the nut cover back into position.

15 Windscreen wiper motor and linkage – removal and refitting

Removal

1 Remove the windscreen cowl panel and bulkhead closure panel as described in Chapter 11, Section 20.

2 Undo the 3 bolts securing the wiper motor and linkage assembly to the scuttle (see illustration).

3 Withdraw the motor and linkage assembly from its location, disengage the locating grommet as the assembly is withdrawn (see illustration).

4 Extract the two wiring harness support clips from the linkage frame, then disconnect the wiring connector from the motor. Remove the assembly from the car.

5 Note the fitted position of the wiper motor arm (typically, it will be horizontally aligned, along the axis of the linkage frame). Undo the motor arm retaining nut and lift off the arm, then unscrew the three bolts and remove the motor from the frame (see illustration).

Refitting

6 Refitting is a reversal of removal, bearing in mind the following points:

a) Ensure that the motor is in the 'parked' position before refitting.

b) Set the motor arm to the position noted prior to removal, then refit the arm and tighten the retaining nut securely.

c) Refit the bulkhead closure panel and windscreen cowl panel as described in Chapter, Section.

14.4 Using a small puller to free the wiper arm from the spindle

15.3 The grommet on the linkage aligns with the slot in the body bracket

16 Tailgate wiper motor – removal and refitting

Removal

1 Remove the tailgate trim panel as described in Chapter 11, Section 23.

2 Ensure the wiper arm is in the 'at-rest' position, then remove it (see illustrations).

3 Disconnect the wiper motor wiring plug.

4 Remove the 3 motor mounting bolts, recover the washers, and withdraw the motor from the tailgate (see illustration).

Refitting

5 Refitting is a reversal of removal. Ensure that the wiper motor spindle grommet stays

15.2 Undo the 3 bolts securing the wiper motor and linkage assembly to the scuttle

15.5 Unscrew the motor arm retaining nut and the motor retaining bolts

in place in the tailgate as the spindle is fitted back through.

17 Windscreen/tailgate washer system components – removal and refitting

Washer fluid reservoir

Removal

1 The windscreen washer fluid reservoir is located behind the front bumper on the left-hand side.

2 Remove the front bumper as described in Chapter 11, Section 6.

3 Disconnect the wiring plug and the washer hoses from the washer pump (see

16.2a Unscrew the retaining nut ...

16.2b ... and remove the wiper arm

16.4 Remove 3 motor mounting bolts

17.3 Disconnect the wiring plug (A) and the washer hoses (B) from the washer pump

17.4 Washer reservoir retaining bolts

17.13 Prise out the plastic studs and remove the sound deadening pad from inside the bonnet

17.14 Pull the T-piece hose connector off the end of the washer jet

17.15a Depress the tab at the top of the jet body…

17.15b … then remove the jet from the outside of the bonnet

illustration). Anticipate some spillage of washer fluid (have a suitable container ready).
4 Undo the two reservoir retaining bolts, disengage the locating peg and remove the reservoir from the car (see illustration).

Refitting

5 Refitting is a reversal of removal. Make sure the washer hoses are securely reconnected to their original positions.

Washer fluid pump
Removal

6 If possible, siphon the fluid from the reservoir into a suitable container using a long tube inserted through the filler neck.
7 Slacken the left-hand front wheel retaining nuts, raise the front of the vehicle and support it securely on axle stands (see *Jacking and vehicle support*). Remove the roadwheel.
8 Undo the fasteners and pull back the front section of the wheelarch liner.
9 Disconnect the wiring plug, prise the pump from the reservoir, and recover the rubber sealing grommet (see illustration 17.2). If all the fluid was not removed, position a container beneath the reservoir.

Refitting

10 Examine the rubber sealing grommet, and renew if necessary.
11 Refitting is a reversal of removal, but take care not to push the grommet into the reservoir when refitting the pump. Make sure that the pump is securely fitted in its sealing grommet, and make sure that the fluid hose(s) are securely reconnected.

Windscreen washer jet
Removal

12 Open the bonnet, and support it on its stay.
13 Prise out the plastic studs and remove the sound deadening pad from inside the bonnet (see illustration).
14 Pull the T-piece hose connector off the end of the washer jet (see illustration).
15 Depress the tab at the top of the jet body, then remove the jet from the outside of the bonnet (see illustrations).

Refitting

16 Refitting is a reversal of removal.

Tailgate washer jet

17 The washer jet is an integral part of the high-level brake light and cannot be individually removed. Removal of the high-level brake light is described in Section 7.

18.2 Slide the audio unit rearwards

18 Facia-mounted audio unit – removal and refitting

Note: *If a Ford 'Keycode' unit is fitted, and the battery is disconnected, the unit may not function again on reconnection until the correct security code is entered,*

Removal

1 Remove the facia upper centre switch/vent panel as described in Section 4.
2 Slide the audio unit from its location in the facia for access to the rear wiring and aerial (see illustration).
3 Disconnect the wiring connectors and aerial lead then remove the unit from the car (see illustration).

18.3 Disconnect the wiring connectors and aerial lead at the rear

Refitting

4 Refitting is a reversal of removal.

---

19 Loudspeakers – removal and refitting

Removal

1 Remove the relevant door inner trim panel as described in Chapter 11 Section 11, or rear quarter panel as described in Chapter 11 Section 23 (as applicable).
2 Unscrew the three main loudspeaker securing screws, then withdraw the loudspeaker and disconnect the wiring plug (see illustration).

Refitting

3 Refitting is a reversal of removal.

---

20 Radio aerial – removal and refitting

Removal

1 If only the aerial mast is to be removed, this can be unscrewed from the aerial base. To remove the base, proceed as follows.
2 Remove the interior light as described in Section 6.
3 Working through the interior light aperture, unscrew the bolt, and disconnect the aerial cable (see illustration). Remove the aerial from the roof, and recover the sealing grommet.

Refitting

4 Refitting is a reversal of removal.

---

21 Anti-theft alarm system and engine immobiliser – general information

---

1 Certain models are equipped with an anti-theft alarm system, in addition to the engine immobiliser fitted to all models. Various types of system may be fitted, depending on specification and market.
2 The anti-theft alarm system is automatically activated by the central locking system

19.2 Loudspeaker securing screws

(manually, or via the remote control, where applicable). The engine immobiliser system is operated by a coded unit in the ignition key – the engine can only be started using one of the ignition keys originally supplied with the car when new.
3 The alarm system uses the courtesy light switches built into the door lock assemblies.
4 Any faults with the system should be referred to a Ford dealer.

Immobiliser system

5 An engine immobiliser system is fitted as standard to all models, and the system is operated automatically every time the ignition key is inserted/removed.
6 The immobiliser system ensures that the car can only be started using the original Ford ignition key. The key contains an electronic chip (transponder) which is programmed with a code. When the key is inserted into the ignition switch, it uses the current present in the sensor coil (which is fitted to the switch housing) to send a signal to the Body Control Module (BCM). The BCM checks this code every time the ignition is switched on. If the key code does not match the BCM code, the BCM will disable the starter circuit to prevent the engine being started.
7 If the ignition key is lost, a new one can be obtained from a Ford dealer. They have access to the correct key code for the immobiliser system of your car, and will be able to supply a new coded key.
8 If you have any spare keys cut, if they are not coded correctly, they will only open the doors, etc, and will not be capable of starting the engine. For this reason, it may be best to have any spare keys supplied by your Ford dealer, who will also be able to advise you on coding the keys. The key coding procedure for new keys is given in the car's handbook.

---

22 Airbag system – general information, precautions and system de-activation

---

General information

1 Driver's and front seat passenger's airbags are fitted as standard equipment on all models. The driver's airbag is fitted to the steering

20.3 Unscrew the aerial base retaining bolt and disconnect the aerial cable

wheel centre pad, while the passenger's unit is fitted to the top of the facia.
2 Models equipped with higher specification equipment packages also have side airbags, which fire from modules built into the front seats, side curtain airbags, which are deployed from modules in the headlining and a driver's knee airbag deployed from a module under the facia.
3 The system is armed only when the ignition is switched on, however, a reserve power source maintains a power supply to the system in the event of a break in the main electrical supply. The system is activated by a 'g' sensor (deceleration sensor), incorporated in the Restraints Control Module (RCM), a front impact sensor located on the bonnet slam panel, and side impact sensors located in the 'B' pillar each side. Note that the RCM also controls the front seat belt tensioners, fitted to all models.
4 The airbags are inflated by gas generators, which force the bags out from their locations. Although these are safety items, their deployment is violently rapid, and this may cause injury if they are triggered unintentionally.

Precautions

 Warning: The following precautions must be observed when working on vehicles equipped with an airbag system, to prevent the possibility of personal injury.

General precautions

5 The following precautions must be observed when carrying out work on a vehicle equipped with an airbag:
a) *Do not disconnect the battery with the engine running.*
b) *Before carrying out any work in the vicinity of the airbag, removal of any of the airbag components, or any welding work on the car, de-activate the system as described in the following sub-Section.*
c) *Do not attempt to test any of the airbag system circuits using test meters or any other test equipment.*
d) *If the airbag warning light comes on, or any fault in the system is suspected, consult a Ford dealer without delay. Do not attempt to carry out fault diagnosis, or any dismantling of the components.*

Precautions when handling an airbag

a) *Transport the airbag by itself, bag upward.*
b) *Do not put your arms around the airbag.*
c) *Carry the airbag close to the body.*
d) *Do not drop the airbag or expose it to impacts.*
e) *Do not attempt to dismantle the airbag unit.*
f) *Do not connect any form of electrical equipment to any part of the airbag circuit.*

Precautions when storing an airbag

a) *Store the unit in a cupboard with the airbag upward.*

b) *Do not expose the airbag to temperatures above 80ºC.*
c) *Do not expose the airbag to flames.*
d) *Do not attempt to dispose of the airbag – consult a Ford dealer.*
e) *Never refit an airbag which is known to be faulty or damaged.*

De-activation of airbag system

6 The system must be de-activated as follows, before carrying out any work on the airbag components or surrounding area.
a) *Switch off the ignition.*
b) *Remove the ignition key.*
c) *Switch off all electrical equipment.*
d) *Disconnect the battery negative lead as described in Chapter 5A Section 4.*
e) *Insulate the battery negative terminal and the end of the battery negative lead to prevent any possibility of contact.*
f) *Wait for at least three minutes before carrying out any further work.*

23 Airbag system components – removal and refitting

⚠ *Warning: Refer to the precautions given in Section 22 before attempting to carry out work on the airbag components.*

Driver's airbag unit

Removal

1 De-activate the airbag system as described in Section 22. The airbag unit is an integral part of the steering wheel centre pad.
2 Locate the two airbag retaining wire spring access points on the back of the steering wheel. These will be visible as a slight mark or indentation in the steering wheel hub **(see illustration)**.
3 Using a sharp knife, make a slit at the access point on each side **(see illustration)**.
4 Using a 3 mm diameter Torx screwdriver or rod inserted through the hole now created, engage the end of the screwdriver/rod with the airbag retaining wire spring. Push up on the wire spring while at the same time pulling the airbag module to release it from the steering

23.2 Airbag retaining wire spring access point on the back of the steering wheel

23.4a Insert a 3 mm rod/screwdriver/punch through the hole…

wheel **(see illustrations)**. Once the airbag is released on one side, repeat the procedure on the other side.
5 Once the airbag retaining wire springs have been released, withdraw the airbag from the steering wheel and disconnect the main wiring plug and the two earth leads **(see illustrations)**. Remove the airbag and store it in a safe place, with reference to the precautions in Section 22.

Refitting

6 Refitting is a reversal of removal, noting the following points:
a) *The battery must still be disconnected when reconnecting the airbag wiring.*
b) *Ensure that the airbag wiring plug is securely reconnected.*
c) *The airbag must be firmly pressed into place to secure the retaining wire spring.*

23.3 Using a sharp knife, make a slit at the access point on each side

23.4b …compress the spring to release the airbag catch

Passenger's airbag unit

Removal

7 De-activate the airbag system as described in Section 22.
8 Remove the glovebox as described in Chapter 11, Section 23.
9 Disconnect the airbag wiring connector, then undo the two nuts securing the airbag support bracket to the facia crossmember **(see illustration)**.
10 Undo the remaining 6 retaining nuts securing the airbag to the facia and remove the unit from below.

Refitting

11 Refitting is a reversal of removal, bearing in mind the following points:
a) *The battery must still be disconnected when reconnecting the airbag wiring.*

23.5a Squeeze together the tabs, disconnect the airbag wiring plug…

23.5b … and the two earth leads

23.9 Passenger's airbag wiring connector (A) and airbag support bracket retaining nuts (B)

23.17 Fold over the locking bars and disconnect the wiring plugs

23.24a Release the tabs on the rear face of the clockspring...

23.24b ...and the tab on the front

23.28 Align the arrow mark with the raised V on the outer cover

b) Make sure that the wiring connector is securely reconnected.
c) Tighten the mounting nuts to the specified torque.

Driver's knee airbag unit

12 De-activate the airbag system as described in Section 22.
13 Remove the driver's lower facia trim panel as described in Chapter 11, Section 23. The knee airbag is an integral part of the lower facia trim panel and cannot be individually removed.

Restraints Control Module (RCM)

Removal

14 De-activate the airbag system as described in Section 22.
15 Remove the centre console as described in Chapter 11, Section 24.
16 Free the handbrake warning switch wiring from the clips on the plastic cover over the RCM.

17 Lift off the cover (where fitted) over the RCM and disconnect the wiring plugs **(see illustration)**.
18 Undo the 3 retaining nuts and remove the RCM from the car.

Refitting

19 Refitting is a reversal of removal. Tighten the RCM retaining nuts to the specified torque.

Airbag clockspring (rotary connector)

Removal

20 De-activate the airbag system as described in Section 22.
21 Remove the steering wheel as described in Chapter 10 Section 14.
22 Remove the steering column shrouds as described in Chapter 11, Section 23.
23 Disconnect the wiring connector from the base of the clockspring.
24 Using a small screwdriver, lift the three

locating tabs and withdraw the unit from the steering column **(see illustrations)**.

Refitting

25 Refitting is a reversal of removal.
26 Before refitting the steering column shrouds, the clockspring unit should be centralised (unless it is known absolutely that the steering wheel was centralised before removal, and that the clockspring has not been turned during or since its removal).
27 The procedure for centralising should be written on the clockspring itself. If this procedure conflicts significantly with what appears below, consult a Ford dealer for the latest information.
28 First, turn the clockspring anti-clockwise gently, until resistance is felt. Now turn the clockspring about two and a half turns clockwise, until the arrow marking on the front face aligns with the raised V marking on the clockspring's outer cover **(see illustration)**.
29 Refit the steering column shrouds and

23.34 Front crash sensor

23.38 Side crash sensor retaining nut

23.42 Undo the Torx bolts and remove the sensor

steering wheel as described in Chapters 11 and 10.

Side airbags

30 The side airbags are located internally within the front seat backrest, and no attempt should be made to remove them.

Any suspected problems with the side airbag system should be referred to a Ford dealer.

Side curtain airbags

31 The modules for the side curtain airbags are located at the sides of the headlining. It is strongly recommended that any work which requires even just the removal of the headlining, never mind any work on the side curtain airbags, be referred to a Ford dealer.

Front crash sensor

32 The front crash sensor is located behind the bonnet lock assembly.
33 De-activate the airbag system as described in Section 22.
34 Disconnect the wiring plug, undo the retaining nut and remove the sensor from place (see illustration).
35 Refitting is a reversal of removal. Tighten the sensor retaining nut to the specified torque.

Side crash sensors

36 De-activate the airbag system as described in Section 22.

37 Remove the front seat belt inertia reel assembly from B-pillar on the relevant side, as described in Chapter 11 Section 22. Note that there is no need to release the seat belt upper or lower anchorage bolts. Move the inertia reel assembly to one side.
38 Disconnect the wiring plug, undo the retaining nut and remove the sensor (see illustration).
39 Refitting is a reversal of removal. Tighten the sensor retaining nut to the specified torque.

Front door crash sensors

40 De-activate the airbag system as described in Section 22.
41 Remove the door inner trim panel as described in Chapter 11 Section 11.
42 Disconnect the wiring plug, then undo the 2 Torx bolts and remove the sensor (see illustration).
43 Refitting is a reversal of removal.

BATTERY JUNCTION BOX (BJB)

FUSE/RELAY	VALUE	DESCRIPTION	OEM NAME
F1	40 A	Anti-lock Brake system (ABS) module (30A also used)	F1
F2	60 A	High speed cooling fan relay (BJB)	F2
F3	40 A	Cooling fan relay (BJB) (30A also used)	F3
F4	30 A	Blower motor relay (BJB)	F4
F5	60 A	Central Junction Box (CJB), fuses F19, F21 – F24, F28 – F30, F34 – F36, F38	F5
F6	30 A	Body Control Module (BCM) – Locks	F6
F7	60 A	Ignition Relay	F7
F8	50 A	Transmission Control Module (TCM) (available for DPS6)	F8
	60 A	Glow Plug Relay (available for Diesel engines)	
F9	60 A	Heated windshield relay	F9
F10	-	Not used	F10
F11	30 A	Start inhibit relay	F11
F12	10 A	Headlamp assembly LH	F12
F13	10 A	Headlamp assembly RH	F13
F14	10 A	Coolant pump (available for 1.0L GTDI)	F14
F15	10 A	Coil on plugs (available for 1.0L, 1.6L GTDI engines)	F15
F16	15 A	Powertrain Control Module (PCM), Cooling fan relays, Evaporative emission canister purge valve, Fuel injectors and Variable camshaft timing solenoids (available for 1.0L, 1.6L engines) and Fuel pump relay (BJB), Exhaust Gas Recirculation (EGR) cooler bypass valve (available for 1.0L engine)	F16
		Powertrain Control Module (PCM), Fuel metering valve, Mass Air Flow and Temperature (MAFT) sensor, Cooling fan relays (BJB) (15A also used) (available for Diesel engines)	
F17	20 A	Powertrain Control Module (PCM) (15A also used) (available for Diesel engines)	F17
	15 A	Heated oxygen sensors (available for Petrol engines)	
F18	-	Not used	F18

Fuses and relays

F19	7.5 A	Air conditioning (A/C) compressor control solenoid (available for 1.0L engines)	F19
F20	-	Not used	F20
F21	7.5 A	High speed cooling fan relay (available for 1.6L GTDI, DV6 ECO), Fuel pump relay (available for 1.6L GTDI)	F21
F22	20 A	Fuel pump relay	F22
F23	15 A	Front fog lamp relay	F23
F24	15 A	Body Control Module (BCM) – Turn signals	F24
F25	15 A	Body Control Module (BCM) – Exterior lighting LH	F25
F26	15 A	Body Control Module (BCM) – Exterior lighting RH	F26
F27	7.5 A	Powertrain Control Module (PCM), Powertrain Control Module (PCM) relay or Powertrain Control Module (PCM) relay	F27
F28	20 A	Anti-lock Brake system (ABS) module – ESP	F28
F29	10 A	Air conditioning (A/C) clutch relay (BJB) – A/C	F29
F30	-	Not used	F30
F31	15 A	Intercooler fan relay (available for 1.0L GTDI)	F31
F32	20 A	Body Control Module (BCM) – Battery saver/Horn	F32
F33	20 A	Body Control Module (BCM) – Heated backlite	F33
F34	20 A	Fuel pump relay (BJB)	F34
F35	15 A	Anti-theft alarm horn with integral battery	F35
F36	7.5 A	Transmission Control Module (TCM) (available for DPS6)	F36
F37	25 A	Driver Door Module (DDM)	F37
F38	25 A	Passenger Door Module (PDM)	F38
F39	25 A	Rear Door Module (RDM) LH	F39
F40	25 A	Rear Door Module (RDM) RH	F40
R1	-	High speed cooling fan relay or Cooling fan relay	-
R2	-	Heated windshield relay	-
R3	-	Powertrain Control Module (PCM) relay	-
R4	-	Headlamp high beam relay	-
R5	-	Not used	-
R6	-	Not used	-
R7	-	Cooling fan relay (available for 1.25L engine without A/C or twin speed fan)	-
R8	-	Start inhibit relay	-
R9	-	Air conditioning clutch relay (BJB)	-
R10	-	Front fog lamp relay	-
R11	-	Fuel pump relay (available for Petrol engines)	-
	-	Fuel heater relay (available for Diesel engines)	
R12	-	Reversing lamp relay (available for DPS6)	-
R13	-	Blower motor relay	-

Fuses and relays (continued)

CENTRAL JUNCTION BOX (CJB)

FUSE/RELAY	VALUE	DESCRIPTION	OEM NAME
F1	7.5 A	Electric booster heater relays, Air conditioning (A/C) clutch relay, Front interior lamp, Rain sensor module, Auto-dimming interior mirror, Heated windshield relay, Auxiliary power socket relay, Auxiliary relay box – electric booster heater	F1
F2	10 A	Stoplamp switch, Active city stop relay	F2
F3	7.5 A	Reversing lamp switch, Reversing lamp relay (available for DPS6)	F3
F4	7.5 A	Headlamp switch, Headlamp assemblies	F4
F5	20 A	Body Control Module (BCM)	F5
F6	15 A	Body Control Module (BCM)	F6
F7	15 A	Windshield wiper, Washer switch	F7
F8	-	Not used	F8
F9	15 A	Passenger Seat	F9
F10	15 A	Driver Seat	F10
F11	-	Not used	F11

Fuses and relays (continued)

F12	10 A	Restraints Control Module (RCM)	F12
F13	10 A	Body Control Module (BCM), HVAC control module – manual air conditioning, Instrument Panel Cluster (IPC), Power Steering Control Module (PSCM), Blower motor relay and Passive Anti-Theft System (PATS) transceiver, Anti-lock Brake System (ABS) module (without Keyless)	F13
F14	7.5 A	Accelerator Pedal Position (APP) sensor, Powertrain Control Module (PCM), Front fog lamp relay and Transmission Control Module (TCM) (available for DPS6) and Fuel pump relay (available for Petrol engines except 1.0L, 1.6LGTDI) and Fuel heater relay (available for Diesel engines)	F14
F15	7.5 A	Instrument Panel Cluster (IPC), Audio front Control Module (ACM)	F15
F16	-	Not used	F16
F17	-	Not used	F17
F18	-	Not used	F18
F19	15 A	Data Link Connector (DLC)	F19
F20	-	Not used	F20
F21	15 A	Audio front Control Module (ACM)	F21
F22	7.5 A	Instrument Panel Cluster (ICP)	F22
F23	7.5 A	Front Control/Display Interface Module (FCDIM), Driver door window switch and Radio Frequency (RF) Receiver (with Keyless) and Heating Ventilation and Air Conditioning (HVAC) Control Module (available for engines with manual air conditioning) and Electronic Automatic Temperature Control (EATC) Module (available for engines with automatic air conditioning)	F23
F24	10 A	SYNC Module (APIM), Global Positioning System Module (GPSM)	F24
F25	-	Not used	F25
F26	30 A	Heated windshield element LH	F26
F27	30 A	Heated windshield element RH	F27
F28	30 A	Low Voltage Direct Current/Direct Current (DC/DC) Converter (available for Auto-Start-Stop) and Fuses F19, F21, F23, F24 (CJB) (available for engines without Auto-Start-Stop)	F28
F29	20 A	Battery saver relay (CJB) – auxiliary power point	F29
F30	20 A	Auxiliary power socket relay (CJB)	F30
F31	-	Not used	F31
F32	-	Not used	F32
F33	-	Not used	F33
F34	20 A	Remote Function Actuator (RFA) module – Keyless entry	F34
F35	20 A	Remote Function Actuator (RFA) module – Keyless entry	F35
F36	15 A	Ignition Switch (available for engines without Keyless) and Smart keyless entry relays (CJB) (available for engines with Keyless)	F36
F37	-	Not used	F37
F38	7.5 A	Intrusion sensor	F38
F39	-	Not used	F39
F40	-	Not used	F40
F41	-	Not used	F41
F42	7.5 A	Rear Parking Aid Camera	F42
F43	10 A	Active City Stop Module	F43
F44	7.5 A	Passenger Airbag Deactivation (PAD) indicator	F44
F45	-	Not used	F45
F46	-	Not used	F46
F47	-	Not used	F47
F48	-	Not used	F48
F49	-	Not used	F49

Fuses and relays (continued)

R1	-	Auxiliary power socket relay	-
R2	-	Double Lock Relay	-
R3	-	Active City Stop Relay	-
R4	-	Battery Saver Relay	-
R5	-	Smart Keyless Entry Ignition Relay (with Keyless)	-
R6	-	Smart Keyless Entry Accessory Relay (with Keyless)	-
R7	-	Ignition Relay	-
R8	-	Not used	-
R9	-	Not used	-
R10	-	Not used	-
R11	-	Not used	-
R12	-	Not used	-

HIGH CURRENT BATTERY JUNCTION BOX (BJB)

FUSE/RELAY	VALUE	DESCRIPTION	OEM NAME
F1	450 A	Starter motor, Generator	MEGA 1
F2	60 A	Power Steering Control Module (PSCM)	MEGA 2
F3	200 A	BATTERY JUNCTION BOX (BJB)	MEGA 3
F4	70 A	Electric Booster heater relays	MEGA 4
F5	-	Not used	MEGA 5
F6	3 A	Battery monitoring sensor (SRC)	F1

Fuses and relays (continued)

AUXILIARY RELAY BOX

FUSE/RELAY	VALUE	DESCRIPTION	OEM NAME
R1	-	Fuel pump relay	-
R2	-	Electric Booster heater relay 2	-
R3	-	Glow Plug Relay	-
R4	-	Electric Booster heater relay 1	-

Fuses and relays (continued)

*1 Except 1.0L early production
*2 For 1.0L early production
*3 Except 1.6L GTDI
*4 LHD
*5 1.6L TIVCT
*6 1.25L
*7 1.0L
*8 Diesel Stage 5
*9 Diesel Stage 6
*10 Except 1.6L TIVCT
*11 Auto-Start-Stop
*12 1.0L GTDI
*13 Keyless
*14 RHD
*15 Early production
*16 Late production

Starting and charging - with Keyless entry

Starting and Charging – without Keyless entry

Heating and Automatic air conditioning

Heating and Manual air conditioning

Seat heating

*1 LHD
*2 RHD

Power windows

*1 LHD
*2 RHD
*3 3-Door
*4 5-Door
*5 5-Door Double-Locking

Keyless entry

Central locking

Exterior lights - part 1

*1 LHD
*2 RHD
*3 With Active City Stop
*4 Without Active City Stop
*5 For 1.6L
*6 For Diesel Stage 5
*7 For Diesel Stage 6
*8 For 1.25L
*9 For 1.0L
*10 For 1.6L TiVCT
*11 Equipment code: IB5
*12 Equipment code: DPS6

Exterior lights - part 2

Washers and wipers

*1 RHD
*2 LHD
*3 Equipment code: DPS6
*4 Equipment code: IB5
*5 For 1.6L TDCI
*6 Except 1.6L TDCI

Interior lights

*1 LHD
*2 RHD
*3 With Double Locking
*4 Without Double Locking
*5 Early production
*6 Late production

Infotainment - part 1

*1 LHD
*2 RHD
*3 Without SYNC
*4 With SYNC
*5 5-Door
*6 3-Door
*7 Vehicle emergency
*8 Early production
*9 Late production
*10 With 5" display
*11 Without 5" display

Infotainment – part 2

Fuel pump/sender - diesel

Fuel pump/sender - petrol

*1 1.0L GTDI
*2 1.6L TiVCT
*3 1.25L
*4 Equipment code: IB5
*5 Equipment code: DPS6
*6 Late production
*7 LHD
*8 RHD

Notes

Note: *All figures are approximate and may vary according to model. Refer to manufacturer's data for exact figures.*

Dimensions

Overall length	3982 mm
Overall width (including door mirrors)	1978 mm
Overall height (unladen)	1495 mm
Wheelbase	2489 mm
Front track	1492 mm
Rear track	1481 mm

Weights

Kerb weight	Refer to information contained on the vehicle identification plate
Gross vehicle weight	Refer to information contained on the vehicle identification plate
Maximum roof load (including weight of rack)	50 kg

Fuel economy

Although depreciation is still the biggest part of the cost of motoring for most car owners, the cost of fuel is more immediately noticeable. These pages give some tips on how to get the best fuel economy.

Working it out

Manufacturer's figures

Car manufacturers are required by law to provide fuel consumption information on all new vehicles sold. These 'official' figures are obtained by simulating various driving conditions on a rolling road or a test track. Real life conditions are different, so the fuel consumption actually achieved may not bear much resemblance to the quoted figures.

How to calculate it

Many cars now have trip computers which will

display fuel consumption, both instantaneous and average. Refer to the owner's handbook for details of how to use these.

To calculate consumption yourself (and maybe to check that the trip computer is accurate), proceed as follows.

1. Fill up with fuel and note the mileage, or zero the trip recorder.
2. Drive as usual until you need to fill up again.
3. Note the amount of fuel required to refill the tank, and the mileage covered since the previous fill-up.
4. Divide the mileage by the amount of fuel used to obtain the consumption figure.

For example:

   Mileage at first fill-up (a) = 27,903
   Mileage at second fill-up (b) = 28,346
   Mileage covered (b - a) = 443
   Fuel required at second fill-up = 48.6 litres

The half-completed changeover to metric units in the UK means that we buy our fuel in litres, measure distances in miles and talk about fuel consumption in miles per gallon. There are two ways round this: the first is to convert the litres to gallons before doing the calculation (by dividing by 4.546, or see Table 1). So in the example:

   48.6 litres ÷ 4.546 = 10.69 gallons
   443 miles ÷ 10.69 gallons = 41.4 mpg

The second way is to calculate the consumption in miles per litre, then multiply that figure by 4.546 (or see Table 2).

So in the example, fuel consumption is:

   443 miles ÷ 48.6 litres = 9.1 mpl
   9.1 mpl x 4.546 = 41.4 mpg

The rest of Europe expresses fuel consumption in litres of fuel required to travel 100 km (l/100 km). For interest, the conversions are given in Table 3. In practice it doesn't matter what units you use, provided you know what your normal consumption is and can spot if it's getting better or worse.

Table 1: conversion of litres to Imperial gallons

litres	1	2	3	4	5	10	20	30	40	50	60	70
gallons	0.22	0.44	0.66	0.88	1.10	2.24	4.49	6.73	8.98	11.22	13.47	15.71

Table 2: conversion of miles per litre to miles per gallon

miles per litre	5	6	7	8	9	10	11	12	13	14
miles per gallon	23	27	32	36	41	46	50	55	59	64

Table 3: conversion of litres per 100 km to miles per gallon

litres per 100 km	4	4.5	5	5.5	6	6.5	7	8	9	10
miles per gallon	71	63	56	51	47	43	40	35	31	28

Maintenance

A well-maintained car uses less fuel and creates less pollution. In particular:

Filters

Change air and fuel filters at the specified intervals.

Oil

Use a good quality oil of the lowest viscosity specified by the vehicle manufacturer (see *Lubricants and fluids*). Check the level often and be careful not to overfill.

Spark plugs

When applicable, renew at the specified intervals.

Tyres

Check tyre pressures regularly. Under-inflated tyres have an increased rolling resistance. It is generally safe to use the higher pressures specified for full load conditions even when not fully laden, but keep an eye on the centre band of tread for signs of wear due to over-inflation.

When buying new tyres, consider the 'fuel saving' models which most manufacturers include in their ranges.

Driving style

Acceleration

Acceleration uses more fuel than driving at a steady speed. The best technique with modern cars is to accelerate reasonably briskly to the desired speed, changing up through the gears as soon as possible without making the engine labour.

Air conditioning

Air conditioning absorbs quite a bit of energy from the engine – typically 3 kW (4 hp) or so. The effect on fuel consumption is at its worst in slow traffic. Switch it off when not required.

Anticipation

Drive smoothly and try to read the traffic flow so as to avoid unnecessary acceleration and braking.

Automatic transmission

When accelerating in an automatic, avoid depressing the throttle so far as to make the transmission hold onto lower gears at higher speeds. Don't use the 'Sport' setting, if applicable.

When stationary with the engine running, select 'N' or 'P'. When moving, keep your left foot away from the brake.

Braking

Braking converts the car's energy of motion into heat – essentially, it is wasted. Obviously some braking is always going to be necessary, but with good anticipation it is surprising how much can be avoided, especially on routes that you know well.

Carshare

Consider sharing lifts to work or to the shops. Even once a week will make a difference.

Electrical loads

Electricity is 'fuel' too; the alternator which charges the battery does so by converting some of the engine's energy of motion into electrical energy. The more electrical accessories are in use, the greater the load on the alternator. Switch off big consumers like the heated rear window when not required.

Freewheeling

Freewheeling (coasting) in neutral with the engine switched off is dangerous. The effort required to operate power-assisted brakes and steering increases when the engine is not running, with a potential lack of control in emergency situations.

In any case, modern fuel injection systems automatically cut off the engine's fuel supply on the overrun (moving and in gear, but with the accelerator pedal released).

Gadgets

Bolt-on devices claiming to save fuel have been around for nearly as long as the motor car itself. Those which worked were rapidly adopted as standard equipment by the vehicle manufacturers. Others worked only in certain situations, or saved fuel only at the expense of unacceptable effects on performance, driveability or the life of engine components.

The most effective fuel saving gadget is the driver's right foot.

Journey planning

Combine (eg) a trip to the supermarket with a visit to the recycling centre and the DIY store, rather than making separate journeys.

When possible choose a travelling time outside rush hours.

Load

The more heavily a car is laden, the greater the energy required to accelerate it to a given speed. Remove heavy items which you don't need to carry.

One load which is often overlooked is the contents of the fuel tank. A tankful of fuel (55 litres / 12 gallons) weighs 45 kg (100 lb) or so. Just half filling it may be worthwhile.

Lost?

At the risk of stating the obvious, if you're going somewhere new, have details of the route to hand. There's not much point in achieving record mpg if you also go miles out of your way.

Parking

If possible, carry out any reversing or turning manoeuvres when you arrive at a parking space so that you can drive straight out when you leave. Manoeuvering when the engine is cold uses a lot more fuel.

Driving around looking for free on-street parking may cost more in fuel than buying a car park ticket.

Premium fuel

Most major oil companies (and some supermarkets) have premium grades of fuel which are several pence a litre dearer than the standard grades. Reports vary, but the consensus seems to be that if these fuels improve economy at all, they do not do so by enough to justify their extra cost.

Roof rack

When loading a roof rack, try to produce a wedge shape with the narrow end at the front. Any cover should be securely fastened – if it flaps it's creating turbulence and absorbing energy.

Remove roof racks and boxes when not in use – they increase air resistance and can create a surprising amount of noise.

Short journeys

The engine is at its least efficient, and wear is highest, during the first few miles after a cold start. Consider walking, cycling or using public transport.

Speed

The engine is at its most efficient when running at a steady speed and load at the rpm where it develops maximum torque. (You can find this figure in the car's handbook.) For most cars this corresponds to between 55 and 65 mph in top gear.

Above the optimum cruising speed, fuel consumption starts to rise quite sharply. A car travelling at 80 mph will typically be using 30% more fuel than at 60 mph.

Supermarket fuel

It may be cheap but is it any good? In the UK all supermarket fuel must meet the relevant British Standard. The major oil companies will say that their branded fuels have better additive packages which may stop carbon and other deposits building up. A reasonable compromise might be to use one tank of branded fuel to three or four from the supermarket.

Switch off when stationary

Switch off the engine if you look like being stationary for more than 30 seconds or so. This is good for the environment as well as for your pocket. Be aware though that frequent restarts are hard on the battery and the starter motor.

Windows

Driving with the windows open increases air turbulence around the vehicle. Closing the windows promotes smooth airflow and reduced resistance. The faster you go, the more significant this is.

And finally . . .

Driving techniques associated with good fuel economy tend to involve moderate acceleration and low top speeds. Be considerate to the needs of other road users who may need to make brisker progress; even if you do not agree with them this is not an excuse to be obstructive.

Safety must always take precedence over economy, whether it is a question of accelerating hard to complete an overtaking manoeuvre, killing your speed when confronted with a potential hazard or switching the lights on when it starts to get dark.

Conversion factors

Length (distance)

Inches (in)	x 25.4	= Millimetres (mm)	x 0.0394	= Inches (in)
Feet (ft)	x 0.305	= Metres (m)	x 3.281	= Feet (ft)
Miles	x 1.609	= Kilometres (km)	x 0.621	= Miles

Volume (capacity)

Cubic inches (cu in; in³)	x 16.387	= Cubic centimetres (cc; cm³)	x 0.061	= Cubic inches (cu in; in³)
Imperial pints (Imp pt)	x 0.568	= Litres (l)	x 1.76	= Imperial pints (Imp pt)
Imperial quarts (Imp qt)	x 1.137	= Litres (l)	x 0.88	= Imperial quarts (Imp qt)
Imperial quarts (Imp qt)	x 1.201	= US quarts (US qt)	x 0.833	= Imperial quarts (Imp qt)
US quarts (US qt)	x 0.946	= Litres (l)	x 1.057	= US quarts (US qt)
Imperial gallons (Imp gal)	x 4.546	= Litres (l)	x 0.22	= Imperial gallons (Imp gal)
Imperial gallons (Imp gal)	x 1.201	= US gallons (US gal)	x 0.833	= Imperial gallons (Imp gal)
US gallons (US gal)	x 3.785	= Litres (l)	x 0.264	= US gallons (US gal)

Mass (weight)

Ounces (oz)	x 28.35	= Grams (g)	x 0.035	= Ounces (oz)
Pounds (lb)	x 0.454	= Kilograms (kg)	x 2.205	= Pounds (lb)

Force

Ounces-force (ozf; oz)	x 0.278	= Newtons (N)	x 3.6	= Ounces-force (ozf; oz)
Pounds-force (lbf; lb)	x 4.448	= Newtons (N)	x 0.225	= Pounds-force (lbf; lb)
Newtons (N)	x 0.1	= Kilograms-force (kgf; kg)	x 9.81	= Newtons (N)

Pressure

Pounds-force per square inch (psi; lbf/in²; lb/in²)	x 0.070	= Kilograms-force per square centimetre (kgf/cm²; kg/cm²)	x 14.223	= Pounds-force per square inch (psi; lbf/in²; lb/in²)
Pounds-force per square inch (psi; lbf/in²; lb/in²)	x 0.068	= Atmospheres (atm)	x 14.696	= Pounds-force per square inch (psi; lbf/in²; lb/in²)
Pounds-force per square inch (psi; lbf/in²; lb/in²)	x 0.069	= Bars	x 14.5	= Pounds-force per square inch (psi; lbf/in²; lb/in²)
Pounds-force per square inch (psi; lbf/in²; lb/in²)	x 6.895	= Kilopascals (kPa)	x 0.145	= Pounds-force per square inch (psi; lbf/in²; lb/in²)
Kilopascals (kPa)	x 0.01	= Kilograms-force per square centimetre (kgf/cm²; kg/cm²)	x 98.1	= Kilopascals (kPa)
Millibar (mbar)	x 100	= Pascals (Pa)	x 0.01	= Millibar (mbar)
Millibar (mbar)	x 0.0145	= Pounds-force per square inch (psi; lbf/in²; lb/in²)	x 68.947	= Millibar (mbar)
Millibar (mbar)	x 0.75	= Millimetres of mercury (mmHg)	x 1.333	= Millibar (mbar)
Millibar (mbar)	x 0.401	= Inches of water (inH₂O)	x 2.491	= Millibar (mbar)
Millimetres of mercury (mmHg)	x 0.535	= Inches of water (inH₂O)	x 1.868	= Millimetres of mercury (mmHg)
Inches of water (inH₂O)	x 0.036	= Pounds-force per square inch (psi; lbf/in²; lb/in²)	x 27.68	= Inches of water (inH₂O)

Torque (moment of force)

Pounds-force inches (lbf in; lb in)	x 1.152	= Kilograms-force centimetre (kgf cm; kg cm)	x 0.868	= Pounds-force inches (lbf in; lb in)
Pounds-force inches (lbf in; lb in)	x 0.113	= Newton metres (Nm)	x 8.85	= Pounds-force inches (lbf in; lb in)
Pounds-force inches (lbf in; lb in)	x 0.083	= Pounds-force feet (lbf ft; lb ft)	x 12	= Pounds-force inches (lbf in; lb in)
Pounds-force feet (lbf ft; lb ft)	x 0.138	= Kilograms-force metres (kgf m; kg m)	x 7.233	= Pounds-force feet (lbf ft; lb ft)
Pounds-force feet (lbf ft; lb ft)	x 1.356	= Newton metres (Nm)	x 0.738	= Pounds-force feet (lbf ft; lb ft)
Newton metres (Nm)	x 0.102	= Kilograms-force metres (kgf m; kg m)	x 9.804	= Newton metres (Nm)

Power

Horsepower (hp)	x 745.7	= Watts (W)	x 0.0013	= Horsepower (hp)

Velocity (speed)

Miles per hour (miles/hr; mph)	x 1.609	= Kilometres per hour (km/hr; kph)	x 0.621	= Miles per hour (miles/hr; mph)

Fuel consumption*

Miles per gallon, Imperial (mpg)	x 0.354	= Kilometres per litre (km/l)	x 2.825	= Miles per gallon, Imperial (mpg)
Miles per gallon, US (mpg)	x 0.425	= Kilometres per litre (km/l)	x 2.352	= Miles per gallon, US (mpg)

Temperature

Degrees Fahrenheit = (°C x 1.8) + 32   Degrees Celsius (Degrees Centigrade; °C) = (°F - 32) x 0.56

It is common practice to convert from miles per gallon (mpg) to litres/100 kilometres (l/100km), where mpg x l/100 km = 282

Spare parts are available from many sources, including maker's appointed garages, accessory shops, and motor factors. To be sure of obtaining the correct parts, it will sometimes be necessary to quote the vehicle identification number (see Vehicle identification). If possible, it can also be useful to take the old parts along for positive identification. Items such as starter motors and alternators may be available under a service exchange scheme – any parts returned should always be clean.

Our advice regarding spare part sources is as follows.

Officially-appointed garages

This is the best source of parts which are peculiar to your car, and which are not otherwise generally available (eg badges, interior trim, certain body panels, etc). It is also the only place at which you should buy parts if the car is still under warranty.

Accessory shops

These are very good places to buy materials and components needed for the maintenance of your car (oil, air and fuel filters, spark plugs, light bulbs, drivebelts, oils and greases, brake pads, touch-up paint, etc). Components of this nature sold by a reputable shop are of the same standard as those used by the car manufacturer.

Besides components, these shops also sell tools and general accessories, usually have convenient opening hours, charge lower prices, and can often be found not far from home. Some accessory shops have parts counters where the components needed for almost any repair job can be purchased or ordered.

Motor factors

Good factors will stock all the more important components which wear out comparatively quickly, and can sometimes supply individual components needed for the overhaul of a larger assembly (eg brake seals and hydraulic parts, bearing shells, pistons, valves, alternator brushes). They may also handle work such as cylinder block reboring, crankshaft regrinding and balancing, etc.

Tyre and exhaust specialists

These outlets may be independent, or members of a local or national chain. They frequently offer competitive prices when compared with a main dealer or local garage, but it will pay to obtain several quotes before making a decision. When researching prices, also ask what 'extras' may be added – for instance, fitting a new valve and balancing the wheel are both commonly charged on top of the price of a new tyre.

Other sources

Beware of parts or materials obtained from market stalls, car boot sales or similar outlets. Such items are not invariably sub-standard, but there is little chance of compensation if they do prove unsatisfactory. In the case of safety-critical components such as brake pads, there is the risk not only of financial loss but also of an accident causing injury or death.

Second-hand components or assemblies obtained from a car breaker can be a good buy in some circumstances, but this sort of purchase is best made by the experienced DIY mechanic.

Vehicle identification numbers

Modifications are a continuing and unpublicised process in car manufacture, quite apart from major model changes. Spare parts manuals and lists are compiled upon a numerical basis, the individual vehicle identification numbers being essential to correct identification of the component concerned.

When ordering spare parts, always give as much information as possible. Quote the car model, year of manufacture, body and engine numbers as appropriate.

The vehicle identification plate is located at the base of the driver's door B-pillar, and can be viewed with the door open (see illustration). In addition to many other details, it carries the Vehicle Identification Number (VIN), maximum vehicle weight information, and codes for interior trim and body colours.

The Vehicle Identification Number (VIN) is given on the vehicle identification plate. It is also stamped into the driver's-side floor panel beside the front seat, and may also be viewed through the base of the windscreen on the passenger's side (see illustrations).

The engine number is stamped in the following locations, according to engine type:

☐ On petrol engines, it appears at the transmission end of the engine, below the throttle housing (see illustration).
☐ On diesel engines, the number is stamped at the top of the engine, below and in line with the oil filler cap (see illustration).

VIN plate at the base of the driver's door pillar

VIN is visible on the passenger side of the windscreen

VIN is stamped into the driver's side floor panel

On petrol engines, the engine number is under the throttle housing

Engine number location on diesel engines

Whenever servicing, repair or overhaul work is carried out on the car or its components, observe the following procedures and instructions. This will assist in carrying out the operation efficiently and to a professional standard of workmanship.

Joint mating faces and gaskets

When separating components at their mating faces, never insert screwdrivers or similar implements into the joint between the faces in order to prise them apart. This can cause severe damage which results in oil leaks, coolant leaks, etc upon reassembly. Separation is usually achieved by tapping along the joint with a soft-faced hammer in order to break the seal. However, note that this method may not be suitable where dowels are used for component location.

Where a gasket is used between the mating faces of two components, a new one must be fitted on reassembly; fit it dry unless otherwise stated in the repair procedure. Make sure that the mating faces are clean and dry, with all traces of old gasket removed. When cleaning a joint face, use a tool which is unlikely to score or damage the face, and remove any burrs or nicks with an oilstone or fine file.

Make sure that tapped holes are cleaned with a pipe cleaner, and keep them free of jointing compound, if this is being used, unless specifically instructed otherwise.

Ensure that all orifices, channels or pipes are clear, and blow through them, preferably using compressed air.

Oil seals

Oil seals can be removed by levering them out with a wide flat-bladed screwdriver or similar implement. Alternatively, a number of self-tapping screws may be screwed into the seal, and these used as a purchase for pliers or some similar device in order to pull the seal free.

Whenever an oil seal is removed from its working location, either individually or as part of an assembly, it should be renewed.

The very fine sealing lip of the seal is easily damaged, and will not seal if the surface it contacts is not completely clean and free from scratches, nicks or grooves. If the original sealing surface of the component cannot be restored, and the manufacturer has not made provision for slight relocation of the seal relative to the sealing surface, the component should be renewed.

Protect the lips of the seal from any surface which may damage them in the course of fitting. Use tape or a conical sleeve where possible. Where indicated, lubricate the seal lips with oil before fitting and, on dual-lipped seals, fill the space between the lips with grease.

Unless otherwise stated, oil seals must be fitted with their sealing lips toward the lubricant to be sealed.

Use a tubular drift or block of wood of the appropriate size to install the seal and, if the seal housing is shouldered, drive the seal down to the shoulder. If the seal housing is unshouldered, the seal should be fitted with its face flush with the housing top face (unless otherwise instructed).

Screw threads and fastenings

Seized nuts, bolts and screws are quite a common occurrence where corrosion has set in, and the use of penetrating oil or releasing fluid will often overcome this problem if the offending item is soaked for a while before attempting to release it. The use of an impact driver may also provide a means of releasing such stubborn fastening devices, when used in conjunction with the appropriate screwdriver bit or socket. If none of these methods works, it may be necessary to resort to the careful application of heat, or the use of a hacksaw or nut splitter device. Before resorting to extreme methods, check that you are not dealing with a left-hand thread!

Studs are usually removed by locking two nuts together on the threaded part, and then using a spanner on the lower nut to unscrew the stud. Studs or bolts which have broken off below the surface of the component in which they are mounted can sometimes be removed using a stud extractor.

Always ensure that a blind tapped hole is completely free from oil, grease, water or other fluid before installing the bolt or stud. Failure to do this could cause the housing to crack due to the hydraulic action of the bolt or stud as it is screwed in.

For some screw fastenings, notably cylinder head bolts or nuts, torque wrench settings are no longer specified for the latter stages of tightening, "angle-tightening" being called up instead. Typically, a fairly low torque wrench setting will be applied to the bolts/nuts in the correct sequence, followed by one or more stages of tightening through specified angles.

When checking or retightening a nut or bolt to a specified torque setting, slacken the nut or bolt by a quarter of a turn, and then retighten to the specified setting. However, this should not be attempted where angular tightening has been used.

Locknuts, locktabs and washers

Any fastening which will rotate against a component or housing during tightening should always have a washer between it and the relevant component or housing.

Spring or split washers should always be renewed when they are used to lock a critical component such as a big-end bearing retaining bolt or nut. Locktabs which are folded over to retain a nut or bolt should always be renewed.

Self-locking nuts can be re-used in non-critical areas, providing resistance can be felt when the locking portion passes over the bolt or stud thread. However, it should be noted that self-locking stiffnuts tend to lose their effectiveness after long periods of use, and should then be renewed as a matter of course.

Split pins must always be replaced with new ones of the correct size for the hole.

When thread-locking compound is found on the threads of a fastener which is to be re-used, it should be cleaned off with a wire brush and solvent, and fresh compound applied on reassembly.

Special tools

Some repair procedures in this manual entail the use of special tools such as a press, two or three-legged pullers, spring compressors, etc. Wherever possible, suitable readily-available alternatives to the manufacturer's special tools are described, and are shown in use. In some instances, where no alternative is possible, it has been necessary to resort to the use of a manufacturer's tool, and this has been done for reasons of safety as well as the efficient completion of the repair operation. Unless you are highly-skilled and have a thorough understanding of the procedures described, never attempt to bypass the use of any special tool when the procedure described specifies its use. Not only is there a very great risk of personal injury, but expensive damage could be caused to the components involved.

Environmental considerations

When disposing of used engine oil, brake fluid, antifreeze, etc, give due consideration to any detrimental environmental effects. Do not, for instance, pour any of the above liquids down drains into the general sewage system, or onto the ground to soak away, as this is likely to pollute your local environment. Many local council refuse tips provide a facility for waste oil disposal, as do some garages. You can find your nearest disposal point by calling the Environment Agency on 03708 506 506 or by visiting www.oilbankline.org.uk.

Note: It is illegal and anti-social to dump oil down the drain. To find the location of your local oil recycling bank, call 03708 506 506 or visit www.oilbankline.org.uk.

The jack supplied with the car's tool kit should only be used for changing the roadwheels – see Wheel changing at the front of this manual. When carrying out any other kind of work, raise the car using a hydraulic (or 'trolley') jack, and always supplement the jack with axle stands positioned under the jacking/support points **(see illustration)**. If the roadwheels do not have to be removed, consider using wheel ramps – if wished, these can be placed under the wheels once the car has been raised using a hydraulic jack, and then lowered onto the ramps so that it is resting on its wheels.

Only ever jack the car up on a solid, level surface. If there is even a slight slope, take great care that the car cannot move as the wheels are lifted off the ground. Jacking up on an uneven or gravelled surface is not recommended, as the weight of the car will not be evenly distributed, and the jack may slip as the car is raised.

As far as possible, do not leave the car unattended once it has been raised, particularly if children are playing nearby.

Before jacking up the front of the car, ensure that the handbrake is firmly applied. When jacking up the rear of the car, place wooden chocks in front of the front wheels, and engage first gear.

To raise the front and/or rear of the car, use the jacking/support points at the front and rear ends of the door sills, which are located at the places marked by a notch in the sill's lower flange **(see illustration)**. Position a block of wood with a groove cut in it on the jack head to prevent the car's weight resting on the sill edge; align the sill edge with the groove in the wood so that the car's weight is spread evenly over the surface of the block. Supplement the jack with axle stands (also with slotted blocks of wood) positioned as close as possible to the jacking points.

When using a hydraulic jack or axle stands,

always try to position the jack head or axle stand head under one of the relevant jacking points.

Providing care is taken (and a block of wood is used to spread the load), the centre of the front subframe and centre of the rear axle beam, may be used as support points. It may be safe also to use reinforced areas of the floor pan ('chassis legs'), particularly those in the region of suspension mountings, as support points – consult a Ford dealer for advice before using anything other than the approved jacking points, however.

Do not jack the car under any other part of the sill, sump, floor pan, or directly under any of the steering or suspension components.

⚠ *Warning: Never work under, around, or near a raised vehicle, unless it is adequately supported on stands. Do not rely on a jack alone, as even a hydraulic jack could fail under load.*

Sill jacking points

Jacking points on sill flanges are indicated by notches

Introduction

A selection of good tools is a fundamental requirement for anyone contemplating the maintenance and repair of a motor vehicle. For the owner who does not possess any, their purchase will prove a considerable expense, offsetting some of the savings made by doing-it-yourself. However, provided that the tools purchased meet the relevant national safety standards and are of good quality, they will last for many years and prove an extremely worthwhile investment.

To help the average owner to decide which tools are needed to carry out the various tasks detailed in this manual, we have compiled three lists of tools under the following headings: *Maintenance and minor repair*, *Repair and overhaul*, and *Special*. Newcomers to practical mechanics should start off with the *Maintenance and minor repair* tool kit, and confine themselves to the simpler jobs around the vehicle. Then, as confidence and experience grow, more difficult tasks can be undertaken, with extra tools being purchased as, and when, they are needed. In this way, a *Maintenance and minor repair* tool kit can be built up into a *Repair and overhaul* tool kit over a considerable period of time, without any major cash outlays. The experienced do-it-yourselfer will have a tool kit good enough for most repair and overhaul procedures, and will add tools from the *Special* category when it is felt that the expense is justified by the amount of use to which these tools will be put.

Maintenance and minor repair tool kit

The tools given in this list should be considered as a minimum requirement if routine maintenance, servicing and minor repair operations are to be undertaken. We recommend the purchase of combination spanners (ring one end, open-ended the other); although more expensive than open-ended ones, they do give the advantages of both types of spanner.

☐ *Combination spanners:*
  Metric - 8 to 19 mm inclusive
☐ *Adjustable spanner - 35 mm jaw (approx.)*
☐ *Spark plug spanner (with rubber insert) - petrol models*
☐ *Spark plug gap adjustment tool - petrol models*
☐ *Set of feeler gauges*
☐ *Brake bleed nipple spanner*
☐ *Screwdrivers:*
  Flat blade - 100 mm long x 6 mm dia
  Cross blade - 100 mm long x 6 mm dia
  Torx - various sizes (not all vehicles)
☐ *Combination pliers*
☐ *Hacksaw (junior)*
☐ *Tyre pump*
☐ *Tyre pressure gauge*
☐ *Oil can*
☐ *Oil filter removal tool (if applicable)*
☐ *Fine emery cloth*
☐ *Wire brush (small)*
☐ *Funnel (medium size)*
☐ *Sump drain plug key (not all vehicles)*

Repair and overhaul tool kit

These tools are virtually essential for anyone undertaking any major repairs to a motor vehicle, and are additional to those given in the *Maintenance and minor repair* list. Included in this list is a comprehensive set of sockets. Although these are expensive, they will be found invaluable as they are so versatile - particularly if various drives are included in the set. We recommend the half-inch square-drive type, as this can be used with most proprietary torque wrenches.

The tools in this list will sometimes need to be supplemented by tools from the *Special* list:

☐ *Sockets to cover range in previous list (including Torx sockets)*
☐ *Reversible ratchet drive (for use with sockets)*
☐ *Extension piece, 250 mm (for use with sockets)*
☐ *Universal joint (for use with sockets)*
☐ *Flexible handle or sliding T "breaker bar" (for use with sockets)*
☐ *Torque wrench (for use with sockets)*
☐ *Self-locking grips*
☐ *Ball pein hammer*
☐ *Soft-faced mallet (plastic or rubber)*
☐ *Screwdrivers:*
  Flat blade - long & sturdy, short (chubby), and narrow (electrician's) types
  Cross blade – long & sturdy, and short (chubby) types
☐ *Pliers:*
  Long-nosed
  Side cutters (electrician's)
  Circlip (internal and external)
☐ *Cold chisel - 25 mm*
☐ *Scriber*
☐ *Scraper*
☐ *Centre-punch*
☐ *Pin punch*
☐ *Hacksaw*
☐ *Brake hose clamp*
☐ *Brake/clutch bleeding kit*
☐ *Selection of twist drills*
☐ *Steel rule/straight-edge*
☐ *Allen keys (inc. splined/Torx type)*
☐ *Selection of files*
☐ *Wire brush*
☐ *Axle stands*
☐ *Jack (strong trolley or hydraulic type)*
☐ *Light with extension lead*
☐ *Universal electrical multi-meter*

Sockets and reversible ratchet drive

Brake bleeding kit

Torx key, socket and bit

Hose clamp

Angular-tightening gauge

Special tools

The tools in this list are those which are not used regularly, are expensive to buy, or which need to be used in accordance with their manufacturers' instructions. Unless relatively difficult mechanical jobs are undertaken frequently, it will not be economic to buy many of these tools. Where this is the case, you could consider clubbing together with friends (or joining a motorists' club) to make a joint purchase, or borrowing the tools against a deposit from a local garage or tool hire specialist.

The following list contains only those tools and instruments freely available to the public, and not those special tools produced by the vehicle manufacturer specifically for its dealer network. You will find occasional references to these manufacturers' special tools in the text of this manual. Generally, an alternative method of doing the job without the vehicle manufacturers' special tool is given. However, sometimes there is no alternative to using them. Where this is the case and the relevant tool cannot be bought or borrowed, you will have to entrust the work to a dealer.

- ☐ Angular-tightening gauge
- ☐ Valve spring compressor
- ☐ Valve grinding tool
- ☐ Piston ring compressor
- ☐ Piston ring removal/installation tool
- ☐ Cylinder bore hone
- ☐ Balljoint separator
- ☐ Coil spring compressors (where applicable)
- ☐ Two/three-legged hub and bearing puller
- ☐ Impact screwdriver
- ☐ Micrometer and/or vernier calipers
- ☐ Dial gauge
- ☐ Tachometer
- ☐ Fault code reader
- ☐ Cylinder compression gauge
- ☐ Hand-operated vacuum pump and gauge
- ☐ Clutch plate alignment set
- ☐ Brake shoe steady spring cup removal tool
- ☐ Bush and bearing removal/installation set
- ☐ Stud extractors
- ☐ Tap and die set
- ☐ Lifting tackle

Buying tools

Reputable motor accessory shops and superstores often offer excellent quality tools at discount prices, so it pays to shop around.

Remember, you don't have to buy the most expensive items on the shelf, but it is always advisable to steer clear of the very cheap tools. Beware of 'bargains' offered on market stalls, on-line or at car boot sales. There are plenty of good tools around at reasonable prices, but always aim to purchase items which meet the relevant national safety standards. If in doubt, ask the proprietor or manager of the shop for advice before making a purchase.

Care and maintenance of tools

Having purchased a reasonable tool kit, it is necessary to keep the tools in a clean and serviceable condition. After use, always wipe off any dirt, grease and metal particles using a clean, dry cloth, before putting the tools away. Never leave them lying around after they have been used. A simple tool rack on the garage or workshop wall for items such as screwdrivers and pliers is a good idea. Store all normal spanners and sockets in a metal box. Any measuring instruments, gauges, meters, etc, must be carefully stored where they cannot be damaged or become rusty.

Take a little care when tools are used. Hammer heads inevitably become marked, and screwdrivers lose the keen edge on their blades from time to time. A little timely attention with emery cloth or a file will soon restore items like this to a good finish.

Working facilities

Not to be forgotten when discussing tools is the workshop itself. If anything more than routine maintenance is to be carried out, a suitable working area becomes essential.

It is appreciated that many an owner-mechanic is forced by circumstances to remove an engine or similar item without the benefit of a garage or workshop. Having done this, any repairs should always be done under the cover of a roof.

Wherever possible, any dismantling should be done on a clean, flat workbench or table at a suitable working height.

Any workbench needs a vice; one with a jaw opening of 100 mm is suitable for most jobs. As mentioned previously, some clean dry storage space is also required for tools, as well as for any lubricants, cleaning fluids, touch-up paints etc, which become necessary.

Another item which may be required, and which has a much more general usage, is an electric drill with a chuck capacity of at least 8 mm. This, together with a good range of twist drills, is virtually essential for fitting accessories.

Last, but not least, always keep a supply of old newspapers and clean, lint-free rags available, and try to keep any working area as clean as possible.

Micrometers

Dial test indicator ("dial gauge")

Oil filter removal tool (strap wrench type)

Compression tester

Bearing puller

This is a guide to getting your vehicle through the MOT test. Obviously it will not be possible to examine the vehicle to the same standard as the professional MOT tester. However, working through the following checks will enable you to identify any problem areas before submitting the vehicle for the test.

It has only been possible to summarise the test requirements here, based on the regulations in force at the time of printing. Test standards are becoming increasingly stringent, although there are some exemptions for older vehicles.

An assistant will be needed to help carry out some of these checks.

The checks have been sub-divided into four categories, as follows:

1 Checks carried out **FROM THE DRIVER'S SEAT**

2 Checks carried out **WITH THE VEHICLE ON THE GROUND**

3 Checks carried out **WITH THE VEHICLE RAISED AND THE WHEELS FREE TO TURN**

4 Checks carried out on **YOUR VEHICLE'S EXHAUST EMISSION SYSTEM**

---

1 Checks carried out **FROM THE DRIVER'S SEAT**

Handbrake (parking brake)

☐ Test the operation of the handbrake. Excessive travel (too many clicks) indicates incorrect brake or cable adjustment.
☐ Check that the handbrake cannot be released by tapping the lever sideways. Check the security of the lever mountings.

☐ If the parking brake is foot-operated, check that the pedal is secure and without excessive travel, and that the release mechanism operates correctly.
☐ Where applicable, test the operation of the electronic handbrake. The brake should engage and disengage without excessive delay. If the warning light does not extinguish when the brake is disengaged, this could indicate a fault which will need further investigation.

Footbrake

☐ Depress the brake pedal and check that it does not creep down to the floor, indicating a master cylinder fault. Release the pedal, wait a few seconds, then depress it again. If the pedal travels nearly to the floor before firm resistance is felt, brake adjustment or repair is necessary. If the pedal feels spongy, there is air in the hydraulic system which must be removed by bleeding.

☐ Check that the brake pedal is secure and in good condition. Check also for signs of fluid leaks on the pedal, floor or carpets, which would indicate failed seals in the brake master cylinder.
☐ Check the servo unit (when applicable) by operating the brake pedal several times, then keeping the pedal depressed and starting the engine. As the engine starts, the pedal will move down slightly. If not, the vacuum hose or the servo itself may be faulty.

Steering wheel and column

☐ Examine the steering wheel for fractures or looseness of the hub, spokes or rim.
☐ Move the steering wheel from side to side and then up and down. Check that the steering wheel is not loose on the column, indicating wear or a loose retaining nut. Continue moving the steering wheel as before, but also turn it slightly from left to right.

☐ Check that the steering wheel is not loose on the column, and that there is no abnormal movement of the steering wheel, indicating wear in the column support bearings or couplings.
☐ Check that the ignition lock (where fitted) engages and disengages correctly.
☐ Steering column adjustment mechanisms (where fitted) must be able to lock the column securely in place with no play evident.

Windscreen, mirrors and sunvisor

☐ The windscreen must be free of cracks or other significant damage within the driver's field of view. (Small stone chips are acceptable.) Rear view mirrors must be secure, intact, and capable of being adjusted.

☐ The driver's sunvisor must be capable of being stored in the "up" position.

Seat belts and seats

Note: *The following checks are applicable to all seat belts, front and rear.*

☐ Examine the webbing of all the belts (including rear belts if fitted) for cuts, serious fraying or deterioration. Fasten and unfasten each belt to check the buckles. If applicable, check the retracting mechanism. Check the security of all seat belt mountings accessible from inside the vehicle, ensuring any height adjustable mountings lock securely in place.

☐ Seat belts with pre-tensioners, once activated, have a "flag" or similar showing on the seat belt stalk. This, in itself, is not a reason for test failure.

☐ The front seats themselves must be securely attached and the backrests must lock in the upright position.

Doors

☐ Both front doors must be able to be opened and closed from outside and inside, and must latch securely when closed.

Bonnet and boot/tailgate

☐ The bonnet and boot/tailgate must latch securely when closed.

2 Checks carried out WITH THE VEHICLE ON THE GROUND

Vehicle identification

☐ Number plates must be in good condition, secure and legible, with letters and numbers correctly spaced – spacing at (A) should be 33 mm and at (B) 11 mm. At the front, digits must be black on a white background and at the rear black on a yellow background. Other background designs (such as honeycomb) are not permitted.

☐ The VIN plate and/or homologation plate must be permanently displayed and legible.

Electrical equipment

☐ Switch on the ignition and check the operation of the horn.

☐ Check the windscreen washers and wipers, examining the wiper blades; renew damaged or perished blades. Also check the operation of the stop-lights.

☐ Check the operation of the sidelights and number plate lights. The lenses and reflectors must be secure, clean and undamaged.

☐ Check the operation and alignment of the headlights. The headlight reflectors must not be tarnished and the lenses must be undamaged.

☐ Switch on the ignition and check the operation of the direction indicators (including the instrument panel tell-tale) and the hazard warning lights. Operation of the sidelights and stop-lights must not affect the indicators - if it does, the cause is usually a bad earth at the rear light cluster. Indicators should flash at a rate of between 60 and 120 times per minute – faster or slower than this could indicate a fault with the flasher unit or a bad earth at one of the light units.

☐ Check the operation of the rear foglight(s), including the warning light on the instrument panel or in the switch.

☐ The warning lights must illuminate in accordance with the manufacturer's design. For most vehicles, the ABS and other warning lights should illuminate when the ignition is switched on, and (if the system is operating properly) extinguish after a few seconds. Refer to the owner's handbook.

Footbrake

☐ Examine the master cylinder, brake pipes and servo unit for leaks, loose mountings, corrosion or other damage. If ABS is fitted, this unit should also be examined for signs of leaks or corrosion.

☐ The fluid reservoir must be secure and the fluid level must be between the upper (A) and lower (B) markings.

☐ Inspect both front brake flexible hoses for cracks or deterioration of the rubber. Turn the steering from lock to lock, and ensure that the hoses do not contact the wheel, tyre, or any part of the steering or suspension mechanism. With the brake pedal firmly depressed, check the hoses for bulges or leaks under pressure.

Steering and suspension

☐ Have your assistant turn the steering wheel from side to side slightly, up to the point where the steering gear just begins to transmit this movement to the roadwheels. Check for excessive free play between the steering wheel and the steering gear, indicating wear or insecurity of the steering column joints, the column-to-steering gear coupling, or the steering gear itself.

☐ Have your assistant turn the steering wheel more vigorously in each direction, so that the roadwheels just begin to turn. As this is done, examine all the steering joints, linkages, fittings and attachments. Renew any component that shows signs of wear or damage. On vehicles with power steering, check the security and condition of the steering pump, drivebelt and hoses.

☐ Check that the vehicle is standing level, and at approximately the correct ride height.

Shock absorbers

☐ Depress each corner of the vehicle in turn, then release it. The vehicle should rise and then settle in its normal position. If the vehicle continues to rise and fall, the shock absorber is defective. A shock absorber which has seized will also cause the vehicle to fail.

Exhaust system

☐ Start the engine. With your assistant holding a rag over the tailpipe, check the entire system for leaks. Repair or renew leaking sections.

3 Checks carried out **WITH THE VEHICLE RAISED AND THE WHEELS FREE TO TURN**

Jack up the front and rear of the vehicle, and securely support it on axle stands. Position the stands clear of the suspension assemblies. Ensure that the wheels are clear of the ground and that the steering can be turned from lock to lock.

Steering mechanism

☐ Have your assistant turn the steering from lock to lock. Check that the steering turns smoothly, and that no part of the steering mechanism, including a wheel or tyre, fouls any brake hose or pipe or any part of the body structure.
☐ Examine the steering rack rubber gaiters for damage or insecurity of the retaining clips. If power steering is fitted, check for signs of damage or leakage of the fluid hoses, pipes or connections. Also check for excessive stiffness or binding of the steering, a missing split pin or locking device, or severe corrosion of the body structure within 30 cm of any steering component attachment point.

Front and rear suspension and wheel bearings

☐ Starting at the front right-hand side, grasp the roadwheel at the 3 o'clock and 9 o'clock positions and rock gently but firmly. Check for free play or insecurity at the wheel bearings, suspension balljoints, or suspension mount-ings, pivots and attachments.
☐ Now grasp the wheel at the 12 o'clock and 6 o'clock positions and repeat the previous inspection. Spin the wheel, and check for roughness or tightness of the front wheel bearing.

☐ If excess free play is suspected at a component pivot point, this can be confirmed by using a large screwdriver or similar tool and levering between the mounting and the component attachment. This will confirm whether the wear is in the pivot bush, its retaining bolt, or in the mounting itself (the bolt holes can often become elongated).

☐ Carry out all the above checks at the other front wheel, and then at both rear wheels.

Springs and shock absorbers

☐ Examine the suspension struts (when applicable) for serious fluid leakage, corrosion, or damage to the casing. Also check the security of the mounting points.
☐ If coil springs are fitted, check that the spring ends locate in their seats, and that the spring is not corroded, cracked or broken.
☐ If leaf springs are fitted, check that all leaves are intact, that the axle is securely attached to each spring, and that there is no deterioration of the spring eye mountings, bushes, and shackles.

☐ The same general checks apply to vehicles fitted with other suspension types, such as torsion bars, hydraulic displacer units, etc. Ensure that all mountings and attachments are secure, that there are no signs of excessive wear, corrosion or damage, and (on hydraulic types) that there are no fluid leaks or damaged pipes.
☐ Inspect the shock absorbers for signs of serious fluid leakage. Check for wear of the mounting bushes or attachments, or damage to the body of the unit.

Driveshafts (fwd vehicles only)

☐ Rotate each front wheel in turn and inspect the constant velocity joint gaiters for splits or damage. Also check that each driveshaft is straight and undamaged.

Braking system

☐ If possible without dismantling, check brake pad wear and disc condition. Ensure that the friction lining material has not worn excessively, (A) and that the discs are not fractured, pitted, scored or badly worn (B).

☐ Examine all the rigid brake pipes underneath the vehicle, and the flexible hose(s) at the rear. Look for corrosion, chafing or insecurity of the pipes, and for signs of bulging under pressure, chafing, splits or deterioration of the flexible hoses.
☐ Look for signs of fluid leaks at the brake calipers or on the brake backplates. Repair or renew leaking components.
☐ Slowly spin each wheel, while your assistant depresses and releases the footbrake. Ensure that each brake is operating and does not bind when the pedal is released.

□Examine the handbrake mechanism, checking for frayed or broken cables, excessive corrosion, or wear or insecurity of the linkage. Check that the mechanism works on each relevant wheel, and releases fully, without binding.

□It is not possible to test brake efficiency without special equipment, but a road test can be carried out later to check that the vehicle pulls up in a straight line.

Fuel and exhaust systems

□Inspect the fuel tank (including the filler cap), fuel pipes, hoses and unions. All components must be secure and free from leaks. Locking fuel caps must lock securely and the key must be provided for the MOT test.

□Examine the exhaust system over its entire length, checking for any damaged, broken or missing mountings, security of the retaining clamps and rust or corrosion.

Wheels and tyres

□Examine the sidewalls and tread area of each tyre in turn. Check for cuts, tears, lumps, bulges, separation of the tread, and exposure of the ply or cord due to wear or damage. Check that the tyre bead is correctly seated on the wheel rim, that the valve is sound and properly seated, and that the wheel is not distorted or damaged.

□Check that the tyres are of the correct size for the vehicle, that they are of the same size and type on each axle, and that the pressures are correct.

□Check the tyre tread depth. The legal minimum at the time of writing is 1.6 mm over the central three-quarters of the tread width. Abnormal tread wear may indicate incorrect front wheel alignment or wear in steering or suspension components.

□If the spare wheel is fitted externally or in a separate carrier beneath the vehicle, check that mountings are secure and free of excessive corrosion.

Body corrosion

□Check the condition of the entire vehicle structure for signs of corrosion in load-bearing areas. (These include chassis box sections, side sills, cross-members, pillars, and all suspension, steering, braking system and seat belt mountings and anchorages.) Any corrosion which has seriously reduced the thickness of a load-bearing area (or is within 30 cm of safety-related components such as steering or suspension) is likely to cause the vehicle to fail. In this case professional repairs are likely to be needed.

□Damage or corrosion which causes sharp or otherwise dangerous edges to be exposed will also cause the vehicle to fail.

Towbars

□Check the condition of mounting points (both beneath the vehicle and within boot/hatchback areas) for signs of corrosion, ensuring that all fixings are secure and not worn or damaged. There must be no excessive play in detachable tow ball arms or quick-release mechanisms.

4 Checks carried out on **YOUR VEHICLE'S EXHAUST EMISSION SYSTEM**

Petrol models

□The engine should be warmed up, and running well (ignition system in good order, air filter element clean, etc).

□Before testing, run the engine at around 2500 rpm for 20 seconds. Let the engine drop to idle, and watch for smoke from the exhaust. If the idle speed is too high, or if dense blue or black smoke emerges for more than 5 seconds, the vehicle will fail. Typically, blue smoke signifies oil burning (engine wear); black smoke means unburnt fuel (dirty air cleaner element, or other fuel system fault).

□An exhaust gas analyser for measuring carbon monoxide (CO) and hydrocarbons (HC) is now needed. If one cannot be hired or borrowed, have a local garage perform the check.

CO emissions (mixture)

□The MOT tester has access to the CO limits for all vehicles. The CO level is measured at idle speed, and at 'fast idle' (2500 to 3000 rpm). The following limits are given as a general guide:

At idle speed – Less than 0.5% CO
At 'fast idle' – Less than 0.3% CO
Lambda reading – 0.97 to 1.03

□If the CO level is too high, this may point to poor maintenance, a fuel injection system problem, faulty lambda (oxygen) sensor or catalytic converter. Try an injector cleaning treatment, and check the vehicle's ECU for fault codes.

HC emissions

□The MOT tester has access to HC limits for all vehicles. The HC level is measured at 'fast idle' (2500 to 3000 rpm). The following limits are given as a general guide:

At 'fast idle' – Less then 200 ppm

□Excessive HC emissions are typically caused by oil being burnt (worn engine), or by a blocked crankcase ventilation system ('breather'). If the engine oil is old and thin, an oil change may help. If the engine is running badly, check the vehicle's ECU for fault codes.

Diesel models

□The only emission test for diesel engines is measuring exhaust smoke density, using a calibrated smoke meter. The test involves accelerating the engine at least 3 times to its maximum unloaded speed.

Note: *On engines with a timing belt, it is VITAL that the belt is in good condition before the test is carried out.*

□With the engine warmed up, it is first purged by running at around 2500 rpm for 20 seconds. A governor check is then carried out, by slowly accelerating the engine to its maximum speed. After this, the smoke meter is connected, and the engine is accelerated quickly to maximum speed three times. If the smoke density is less than the limits given below, the vehicle will pass:

Non-turbo vehicles: 2.5m-1
Turbocharged vehicles: 3.0m-1

□If excess smoke is produced, try fitting a new air cleaner element, or using an injector cleaning treatment. If the engine is running badly, where applicable, check the vehicle's ECU for fault codes. Also check the vehicle's EGR system, where applicable. At high mileages, the injectors may require professional attention.

Engine

- [ ] Engine fails to rotate when attempting to start
- [ ] Engine rotates, but will not start
- [ ] Engine difficult to start when cold
- [ ] Engine difficult to start when hot
- [ ] Starter motor noisy or excessively-rough in engagement
- [ ] Engine starts, but stops immediately
- [ ] Engine idles erratically
- [ ] Engine misfires at idle speed
- [ ] Engine misfires throughout the driving speed range
- [ ] Engine hesitates on acceleration
- [ ] Engine stalls
- [ ] Engine lacks power
- [ ] Engine backfires
- [ ] Oil pressure warning light illuminated with engine running
- [ ] Engine runs-on after switching off
- [ ] Engine noises

Cooling system

- [ ] Overheating
- [ ] Overcooling
- [ ] External coolant leakage
- [ ] Internal coolant leakage
- [ ] Corrosion

Fuel and exhaust systems

- [ ] Excessive fuel consumption
- [ ] Fuel leakage and/or fuel odour
- [ ] Excessive noise or fumes from exhaust system

Clutch

- [ ] Pedal travels to floor – no pressure or very little resistance
- [ ] Clutch fails to disengage (unable to select gears)
- [ ] Clutch slips (engine speed increases, with no increase in vehicle speed)
- [ ] Judder as clutch is engaged
- [ ] Noise when depressing or releasing clutch pedal

Manual transmission

- [ ] Noisy in neutral with engine running
- [ ] Noisy in one particular gear
- [ ] Difficulty engaging gears
- [ ] Jumps out of gear
- [ ] Vibration
- [ ] Lubricant leaks

PowerShift transmission

- [ ] Fluid leakage
- [ ] General gear selection problems
- [ ] Transmission will not downshift (kickdown) with accelerator pedal fully depressed
- [ ] Engine will not start in any gear, or starts in gears other than Park or Neutral
- [ ] Transmission slips, shifts roughly, is noisy, or has no drive in forward or reverse gears

Driveshafts

- [ ] Vibration when accelerating or decelerating
- [ ] Clicking or knocking noise on turns (at slow speed on full-lock)

Braking system

- [ ] Vehicle pulls to one side under braking
- [ ] Noise (grinding or high-pitched squeal) when brakes applied
- [ ] Excessive brake pedal travel
- [ ] Brake pedal feels spongy when depressed
- [ ] Excessive brake pedal effort required to stop vehicle
- [ ] Judder felt through brake pedal or steering wheel when braking
- [ ] Brakes binding
- [ ] Rear wheels locking under normal braking

Suspension and steering

- [ ] Vehicle pulls to one side
- [ ] Wheel wobble and vibration
- [ ] Excessive pitching and/or rolling around corners, or during braking
- [ ] Wandering or general instability
- [ ] Excessively-stiff steering
- [ ] Excessive play in steering
- [ ] Lack of power assistance
- [ ] Tyre wear excessive

Electrical system

- [ ] Battery will not hold a charge for more than a few days
- [ ] Ignition/no-charge warning light remains illuminated with engine running
- [ ] Ignition/no-charge warning light fails to come on
- [ ] Lights inoperative
- [ ] Instrument readings inaccurate or erratic
- [ ] Horn inoperative, or unsatisfactory in operation
- [ ] Windscreen wipers inoperative, or unsatisfactory in operation
- [ ] Windscreen washers inoperative, or unsatisfactory in operation
- [ ] Electric windows inoperative, or unsatisfactory in operation
- [ ] Window glass fails to move
- [ ] Central locking system inoperative, or unsatisfactory in operation

Introduction

The vehicle owner who does his or her own maintenance according to the recommended service schedules should not have to use this section of the manual very often. Modern component reliability is such that, provided those items subject to wear or deterioration are inspected or renewed at the specified intervals, sudden failure is comparatively rare. Faults do not usually just happen as a result of sudden failure, but develop over a period of time. Major mechanical failures in particular are usually preceded by characteristic symptoms over hundreds or even thousands of miles. Those components which do

occasionally fail without warning are often small and easily carried in the vehicle.

With any fault-finding, the first step is to decide where to begin investigations. Sometimes this is obvious, but on other occasions, a little detective work will be necessary. The owner who makes half a dozen haphazard adjustments or replacements may be successful in curing a fault (or its symptoms), but will be none the wiser if the fault recurs, and ultimately may have spent more time and money than was necessary. A calm and logical approach will be found to be more satisfactory in the long run.

Always take into account any warning signs or abnormalities that may have been noticed in the period preceding the fault – power loss, high or low gauge readings, unusual smells, etc – and remember that failure of components such as fuses or spark plugs may only be pointers to some underlying fault.

The pages which follow provide an easy-reference guide to the more common problems which may occur during the operation of the vehicle. These problems and their possible causes are grouped under headings denoting various components or systems, such as Engine, Cooling system, etc. The general Chapter which deals with the problem is also shown in brackets; refer to the relevant part of that Chapter for system-specific information. Whatever the fault, certain basic principles apply. These are as follows:

Verify the fault. This is simply a matter of being sure that you know what the symptoms are before starting work. This is particularly important if you are investigating a fault for someone else, who may not have described it very accurately.

Don't overlook the obvious. For example, if the vehicle won't start, is there fuel in the tank? (Don't take anyone else's word on this particular point, and don't trust the fuel gauge either!) If an electrical fault is indicated, look for loose or broken wires before digging out the test gear.

Cure the disease, not the symptom. Substituting a flat battery with a fully-charged one will get you off the hard shoulder, but if the underlying cause is not attended to, the new battery will go the same way. Similarly, changing oil-fouled spark plugs for a new set will get you moving again, but remember that the reason for the fouling (if it wasn't simply

an incorrect grade of plug) will have to be established and corrected.

Don't take anything for granted. Particularly, don't forget that a 'new' component may itself be defective (especially if it's been rattling around in the boot for months), and don't leave components out of a fault diagnosis sequence just because they are new or recently-fitted. When you do finally diagnose a difficult fault, you'll probably realise that all the evidence was there from the start.

Consider what work, if any, has recently been carried out. Many faults arise through careless or hurried work. For instance, if any work has been performed under the bonnet, could some of the wiring have been dislodged or incorrectly routed, or a hose trapped? Have all the fasteners been properly tightened? Were new, genuine parts and new gaskets used? There is often a certain amount of detective work to be done in this case, as an apparently-unrelated task can have far-reaching consequences.

Diesel fault diagnosis

The majority of starting problems on small diesel engines are electrical in origin. The mechanic who is familiar with petrol engines

but less so with diesel may be inclined to view the diesel's injectors and pump in the same light as the spark plugs and distributor, but this is generally a mistake.

When investigating complaints of difficult starting for someone else, make sure that the correct starting procedure is understood and is being followed. Some drivers are unaware of the significance of the preheating warning light – many modern engines are sufficiently forgiving for this not to matter in mild weather, but with the onset of winter, problems begin. Glow plugs in particular are often neglected – just one faulty plug will make cold-weather starting very difficult.

As a rule of thumb, if the engine is difficult to start but runs well when it has finally got going, the problem is electrical (battery, starter motor or preheating system). If poor performance is combined with difficult starting, the problem is likely to be in the fuel system. The low-pressure (supply) side of the fuel system should be checked before suspecting the injectors and high-pressure pump. The most common fuel supply problem is air getting into the system, and any pipe from the fuel tank forwards must be scrutinised if air leakage is suspected.

Engine

Engine fails to rotate when attempting to start

☐ Battery terminal connections loose or corroded (see *Weekly checks*)
☐ Battery discharged or faulty (Chapter 5A Section 3)
☐ Broken, loose or disconnected wiring in the starting circuit (Chapter 5A Section 10)
☐ Defective starter solenoid or ignition switch (Chapter 5A or 12)
☐ Defective starter motor (Chapter 5A Section 9)
☐ Starter pinion or flywheel ring gear teeth loose or broken (Chapter 2A Section 16, Chapter 2B Section 17, Chapter 2C Section 15, Chapter 2D Section 15 or Chapter 5A Section 9)
☐ Engine earth strap broken or disconnected (Chapter 12 Section 2)
☐ Engine suffering "hydraulic lock" (eg from water drawn into the engine after traversing flooded roads, or from a serious internal coolant leak) – consult a main dealer for advice

Engine rotates, but will not start

☐ Fuel tank empty
☐ Battery discharged (engine rotates slowly) (Chapter 5A Section 3)
☐ Battery terminal connections loose or corroded (see *Weekly checks*)
☐ Ignition components damp or damaged – petrol models (Chapter 1A or 5B)l
☐ mmobiliser fault, or "uncoded" ignition key being used (Chapter 12 or *Roadside repairs*)
☐ Broken, loose or disconnected wiring in the ignition circuit – petrol models (Chapter 1A or 5B)
☐ Worn, faulty or incorrectly-gapped spark plugs – petrol models (Chapter 1A Section 21)
☐ Preheating system faulty – diesel models (Chapter 5A Section 11)
☐ Fuel injection/engine management system fault (Chapter 4A or Chapter 4B)
☐ Air in fuel system – diesel models (Chapter 4B Section 3)
☐ Major mechanical failure (eg. timing belt/chain) (Chapter 2A, Chapter 2B, Chapter 2C or Chapter 2D)

Engine difficult to start when cold

☐ Battery discharged (Chapter 5A Section 3)

☐ Battery terminal connections loose or corroded (see *Weekly checks*)
☐ Worn, faulty or incorrectly-gapped spark plugs – petrol models (Chapter 1A Section 21)
☐ Other ignition system fault – petrol models (Chapter 1A or 5B)
☐ Preheating system faulty – diesel models (Chapter 5A Section 11)
☐ Fuel injection/engine management system fault (Chapter 4Aor Chapter 4B)
☐ Wrong grade of engine oil used (*Weekly checks*, Chapter 1A or 1B)
☐ Low cylinder compression (Chapter 2A Section 2, Chapter 2B Section 2, Chapter 2C Section 2 or Chapter 2D Section 2)

Engine difficult to start when hot

☐ Air filter element dirty or clogged (Chapter 1A Section 22 or Chapter 1B Section 23)
☐ Fuel injection/engine management system fault (Chapter 4A or Chapter 4B)
☐ Low cylinder compression (Chapter 2A Section 2, Chapter 2B Section 2, Chapter 2C Section 2 or Chapter 2D Section 2)

Starter motor noisy or excessively-rough in engagement

☐ Starter pinion or flywheel ring gear teeth loose or broken (Chapter 2A Section 16, Chapter 2B Section 17, Chapter 2C Section 15, Chapter 2D Section 15 or Chapter 5A Section 9)
☐ Starter motor mounting bolts loose or missing (Chapter 5A Section 9)
☐ Starter motor internal components worn or damaged (Chapter 5A Section 10)

Engine starts, but stops immediately

☐ Loose or faulty electrical connections in the ignition circuit – petrol models (Chapter 1A or 5B)
☐ Vacuum leak at the throttle housing or inlet manifold – petrol models (Chapter 4A or 4B)
☐ Blocked injectors/fuel injection system fault (Chapter 4A or 4B)

Engine (continued)

Engine idles erratically

- [ ] Air filter element clogged (Chapter 1A Section 22 or Chapter 1B Section 23)
- [ ] Vacuum leak at the throttle housing, inlet manifold or associated hoses – petrol models (Chapter 4A or 4C)
- [ ] Worn, faulty or incorrectly-gapped spark plugs – petrol models (Chapter 1A Section 21)
- [ ] Uneven or low cylinder compression (Chapter 2A Section 2, Chapter 2B Section 2, Chapter 2C Section 2 or Chapter 2D Section 2)
- [ ] Camshaft lobes worn (Chapter 2A Section 10, Chapter 2B Section 11, Chapter 2C Section 9 or Chapter 2D Section 9)
- [ ] Blocked injectors/fuel injection system fault (Chapter 4A, or 4B)

Engine misfires at idle speed

- [ ] Worn, faulty or incorrectly-gapped spark plugs – petrol models (Chapter 1A Section 21)
- [ ] Vacuum leak at the throttle housing, inlet manifold or associated hoses – petrol models (Chapter 4A or 4C)
- [ ] Blocked injectors/fuel injection system fault (Chapter 4A, 4B or 4C)
- [ ] Faulty injector(s) – diesel models (Chapter 4B Section 11)
- [ ] Uneven or low cylinder compression (Chapter 2A Section 2, Chapter 2B Section 2, Chapter 2C Section 2 or Chapter 2D Section 2)
- [ ] Disconnected, leaking, or perished crankcase ventilation hoses (Chapter 4C)

Engine misfires throughout the driving speed range

- [ ] Fuel filter choked (Chapter 1B Section 22)
- [ ] Fuel pump faulty, or delivery pressure low – petrol models (Chapter 4A Section 8)
- [ ] Fuel tank vent blocked, or fuel pipes restricted (Chapter 4A or 4B)
- [ ] Vacuum leak at the throttle housing, inlet manifold or associated hoses – petrol models (Chapter 4A or 4C)
- [ ] Worn, faulty or incorrectly-gapped spark plugs – petrol models (Chapter 1A Section 21)
- [ ] Faulty injector(s) – diesel models (Chapter 4B Section 11)
- [ ] Faulty ignition module – petrol models (Chapter 5B Section 2)
- [ ] Uneven or low cylinder compression (Chapter 2A Section 2, Chapter 2B Section 2, Chapter 2C Section 2 or Chapter 2D Section 2)
- [ ] Blocked injector/fuel injection system fault (Chapter 4A or 4B)
- [ ] Blocked catalytic converter (Chapter 4A, 4B or 4C)
- [ ] Engine overheating (Chapter 3)

Engine hesitates on acceleration

- [ ] Worn, faulty or incorrectly-gapped spark plugs – petrol models (Chapter 1A Section 21)
- [ ] Vacuum leak at the throttle housing, inlet manifold or associated hoses – petrol models (Chapter 4A or 4C)
- [ ] Blocked injectors/fuel injection system fault (Chapter 4A or 4B)
- [ ] Faulty injector(s) – diesel models (Chapter 4B Section 11)

Engine stalls

- [ ] Vacuum leak at the throttle housing, inlet manifold or associated hoses – petrol models (Chapter 4A or 4C)
- [ ] Fuel filter choked (Chapter 1B Section 22)
- [ ] Fuel pump faulty, or delivery pressure low – petrol models (Chapter 4A Section 8)
- [ ] Fuel tank vent blocked, or fuel pipes restricted (Chapter 4A or 4B)
- [ ] Blocked injectors/fuel injection system fault (Chapter 4A or 4B)
- [ ] Faulty injector(s) – diesel models (Chapter 4B Section 11)

Engine lacks power

- [ ] Air filter element blocked (Chapter 1A Section 22 or Chapter 1B Section 23)
- [ ] Timing belt incorrectly fitted (Chapter 2A Section 8, Chapter 2B Section 8, Chapter 2C Section 7 or Chapter 2D Section 7)
- [ ] Fuel filter choked (Chapter 1B Section 22)
- [ ] Fuel pipes blocked or restricted (Chapter 4A or 4B)
- [ ] Worn, faulty or incorrectly-gapped spark plugs – petrol models (Chapter 1A Section 21)
- [ ] Engine overheating (Chapter 3)
- [ ] Fuel tank level low – diesel models (Chapter 4B Section 7)
- [ ] Accelerator pedal position sensor faulty (Chapter 4A Section 6 or Chapter 4B Section 5)
- [ ] Vacuum leak at the throttle housing, inlet manifold or associated hoses – petrol models (Chapter 4A or 4C)
- [ ] Blocked injectors/fuel injection system fault (Chapter 4A or 4B)
- [ ] Faulty injector(s) – diesel models (Chapter 4B Section 11)
- [ ] Fuel pump faulty, or delivery pressure low – petrol models (Chapter 4A Section 8)
- [ ] Uneven or low cylinder compression (Chapter 2A Section 2, Chapter 2B Section 2, Chapter 2C Section 2 or Chapter 2D Section 2)
- [ ] Blocked catalytic converter (Chapter 4A, 4B or 4C)
- [ ] Brakes binding (Chapter 1A, 1B or 9)
- [ ] Clutch slipping (Chapter 6 Section 6)
- [ ] Faulty turbocharger (Chapter 4A Section 15 or Chapter 4B Section 16)
- [ ] Leaking intercooler (Chapter 4A Section 14 or Chapter 4B Section 17)

Engine backfires

- [ ] Vacuum leak at the throttle housing, inlet manifold or associated hoses – petrol models (Chapter 4A)
- [ ] Blocked injectors/fuel injection system fault (Chapter 4A or 4B)
- [ ] Blocked catalytic converter (Chapter 4A, 4B or 4C)
- [ ] Faulty ignition module – petrol models (Chapter 5B Section 2)

Oil pressure warning light illuminated with engine running

- [ ] Low oil level, or incorrect oil grade (see *Weekly checks*)
- [ ] Faulty oil pressure switch, or wiring damaged (Chapter 2A Section 14, Chapter 2B Section 15, Chapter 2C Section 14 or Chapter 2D Section 14)
- [ ] Worn engine bearings and/or oil pump (Chapter 2A Section 13, Chapter 2B Section 14, Chapter 2C Section 12, Chapter 2D Section 12 or Chapter 2E)
- [ ] High engine operating temperature (Chapter 3)
- [ ] Oil pump pick-up strainer clogged (Chapter 2A Section 12, Chapter 2B Section 13, Chapter 2C Section 11 or Chapter 2D Section 11)

Engine runs-on after switching off

- [ ] Excessive carbon build-up in engine (Chapter 2E Section 8)
- [ ] High engine operating temperature (Chapter 3)
- [ ] Fuel injection/engine management system fault (Chapter 4A or Chapter 4B)

Engine noises

Pre-ignition (pinking) or knocking during acceleration or under load

- [ ] Ignition timing incorrect/ignition system fault – petrol models (Chapter 1A or 5B)
- [ ] Incorrect grade of spark plug – petrol models (Chapter 1A Section 21)
- [ ] Incorrect grade of fuel (Chapter 4A or 4B)
- [ ] Knock sensor faulty – petrol models (Chapter 5B Section 6)
- [ ] Vacuum leak at the throttle housing, inlet manifold or associated hoses – petrol models (Chapter 4A or 4C)
- [ ] Excessive carbon build-up in engine (Chapter 2E Section 8)
- [ ] uel injection/engine management system fault (Chapter 4A or Chapter 4B)
- [ ] Faulty injector(s) – diesel models (Chapter 4B Section 11)

Whistling or wheezing noises

- [ ] Leaking inlet manifold or throttle housing gasket – petrol models (Chapter 4A)

Engine (continued)

☐ Leaking exhaust manifold gasket or pipe-to-manifold joint (Chapter 4A or 4B)
☐ Leaking vacuum hose (Chapter 4A, 4B, 4C or 9)
☐ Blowing cylinder head gasket (Chapter 2A Section 11, Chapter 2B Section 12, Chapter 2C Section 10 or Chapter 2D Section 10)
☐ Leaking turbocharger or intercooler hoses (Chapter 4A or Chapter 4B)
☐ Partially blocked or leaking crankcase ventilation system (Chapter 4C)

Tapping or rattling noises

☐ Worn valve gear or camshaft (Chapter 2A Section 10, Chapter 2B Section 11, Chapter 2C Section 9 or Chapter 2D Section 9)
☐ Ancillary component fault (coolant pump, alternator, etc) (Chapter 3, 5A, etc)

Knocking or thumping noises

☐ Worn big-end bearings (regular heavy knocking, perhaps less under load) (Chapter 2E Section 13)
☐ Worn main bearings (rumbling and knocking, perhaps worsening under load) (Chapter 2E Section 15)
☐ Piston slap – most noticeable when cold, caused by piston/bore wear (Chapter 2E Section 13)
☐ Ancillary component fault (coolant pump, alternator, etc) (Chapter 3, 5A, etc)
☐ Engine mountings worn or defective (Chapter 2A Section 17, Chapter 2B Section 18, Chapter 2C Section 16 or Chapter 2D Section 16)
☐ Front suspension or steering components worn (Chapter 10)

Cooling system

Overheating

☐ Insufficient coolant in system (see *Weekly checks*)
☐ Thermostat faulty (Chapter 3 Section 4)
☐ Radiator core blocked, or grille restricted (Chapter 3 Section 3)
☐ Cooling fan faulty, or resistor pack fault (Chapter 3 Section 5)
☐ Inaccurate coolant temperature sensor (Chapter 3 Section 6)
☐ Airlock in cooling system (Chapter 1A, 1B or 3)
☐ Expansion tank pressure cap faulty (Chapter 3 Section 1)
☐ Engine management system fault (Chapter 4A or Chapter 4B)

Overcooling

☐ Thermostat faulty (Chapter 3 Section 4)
☐ Inaccurate coolant temperature sensor (Chapter 3 Section 6)
☐ Cooling fan faulty (Chapter 3 Section 5)
☐ Engine management system fault (Chapter 4A or Chapter 4B)

External coolant leakage

☐ Deteriorated or damaged hoses or hose clips (Chapter 1A or 1B)
☐ Radiator core or heater matrix leaking (Chapter 3 Section 3)
☐ Expansion tank pressure cap faulty (Chapter 1A or 1B)
☐ Coolant pump internal seal leaking (Chapter 3 Section 7)
☐ Coolant pump gasket leaking (Chapter 3 Section 7)
☐ Boiling due to overheating (Chapter 3 Section 1)
☐ Cylinder block core plug leaking (Chapter 2E Section 12)

Internal coolant leakage

☐ Leaking cylinder head gasket (Chapter 2A Section 11, Chapter 2B Section 12, Chapter 2C Section 10 or Chapter 2D Section 10)
☐ Cracked cylinder head or cylinder block (Chapter 2E)

Corrosion

☐ Infrequent draining and flushing (Chapter 1A or 1B)
☐ Incorrect coolant mixture or inappropriate coolant type (see *Weekly checks*)

Fuel and exhaust systems

Excessive fuel consumption

☐ Air filter element dirty or clogged (Chapter 1A Section 22 or Chapter 1B Section 23)
☐ Fuel injection system fault (Chapter 4A or Chapter 4B)
☐ Engine management system fault (Chapter 4A or Chapter 4B)
☐ Crankcase ventilation system blocked (Chapter 4C)
☐ Tyres under-inflated (see *Weekly checks*)
☐ Brakes binding (Chapter 1A, 1B or 9)
☐ Fuel leak, causing apparent high consumption (Chapter 1A, 1B, 4A or 4B)

Fuel leakage and/or fuel odour

☐ Damaged or corroded fuel tank, pipes or connections (Chapter 4A, 4B or 4C)
☐ Evaporative emissions system fault – petrol models (Chapter 4C Section 2)

Excessive noise or fumes from exhaust system

☐ Leaking exhaust system or manifold joints (Chapter 4A or Chapter 4B)
☐ Leaking, corroded or damaged silencers or pipe (Chapter 4A Section 13 or Chapter 4B Section 18)
☐ Broken mountings causing body or suspension contact (Chapter 1A or 1B)

Clutch

Pedal travels to floor – no pressure or very little resistance

☐ Air in hydraulic system/faulty master or slave cylinder (Chapter 6)
☐ Faulty hydraulic release system (Chapter 6 Section 4)
☐ Clutch pedal return spring detached or broken (Chapter 6 Section 5)
☐ Broken diaphragm spring in clutch pressure plate (Chapter 6 Section 6)

Clutch fails to disengage (unable to select gears)

☐ Air in hydraulic system/faulty master or slave cylinder (Chapter 6 Section 4)
☐ Faulty hydraulic release system (Chapter 6 Section 3)
☐ Clutch disc sticking on transmission input shaft splines (Chapter 6 Section 6)
☐ Clutch disc sticking to flywheel or pressure plate (Chapter 6 Section 6)
☐ Faulty pressure plate assembly (Chapter 6 Section 6)
☐ Clutch release mechanism worn or incorrectly assembled (Chapter 6 Section 7)

Clutch slips (engine speed increases, with no increase in vehicle speed)

☐ Faulty hydraulic release system (Chapter 6 Section 4)
☐ Clutch disc linings excessively worn (Chapter 6 Section 6)

☐ Clutch disc linings contaminated with oil or grease (Chapter 6 Section 6)
☐ Faulty pressure plate or weak diaphragm spring (Chapter 6 Section 6)

Judder as clutch is engaged

☐ Clutch disc linings contaminated with oil or grease (Chapter 6 Section 6)
☐ Clutch disc linings excessively worn (Chapter 6 Section 6)
☐ Faulty or distorted pressure plate or diaphragm spring (Chapter 6 Section 6).
☐ Worn or loose engine or transmission mountings (Chapter 2A Section 17, Chapter 2B Section 18, Chapter 2C Section 16 or Chapter 2D Section 16)
☐ Clutch disc hub or transmission input shaft splines worn (Chapter 6)

Noise when depressing or releasing clutch pedal

☐ Faulty hydraulic release system (Chapter 6 Section 4)
☐ Worn or dry clutch pedal bushes (Chapter 6 Section 5)
☐ Worn or dry clutch master cylinder piston (Chapter 6 Section 2)
☐ Faulty pressure plate assembly (Chapter 6 Section 6)
☐ Pressure plate diaphragm spring broken (Chapter 6 Section 6)
☐ Broken clutch disc cushioning springs (Chapter 6 Section 6)

Driveshafts

Vibration when accelerating or decelerating

☐ Worn inner constant velocity joint (Chapter 8 Section 4, 5)
☐ Bent or distorted driveshaft (Chapter 8 Section 5)
☐ Worn intermediate bearing (Chapter 8 Section 5)

Clicking or knocking noise on turns (at slow speed on full-lock)

☐ Worn outer constant velocity joint (Chapter 8 Section 5)
☐ Lack of constant velocity joint lubricant, possibly due to damaged gaiter (Chapter 8)

Manual transmission

Noisy in neutral with engine running

☐ Lack of oil (Chapter 1A Section 28 or 1B Section 28)
☐ Input shaft bearings worn (noise apparent with clutch pedal released, but not when depressed) (Chapter 7A)*
☐ Clutch release bearing system (noise apparent with clutch pedal depressed, possibly less when released) (Chapter 6 Section 7)

Noisy in one particular gear

☐ Worn, damaged or chipped gear teeth (Chapter 7A Section 7)*

Difficulty engaging gears

☐ Clutch fault (Chapter 6)
☐ Worn, damaged, or poorly-adjusted gearchange (Chapter 7A Section 2)
☐ Lack of oil (Chapter 7A)
☐ Worn synchroniser units (Chapter 7A Section 7)*

Jumps out of gear

☐ Worn, damaged, or poorly-adjusted gearchange (Chapter 7A Section 2)
☐ Worn synchroniser units (Chapter 7A Section 7)*
☐ Worn selector forks (Chapter 7A Section 7)*

Vibration

☐ Lack of oil (Chapter 7A)
☐ Worn bearings (Chapter 7A Section 7)*

Lubricant leaks

☐ Leaking driveshaft or selector shaft oil seal (Chapter 7A Section 5)
☐ Leaking housing joint (Chapter 7A Section 7)*
☐ Leaking input shaft oil seal (Chapter 7A Section 5)*

PowerShift transmission

Fluid leakage

Note: *Due to the complexity of the PowerShift transmission, it is difficult for the home mechanic to properly diagnose and service this unit. For problems other than the following, the vehicle should be taken to a dealer service department or transmission specialist. Do not be too hasty in removing the transmission if a fault is suspected, as most of the testing is carried out with the unit still fitted.*

The transmission fluid is usually dark in colour. Fluid leaks should not be confused with engine oil, which can easily be blown onto the transmission by airflow.

To determine the source of a leak, first remove all built-up dirt and grime from the transmission housing and surrounding areas using a degreasing agent, or by steam-cleaning. Drive the vehicle at low speed, so airflow will not blow the leak far from its source. Raise and support the vehicle, and determine where the leak is coming from.

General gear selection problems

☐ Chapter 7B deals with checking and adjusting the selector mechanism. The following are common problems which may be caused by a poorly-adjusted mechanism:
Engine starting in gears other than Park or Neutral.
Indicator panel indicating a gear other than the one actually being used.

Vehicle moves when in Park or Neutral.
Poor gear shift quality or erratic gear changes.
☐ Refer to Chapter 7B Section 3 for the selector mechanism adjustment procedure.

Transmission will not downshift (kickdown) with accelerator pedal fully depressed

☐ Low transmission fluid level (Chapter 7B Section 2).
☐ Incorrect selector mechanism adjustment (Chapter 7B Section 3).

Engine will not start in any gear, or starts in gears other than Park or Neutral

☐ Incorrect selector mechanism adjustment (Chapter 7B Section 3).

Transmission slips, shifts roughly, is noisy, or has no drive in forward or reverse gears

☐ There are many probable causes for the above problems, but unless there is a very obvious reason (such as a loose or corroded wiring plug connection on or near the transmission), the car should be taken to a franchise dealer or specialist for the fault to be diagnosed. The transmission control unit incorporates a self-diagnosis facility, and any fault codes can quickly be read and interpreted by a dealer with the proper diagnostic equipment.

Braking system

Vehicle pulls to one side under braking

Note: *Before assuming that a brake problem exists, make sure that the tyres are in good condition and correctly inflated, that the front wheel alignment is correct, and that the vehicle is not loaded with weight in an unequal manner. Apart from checking the condition of all pipe and hose connections, any faults occurring on the anti-lock braking system should be referred to a Ford dealer for diagnosis.*

☐ Worn, defective, damaged or contaminated brake pads/shoes on one side (Chapter 1A, 1B or 9)
☐ Seized or partially-seized brake caliper or wheel cylinder piston (Chapter 1A, 1B or 9)
☐ A mixture of brake pad/shoe lining materials fitted between sides (Chapter 1A, 1B or 9)
☐ Brake caliper or backplate mounting bolts loose (Chapter 9 Section 5)
☐ Worn or damaged steering or suspension components (Chapter 1A, 1B or 10)

Noise (grinding or high-pitched squeal) when brakes applied

☐ Brake pad/shoe friction lining material worn down to metal backing (Chapter 1A, 1B or 9)
☐ Excessive corrosion of brake disc/drum (may be apparent after the vehicle has been standing for some time (Chapter 1A, 1B or 9)
☐ Foreign object (stone chipping, etc) trapped between brake disc and shield (Chapter 1A, 1B or 9)

Excessive brake pedal travel

☐ Faulty master cylinder (Chapter 9 Section 10)
☐ Air in hydraulic system (Chapter 9 Section 2)
☐ Faulty vacuum servo unit (Chapter 9 Section 12)

Brake pedal feels spongy when depressed

☐ Air in hydraulic system (Chapter 9 Section 2)
☐ Deteriorated flexible rubber brake hoses (Chapter 1A, 1B or 9)

master cylinder mounting nuts loose (Chapter 9 Section 10)
☐ Faulty master cylinder (Chapter 9 Section 10)

Excessive brake pedal effort required to stop vehicle

☐ Faulty vacuum servo unit (Chapter 9 Section 12, 13)
☐ Faulty vacuum pump (Chapter 9 Section 21)
☐ Disconnected, damaged or insecure brake servo vacuum hose (Chapter 9 Section 13)
☐ Primary or secondary hydraulic circuit failure (Chapter 9)
☐ Seized brake caliper or wheel cylinder piston (Chapter 9)
☐ Brake pads/shoes incorrectly fitted (Chapter 9)
☐ Incorrect grade of brake pads/shoes fitted (Chapter 9)
☐ Brake pad/shoe linings contaminated (Chapter 1A, 1B or 9)

Judder felt through brake pedal or steering wheel when braking

Note: *Under heavy braking on models equipped with ABS, vibration may be felt through the brake pedal. This is a normal feature of ABS operation, and does not constitute a fault.*

☐ Excessive run-out or distortion of discs/drums (Chapter 9)
☐ Brake pad/shoe linings worn (Chapter 1A, 1B or 9)
☐ Brake caliper/backplate mounting bolts loose (Chapter 9)
☐ Wear in suspension or steering components or mountings (Chapter 1A, 1B or 10)
☐ Front wheels out of balance (see *Weekly checks*)

Brakes binding

☐ Seized brake caliper or wheel cylinder piston (Chapter 9)
☐ Incorrectly-adjusted handbrake mechanism (Chapter 9 Section 14)
☐ Faulty master cylinder (Chapter 9 Section 10)

Rear wheels locking under normal braking

☐ Rear brake shoe linings contaminated or damaged (Chapter 1A or 9)
☐ Rear brake drums warped (Chapter 1A, 1B or 9)

Suspension and steering

Vehicle pulls to one side

Note: *Before diagnosing suspension or steering faults, be sure that the trouble is not due to incorrect tyre pressures, mixtures of tyre types, or binding brakes.*

- [ ] Defective tyre (see *Weekly checks*)
- [ ] Excessive wear in suspension or steering components (Chapter 1A, 1B or 10)
- [ ] Incorrect front wheel alignment (Chapter 10 Section 20)
- [ ] Accident damage to steering or suspension components (Chapter 1A or 1B)

Wheel wobble and vibration

- [ ] Front wheels out of balance (vibration felt mainly through the steering wheel) (see *Weekly checks*)
- [ ] Rear wheels out of balance (vibration felt throughout the vehicle) (see *Weekly checks*)
- [ ] Roadwheels damaged or distorted (see *Weekly checks*)
- [ ] Faulty or damaged tyre (see *Weekly checks*)
- [ ] Worn steering or suspension joints, bushes or components (Chapter 1A, 1B or 10)
- [ ] Wheel nuts loose (Chapter 1A or 1B)

Excessive pitching and/or rolling around corners, or during braking

- [ ] Defective shock absorbers (Chapter 1A, 1B or 10)
- [ ] Broken or weak spring and/or suspension component (Chapter 1A, 1B or 10)
- [ ] Worn or damaged anti-roll bar or mountings (Chapter 1A, 1B or 10)

Wandering or general instability

- [ ] Incorrect front wheel alignment (Chapter 10 Section 20)
- [ ] Worn steering or suspension joints, bushes or components (Chapter 1A, 1B or 10)
- [ ] Roadwheels out of balance (see *Weekly checks*)
- [ ] Faulty or damaged tyre (see *Weekly checks*)
- [ ] Wheel nuts loose (Chapter 1A or 1B)
- [ ] Defective shock absorbers (Chapter 1A, 1B or 10)
- [ ] Electric power steering system fault (Chapter 10 Section 16)

Excessively-stiff steering

- [ ] Seized steering linkage balljoint or suspension balljoint (Chapter 1A, 1B or 10)
- [ ] Incorrect front wheel alignment (Chapter 10 Section 20)
- [ ] Steering rack damaged (Chapter 10 Section 18)
- [ ] Electric power steering system fault (Chapter 10 Section 15)

Excessive play in steering

- [ ] Worn steering column/intermediate shaft joints (Chapter 10 Section 15)
- [ ] Worn track rod end balljoints (Chapter 1A, 1B or 10)
- [ ] Worn steering rack (Chapter 10 Section 18)
- [ ] Worn steering or suspension joints, bushes or components (Chapter 1A, 1B or 10)

Lack of power assistance

- [ ] Electric power steering system fault (Chapter 10 Section 15)
- [ ] Faulty steering rack (Chapter 10 Section 18)

Tyre wear excessive

Tyres worn on inside or outside edges

- [ ] Tyres under-inflated (wear on both edges) (see *Weekly checks*)
- [ ] Incorrect camber or castor angles (wear on one edge only) (Chapter 10 Section 20)
- [ ] Worn steering or suspension joints, bushes or components (Chapter 1A, 1B or 10)
- [ ] Excessively-hard cornering or braking
- [ ] Accident damage

Tyre treads exhibit feathered edges

- [ ] Incorrect toe-setting (Chapter 10 Section 20)

Tyres worn in centre of tread

- [ ] Tyres over-inflated (see *Weekly checks*)

Tyres worn on inside and outside edges

- [ ] Tyres under-inflated (see *Weekly checks*)

Tyres worn unevenly

- [ ] Tyres/wheels out of balance (see *Weekly checks*)
- [ ] Excessive wheel or tyre run-out
- [ ] Worn shock absorbers (Chapter 1A, 1B or 10)
- [ ] Faulty tyre (see *Weekly checks*)

Electrical system

Battery will not hold a charge for more than a few days

Note: *For problems associated with the starting system, refer to the faults listed under "Engine" earlier in this Section.*

- [ ] Battery defective internally (Chapter 5A Section 3)
- [ ] Battery terminal connections loose or corroded (see *Weekly checks*)
- [ ] Auxiliary drivebelt worn or incorrectly adjusted (Chapter 1A Section 9 or Chapter 1B Section 10)
- [ ] Alternator not charging at correct output (Chapter 5A Section 5)
- [ ] Alternator or voltage regulator faulty (Chapter 5A Section 5)
- [ ] Short-circuit causing continual battery drain (Chapter 5A or Chapter 12 Section 2)

Ignition/no-charge warning light remains illuminated with engine running

- [ ] Auxiliary drivebelt broken, worn, or incorrectly adjusted (Chapter 1A Section 9 or Chapter 1B Section 10)
- [ ] Internal fault in alternator or voltage regulator (Chapter 5A Section 5)
- [ ] Broken, disconnected, or loose wiring in charging circuit (Chapter 5A or 12)

Ignition/no-charge warning light fails to come on

- [ ] Broken, disconnected, or loose wiring in warning light circuit (Chapter 5A or 12)
- [ ] Alternator faulty (Chapter 5A Section 5)

Electrical system (continued

Lights inoperative
- [ ] Bulb blown (Chapter 12)
- [ ] Corrosion of bulb or bulbholder contacts (Chapter 12)
- [ ] Blown fuse (Chapter 12 Section 3)
- [ ] Faulty relay (Chapter 12 Section 3)
- [ ] Broken, loose, or disconnected wiring (Chapter 12)
- [ ] Faulty switch (Chapter 12 Section 4)

Instrument readings inaccurate or erratic

Fuel or temperature gauges give no reading
- [ ] Faulty gauge sender unit (Chapter 3 Section 6, Chapter 4A Section 8 or Chapter 4B Section 7)
- [ ] Wiring open-circuit (Chapter 12 Section 2)
- [ ] Faulty gauge (Chapter 12 Section 10)

Fuel or temperature gauges give continuous maximum reading
- [ ] Faulty gauge sender unit (Chapter 3 Section 6, Chapter 4A Section 8 or Chapter 4B Section 7)
- [ ] Wiring short-circuit (Chapter 12 Section 2)
- [ ] Faulty gauge (Chapter 12 Section 10)

Horn inoperative, or unsatisfactory in operation

Horn operates all the time
- [ ] Horn push either earthed or stuck down (Chapter 12 Section 4)
- [ ] Horn cable-to-horn push earthed (Chapter 12 Section 2)

Horn fails to operate
- [ ] Blown fuse (Chapter 12 Section 3)
- [ ] Cable or connections loose, broken or disconnected (Chapter 12 Section 2)
- [ ] Faulty horn (Chapter 12 Section 13)

Horn emits intermittent or unsatisfactory sound
- [ ] Cable connections loose (Chapter 12 Section 2)
- [ ] Horn mountings loose (Chapter 12 Section 13)
- [ ] Faulty horn (Chapter 12 Section 13)

Windscreen wipers inoperative, or unsatisfactory in operation

Wipers fail to operate, or operate very slowly
- [ ] Wiper blades stuck to screen, or linkage seized or binding (Chapter 12 Section 15)
- [ ] Blown fuse (Chapter 12 Section 3)
- [ ] Battery discharged (Chapter 5A Section 3)
- [ ] Cable or connections loose, broken or disconnected (Chapter 12 Section 2)
- [ ] Faulty relay (Chapter 12 Section 3)
- [ ] Faulty wiper motor (Chapter 12 Section 15)

Wiper blades sweep over too large or too small an area of the glass
- [ ] Wiper blades incorrectly fitted, or wrong size used (see *Weekly checks*)
- [ ] Wiper arms incorrectly positioned on spindles (Chapter 12 Section 14)
- [ ] Excessive wear of wiper linkage (Chapter 12 Section 15)
- [ ] Wiper motor or linkage mountings loose or insecure (Chapter 12 Section 15)

Wiper blades fail to clean the glass effectively
- [ ] Wiper blade rubbers dirty, worn or perished (see *Weekly checks*)
- [ ] Wiper blades incorrectly fitted, or wrong size used (see *Weekly checks*)

- [ ] Wiper arm tension springs broken, or arm pivots seized (Chapter 12 Section 14)
- [ ] Insufficient windscreen washer additive to adequately remove road film (see Weekly checks 0 Section 5)

Windscreen washers inoperative, or unsatisfactory in operation

One or more washer jets inoperative
- [ ] Blocked washer jet
- [ ] Disconnected, kinked or restricted fluid hose (Chapter 12)
- [ ] Insufficient fluid in washer reservoir (see *Weekly checks*)

Washer pump fails to operate
- [ ] Broken or disconnected wiring or connections (Chapter 12 Section 2)
- [ ] Blown fuse (Chapter 12 Section 3)
- [ ] Faulty washer switch (Chapter 12 Section 4)
- [ ] Faulty washer pump (Chapter 12 Section 17)

Washer pump runs for some time before fluid is emitted from jets
- [ ] Faulty one-way valve in fluid supply hose (Chapter 12)

Electric windows inoperative, or unsatisfactory in operation

Window glass will only move in one direction
- [ ] Faulty switch (Chapter 12 Section 4)

Window glass slow to move
- [ ] Battery discharged (Chapter 5A Section 3)
- [ ] Regulator seized or damaged, or in need of lubrication (Chapter 11 Section 13)
- [ ] Door internal components or trim fouling regulator (Chapter 11 Section 13)
- [ ] Faulty motor (Chapter 11 Section 13)

Window glass fails to move
- [ ] Blown fuse (Chapter 12 Section 3)
- [ ] Faulty relay (Chapter 12 Section 3)
- [ ] Broken or disconnected wiring or connections (Chapter 12 Section 2)
- [ ] Faulty motor (Chapter 11 Section 13)

Central locking system inoperative, or unsatisfactory in operation

Complete system failure
- [ ] Remote handset battery discharged, where applicable (Chapter 1A or 1B)
- [ ] Blown fuse (Chapter 12 Section 3)
- [ ] Faulty relay (Chapter 12 Section 3)
- [ ] Broken or disconnected wiring or connections (Chapter 12)
- [ ] Faulty motor (Chapter 11 Section 14)

Latch locks but will not unlock, or unlocks but will not lock
- [ ] Remote handset battery discharged, where applicable (Chapter 1A or 1B)
- [ ] Faulty master switch (Chapter 12 Section 4)
- [ ] Broken or disconnected latch operating rods or levers (Chapter 11 Section 14)
- [ ] Faulty relay (Chapter 12 Section 3)
- [ ] Faulty motor (Chapter 11 Section 17)

One solenoid/motor fails to operate
- [ ] Broken or disconnected wiring or connections (Chapter 12 Section 2)
- [ ] Faulty operating assembly (Chapter 11 Section 17)
- [ ] Broken, binding or disconnected latch operating rods or levers (Chapter 11 Section 14)
- [ ] Fault in door latch (Chapter 11 Section 14)

Note: *References throughout this index are in the form "Chapter number" • "Page number". So, for example, 2C•15 refers to page 15 of Chapter 2C.*

Note: *References throughout this index are in the form "**Chapter number**" • "**Page number**". So, for example, 2C•15 refers to page 15 of Chapter 2C.*

Note: *References throughout this index are in the form "Chapter number" • "Page number". So, for example, 2C•15 refers to page 15 of Chapter 2C.*

Note: *References throughout this index are in the form "**Chapter number**" • "**Page number**". So, for example, 2C•15 refers to page 15 of Chapter 2C.*

Preserving Our Motoring Heritage

> The Model J Duesenberg Derham Tourster. Only eight of these magnificent cars were ever built – this is the only example to be found outside the United States of America

Almost every car you've ever loved, loathed or desired is gathered under one roof at the Haynes Motor Museum. Over 300 immaculately presented cars and motorbikes represent every aspect of our motoring heritage, from elegant reminders of bygone days, such as the superb Model J Duesenberg to curiosities like the bug-eyed BMW Isetta. There are also many old friends and flames. Perhaps you remember the 1959 Ford Popular that you did your courting in? The magnificent 'Red Collection' is a spectacle of classic sports cars including AC, Alfa Romeo, Austin Healey, Ferrari, Lamborghini, Maserati, MG, Riley, Porsche and Triumph.

A Perfect Day Out

Each and every vehicle at the Haynes Motor Museum has played its part in the history and culture of Motoring. Today, they make a wonderful spectacle and a great day out for all the family. Bring the kids, bring Mum and Dad, but above all bring your camera to capture those golden memories for ever. You will also find an impressive array of motoring memorabilia, a comfortable 70 seat video cinema and one of the most extensive transport book shops in Britain. The Pit Stop Cafe serves everything from a cup of tea to wholesome, home-made meals or, if you prefer, you can enjoy the large picnic area nestled in the beautiful rural surroundings of Somerset.

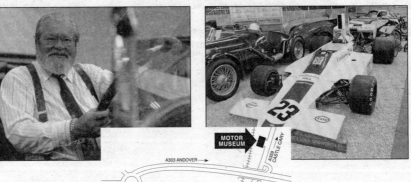

> John Haynes O.B.E., Founder and Chairman of the museum at the wheel of a Haynes Light 12.

> Graham Hill's Lola Cosworth Formula 1 car next to a 1934 Riley Sports.

The Museum is situated on the A359 Yeovil to Frome road at Sparkford, just off the A303 in Somerset. It is about 40 miles south of Bristol, and 25 minutes drive from the M5 intersection at Taunton.

Open 9.30am - 5.30pm (10.00am - 4.00pm Winter) 7 days a week, *except Christmas Day, Boxing Day and New Years Day*

Special rates available for schools, coach parties and outings Charitable Trust No. 292048